THE OXFORD HANDBOOK OF

CORPORATE
REPUTATION

THE OXFORD HANDBOOK OF

CORPORATE

REPUTATION

Edited by

MICHAEL L. BARNETT
and
TIMOTHY G. POLLOCK

OXFORD
UNIVERSITY PRESS

UNIVERSITY PRESS

Great Clarendon Street, Oxford, ox2 6DP,
United Kingdom

Oxford University Press is a department of the University of Oxford.
It furthers the University's objective of excellence in research, scholarship,
and education by publishing worldwide. Oxford is a registered trade mark of
Oxford University Press in the UK and in certain other countries

First Edition published in 2012
First published in paperback 2014
Impression: 1

British Library Cataloguing in Publication Data
Data available

Library of Congress Cataloging in Publication Data
Data available

ISBN 978–0–19–959670–6 (hbk)
ISBN 978–0–19–870461–4 (pbk)

Printed in Great Britain on acid-free paper by
CPI Group (UK) Ltd, Croydon, CR0 4YY

ACKNOWLEDGMENTS

There are a number of individuals without whom this book would not have been possible. First and foremost are the wonderful group of scholars who have contributed its content. We truly appreciate the time and effort they put into crafting their chapters, as well as their tolerance and good humor in the face of our nattering and pestering them about style, length, and all manner of other issues across multiple rounds of revision. We would also like to thank Rupert Younger and the folks in the Oxford University Centre for Corporate Reputation for providing the financial resources to put on a conference for our authors, and for helping organize the conference. It was a great event that helped immeasurably to improve the quality and increase the coherence of the *Handbook*. We of course would also like to thank the folks at Oxford University Press, particularly David Musson, Emma Lambert, and Rachel Platt, for publishing the book, and for their help, guidance, and expertise as we wended our way through our maiden voyage in the book publishing world. Last, but certainly not least, we would like to thank our families—Mike's wife Lisa and his children Lauren and Jack, and Tim's wife Sarah—for their support throughout this process, and their tolerance with the substantial time and occasional absences that this book necessitated. Finally, Tim would like to thank his late dog Annie, the best companion a guy could ever have, who survived cancer long enough to see the full manuscript submitted to the publisher. I miss you.

Mike Barnett
Tim Pollock

August, 2011

CONTENTS

LIST OF FIGURES

LIST OF TABLES

SUMMARIES OF CORE LITERATURE

LIST OF CONTRIBUTORS

Nick Adams is Vice President of Corporate Branding at Novo Nordisk A/S. Nick is a brand and marketing strategist with extensive experience in international brand development and implementation. Before joining Novo Nordisk, he spent a decade as a brand consultant working extensively with healthcare, manufacturing and FMCG brands. As Head of Corporate Branding at Novo Nordisk, Nick is responsible for global brand strategy, reputation management, corporate campaigns, digital communications and brand identity. Nick is a graduate of the University of Humberside and an Executive Master of Corporate Communications from Copenhagen Business School.

Michael L. Barnett is Professor and Vice Dean for Academic Programs at Rutgers Business School. Mike's research focuses on the firm-stakeholder interface. In particular, he studies how firms individually and collectively manage their relationships with stakeholders, and how their efforts at stakeholder management influence their reputations and financial performance. Mike's scholarship has won numerous honors, to include the 2008 Academy of Management Journal Best Paper Prize and the 2006 Best Article Award from the International Association for Business & Society. Mike serves on the editorial boards of *Academy of Management Journal, Academy of Management Review, Academy of Management Perspectives, Business & Society, Long Range Planning,* and *Strategic Management Journal.*

David N. Barron is Rhodes Trust Reader in Organizational Sociology at the Saïd Business School, University of Oxford, and a Fellow of Jesus College, Oxford. His research interests include organization theory, health care management, quantitative research methods, and corporate reputation. He has published widely in leading sociological and health care management journals and presented his work at numerous international conferences.

Stephen Brammer is Professor of Strategy and Director of Faculty at Birmingham Business School. His research explores firm-stakeholder relationships, the strategic management of these, and the impacts of these upon company performance and reputation. His research has been widely published in leading journals such as the *Strategic Management Journal, Journal of Management Studies,* and *Organisation Studies.* He is a member of the Academy of Management and has served as the President of the International Association for Business and Society.

Jay Inghwee Chok is Assistant Professor of Strategy and Entrepreneurship at the Keck Graduate Institute, Claremont Colleges. His research interests lie at the intersection of the sociology of professions, academic entrepreneurship, and network strategy.

Cynthia E. Devers is an Associate Professor of Strategic Management in the Broad College of Business at Michigan State University. She is also an Associate Editor of *Academy of Management Review* and a Fellow at the University of Oxford's Centre for Corporate Reputation. In her research, she draws on behavioral decision and social psychological perspectives to examine the roles formal and informal governance mechanisms and social evaluations play in individual perceptions, and in individual, group, and organizational behavior and outcomes.

Grahame R. Dowling, after a 30-year career at the University of New South Wales, first at the Australian Graduate School of Management, and then after its dissolution at the Australian School of Business, was made an Emeritus Professor on his retirement in 2009. He currently has a part-time appointment in the Faculty of Business at the University of Technology, Sydney. Since his retirement Grahame has remained an active researcher.

Kimberly D. Elsbach is Professor of Management and Stephen G. Newberry Chair in Leadership at the Graduate School of Management, University of California, Davis. She received her Ph.D. in Industrial Engineering from Stanford University. Kim's research focuses on perception—specifically how people perceive each other and their organizations. She has studied these perceptual processes in a variety of contexts ranging from the California cattle industry, and the National Rifle Association, to Hollywood screenwriters. She is currently studying how crying at work affects images of professional women and why fans identify with NASCAR.

Charles J. Fombrun is Chairman of the Reputation Institute, a global research and consulting firm specializing in the development and management of reputational assets. Dr Fombrun is a former Professor of Management at the Wharton School (1979–84) and at New York University's Stern School of Business (1984–2004). He is the author of six books, including the pioneering *Reputation: Realizing Value from the Corporate Image* (1996) and *Fame and Fortune: How Global Companies Create Value from Reputation* (2004). Dr Fombrun has also written hundreds of articles and chapters in academic and practitioner publications and is the creator of reputation management systems used by many of the world's largest companies.

Peter O. Foreman is Associate Professor of Management at Illinois State University. His research interests are in organizational identity, image, and reputation, with a particular focus on multiple identity organizations and the management of identity complexity and conflict. His work has examined these topics in a range of organizational settings, including rural cooperatives, health care systems, sporting events, universities, and insurance companies. His most current research explores the temporally related issues of identity construction, maintenance, and change.

Naomi A. Gardberg is a tenured Associate Professor in the Department of Management, Baruch College—City University of New York. She earned her Ph.D. from New York

University. Dr Gardberg's research interest is in nonmarket competition and the creation, transfer, and dissipation of intangible assets, such as corporate reputation. Her work in these areas has been published in the field's major journals, such as *Academy of Management Review, Business & Society* and the *Journal of International Business Studies*. She also has several cases to her credit.

Sharon Gilad is a Senior Lecturer at the Department of Political Science and the Federman School of Public Policy at the Hebrew University of Jerusalem. Her research contributes a New Institutional perspective to the analysis of regulatory agencies' interaction with their multiple audiences, and of firms' responses to regulation.

Scott D. Graffin is Assistant Professor at the Terry College of Business at the University of Georgia. He received his Ph.D. in strategic management from the University of Wisconsin, Madison. His research interests include corporate governance, and the impact of reputation, status, and the financial press on organization outcomes. Scott's research has been published in the *Strategic Management Journal*, the *Academy of Management Journal, Organization Science, Strategic Organization*, and other outlets.

William S. Harvey is a Senior Lecturer at the University of Exeter Business School, an Associate Fellow in the Centre for Corporate Reputation at the University of Oxford and an Honorary Senior Lecturer at the University of Sydney. Will's research focuses on three areas. First, on how reputation is built and sustained within professional service firms. Second, on the mobility, economic impact and social networks of highly skilled migrants. Third, on some of the methodological, fieldwork and practical challenges with interviewing elite business professionals. Will has published in a range of journals in business and management, sociology, geography and industrial relations including: *Journal of Management Development, Work and Occupations, Employee Relations, Population, Space and Place, Qualitative Research, Global Networks, Asian Population Studies* and *Geoforum*. He has also recently co-edited a book with Cambridge University Press on International Human Resource Management.

Mary Jo Hatch works freelance as an organizational theorist, having formally retired from academia in 2007, but acts as visiting professor at Copenhagen Business School and Gothenburg University for some months of each year. She writes and lectures on branding (from an organizational point of view), organizational culture and identity, and on art and design in organizations, and does consulting. She spends the rest of her time writing and painting on Boston's North Shore. Check out her most recent book *Organizations: A Very Short Introduction* (2011) from Oxford University Press.

Michael W. Hill is a Ph.D. student at the Terry College of Business at the University of Georgia. He studies strategic management and his research interests include intangible assets, top management teams, and boards of directors.

Paul Ingram is the Kravis Professor of Business at the Columbia Business School, and Faculty Director of the Columbia Senior Executive Program. His Ph.D. is from Cornell

University, and he was on the faculty of Carnegie Mellon University before coming to Columbia. He has served as a consulting editor for the *American Journal of Sociology*, a senior editor for *Organization Science*, an associate editor for *Management Science*, and on the editorial boards of *Administrative Science Quarterly* and *Strategic Organization*.

Gregory Jackson is Professor of Management at the Freie Universität Berlin and chief editor of *Socio-Economic Review*. His research examines how corporate governance is influenced by diverse organizational and institutional contexts. His comparative studies have focused on Germany, Japan, the UK, and the US, and integrated disparate fields of scholarship, including institutional theory, international business, economic sociology, and comparative political economy. His current projects look at corporate responsibility in different countries, and apply qualitative comparative analysis (QCA) to understanding organizational configurations.

Michael Jensen is Associate Professor at the University of Michigan, Ross School of Business. His main research focuses on the role of social structures and dynamics in markets, and his current projects include work on identity and status.

Jonathan M. Karpoff is the Washington Mutual Endowed Chair in Innovation and Professor of Finance at the University of Washington. Jon's research seeks to understand how Adam Smith's Invisible Hand works, or does not work, to coordinate economic activities ranging from fisheries management to Arctic exploration to corporate governance. Jon teaches and seeks to inspire Executive, MBA, and Ph.D. finance students. He also serves as associate editor for several research journals, is past president of The Financial Management Association, and past director of the Univeristy of Washington's CFO Forum and Environmental Management Program.

Mark Thomas Kennedy is Assistant Professor of Strategy in the Department of Management and Organizations at University of Southern California's Marshall School of Business. His research focuses on the emergence of new organizational phenomena— categories, identities, forms, strategies, practices, reputation criteria, and so on—with particular attention to meaning construction processes.

Bo Kyung Kim is Assistant Professor at, Edwin L. Cox School of Business, Southern Methodist University. Her current research focuses on market identity and social structure, with emphasis on the interaction between them over time.

Heeyon Kim is Assistant Professor at the National University of Singapore Business School (starting summer of 2014). Her research interests are in the areas of organizational identity and status, with current projects focusing on the mobility of status and identity. She received her Ph.D. from the University of Michigan, Ross School of Business.

Tohyun Kim is Assistant Professor at the SKKU Business School, Sungkyunkwan University. His research interests include organizational learning, organizational identity, social networks, and institutional logics. His recent publication appeared in

Strategic Organization. He received his Ph.D. from the Shidler College of Business at the University of Hawaii.

Jingfang Liu is a Ph.D. candidate at the Annenberg School for Communication and Journalism at the University of Southern California. Her research lies at the intersection of information technology innovation, sustainability, as well as organizational change and communication. She has complementary interests in corporate social responsibility, environmental communication, new media and technology for social change, international business and global communication, and critical theory.

Alison Mackey is Assistant Professor of Management at the Orfalea College of Business at California Polytechnic State University. Her research is related to executive labor markets, executive compensation, and corporate social responsibility. Her research has been published in *Academy of Management Review*, the *Strategic Management Journal*, and *Business & Society*. She received the Wiley Blackwell Outstanding Dissertation award from the Academy of Management. She serves on the editorial boards at the *Strategic Management Journal* and *Journal of Management*. She earned her Ph.D. from the Ohio State University.

Luis L. Martins is Associate Professor of Management at the McCombs School of Business, the University of Texas at Austin. He received a Ph.D. in Management and Organizational Behavior from the Stern School of Business, New York University. His research interests include identity processes in organizations, managerial cognition, and organizational change.

Christopher McKenna is University Reader in Business History and Strategy at the Saïd Business School, a Fellow of Brasenose College, and an Academic Programme Director in the Centre for Corporate Reputation, all within the University of Oxford. His research focuses on the historical development and evolving strategies of professional firms and their role in the global transformation of business, nonprofits, and the state. He is currently researching the international history of white-collar crime.

Yuri Mishina is Assistant Professor of Organisational Behaviour/Strategy at Imperial College London. He received his Ph.D. from the University of Illinois at Urbana-Champaign. His work has been published in the *Academy of Management Journal, Organization Science*, and the *Strategic Management Journal*, and his research examines how top management team and stakeholder belief systems, including reputations, stigma, expectations, and cognitive biases, influence a firm's strategic choices and outcomes.

Timothy Morris is Professor of Management Studies at the University of Oxford and a Programme Director in the Centre for Corporate Reputation. His current work on reputation focuses on the processes of reputation production and maintenance in consulting firms and links to his interests in innovation, change, and decision-making in professional service firms. Timothy's research has been published in journals such as the *Academy of Management Journal, Journal of Management Studies*, and *Organization Studies*.

William Newburry is Associate Professor and SunTrust Bank Professor at Florida International University in the Department of Management and International Business. He received his Ph.D. from the University of New York in 2000. His current research examines how foreign subsidiaries, their current and potential employees, and other local stakeholders perceive issues related to firm globalization, such as firm reputation. He has published over 25 papers in top-tier, peer-reviewed journals, such as the *Journal of International Business Studies, Strategic Management Journal*, and *Journal of Management Studies*, among others.

Thomas Noe is the Ernest Butten Professor of Management Studies at the Saïd Business School and a Professorial Fellow at Balliol College, University of Oxford. He received his Ph.D. from the University of Texas at Austin. Professor Noe's research has focused on developing and experimentally validating rational choice models of financing, investment, governance, and management compensation. His current research focuses on the role of learning in executive compensation determination, the inherent limitations of shareholder democracy, and the role of intra-family altruism in family firm governance. He has served or is serving on numerous panels, program committees, and editorial boards, including for the *Review of Financial Studies* and the *Review of Corporate Finance Studies*.

Rowena Olegario is the author of *A Culture of Credit: Embedding Trust and Transparency in American Business* (2006). She is co-author (with Davis Dyer and Frederick Dalzell) of *Rising Tide: Lessons from 165 Years of Brand Building at Procter & Gamble* (2004). She is currently writing a history of business and household credit in the United States. Olegario is a Senior Research Fellow at the Oxford University Centre for Corporate Reputation. She is also the Research Coordinator of the Centre.

Antoaneta P. Petkova is Associate Professor of Management and Organization at San Francisco State University, California. She earned her doctorate in strategic management from the University of Maryland—College Park in 2006. Her current research focuses on the processes of reputation accumulation by young organizations and the role of reputation for increasing organizational innovation and entrepreneurship.

Michael D. Pfarrer is Associate Professor at the Terry College of Business at the University of Georgia. He received his Ph.D. in strategic management from the University of Maryland. His research focuses on external perceptions of firm behaviors and how firms manage these interpretations to create value. His specific interests include positive and negative social evaluations (e.g., firm celebrity, legitimacy, reputation, and stigma), impression and crisis management, media accounts, and the role of business in society.

Timothy G. Pollock is the Farrell Professor of Entrepreneurship in the Smeal College of Business at Penn State University. His research focuses on the social construction of value in uncertain and ambiguous circumstances, particularly the contexts of corporate governance, executive compensation, and entrepreneurial market environments. He has published articles in all the major management journals and his research has won numerous awards, most recently receiving the Oxford University Centre for Corporate Reputation's Award for Best Published Article in 2010. Tim has recently completed his term as an Associate Editor for the *Academy of Management Journal*, has served on numerous editorial boards and the executive committees of the Organization Science Division of INFORMS and the OMT Division of the Academy of Management, and is an International Research Fellow of the Oxford Centre for Corporate Reputation.

Mooweon Rhee is the Hyundai Motor Company and YSB Research Chair Professor and Professor of Management at the School of Business, Yonsei University in Korea. His research interests revolve around organization learning, corporate reputation, and social networks. He is also interested in constructing Asia-based theories of organizations. In 2009 he was selected as an Ascendant Scholar by the Western Academy of Management. He obtained his Ph.D. from the Stanford Graduate School of Business.

Violina P. Rindova is the Ralph B. Thomas Professor of Business at the McCombs School of Business, University of Texas at Austin and a Fellow of the IC² Institute of the University of Texas at Austin. She received a JD from Sofia University, Bulgaria, an MBA from Madrid Business School—University of Houston, Spain, and a Ph.D. from The Stern School of Business, New York University. Her research focuses on value creation, intangible assets, and the dynamics of competitive advantage in a variety of industries.

Meredith Rolfe held a Nuffield College Postdoctoral Prize Research Fellowship before joining Saïd Business School (University of Oxford) as Senior Research Fellow. Her Ph.D. was earned at the University of Chicago. She was an invited contributor to the *Oxford Handbook of Analytical Sociology*, and has been awarded grants by the National Science Foundation, British Academy, Oxford University Press John Fell Fund, the EU-sponsored EQUALSOC Framework, and the Oxford University Centre for Corporation Reputation. Her dissertation received the Mancur Olson Award from the APSA Political Economy section.

Majken Schultz is Professor at Copenhagen Business School, senior advisor at The Reputation Institute, and International Research Fellow at Oxford University Centre for Corporate Reputation. Her research interests are located at the interfaces between organizational culture, organizational identity and image, corporate branding, and reputation. Majken has published more than 50 articles in international journals and written multiple books on these topics. She serves on several company boards, the Board of Governors for the Academy of Management, and is a regular columnist in the local newspapers.

David A. Whetten is the Jack Wheatley Professor of Organizational Studies and Director of the Faculty Development Center at Brigham Young University, Provo, Utah,

US. He received his Ph.D. from Cornell. His recent scholarship has focused on organizational identity and identification, theory development, and management education. He has served as president of the Academy of Management and as editor of the *Foundations for Organizational Science*, an academic book series, and the *Academy of Management Review*.

Richard Whittington is Professor of Strategic Management at the Saïd Business School and Millman Fellow at New College, University of Oxford. His main research interest is in strategy-as-practice, with projects on strategy communications and the history of strategic planning. He has authored or co-authored nine books, including *Exploring Strategy* (9th edition, 2010), *Strategy as Practice: Research Directions and Resources* (2007), and *The European Corporation* (2000). He has published articles in leading journals such as the *Journal of Management Studies, Organization Science, Organization Studies*, and the *Strategic Management Journal*. He has held visiting or full positions at the Harvard Business School, Imperial College, the University of Toulouse, and the University of Warwick.

Basak Yakis-Douglas is Lecturer of Management at New College and Research Fellow at the Centre for Corporate Reputation at Saïd Business School, University of Oxford. Her main research interests are in corporate reputation and building a "practice" perspective on strategy. Her ongoing projects on corporate reputation focus on how corporations build, manage, or destroy their reputations through the external formal communication of their strategies. Regarding strategy as practice, her main project from within this perspective is on the evolution of strategy practice. She is a regular contributor to main strategy textbooks including *Exploring Strategy: Text and Cases*.

Tamar Yogev is Lecturer at The Faculty of Management, University of Haifa. She is Associate Fellow of the Said Business School, University of Oxford and Associate Member of Nuffield College, University of Oxford. Her Ph.D. was earned at the University of Oxford. Tamar's main research interests include economic sociology, organization studies, social networks, and sociology of culture and art. Her research has been published in journals such as *Socio-Economic Review, Social Networks and The American Journal of Epidemiology*. She is a contributor to various books, and has been awarded a grant by the Oxford Centre for Corporate Reputation.

Lori Qingyuan Yue is Assistant Professor at the USC Marshall School of Business. She received her Ph.D. in business administration from Columbia University. She studies evolutions of market institutions and market structures. Her recent research topics include the endogenous institutional failure in generating market dynamics, the incomplete information model in private politics, and the asymmetric effects of fashions on the formation and dissolution of interorganizational networks. Her research has been published in journals such as *American Journal of Sociology, American Sociological Review*, and *Organization Science*.

CHAPTER 1

··

CHARTING THE LANDSCAPE OF CORPORATE REPUTATION RESEARCH

··

MICHAEL L. BARNETT
TIMOTHY G. POLLOCK

In this chapter we discuss the motivation behind the *Handbook* and why the timing is right for such a compendium. We also explain how the book is organized and to be used, offer brief summaries of the chapters, and discuss the future directions corporate reputation research can take.

WHAT does it mean to have a "good" or "bad" reputation? How does it create or destroy value, or shape chances to pursue particular opportunities? Where do reputations come from? How do we measure them? How do we build and manage them?

Over the last twenty years the answers to these questions have become increasingly important—and increasingly problematic—for scholars and practitioners seeking to understand the creation, management, and role of reputation in corporate life. As documented by Fombrun in this volume (Chapter 5), there has been an explosion of interest in both the scholarly literature and popular press in corporate reputation. Various reputation rankings by business press publications have emerged to parse, order, and rate corporations both generally (e.g., *Fortune*'s rankings of "America's (now the World's) Most Admired Companies") and based on their reputations for different things with different stakeholder groups (e.g., *Fortune*'s "Best Places to Work" and *Businessweek*'s "Most Innovative Companies"). Scholars have used many of these measures, as well as created new measures of their own, to understand what corporate reputation is, where it comes from, and to offer guidance to practitioners about how best to manage it to create value for their companies (see Dowling & Gardberg, Chapter 3, this volume). *Corporate Reputation Review*, a journal founded solely to promote scholarship on corporate reputation, is entering its fifteenth year of publication as of the printing of this book, and Oxford University has a research center dedicated to the production and dissemination of knowledge about corporate reputation.

At the same time, this explosion of interest has also spawned a thicket of problems. Different definitions of corporate reputation have proliferated (see Barnett, Jermier, & Lafferty, 2006; King & Whetten, 2008; Lange, Lee, & Dai, 2011; and Rindova et al., 2005 for recent reviews); distinct theoretical constructs such as image, identity, brand, status, and legitimacy have been either conflated with reputation or treated synonymously; and a plethora of measures—many of dubious quality, or which have also been used to operationalize different constructs—have been used to operationalize corporate reputation. Indeed, even the nature of what constitutes a corporate reputation, whether or not it is an asset of the firm, who creates it, and who controls it, have all been open for debate (Pfarrer, Pollock, & Rindova, 2010).

Given the concomitant levels of interest in and confusion about corporate reputation, it seemed a good time to write this *Handbook*, which is intended to bring definitional clarity to these issues, chronicle where we have been, and offer guidance about where scholarship on corporate reputation might most profitably head. The eminent scholars from a variety of disciplines who have contributed to this *Handbook* provide state-of-the-art definitions of corporate reputation; differentiate reputation from other constructs and intangible assets; offer guidance on measuring reputation; consider the role of reputation as a corporate asset and how a variety of factors, including stage of life, nation of origin, and the stakeholders considered affect its ability to create value; and explore corporate reputation's role more broadly as a regulatory mechanism. Finally, they also discuss how to manage and grow reputations, as well as repair them when they are damaged. In discussing these issues we hope this *Handbook* moves the field of corporate reputation research forward by demonstrating where the field is now, addressing some of the perpetual problems of definition and differentiation, identifying areas that have been resolved and so do not need more research, and suggesting future research directions that have gone unconsidered, are under-considered, or that require continued attention.

In the remainder of this chapter we identify and discuss the four overarching questions that have been used to structure the *Handbook*, identify points of consensus across chapters, points of controversy that merit continued exploration, and the unanswered questions that can inspire and guide future research on corporate reputation.

THE STRUCTURE OF THE *HANDBOOK*

A handbook is a reference resource. Our intent is that researchers and thoughtful practitioners be able to pick up this *Handbook* and quickly find the information they seek. Each chapter addresses a specific topic that can be discerned easily from its title and abstract. Each chapter contains a table that lists the references and core contributions of a handful of the most influential studies in the relevant literature. And each chapter outlines questions that remain open within this particular literature and suggests means of addressing them. Thus, each chapter provides both a robust sense of the current state of the literature and a clear path forward for contributing to its development.

Of course, reputation is a diverse topic with many intertwined levels, disciplines, and theoretical perspectives. Any single chapter will not provide the entire picture. We encourage you to read the *Handbook* cover to cover to obtain a full appreciation of this diversity. Should you not have this luxury, however, please note that the chapters are arranged to correspond with four fundamental questions: (1) What is corporate reputation?; (2) What *isn't* corporate reputation?; (3) Why is corporate reputation important?; and (4) How can corporate reputation be managed?

The first two questions are fundamental to developing theoretical and empirical understandings of the corporate reputation construct, the role it plays in organizational life, and how to measure it effectively. These questions push us to understand the key dimensions of corporate reputation and how they differ from the dimensions of other, related constructs such as status, image, identity, celebrity, legitimacy, and brand. Along with corporate reputation, these constructs are all part of the class of intangible assets identified as "social approval assets," because they "derive their value from favorable collective perceptions" (Pfarrer, Pollock, & Rindova, 2010: 1131). They also allow us to differentiate between a bad reputation and stigma (Devers et al., 2009; Pozner, 2008; Wiesenfeld, Wurthmann, & Hambrick, 2008), and to differentiate between the reputation of the organization and the reputations of the organization's executives, its industry, and the nation in which it is domiciled.

The first two questions are also fundamental to answering the second two questions, because if you do not know what corporate reputation is and how it is different from other social approval assets, then it is difficult to assess its importance and role, or understand how to manage it effectively. These latter two questions are also important to scholars who wish to understand the broader role of reputation at the industry and field levels of analysis, and its role—and limitations—as a regulatory mechanism in markets. These questions are also valuable to those who want to understand the processes through which reputation is built, managed, and repaired. They are also of considerable interest to thoughtful practitioners who want to better understand the implications and value of their corporations' reputations, and how to manage them more effectively.

Below, we address each of these questions in more detail, and briefly describe how the associated chapters in this *Handbook* help to answer them.

WHAT IS CORPORATE REPUTATION?

Though there has been a sharp spike in studies of corporate reputation in recent years, the spike in cumulative understanding of corporate reputation has been, well, less sharp. There is no stronger prescription for blunted research progress than poor construct clarity. It is impossible to build on the work of others if you are working from a completely different blueprint. Yet researchers have, sometimes explicitly but often implicitly, used differing conceptualizations of corporate reputation in their studies. To move forward we need a clear understanding of what each of us means when we say we are studying corporate reputation. This does not mean that all of us must agree on a single definition. This *Handbook* is not intended to impose a standard on the field. But it does mean that researchers need to be explicit about how they conceptualize reputation, and cognizant of how their conceptualization compares and contrasts with that of others. Else, we will remain stuck in the trap of creating isolated islands of partial insights.

Rindova and Martins (Chapter 2) jumpstart the *Handbook* by explicating the features of corporate reputation that make it an intangible asset. Firms often claim their reputations are one of their most, if not *the* most, valued of assets. But what makes reputation such a valued asset? Rindova and Martins develop a multidimensional conceptualization that combines the insights of game-theoretic, social constructionist, and institutional perspectives regarding the ways in which observers perceive firms' signals, prominence, and standing to identify four dimensions of corporate reputation that make it an intangible asset: specificity, accumulation, breadth of appeal, and codification. The resulting model provides a framework that can aid in measuring a firm's valuable reputational assets, though the task is not an easy one, as Chapter 2 attests.

Researchers have been known to adopt measures of corporate reputation based more on data availability than on fit with the underlying construct. While trying to perfectly measure reputation may be a Sisyphean task given its intangible and multidimensional nature, it is important that we come as close as possible, because what gets measured gets done. If the wrong things are measured, then scholars may provide a faulty understanding of what reputation is and how it creates value, and firms may do the wrong things as they try to build and protect this valuable intangible asset.

Dowling and Gardberg (Chapter 3) take a close look at extant measures of corporate reputation and find them both varied and lacking in construct validity. They review ten measures that have been used in prior studies, sorting them according to unit of measurement (individuals or firms) and data source (primary or secondary), and list their strengths and weaknesses relative to ten specific measurement challenges. They further list seven recommendations for those who seek to create new measures of corporate reputation. Of course, no perfect measure can be developed. All measures entail trade-offs, so Dowling and Gardberg recommend triangulation by using more than one measure to capture the multidimensional nature of reputation. To help with this, they provide a comprehensive and exhaustive appendix of reputation measures from around the world.

Dowling and Gardberg conclude their chapter by identifying two trends—advances in technology and "gamma change"—that will exert major influences on measurement in the years ahead. Technology makes it easier to access people and collect data in new and sophisticated ways, but it also brings biases that need to be considered. Gamma change is a change in the criteria by which observers evaluate firms. As the criteria used to assess firms change, so do perceptions of how well or poorly they perform. Thus, a highly regarded firm of yesteryear may be viewed as a menace by contemporary standards, even if its behaviors have not materially changed. For example, firms' social and environmental practices are now more closely scrutinized, leading to new and more sophisticated measures of these practices, and scandals in accounting and banking have led to increased monitoring of corporate governance and transparency. The next chapter describes the process by which these new criteria arise and become part of how observers assess a firm's reputation.

Kennedy, Chock, and Liu (Chapter 4) adopt a social constructionist perspective to explain how critics and corporations engage in competition and contestation to converge on a common set of criteria to judge corporations. They analyze the content of corporate press releases and contrast it with the content of media coverage to show how corporate environmental responsibility criteria emerged and were challenged, influenced, and finally embraced by corporations. Kennedy et al. make the interesting observation that firms can act to create the scorecard by which they are assessed, rather than acting only to influence their score. They describe a theoretical approach and methodology that can be used to assess not only how reputation criteria emerge, but also how they fade away.

Fombrun (Chapter 5) takes on a different type of contestation—that of construct definition among reputation scholars—and seeks to find a common ground, as well. He reviews the various definitions that scholars have used in approaching corporate reputation from the vantage of some seven different conceptual frameworks. He notes a variety of shortcomings in these definitions, including the muddling of antecedents and consequences with the construct itself, and suggests a new definition that is narrower and deeper in focus because, he argues, reputation needs to be defined in terms of both a specific stakeholder group and a specific reference group. To achieve this, Fombrun calls for researchers to interact more with practitioners on thick descriptions and contextualized case studies. This call is laudable, as such work will no doubt help dimensionalize reputation; at the same time it will present significant challenges for the development of large data sets that can be used to assess the generalizability of reputation's effects. As the next chapter highlights, there are trade-offs between the richness of description and the ability to model the mechanisms at work.

Noe (Chapter 6) explains how economists model a firm's reputation. He argues that reputation is based on the firm's past behavior, and it represents the stakeholder's assessment of the probability that a firm is of a particular type: the type that will behave opportunistically in future transactions or not. As new information is revealed through new behaviors and stakeholders become more certain about the type of firm they are dealing with, they become more or less willing to engage in transactions with the firm under more or less favorable conditions. Noe argues that though economic modeling requires simplifying assumptions that are violated in reality, the predictions of these models are nonetheless often accurate. Further, Noe suggests a path forward wherein the beneficial rigor of economic modeling can be retained while the richness of the models are enhanced, so long as researchers are willing to pay the "tariff" inherent in increasing the sophistication and complication of their models. Noe encourages incorporation of the accumulating insights from the management and psychology literatures into economic models to further reduce the gap between economic conceptualization and managerial reality regarding the management of corporate reputation.

Of course, economic activity is embedded in a social context (Granovetter, 1985). In Chapter 7, Jensen, Kim, and Kim account for the social context missing in purely economic theorizing. They put forth a role-theoretic perspective of corporate reputation, arguing that stakeholders interpret a firm's behavior in light of the role that the firm is expected to play given its status in a particular social context. Meeting role expectations is the key inflection point from which positive or negative reputations are formed. Stakeholders may expect different things of different firms, and so the same type of behavior can produce different reputational consequences for different organizations. This helps explain, for example, the extra burden that high-status firms may face; stakeholders have higher expectations of them than they do of lower-status firms and so they must do more to simply meet expectations and so maintain a favorable reputation.

In developing their arguments Jensen et al. draw on the concept of status, one of several constructs that many have conflated with corporate reputation. Thus, this chapter provides a bridge to this *Handbook*'s second organizing question: What *isn't* corporate reputation?

What *isn't* Corporate Reputation?

Status often is conflated with reputation because both constructs deal with how observers assess a firm's characteristics and form expectations of its likely future behaviors. But, as Barron and Rolfe (Chapter 8) point out, they differ in terms of how these assessments and expectations are formed. Reputation is commonly viewed as arising from observation of a firm's behaviors, while status is commonly viewed as arising from observation of a firm's affiliations. That is, status can be untethered from behavior, and may be deemed an unearned privilege based on the company one keeps. As Jensen et al. point out, status can bring burdens, but as Barron and Rolfe identify here, it can also be a boon. They further note that though there is a clear conceptual distinction to be made, these two constructs may be indistinguishable in certain settings, such as for new firms with no performance history. They may also be used in tandem, such as with customers who might use status as an initial screen (I want a car of a certain status) and then reputation to choose within a status grouping (I want the high-status car that has the best performance record) (cf. Jensen & Roy, 2008). Thus, they call for more research that simultaneously employs measures of both reputation and status to distinguish the underlying cognitive mechanisms by which stakeholders assess firms.

Foreman, Whetten, and Mackey (Chapter 9) take on the formidable task of distinguishing reputation from image and legitimacy. Image and legitimacy are common constructs that are open to numerous conceptualizations, some more muddled with reputation than others. Foreman et al. describe the distinctions and interrelationships amongst them from an identity-based view. An organization's identity is composed of its central, enduring, and distinctive characteristics (Albert & Whetten, 1985). Image, then, may be viewed as stakeholder perceptions of an organization's identity, and legitimacy as the appropriateness of this identity within some social system. They extend the identity view to stakeholders as well as organizations in order to flesh out their conceptualization of reputation. Stakeholders also have identities and these shape what they expect of a firm and influence how they attend to and perceive a firm's actions.

Mishina and Devers (Chapter 10) untangle corporate reputation from a construct that is a relatively new entrant to the business literature: stigma. Stigmas have been associated with individuals for a long while, but this concept has only been adapted to organizations in recent years. Mishina and Devers note that though stigma can easily be confused with a bad reputation, the two constructs arise in different ways and have different effects on organizations. Whereas reputation is multidimensional, stigma is one-dimensional, permeating the entire organization and stripping it of its unique characteristics such that the firm is "tainted" in its totality. Further, societal expectations, not a history of performance, determine who is and is not stigmatized. Thus, stigma is a label used as a form of social control, as opposed to a tool providing the ability to predict how a firm will behave. Differentiating between stigma and a bad reputation can have a bearing on the reversibility of a negative event, or lack thereof, described by Noe (Chapter 6), and to the role of expectations articulated by Jensen et al. (Chapter 7). Given the relative novelty of work in this area, there remains quite fertile ground for further research sorting out the nature, causes, and consequences of stigma.

Graffin, Pfarrer, and Hill (Chapter 11) shift the focus of attention inward, and aim to separate the man (typically) from the monolith by identifying the boundaries and inter-relationships between executive and corporate reputation. As the visible face of the organization, an executive's reputation can be closely associated with or subsumed within the firm's reputation. Indeed, as Graffin et al. note, executive and firm reputations tend to move in tandem, converging and co-evolving over time. An executive's reputation also serves a similar purpose to that of a firm's reputation by providing stakeholders with a guide to predict the individual's behavior. And like a firm's reputation, an executive's reputation can serve as a valuable intangible asset. However, there are significant differences. Graffin et al. suggest these differences become most apparent when shocks occur that decouple executive and firm reputations. Moreover, there are many interesting issues regarding who captures the rents from firm and executive reputations, as well as the potential for celebrity CEOs to generate negative firm performance. Overall, this area of research on reputation remains in its infancy and so Graffin et al. outline a variety of opportunities for scholars to advance it.

Newburry (Chapter 12) reverses course and shifts the level of analysis well beyond the firm, to that of the country. Newburry notes that whereas the effects of country of origin (COO) on consumer perceptions of products have been studied extensively, COO's influence on a firm's overall reputation has not received much attention, although COO can serve as a simplifying heuristic that affects a firm's reputation. Consider the differing assessments a stakeholder might make of a manufacturing firm located in China versus Germany, irrespective of the actual manufacturing operations in place. Newburry suggests, though, that when stakeholders have more specific knowledge of a firm's characteristics and behaviors, the effects of COO may be diminished. Thus, a key issue is when will stakeholders search beyond country effects to assess individual firm behavior, and when will they just rely on COO as a convenient reputational heuristic? Indeed, Newburry points out that the heuristic can be even broader than country, using even more general classifications such as "developing countries" to group multiple nations together. Thus, COO can stigmatize firms from certain regions (cf. Mishina and Devers, Chapter 10), while yielding benefits to those from higher-status classifications (cf. Jensen, Kim, and Kim, Chapter 7, and Barron and Rolfe, Chapter 8). Whatever the case, it seems that the residents of a country are poor judges of how others view their country, which is an interesting identity versus image puzzle to sort out. Further, Newburry calls for longitudinal work to explore the recursive relationship between firm and country reputation, and how they mutually influence each other over time.

Surely there are many other things that are *not* reputation but have been confounded with reputation, but the chapters in this section address the most common confounds. Having brought a bit more breathing room and clarity to our core construct, in the next section of the *Handbook* we tackle the question: Why is corporate reputation important?

Why is Corporate Reputation Important?

The chapters in the *Handbook* addressing this question argue that reputation is important because it facilitates economic transactions where markets might otherwise fail by providing incentives for firms to behave in certain predictable ways. As such, it functions as a form of non-governmental regulation. Firms regulate their behaviors because they recognize that there are financial, social, and even psychological penalties that accrue to the executives, firm, and/or industry that exceed any potential benefit from behaving in unconstrained ways. But how and how well does this self-regulatory mechanism work?

McKenna and Olegario (Chapter 13) reach back in time to provide a historical perspective on how corporate reputation has been intertwined with, and even reliant upon, formal regulation, and how the nature of this relationship has oscillated over time. Skepticism of corporations has run high at various points in history, often on the heels of scandals. McKenna and Olegario argue that though reputation can bolster markets, stakeholders seem to have stronger beliefs in the power of regulators to secure their safety than they do in firms to self-regulate. Thus, firms have welcomed formal regulation from time to time to maintain public trust in enterprise. Reputation, although a less convincing means of forging trust with stakeholders, effectively functions to fill the gaps where formal regulation and direct interaction are lacking. McKenna and Olegario encourage scholars to take better account of historical circumstance when studying corporate reputation, to consider more fully the specific relationship between reputation and regulation during the period studied and how it might differ during other periods, and to treat this relationship as dynamic and evolving.

Yue and Ingram (Chapter 14) also use a historical example, the New York Clearing House Association, to address how firms rely on reputational solutions to fill the "institutional vacuum" left by lack of formal regulation, but they examine these dynamics at the industry level. Whereas Rindova and Martins (Chapter 2) started us off by delineating the intangible asset qualities of a *firm's* reputation, Yue and Ingram note that firms across an industry can share a common reputation, and the desire to protect this valuable *collective* intangible asset can shape how member firms behave and self-regulate. This "reputation commons" (Barnett & King, 2008) can be damaged by the actions of any individual member firm and requires cooperation across the industry to protect it. Commons are notoriously difficult to manage given the free-rider problem, but under certain conditions firms do come together to create industry-wide, self-regulatory institutions. Industry self-regulation has been criticized for being a country club, with enforcement that lacks teeth. However, as Yue and Ingram illustrate, industry self-regulation can also be an "iron fist." Yue and Ingram call for more research on the role and functioning of the reputation commons, and how industry self-regulatory programs can accomplish this yet not run afoul of antitrust laws.

Brammer and Jackson (Chapter 15) also note that reputation may substitute for formal regulation, but they further clarify that the relationship is more complicated than just substitution. Reputation is also interdependent with regulation because regulatory institutions shape what stakeholders expect of firms. These regulatory institutions vary across countries, with some countries having very involved and established regulatory regimes and others suffering institutional voids. Brammer and Jackson explore the implications of variation in country regulatory institutions for how firms manage their reputations. They urge researchers to attend more closely to cross-country differences and suggest a research agenda that takes a comparative institutional approach.

Gilad and Yogev (Chapter 16) flip the focus between regulators and the reputations of the regulated, and make the interesting observation that regulators also have reputations that they may struggle to manage. Gilad and Yogev question the assumption that formal regulation need be a strong form of regulation, and note that regulatory authority and ability can be called into question. Regulators must manage how they are perceived if they are to fulfill their duties effectively and survive. To avoid blame for ineffective regulation, regulators may seek to forge a narrow domain of responsibility, thereby limiting their exposure and responsibility for areas outside their direct expertise. This provides an interesting counterweight to the well-established idea of mission creep in bureaucratic organizations; cognizance of the dangers of being exposed to blame may serve as a brake on managerial tendencies toward empire building. Gilad and Yogev illustrate these dynamics through a study of the British Financial Ombudsman Service, and develop a framework for understanding how regulators manage their reputations across three broad spheres of task boundaries, communication, and operation.

While the preponderance of reputation research has focused on how corporate reputation affects customers, Harvey and Morris (Chapter 17) build on the notion that reputations can vary across different stakeholder groups, and highlight the importance of reputation in one particular domain—labor markets—especially as it applies to professional service firms. Firms vie for employee talent, and a firm's ability to attract and retain talent depends upon its reputation in the labor market. This is particularly true in professional service firms, where firm performance is directly attributable to the talent of the firm's labor force. As they explain, "employees can both create and evaluate the organization's reputation simultaneously." Thus, Harvey and Morris illustrate the need for ongoing research that considers how reputation differs across stakeholder groups, and the indirect effects that a firm's reputation with one set of stakeholders has on its reputation in other domains.

Karpoff (Chapter 18) wraps up this section by attempting to answer a fundamental question about the importance of reputation: Does it actually work to discipline firm misconduct? If firms do not lose or suffer damage to this valuable intangible asset when they behave badly, then its utility as a means of regulation is limited. Karpoff reviews the literature testing for reputational penalties in financial markets, and comes to the conclusion: sometimes reputation works to discipline misconduct, and sometimes it doesn't. Whether it does or does not work is contingent on who is harmed. He finds that penalties are imposed if the misconduct affects those with whom the offending firm has a business relationship, but not if the misconduct affects parties with whom the firm has no business relationship. For example, instances of financial misconduct tend to incur significant reputational penalties, whereas, "on average, the reputational loss from harming the environment is negligible."

Though not ethically appealing, these findings nonetheless provide a functional and realistic answer that brings into sharp focus the differing tasks performed by formal regulation and informal regulation through reputation. Reputation works as a regulatory mechanism in settings where the party harmed has a direct business relationship with the offending firm and can in turn do direct harm to its reputation; however, reputation does not regulate behavior that causes harm to those who cannot return the favor. But, as Karpoff notes, firms that harm non-transacting parties may still suffer significant *regulatory* penalties, even if they do not suffer reputational penalties. Thus, thoughtful, targeted government regulation is still required.

Karpoff provides evidence of the monetary costs of reputational damage. So how do you create this valuable asset, and how do you manage it and protect it thereafter? The final set of chapters address precisely this.

How can Corporate Reputation be Managed?

Petkova (Chapter 19) starts us off from ground zero, explaining how new firms, with limited or no history upon which observers can rely to make assessments, develop a reputation. She argues that new firms can develop a reputation via three mechanisms: (1) reputation borrowing, which ties to prior discussions of status (Chapters 7 and 8) as it is based on affiliation with others; (2) reputation building, which requires significant time and effort to create a performance history; and (3) reputation by endowment, which ties to prior discussions of how a firm's reputation is intertwined with that of its executives (Chapter 11). Petkova further argues that the process of creating a reputation occurs in three stages: (1) attention generation, in which the new firm develops a public profile; (2) uncertainty reduction, in which it explains its function—and, if necessary, that of its industry—to stakeholders; and (3) evaluation, in which it demonstrates the competence with which it fulfills its function. Thus, although the mechanisms employed by new firms can also be used, although perhaps to a lesser extent, by established firms, the process through which a new firm's reputation is created varies in both focus and kind from that of established companies.

In Chapter 20, Whittington and Yakis-Douglas note that when stakeholders evaluate a firm, new or old, they evaluate not just the way the firm has acted, but also the way it communicates these actions. That is, the process by which information about a firm is disclosed affects how that information is perceived, and thus the influence it has on the firm's reputation. Some firms and their managers are able to build trust and understanding with stakeholders through their "performances," while others, as a result of their manner of speaking, dress, body language, and other symbolic actions, breed distrust and misunderstanding. Yet these nonverbal aspects of communication and reputation management are often ignored. Whittington and Yakis-Douglas explore both the form and content of firms' communications, and note how variations in the skill with which firms communicate their strategies influence a firm's reputation. They recommend corporate reputation research be enriched by more study of the practice and praxis of strategy communications through such methods as discourse analysis and dramaturgy.

Schultz, Hatch, and Adams (Chapter 21) continue the focus on symbolic management by explicating the role of corporate branding in managing corporate reputation, using Novo Nordisk as a case study. Brand and reputation are often conflated, although they are distinct constructs. Schultz et al. distinguish between these constructs, not just in terms of who on the organizational chart is responsible for them (e.g., marketing vs. PR or corporate communications), but in their processes and in their distinctive yet intertwined aims. They argue that branding is more of an affective reaction to the various aspects of a firm, rather than an assessment of the firm's past behaviors, and that these affective responses arise from interacting with the symbols and practices associated with the products and/or services provided. Because it is about meaning making and experiences, managing the corporate brand entails a process of co-creation with stakeholders that Schultz et al. illustrate through the Novo Nordisk example. They further make the case that, although they are distinct constructs, firms can manage their reputation by managing their brand. This interdependent relationship between brand and reputation is moderated by management practices, and they urge future research on corporate reputation management to consider brand management as an important part of the process.

Rhee and Kim (Chapter 22) tackle perhaps the most awkward phase of reputation management, that of repairing a damaged reputation. Whereas Noe (Chapter 6) recognized economic models' unrealistic limiting assumption that reputation is not recoverable, Rhee and Kim describe the process by which firms attempt to repair their reputations. They develop a model embedded in the behavioral theory of the firm (Cyert & March, 1963) that explains how firms recognize that a problem exists and then search for and implement a solution. The specific characteristics of the problem, the organization, and stakeholders shape how this process unfolds. They recognize that depending upon how these factors play out, this process can go astray in such a way that a firm may implement an ineffective, superficial solution to the problem.

Elsbach (Chapter 23) closes out the *Handbook* by bringing temporality to reputation management, looking beyond how firms respond to the reputational challenges brought about by a single event to examine the process by which firms manage reputation-affecting events that are both anticipated and unanticipated, as well as positive and negative. She uses the controversy over Apple's iPhone 4, starting with how it handled the premature leak of its characteristics and the subsequent problem with its antenna, as a case study to demonstrate both the right and wrong ways of managing unfolding events of different sorts and develops a prescriptive framework for properly managing these events in ways to safeguard the company's reputation. The resulting framework recognizes that the solutions are situational and that managers must account for myriad contextual dimensions, including the timing and valence of the event and the sequence of communications. However, as Elsbach recognizes and as played out in the Apple case, though there may be somewhat objective solutions to such challenges, a firm's identity, perhaps intertwined with that of its CEO, can limit its ability to recognize and implement these solutions and instead bias it toward non-optimal managerial actions.

FUTURE DIRECTIONS FOR CORPORATE REPUTATION RESEARCH

All of the chapters in this *Handbook* provide guidance on productive directions for future research within each of their topic domains. Going into this project we initially expected this section of the introduction would discuss "dry holes" that do not require more research attention, as well as those areas that do. However, after working with all the authors to develop their chapters, it has become clear to us that, with one exception (we don't need more research establishing that corporate reputation is an asset for firms—it is), the garden of research topics remains fecund and ongoing opportunities exist in virtually every area of inquiry.

In reviewing our authors' recommendations, we have identified five broad areas that offer the most promising possibilities for future research on corporate reputation: (1) The construct validity of corporate reputation; (2) Microfoundations of corporate reputation; (3) Levels of analysis other than the firm and multilevel modeling; (4) Temporality and dynamism; and (5) Process research.

Construct validity. Although significant advances have been made in defining and dimensionalizing corporate reputation, differentiating it from related constructs, and developing empirical measures, much work still needs to be done. Definitional debates rage on, and scholars continue to identify, test, and refine the dimensions of corporate reputation. Since definitional clarity is a necessary component of measurement precision, research that resolves or at least clarifies the boundary conditions of the definitional debate, and the concurrent development of reputation measures that explicitly acknowledge the definitions and assumptions that underlie them, will continue to yield value. Similarly, research that empirically differentiates reputation, status, identity, image, legitimacy, celebrity, and brand, as well as explores the relationships among these constructs, will also be theoretically and practically valuable.

Microfoundations. Part and parcel with defining reputation, more work is needed to understand the underlying behavioral antecedents; that is, how reputation is created, the underlying cognitive processes that allow it to create value for firms, and the relative influence of the perceptions, actions, and reports of those who have direct versus indirect experience with the focal firm. Not only will such research be useful for increasing our understanding of how to create value, and thus to manage it more effectively, it will also help in differentiating reputation from other constructs (e.g., Pfarrer, Pollock, & Rindova, 2010). In order to get inside the heads of those whose perceptions determine reputation, scholars will also need to broaden their methodological repertoire and develop research designs that incorporate methods such as lab experiments and policy capturing into their toolkits.

Different levels of analysis. Given that corporate reputation is a firm-level construct, most research today has been—as one would expect—at the firm level of analysis. However, as the scholars contributing to this volume have demonstrated, corporate reputation can affect, and be affected by, the firm's industry and country of origin, or, more broadly, by the institutional field in which it exists. Likewise, little research has dropped down levels of analysis from the firm, and considered how business units within the firm, or how stakeholder interactions at the individual level, influence and are influenced by corporate reputation. We also still know little about the extent to which reputational concerns can protect stakeholders, and the circumstances that lead to different mixes of reputational and regulatory protections. Further, to the extent that such research has been conducted, the analyses rarely if ever employ multilevel theorizing or analytical techniques. Future research that takes advantage of these emerging theoretical and methodological approaches can enhance our understanding of the rich interplay of corporate reputation across levels of analysis.

Temporality and dynamism. To date, most research on corporate reputation has been static and has given limited attention to issues of temporality, both in the short and long term. However, reputations are not static, and reputation's role as a value-creating asset and regulatory mechanism varies over time. Future theorizing and empirical research must pay greater heed to the role of time in designing studies, and consider how and why firms have specific reputations in particular time periods, how and why reputations change and evolve over time, how the changes in the roles firms play affect their reputations, and how different macro-social factors influence corporate reputations and their effects in different historical periods.

Process research. Finally, while scholars have begun to explore the processes through which corporate reputations are built, maintained, and repaired, more work needs to be done to fully understand how to manage reputation effectively. To date, much of this research has been qualitative, offering the benefits of thick description and inductive theorizing. Going forward, research in this area would also benefit greatly from other methodological approaches, such as field quasi-experiments (Grant & Wall, 2009) that systematically test the benefits and efficacy of different reputation management practices. Given the high level of interest in this issue among practitioners, the time may be right to forge relationships that allow this kind of research to be conducted, thereby enhancing the practical importance, as well as the theoretical rigor, of corporate reputation research in this area.

CONCLUSION

Corporate reputation research reflects the essence of "Pasteur's Quadrant" (Stokes, 1997) in the social sciences: It is theoretically meaningful because it contributes to our basic understanding of fundamental social processes and resources, and it is practically important because reputations create substantial value for companies. But we still lack a thorough understanding of the processes through which this important intangible asset should be managed, and we still lack clarity regarding how that value is created. For this *Handbook* we collected scholars from some of the diverse disciplines that have endeavored to better understand corporate reputation—management, sociology, economics, finance, history, marketing, and psychology—and asked them to discuss the state-of-the-art in their domain, and to offer guidance that facilitates future inquiry. We hope you find their insights both theoretically enriching and practically useful in guiding future research and practice.

REFERENCES

Albert, S. A. & Whetten, D. A. (1985). "Organizational identity." In L. L. Cummings & B. M. Staw (Eds.), *Research in Organizational Behavior*, Vol. 7. Greenwich, CT: JAI, 263–295.

Barnett, M. L. & King, A. (2008). "Good fences make good neighbors: A longitudinal analysis of an industry self-regulatory institution." *Academy of Management Journal*, 51(6): 1150–1170.

——, Jermier, J. M., & Lafferty, B. A. (2006). "Corporate reputation: The definitional landscape." *Corporate Reputation Review*, 9(1): 26–38.

Cyert, R. M. & March, J. G. (1963). *A Behavioral Theory of the Firm*. Englewood Cliffs, NJ: Prentice-Hall.

Devers, C. E., Dewett, T., Mishina, Y., & Belsito, C. A. (2009). "A general theory of organizational stigma." *Organization Science*, 20(1): 154–171.

Granovetter, M. (1985). "Economic action and social structure: The problem of embeddedness." *American Journal of Sociology*, 91: 481–510.

Grant, A. M. & Wall, T. D. (2009). "The neglected science and art of quasi-experimentation: Why-to, when-to, and how-to advice for organizational researchers." *Organizational Research Methods*, 12: 653–686.

Jensen, M. & Roy, A. (2008). "Staging exchange partner choices: When do status and reputation matter?" *Academy of Management Journal*, 51: 495–516.

King, B. G. & Whetten, D. A. (2008). "Rethinking the relationship between reputation and legitimacy: A social actor conceptualization." *Corporate Reputation Review*, 11: 192–208.

Lange, D., Lee, P. M., & Dai, Y. (2011). "Organizational reputation: A review." *Journal of Management*, 37(1): 153–184.

Pfarrer, M., Pollock, T., & Rindova, V. (2010). "A tale of two assets: The effects of firm reputation and celebrity on earnings surprises and investors' reactions." *Academy of Management Journal*, 53(5): 1131–1152.

Pozner, J. E. (2008). "Stigma and settling up: An integrated approach to the consequences of organizational misconduct for organizational elites." *Journal of Business Ethics*, 80: 141–150.

Rindova, V., Williamson, I., Petkova, A., & Sever, J. (2005). "Being good or being known: An empirical examination of the dimensions, antecedents, and consequences of organizational reputation." *Academy of Management Journal*, 48(6): 1033–1049.

Stokes, D. (1997). *Pasteur's quadrant: Basic Science and Technological Innovation*. Washington, DC: Brookings Institution Press.

Wiesenfeld, B. M., Wurthmann, K., & Hambrick, D. C. (2008). "The stigmatization and devaluation of elites associated with corporate failures: A process model." *Academy of Management Review*, 33(1): 231–251.

....

CHAPTER 2

SHOW ME THE MONEY: A MULTIDIMENSIONAL PERSPECTIVE ON REPUTATION AS AN INTANGIBLE ASSET

....

VIOLINA P. RINDOVA
LUIS L. MARTINS

This chapter articulates a multidimensional perspective on reputation as a strategic intangible asset of firms. First, we identify three distinct conceptualizations of reputation—as a signal, as an amalgamation of collective perceptions, and as a position in reputational rankings—that have been advanced by the three major perspectives in management research on reputation. We examine how each perspective defines reputation and argues its effects. Based on the different characteristics of reputation highlighted by the three perspectives, we propose an integrative, multidimensional view of reputation that articulates four dimensions that characterize reputational assets: specificity, accumulation, breadth of appeal, and codification. These dimensions together define the extent to which reputation is a strategic intangible asset for a firm. The multidimensional view we propose has important implications for the specificity with which the functioning of reputation as a strategic asset is understood theoretically and measured empirically in future research. It also suggests that assessing their reputational assets using these four dimensions can help managers strategize about which specific action levers can be mobilized to enhance the strategic value of their corporate reputation.

OVER the last two decades the concept of organizational reputation has attracted scholarly attention from a diverse set of disciplines, including economics, sociology, marketing, public relations, communications, and management. Much of the management research on reputation has been motivated by the idea that it is an intangible asset in that it generates economic benefits for the firm (Barney, 1991; Dierickx & Cool, 1989; Fombrun, 1996). This intuition appears to be broadly accepted and has generated a large body of research demonstrating the effects of firm reputations on firm performance (Deephouse, 2000; Rao, 1994; Roberts & Dowling, 2002; and Rindova et al., 2005 provide extensive discussions of this research).

While the research demonstrating that firm reputations have positive performance consequences confirms the basic idea that a firm's reputation is a strategic asset, little theoretical progress has been made toward understanding the attributes that make a firm's reputation an asset. The current view of reputation as an asset relies on two empirical strategies for assessing the extent to which reputations create value, and therefore can be considered an intangible asset. The first strategy is to track the observed empirical relationships between firms' positions in various reputational rankings and firm performance as a measure of the value of a firm's reputation. The second is to track the extent to which a firm exhibits the strategic behaviors that are expected to generate positive reputations, for example high levels of advertising (Shapiro, 1983) or investments in quality inputs (Rindova et al., 2005), and to attribute the effect of these investments to the development of a reputational asset. By inferring that a firm's reputation is an asset from a set of outcomes, these approaches do not provide a theoretical basis for understanding which attributes give corporate reputations their quality of intangible assets.

The theoretical framework that has provided the most explicit discussion of reputation as an intangible asset that confers competitive advantage on firms is the resource-based view (RBV) of the firm (Dierickx & Cool, 1989; Barney, 1991). In their seminal contribution to the theory of intangible assets, Dierickx and Cool (1989: 1506) argued that: "A reputation for quality may be built (rather than bought) by following a consistent set of production, quality control etc. policies over some period of time. Similarly, a reputation for 'toughness' (readiness to retaliate) is established through a history of aggressive behavior, and so on... The common element in all of these cases is that the strategic asset is the cumulative result of adhering to a set of consistent policies over a period of time. Put differently, strategic asset stocks are accumulated by choosing appropriate time paths of flows over a period of time." A core implication of these arguments is that reputation becomes an asset through processes of accumulation that are based on consistent and sustained policies, practices, and actions. Similarly, Barney (1991) also argued that reputation is a strategic asset. He emphasized that reputations are built through socially complex processes, which make their accumulation difficult to imitate or replicate, and therefore make them central to the sustainability of firms' competitive advantages.

These contributions emphasize the importance of reputational assets for the sustainability of competitive advantage but do not articulate the attributes that give reputations their value as intangible assets in the first place. Thus, while highlighting attributes such as relative inimitability arising from time compression diseconomies (Dierickx & Cool, 1989), social complexity, and causal ambiguity (Barney, 1991), that determine the impact of reputation on the sustainability of advantage, researchers remain largely silent about the attributes that give reputation its asset value.

The answer to the question of which attributes make reputations intangible assets is far from apparent. As we will discuss later, scholars debate intensely whether reputation consists of specific perceptions about an organization's strategic type (e.g., ability to deliver quality) (Shapiro, 1983; Weigelt & Camerer, 1988) or whether it encompasses broad collective knowledge and recognition (Fombrun, 1996; King & Whetten, 2008; Rao, 1994; Rhee & Valdez, 2009). They also debate whether reputation comprises the perceptions of a particular stakeholder group, such as customers (Shapiro, 1983) or alliance partners (Dollinger, Golden, & Saxton, 1997), or whether it combines and integrates perceptions across stakeholder groups (Fombrun & Shanley, 1990; King & Whetten, 2008). In Chapter 5 of this *Handbook*, Fombrun provides a comprehensive discussion of some of the debates and ambiguities surrounding the definition of corporate reputation as well as its antecedents and consequences.

What is clear, however, is that questions about the attributes of reputations that make them strategic intangible assets need to be addressed in order to fully develop our understanding of reputation as a strategic intangible asset of the firm. The current literature addressing these issues has developed in a fragmentary fashion, with each theoretical perspective focusing on a different aspect of reputation. Each of these perspectives is individually incomplete in accounting for the complexity of the social processes through which reputations develop and affect firm outcomes. To redress this problem, a multidimensional conceptualization that builds on, and integrates, the various perspectives on reputations presented in the literature is needed (Lange, Lee, & Dai, 2011). A multidimensional conceptualization can simultaneously present a more comprehensive view of how reputations create value, and specify distinct dimensions along which value-creating effects can be measured and studied. Such an approach will enable both scholars and managers to better understand how different strategies affect their reputational assets, what the compositional attributes of these assets may be, and whether different attributes are differentially valuable under different circumstances.

In this chapter we examine the different conceptualizations of reputation offered by three distinct perspectives: game-theoretic, social-constructionist, and institutional. These three perspectives have conceptualized reputation as a signal, an amalgamation of collective perceptions, and a position in reputational rankings, respectively. For each of these perspectives, we articulate the logic through which reputation generates economic benefits for firms. We focus on economic effects in order to uncover how a particular perspective implicitly conceives of reputation as an intangible asset that creates economic value for firms. Then, integrating across the three perspectives, we develop a four-dimensional framework characterizing reputational assets in terms of: (a) asset *specificity* based on the signaling value of a firm's reputation with regard to its strategic character; (b) asset *accumulation* based on the firm's level of visibility or prominence; (c) asset *breadth of appeal* represented in the degree of favorability of assessments among a broad set of stakeholders; and (d) asset *codification* based on the relative position assigned to the firm in reputational rankings created by third-party institutional intermediaries. The links between the three perspectives on reputation, their underlying

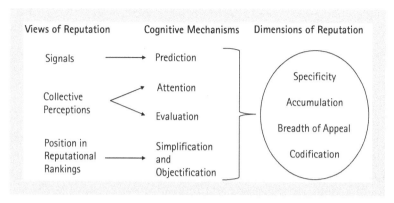

FIGURE 2.1 A multidimensional conceptualization of reputation as a strategic intangible asset.

logics of the economic effects of reputation, and our integrated multidimensional conceptualization of reputation are depicted in Figure 2.1.

THEORETICAL PERSPECTIVES ON REPUTATION

In this section, we briefly summarize the three major theoretical perspectives that have been advanced to understand reputations. For each of the perspectives, we also articulate the cognitive mechanisms it emphasizes in relating reputation to firm performance. Table 1 summarizes key contributions of selected research within each perspective.

The Game-Theoretic View: Reputation as a Signal

Much of the earliest work on reputation that influenced management scholarship came from economics research using game-theoretic perspectives to study how the past behaviors of players affect future strategic interactions (Milgrom & Roberts, 1982; Shapiro, 1983). Scholars working from this perspective define reputation as beliefs about an organization's strategic type, such as its competitive toughness or ability to produce quality (Milgrom & Roberts, 1982; Shapiro, 1983; Weigelt & Camerer, 1988). Reputations as signals are based on observations of firms' actions over time and under particular conditions (Weigelt & Camerer, 1988; Rindova, Petkova, & Kotha, 2007). Actions reveal information about the underlying unobservable attributes of firms because different attributes lead to different incentives and/or capabilities to take particular types of actions (Basdeo et al., 2006; Rindova, Petkova, & Kotha, 2007).

This perspective therefore emphasizes that reputations create value by providing information about otherwise unobservable firm attributes. This information enhances the predictability of economic exchanges between the firm and a specific set of players or stakeholders interested in predicting the behavior of the firm with regard to a specific attribute they value. For instance, firms' reputations for quality among buyers are based on the experiences of other buyers, and are useful to buyers seeking to select exchange partners that are capable of meeting their quality expectations (Nayyar, 1990). Perceived quality, therefore, reflects buyers' predictions about whether a firm's products are likely to meet their performance expectations.

To summarize, the signaling perspective emphasizes that firms have reputations about specific attributes with particular stakeholder groups, based on past actions of a given type. Depending on the type of actions being tracked, the same firm can have different reputations for different attributes with different stakeholders because specific types of actions are perceived and valued differently by different stakeholder groups. The economic value of reputation from this perspective depends on the specificity of perceptions held within a given stakeholder group that is concerned with the particular attribute along which reputation is deduced from prior behavior. This perspective suggests that the locus of control over a firm's reputation lies largely within the firm, in that it chooses what actions to take and therefore, what reputational signal it will send.

While the view of reputation as perceptions about the firm's type or character is important for understanding how a firm may be viewed by a particular stakeholder group, it leaves unanswered questions about spillover effects of a particular reputation from one stakeholder group to another, as well as interference effects that may result from having different and potentially contradictory reputations. Thus, while emphasizing the consequences of specific reputations with specific stakeholder groups, this view does not effectively address the effect of linkages among stakeholders on the formation of broader, higher-level general reputations that may only partially overlap with lower-level specific, stakeholder-centric reputations. These issues are addressed by the social constructionist perspective, which views reputations as amalgamations of collective perceptions, and is discussed next.

The Social-Constructionist View: Reputation as an Amalgamation of Collective Perceptions

A second body of work, which can be characterized as social-constructionist in its assumptions, emphasizes the diversity of perceptions and cognitions that amalgamate into the construction of reputations in organizational fields. These perceptions and cognitions can vary from simple awareness, to general impressions, to attribute-specific knowledge. Importantly, these perceptions are held in the organizational field, defined as a set of interacting stakeholder audiences who are aware of each other (see Dimaggio & Powell, 1983). A key contribution of this perspective, therefore, is that it emphasizes the diversity of perceptions and the collective, socially constructed nature of firm reputations.

The social-constructionist perspective also recognizes that perceptions about firms in the marketplace can be derived from a variety of sources, and not only from the set of actions that economic theory qualifies as valid signals. For example, the Four Seasons—a hotel management company with a stellar reputation for service—is often perceived as a US company, when in fact it is headquartered in Canada. Even though this perception is inaccurate, and irrelevant with respect to the perceived quality of the firm's services, it has consequences for how stakeholders in different locations around the world respond to the firm.

By concerning itself with a broader range of perceptions about firms, the view of reputations as amalgamations of different stakeholders' cognitions and perceptions accounts more fully for the nature of information exchanges about firms in the marketplace (Pollock, Rindova, & Maggitti, 2008). Yet, it can also appear atheoretical and imprecise, because scholars often refer to fundamentally different cognitions and perceptions with the common term "reputation." For example, reputation has been defined in terms of *evaluative judgments* (Rindova et al., 2005), *salient attributes* ascribed to firms (Fombrun & Shanley, 1990), observers' *impressions* of a firm's disposition to behave in a certain manner (Clark & Montgomery, 1998), as well as *general awareness* (Shamsie, 2003), *fame* (Hall, 1992), and *esteem* (Fombrun, 1996).

In an effort to increase clarity and precision in this regard, recent work in the area has begun to dimensionalize reputation in an effort to distinguish the effects of different types of collective perceptions on firm outcomes. For example, Rindova et al. (2005) argue that reputation manifests itself along two dimensions—prominence and perceived quality. Prominence refers to the overall level of recognition given to a firm in the collective cognitive and interpretive space of an organizational field, whereas perceived quality reflects the relative favorability of stakeholders' evaluations. The concept of prominence bears some similarity to the concept of visibility (Fombrun & Shanley, 1990; Deephouse, 2000; Rindova, Petkova, & Kotha, 2007), which refers to the level of attention that a firm commands in the media. To the degree that the media reflect the perspective and viewpoints of a broad cross-section of stakeholders (Deephouse, 2000), media visibility may be a representative measure of a firm's prominence.

The more commonly studied aspect of the collective perceptions about a firm is their favorability (Deephouse, 2000; Greenwood et al., 2005; Rindova, Petkova, & Kotha, 2007). In fact, for many students of reputation, the favorability of perceptions about a firm's ability to create value is the defining attribute of corporate reputations and is the key mechanism through which reputations affect economic exchanges (Fombrun, 1996). However, while the favorability of evaluations is a much emphasized dimension of reputation, the nature of the perceptions that underlie the favorability of reputations is poorly understood. It is important to distinguish the various aspects of favorability since they affect the value of reputational assets in different ways.

First, as discussed earlier, stakeholders may evaluate favorably a specific attribute of the firm, such as its ability to deliver quality or its capability to manage effectively strategic alliances. This favorable perception affects the stakeholders' exchanges with the firm in areas related to that specific attribute. Second, stakeholders may hold a general favorable impression of the firm, which may include references to specific actions and attributes, but does not have to. This second type of favorability is particularly interesting and important for understanding the value of reputation, as it is not necessarily traceable to specific actions and observations, even if in general it tends to reflect the patterns in the history of a firm's actions (Suchman, 1995). As such, it becomes decoupled from specific actions and investments, and may provide the firm with more "leverage" in its reputation management.

Furthermore, leverage is gained from the fact that such generalized, non-attribute-specific positive attitudes tend to transcend stakeholder group boundaries. Thus, as the favorability of stakeholder perceptions of a firm expands from attribute-specific to generalized perceptions, firm reputations acquire a higher-level quality associated with economic effects that are different from those of attribute-specific reputations. Third, favorability is sometimes confounded with stakeholders having a positive emotional response to a firm. While judgments and impressions may have an implicit affective aspect to them (Fiske & Taylor, 1991), rational and affective information processing are two distinct modes through which people manage and organize information (see Pfarrer, Pollock, & Rindova, 2010 for a detailed discussion). Therefore, emotional responses to firms are distinct from favorable evaluations, and have been theorized as constituent of a different intangible asset—namely, firm celebrity (Rindova, Pollock, & Hayward, 2006; Pfarrer, Pollock, & Rindova, 2010).

In sum, the social-constructionist perspective highlights two aspects of reputation that exist at the collective stakeholder level. The prominence or visibility of a firm captures the collective attention paid to the firm, and the favorability of perceptions of the firm across stakeholders reflects the favorability of collective evaluations across stakeholders within an organizational field, or in a society at large. This perspective emphasizes that firm reputations are affected not only by a firm's actions but also by interactions and information exchanges among the firm's stakeholders, and that the locus of control over a firm's reputation is outside the firm's boundary and is distributed among diverse and interacting stakeholders.

The Institutional View: Reputation as a Position in Reputational Rankings

A third perspective on reputation, rooted in institutional theory, characterizes it as the relative position of a firm in explicit rankings created by powerful institutional intermediaries in organizational fields. Institutional intermediaries include the media, financial analysts, and monitoring organizations (Fombrun & Shanley, 1990; Pollock & Rindova, 2003; Rao, 1998). Institutional intermediaries are integral players in a process of social construction of reputations because they specialize in the generation and presentation of information about firms to large stakeholder audiences (Fombrun & Shanley, 1990; Rao, 1994). Within this function, intermediaries generate various lists, which specify the

standing of an organization relative to others based on criteria determined by the information intermediary (Martins, 2005). For example, *Fortune* magazine publishes a
ranking of the best places to work, and the *Financial Times* publishes a ranking of the
best business schools. These rankings are recognized by various actors and stakeholder
audiences as explicit reputational orderings, and firms' positions in them are seen as a
reflection of a firm's reputation for one or multiple attributes. These hierarchical orderings may reflect objective indicators of past performance (e.g., the largest firms by revenues) or subjective evaluative judgments (e.g., rankings based on surveys of certain
stakeholders). They may focus on firms in a particular industry or may be broad cross-
industry lists.

Viewed as a position in a reputational hierarchy, reputation is understood as acquiring a more objective status as a "social fact," that is, a socially produced artifact that is
treated as an objective fact (Martins, 2005; Rao, 1994). This is because reputational rankings are believed to contain information that otherwise may be private or available to a
limited set of privileged actors. They also are seen as making information more comparable and reliable across firms. Finally, reputational rankings are seen as providing stakeholders with independent "third-party" certifications of various firm attributes.
Consistent with these ideas that reputational rankings objectify a firm's reputation,
researchers in the area have used reputational rankings extensively as the measure of a
firm's reputation (e.g., Fombrun & Shanley, 1990; Pfarrer, Pollock, & Rindova, 2010;
Roberts & Dowling, 2002).

However, because firms' positions in rankings depend on numerous measurement
choices, reputations defined by reputational hierarchies are often subject to debate and
controversy (Gioia & Corley, 2002; Chandler & Rindova, 2008). Scholars have shown
that a firm's position in a reputational hierarchy can be relatively arbitrary (Dichev, 1999)
and very different from the reputation based on the collective perceptions discussed
above. This is because a firm's standing in a reputational ranking depends entirely on the
criteria, methodology, comparison set of firms, and perhaps the biases of the institutional intermediary producing the ranking.

Despite the controversies surrounding rankings as measures of firm reputation, they
have been consistently found to affect both firms' actions (Martins, 2005), and their
stakeholders' and employees' experiences (Elsbach & Kramer, 1996). Their impact
derives from the fact that they capture in a concrete, externally validated way the complex and diverse perceptions that make up firm reputations. As such they can be seen as
codifications of otherwise tacit and diffused perceptions and beliefs. The reputational
hierarchies created by information intermediaries also carry institutional validity since
information intermediaries are "social control specialists who institutionalize distrust
of agents by inspecting their performance... and who sustain social order" (Rao, 1998:
914). Having acquired this objectification, firms' reputations are more available to
stakeholders and become the de facto reputations of firms. As a result, reputation as
position in a reputational ranking is treated by many as the most important assessment
of reputation, one that is a closely guarded and furiously defended asset (Fombrun &
Shanley, 1990; Martins, 2005). For this reason, a firm's reputation defined as a position

in a reputational ranking is a distinct dimension of reputation with distinct economic impact.

To summarize, the institutional perspective emphasizes the codification of the relative standing of a firm, relative to its competitors or a broad cross-section of other firms. The importance of this aspect of reputation, and its value to stakeholders, derives from the fact that rankings summarize, simplify, and objectify information about competing firms and thereby reduce stakeholder uncertainty with regard to exchanges with these firms. This perspective suggests that the locus of control over a firm's reputation lies among institutional intermediaries in the organizational field who assess firms within the field using certain criteria, and in doing so define the reputation of the firms.

FROM MULTIPLE PERSPECTIVES TO A MULTIDIMENSIONAL CONCEPTUALIZATION OF REPUTATION AS AN ASSET

Our review of the management research on reputation above identifies three perspectives that have evolved relatively separately and propose distinct views of what reputation is and how it affects economic exchanges. Whereas the three perspectives have made significant contributions to our understanding of reputations, they are individually incomplete in terms of capturing the various characteristics that make reputations strategic intangible assets. First, the perspectives are fragmented in their analyses, with each theory focusing on a different dimension of reputation as an asset. Indeed, the differences in theoretical approaches to the conceptualization of reputation that they use reveal why reputation research has engaged in a number of debates about the phenomenological status of reputation. Second, each of the perspectives on its own does not incorporate the complexity of the social processes through which reputations are developed.

In order to address these concerns and to develop a comprehensive understanding of the characteristics that make reputations strategic assets, we need an integrated view that addresses the multiple dimensions that make corporate reputations intangible assets (Lange, Lee, & Dai, 2011). Our discussion of the theoretical logic and implications of each of the three perspectives suggests that rather than seeking a theoretically "correct" approach to analyzing corporate reputation, future research will benefit from an integrative conceptualization of reputation that captures the different aspects of audience perceptions about a firm and the effects of these different perceptions on economic exchanges.

Specifically, across the three perspectives, the following integrated understanding of reputation can be articulated. First, phenomenologically speaking, a firm's reputation incorporates many different types of perceptions that circulate among different actors interacting in the marketplace. Second, for each firm, these perceptions may have a different, firm-specific configuration. This configuration defines the composition and the value of its reputation as a strategic intangible asset. Third, reputation as an asset can be characterized in terms of four distinct dimensions, each of which captures the defining notions of reputation espoused by each of the three perspectives. The clarity and specificity of reputation emphasized by the signaling perspective define the asset specificity dimension of reputational assets. The prominence and visibility of the firm emphasized by the reputation research focusing on the collective social-construction of reputations define the asset accumulation dimension. The development of generalized favorable attitudes and beliefs toward the firm—also emphasized by the collective social-constructionist view—defines the asset breadth of appeal. Finally, the positions of the firm in reputational rankings produced by institutional intermediaries emphasized by the institutional perspective define the asset codification dimension of reputation. Each of these dimensions of reputation as a strategic asset affects different aspects of value creation and a combination of the levels of each dimension determines the overall value of a firm's reputation as a strategic intangible asset. We discuss the distinct economic, value-creation effects of the various dimensions of reputation, next.

Asset specificity. The clarity and strength of a firm's reputation for specific attributes valued by specific stakeholder groups determines the *specificity of its reputational asset.* When scholars and managers ask the question "reputation for what" they are concerned with one characteristic of reputational assets—the clarity of stakeholders' understanding about the quality of the firm's products, or the nature of its competitive strategies, or the persistence in its performance results. Firms strive for accuracy in the perceptions that their stakeholders hold of relevant firm attributes, and stakeholders benefit from such accuracy because it reduces their search and monitoring costs. Importantly, the more specific the perceptions are with regard to the relevant attribute, the more useful they are in facilitating economic exchanges between the firm and the stakeholder group or groups that value this attribute. We term this dimension of reputation asset specificity to capture the extent to which firms vary in their desire to shape the perceptions of specific stakeholders and in their willingness to make costly investments to do so. The more firms target a particular stakeholder group, and the more they focus their investments on signaling information to this stakeholder group, the higher the level of specificity that their reputational assets are likely to have. Of course, firms may choose to target multiple groups, in which case they need to manage the specificity of their assets similarly to their management of the specificity of other types of intangible assets, such as R&D or umbrella versus product-level branding.

Specificity is an important characteristic that affects the economic value of reputational assets because it determines the extent to which a firm's reputation facilitates its exchanges or interactions with a particular stakeholder group, such as customers, investors, or competitors. For example, the stability of competitive interactions that arises from the specificity of competitive reputations has long been emphasized as a key predictor of firm, as well as industry, profitability (e.g. Porter, 1980; Milgrom & Roberts, 1982). Similarly, specific reputations for quality, reliability, or innovativeness enable customers to select more clearly among multiple differentiated offerings in a given industry. Therefore, reputational assets with a high degree of specificity increase the efficiency of economic exchanges and increase the attractiveness of a firm as an exchange partner for a given stakeholder group.

Asset accumulation. In contrast to asset specificity, which emphasizes the individual perceptions of distinct stakeholder groups, the asset accumulation quality characterizes the level of accumulation of reputation by a firm within its organizational field. As such it characterizes the degree of recognition and attention among diverse stakeholder groups who interact with each other and with the firm within a given organizational field (see Rindova & Fombrun, 1999). Two concepts in extant reputation research capture the idea of accumulation of reputational assets: prominence and visibility (Deephouse, 2000; Pollock & Rindova, 2003; Rindova et al., 2005; Rindova, Petkova, & Kotha, 2007; Pfarrer, Pollock, & Rindova, 2010). Both concepts refer to the level of attention focused on the firm, but the concept of visibility is primarily used in research focusing on reputation-making in the media, as media attention provides the firm with visibility.

The asset accumulation of firm reputations is defined by the size of the audience that is focused on a given firm, as well as the relative salience of the firm in the collective attention of the audience. Research on information flows in markets shows that firms that enjoy high levels of prominence attract disproportionately more attention from the media and other stakeholders. This is because attention in markets is often limited to a subset of companies that are "chronically available" in the media and in the public discourse (see Pollock, Rindova, & Maggitti, 2008 for a discussion of availability cascades in markets). Organizations about which stakeholders encounter information more frequently are likely to be more focal in their attention. As a result, they are evoked, recognized, and acted upon more frequently, as information about them is recalled more easily. Such organizations are more likely to be considered and selected as exchange partners, and therefore will benefit from stakeholders' awareness of them.

The asset accumulation of a reputational asset therefore has distinct and important value-creating effects. In general, the degree of accumulation of an asset, that is, its asset mass, enhances economic performance through scale effects. For example, Coke's accumulated brand equity increases the efficiency of its current advertising spending. This example also illustrates how asset accumulation facilitates further asset growth, as adding increments to an existing asset may be facilitated by possessing high prior levels of it. Dierickx & Cool (1989: 1507) term this effect "asset mass efficiencies" and identify it as an important determinant of sustaining privileged asset positions.

Asset breadth of appeal. In addition to asset mass, the heterogeneous perceptions that constitute firms' reputations affect the scope of applicability of the asset—that is, its breadth of appeal. Reputational assets have high degrees of attractiveness when the invariable heterogeneous perceptions that surround firms are anchored in predominantly positive general opinions, beliefs, and assessments. We characterize this characteristic of breadth of appeal of a reputation as a generalized positive attitude to distinguish it from the specific evaluative judgments that underlie the asset specificity dimension.

The generalized nature of favorable perceptions is important in characterizing the value of a firm's reputation as an asset. As firm reputations become generalized, they also become increasingly decoupled from the specific investments and actions that generated them in the first place. From a firm point of view, generalized reputations require less investment in maintenance and can be leveraged across a broader variety of situations. For example, research shows that consumers are more willing to try new products introduced by well-regarded firms. The positive regard for the firm generalizes to the context of a new and unproven product or technology. From stakeholders' points of view, generalized reputations reduce monitoring costs, as generalized beliefs reduce the attention paid to specific occurrences, and predispose observers to integrate current information to fit with pre-existing beliefs (Fiske & Taylor, 1991). This reduction in monitoring, however, may be either efficient or inefficient for a particular stakeholder, depending on whether the generalized reputation of a firm continues to reflect accurately the relevant unobservable attributes.

Asset codification. Finally, the position of a firm in reputational rankings defines a distinct quality of reputational assets, which we term asset codification. As discussed earlier, codification of a firm's reputation through the designation of a position in a reputational ranking gives the reputation a social facticity that increases stakeholder reliance on it in decision-making. Rankings are essentially socially constructed cognitive shortcuts available to the firm and its stakeholders in assessing or discussing its reputation. For example, being billed as a "Big Four" accounting firm or a "Top 20" business school immediately indicates the relative standing of the particular organization to its stakeholders, with consequent implications for their economic exchanges with it. Not only can a firm's position in a reputational ranking affect its dyadic exchanges with individual stakeholders, but it may also affect the information carried in the interactions among its stakeholders. A firm can therefore trade on its position within a reputational ranking to the extent that its stakeholders perceive the position to be a credible indicator of the true characteristics of the firm. The empirical evidence suggests that despite continued debates about the validity of rankings among academics and practicing managers, both sets of actors continue to act on the information derived from rankings due to their instutitonalization as measures of firm reputation (Dichev, 1999; Martins, 2005).

Conclusions and Implications

In the previous section, we developed a multidimensional conceptualization of reputation as a strategic intangible asset, by integrating the three dominant perspectives within research on reputation. The integrated, multidimensional view we propose can advance research and practice in the area of corporate reputations by integrating currently disparate views of corporate reputations, and by bringing greater clarity to the distinct effects of different characteristics of reputations as well as to the mechanisms through which they generate economic benefits. It further contributes to an understanding of reputations as intangible assets by relating the disparate characteristics of reputations emphasized by different strands of research to specific asset characteristics with distinct economic effects. Our hope is that the approach we offer will both increase the precision with which reputation is studied in future empirical studies, and provide practicing managers with a guide for making meaningful assessments of their reputational assets.

The multidimensional composite view of reputations and their asset qualities that we propose has three significant implications for research on, and management of, reputations. First, a multidimensional approach can increase the validity of empirical investigations about firms' reputations by enabling researchers to better account for the complexity of the phenomenon. Second, a multidimensional approach suggests the need for more sophisticated construct measurement to understand the effects of specific dimensions of reputations, and for configurational approaches to assess the effects of various combinations of the dimensions. Third, a multidimensional approach calls for more fine-grained and longitudinal analysis of the strategies through which firms develop their reputational assets along these dimensions. We elaborate on each of these opportunities for future research below.

By emphasizing the importance of understanding how reputations function as intangible assets and suggesting multiple asset attributes that need to be considered and empirically measured, our approach encourages future research to take a more pragmatic approach to understanding the phenomenon of corporate reputation in markets. Such an approach has an advantage over purely theory-driven approaches to reputation in that it enables researchers to deal with the complexity of the phenomenon in a comprehensive and structured fashion. As we discussed, theory-driven approaches tend to emphasize one or two dimensions, whereas in reality reputations are complex and multidimensional. A multidimensional approach provides a structure, within which firm reputations can be compared more systematically. Currently, such comparisons are relegated to the authority of organizations that produce reputational rankings, which often enact their own interests and agendas in the process. In contrast, a multidimensional approach using the four dimensions we propose enables researchers to systematically compare reputations across firms in a more rigorous manner that is applicable to a wide set of reputational assets.

The complexity of corporate reputations is well understood among researchers working in the area (see Lange, Lee, & Dai, 2011 for a review), yet limited work has been done on the measurement and dimensionalization of the construct. Our approach highlights the need for sophisticated analytical approaches capable of capturing the different types of perceptions and cognitions that simultaneously surround firms. Toward this end, we suggest that researchers should consider more extensively the use of rich combinations of psychometric approaches developed by cognitive, social, and organizational psychologists. Further, we recommend that researchers consider the use of configurational models to understand: (a) the effects of the different dimensions on firm performance, and (b) the performance outcomes of possessing reputational assets with different compositions along these dimensions.

Finally, our multidimensional view suggests the need for more differentiated theory and empirical work on the strategies through which firms build reputational assets with different compositions. For example, in a study of the development of reputations by new firms in nascent markets, Rindova and colleagues (2007) observed that reputations have different components and that these different components accumulate through different processes, generating reputational assets with different compositions. For example, taking many market actions appears to increase the salience of a firm, resulting in higher levels of visibility, whereas taking novel actions appears to signal high performance potential, resulting in higher favorability of evaluations. Further, while the totality of actions increases a firm's visibility, the composition of the action repertoire, that is, the extent and consistency with which a firm takes actions of a given type, determines the attributes that a new firm becomes known for, or its asset specificity. These observations derived from an inductive qualitative study of three new entrants in a nascent market highlight the significant opportunities that exist for expanding our understanding of the development of reputational assets and their various qualities through longitudinal analyses that systematically track firm actions and interactions with their environments.

To summarize, our discussion in this chapter suggests that research on firm reputation has evolved along three different lines represented in three perspectives, each offering its own hints about the characteristics of reputation that make it a strategic asset. We drew on these perspectives to develop a multidimensional view of reputation that elucidates several qualities of reputational assets that define their economic value. Our proposal suggests the need for more complex and specific theory and empirical measurement in the study of the relationships between firm reputation and firm performance. Whereas that will take greater effort than the narrower conceptualizations used in the past, it will get us closer to understanding the underlying characteristics that make reputation a strategic asset. In so doing, it will not only address a critical gap in research on reputation, but will also provide more concrete guidance for managers on how to manage and capitalize on their firms' reputations.

Key Contributions on Reputation

Reference	Key Constructs and Findings
Game-Theoretic View: Reputation as a Signal	
Milgrom & Roberts (1982)	• Reputation of a player is defined as "the beliefs that other players hold about his unknown characteristics and on the basis of which they predict his behavior." (p. 283) • Reputational beliefs are derived from past behavior. • The paper models how predatory pricing behavior can generate a reputation for competitive toughness that deters potential entrants from entering the market.

(Continued)

Table Continued

Reference	Key Constructs and Findings
Shapiro (1983)	• "reputation formation is a type of signaling activity: the quality of items produced in previous periods serves as a signal of the quality of those produced during the current period." (p. 660) • A reputation for high quality allows sellers to earn a premium on their products. • There are costs to developing a reputation for quality; as a result, reputation becomes a cost/barrier to entry into a market.
Weigelt & Camerer (1988)	• Reputation defined as "a set of attributes ascribed to a firm, inferred from the firm's past actions." (p. 443) • Reputation can help predict competitor behavior in game-theoretic models and decision-makers' motives in strategy research.

Social-Constructionist View: Reputation as an Amalgamation of Collective Perceptions

Reference	Key Constructs and Findings
Deephouse (2000)	• Reputation framed as "media reputation" and defined as "an overall evaluation of a firm presented in the media." (p. 1091) • The media play a critical role in the generation and distribution of information about a firm, and influence public opinion about the firm. • Media reputation was found to be positively related to firm performance in a sample of banks.
Rao (1994)	• Reputation defined as "an outcome of the process of legitimation" (p. 31) and is, therefore, socially constructed. • The study demonstrates that victories in certification contests confer legitimacy and generate positive reputations.
Rindova, Petkova, & Kotha (2007)	• Reputation "refers to the regard that stakeholders hold a firm in based on expectations that it can deliver value along key dimensions of performance." (p. 33) • New firms develop reputations that reflect the level, diversity, and type of visible market actions they take. High level of actions generates visibility, the composition of types of actions taken defines what a firm is known for, and novel and symbolic actions generate favorability and esteem. • Reputations reflect the strategic actions of firms, as interpreted and reported by the media.
Rindova, Williamson, Petkova, & Sever (2005)	• Reputation "can be conceptualized as comprising two dimensions: (1) a perceived quality dimension, which captures the degree to which stakeholders evaluate an organization positively on a specific attribute, such as ability to produce quality products, and (2) a prominence dimension, which captures the degree to which an organization receives large-scale collective recognition in its organizational field." (p. 1035) • The two dimensions of reputation have distinct antecedents and consequences. Perceived quality is influenced by resource signals, whereas prominence is influenced by institutional signals. In the context of US business schools prominence has a direct effect on the price premia that graduates command, whereas perceived quality has an indirect effect through its effect on prominence.

Reference	Key Constructs and Findings
Institutional View: Reputation as a Position in Reputational Rankings	
Elsbach & Kramer (1996)	• Reputation, defined as position in reputational rankings, used as an external indication of an organization's identity.
	• Found that an organization's position in reputational rankings questioned the beliefs of organizational members, who then engaged in sensemaking to resolve dissonance between their identity and their reputation.
Fombrun & Shanley (1990)	• Reputation is determined by an organization's stakeholders based on "information about firms' relative structural positions within organizational fields, specifically using market and accounting signals indicating performance, institutional signals indicating conformity to social norms, and strategy signals indicating strategic postures." (p. 233)
	• Reputations emerge from an interplay of firms, stakeholders, and the media in an institutional field.
Martins (2005)	• Reputation defined as "an external image" of an organization, as represented in a position in a reputational ranking. (p. 703)
	• A perception of a discrepancy between an organization's position in reputational rankings and its own estimation of its standing in the industry prompted organizational change in conformity with action criteria emphasized by the rankings.
	• Perceptions of impact and an externally focused organizational identity made change in response to a perceived identity-reputation discrepancy more likely.

REFERENCES

Barney, J. B. (1991). "Firm resources and sustained competitive advantage." *Journal of Management*, 17: 99–120.

Basdeo, D., Smith, K. G., Grimm, C., Rindova, V. P., & Derfus, P. (2006). "The impact of market actions on firm reputation." *Strategic Management Journal*, 27: 1205–1219.

Chandler, D. & Rindova, V. P. (2008). "Would you like fries with that? Producing and consuming social measures of firm value." *Academy of Management Annual Meeting Proceedings*, 1–6.

Clark, B. H. & Montgomery, D. B. (1998). "Deterrence, reputations, and competitive cognition." *Management Science*, 44(1): 62–82.

Deephouse, D. L. (2000). "Media reputation as a strategic resource: An integration of mass communication and resource-based theories." *Journal of Management*, 26(6): 1091–1112.

Dichev, I. D. (1999). "How good are business school rankings?" *Journal of Business*, 72: 201–213.

Dierickx, I. & Cool, K. (1989). "Asset stock accumulation and sustainability of competitive advantage." *Management Science*, 35: 1504–1511.

Dimaggio, P. J. & Powell, W. W. (1983). "The iron cage revisited: Institutional isomorphism and collective rationality in organizational fields." *American Sociological Review*, 48: 147–160.

Dollinger, M., Golden, P., & Saxton, T. (1997). "The effects of reputation on the decision to joint venture." *Strategic Management Journal*, 18(2): 127–140.

Elsbach, K. D. & Kramer, R. M. (1996). "Members' responses to organizational identity threats: Encountering and countering the *Business Week* rankings." *Administrative Science Quarterly*, 41: 442–476.

Fiske, S. T. & Taylor, S. E. (1991). *Social cognition* (2nd edn). New York: McGraw-Hill.

Fombrun, C. J. (1996). *Reputation: Realizing Value from the Corporate Image*. Boston: Harvard Business School Press.

—— &Shanley, M. (1990). "What's in a name? Reputation building and corporate strategy." *Academy of Management Journal*, 33: 233–258.

Gioia, D. & Corley, K. G. (2002). "Being good versus looking good: Business school rankings and the Circean transformation from substance to image." *Academy of Management Learning and Education*, 1: 107–120.

Greenwood, R., Li, S. X., Prakash, R., & Deephouse, D. L. (2005). "Reputation, diversification and organizational explanations of performance in professional service firms." *Organization Science*, 16: 661–675.

Hall, R. (1992). "The strategic analysis of intangible resources." *Strategic Management Journal*, 13: 135–144.

King, B. G. & Whetten, D. A. (2008). "Rethinking the relationship between reputation and legitimacy: A social actor conceptualization." *Corporate Reputation Review*, 11: 192–208.

Lange, D., Lee, P. M., & Dai, Y. (2011). "Organizational reputation: A review." *Journal of Management*, 37(1): 153–184.

Martins, Luis L. (2005). "A model of the effects of reputational rankings on organizational change." *Organization Science*, 16(6): 701–720.

Milgrom, P. & Roberts, J. (1982). "Predation, reputation and entry deterrence." *Journal of Economic Theory*, 27(2): 280–312.

Nayyar, P. R. (1990). "Information asymmetries: A source of competitive advantage for diversified service firms." *Strategic Management Journal*, 11: 513–519.

Pfarrer, M., Pollock, T., & Rindova, V. (2010). "A tale of two assets: The effects of firm reputation and celebrity on earnings surprises and investors' reactions." *Academy of Management Journal*, 53(5): 1131–1152.

Pollock, T. & Rindova, V. (2003). "Media legitimation effects in the market for initial public offerings." *Academy of Management Journal*, 46: 631–642.

——, ——, & Maggitti, P. (2008). "Market watch: Information and availability cascades among the media and investors in the US IPO market." *Academy of Management Journal*, 51(2): 335–358.

Porter, M. (1980). *Competitive Strategy*. New York: Free Press.

Rao, H. (1994). "The social construction of reputation: Certification contests, legitimation, and the survival of organizations in the American automobile industry: 1895–1912." *Strategic Management Journal*, 15: 29–44.

—— (1998). "Caveat emptor: The construction of nonprofit consumer watchdog organizations." *American Journal of Sociology*, 103(4): 912–961.

Rhee, M. & Valdez, M. E. (2009). "Contextual factors surrounding reputation damage with potential implications for reputation repair." *Academy of Management Review*, 34: 146–168.

Rindova, V. P. & Fombrun, C. J. (1999). "Constructing competitive advantage: The role of firm-constituent interactions." *Strategic Management Journal*, 20: 691–710.

——, Pollock, T., & Hayward, M. (2006). "Celebrity firms: The social construction of market popularity." *Academy of Management Review*, 31(1): 50–71.

——, Petkova, A., & Kotha, S. (2007). "Standing out: How new firms in emerging markets build reputation." *Strategic Organization*, 5(1): 31–70.

——, Williamson, I., Petkova, A., & Sever, J. (2005). "Being good or being known: An empirical examination of the dimensions, antecedents, and consequences of organizational reputation." *Academy of Management Journal*, 48(6): 1033–1049.

Roberts, P. W. & Dowling, G. R. (2002). "Corporate reputation and sustained superior performance." *Strategic Management Journal*, 23: 1077–1093.

Shamsie, J. (2003). "The context of dominance: An industry driven framework for exploiting reputation as a resource." *Strategic Management Journal*, 24(3): 199–215.

Shapiro, C. (1983). "Premiums for high quality products as returns to reputations." *Quarterly Journal of Economics*, 98: 659–680.

Suchman, M. C. (1995). "Managing legitimacy: Strategic and institutional approaches." *Academy of Management Review*, 20: 571–610.

Weigelt, K. & Camerer, C. (1988). "Reputation and corporate strategy: A review of recent theory and applications." *Strategic Management Journal*, 9: 443–454.

CHAPTER 3

....

KEEPING SCORE: THE CHALLENGES OF MEASURING CORPORATE REPUTATION

....

GRAHAME R. DOWLING

NAOMI A. GARDBERG

While corporate reputation's (CR) benefits are known and lauded, its nature as an intangible asset causes its measurement to remain elusive. We describe methodological issues faced by CR researchers, including the thorny issues of construct definition, conceptualization as a formative and/or reflective construct, item breadth, sampling frames, scales' psychometric properties, and their appropriateness for measurement across industry, national, and ownership contexts.

We also discuss the appropriateness of various methodologies such as survey, content analysis, and archival data. We then review the most visible academic and practitioner quantitative measures of CR from Fortune's "America's Most Admired Companies" to the Reputation Institute's RepTrak Pulse that have been published by consultants or business media outlets in over fifty countries.

Overall, CR measurement has improved, providing better tools for both academic research and practice. We emphasize the need for multiple methodologies to facilitate triangulation, and conclude with suggestions for future operationalizations of corporate reputation.

A fundamental tenet of good research and management practice is that of sound measurement. Poor measures hinder theory development and testing, and they obscure the evaluation of organizational performance. In both management science and practice, measurement is a vexing problem. The constructs we seek to measure are often difficult to define and operationalize within a business context. Notwithstanding this, measures proliferate and some measurement methodologies become accepted to the point that their formalistic nature shapes the research performed (Starbuck, 1993). The field of corporate reputation is not immune from such measurement problems (see for example,

Brown & Perry, 1994; Baucus, 1995; Eidson & Master, 2000; Bromley, 2002; Wartick, 2002; Berens & Van Riel, 2004; Chun, 2005; Helm, 2005).

Other chapters in this volume address the nomological network in which the construct *corporate reputation* (CR) exists, the theories that frame it, and the construct's definitional web. Thus we focus on operationalization and measurement. As these chapters attest, corporate reputation is a valuable intangible asset. While this intangible nature enhances its role in creating sustainable competitive advantage it also hinders its measurement. We review the topic of measurement to help guide those who desire to create a new measure of corporate reputation, those choosing among extant operationalizations and measures, as well as companies interpreting their various reputation scores.

This chapter describes a variety of corporate reputation measures to highlight the methodological issues faced by researchers and practitioners. Our goal is to identify the principal issues that researchers need to consider when creating the next generation of reputation measures. Of particular interest are those reputation rankings of companies and universities that make their way into the media. Despite attracting academic scorn, some of these have played a significant role in shaping empirical research and guiding management practice. These measures are extensively reviewed and summarized in our appendix.

The chapter starts with an overview of the issues that bedevil the measurement of corporate reputation. Then we describe four principal types of reputation measure. To illustrate the issues raised in these two sections we review and discuss the strengths and weaknesses of a number of prominent measures of corporate reputation. We conclude with suggestions for creating more valid and reliable measures of corporate reputations.

MEASUREMENT CHALLENGES

While the notion of reputation has been discussed for centuries, it is only recently that management scholars have sought to develop a more formal and measurable notion of the construct. From our reading of the literature we identify ten issues that have hindered progress during this period.

1. *Construct confusion* stems from the emergence of numerous similar overlapping constructs that are sometimes used interchangeably across disciplines. For example, there is corporate—brand (in marketing), identity (marketing and graphic design), image (marketing and psychology), reputation (economics, organizational behavior, and strategy), and celebrity and status (organizational behavior, sociology, and strategy). These constructs are designed to focus on different viewpoints of a company (Brown et al., 2006), for example:
    (a) Who do we want to be (e.g., corporate identity and corporate brand)?
    (b) What do people actually think about us (e.g., corporate image and corporate reputation)?

Because these closely related constructs are introduced and developed in different disciplines, their measurement often has adopted different techniques and methodologies. Thus even earnest researchers find it difficult to examine discriminant validity among these constructs and their measures.

2. *Definitions* of corporate reputation create a related obstacle in the development of rigorous measures. As Barnett, Jermier, & Lafferty (2006: 35) write, "It would be inaccurate to claim that there is something of an emerging consensus among researchers when it comes to defining corporate reputation because many do not appear to define the term or do not appear to be aware of how others are handling the concept." It is puzzling why researchers are confusing some established constructs and why journal reviewers and editors are not challenging this research.

3. *The time of the measure* is often confusing. Scholars can measure CR as either a forward-looking, contemporary, or backwards-looking construct. For example, defining CR in terms of admiration and respect is essentially a backwards-looking measure because a respondent is reflecting on the past behavior of the firm. Defining CR in terms of firm characteristics like distinctiveness and transparency is a contemporary measure. And defining CR in terms of trustworthiness is a forwards-looking measure because the respondent is forecasting some future behavior of the firm. Some measures combine two or more time frames in the one measure.

4. *Unit of measurement and the unit of analysis* are confounded by some scholars. As noted throughout this book, sometimes CR is conceptualized as an individual phenomenon and sometimes it is a group or shared phenomenon. For example, as a group phenomenon reputation can be measured as a set of homogeneous evaluations or as individuals' perceptions of how they believe other types of people think about the company. For some group advocates the unit of analysis is a single group, such as employees or customers, while for others reputation perceptions converge across different groups. A problem occurs when scholars who postulate reputation as a group phenomenon measure it as an individual perception with no reference to how other (similar) people might share a value system that drives their common perceptions. Thus, if corporate reputation is defined as a group-level construct there needs to be either an *ex ante* "theory of the group" or an *ex post* "statistical theory" to capture reputation's "shared" or "common" aspect. For example, stakeholder theory and social identity theory have been used as *ex ante* group theories.

Alternatively, reputation can be measured as individuals' perceptions of what they think about the company. Here, respondent perceptions can be aggregated *ex post* into what Bromley (2002: 36) calls a "meta reputation" and Safón (2009: 205) calls a "grand reputation." A key issue is that many reputation measures are reported as the aggregated perceptions of a large group of respondents. Statistics have long recognized that when a big heterogeneous group is decomposed into smaller, more homogeneous groups, these groups' means often have little relationship to those of the larger group. Better still is for respondents to be clustered into homogeneous groups for reporting and further statistical analysis. This *ex post* statistical grouping is analogous to the idea of customer segmentation in marketing.

5. *Breadth of measure* refers to whether corporate reputations should be measured as an attribute based or an overall assessment of an organization (Barnett, Jermier, & Laffery, 2006). Attribute-based approaches ask individuals to rate a set of attributes that are then aggregated to (a) form "dimensions of judgment", or (b) an overall reputation score, or (c) used as the indicators of a latent CR variable. In this chapter we will use "attribute" to describe specific organizational characteristics used in survey questions to respondents, and "dimension" to describe clusters of related attributes specified by the researcher or uncovered through statistical analysis. Multi-attribute measures present researchers with a number of issues to consider:

(a) The attributes can be conceptualized as cognitive (descriptors), affective (evalua-tions), or conative (intentions to engage with) dimensions of judgment. The issue here is whether these different types of attributes (dimensions) are considered as inde-pendent or causally related. For example, a person could admire a company (affect) because (s)he believes it to be trustworthy (cognition) and thus be willing to buy its products (conation). The assumption of independence or causal relationship will affect how the attributes are combined (Wong, Law, & Huang, 2008).

(b) Many measures implicitly assume that all attributes (dimensions) are equally important. Given that this is often unjustified, their relative importance can be determined either by respondent self-rating or statistical estimation.

(c) If a company's reputation is composed of both positive and negative attributes (dimensions), then aggregating these assessments to form an overall reputation "number" will obscure key aspects of the construct.

(d) If the attributes (dimensions) that create a good reputation are different from those that destroy such reputations, averaging across these compromises the measure's efficacy.

(e) When researchers ask respondents to assess multiple attributes of reputation, they assume that either their respondents are knowledgeable enough to pro-vide valid assessments, or their measurement model can accommodate some poor quality assessments.

Alternatively, an overall assessment of reputation (such as "Company X has a good or bad reputation") presents an easier task for respondents. If they are also asked to com-pare the similarity of reputations across companies, statistical routines can be used to discover the dimensions of judgment that discriminate amongst the companies (Dowling, 1988; Jaworska & Chupetlovska-Anastasova, 2009). While these decomposi-tional techniques are particularly well suited to measuring both the competitive and sta-tus differences in reputation, they are seldom used.

6. *The structural model of reputation* refers here to the selection of the attributes (and dimensions) that form, or are reflected by, CR. For example, after *Fortune*'s "America's

Most Admired Companies" (AMAC) ranking became well established, many research-ers used these attributes as the basis for their measure without due regard to whether a respondent might know about all these characteristics. (The justification here was to build on prior research.) Alternatively, a panel of experts was asked to generate a list, and/or a literature search was used to identify attributes used by other researchers. This approach to CR measurement assumes that if a company can improve, say, its social responsibility it will enhance its corporate reputation, and possibly its ranking against its peers.

The "literature search" process to attribute selection stands in contrast to a definition-based approach. Here the list of attributes is derived according to a well-constructed definition of CR. Rossiter (2002) and Mackenzie (2003) suggest that such a definition would include:

  (a) an object—the company being measured;
  (b) dimensions of judgment (such as social responsibility);
  (c) a rater entity, namely, a specific group of people (such as consumers);
  (d) the construct's conceptual theme (such as the company's overall appeal); and
  (e) how the construct is expected to differ across cases and contexts (such as CR being damaged in a crisis).

Definition-based attribute selection starts with considering how the rater entity would construct their reputation of the target object. This will rely on assumptions about the knowledge structures of the individuals and/or the shared perceptions of the group.
    Sometimes the two approaches to CR measurement converge, but often they do not. When they do, the CR measure informs management action because individual evalua-tions suggest what managers should change to improve their company's desired reputa-tion. A good example of the struggle to get such alignment is provided in Fombrun and van Riel's book *Fame & Fortune* (2004). Here, the authors describe two different struc-tural models of reputation formation—one to determine a reputation ranking (chap-ter 3), the other to suggest a set of actions managers should follow to enhance their company's reputation (chapter 5). The "ranking model" is derived from past scholarship, while the "management model" seems to be derived from how individuals would assess a company. There is no overlap of the variables used in the two models.

    7. *The measurement model* specifies the relationship between the CR construct and its measures, namely, whether these are effect indicators (a reflective scale) or causal indicators (a formative index). In the late 1970s and early 1980s a small group of influ-ential scholars in psychology, management, and marketing berated their peers about failing to pay enough attention to the issue of construct validity and its associated measurement issues (for a review see Bromley, 2002; Jarvis, Mackenzie, & Podsakoff, 2003). Based on classical test theory these scholars then proposed a series of measure-ment protocols that were subsequently adopted by most journal editors. The issue here

was that classic test theory was only one approach to measurement. It assumes that the variations in the measured scores of a latent construct such as CR are made up of the true score, plus error. Here, a change in the measured score (the indicator) *reflects* a change in the (latent) construct. Thus, the construct is assumed to cause its measures. *Reflective* measures have the character of "(reputation) defines what you should measure" its indicators to be. In this protocol, a construct should be measured with a battery of positively correlated items. The calibration of reliability (via, say, coefficient alpha) and various types of validity (content, face, criterion-related, concurrent, predictive, construct, convergent, and discriminant) test the efficacy of the measure. No scholar ever conducts all these tests, nor is it expected that a measure will pass them all. Judgments are routinely made about what is "good enough" (such as an alpha > 0.7) in order to use the measure in a structural model.

While this reflective style of measure is popular with many scholars, some in economics and sociology, and many practicing market researchers, adopt a different approach. They combine a number of indicators to form the measure of a construct without any assumptions about the correlations amongst these indicators. In essence, the indicators *form* the latent construct. In contrast to a reflective measure, here the causality flows from each indicator to the construct. These *formative* measures have the character of "define what you mean" (reputation to be). The set of indicators chosen are typically aggregated into an index measure.

Because constructs themselves exist apart from their measurement, CR can be measured as either a formative or reflective construct (Wilcox, Howell, & Breivik, 2008). The challenge for the researcher is to argue his or her case (see, for example, Schwaiger, 2004; Helm, 2005; Safón, 2009). While guidance is available (see, for example, Jarvis, Mackenzie, & Podsakoff, 2003), the task can be challenging. Also, while the protocols for constructing reflective measurement models are well understood, those for formative models are still emerging. Papers by Rossiter (2002), Diamantopoulos and Siguaw (2006), and those in the special issue of the *Journal of Business Research* catalog progress to date (Diamantopoulos, Riefler, & Zeugner-Roth, 2008). This chapter will not attempt to summarize the technicalities of this developing measurement protocol. Rather, we note how some of the more popular measures of reputation seem to be measured as reflective or formative constructs.

8. *Sample frame & selection* is a two part measurement issue that refers to both organizations and informants. In all types of CR studies the company sampling frame can influence interpretation of the outcomes. For example, some ranking-style measures of reputation use a narrow selection of companies, namely, only those that are very large or familiar. These are particularly prone to having reputations composed of both positive and negative attributes (Brooks et al., 2003). Thus, any equally weighted, aggregate reputation score will obscure the complexity of their reputation. Another issue is whether the companies selected compete with each other. When they don't, many managers regard the comparison of a disparate list of companies as a "beauty contest."

A related issue is whether different types of companies may have quite different types of reputation. For example, will the same set of attributes be equally effective in describing the reputation of a service company and a manufacturing company (Walsh & Beatty, 2007). Also, will stigmatized companies (such as cigarette manufacturers) (Chapter 10, this volume) and lionized companies (such as health care institutions) share a common set of reputation attributes? These remain largely unexplored questions.

For surveys the choice of respondents also is critical. For example, should the sample be broadly based or narrowly focused? This decision should be guided by the construct definition. Some scholars view corporate reputation as an aggregate of public or external stakeholder perceptions. Their methodology often builds on opinion polling methods. Other scholars argue that employees, customers, business partners, and the general public have differing needs from, and relationships with, companies such that their views of the same company will differ substantially (e.g., Dowling, 2001; Wartick, 2002; Walsh & Beatty, 2007). This also raises the question of whether a single measure of reputation can "work" with different groups and/or across different cultures. And, can the now widely used Internet panels provide a representative sample of a particular group?

The key issue here is the nature of the sampling frame and whether or not the final selection of respondents or firms is appropriate for theory testing or an effects application style of research (Calder, Phillips, & Tybout, 1981).

9. *Research context* relates to how the context in which reputation judgments are elicited from respondents may affect the measure's efficacy. In any form of opinion research it is well established that the nature of the task and the context in which people find themselves significantly shape how beliefs are reported (Devinney, 2007). For example, if a survey respondent has little direct knowledge of a company, then the context in which they make their evaluations will be primed by the research setting. These people do not formally construct an attribute-based evaluation of the company's reputation as presented by a polling organization. Also, in many survey contexts there is little incentive for the respondent to reveal information that is truthful. And especially in long surveys when fatigue sets in, many respondents take little care with their responses. Finally, when there is no direct "line of sight" between respondents' reputation judgments and how these might influence their subsequent behavior, there is little incentive to evaluate a company in a way that informs this behavior. The theory of planned behavior, which deals with the conditions under which attitudes are likely to predict behavior, suggests that context effects are very important (Wilson & Hodges, 1992; Albarracin et al., 2001). Thus, the predictive validity of specific reputation outcomes for many corporate reputation measures will be low (e.g. Page & Fearn, 2005).

10. *Measuring changes in corporate reputations* has been almost completely ignored. To stimulate more interest in this topic we describe how scholars might approach measuring change. Consider the situation where a company seeks to improve its corporate reputation. For example, many corporate social responsibility (CSR) initiatives have been proposed as a way to either improve a company's standing in the societies in

which it operates and/or to counter adverse perceptions of its operations. Likewise, corporate branding initiatives may be designed to improve employee and customer perceptions. Shareholder communication programs target this group. The question of interest then becomes do such programs improve the company's desired reputation? That is, do they improve respondents' self-reported attribute scores of CR? It turns out that simple ideas of how to measure change in these perceptions can result in ambiguous and sometimes incorrect conclusions being drawn.

Golembiewski, Billingsley, & Yeager (1976) conceptualize three kinds of change that a management intervention such as a reputation improvement program may achieve. Alpha change occurs when the meaning of the attributes (reputation construct) to the respondent and the psychological interpretation of the units of measurement on the attribute scales stay the same, but the level of the measurement on the scales changes. For example, suppose that the shareholder communication program noted above involved merely providing information to shareholders on a quarterly rather than half-yearly basis. It would be reasonable to assume that change differences in rating scale scores for the same set of attribute scales would accurately measure any improvement. In this case, the intervention is designed to leave the "measurement rule" unchanged but increase the level on this rule.

Now consider the corporate branding initiative. Assume that this entailed a new creative execution of an existing position statement. The idea here is to improve the "wow factor" associated with the position statement. This is an example of beta change. It occurs when the meaning of the construct (in this case the corporate slogan) to the respondent stays the same, but the respondent subjectively recalibrates their "measurement rule." What they previously considered to be, say, "very good" on the measurement scale(s) now shifts up or down depending on how they liked the new execution. This is a similar problem to aggregating the rating scale values of people who interpret the values and/or intervals between them differently. To compare pre- and post-measures now requires some type of psychometric adjustment of one or both of the sets of scales.

Now consider the CSR initiative. Assume that this was the first time that the company had undertaken such a program and its motivation was to add a new dimension to the company's reputation profile. This is an example of gamma change. It occurs when the conceptual domain of the construct (attributes and/or dimensions) is radically altered in such a way as to make the previous set of attribute scales unreliable. In this case the meaning of the "measurement rule" has been changed by the intervention. No amount of psychometric rescaling can adjust the pre- and post-scales such that a simple difference score is meaningful.

Since Golembiewski, Billingsley, & Yeager (1976) introduced these ideas there has been some work in the discipline of organizational behavior to determine which approaches are needed to reliably measure each type of change (Thompson & Hunt, 1996; Riordan et al., 2001). This is an area that needs further consideration.

Taken together, these measurement issues constitute a considerable set of challenges for researchers seeking to operationalize corporate reputation and understand its impact on organizational performance and stakeholder relationships. And the combination of a variety of similar constructs, often measured differently across disciplines, makes the accumulation of knowledge problematic. To help a better understanding of these challenges we now describe four different types of reputation measure. Because specific measurement issues vary among these categories, we discuss them separately. By far the largest category involves ranking-style indices. The popular *Fortune* AMAC measure is covered in this section.

EXEMPLARY CORPORATE REPUTATION MEASUREMENT

Our thesis is that the way that the CR construct is measured is a choice of the researcher, albeit one that is based on a clear definition of reputation, which in turn is based on, or informs, a theory of reputation formation and change. At the heart of this process and the challenges just described are decisions about the unit of measurement and the source of data. Figure 3.1 uses these two factors to profile four different types of measure: Attitude, Ranking, Qualitative, and Surrogate. We now describe Figure 3.1 and present exemplary measures from each quadrant.

Primary Versus Secondary Sources of Data

Corporate reputation research is rich with different data collection methodologies. In the social sciences much has been published on best practices for each methodology so

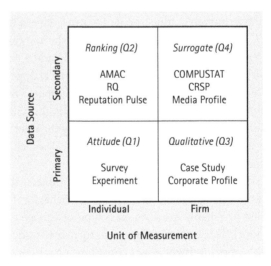

FIGURE 3.1 Categories of reputation measurement.

we concentrate on how the data collection shapes CR measurement. Primary research includes experiments, surveys, and case analyses conducted by the researcher. These may be obtrusive. Secondary research refers to the use of archival data such as published corporate reputation rankings, financial and accounting data, and media coverage. These tend to be unobtrusive. The research question should inform the selection of an existing data set or the development of a new measure of CR.

Although secondary data can provide opportunities for longitudinal or cross-national research based on so-called validated measures, we encourage researchers to review critically the methods employed during the initial data collection when considering secondary data. These include sampling frame(s), consistency in the criteria or items over time, artifacts from data collection such as halo effects, aggregation method, and the motivation of institutional intermediaries that collected the data. For example, to reflect a more global outlook (and perhaps to save money) *Fortune* ceased collecting and publishing its AMAC data set in favor of its "World's Most Admired Companies" data set. We have observed inappropriate generalization from samples, the combination of archival data sources in such a way that the remaining sample is not representative of anything, and the use of financial data to create inappropriate surrogate measures of CR.

Individual Evaluations Versus Firm Characteristics

As we noted above, researchers must determine both their unit of measurement and unit of analysis. Individual-based measurement includes experiments and surveys of individuals. However, sometimes these evaluations are aggregated to form firm-based measures for firm-level analysis (such as those in quadrant 2 of Figure 3.1). Firm-based measurement also includes financial or accounting data, media stories, and case studies. These profile corporate characteristics, behaviors, and/or performance that signal corporate reputation to stakeholders. For firm-based measures the decision to sample according to salience, size, industry, or region greatly affects the validity and generalizability of the findings.

Next we describe each of the quadrants in Figure 3.1 with examples of each measure. Table 3.1 contains a summary of these operationalizations and examples.

Attitude (Q1): Primary Data at the Individual Unit of Measurement

Most of the measures in Quadrants 1 and 2 are made up of multi-item scales and indices that are thought to improve the reliability of the measure and reduce the effects of random error. They are preferred to single-item measures despite recent papers that illustrate that in many circumstances these are just as reliable (Bergkvist & Rossiter, 2007). The Attitude Quadrant (1) includes CR measures based on individual-level data via surveys and experiments. Survey-based measures include individual efforts for the purpose of a single study (Helm, 2005), to create a scale for others' use (Walsh & Beatty, 2007), or the creation of a data set of rankings to be published for others' use. Because the latter measures occupy the Ranking Quadrant (2) we discuss these in the next section.

Walsh & Beatty (2007: 129) created a customer-based reputation (CBR) instrument where CBR is defined as "the customer's overall evaluation of a firm based on his or her reactions to the firm's goods, services, communication activities, interactions with the firm and/or its representatives or constituencies (such as employees, management, or other customers) and/or known corporate activities." CBR was conceptualized as an attitude-like judgment and measured using the classical test approach. The "problem" here is that its definition implies (to us) that the attributes of the company will cause CBR and thus their scale is formed not reflective. The scale is composed of 28 items that are organized into 5 dimensions. It was tested in the US. A variable measuring overall reputation was regressed on the CBR scale and had an R^2 of 0.66. Nomological validity was established by correlating it with the outcome variables of customer satisfaction—loyalty, trust, and word of mouth. Walsh, Beatty, & Shiu (2009) abridged their CBR scale to 15 items and validated it in Germany and the UK. It retains the same dimensions and when the overall scale is regressed against an overall measure of reputation, its R^2 for the UK was 0.46 and for Germany 0.53. In both contexts CBR was associated with the outcome variables noted above.

Helm (2005: 100) developed a 10-attribute formative measure based on a definition of corporate reputation as "a single stakeholder's perception of the estimation in which a certain firm is held by its stakeholders in general." This definition requires the reputation measure to calibrate how an individual thinks other similar people regard a particular firm. Thus, Helm asked her German respondents what they believed "the public" thought about ten characteristics of an international consumer goods producer. These people were consumers who said they knew about the target company. The question here, however, is how would consumers know what "the public" (a very heterogeneous group) thought about ten attributes of a company?

When developing her reputation measure using open-ended interviews of customers, employees, and shareholders, Helm found that all groups used the same descriptive attributes. However, when the reputation measure was later used with a group of consumers, she found that only five of her ten attributes were significant. These were product quality, commitment to the environment, customer orientation, value for money products, and advertising credibility. The non-significant attributes were things that only employees and shareholders would be aware of (namely, corporate success, treatment of employees, commitment to charitable and social issues, financial performance, and the qualifications of management). Thus, if groups are expected to differ, their reputations will best be profiled with different sets of attributes, otherwise there will be substantial redundancy in the measure. That is, each stakeholder group effectively creates a different CR construct (Rossiter, 2002: 309).

In a study of journalists' evaluations of prominent Australian companies Dowling (2004) used a combination of theory-driven and data investigation techniques to create a 25-attribute scale that forms into 5 dimensions of judgment (namely, social accounta-bility—made up of 4 attributes; corporate capability—8 attributes; media relations—3 attributes; market presence—4 attributes; and corporate personality—6 attributes). The aim of the study was to better understand how these characteristics predicted why 25 business journalists would believe what the companies they reported on were saying, and trust, admire, respect, and be confident about the future actions of these companies. These synonyms were used as a measure of the journalists' perception of the reputations of the companies that they evaluated. Together these five dimensions explained 83 per-cent of the variance in the journalists' reputation scores.

In an experimental setting designed to test the effects of advertiser reputation on advertising effectiveness, Goldberg & Hartwick (1990) used word descriptions of a posi-tive and negative advertiser reputation. They consisted of attributes such as the number of employees, the number of years the firm had been in business, past success, and whether or not the Securities and Exchange Commission had the firm under investiga-tion. As a manipulation check, subjects were asked to rate what sort of reputation they thought the firm had with its employees, investors, and with the US and Canadian pub-lics. Answers were averaged to form a reputation index. The two descriptions resulted in significantly different reputations.

In summary, what we see from these CR measures is that each has shown promising results. However, what is also noticeable is that most of these and many other similar measures are developed without adequate discussion of their measurement model. This is understandable given the only recent availability of articles about formative versus reflective measurement and the widespread assumption amongst the community of journal editors and reviewers regarding the appropriateness of reflective measurement.

Ranking (Q2): Secondary Data at the Individual Unit of Measurement

The Ranking Quadrant (2) contains the rankings-style measures, which are some of the oldest and most used measures in both the fields of scholarship and practice. Most are formative measures that define reputation as a multi-attribute construct composed of typically between 5 and 20 items. Attribute scores are generally aggregated into an over-all index score which is then used for inter-company comparison. Some of the more popular business school ranking schemes have come under academic scrutiny and have been found to be of suspect validity (see Devinney, Dowling, & Perm-Ajchariyawong, 2008). However, these rankings have gained enough traction to motivate deans and administrators to "manage to these measures." Others like Fortune's AMAC measure are thought to have been used by a handful of companies to help appraise CEO perform-ance. So whether or not we think that these rankings reflect what they purportedly set out to measure, the fact is that they cannot be ignored.

The modern era of public rankings of organizations began with Fortune's AMAC rankings in 1984, and Business Week's rankings of US business schools in 1988. Since then, many other ranking schemes have been developed by academics, consultants, media outlets, and research institutes. The Reputation Institute has identified 183 public lists of corporate reputation ratings in 38 countries (Fombrun, 2007). Of these 183 lists, 61 convey a rating and/or ranking of a set of firms based on an index measure of corporate reputation. Since the measures vary in the number of items used and sampling frames employed, comparing the results across studies or cross-nationally is problematic (Fombrun, Gardberg, & Sever, 2000). Our appendix, which lists about 30 different measures in over 50 countries, illustrates the challenge in using archival data for cross-national research and comparison.

The examination of any reputation ranking scheme starts with a definition of what it sets out to measure. And here lies a major problem. The media organizations that have created the most popular schemes, namely, *Business Week*, *Financial Times*, and *Fortune*, do not provide a clear definition of what is measured. For example, even after an extensive investigation of the *Financial Times* ranking of business schools it was impossible to describe exactly what was being measured (Devinney, Dowling, & Perm-Ajchariyawong, 2008). When no definition is provided one is forced to work backwards using the item scales, sampling frame, and methodology to infer what is meant.

In the case of *Fortune*'s AMAC measure we see that executives, directors, and security analysts are asked to select ten companies they admire most from a list of last year's top ranked companies. These are the sampling frames of rater entities and companies. An interesting artifact of this process is that poorly ranked companies should be regarded as "the worst of the best." Also, this "good reputation bias" helps to explain why many studies that use the AMAC data find statistically significant but only marginally important results. Respondents then rate companies in their own industry on eight items covering financial soundness, investment value, use of corporate assets, innovativeness, management, products and services, employees, and social responsibility, which *Fortune* argues describe the reputation of large companies. Nine attributes are used in their World's Most Admired Companies survey. The ninth item is global competitiveness. Thus, an overall (reflective) measure is used to select companies and a formative index to measure corporate reputation. Also, *Fortune* reports reputation scores by industry group. Thus, "industry rivalry" is supposedly their "theory of the group."

Over the years the AMAC measure has been criticized by some (e.g., Brown & Perry, 1994; Fryxell & Wang, 1994; Caruana, 1997) and defended by many (namely, the scholars who have published papers using the data). Some criticism is justified, and some is misguided. For example, if the AMAC measure is used as a measure of the corporate reputation of anybody other than industry people and large companies, it will be of questionable validity. *Fortune* does not advocate generalizing beyond its sample frames. The AMAC measure is a specific constituency-based measure of reputation, one that strategy researchers have used to search for a relationship between reputation and financial performance (e.g., Shanley & Fombrun, 1993; Roberts & Dowling, 2002).

Now consider the claim that the AMAC measure's eight attributes are so highly correlated that when factor analyzed, they all load on one factor. And, that the financial performance attributes are by far the most dominant. This effect has been called a financial halo and AMAC's most ardent critics suggest that effectively it invalidates the measure. There are a number of ways to assess this claim. First, a company's financial performance is likely to be driven by, and thus correlated with, the other attributes used in the measure. Thus, the overall index is not a good proxy measure of any of its components and should not be used as such (Fryxell & Wang, 1994). Also, if we accept that AMAC is a formative measure, then by definition the correlations among the dimensions are irrelevant to both the content and predictive validity of the overall measure. Second, Capraro & Srivastava (1997) have found that the financial halo effect is likely to be overstated. And, as Roberts & Dowling (2002) illustrate, if the researcher is worried that this is a measurement bias, it can be parceled out during statistical analysis.

Inspired by the AMAC ranking, several academics set out to develop better multi-attribute formative measures of corporate reputation. For example, since 1999 the Reputation Institute, with the market research firm Harris Interactive, has conducted studies of corporate reputation in the US and other countries (Fombrun, Gardberg, & Sever, 2000; Gardberg, 2006). The studies used the Reputation Quotient (RQ), a 20-attribute, cross-national, standardized measure of reputation where each company is scored out of 100. An organization's absolute score calibrates its reputation, while its relative score reveals its positional status.

The RQ was grounded in public polling theory and practice. Respondents are consumers/members of the general public selected by Harris Interactive from their various country online databases. As with its opinion polling, Harris collects demographic and behavioral data, which are used as a surrogate for stakeholder type to propensity weight responses. Because this is a proprietary procedure it is not clear which "theory of the group" guides selection of the multiple stakeholder groups or how their aggregation produces a "collective representation." The company sampling frame is based on salient reputations. Respondents nominate two companies that they consider to have the best and two the worst overall reputations. While this data collection screen is designed to ensure that respondents are familiar (enough) with the companies they rate in order to avoid the GIGO (garbage-in, garbage-out) trap, it leaves the RQ open to criticism by managers that their company has no meaningful comparator.

Until 2005, the Reputation Institute and affiliated academics conducted a global project to measure the reputations of the world's most visible companies in Australia, Denmark, Germany, Italy, Japan, the UK, and the US, among others. Although Gardberg (2006) established that the CR construct had conceptual and functional equivalence (Singh, 1995), her research exposed the fact that the RQ instrument lacked some kinds of instrument equivalence, which refers to whether "the scale items, response categories and questionnaire stimuli [are] interpreted identically across nations" (Singh, 1995: 605). Also, some items lacked relevance in specific contexts. This and a review by the Reputation Institute prompted the development of the measure called RepTrak™.

RepTrak™ is another Reputation Institute measure. It combines 23 company performance attributes into 7 dimensions (namely, products and services, innovation, workplace, governance, citizenship, leadership, and performance) that form a standardized, cross-national measure. The dimension scores are regressed against a four-part measure of reputation comprised of the reputation synonyms—trust, admiration, good feeling, and high esteem. This measure is called RepTrak Pulse™, and was validated in 41 countries. While the Pulse avoids the issue of measure breadth such as varying item valence (Ponzi, Fombrun, & Gardberg, 2011), it is captured by the time issue noted earlier, namely, it combines a past, present, and future measure of CR into a single score. However, like the MIMIC (multiple indicators and multiple causes) approach adopted by Safón (2009), a strength of this two-part measurement model is the diagnostic insights gained by comparing the two sets of measures. Also, when scholars are not interested in the drivers of reputation, they can use the short-form measure as a dependent, independent, or control variable in their models.

In summary, corporate reputation measurement has advanced since the launch of *Fortune*'s ratings of "America's Most Admired Companies." The new instruments vary in their sampling frames, items, and length. Few other than the RQ and RepTrak™ have been validated in countries beyond Germany, the UK and the US. While there is a friendly rivalry amongst the various groups that create these ranking schemes (e.g., Eidson & Master, 2000), there is some criticism of this general approach to reputation measurement.

Qualitative (Q3): Primary Data at the Firm Unit of Measurement

Case studies and corporate profiles (defined here as a description of a company containing information about its reputation or standing amongst its peers) are descriptive measures of reputation. They can provide an in-depth description of the attributes and actions of companies and the reputations held by various stakeholder groups. While these are not a quantitative measure of reputation like those described elsewhere in this chapter, nevertheless these literary descriptions provide a valuable record of, and insight into, corporate admiration and respect.

Information about the reputation of a company can be self-generated (such as that appearing on the corporate website), sponsored (such as an "official" corporate history), or opinion-based (such as the comments of a company analyst, a journalist, or people on Internet sites). For example, business schools often tout their reputations to potential students using a combination of quality indicators, institutional ratings, and endorsements by satisfied customers. The combination of information used reflects the supposedly important dimensions of reputation. Internet auction sites often report the satisfaction of buyers as a way to signal their reputation.

More extensive versions of cases are written by academics as company profiles and descriptions of practice, CEOs as company histories (e.g., Anita Roddick's *Body and Soul: Profits with Principles*), journalists as business books (e.g., Matt Peacock's *Killer Company*—the story of the James Hardie company and its long-running asbestos crisis), and television and video producers as documentaries (e.g., *Enron, The Smartest Guys in the Room*). The advantage of these is a rich and interesting storyline. The disadvantage is that the dimensions and levels of reputation are based on the author's opinion. Notwithstanding the "biased" nature of the reporting sometimes, these cases have a profound effect on the consulting opportunities of the authors, and occasionally public policy because the issues raised trigger new laws and regulations.

The corporate reputation scholarly literature contains relatively few in-depth case studies (see, for example, Carroll, 2009). Many of those that get published appear mainly in the management literature (e.g., Balmer, Stuart, & Greyser, 2009). Some of the more prominent of these deal with the construct known as organizational identity and have appeared in *Academy of Management Review* and *Administrative Science Quarterly* (e.g., Dutton, Dukerich, & Harquail, 1994). There is an opportunity here for more scholarly company descriptions.

Surrogate (Q4): Secondary Data at the Firm Unit of Measurement

Several different types of studies use secondary data at the firm-level of measurement. These include media content analysis, (certified) reports of activities such as corporate social responsibility and philanthropy, "wins" in certification contests, market share, capital assets, and financial and accounting data. Because some of these *surrogate* measures can be regarded as antecedents or consequences of reputation they need to be used with care.

Deephouse (2000: 1091) proposes a construct called "media reputation," defined as "the overall evaluation of a firm presented in the media." This definition reflects the belief in the media's influence on the social construction of reality. It is consistent with many definitions of corporate reputation in this book. Media research also suggests that the reputation of an organization is both formed and reflected by the media coverage it receives. Media measures, however, assume that this commentary helps people to form their reputation of a company by creating or updating the dimensions of judgment used. The rationale here is that media coverage helps to define what is important for many people to believe about companies and what aspects of companies' character and performance should be used to evaluate them (Carroll & McCombs, 2003; Einweller, Carroll, & Korn, 2010).

In scholarly as opposed to practitioner research media reputation is mostly measured as an index of the amount of media exposure and its (un)favorableness (e.g., Wartick, 1992; Deephouse, 2000; Deephouse & Carter, 2005; Greenwood et al., 2005; Wry, Deephouse, & McNamara, 2006; Eccles, Newquist, & Schatz, 2007). These indices are typically independent variables in studies of corporate performance. Deephouse and his colleagues have found that the predictive validity of favorable media coverage is greater than the total media coverage received. Many companies use the services of a media analytics firm as the prime (and only) scorecard of their reputation.

Dowling & Weeks (2008) identify several reasons why media measures are useful. As well as overall "counts" of favorable and unfavorable media items, dimensions of judgment are revealed. These emerge from the natural language of journalists and the people who comment on the companies, as opposed to being prescribed by the researcher. They are also described in terms of themes (consistent coverage) and contradictions (mixed coverage). The dimensions of judgment can be profiled by different rater entities, such as journalist, website, time period, competitor, and so on. Typically, each of the dimensions of judgment will be "unpacked" (reported as a profile) when reported to management. Thus, they can inform remedial action for a company in a way that opinion poll-style reputation ranking schemes cannot. Hence, all the major companies in the world use some type of media analysis.

In another surrogate measure of reputation Karpoff and associates use event study analysis to compute reputational penalties resulting from corporate misbehavior. For example, in a study of the cost to companies of being caught cooking the books, Karpoff, Lee, & Martin (2008) computed the reduction in net present value of the company's cash flows as a measure of "lost reputation." Karpoff presents more details of his methods in Chapter 18 of this volume. Ratings agencies like Moody's and Standard & Poors also use financial metrics as surrogate reputation measures.

Lee, Pollock, & Jin (2011) created a multi-item index to measure venture capital (VC) firms' reputations. They focused their index on the specific attributes that signal a VC firm's ability to raise its own investment capital and successfully take its holdings public. The attributes are based on the five years prior to the focal year and include the total number of portfolio companies in which the VC invested; the total funds invested in portfolio firms; the total dollar amount of funds raised; the number of individual funds raised; the number of portfolio firms taken public; and the VC's age in the focal year. Although the index appears to be formative, the authors used methods for examining the reliability of reflective scales to create it.

Sometimes surrogates like the structural factors of a company (such as its size) or environmental factors (such as its perceived country of origin) correlate with reputation-like effects. These measures are used as surrogates for reputation whereby the researcher (often boldly) claims that they capture the essence of the construct. However, often the estranged nature of these measures means that more than one variable will be used to measure reputation. While it is easy to be critical of these measures, they can be useful if postulated as an alternative model of the reputation effects. For example, few scholars test their more direct measure of reputation against an alternative model comprised of structural and environmental variables. In one study that did, Devinney, Dowling, & Perm-Ajchariyawong (2008) found that they could substantially reproduce the *Financial Times* ranking of business schools with a set of these factors.

Another type of measure involves measuring reputation by a company's association with other similar companies. This is common in the field of Initial Public Offerings (IPOs) where the underwriter's relative placement (market share) in stock offering "tombstone" announcements serves as a surrogate for reputation. However, these are as much measures of prestige as they are of reputation (e.g., Carter, Dark, & Singh, 1998).

GOING FORWARD

We conclude with suggestions for creating more valid and reliable measures of corporate reputations. Looking back across the various measures described here we note that too few (including our own) address all the key measurement challenges (MC) described at the beginning of the chapter. This has meant that many measures are poorly formulated. And with a variety of definitions of corporate reputation and a variety of measures, it is little wonder that many scholars periodically express their frustration with the field of reputation research. Based on the previous measurement challenges, our recommendations for creating new measures of corporate reputation are:

1. Derive a measure of CR from a well-constructed definition of the construct such that the object, attributes of judgment, rater entity, conceptual theme, and context are clear. (MCs 1, 2, 3, and 6.)
2. If the definition specifies that corporate reputation is a shared estimation, describe the "theory of the group" on which it is based, otherwise describe the rationale for the data aggregation and reporting procedure. For all group or shared reputations report a measure of heterogeneity. (MC 4.)
3. Ensure that it is clear how the rater entities (companies and respondents), and their sampling frame and selection procedure, support theory testing or effect application research. (MC 8.)
4. If CR is conceptualized as a multidimensional construct, explain the relationship between the dimensions and the overall CR construct. (MC 5.)
5. Describe the reasoning behind choosing to measure CR as either a reflective or formative construct. Then use appropriate procedures to create and validate the measure (e.g., Safón, 2009). (MC 7.)
6. For survey-based measures, describe how context effects have been addressed. (MC 9.)
7. If the CR measure is to be used to test differences in scores across time or in different contexts (such as countries), specify the type of change expected and how differences will be measured. (MC 10.)

As Barnett, Jermier, & Lafferty (2006) note, interest in corporate reputation has been growing as a subfield of organization science. Our review of the literature for this chapter suggests that future research might be influenced by two factors: technology and gamma change.

Technology has the potential to change many elements of corporate reputation measurement. Internet-based technologies, together with the more widespread use of smart phones and tablets, can reduce the cost of surveys and increase their frequency. However, this will come at a cost, namely, the nature of the people polled. At present there are many groups that do not engage with these technologies. Thus, while the timeliness of response and the number of people who might reply to short surveys seem impressive, how generalizable the findings are is still unclear. Technology, especially when leveraged through social media, is also changing the conversations about, and interactions with, companies. Specialist consultancies are emerging to monitor this traffic and to help companies respond in appropriate ways. A natural outgrowth of this is website measures of reputation. Toms & Taves (2004) describe various approaches. This is an interesting and evolving area of inquiry.

The previous discussion of gamma change focuses attention on how the criteria used by stakeholders to evaluate companies evolve over time. For example, in the years between developing the RQ and RepTrak™, Charles Fombrun and his associates observed a greater emphasis on communication, governance, and transparency as determinants of reputation. The global financial crisis has also changed the criteria many people use to evaluate companies, especially financial institutions. And as more media and political attention is directed towards the issues of sustainability and environmentalism we see that the meaning of these changes over time (Chapter 4, this volume). Media analysis is a good way for researchers to monitor CR when such potential changes occur. And when they do, new measures may need to be developed.

In conclusion, while CR measurement has shown signs of improvement over the last few years, it is now at a watershed. If academic research and practice continues on its present course further improvement will be gradual. What is needed to further our knowledge is a variety of well-constructed measures using multiple methodologies in all four quadrants of Figure 3.1.

Acknowledgment

This work was supported in part by a grant from the City University of New York PSC-CUNY Research Award Program and the Weissman Center for International Business at Baruch College. Authors contributed equally to this chapter.

Exemplar Corporate Reputation Operationalization

Reference	Components

Attitude (Q1): Primary Data at the Individual–Unit of Measurement

Dowling (2004)	*Definition:* The overall estimation in which a company is held (p. 196).
	Unit of analysis/measurement: Individual
	Measurement theory: Attitudinal formative measure
	Breadth of measure: Social accountability, corporate capability, media relations, market presence, personality (25 items)
	Sample frame(s): Business journalists
	Research context: Personal interviews
	Measuring change: NA
Helm (2005)	*Definition:* A single stakeholder's perception of the estimation in which a certain firm is held by its stakeholders in general (p. 100).
	Unit of analysis/measurement: Individual
	Measurement theory: Attitudinal formative measure
	Breadth of measure: 10 items across performance domains
	Sample frame(s): Consumers
	Research context: Personal interviews, focus groups
	Measuring change: NA
CBR Walsh & Beatty (2007)	*Definition:* The customer's overall evaluation of a firm based on his or her reactions to the firm's goods, services, communication activities, interactions with the firm and/or its representatives or constituencies (such as employees, management, or other customers), and/or known corporate activities (p. 129).
	Unit of analysis/measurement: Individual
	Measurement theory: Attitudinal reflective measure
	Breadth of measure: Customer orientation, good employer, reliable and financially strong, product and service quality, social and environmental responsibility (28 items)
	Sample frame(s): Customers
	Research context: Personal interviews, expert evaluations, online customer survey
	Measuring change: NA

Ranking (Q2): Secondary Data at the Individual—Unit of Measurement

Reputation Quotient (RQ)	*Definition:* A collective representation of a firm's past behavior and outcomes that depicts its ability to render valued results to multiple stakeholders (p. 243).
	Unit of analysis/measurement: Individual
	Measurement theory: Ranking formative and reflective scale
Fombrun, Gardberg & Sever (2000)	*Breadth of measure:* Emotional appeal, financial performance, products and services, social and environmental responsibility, vision and leadership, workplace environment (20 items)
	Sample frame(s): Visible companies/general public and stakeholders
	Research context: Online survey
	Measuring change: Alpha change

(Continued)

Table Continued

Reference	Components
Goldberg & Hartwick (1990)	*Definition:* The consumer's impression of the company that is producing and selling a given product or brand (p. 173). *Unit of analysis/measurement:* Individual *Measurement theory:* Qualitative literary description *Breadth of measure:* Expertise, success, contributions to industry and society *Sample frame(s):* Undergraduate students *Research context:* Experiment *Measuring change:* NA
RepTrak Pulse	*Definition:* Beliefs about companies' past and future actions that shape how stakeholders interact with them (p. 30). *Unit of analysis/measurement:* Individual *Measurement theory:* Ranking reflective scale
Ponzi, Fombrun, & Gardberg (2011)	*Breadth of measure:* 4 items *Sample frame(s):* Large companies/general public *Research context:* Online survey *Measuring change:* Alpha change
Qualitative (Q3): Primary Data at the Firm—Unit of Measurement	
James Hardie	*Definition:* Natural language meaning of reputation *Unit of analysis/measurement:* Company *Measurement theory:* Qualitative literary description
Peacock (2009)	*Breadth of measure:* Many dimensions *Sample frame(s):* James Hardie company *Research context:* Personal interviews, reports and archival documents *Measuring change:* NA
Surrogate (Q4): Secondary Data at the Firm—Unit of Measurement	
Media Reputation	*Definition:* The overall evaluation of a firm by its stakeholders presented in the media (p. 1091, 1093). *Unit of analysis/measurement:* Bank *Measurement theory:* Surrogate—articles about a bank
Deephouse (2000)	*Breadth of measure:* Favorable, unfavorable, or neutral *Sample frame(s):* Newspapers *Research context:* Media content analysis *Measuring change:* NA
Reputational Penalty	*Definition:* The expected loss in the present value of future cash flows due to lower sales and higher contracting and financing costs (p. 581). *Unit of analysis/measurement:* Company
Karpoff, Lee, & Martin (2008)	*Measurement theory:* Surrogate—share price movements *Breadth of measure:* Share value *Sample frame(s):* Companies *Research context:* Corporate valuation (CRSP and Compustat databases) *Measuring change:* Alpha change

Reference	Components
VC Reputation Lee, Pollock, & Jin (2011)	*Definition:* An intangible asset based on broad public recognition of the quality of a firm's activities and outputs (p. 35). *Unit of analysis/measurement:* Venture capital firm *Measurement theory:* Surrogate—time varying, multi-item, formative index *Dimensions of measure:* Prominence and quality of outputs *Sample frame(s):* Venture capital firms, IPOs *Research context:* Firm valuation *Measuring change:* Alpha change

REFERENCES

Albarracin, D., Johnson, B. T., Fishbein, M., & Muellerleile, P. A. (2001). "Theories of reasoned action and planned behavior as models of condom use: A meta-analysis." *Psychological Bulletin*, 127(1): 142–161.

Balmer, J. M., Stuart, H., & Greyser, S. A. (2009). "Aligning identity and strategy." *California Management Review*, 51: 6–23.

Barnett, M. L., Jermier, J. M., & Lafferty, B. A. (2006). "Corporate reputation: The definitional landscape." *Corporate Reputation Review*, 9(1): 26–38.

Baucus, M. S. (1995). "Halo-adjusted residuals: Prolonging the life of a terminally ill measure of corporate social performance." *Business & Society*, 34: 227–235.

Berens, G. & Van Riel, C. B. M. (2004). "Corporate associations in the academic literature: Three main streams of thought in the reputation measurement literature." *Corporate Reputation Review*, 7(2): 161–178.

Bergkvist, L. & Rossiter, J. J. (2007). "The predictive validity of multiple-item versus single-item measures of the same constructs." *Journal of Marketing Research*, 44: 175–184.

Bromley, D. (2002). "Comparing corporate reputations: League tables, quotients, benchmarks or case studies." *Corporate Reputation Review*, 5(1): 35–50.

Brooks, M. E., Highhouse, S., Russell, S. S., & Mohr, D. C. (2003). "Familiarity, ambivalence and firm reputation: Is corporate fame a double-edged sword?" *Journal of Applied Psychology*, 88(5): 904–914.

Brown, T. J., Dacin, P. A., Pratt, M. G., & Whetten, D. A. (2006). "Identity, intended image, construed image and reputation: An interdisciplinary framework and suggested terminology." *Journal of the Academy of Marketing Science*, 34(2): 99–106.

Brown, B. & Perry, S. (1994). "Removing the financial performance halo from Fortune's 'most admired' companies." *Academy of Management Journal*, 37: 1347–1359.

Calder, B., Phillips, L., & Tybout, A. 1981. "Designing research for application." *Journal of Consumer Research*, 8(3): 197–207.

Capraro, A. J. & Srivastava, R. K. (1997). "Has the influence of financial performance on reputation measures been overstated?" *Corporate Reputation Review*, 1(1–2): 86–92.

Carroll, C. (2009). "Defying a reputational crisis—Cadbury's salmonella scare: Why are customers willing to forgive and forget?" *Corporate Reputation Review*, 12(1): 64–82.

Carroll, G. E. & McCombs, M. (2003). "Agenda-setting effects of business news on the public's images and opinions about major corporations." *Corporate Reputation Review*, 6(1): 36–46.

Carter, R. B., Dark, F. H., & Singh, A. K. (1998). "Underwriter reputation, initial returns and the long-run performance of IPO stocks." *The Journal of Finance*, 53(1): 285–311.

Caruana, A. (1997). "Corporate reputation: Concept and measurement." *The Journal of Product and Brand Management*, 6 (2): 109–118.

Chun, R. (2005). "Corporate reputation: Meaning and measurement." *International Journal of Management Reviews*, 7(2): 91–109.

Deephouse, D. L. (2000). "Media reputation as a strategic resource: An integration of mass communication and resource-based theories." *Journal of Management*, 26(6): 1091–1112.

—— & Carter, S. M. (2005). "An examination of differences between organizational legitimacy and organizational reputation." *Journal of Management Studies*, 42(2): 329–360.

Devinney, T. (2007). "A penny for your uninformed opinion." *Living Ethics*, 69: 6.

——, Dowling, G. R., & Perm-Ajchariyawong, N. (2008). "The Financial Times business schools rankings: What quality is this signal of quality?" *European Management Review*, 5(4): 195–208.

Diamantopoulos, A. and Siguaw, J. A. (2006). "Formative versus reflective indicators in organizational measure development: A comparison and empirical illustration." *British Journal of Management*, 17(4): 263–282.

——, Riefler, P., & Zeugner-Roth, K. P. (2008). "Advancing formative measurement models." *Journal of Business Research*, 61(12): 1203–1218.

Dowling, G. R. (1988). "Measuring corporate images: A review of alternative approaches." *Journal of Business Research*, 17(1): 27–34.

—— (2001). *Creating Corporate Reputations*. Oxford: Oxford University Press.

—— (2004). "Journalists' evaluations of corporate reputations." *Corporate Reputation Review*, 7(2): 196–205.

—— & Weeks, W. (2008). "What the media is really telling you about your brand." *Sloan Management Review*, 49(3): 28–34.

Dutton, J. E., Dukerich, J. M., & Harquail, C. V. (1994). "Organizational images and member identification." *Academy of Management Review*, 34: 517–554.

Eccles, R. G., Newquist, S. C., & Schatz, R. (2007). "Reputation and its risks." *Harvard Business Review*, February: 104–114.

Eidson, C. & Master, M. (2000). "Most respected: Who makes the call?" *Across the Board*, 37(3): 17–22.

Einweller, S. A., Carroll, C. E., & Korn, K. (2010). "Under what conditions do the news media influence corporate reputation? The roles of media dependency and need for orientation." *Corporate Reputation Review*, 12(4): 299–315.

Fombrun, C. J. (2007). "List of lists: A compilation of international corporate reputation ratings." *Corporate Reputation Review*, 10(2): 144–153.

—— & Van Riel, C. B. M. (2004). *Fame & Fortune*. New York: FT Prentice Hall.

——, Gardberg, N. A., & Sever, J. M. (2000). "The reputation quotient: A multi-stakeholder measure of corporate reputation." *The Journal of Brand Management*, 7(4): 241–254.

Fryxell, G. E. & Wang, J. (1994). "The Fortune reputation index: Reputation for what?" *Journal of Management*, 20(1): 1–14.

Gardberg, N. (2006). "Reputatie, Reputation, Réputation, Reputazione, Ruf: A cross-cultural qualitative analysis of construct and instrument equivalence." *Corporate Reputation Review*, 9 (1): 39–61.

Goldberg, M. E. & Hartwick, J. (1990). "The effects of advertiser reputation and extremity of advertising claim on advertising effectiveness." *Journal of Consumer Research*, 17(2): 172–179.

Golembiewski, R. T., Billingslet, K., & Yeager, S. (1976). "Measuring change and persistence in human affairs: Types of change generated by OD designs." *Journal of Applied Behavioral Science*, 12(2): 133–157.

Greenwood, R., Li, S. X., Prakash, R., & Deephouse, D. L. (2005). "Reputation, diversification and organizational explanations of performance in professional service firms." *Organization Science*, 16(6): 661–673.

Helm, S. (2005). "Designing a formative measure for corporate reputation." *Corporate Reputation Review*, 8(2): 95–109.

Jarvis, C. B., Mackenzie, S. B., & Podsakoff, P. M. (2003). "A critical review of construct indicators and measurement model specification in marketing and consumer research." *Journal of Consumer Research*, 30: 199–218.

Jaworska, N. & Chupetlovska-Anastasova, A. (2009). "A review of multidimensional scaling (MDS) and its utility in various psychological domains." *Tutorials in Quantitative Methods for Psychology*, 5(1): 1–10.

Karpoff, J. M., Lee, D. S., & Martin, G. S. (2008). "The cost to firms of cooking the books." *Journal of Financial and Quantitative Analysis*, 43 (3): 581–612.

Lee, P. M., Pollock, T. G., & Jin, K.(2011). "The contingent value of venture capitalist reputation." *Strategic Organization*, 9(1): 33–69.

Mackenzie, S. B. (2003). "The damagers of poor construct conceptualization." *Journal of the Academy of Marketing Science*, 31(3): 323–326.

Page, G. & Fearn, H. (2005). "Corporate reputation: What do consumers really care about?" *Journal of Advertising Research*, 45(3): 305–313.

Peacock, M. (2009). *Killer Company: James Hardie Exposed*. Sydney: ABC Books.

Ponzi, L. J., Fombrun, C. J., & Gardberg, N. A. (2011). "RepTrak Pulse: Conceptualizing and validating a short-form measure of corporate reputation." *Corporate Reputation Review*, 14: 15–35.

Riordan, C. M., Richardson, H. A., Schaffer, H., & Vandenberg, R. J. (2001). "Alpha, beta and gamma change: A review of past research with recommendations for new directions." In C. A. Schriesheim & L. L. Neider (Eds.), *Equivalence in Measurement Vol. 1: Research in Management*. Greenwich, CT: Information Age Publishing, 51–98.

Roberts, P. W. & Dowling, G. R. (2002). "Corporate reputation and sustained superior financial performance." *Strategic Management Journal*, 23(12): 1077–1093.

Rossiter, J. R. (2002). "The C-OAR-SE procedure for scale development in marketing." *International Journal of Research in Marketing*, 19(4): 305–336.

Safón, V. (2009). "Measuring the reputation of top US business schools: A MIMIC modeling approach." *Corporate Reputation Review*, 12(3): 204–228.

Schwaiger, M. (2004). "Components and parameters of corporate reputation—An empirical study." *Schmalenbach Business Review*, 56 (January): 46–71.

Shanley, M. & Fombrun, C. (1993). "The market impact of reputational rankings." New York University, Stern School of Business, Working Paper. In C. J. Fombrun (1996), *Reputation*. Harvard: Harvard Business School Press, 188.

Singh, J. (1995). "Measurement issues in cross-national research." *Journal of International Business Studies*, 26(3): 597–618.

Starbuck, W. H. (1993). "Keeping a butterfly and an elephant in a house of cards." *Journal of Management Studies*, 30(6): 885–921.

Thompson, R. C. & Hunt, J. G. (1996). "Inside the black box of alpha, beta and gamma change: Using a cognitive-processing model to assess attitude structure." *Academy of Management Review*, 21(3): 655–690.

Toms, E. G. & Taves, A. R. (2004). "Measuring user perceptions of web site reputation." *Information Processing and Management*, 40: 291–317.

Walsh, G. & Beatty, S. E. (2007). "Customer-based corporate reputation of a service firm: Scale development and validation." *Journal of the Academy of Marketing Science*, 35(1): 127–143.

——,——,& Shiu, E. M. K. (2009). "The customer-based corporate reputation scale: Replication and short form." *Journal of Business Research*, 62(10): 924–930.

Wartick, S. L. (2002). "Measuring corporate reputation: Definition and data." *Business & Society*, 41(4): 371–392.

Wilcox, J. B., Howell, R. D., & Breivik, E. (2008). "Questions about formative measurement." *Journal of Business Research*, 61(12): 1219–1228.

Wilson, T. D. & Hodges, S. D. (1992). "Attitudes as temporary constructions." In L. L. Martin and A. Tesser (Eds.), *The Construction of Social Judgments*. Hillsdale, NJ: Erlbaum, 37–65.

Wong, C. S., Law, K. S., & Huang, G-h. (2008). "On the importance of conducting construct-level analysis for multidimensional constructs in theory development and testing." *Journal of Management*, 34: 744–764.

Wry, T., Deephouse, D. L., & Mcnamara, G. (2006). "Substantive and evaluative media reputations among and within cognitive strategic groups." *Corporate Reputation Review*, 9(4): 225–242.

Appendix (Table 3.1) Summary of Available Corporate Reputation Measures and Resources

Measure[a]	Sponsor/Media Partner/ Market Research Firm[b]	Time Frame[c]	Sampling Frame[d]		Accessibility[e]
			Company	Informant	
Global					
Global RepTrak Pulse	Reputation Institute (RI) Forbes	2000–11	Largest firms from 15 (inc. G8 and BRIC) countries	General public	*Forbes*/RI
World's Best Banks	Global Finance	2002–11	Banks worldwide	Unclear	http://www.gfmag.com/tools/best-banks. html#axzz1S7YE5big
World's Most Admired Companies	Fortune/Hay Group	1997–2011	Fortune 1000 and Global 500 Foreign firms in US	Sample firm's executives and directors plus analysts	*Fortune*
World's Most Respected Companies	Barron's	2005–11	World's 100 largest firms by market capitalization	Professional money managers	*Barron's*/*Barron's* online for last 5 years
World's Most Respected Companies	Financial Times PriceWaterhouseCo- ope-s (PWC)	1998–2005	Nominations	Chief executive officers	*Financial Times*
Regional					
East Africa's Most Respected Companies Survey	PWC/Nations Media Group/Steadman Synovate	2000–10 2008 Rwanda	Nominations in Kenya, Rwanda, Tanzania, and Uganda. Separate survey in Ghana and Nigeria	CEOs and business leaders	PWC website—partial

(Continued)

Appendix (Table 3.1) Continued

Measure[a]	Sponsor/Media Partner/ Market Research Firm[b]	Time Frame[c]	Sampling Frame[d]		Accessibility[e]
			Company	Informant	
Asia 200	*Far Eastern Economic Review*	1993–2005	Largest 40 firms in DJ Indices in Australia, China, Hong Kong, India, Indonesia, Japan, Malaysia, Philippines, Singapore, S. Korea, Taiwan, and Thailand	Executives and professionals	Partial results on WSJAsia.com
Asia 200	WSJ/Nielson	2006–10	Same as above	2,500 + Executives and professionals	Partial results on WSJAsia.com
Argentina					
Monitor Empresarial de Reputación Corporativa (MERCO)	Villafañe & Associates/ *Clarin*/Universidad Tres de Febrero	2010 (first)	100 large firms	5,000 + (Expert and Public)	www.merco.info/es additional data for sale iEco
Prestigio Empresario/Las 100 empresas más admiradas	*Clarin*/CEOP	2004–07	Large firms operating in Argentina	Executives of the same large firms	Top 10 online at *Clarin* CEOP.com.ar–partial
Prestigio Empresario	*Prensa Económica*	2003–11	Large firms operating in Argentina	Executives	2010 available on CD from *Prensa Económica*
RepTrak Pulse	RI	2006–11	10 + large Argentinian firms	Public	RI
Australia					
Corporate Reputation Index (RepTrak)	RI/amrinteractive	2006–11	60 largest firms from BRW Top 100 list	Public	RI

Good Reputation Guide	RepuTex (formerly Reputation Measurement)/ Fairfax Publications: *Sydney Morning Herald* and *The Age*	2001–05	100 largest	Executives surveyed about their own firm/21 NGOs.	NA
Good Reputation Index/St James Ethics	Fairfax Publications	2000–02	100 largest	Experts and Research Groups (NGOs)	Newspaper archives
Reputation Quotient (RQ)	RI/*Financial Review*/ aminteractive	2000–07	Nominations	Public	RI
Austria					
RepTrak Pulse	RI	2009–11	5 + largest firms	Public	RI
Belgium					
RepTrak	RI/akkanto	2009–11	30 largest from Bel20Index	Public	RI/http://akkan.to/ RepTrak
Bolivia					
RepTrak Pulse	RI	2011	70 + firms listed as contributing to Bolivian economy by *Nueva Economia*	Public	RI
Brazil					
Most Admired Companies in Brazil/Empresas Mais Admiradas no Brasil	TNS InterScience/*CartaCapital* magazine	1998–2010	Size	Executives	Full list in hard copy only
RepTrak Pulse	RI	2006–11	25 + largest and visible from Exame's "500 Best & Largest"	Public	Not published/RI
Canada					
Canada's Top 25 Most Respected Corporations	KPMG/*The Globe and Mail*/Ipsos-Reid	1994–2005	NA	250 CEOs	2000–2005 RI List of lists

(Continued)

Appendix (Table 3.1) Continued

Measure[a]	Sponsor/Media Partner/Market Research Firm[b]	Time Frame[c]	Sampling Frame[d]		Accessibility[e]
			Company	Informant	
RepTrak Pulse	RI	2006–11	50 largest (revenue) public and private	Public	RI
Chile					
Monitor Empresarial de Reputación Corporativa (MERCO)	Villafañe & Associates	2010	100 largest	5,000 + experts, corporate directors, and public	www.merco.info/es Additional data for sale
Hill & Knowlton Reputation Study	Hill & Knowlton/*La Tercera*	2002–10	70 + companies	3,500 public	NA
RepTrak Pulse	RI	2006–11	5 + largest (revenue) firms	Public	RI
China					
中國最受尊敬企業十年 10th Anniversary of The Most Respected Companies of China	*Economic Observer* Newspaper/Peking University	2001–11 (Cumulative List)	Nominations	Experts	*Economic Observer* newspaper
RepTrak Pulse	RI	2006–11	40 + largest (revenue) firms	Public	RI
Colombia					
Monitor Empresarial de Reputación Corporativa (MERCO)	Villafañe & Associates	2008–10	100 largest	1,000 + Experts, executives, and public	www.merco.info/es Additional data for sale
RepTrak Pulse	RI	2011	100 + largest (revenue) firms	Public	RI
Denmark					
RepTrak	RI	2006–11	Top 40 most visible firms	Public	RI
Reputation Quotient (RQ)	RI/Harris Interactive	2002–05	15 most nominated for good and bad reputations	Public	*WSJEurope* (2004)/RI

Finland					
RepTrak	RI	2006–11	65 largest firms	Public	RI/*Talouselama*
France					
Barometre d'Image des Grandes Entreprises	*Europe 1, Le Nouvel Economiste, Le Point, Le Parisien, Le JDD* (partners changed over time)/Ipsos France	1999–2011	Size	Public	http://www.ipsos.fr/ipsos-public-affairs
Ipsos Reputation Index	Ipsos	2009–11	100 largest in 10 industries	Public	http://www.ipsos.fr/
Reputation Quotient (RQ)	RI/*WSJ Europe & La Tribune*/ Harris Interactive	2004	15 most nominated for good and bad reputations	Public	RI/*WSJ Europe* (2004)
Réputation des Entreprises du CAC 40	Observatoire de la Reputation/Datops	1994, 2000, 2005	CAC 40	300 French executives, senior executives, and directors	archives
Réputation des Entreprises du CAC 40 (RepTrak Pulse)	RI/*i-Ète*	2006–11	CAC 40	Public	www.management-reputation.fr/RI
Germany					
Best Companies/Image Profile	*Manager Magazin*	1988–2008 biannual	170 + DAX-listed firms	2,500 + CEOs, board members, and top managers	*Manager-Magazin.de*
RepTrak Pulse	RI	2006–11	150 largest (revenue) firms	Public	RI/*The Frankfurter*
Reputation Quotient (RQ)	RI/*WSJ Europe & Handelsblatt*/Harris Interactive	2004	15 most nominated for good and bad reputations	Public	RI/*WSJ Europe* (2004)

(Continued)

Appendix (Table 3.1) Continued

Measure[a]	Sponsor/Media Partner/ Market Research Firm[b]	Time Frame[c]	Sampling Frame[d]		Accessibility[e]
			Company	Informant	
Greece					
RepTrak Pulse	RI	2006, 2008–11	20 largest (revenue) firms	Public	Not published/RI
Reputation Quotient (RQ)	RI/Harris Interactive	2003–04	Nominations	Public	RI
Hungary					
RepTrak Pulse	RI	2010–11	10 largest firms by revenue	Public	RI
India					
India's Most Respected Companies	*BusinessWorld*/Ipsos Indica Research	1983–2011 about biannually	Leading listed firms and significant private firms	1,000 + business leaders, general managers to CEOS	www.businessworld.in
RepTrak Pulse	RI	2006–11	20 largest (revenue) firms	Public	RI
Ireland					
RepTrak Pulse	RI	2006–11	Largest and most visible firms	Public	RI/http://www. corporatereputations.ie/
Italy					
RepTrak Pulse	RI	2006–11	20 firms in Mediobanca's ranking by revenue	Public	RI
Reputation Quotient (RQ)	RI/*WSJEurope*/ Harris Interactive	2004	15 most nominated for good and bad reputations	Public	RI/*WSJEurope*
Japan					
RepTrak Pulse	RI	2006–11	20 largest (revenue) firms	Public	RI
RQ	RI/Harris Interactive/ Dentsu	2004	NA	NA	NA
Mexico					
RepTrak Pulse	RI	2006–11	70 + most visible and largest (revenue) firms	Public	RI

Netherlands					
RepTrak Pulse	RI	2006–11	30 largest (revenue) B2C firms	Public	RI
Reputation Quotient (RQ)	RI/Harris Interactive	2001–05	15 most nominated for good and bad reputations	Public	RI/*WSJEurope* (2004)
New Zealand					
Corporate Reputation Index (RepTrak Pulse)	RI/amrinteractive	2010–11	25 largest (revenue) firms	Public	Ranks–nzhearald.com RI
Norway					
Reputation Quotient (RQ)	RI Harris Interactive	2004	15 most nominated for good and bad reputations	Public	RI/*WSJEurope* (2004)
Dagens Næringsliv (RepTrak Pulse)	RI	2006–11	40 most visible firms	Public	RI
Peru					
RepTrak Pulse	RI	2010–11	50 + most visible and largest (revenue) firms	Public	RI
Poland					
RepTrak Pulse	RI	2006–11	10 largest (revenue) firms	Public	RI
Portugal					
RepTrak Pulse	RI	2007–11	152 largest (revenue) firms including PSI 20	Public	RI
Russian Federation					
RepTrak Pulse	RI	2006–11	20 + largest firms	Public	RI
Reputation-2010 Репутация-2010	W-City	2010	Size	1,000 middle-class members & business leaders	http://w-city.net/anonsyi/reyting-kompaniy-rossii-reputat-siya-2010-2.html

(Continued)

Appendix (Table 3.1) Continued

Measure[a]	Sponsor/Media Partner/Market Research Firm[b]	Time Frame[c]	Sampling Frame[d]		Accessibility[e]
			Company	Informant	
Singapore					
Corporate Reputation Index	Reputation Management Associates	2005–11	5 industries & SMEs	Public	www.reputation.asia
RepTrak Pulse	RI	2009–11	5 largest firms by revenue	Public	RI
South Africa					
SA Top Companies Global Awards	Business Report/PWC/Barloworld	1997–2004	Largest 100 (market cap)	Firms complete questionnaire	Business Report–partial results
FN Top 100	Financial Mail	2003–09	200 of the listed firms	Not clear	www.topcompanies.co.za
RepTrak Pulse	RI	2006–11	15 + largest firms by revenue	Public	lafrica.com/RI
RQ	RI/Harris Interactive	2003	Most visible	Public	NA
South Korea					
RepTrak Pulse	RI	2006–11	15 + largest firms	Public	RI
Spain					
Monitor	Villafañe & Associates, Catedrático de la Universidad/Complutense de Madrid;	2001–11	100 firms operating in Spain with annual revenue greater than 50 million euros	Expert and public	www.merco.info/es
Empresarial de Reputación Corporativa (MERCO)	El País/KPMG (since 2010)				Data for sale
RepTrak Pulse	RI	2006–11	125 most visible and largest (revenue) firms	Public	www.Publico.es/es
Sweden					
RepTrak Pulse	RI	2006–11	50 most visible firms	Public	RI

Reputation Quotient (RQ)	FI/WSJEurope/ Harris Interactive	2004	15 most nominated for good and bad reputations	Public	RI/WSJEurope
Switzerland					
RepTrak Pulse	RI	2006–11	60 + largest firms	Public	RI
Taiwan					
2010天下企業公民 TOP 50 2010 Excellence in Corporate Social Responsibility Top 50	CommonWealth Magazine	2009–11	Nominations	Experts and industry insiders	CommonWealth Magazine http://issue.cw.com.tw/ issue/2010csr/ e2010report-1.jsp
RepTrak Pulse	RI	2006–11	5 largest (revenue) firms	Public	RI
Thailand					
RepTrak Pulse	R	2009–11	5 + largest (revenue) firms	Public	RI
Turkey					
Most Admired Companies in 36 Sectors and The Most Admired of Turkey	Capital magazine/Adecco	1999–2010	Nominations	1,300 + medium- and senior-level managers	Capital
RepTrak Pulse	RI	2009–11	10 largest (revenue) firms	Public	RI
United Kingdom					
Britain's Most Admired Companies (BMAC)	Management Today	1990–2010 Except 1993	10 largest firms in 20+ sectors	Executives	Managementtoday.co.uk
RepTrak Pulse	RI	2006–11	300 largest firms by market cap and revenue	Public	RI
Reputation Quotient (RQ)	RI/WSJEurope/Harris Interactive	2004–05	15 most nominated for good and bad reputations	Public	RI/WSJEurope
United States					
Airline RQ	RI/WSJ/Harris Interactive	2000	Largest 25 airlines serving US	Public	www.wsj.com
America's Most Admired Companies	Fortune, Hay Group (since 2001)	1984–2008	Size	Analysts and industry insiders	Fortune

(Continued)

Appendix (Table 3.1) Continued

Measure[a]	Sponsor/Media Partner/ Market Research Firm[b]	Time Frame[c]	Sampling Frame[d] Company	Informant	Accessibility[e]
America's Most Reputable Companies: The Rankings (RepTrak Pulse)	Reputation Institute/Forbes	2006–11	150 most visible firms and (revenue) largest	Public	Forbes/RI
RepTrak Pulse–Puerto Rico	RI	2011	65 + most visible and (revenue) largest	Public	RI
FSRQ: The Reputations of Financial Firms	RI/American Banker Harris Interactive	2001	Nominations of financial service firms (40 firms)	Public	www.americanbanker.com
Reputation Quotient (RQ)	RI/WSJ/Harris Interactive	2000–05	60 most nominated for good and bad reputations	Public	www.wsj.com through 2005
Reputation Quotient (RQ)	Harris Interactive WSJ (2006 only)	2006–11	60 most nominated for good and bad reputations	Public	www.harrisinteractive.com/www.wsj.com through 2006
RQ Digital	RI/WSJ/Harris Interactive	1999	40 most nominated for good and bad reputations	Public	www.wsj.com
Pharma RQ: The Reputations of Life Science Firms	RI/WSJ/Harris Interactive	2000	Large pharma firms	Medical professionals	NA
Venture Capitalist Reputation Index	Strategic Organization Lee, Pollock & Jin (2011)	1990–2000	500 to 1,500 VC firms depending on the year	Archival data	http://www.timothypollock.com/vc_reputation.htm

[a] Local language if available and English.

[b] Strategic alliance among sponsors, media partners, and research firms change over time. The list reflects recent relationships.

[c] Denotes start date. Some countries may have fewer years of data.

[d] Some sampling frames changed and sample sizes tend to increase over time.

[e] Print media includes their websites and archives. Most of the media archives and the Reputation Institute's List of Lists, which tracks many ratings, require subscriptions. Data also can be available from media partner and/or sponsor.

CHAPTER 4

··

WHAT DOES IT MEAN TO BE GREEN? THE EMERGENCE OF NEW CRITERIA FOR ASSESSING CORPORATE REPUTATION

··

MARK THOMAS KENNEDY

JAY INGHWEE CHOK

JINGFANG LIU

This research theorizes how new criteria for corporate reputations emerge and, as a case study, uses the concept of "green" as applied to business as an illustration. Defining corporation reputation as a collective perception of how organizations of a given type or identity measure up on standards used to judge their quality, we argue that new reputation criteria become real for corporations when those who propose them find common ground either with corporations themselves or with parties capable of exerting pressure on corporations. Compared with ignoring critics calling for new criteria, corporate engagement of ensuing debates is a double edge sword: it makes nascent criteria seem more real while also affording opportunities to shape them. To illustrate this argument, we use the case of what it means for corporations to be green. In analyses of which attributes of green are most central to its usage in organizations' press releases and journalists' news stories for 2001 and 2009, we find what it means to be green shifted to reflect green's usage in press releases, but not vice versa. We conclude by observing the opportunity for future research to decompose reputation's major components, treat them as dynamic rather than fixed, and trace the interactions that contribute to their dynamics.

INTRODUCTION

THE criteria used to determine corporate reputations change often and dramatically. Only a generation ago, having a well-diversified business portfolio was synonymous with being a well-run modern corporation. When so-called "corporate raiders" began to make money by breaking up conglomerates, however, their profits finally sold theory that debunked their dividend-smoothing logic (Modigliani & Miller, 1958), and once feted conglomerates were denounced and dismantled (Davis, Diekmann, & Tinsley, 1994). At first, these "hostile takeovers" were undertaken only by low-status actors, but such tactics quickly became staples of legitimate investment banking deals now known simply as mergers and acquisitions (Hirsch, 1986). Eschewing unrelated diversification, corporations were lauded for combining businesses in related industries (Bettis, 1981) and cultivating capabilities that created "synergies" between them (Barney, 1991). With recognition that profits can be made through unowned assets or outsourced operations (Williamson, 1975), managers developed more strategic partnerships and alliance networks (Stuart, 1999).

With such changes, ideas about what makes a good leader can also change dramatically. Whereas careers in finance were once all but required for becoming a CEO (Hambrick & Mason, 1984), promotion paths diversified as more charismatic and visionary leadership styles gained popularity (Conger, 1989). As shareholders came to see downsides of CEO power (Beatty & Zajac, 1994; Lipton & Lorsch, 1992), however, good governance came to require reining in even the most charismatic leaders by separating the CEO and Board Chair roles (e.g., see Stewart, 2005). More recently, investors have seen the difficulties of distinguishing constructive innovations of visionary leaders from destructive ones that cause market crises. For example, consider the Enron scandal and the 2008 recession. Since Enron executives used exotic financing strategies to disguise fraudulent reporting of corporate financial results (Boyd, 2004), investors are less enthusiastic about visionary innovators and complex finance schemes. Similarly, the recession of 2008 gave investors reason to be leery of strategies based on complex investment vehicles capable of hiding elaborate rip-off schemes (Powell, 2010; Tett, 2009).

The profound social and economic consequences of changing criteria for corporate reputation raise a difficult but important question: how do such criteria emerge? That is, how do new ideas raised by competitors or activists become institutionalized aspects of the standards against which corporations are judged? Is it possible to tell when such ideas are failing or succeeding as attempts to establish a new reputation criterion? How and why do nascent reputation criteria become social realities organizations must meet?

In this chapter, we draw on relational sociology and developments in content analysis to both theorize emergence of new criteria of corporate reputation and illustrate a practical research design for observing such change. To summarize our argument, nascent reputation criteria become social realities through development of common ground between corporations and those who judge their value—not only investors and analysts, but also critics in the media and activists seeking corporate reforms. To illustrate our argument, we explore what it means for businesses to be "green," a case that reveals an idea in motion and suggests the importance of common ground in working out both whether it matters and what it means.

DEFINITIONS: REPUTATION AND CRITERIA

Our theory about how reputation criteria emerge is founded on the corporation reputation literature's assessment-oriented view of reputation (see Barnett, Jermier, & Lafferty, 2006). As opposed to mere awareness or recognition, this view links reputation to collective assessments, or judgments, of quality (Rindova et al., 2005). That is, corporate reputations reflect socially accepted standards about what counts as quality for a given type of organization.

Thus, corporate reputation is different from organizational legitimacy and identity. Whereas legitimacy is about meeting expectations for a given type of organization, reputation is a relative measure of standing versus other firms of that type. That is, organizations have "good reputations when they are viewed favorably relative to the ideal standard for a particular social identity" (King & Whetten, 2008: 192), and they have bad reputations when they stand out for contradicting or falling short of expectations for various elements of the standard—especially those most central.

Since this definition emphasizes collective assessments of firms, it makes media coverage quite important to reputation (Hayward, Rindova, & Pollock, 2004; Rindova, Pollock, & Hayward, 2006). Positive media coverage can accumulate to become a source of advantage (Deephouse, 2000), even making celebrities of managers and firms (Rindova, Petkova, & Kotha, 2007; Rindova et al., 2005). Conversely, negative coverage can undermine and even destroy a firm's reputation.

Criteria, Movements, and Categorization

Linking reputation to quality judgments raises two questions about how media coverage affects a nascent reputation criterion. First, when does increasing coverage have the effect of affirming an issue as a real concern for corporations? While highly cited studies of institutionalization link legitimacy of a new thing to its adoption and diffusion (Tolbert & Zucker, 1983; Westphal, Gulati, & Shortell, 1997), that linkage is probably overstated by over-sampling cases of legitimation (Denrell & Kovács, 2008). Indeed, adoption and diffusion occur with quickly rejected fads (Abrahamson & Fairchild, 1999; Strang & Macy, 2001). Accordingly, Colyvas and Jonsson (2011) suggest new theorizing is needed to explain cases where legitimacy occurs without ubiquity, and vice versa.

Second, when does increased visibility of an issue lead the public to embrace rather than reject it? The social movements literature (for an overview, see Snow, Soule, & Kriesi, 2004) provides clues by linking policy changes to organizers' strategic efforts to present their concerns using words and images that "frame" causes by bringing certain ideas into focus while leaving others unaddressed (Snow et al., 1986). Whereas corporate reputation studies tend to relate new criteria to organizational decisions (King, Lenox,

& Barnett, 2002), social movement studies focus more on the effects of activist pressure (King, 2008; Rao, Yue, & Ingram, 2010).

While it is not yet clear when activist pressure on corporations leads to change or resistance, answers to this question can be found in the growing literature on the role of categorization in organizations and markets (for an overview, see Hsu, Koçak, & Negro, 2010). This literature links institutional pressures on firms to expectations associated with particular types, or categories, of firms, and the shared prototypes or ideals people use to judge category membership (Rosch & Lloyd, 1978). While prototypes have many attributes, cognitive limits restrict those that define category meaning. A category's defining attributes are therefore those (a) most central to its meaning and (b) most salient as points of contrast with an alternative or superordinate category.

Applied to corporate reputation, reputation criteria are category-specific standards for evaluating the quality or worth of firms. As Zuckerman (1999) shows in the context of securities markets, failing to fit any recognized category well leads firms to be overlooked, dismissed, and devalued because such "straddling" of multiple categories reduces the appeal of audiences primarily interested in just one of them (Hsu, 2006; Negro, Hannan, & Rao, 2010). Of course, categories can and do change, so the value of fitting an established category closely versus straddling several others less neatly depends on (1) whether such a straddle is on its way to being viewed as a category in its own right and (2) trends in the relative appeal of a potentially new category versus those that are more established. That is, the effects of category conformity depend on the currency of a category and how it changes over time (Kennedy, Lo, & Lounsbury, 2010). Thus, fitting the slide rule category perfectly was a problem for slide rule makers when electronic calculators were replacing slide rules.

Categories and Frames versus Reputation Criteria and Memes

It is important to distinguish categories, frames, and framing from reputation criteria. Categories are shared definitions of persons, places, or things deemed sufficiently distinct and important to be worth naming; they conserve cognitive effort by emphasizing the common properties of their members (Zerubvael, 1993). Frames are shared understandings of situations that supply answers to questions about what is going on and what is expected (Goffman, 1974: 21), and framing is the process of defining a situation by selecting from among potentially applicable frames the one particular frame as the most apt or desirable way to define and govern the situation. Criteria are category- or situation-specific standards of judgment that include a set of attributes and expectations for each.

While categories and frames depend on common knowledge and often map onto each other quite closely, knowing what a category means is knowing what belongs to it and why, but knowing what a frame means includes understanding principles of action. For example, the category "games" refers to activities as varied as poker, football, and chess but not generally to activities such as deal-making. Nonetheless, dealmakers sometimes frame bargaining situations as "games"—especially when they are inclined to "game" things, or cheat a bit—because the "game" framing permits cheating more readily than the "deal" frame. (Think, "a deal is a deal.") While "honesty" is generally important to positive reputations for "dealmakers," it contributes less to the reputations of "gamers." While categories and frames generally map onto each other quite closely, these mappings leave room for creativity and "framing contests" in which actors compete to frame situations to their liking (Kaplan, 2008). Thus, framing involves selecting from a set of existing shared understandings of situations potentially applicable to a focal kind—or category— of situation, but the emergence of new reputation criteria requires developing the same kind of shared understandings of subjective elements of value that are important to the construction of new product market categories (Khaire & Wadhwani, 2010).

For making sense of emergent and constructed meanings of reputation criteria, we believe "meme" (Dawkins, 1976) is a helpful word and idea. Inspired by genes and their role in evolutionary biology, the term meme was coined to relate the evolution of culture to ideas' unfolding impact on each other, not human agency. As originally conceived, the idea of a meme pinned the fate of new ideas on their fit with existing theories (Dawkins, 1976: 209). In our view, meme echoes a similar, yet better-theorized idea developed in structuralism, the school of thought inspired by de Sassure (1966) and Lévi-Strauss (1969). De Sassure argued that words of natural language vocabularies encode the kinds of changes possible within the cultures they belong to, and vice versa. Similarly, Lévi-Strauss argued that both cultural persistence and change are dictated by the logic of a culture's basic social structures and the rules that govern interactions among the roles they define and reinforce. In structuralism, words—like memes—are elements of culture whose definitions imply interactions that can produce new words and changes in the meanings of existing ones.

The definition of the meme concept has changed as it has spread, particularly with its recent usage to describe rapid diffusion of new ideas through word and image on the Internet (e.g., see Leskovec, Beckstrom, & Kleinberg, 2009). To add our own spin to its continuing evolution, we see memes as a set of both choices and constraints provided by available cultural toolkits (Swidler, 1986; Weber, 2005). Memes are not only words used in public discourse, but also elements of culture they refer to—identities, categories, genres, fields, and for organizations, forms, strategies, and practices. While some nascent memes never catch on, others spread like wildfire but burn out just as fast, and still others come to matter enormously. In the context of corporate reputation, we seek to highlight several factors that help explain these differences.

THEORY

To understand how nascent reputation criteria become real enough to effect organizational change, we need to understand how controversies about quality standards are settled. For that, we turn to social movements and the relational foundations of culture for two ideas that help explain when and why such controversies actually affect a targeted class of organizations (for an overview of each literature, see, respectively, McAdam & Snow, 2009; Mische, 2011).

From social movements: the importance of language

First, from studies of social movements, we take the idea that savvy use of language is a tool for mobilizing support for an agenda. The framing of a nascent reputation criterion contributes to its acceptance when it resonates with existing values and ideas for assessing the quality of firms (Snow & Benford, 1988). Thus, framing contributes to the social forces of new ideas by winning support for passage of new laws, articulating new rules of market competition, or suggesting appropriate legitimacy standards. As such outcomes institutionalize quality standards, they create pressures for conformity that can eventually become taken for granted (DiMaggio, 1997; see also Scott, 2001).

This makes media coverage important to criteria emergence because it distributes and weighs the language choices of actors important to legitimating new kinds of organizational and market categories, forms, and practices (Fligstein, 1996). Also, it shapes impressions of political opportunity (Diani, 1996; Gamson & Meyer, 1996; Zald, 1996) by reporting on legitimating events, often with legitimating rhetoric (Green, 2004; Suddaby & Greenwood, 2005).

Historically, mass media outlets were the most influential sources of news relevant to changing corporate reputation criteria, but so-called "new media" have become more important to public discourse in the last decade or so. Although the Internet expands the range of voices that can participate in public discourse, pre-Internet evidence suggests firms' attempts to attract media coverage were effective at shaping emerging market categories (Kennedy, 2005).

From Cultural Sociology: a Relational Approach to Meaning Construction

Second, from relational sociology (for an overview, see Mische, 2011), we take the idea that the legitimacy of nascent quality standards is determined by whether and how they are seen as connecting to elements of existing standards and values. Echoing Stinchcombe's (1968) definition of a mechanism, the heart of the relational approach to culture is that it links the pressures exerted by social structures to the dynamics of patterns of association observed at lower levels of analysis (e.g., see Breiger & Mohr, 2004; Mohr, 1998; Tilly, 1998; White et al., 2004; White, 2002). The relational view thus lends itself to empirical analysis by conceptualizing meaning—and changes to it—as the product of discursively observed connections among memes and words that refer to the defining attributes and instances of memes (Mohr, 1998). In this spirit, Kennedy

(2008) relates emergence of new product market categories to collective inference about the ontological status of new kinds of organizations by linking survival outcomes to producers' positions in networks based on who is co-mentioned with whom in media coverage and press releases. These connections produce cognitive embeddedness (Porac & Rosa, 1996; Zukin & Dimaggio, 1990) through a process that has been called cognitive embedding (Kennedy, 2008).

Applying these ideas to nascent reputation criteria, public discourse shapes and reflects their emergence by relating targeted firms to words that define and explain the new criterion. For a new meme to be taken seriously as a new social reality, its usage in public discourse must link it to its defining attributes in increasingly convergent ways. Such convergence can be observed by mining public discourse for networks that model the relative centrality of various elements of a meme's potential meaning. We refer to such a model as a concept network.

New Reputation Criteria

Combining the movement-like qualities of corporate reputation controversies with a relational approach to understanding their dynamics highlights three insights that lay a foundation for theorizing how corporate reputation criteria emerge.

Critics

Actors who stand between organizations and consumers by serving as third-party evaluators of their dealings are "critics" who effectively also serve as brokers in the process of determining whether nascent corporate reputation criteria will become real—that is, forceful standards against which corporations are judged. White and White (1965) argue that critics are important mediators of change in French fine art. In the context of markets, journalists mediate collective agreement about what nascent product market categories will mean (Kennedy, 2005; Rosa et al., 1999). In securities markets, financial analysts are arbiters of value by sorting themselves and the firms they cover into industry and market categories used to value firms (Zuckerman, 1999).

As mentioned above, journalists in traditional media now compete for influence with new kinds of critics, including independent bloggers and producers or authors of web-only media outlets. While questions about the legitimacy of this expanded array of different types of critics have yet to be answered, bloggers and online-only publications have siphoned audiences away from outlets and journalists that conform to the institutions of journalism that dominated the latter half of the twentieth century. Given these shifts, the work of bloggers, activists, and other stakeholders is increasingly important for the emergence of reputation criteria.

When critics of various types cover a new idea for how corporations ought to behave with increasing frequency and increasingly similar interpretations of its meaning, their voices strengthen claims that the idea has become a real criterion for corporate reputation.

Competition and Contestation

Nascent reputation criteria become social realities for organizations both by political contest and market competition. Obviously, new criteria become more real when new regulations force firms to meet new standards, but ordinary competition also produces reputation criteria when diffusion of a new capability creates isomorphic pressures to adopt it. One way such pressures arise is through emergence of a dominant design (Anderson & Tushman, 1990; Suarez & Utterback, 1995). As competition sifts and sorts competing approaches to building a product or delivering a service, the emergence of a clear winner makes its features part of a reputation criterion against which quality is judged. This parallels a very similar argument made in organizational ecology (Hannan & Freeman, 1977; Hannan, Pòlos, & Carroll, 2007), which is that organizations of a particular type face environmental selection pressures that push them to adopt a family of strategies that bear a strong resemblance to one another.

To explain how organizations respond to activist-led calls for change, King (2008) develops a political mediation model that relates organizational concessions to media exposure and tarnished reputations. In the context of boycotts, King finds that targeted companies are most likely to concede to activist demands when activists have gained significant media attention, or when targeted companies have suffered recent setbacks that tarnish their reputations.[1] Similarly, King and Soule (2007) show that protest activity affects corporate stock prices adversely when tied to issues of importance to critical stakeholder groups and when there is substantial media coverage of the protest— provided, that is, the target organization was not covered closely prior to the protest event. Flipping the question to ask why some activists get more response from their targets, Rao, Yue, and Ingram (2010) use analyses of protests against Wal-Mart stores to argue and show that protest activity is more likely in racially homogeneous communities, an effect they attribute to homogeneity's generally positive effect on solidarity.

Thus, new reputation criteria emerge through competition and contestation that combine to establish new dimensions of quality as standards against which members of a particular organization or type of organization will be judged.

Common Ground

A nascent reputation criterion is unlikely to affect firms of the relevant type until there is a modicum of agreement about what it means and how to assess it. Absent such agreement, the shared prototypes used to recognize categories (Rosch, 1978, 1983) cannot exist. In an analysis of the emerging market for mini-vans, Rosa et al. (1999) related the rationalization of competing definitions for the mini-van to reduced market uncertainty and, in turn, growing sales. More generally, philosophers link the meaning of a word to shared usage in everyday conversation (see Rorty, 1992). Applying this insight to

[1] This complements the proposition that firms in concentrated industries are apt to try to ride out protest rather than respond, especially when their reputations are tied to the industry (King, Lenox, & Barnett, 2002).

memes, a meme cannot become a recognized element of culture unless the word is used reliably to refer largely to the same sets of attributes or instances that define a new identity or category.

Neither entrepreneurial firms nor would-be corporate reformers can establish new reputation criteria unless they find common ground with at least one of the following: the targeted businesses themselves, customers, or the state. By common ground, we mean that change advocates and at least one of these constituents must define the new idea similarly. For example, activists achieve change not by merely getting firms, the public, or lawmakers to talk about the proposed criterion, but by getting them to define the issue in increasingly similar ways. That is what we mean by common ground.

Case Illustration: What Does it Mean to be Green?

To illustrate our theoretical argument about how corporate reputation criteria emerge, we turn now to the case of what it means to be green. There are two reasons this case is excellent for illustrating our theory. First, the history of antipathy between corporations and environmentalists makes the "greening" of corporations somewhat remarkable. Second, continuing ambiguity about what it means to be green makes it hard to distinguish genuinely "green" practices from mere greenwashing—situations where businesses put green labels on things they already do.

We present the green case in two parts: (1) a brief review of the environmental movement that inspired the "green" business idea and (2) a qualitative exploration of whether and how corporations and their media critics found common ground about what it means to be green.

Getting to green: a brief review of environmentalism

American environmentalism owes a great debt to Rachel Carson's *Silent Spring*, the 1962 bestseller that linked business practices to die-offs of birds whose calls historically heralded the yearly arrival of spring. Even as *Silent Spring* raised consciousness of the negative side effects of agriculture and manufacturing, American businesses generally viewed early activists as alarmist and anti-progress. It took considerable change for corporations to go from reactionary resistance to embracing the green concept.

Alarm and Distrust

Thanks to the efforts of early activists, awareness of environmental issues—especially pollution—increased throughout the 1960s. The environmental movement gathered momentum as students, public health workers, and newly formed activist groups found common cause in various issues. As indicators of this momentum, the Environmental Defense Fund was founded in 1967 and the National Resources Defence Council (NRDC), in 1970. The year 1970 also saw passage of the National Environmental Policy Act (NEPA) and the first "Earth Day." By 1980, the movement had become powerful enough to merit a cabinet-level officer in the executive branch of the US federal government, a move that coincided with that year's passage of the Clean Air Act, the Clean Water Act, and the Superfund law that authorized the new Environmental Protection Agency (EPA) to prosecute egregious polluters. To the extent that these laws and policies gave regulators the power to bring criminal charges against business, the EPA's "command and control" approach tended to alienate not only the business community, but also potential "green" entrepreneurs (Anderson & Huggins, 2008).

High-profile environmental problems and disasters contributed further momentum to the environmental movement. Dying trees in the forests of the American Northeast made a visible case for reining in emissions of power generators and automobiles that lead to acid rain. In 1978, the dire health problems of residents in New York's Love Canal led the federal government to buy out and evacuate an entire neighborhood built over a toxic waste dump. A disastrous chemical leak at the Union Carbide plant in Bhopal, India, killed 1,500 people and injured thousands more in 1984. After large corporations had long been seen as engines of progress, ecological problems like these gave big business a black eye.

As growing distrust of business fueled public support for regulations requiring corporations to pay for the cleanup both of past messes and ongoing operations, many corporations met these reforms with denials of the problem, denials of responsibility, or both. When corporations spent money to respond to new demands, no small portion of it went toward lobbyists hired to minimize the costs of compliance or to what came to be called "greenwashing" (Greer & Bruno, 1996)—relatively shallow environmental initiatives that effectively hide deeper ongoing problems.

Rapprochement

As the environmentalism meme was increasingly accepted—or cognitively embedded—into American culture, corporations began taking more proactive approaches to environmental issues. Business thinking began to reflect the mainstreaming of environmentalist sensibilities, and corporations responded not just by righting past wrongs, but also by participating in the creation of new social values and expectations—even though many of these values and expectations directly challenged their traditional profit focus and the argument that externalities are best handled by market forces rather than by government regulation (Livesey & Graham, 2007).

The idea of "sustainable development" is perhaps the earliest clear expression of this new corporate engagement with environmentalism. A concept that emerged in the late 1980s, sustainability became the theme of several rounds of international diplomacy focused on articulating new principles for what business should do rather than on what it should not do. Specifically, sustainable development was a major topic at the 1992

Earth Summit held in Rio de Janeiro, Brazil. Summit participants developed a new and still highly ambiguous definition of sustainability as a long-term goal for business organizations. The summit resulted in the formation of the Business Council for Sustainable Development, a body that was renamed the World Business Council at the 2002 Earth Summit (Bullis & Ie, 1997).

A key point of these developments is that the sustainability meme suited business better because it focused less on fixing the past than on creating a better future (Hall, 1997). As this shift occurred, organizational research began to show evidence suggesting that environmental stewardship could be compatible with business performance (Hart & Ahuja, 1996; King & Lenox, 2001), competitive advantage (Hart, 1995), and innovation (Porter & van Der Linde, 1995). Gradually, managers also linked environmentalism to more positive organizational outcomes, not just fines or profit-eroding regulations. Efforts to cut waste and improve quality—already major features of the total quality management movement of the 1980s and 1990s (Green, Li, & Nohria, 2009)—were obvious fits with the idea of reducing the negative environmental impact of business. Reflecting this new sensibility, the US EPA instituted guidelines for voluntary adoption of environmental management system (EMS) programs, and the ISO 14000 family standard was developed to observe and publicize these changes (Bullis & Ie, 1997).

The "Green" Meme

As a way to refer to positive environmental practices of business, the term "green" began appearing in major news articles around the year 2000. At that time, some corporations began to establish collaborative partnerships with non-governmental organizations (NGOs) that focused on environmental issues. In many cases, this meant allowing former foes a measure of access and even influence in decisions that impact business processes. For example, McDonald's collaborated with the Environmental Defense Fund to redesign its packaging, and the California Rice Industry Association worked with activists and NGOs to form the Ricelands Habitat Partnership. Such cases suggested that collaboration between business and environmentalist NGOs could lead to changes that achieve environmentalists' goals while either improving corporate financial performance, cultivating a better image, or both (Livesey & Graham, 2007).

As the green meme diffused, however, some adopters were insincere about pursuing the tangible benefits realized by similar-sounding programs of green pioneers. Consistent with later adopters' increased likelihood of announcing more than they actually implement (Tolbert & Zucker, 1983), the decoupling of rhetoric and practice is commonplace among corporations that announce green initiatives. In a study of the green-related claims made by 20 transnational companies in 9 countries and 4 continents, for example, Greer and Bruno found cases in which corporations portray their actions as saving the environment while, in reality, they "remain the primary creators and peddlers of dirty, dangerous, and unsustainable technologies" (Greer & Bruno, 1996: 12). Obviously, this creates uncertainty about what green means.

Empirical Observations

With this history as context, we turn now to exploring public discourse that speaks to emergence of common ground between corporations and their media-based critics. Specifically, we explored differing notions of green found in press releases and news stories for the years 2001 and 2009,[2] and consistent with the "common ground" theme we articulated above, we looked for evidence that corporate versus media takes on "green" either converged or diverged over this period.

Informed by the relational approach to meaning described above, we extended Kennedy's approach to observing the changing meaning of a new product market category (see Kennedy, 2008, Appendix A) to more closely observe the changing meaning of "green" as a potential criterion of corporate reputation. As opposed to the within-story co-mentions of producers used to study market formation in Kennedy (2008), we used MemeStat (Kennedy, 2011), a new tool that extends Kennedy's prior work, to produce and explore concept networks for green that were based on within-*sentence* co-mentions of a list of terms ("attributes") we identified as potentially relevant to what it means to be green. By producing such concept networks for corpora representing different times and perspectives, it is possible to examine both the extent of and changes in centrality of the concept's various attributes as seen over time and between perspectives. Although this approach distills a large volume of discourse to numeric data, it is still fundamentally a qualitative search for patterns that suggest two interpretations of a concept are converging, diverging, or neither.

To start, we read all the news stories and press releases to develop a list of potentially relevant attributes, or elements, of what it means to be green; these are listed in Figure 4.1. Next, we used MemeStat to extract networks that model green's usage in news stories and press releases for the 2001 and 2009, respectively, by linking Figure 4.1's concept elements based on within-sentence co-mentions. We then used the network data to rank concept elements by degrees centrality—producing what we call concept element centrality vectors—and compare these rankings to observe both (1) differences in how green is used in press releases versus news stories and (2) how those differences change over time.

Table 4.1 summarizes what we observed. Columns 1–4 contain concept element centrality vectors in which concept elements (referenced by ID numbers shown in Figure 4.1) are ranked in descending order based on centrality in the concept networks

---

[2] We used Lexis-Nexis to search for items in which "green" is used in a sentence with business, corporation, management, or technology in press releases and news stories to represent the corporate and media perspectives respectively. We collected press releases from the BusinessWire and PR NewsWire services. So that we would not too easily find common ground between business and the media, we collected news stories from outlets with, if anything, a pro-environment slant: the *New York Times, Washington Post, BusinessWeek, Forbes, Los Angeles Times, Orange County Register, San Francisco Chronicle, San Diego Union-Tribune, Oakland Tribune, San Jose Mercury News, Sacramento Bee,* and *Fresno Bee.* These searches yielded a media corpus of 2,830 stories and a PR corpus of 4,219 releases. The ratios of stories and releases found for 2001 and 2009 were 1:3 and 1:2, respectively.

Index: ID Numbers for Term(s) Referring to Potential Attributes of Green		
1 "affordable"	15 "energy-efficient"	29 "environmental management"
2 "alternative"	16 "energy-saving"	30 "carbon emissions"
3 "anti-pollution"	17 "footprint"	31 "carbon footprint"
4 "budget"	18 "geothermal"	32 "sustainable development"
5 "carbon"	19 "health"	33 "energy-*"
6 "clean"	20 "management"	34 "conservatio{n|nist}"
7 "conscious"	21 "renewable"	35 "efficien{t|cy}"
8 "conversation"	22 "responsible"	36 "sustainab{le|ility|ly}"
9 "ecofriendly"	23 "safe"	37 "environmen{t|tal|talist}"
10 "economical"	24 "solar"	38 "recycl{e|ing|ed|able}"
11 "ecosystem"	25 "system"	39 "reus{able|ed}"
12 "emissions"	26 "waste"	40 "sensitiv{e|ity}"
13 "EMS"	27 "wind"	41 "transparen{t|cy}"
14 "energy"	28 "waste management"	
(List developed from reading the corpora)		

FIGURE 4.1 "Green" concept element centrality in 2001 press releases and news stories.

extracted as described above. Columns 5–8 summarize differences in concept element centrality obtained by comparing usages of green in news stories versus press releases for 2001 (column 5) and 2009 (column 6), respectively, and by comparing early versus late usage in news stories (column 7) and press releases (column 8).

Looking closely at changes in the centrality of "energy" versus "carbon emissions" and "carbon footprint" illustrates what these vectors reveal. The word "energy" (ID = 14) is 24th in centrality in news stories for 2001 (see column 1, row 24), but it moves up 18 places to 6th in 2009 (see column 3, row 6)—hence the +18 in the first row of column 7. That is, the full word "energy" became more central to news stories about green from 2001 to 2009. In contrast, the centrality of "energy" changed far less in press releases: as seen in column 8, it dropped only 1 place from 2001 to 2009—hence the –1 in the first row of column 8. Thus, energy was and remained important to organizations issuing press releases, and news stories changed to roughly match that. Over the same period, the centrality of "carbon emissions" (ID = 30) and "carbon footprint" (ID = 31) as used in the news story corpus dropped 13 places to end up very close in rank to

Table 4.1 "Green" Concept Element Centrality Data

	(1)	(2)	(3)	(4)		(5)	(6)	(7)	(8)
	Concept Element Centrality Ranking*					Comparison Data (# Places Different)			
	2001		2009			Media v Releases		2001 vs 2009	
Rank	Media	Releases	Media	Releases	ID	2001	2009	Media	Releases
1	37	33	33	33	14	+18	+1	+18	−1
2	35	37	37	37	28	−17	+1	−13	+3
3	36	35	35	35	29	−15	+1	−13	+1
4	38	36	36	24	21	+13		+13	
5	34	21	21	21	30	−13	+1	−13	−1
6	33	14	14	27	34	−12	+3	−12	−3
7	28	24	24	14	31	−11	+1	−13	−3
8	29	25	25	19	32	−9	+1	−13	−5
9	30	27	27	25	38	−9	−2	−9	+2
10	31	26	26	36	20	+8	+2	+8	−2
11	32	20	20	38	24	+8	−3	+8	+3
12	27	22	22	26	17	+7	+1	+7	−1
13	26	38	38	20	15	+6	−2	+6	+2
14	25	23	23	22	25	+6	+1	+6	−1
15	24	17	17	18	41	+6	+5	+6	−5
16	23	19	19	17	6	+5	−1	+5	+1
17	22	34	34	15	22	+5	+2	+5	−2
18	21	18	18	16	33	+5		+5	
19	20	15	15	23	19	+4	−8	+4	+8
20	19	32	28	34	1	−3		−3	
21	18	31	29	28	18	+3	−3	+3	+3
22	17	30	30	29	26	+3	+2	+3	−2
23	16	29	31	30	27	+3	−3	+3	+3
24	14	28	32	31	11	−2	+1	−2	−1
25	15	16	16	32	16	−2	−7	−2	+7
26	12	12	12	12	23	+2	+5	+2	−5
27	13	13	13	6	2	−1		−1	
28	11	6	6	13	3	−1		−1	
29	10	10	10	7	4	−1	−1	−1	+1
30	7	11	11	8	7	−1	−2	−1	+2
31	8	7	7	11	8	−1	−2	−1	+2
32	9	8	8	9	9	−1	−1	−1	+1
33	6	9	9	10	35	−1		−1	
34	5	5	5	5	36	−1	+6	−1	−6
35	4	41	41	4	37	−1		−1	
36	2	4	4	39	39	−1	−4	−1	+4

	(1)	(2)	(3)	(4)		(5)	(6)	(7)	(8)
	Concept Element Centrality Ranking*					Comparison Data (# Places Different)			
	2001		2009			Media v Releases		2001 vs 2009	
Rank	Media	Releases	Media	Releases	ID	2001	2009	Media	Releases
37	3	2	2	2	40	+1		+1	
38	1	3	3	3	5				
39	39	40	40	40	10		+4		−4
40	40	39	39	41	12				
41	41	1	1	1	13		+1		−1
	* Columns contain element IDs				Tot.	206	78	206	86
					S	0.75	0.91	0.75	0.90

its centrality to press release usage of green. Overall, the elements most central to green usage changed more in news stories than in press releases between 2001 and 2009 (column 7's numbers are larger than column 8's), and differences in how green was used in news stories versus press releases shrunk over the same period (column 6's numbers are smaller than column 5's). This indicates that between 2001 and 2009, press release issuers—mostly corporations—exerted relatively more influence than journalists over how important the different elements of the green concept were to what its meaning became.

To understand these differences more clearly, we developed a measure of meaning similarity and used it to assess the relative influence of news stories versus press releases over what green came to mean. We reasoned that centrality rankings for concept elements as they appear in two different corpora should be similar when the concept is used similarly in the texts of both. Since differences in such rankings should reflect differences in what is most essential to a concept, summing them across all concept elements should measure how similar a concept's meaning is in two corpora. Procedurally, this translates into creating concept element centrality vectors for two corpora to compare and then summing the number of vector positions that the elements of one vector must be shifted to match the other one exactly, dividing them by the maximum number of shifts possible, and subtracting this quantity from 1. For two vectors $v1$ and $v2$ with the same set of N elements $E = \{e1, e2, \ldots, e_N\}$ with each element having position $p(vn, en)$, we compute their similarity as follows:

$$S = 1 - \frac{\sum_{i=1}^{N}[p(v_1, e_i) - p(v_2, e_i)]}{N(N-1)}$$

(4.1)

Table 4.1 summarizes the four values of S obtained by comparing usage of "green" in our news story and press release corpora for 2001 and 2009. Comparing green's usage in news stories versus press releases shows that it became more similar from 2001 to 2009, with S values going from 0.75 in 2001 (bottom of column 1) to 0.91 in 2009 (bottom of column 2). These comparisons indicate converging interpretations of green and enlarged common ground between journalists and press release issuers—at least on questions about green's import and meaning. Comparing early versus late usage of green shows that green's usage changed more in news stories than it did in press releases, with S for early versus late news releases being only 0.75 (bottom of column 3) versus 0.90 for early versus late press releases (bottom of column 5). That is, journalists' usage of green shifted during this time more than press release issuers' usage did, and it shifted toward press release usage.

DISCUSSION

When activists push for new standards for assessing the quality and value of corporations, their proposed criteria for corporation reputation become forceful when activists find common ground with customers, the state, corporations themselves, or some combination. Such common ground becomes a source of isomorphic pressures on corporate structure and operational routines by shaping how customers think about what they want, winning political support for new regulations, or establishing new rules of competition—informal ones, that is. This common ground is, in other words, a source of what institutional theorists call cognitive, regulative, and normative isomorphism (Scott, 1991).

The case of what it means to be green illustrates our theory. As public discourse about the green concept grew in volume, corporations and their media-based critics found enlarged common ground about what it means to be green, just as we argued is necessary for new reputation criteria to exert pressures on corporations. That journalists apparently followed issuers of press releases in their usage of the term suggests these organizations—mostly corporations—had more influence on the meaning of green than journalists did, at least in this period.

Such corporate influence on environmentalism is not new with what it means to be green. Donovan Hohn (2011) sketches its history in *Moby Duck,* the story of his search for a container's worth of "rubber ducky" bath toys lost at sea in the Northeast Pacific. This quest led Hohn to Alaskan beachcombers, sentinels of the ocean's health, whose debris collections he came to see as cryptic postcards from the ocean about how it is faring. Hohn tells of surprise at learning from one beachcomber that volunteer beach cleanups had a long history of corporate sponsorship. On Earth day in 1971, the corporate-backed "Keep America Beautiful" campaign began airing a series of poignant ads in which a man dressed in American Indian garb surveys environmental spoilage sadly and finally sheds a single tear in response to thoughtless littering, all to a sonorous voiceover that says, "People start pollution, and people can stop it." In other words, ordinary people are responsible for the kind of spoilage shown in the ad. To Hohn's informant, corporations and politicians love beach cleanups not only because they yield great photo opportunities, but also because they produce impressive statistics that shift attention away from things corporations do to harm the environment. Similarly, press releases about corporate green initiatives shift attention away from, for example, carbon emissions and toward things corporations do to be friendlier to it—things like saving money for being more efficient in their energy usage. That may be progress.

Nonetheless, we do not mean to suggest that journalists simply follow corporations when trying to discern the import and meaning of a new meme like green. What makes the green case remarkable is not only its corporate influence over a reputation criterion first urged by passionate critics, but also that this influence required setting aside deep-seated antipathy between corporations and environmental activists. How did this reversal happen?

Combining our account of reputation criteria emergence with King's (2008) political mediation model of activist influence suggests a possible answer worth further study. Our theory, to recap it briefly, is that emergence of new reputation criteria requires development of common ground between critics of corporations and the corporations themselves, and that while such common ground can be forcibly created by legislation, it also emerges voluntarily when corporations engage in debates raised by their critics. But if merely joining the debate effectively dignifies standards corporations might prefer to reject, why would they ever do so?

This is where King's work on the mediated nature of activist influence is useful. To explore when and why corporations respond to activist-initiated change, he analyzes corporate responses to boycotts to show activists, and finds activists are more likely to get concessions from corporations when they are first successful in getting their causes before the public by attracting large amounts of media coverage. Thus, King argues, activist influence is mediated by media coverage and public awareness of their causes, especially when their corporate targets have recently suffered declines in reputation. This argument puts reputation concerns at the center of corporate responses to activist protest.

Because activists' causes do not become instrumental concerns for corporations until they are widely seen as reputation criteria, however, media coverage creates pressure for corporate change by contributing to the emergence and acceptance of new criteria. In debates over whether shareholder value maximization should be the only concern of a corporation (Fiss & Zajac, 2004), for example, spending on green initiatives can be framed as charitable donations to an environmental cause and dismissed by the argument that shareholders are better off doing this for themselves. To the extent that a potential reputation criterion like being green becomes part of assessing the quality of a corporation, however, it becomes part of valuation and therefore of central concern to shareholders. As new reputation criteria emerge and become widely accepted, therefore, the expenditures required to meet them go from being like taxes to being like investment.

Implications for Theory

There are three major implications of studying emerging corporate reputation criteria. First, looking into reputation criteria breaks down the omnibus reputation concept into components. Second, studying emerging criteria highlights the fact that they are dynamic, not static. Third, these two ideas together suggest that the value of reputation depends not only on how positive it is, but also on how it is constructed. Reputations heavily staked on a narrow set of criteria, for example, are only as good as the continued desirability and importance of those criteria. Thus, positive reputations staked on excellence at producing soon-to-be-obsolete products are of lesser value than similarly positive reputations based on more durable criteria. Just as categories have currency trends that rise and fall as their standards come into and go out of fashion (Kennedy, Lo, & Lounsbury, 2010), reputation criteria also have currency. More generally, memes have currency. That is, being known as one of the world's best-managed conglomerates is a tenuous claim when, as did occur, leading academics reject the idea that well-managed corporations ought to diversify their holdings to manage risk.

Thus, corporate reputations reflect discursive sensemaking about how well firms measure up on a dynamic array of impermanent criteria. This view implies fruitful linkages between organization theory linking corporate reputation to its discursive foundations and work in financial economics that also links text to valuation (see Hoberg & Phillips, 2010). When the emergence of a new corporate reputation criterion leads to rejection of an established one that was important to many firms, the result is the dismantling of a whole regime of valuation and the construction of a new one. As we have argued, a relational approach to culture suggests factors and methods important to developing and measuring growing support for new ideas. In particular, it suggests identifying opposing positions and devising analyses of their respective discourses on nascent memes that can reveal whether they converge. It is our hope that the theory and case we have presented in this chapter will inform and inspire such developments.

Directions for Future Research

These implications raise questions about the durability of corporate reputations. Are reputations destined to deteriorate when based on criteria that lose currency, or do they sometimes persist even as new criteria emerge and formerly important ones fall out of favor? Answering such questions requires decomposing reputation into its most important criteria, treating these as dynamic rather than stable, and tracing out the arguments and relations that establish and support the institutionalization of these criteria. Such work holds the promise of helping to disentangle corporation reputation and status.

In the process of institutionalizing reputation criteria, "common" ground between corporations and their critics suggests integrative bargains between them, but such bargains may not provide equal benefits to all parties. As activist adoption of collaborative influence strategies has drawn corporations into being greener, corporations have shifted talk about being green to emphasize sources of efficiency—and profitability. Further research should address whether and when such common ground benefits corporations, their critics, or society. Our case study of green suggests the stories of media "critics" are sometimes more reporting than criticism.

While we have focused on the emergence of new criteria for corporate reputation, the deinstitutionalization of established reputation criteria deserves equal attention. The relational approach sketched in this chapter could be used to examine, for example, the fall of conglomerates (Davis, Diekmann, & Tinsley, 1994), the diffusion of corporate governance practices (Davis & Greve, 1997; Westphal & Zajac, 1994; Zajac & Westphal, 1998, 2004), and the spread of various forms of globalization (Fiss & Zajac, 2004).

Finally, relational analyses of new phenomena should also account for the tone or valence of text—that is, whether it is positive, neutral or negative (see Pollock, Rindova, & Maggitt, 2008). Valence can be captured by extracting two-mode graphs based on co-mentions of, for example, emotion words (see Pennebaker, Mehl, & Niederhoffer, 2003) and concept elements. Multiplying such a graph by its transpose yields an adjacency matrix in which links among concept elements reflect connections to similar emotion words. The result would be a more refined view of concept meanings and a clearer view of the presence or absence of common ground between critics and their targets.

Conclusion

Exploring how new corporate reputation criteria emerge through public discourse contributes to the more general topic of the currency of categories, identities, and memes underlying the social standing of organizations, which in turn should link the discursive foundations of corporate reputation to the financial economics of corporate valuation. Moreover, linking emerging standards of quality to relations among corporations and their critics advances understanding of how ongoing meaning construction affects the fates of social movements that target corporations for change, corporations themselves, and society more broadly.

Keys for Understanding the Emergence of Reputation Criteria

References	Key Concepts and Findings
Barnett et al. (2006), Rindova et al. (2005)	*Corporate Reputation*—a collective judgment of quality according to accepted standards that affects performance, survival
Snow et al. (1986), Snow et al. (2004)	*Social Movements*—movement organizers mobilize various kinds of resources to effect social change
Mische (2011), Mohr (1998), White (1981), Tilly (1998), Powell et al. (2005)	*Relational Sociology*—an approach to culture that uses the dynamics of relations among actors, usually modeled as networks, to explore and explain social durability and change
Dawkins (1976) (echoes Lévi-Strauss 1969, 1983)	*Meme*—Named elements of culture (or social structure) produced by interactions among memes (text)
Swidler (1986)	*Cultural Toolkit*—culturally available collections of habits, skill, and styles that enable various strategies of action
DiMaggio & Powell (1983), Zuckerman (1999)	*Isomorphism*—Because organizational categories include norms and rules that create pressures for conformity, deviation is sanctioned; conformity, rewarded
Zukin & Dimaggio (1990), Porac & Rosa (1996)	*Cognitive Embeddedness*—shared cognitive associations that contribute to widespread perceptions of (il)legitimacy
Kennedy (2008)	*Cognitive Embedding*—network models of discursively observed connections support observation and explanation of emergence of new ideas, entities
Kennedy, Lo and Lounsbury (2010)	*Category Currency*—The extent to which a category (or criterion) is seen as having clear meaning & positive appeal; affects the value of meeting or exceeding standards

References

Abrahamson, E. & Fairchild, G. (1999). "Management fashion: Lifecycles, triggers, and collective learning processes." *Administrative Science Quarterly*, 44: 708–740.

Anderson, P. & Tushman, M. L. (1990). "Technological discontinuities and dominant designs: A cyclical model of technological change." *Administrative Science Quarterly*, 35: 604–633.

Anderson, T. L. & Huggins, L. E. (2008). *Greener than Thou: Are You Really an Environmentalist?* Stanford, CA: Hoover Institution Press.

Barnett, M. L., Jermier, J. M., & Lafferty, B. A. (2006). "Corporate reputation: The definitional landscape." *Corporate Reputation Review*, 9: 26–38.

Barney, J. (1991). "Firm resources and sustained competitive advantage." *Journal of Management*, 17: 99–120.

Beatty, R. P. and Zajac, E. J. (1994). "Managerial incentives, monitoring, and risk bearing: A study of executive compensation, ownership and board structure in initial public offerings." *Administrative Science Quarterly*, 39: 313–335.

Bettis, R. A. (1981). "Performance differences in related and unrelated diversified firms." *Strategic Management Journal*, 2: 379–393.

Boyd, C. (2004). "The structural origins of conflicts of interest in the accounting profession." *Business Ethics Quarterly*, 14: 377–398.

Breiger, R. L. and Mohr, J. W. (2004). "Institutional logics from the aggregation of organizational networks: Operational procedures for the analysis of counted data." *Computational & Mathematical Organization Theory*, 10: 17–43.

Bullis, C. and Ie, F. (1997). "Corporate environmentalism." In S. May, G. Cheney, & J. Roper (Eds.), *The Debate over Corporate Social Responsibility*. New York: Oxford University Press, 321–335.

Colyvas, J. and Jonsson, S. (2011). "Ubiquity and legitimacy: Disentangling diffusion and institutionalization." *Sociological Theory*, 29: 27–53.

Conger, J. A. (1989). *The Charismatic Leader*. San Francisco: Jossey-Bass.

Davis, G. F., Diekmann, K. A., & Tinsley, C. H. (1994). "The decline and fall of the conglomerate form in the 1980s: The deinstitutionalization of an organizational form." *American Sociological Review*, 59: 547–570.

—— & Greve, H. R. (1997). "Corporate elite networks and governance changes in the 1980s." *American Journal of Sociology*, 103: 1–37.

Dawkins, R. (1976). "Memes and the evolution of culture." *New Scientist*, 21 October: 208.

de Saussure, F. (1966). *Course in General Linguistics*. New York: McGraw-Hill.

Deephouse, D. L. (2000). "Media reputation as a strategic resource: An integration of mass communication and resource based theories." *Journal of Management*, 26: 1091–1112.

Denrell, J. & Kovács, B. (2008). "Selective sampling of empirical settings in organizational studies." *Administrative Science Quarterly*, 53: 109–144.

Diani, M. (1996). "Linking mobilization frames and political opportunities: Insights from regional populism in Italy." *American Sociological Review*, 61: 1053–1069.

DiMaggio, P. (1997). "Culture and cognition." *Annual Review of Sociology*, 23: 263–287.

Fiss, P. and Zajac, E. J. (2004). "The diffusion of ideas over contested terrain: The (non)adoption of a shareholder value orientation among German firms." *Administrative Science Quarterly*, 49: 501–534.

Fligstein, N. (1996). "Markets as politics: a political-cultural approach to market institutions." *American Sociological Review*, 61: 656–673.

Gamson, W. A. & Meyer, D. S. (1996). "Framing political opportunity." In D. McAdam, J. D. McCarthy, & M. N. Zald (Eds.), *Comparative Perspectives on Social Movements*. New York: Cambridge University Press, 275–290.

Goffman, E. (1974). *Frame Analysis: An Essay on the Organization of Experience*. New York: Harper and Row.

Green, S. (2004). "A rhetorical theory of diffusion." *Academy of Management Review*, 29: 653–669.

——, Li, Y., & Nohria, N. (2009). "Suspended in self-spun webs of significance: A rhetorical model of institutionalization and institutionally embedded agency." *Academy of Management Journal*, 52: 11–36.

Greer, J. & Bruno, K. (1996). *Greenwash: The Reality behind Corporate Environmentalism*. Penang, Malaysia: Third World Network.

Hall, S. L. (1997). "Beyond Greening: Strategies for a sustainable world." *Harvard Business Review*, January: 66–76.

Hambrick, D. C. & Mason, P. A. (1984). "Upper echelons: The organization as a reflection of its top managers." *Academy of Management Journal*, 9: 193–206.

Hannan, M. T. & Freeman, J. (1977). "The population ecology of organizations." *American Journal of Sociology*, 82: 929–964.

——, Pòlos, L., & Carroll, G. R. (2007). *Logics of Organization Theory: Audiences, Codes, and Ecologies*. Princeton: Princeton University Press.

Hart, S. L. (1995). "A natural-resource-based view of the firm." *Academy of Management Review*, 20: 986–1014.

—— & Ahuja, G. (1996). "Does it pay to be green? An empirical examination of the relationship between emission reduction and firm performance." *Business Strategy and the Environment*, 5: 30–37.

Hayward, M. L. A., Rindova, V. P., & Pollock, T. G. (2004). "Believing one's own press: The causes and consequences of CEO celebrity." *Strategic Management Journal*, 25: 637–653.

Hirsch, P. M. (1986). "From ambushes to golden parachutes: corporate takeovers as an instance of cultural framing and institutional integration." *American Journal of Sociology*, 91: 800–837.

Hoberg, G. & Phillips, G. (2010). "Product market synergies and competition in mergers and acquisitions: A text-based analysis." *Review of Financial Studies*, 23: 3773–3811.

Hohn, D. (2011). *Moby Duck: The True Story of 28,800 Bath Toys Lost at Sea and of the Beachcombers, Oceanographers, Environmentalists and Fools, Including the Author, Who Went in Search of Them*. New York: Viking.

Hsu, G. (2006). "Jacks of all trades and masters of none: Audiences' reactions to spanning genres in feature film production." *Administrative Science Quarterly*, 51: 420–450.

——, Koçak, Ö., & Negro, G. (2010). "Categories in markets: Origins and evolution." In M. Lounsbury (Ed.), *Research in the Sociology of Organizations*, vol. 31. Emerald.

Kaplan, S. (2008). "Framing contests: Strategy making under uncertainty." *Organization Science*, 19: 729–752.

Kennedy, M. T. (2005). "Behind the one-way mirror: Refraction in the construction of product market categories." *Poetics*, 33: 201–226.

—— (2008). "Getting counted: Markets, media, and reality." *American Sociological Review*, 73: 270–295.

—— (2011). "MemeStat (Ver. 1.0)." Pasadena, CA: Associative Labs.

——, Lo, Y.-C., & Lounsbury, M. (2010). "Category currency: The changing value of conformity as a function of ongoing meaning construction." *Research in the Sociology of Organizations*, 31: 369–397.

Khaire, M. & Wadhwani, R. D. (2010). "Changing landscapes: The construction of meaning and value in a new market—modern Indian art." *Academy of Management Journal*, 53: 1281–1304.

King, A. A. & Lenox, M. J. (2001). "Does it really pay to be green?" *Journal of Industrial Ecology*, 5: 105–116.

King, A. A., Lenox, M., & Barnett, M. L. (2002). "Strategic responses to the reputation commons problem." In A. Hoffman and M. Ventresca (Eds.), *Organizations, Policy, and the Natural Environment: Institutional and Strategic Perspectives*. Palo Alto, CA: Stanford University Press.

King, B. (2008). "A political mediation model of corporate response to social activism." *Administrative Science Quarterly*, 53: 395–421.

King, B. G. & Soule, S. A. (2007). "Social movements as extra-institutional entrepreneurs: The effect of protests on stock price returns." *Administrative Science Quarterly*, 52: 413–442.

—— & Whetten, D. A. (2008). "Rethinking the relationship between reputation and legitimacy: A social actor conceptualization." *Corporate Reputation Review*, 11: 192–207.

Leskovec, J., Beckstrom, L., & Kleinberg, J. (2009). "Meme-tracking and the dynamics of the news cycle." *Proceedings of the 15th ACM SIGKDD International Conference on Knowledge Discovery and Data Mining*. June 28–July 1, Paris, France, 497–505.

Lévi-Strauss, C. (1969). *The Elementary Structures of Kinship*. Translated by J. Bell and J. von Sturmer. Boston: Beacon Press.

Lipton, M. & Lorsch, J. W. (1992). "A modest proposal for improved corporate governance." *Business Lawyer*, 48: 59–77.

Livesey, S. M. & Graham, J. (2007). "Greening of corporations? Eco-talk and the emerging social imaginary of sustainable development." In S. May, G. Cheny, & J. Roper (Eds.), *The Debate over Corporate Social Responsibility*. New York: Oxford University Press, 336–350.

McAdam, D. and Snow, D. A. (2009). "Introduction." In D. McAdam & D. A. Snow (Eds.), *Readings in Social Movements: Origins, Dynamics and Outcomes*. New York: Oxford University Press.

Mische, A. (2011). "Relational sociology, culture, and agency." In J. Scott & P. Carrington (Eds.), *Sage Handbook of Network Analysis*. New York: Sage.

Modigliani, F. & Miller, M. H. (1958). "The cost of capital, corporation finance and the theory of investment." *American Economic Review*, 48: 261–297.

Mohr, J. W. (1998). "Measuring meaning structures." *Annual Review of Sociology*, 24: 345–370.

Negro, G., Hannan, M. T., and Rao, H. (2010). "Categorical contrast and audience appeal: Niche width and critical success in winemaking." *Industrial and Corporate Change*, 19: 1397–1425.

Pennebaker, J. W., Mehl, M. R., & Niederhoffer, K. G. (2003). "Psychological aspects of natural language use: Our words, our selves." *Annual Review of Psychology*, 54: 547–577.

Porter, M. E., van der Linde, C. (1995). "Toward a New Conception of the Environment-Competitiveness Relationship." *Journal of Economic Perspectives*, 9: 97–118.

Pollock, T. G., Rindova, V. P., & Maggitt, P. G. (2008). "Market watch: Information and availability cascades among the media and investors in the U.S. IPO market." *Academy of Management Journal*, 51: 335–358.

Porac, J. F. & Rosa, J. A. (1996). "Rivalry, industry models, and the cognitive embeddedness of the comparable firm." In J. A. C. Baum & J. E. Dutton (Eds.), *Advances in Strategic Management*, vol. 13. Greenwich, CT: JAI Press, 363–388.

Powell, M. G. (2010). "Anthropologist as prognosticator: Gillian Tett and the credit derivatives market." *American Anthropologist*, 112: 142–143.

Rao, H., Yue, Q. L., & Ingram, P. (2010). "Activists, categories and markets: Racial diversity and protests against Walmart store openings in America." In G. Negro, Ö. Koçak, & G. Hsu (Eds.), *Research in the Sociology of Organizations*, vol. 31. London: Emerald.

Rindova, V. P., Pollock, T. G., & Hayward, M. L. A. (2006). "Celebrity firms: The social constructions of market popularity." *Academy of Management Review*, 31: 50–71.

——, Petkova, A. P., & Kotha, S. (2007). "Standing out: How new firms in emerging markets build reputation." *Strategic Organization*, 5: 31–70.

——, Williamson, I. O., Petkova, A. P., & Sever, J. M. (2005). "Being good or being known: An empirical examination of the dimensions, antecedents, and consequences of organizational reputation." *Academy of Management Journal*, 48: 1033–1049.

Rorty, R. M. (1992). *The Linguistic Turn: Essays in Philosophical Method With Two Retrospective Essays*. Chicago: University of Chicago.

Rosa, J. A., Porac, J. F., Runser-Spanjol, J., & Saxon, M. S. (1999). "Sociocognitive dynamics in a product market." *Journal of Marketing*, 63: 64–77.

Rosch, E. (1978). "Principles of categorization." In E. Rosch & B. B. Lloyd (Eds.),*Cognition and Categorization*. Hillsdale, NJ: Lawrence Erlbaum Associates, 27–48.

——— (1983). "Prototype classification and logical classification: The two systems." In E. F. Scholnick (Ed.), *New Trends in Conceptual Representation: Challenges to Piaget's Theory?* Hillsdale, NJ: Erlbaum.

——— & Lloyd, B. B. (1978). *Cognition and Categorization*. Hillsdale, NJ: Erlbaum.

Scott, W. R. (1991). "Unpacking institutional analysis." In W. W. Powell & P. J. DiMaggio (Eds.), *The New Institutionalism in Organizational Analysis*. Chicago: University of Chicago Press, 164–182.

——— (2001). *Institutions and Organizations*. Thousand Oaks: Sage.

Snow, D. A. & Benford, R. D. (1988). "Ideology, frame resonance, and participant mobilization." In B. Klandermans, H. Kriesi, & S. Tarrow (Eds.), *From Structure to Action: Social Movement Participation Across Cultures*. Greenwich, CT: JAI Press, 191–217.

———, Burke Rochford, Jr., E., Worden, S. K., & Benford, R. D. (1986). "Frame alignment processes, micromobilization, and movement participation." *American Sociological Review*, 51: 464–481.

———, Soule, S. A., & Kriesi, H. (2004). *The Blackwell Companion to Social Movements*. Oxford: Blackwell.

Stewart, J. (2005). *Disney War*. New York: Simon & Schuster.

Stinchcombe, A. L. (1968). *Constructing Social Theories*. New York: Harcourt Brace & World.

Strang, D. & Macy, M. W. (2001). "In search of excellence: Fads, success stories, and adaptive emulation." *American Journal of Sociology*, 107: 147–182.

Stuart, T. E. (1999). "Interorganizational alliances and the performance of firms: A study of growth and innovaton rates in a high-technology industry." *Strategic Management Journal*, 21: 791–811.

Suarez, F. F. & Utterback, J. M. (1995). "Dominant designs and the survival of firms." *Strategic Management Journal*, 16: 415–430.

Suddaby, R. & Greenwood, R. (2005). "Rhetorical strategies of Legitimacy." *Administrative Science Quarterly*, 50: 35–67.

Swidler, A. (1986). "Culture in action: symbols and strategies." *American Sociological Review*, 51: 273–86.

Tett, G. (2009). *Fool's Gold: How the Bold Dream of Small Tribe at J.P. Morgan Was Corrupted by Wall Street Greed and Unleashed a Catastrophe*. New York: Free Press.

Tilly, C. (1998). *Durable Inequality*. Berkeley: University of California Press.

Tolbert, P. S. & Zucker, L. G. (1983). "Institutional sources of change in the formal structure of organizations: The diffusion of civil service reform, 1880-1935." *Administrative Science Quarterly*, 28: 22–39.

Weber, K. (2005). "A toolkit for analyzing corporate cultural toolkits." *Poetics*, 33: 227–52.

Westphal, J. D. & Zajac, E. J. (1994). "Substance and symbolism in CEOs' long-term incentive plans." *Administrative Science Quarterly*, 39: 367–390.

Westphal, J., Gulati, R., & Shortell, S. (1997). "Customization or conformity? An institutional and network perspective on the content and consequences of TQM adoption." *Administrative Science Quarterly*, 42: 366–392.

White, D. R., Owen-Smith, J., Moody, J., & Powell, W. W. (2004). "Networks, fields and organizations: Micro-dynamics, scale and cohesive embeddings." *Computational & Mathematical Organization Theory*, 10: 95–117.

White, H. C. (2002). *Markets from Networks: Socioeconomic Models of Production*. Princeton: Princeton University Press.

—— & White, C. A. (1965). *Canvases and Careers: Institutional Change in the French Painting World*. New York: Wiley.

Williamson, O. E. (1975). *Markets and Hierarchies: Analysis and Antitrust Implications*. New York: Free Press.

Zajac, E. J. & Westphal, J. (1998). "Symbolic management of stockholders: Corporate governance reforms and shareholder reactions." *Administrative Science Quarterly*, 43:127–153.

—— & Westphal, J. D. (2004). "The social construction of market value: Institutionalization and learning perspectives on stock market reactions." *American Sociological Review*, 69: 433–457.

Zald, M. N. (1996). "Culture, ideology, and strategic framing." In D. McAdam, J. D. McCarthy, & M. N. Zald (Eds.),*Comparative Perspectives on Social Movements*. New York: Cambridge University Press, 261–274.

Zerubvael, E. (1993). *The Fine Line: Making Distinctions in Everyday Life*. Chicago, IL: University of Chicago Press.

Zuckerman, E. W. (1999). "The categorical imperative: Securities analysts and the illegitimacy discount." *American Journal of Sociology*, 104: 1398–1438.

Zukin, S. & DiMaggio, P. (1990). *Structures of Capital: The Social Organization of the Economy*. Cambridge and New York: Cambridge University Press.

....

CHAPTER 5

THE BUILDING BLOCKS OF CORPORATE REPUTATION: DEFINITIONS, ANTECEDENTS, CONSEQUENCES

....

CHARLES J. FOMBRUN

What are corporate reputations? Where do corporate reputations come from? What effects do corporate reputations have on individuals, companies, and industries? These three questions have been central themes of the academic literature since its inception. They are addressed in different ways by researchers whose roots are mainly in marketing, organization science, economics, and finance. This chapter begins by examining seven principal reference frames that have guided theorizing about corporate reputations. The second section shows how these reference frames have influenced the answers that theorists give to the three fundamental questions posed above. In the third section, I present an integrative model that outlines the key components of an emerging theory of corporate reputations, one that identifies their causal drivers and links them to organizational-level and individual-level outcomes. I conclude by suggesting steps researchers can take to enhance ongoing learning about corporate reputations.

> "Today we are in an all out war for reputation. Our companies are battling, to an unprecedented extent, for our most vital assets: our own identities."
>
> *Miles D. White*
> *Chairman & CEO, Abbott Laboratories*

> "We only serve two masters: revenue and reputation."
>
> *Morten Albaek*
> *Senior VP, Vestas*

A growing literature focuses on the concept of corporate reputation. Barnett et al. (2006) pointed to the rapid growth in research articles published in peer-reviewed journals between 1984 and 2003. Growth in scholarship has been matched by a rising tide of media coverage that directly references "corporate reputation" and related constructs of "identity" and "image." A search of both scholarly articles and online media coverage demonstrates a rising tide of interest in these constructs in discourse about companies (see Figure 5.1). It helps explain managers' verbalized acknowledgments of the importance of reputation issues to their companies, as the opening quotes to this chapter illustrate.

Closer inspection of these accounts indicates that three fundamental questions have been central themes of published literature over the years. What are corporate reputations? Where do corporate reputations come from? What effects do corporate reputations have? They are addressed in different ways by researchers whose roots lie principally in marketing and organization science, with strong influences from the disciplines of sociology and economics (Fombrun, 2001; Fombrun & van Riel, 1997).

This chapter begins by examining seven reference frames that have guided theorizing about corporate reputations. The second section shows how these conceptual lenses have influenced the answers that theorists give to the three fundamental questions posed above. In the process, I address ongoing points of construct definition, as well as the antecedents and consequences of reputation. In the third section, I present an integrative model for studying corporate reputations that links it to a set of prior antecedents as well as to organizational-level performance outcomes. I conclude this chapter by

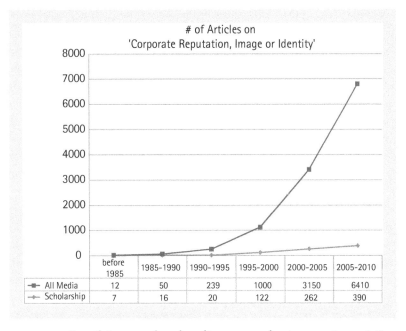

	before 1985	1985-1990	1990-1995	1995-2000	2000-2005	2005-2010
All Media	12	50	239	1000	3150	6410
Scholarship	7	16	20	122	262	390

FIGURE 5.1 Growth in research and media coverage about corporate reputation.

suggesting steps researchers and practitioners can take to enhance ongoing theory-building about corporate reputations.

BIT BY BIT: FRAMING THE REPUTATION LANDSCAPE

Seven conceptual frameworks have had disproportionate influence on theorizing about corporate reputations: Institutional Theory, Agenda-Setting Theory, Stakeholder Theory, Signaling/Impression Theory, Identity Theory, Resource-Based Theory, and Social Construction Theory.

Institutional Theory speaks to the context within which corporate reputations develop. The theory is generally called upon to explain how firms gain legitimacy and social support by developing privileged positions in the social order (Suchman, 2005). Firms' actions are driven partly by social pressures to conform to existing norms and regulations, and motivated by the desire to be regarded as legitimate and thereby secure a continuing license to operate (DiMaggio & Powell, 1996; Oliver, 1997). Institutional thinking calls attention to the importance of the "macro-culture" of the industry and the transactional network from which it derives (Abrahamson & Fombrun, 1994). A macro-culture arises from interactions between organizations and stakeholders, mediated by institutional intermediaries, such as the media and various specialized organizations (Hill & Jones, 1992; Fombrun, 1996). Conformity to the macro-culture generates isomorphism and firms' initiatives come to look more similar over time (DiMaggio & Powell, 1983). For example, the exponential growth in social responsibility reports companies have issued in the past decade is an indicator of institutionalization and an acknowledgment by companies that maintaining favorable stakeholder relationships is of strategic value.

Agenda-Setting Theory suggests that the mass media play a powerful role in setting the agenda of public discourse and directing the public's attention toward particular actors and issues (Carroll & McCombs, 2003; Wartick, 2002). The media are central to the process of creating reputations because they control both the technologies that disseminate information about firms to large audiences and the content of the information that gets disseminated (Rindova et al., 2006). The media inform the public about issues and events and thereby influence stakeholders' impressions of firms (Deephouse, 2000). The media tend to highlight firms that take bold or unusual actions and display distinctive identities. The more visible companies are in the media, the more likely are those companies to be remembered. The more favorable their coverage, the more positively consumers will judge them. And the more salient are the specific features of companies that journalists highlight, the more likely are consumers to associate them with those companies (Carroll & McCombs, 2003).

Stakeholder Theory invites us to identify those groups of people who have a stake in the company's actions and the outcomes they produce (Freeman, 1984). These stakeholders are individuals or statutory groups in the environment within which firms operate, and who are therefore conceived as the direct and indirect targets of actions or communications firms should make to attract resources, or to build and sustain their legitimacy. Stakeholders have differential power in affecting an organization's ability to achieve its objectives, and so their preferences must be regularly assessed and monitored if companies are to succeed in implementing their strategies (Jones, 1995). Companies do so for either or both instrumental and normative purposes—to deliver improved bottom-line performance and to fulfill ethical obligations (Donaldson, 1999). Investors, customers, and employees are generally viewed as primary stakeholders because of their power and legitimacy, as well as their ability to make urgent demands on companies. Suppliers and communities are viewed as either primary or secondary depending on their ability to affect corporate performance (Mitchell, Agle, & Wood, 1997).

Signaling/Impression Theory calls attention to the efforts companies make to influence their stakeholders and build support for their preferred initiatives and interests. Corporate communication, lobbying, and other social interactions/initiatives are considered strategic signals or impressions that companies broadcast in order to inform important resource providers or rivals about key features of their firms (Weigelt & Camerer, 1988). These signals are therefore marketing messages projected to stakeholders to convey either a desired or a desirable image of the company (Basdeo et al., 2006; Fombrun & Shanley, 1990; Turban & Greening, 1997). Firms also contribute to the construction of their reputations by targeting important intermediaries and seeking to manage the impressions about themselves that analysts and journalists portray to their respective audiences (Elsbach, 1994). In their communications, firms often help journalists to construct a "dramatized reality" that is designed to engage stakeholders emotionally (Bryant et al., 2002).

Identity Theory focuses on the interdependent characteristics of the organization that give it specificity, stability, and coherence, and thus make it identifiable. At its core, identity theory raises self-referential questions such as "who am I?" and "who are we?" and calls attention to an entity's attempts to define itself (Albert & Whetten, 1985). Applied to organizations, identity theory seeks to capture the collective self-understandings of organizational members, be they tacit or explicit, taken for granted or more consciously available (Corley & Gioia, 2004). For identity theorists, corporate reputations are partly accurate but partly warped or distorted interpretations that stakeholders make about the main features of a company's identity (Whetten & Godfrey, 1998).

Resource-Based Theory sets out to identify those resources that lead firms to develop a sustained competitive advantage in their industries (Barney, 1991). A firm builds advantage in an industry by gaining control over material, human, organizational, and locational resources and skills that enable it to develop a unique value-creating strategy. Heterogeneous resources create distinct strategic options for a firm that, over time, enable its managers to exploit different levels of economic rent (Peteraf, 1993). A firm's resources are said to be a source of competitive advantage to the degree that they are scarce, specialized, appropriable, valuable, rare, and difficult to imitate or substitute (Amit & Schoemaker, 1993). Reputations are in and of themselves a cognitive source of competitive advantage because they are unique, causally ambiguous to observers, and inimitable (Deephouse, 2000; Rao, 1994; Roberts & Dowling, 2002). The greater the ambiguity experienced by constituents, the greater the importance of reputation as it reduces uncertainty by signaling attractive features of companies such as their product quality or innovativeness. Insofar as stakeholders develop favorable interpretations and preferences for one organization over another (its products, jobs, or shares), their favorable perceptions of a company become a source of competitive advantage (Rindova & Fombrun, 1999).

Ultimately, *social construction theory* underlies much of the discussion taking place in reputation research. It comes from a more sophisticated view of an organization's managers and stakeholders as intimately involved in a reciprocal process of social construction (Berger & Luckman, 1966). Managers and stakeholders co-create shared understandings of their respective roles and involvements as they participate in social and informational exchanges. As stakeholders, intermediaries, and organizations interact, they construct a web of interpretations characterized by: (1) a widespread exchange of information and interpretations among firms and constituents; (2) varying degrees of knowledge and understanding about the industry and the firms inside it; (3) a multiplicity of interpretations, many of which are of a persuasive, self-serving nature; (4) some degree of agreement about standards of performance in an industry; and (5) evaluations of firms relative to these standards and their rivals that give content to their reputations. From these interactions, definitions of success and failure emerge that make of some companies "winners" and others "losers"—and reputations and rankings are created (Rao, 1994; Rindova & Fombrun, 1999).

These seven theoretical frameworks drive much of the conceptual thinking that has taken place in the reputation literature. The first six frames have been used willy-nilly to justify the definitions given to the key constructs we use, and are also regularly called upon to guide the construction of propositions and hypotheses, some of which are then subjected to empirical testing. The seventh frame (social construction theory) provides a context within which to understand reputational dynamics and the evolution of macro-cultural content, but provides little guidance for empirical research.

The next section examines how researchers have relied on these reference frames to address three central questions of particular interest to this *Handbook*, namely: What are corporate reputations? Where do corporate reputations come from? What effects do corporate reputations have on companies and individuals? The table at the end of the chapter summarizes some of the main theories, constructs, and citations examined in this chapter.

WHAT ARE CORPORATE REPUTATIONS?

Various reviewers have pointed to continuing confusion about the concept of corporate reputation, and its misuse in scholarship and research (Walker, 2010; Barnett et al., 2006). Due largely to the diversity of disciplines from which scholarship emerges and the many reference frames they use, the field has taken a long time to converge on a common definition of the reputation construct. The problem is compounded further by practitioners whose applied concepts overlap with, but do not always correspond directly with, those used by scholars. As Pfarrer, Pollock, & Rindova (2010: 1131) point out: "this research has often given different labels to the same types of collective perceptions or has used the same observable proxies to operationalize conceptually distinct constructs…As a result, labels and definitions have proliferated, making it difficult to determine if different studies consider the same or different phenomena, leading to a fragmented body of work and limiting the development of theory that can explain and predict the effects of different intangible assets."

The main points of contention continue to involve overlaps and distinctions between reputation, identity, brand, and image, as well as related constructs such as status, legitimacy, and celebrity. Barnett et al. (2006) examined definitions of corporate reputation in 49 books and articles and found that they grouped around three distinct clusters of meaning: reputation as a state of awareness, reputation as an assessment, and reputation as an asset. They recommend disentangling reputation from related constructs of identity and image in order to minimize confusion. Elsewhere in this *Handbook*, various chapters examine closely these related constructs and their ties to the reputation construct. I dwell here on the reputation construct itself, its definition, antecedents, and consequences.

Drawing on signaling/impression and identity theories, corporate reputation is increasingly conceived as the outcome of identity-consistent initiatives and communications (Whetten, 1997; Barnett et al., 2006) that organizations target to stakeholders, a set of actions generally described as corporate image-building or corporate branding (Hatch & Schultz, 2008; Dowling, 1994). As van Riel and Fombrun (2007: 40) point out, " 'corporate reputation' has gained attention largely because it captures the effects that brands and images have on the overall evaluations which stakeholders make of companies."

Nonetheless, developing a consensus definition of corporate reputation has proven elusive. Barnett et al. (2006: 34) concluded their review of reputation research by recommending that we reserve the construct of "corporate reputation" to describe the judgments made by observers about a firm. They then proposed a definition of corporate reputation as " 'observers' collective judgments of a corporation based on assessments of the financial, social, and environmental impacts attributed to the corporation over time."

I agree with the idea. Unfortunately, the definition they proffer itself falls prey to the criticism that the construct includes not only overall judgments of the company, but also a set of financial, social, and environmental *antecedents* of reputation that confound the construct since those antecedents are many and varied and unlikely to be consensually agreed upon.

In her review, Walker (2010) states that one of the most widely referenced definitions of reputation is the one I originally proposed: "A corporate reputation is a collective representation of a firm's past actions and results that describe the firm's ability to deliver valued outcomes to multiple stakeholders" (Fombrun, 1996). The three key attributes emphasized in that definition were: (1) reputation is based on perceptions; (2) it is a collective judgment of all stakeholders; and (3) it is comparative (Brown & Longsdon, 1997; Wartick, 2002). In addition to these three attributes, Walker (2010) suggested two additional dimensions mentioned in her systematic review of over 62 studies of corporate reputation: (4) it can be positive or negative, and (5) it is stable and enduring. She concluded that these five attributes could form the basis of a definition of corporate reputation as "a relatively stable, issue specific aggregate perceptual representation of a company's past actions and future prospects compared against some standard."

Although there are merits to such a measure, I also believe that both my own original definition, and the refinements proposed by Barnett (2006) and Walker (2010), may be too limiting: For one, building issue-specificity and varying standards into the construct will severely hamper our ability to cumulate research findings. More importantly, however, the more fundamental weakness embedded in all of these prior definitions is that they embed both antecedents and consequences of reputation within the reputation construct itself.

That core weakness is probably the principal factor that has confounded our efforts to define the reputation construct. It suggests the need for a revised approach, one that could enable a more readily accessible understanding—and ultimately measurement—of corporate reputation. To address that issue, I take my cue here from qualitative and quantitative research conducted since 1999 by Reputation Institute. Analyses of empirical measurements of reputation have consistently confirmed that two factors drive stakeholder perceptions of companies: One factor consists of a set of broad emotional attributes that are highly correlated; a second factor is made up of domain-specific perceptions of companies (Fombrun, Gardberg, & Sever, 2000).

Qualitative discussions about "corporate reputation" with different stakeholders, and in various industries and countries, have confirmed these quantitative findings. From answers provided to the question "what do you think of when you think about a company's reputation," we have found that stakeholders regularly interpret the expression "corporate reputation" to be closely associated with emotional reactions that involve "good feeling," "trust," "admiration," "respect," and related synonyms. An analysis of this research by Ponzi, Fombrun, and Gardberg (2011) further tested and confirmed the psychometric properties of an empirical measure of reputation based solely on the emotional factor across a variety of stakeholder groups, countries, and industries.

Following the recommendations of Barnett et al. (2006) to disaggregate constructs, as well as those of Walker (2010) to focus on reputation as stakeholder perceptions—and consistent with survey research conducted by Reputation Institute around the world—I suggest here that it may be worthwhile for scholars to make the construct "corporate reputation" whole again by removing from its definition all reference to antecedents and consequences. Instead, in the construct of corporate reputation, I propose that we retain four components: Reputations are (1) collective assessments (2) of a company's attractiveness (3) to a defined set of stakeholders (4) relative to a reference group of other companies.

> Definition: A corporate reputation is a collective assessment of a company's attractiveness to a specific group of stakeholders relative to a reference group of companies with which the company competes for resources.

This definition suggests that a corporate reputation should always be defined in terms of a specific stakeholder group and a specific reference group. To the question "What is the reputation of this company?," there should be an unambiguous answer: "When compared with a particular reference group of rivals, this company's reputation with stakeholder group X is A, and its reputation with stakeholder group Y is B." Hypothesis development about reputations should therefore always be contextualized in terms of both a stakeholder group and a reference group.

Defined in this way, antecedents and consequences are excluded from the reputation construct itself. Factors that drive a collective view of a company as more or less attractive and appealing to observers can be studied separately from the reputation construct itself. Doing so will facilitate causal examination of the factors that induce reputation, as well as any consequences reputation may have for companies, individuals, and society as a whole. It will also enable segmented comparison and analysis of that company's reputation with investors, customers, employees, managers, the general public, or other specific segments within or across countries. Finally, by disaggregating the construct, a corporate reputation can be developed for the broad ecology that surrounds a company based on an aggregation across relevant stakeholder segments in an industry, a country, or across countries. In this way, we can arrive at a holistic view of the global attractiveness of a firm to all of its constituencies.

A holistic definition of corporate reputation as "attractiveness" is also consistent with the idea that reputation involves a generalized emotional response that stakeholders have to a company's name—its perceived favorability, quality, value, excellence, eminence, distinction, merit, or worth. King and Whetten (2008) described reputation similarly as "a perception that organizations are positively distinctive within their peer group." The measure has both positive and negative components, and can be distinguished clearly from other related constructs.

Clearly there are overlaps between our constructs of "reputation," "identity," "image," "status," "legitimacy," and "celebrity" as many commentators have documented (e.g. Dutton & Dukerich, 1991; Rindova et al., 2006). If identity consists of the features of companies that are distinctive, central, and enduring (Albert & Whetten, 1997), then companies with strong identities are more likely to gain attention and appreciation. If "image" consists of the impression that companies make on external constituents (Bromley, 1993), then companies with a favorable image are more likely to be appreciated and well-regarded. Chapter 9 in this *Handbook* by David Whetten, Peter Foreman, and Alison Mackey addresses one possible way to interpret the complex relationship between identity, image, and reputation.

By contrast, if we view "status" as the relative ranking of a company in a hierarchy, then a company with a high status is more likely to engender respect, develop trust, and become attractive to observers—and so to build reputation. Companies that win repeated contests and consequently appear on multiple "best of" lists build status relative to rivals (Rao, 1994). At the same time, a company that has a strong and favorable reputation is more likely to earn status over time (Abrahamson & Fombrun, 1994).

Chapter 8 in this *Handbook*, by David Barron and Meredith Rolfe, speaks further to the interdependence of the two constructs "status" and "reputation."

A similar relationship binds the concept of reputation to the constructs of "legitimacy" and "celebrity." Rindova et al. (2006) suggest that "legitimacy" focuses on the degree to which a firm's products, practices, and structures are consistent with societal expectations. King and Whetten (2008) argue that both legitimacy and reputation arise from common social comparison processes. If stakeholders use institutionalized standards to assess and compare organizations (Rindova & Fombrun, 1999), then legitimacy may develop from comparisons between organizations that engender appreciation—that is, admiration, trust, and respect—of one company over another, and so build reputation. David Whetten, Peter Foreman, and Alison Mackey (Chapter 9, this volume) speak further to the intertwined processes that link legitimacy and reputation.

Finally, reputation is also tied to the concept of "celebrity." Celebrity results from (1) the amount of public attention a company receives and (2) the positive emotional responses it generates (Rindova et al., 2006; Pfarrer et al., 2010). If corporate reputation is defined, as I have proposed here, in terms of the emotional assessments that stakeholders make about companies, then "celebrity" provides us with an equivalent and more encompassing construct than marketing literature's concept of "brand equity." As Keller (1998: 50) acknowledges: "Customer-based brand equity occurs when the consumer has a high level of awareness and familiarity with the brand and holds some strong, favorable, and unique brand associations in memory." Aaker (1991) operationalized a measure of brand equity in similar ways to the celebrity construct as a product of "familiarity" and "favorability." "Celebrity" is therefore a higher-order interpretation of the concept of "corporate brand equity"—it describes the asset created from the combined visibility and favor in which a stakeholder community or macro-culture regards an organization (Pfarrer et al., 2010).

Other chapters in this *Handbook* examine at greater length the etymology of these related constructs. To make sense of reputation research going forward, it will be important for scholars and practitioners to converge on a shared understanding and definition of these constructs and their ties to the simplified reputation construct I have proposed in this chapter and elsewhere (Ponzi, Fombrun, & Gardberg, 2011). Naomi Gardberg and Grahame Dowling (Chapter 3, this volume) further elaborate on questions of measurement and their institutionalization in the form of reputation ratings and rankings that are consistent with this definition.

WHERE DO CORPORATE REPUTATIONS COME FROM?

Corporate reputations emanate from ontologically prior stakeholder experiences, attitudes, and perceptions of a company. They develop as individual perceptions aggregate into more or less shared understandings with collective properties. A corporate reputation is therefore a feature or property that resides in, and is attached to, an organization. This view is consistent with a concept of the organization as a social actor with a social and legal status whose identity is reflected in the contracts entered into by the organization, and whose reputation emerges from stakeholders' experiences, attitudes, and perceptions of the organization (Scott, 2003; Whetten & Mackey, 2002). Corporate reputations are therefore organizational characteristics that have independent ontological status, which stakeholders may or may not share, and that can be experienced, assessed, valued, and influenced.

Research suggests that corporate reputations develop from three principal sources: The personal experiences that stakeholders have with an organization, the corporate initiatives and communications that managers make to strategically influence stakeholder perceptions, and the specialized coverage the organization receives from influential intermediaries such as analysts, journalists, and other central gatekeepers linked through social networks. Media coverage influences the information held and interpretations made by stakeholders about the validity and merits of the firm's initiatives and communications. They either validate or invalidate the personal experiences of stakeholders and their interpretations of what firms communicate about themselves.

These three principal factors affect corporate reputations through the experiences that stakeholders have of the company's products and services, and the firm itself. Positive experiences generate stakeholder satisfaction, identification with the firm, and engagement, all of which contribute to generating favorable impressions of the firm and making it more attractive—they build reputation.

The marketing literature tells us that the key driver of customer satisfaction itself consists of the personal experiences individuals have with the company and its products (Keller, 1998). Insofar as a company's products become "personalized" to customers, they also identify more strongly with the company. So long as the experience is favorable (the products and the company deliver what they promise), customers are more likely to be satisfied, engaged, and committed, and see the company as more attractive for their own narrow purposes. Extended to the full stakeholder set, those experiences create for customers, employees, and investors more or less favorable perceptions of the company and its products as delivering "value" and "quality," and enable stakeholders to identify more with the company and its products.

Ultimately, a richer understanding of corporate reputations comes from recognizing that their collective properties emerge from a process of social construction. As Hatch (2005) argued in the context of organizational identity, these processes are located in the distributed awareness and collective consciousness of an organization's stakeholders. Just as Czarniawska (1997) proposed for organizational identities, so too can we view reputations as narratives constructed much like novels, with multiple plotlines, characters, and authors who draw on institutionalized discourses to provide the contexts within which meanings are made, and invoke questions about the power and politics through which reputation claims are articulated, negotiated, and substantiated.

WHAT EFFECTS DO CORPORATE
REPUTATIONS HAVE?

A large marketing literature stresses the importance of customer satisfaction as a driver of customer loyalty. Customer loyalty is itself a key factor in creating favorable outcomes for companies, particularly through its effects on building brand equity, employee productivity, revenue growth, and business profitability. The strong link between customer satisfaction and loyalty has been observed in a variety of settings in both offline and online environments. Debate has centered largely on establishing the relative strength of the effect and on explaining how other important factors, such as perceived product quality, brand image, and corporate reputation, influence the relationship between customer satisfaction and loyalty. Implications of that relationship for market segmentation and corporate profitability have also been studied in varying degrees (Keller, 1998). The benefit of having satisfied customers derives from the ability to induce supportive behaviors from customers, employees, and investors that, in turn, have a positive effect on the bottom line.

The link between satisfaction, loyalty, and performance has been extended in varying degrees to other stakeholder groups, including investors and employees. In her study of German investors, Helm (2007) found that satisfied investors were more likely to remain loyal to the company—to hold, invest, and reinvest in the company's shares, as well as to speak more favorably of the company to others. As she reports, this occurred when investors had more favorable regard for the company. Similarly, like investors and customers, satisfied employees, because they find the company attractive, are also more likely to stay with the company, have lower absenteeism, greater productivity and longevity, and therefore contribute to enhancing bottom-line results (Heskett et al., 1997; Reicheld, 1996). Pratt (2000) studied the process through which consumer giant Amway produces identification and engagement in its independent distributor network through both sense-making and sense-breaking initiatives. Research confirms that stakeholder identification has positive benefits: People prefer to buy products from high reputation companies, job-seekers prefer to work for them, and long-term investors favor them as investment vehicles.

Ultimately, stakeholder support makes available a bounty of resources to companies. By appealing to customers, companies grow their top line; by attracting more and better employees, they improve their efficiency and productivity; by drawing support from bankers, they develop lower-cost access to credit; and by attracting investors, they improve the market for their shares. Support therefore translates into better operating results, and has a positive impact on the bottom line (Fombrun & van Riel, 2004).

The long-term effect of having an improved bottom line is growth in the company's pool of intangible assets—the intellectual, organizational, and reputational capital the company gains from having supportive stakeholders (Dowling & Roberts, 2002). Profitable companies generally reinvest at least part of their profits in the development of proprietary products and tools, they reinvest in their people, and they reinvest in their organizational systems—all of which increases their competitive strengths in the marketplace. These reinvestments are intangible assets that create a competitive advantage for companies by erecting mobility barriers that rivals then have difficulty overcoming (Rindova & Fombrun, 1999). In turn, mobility barriers institutionalize reputation, prestige, and celebrity for incumbent firms which reinforces their standing in the industry's pecking order or ranking system (Rao, 1994; Fombrun, 1996), making them appear more legitimate and securing for them a license to operate (Deephouse & Carter, 2005).

Violina Rindova and Luis Martins (Chapter 2, this volume) describe four dimensions of reputation that contribute to their value as intangible assets: specificity, accumulation, breadth of appeal, and codification. These dimensions are directly applicable to our definition of reputation: As a collective assessment of a company's attractiveness to its stakeholders, a reputation can be more or less *specific, visible, appealing*, and *codified*. Aggregation across stakeholders takes place through a process of social construction: Stakeholder-specific reputations become generalized halos with greater or lesser appeal through a process of reciprocal influence that involves signal-producing firms, powerful intermediaries that reflect and refract those signals to others, and social networks and media that interpret those signals and adopt more or less shared understandings of the reputational ordering of firms in a macro-cultural field.

PUTTING IT ALL TOGETHER: AN INTEGRATIVE FRAMEWORK FOR CORPORATE REPUTATION RESEARCH

Several advanced texts on corporate communication describe the interrelationships between brand, identity, image, reputation, and performance (van Riel & Fombrun, 2007; Dowling, 1994). Unfortunately, none have provided us with an integrative framework explaining how these constructs are related. In this section I propose a simple framework for examining corporate reputations, their antecedents, and consequences.

For ease of exposition, the systemic framework described in Figure 5.2 is rooted in causal thinking and suggests that research should flesh out the institutional or contextual factors that induce the development of more or less favorable stakeholder perceptions about a company. In turn, perceptions create corporate reputations, and stimulate stakeholder loyalty and support, from which companies then earn economic, social, and organizational rents. The causal sequencing is not intended to preclude a more complex and systemic grasp of the social construction process through which stakeholders enact their individual understandings of companies and construct interpretations that, in turn, crystallize as collective properties such as "reputations" and rankings. Rather, it calls attention to the aggregate patterning of organizational features that will then be amenable to empirical testing through positivist research designs.

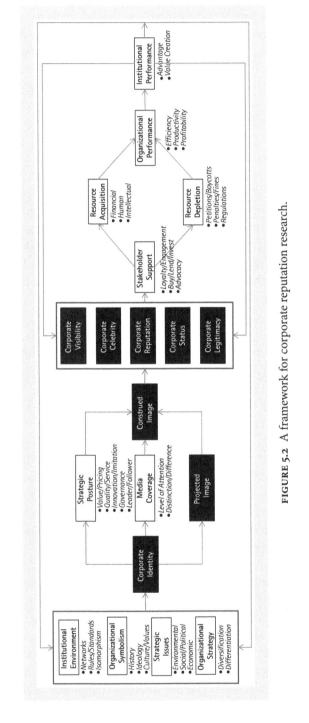

FIGURE 5.2 A framework for corporate reputation research.

Institutional theory calls attention to the context from which reputations develop. The environment consists of stakeholders and role-playing intermediaries linked through networks of influence, whose goal-oriented actions are contextualized by the macro-cultural content they produce and within which firms operate (Abrahamson & Fombrun, 1994). The environment presents firms with strategic issues they must address; it also creates opportunities for diversification and differentiation that firms can elect to pursue in order to create profits (Prahalad & Bettis, 1986; Porter, 1985). The strategic choices companies make are rooted in the unique histories and ideologies that have produced each company's dynamic trajectory through time and space (Dierickx & Cool, 1989).

As a result of the institutional, symbolic, and strategic context within which firms operate, specific companies adopt strategic postures: They elect to inhabit price-value niches that require varying levels of quality and innovation; they also adopt symbolic structures, house styles, brand strategies, and communication practices. As a result of their strategic postures, they prove more or less interesting to media intermediaries and influence journalists' choices of which companies to cover, what level and kind of attention to provide them with, and how they are portrayed (Carroll, 2010).

Identity Theory tells us that, over time, companies develop features that are central, enduring, and distinctive (Albert & Whetten, 1985), and that are contextualized in a system of beliefs, values, and underlying assumptions. Identity expresses cultural understandings at the same time as it mirrors images that outsiders may have of the organization (Hatch & Schultz, 1997: 357). Reputations build as managers convey and communicate their culture-specific, identity-consistent features to stakeholders. They acquire legitimacy by adopting prevailing practices and thereby conforming to established norms, rules, or codes (Suchman, 1995; Scott, 1983).

From Stakeholder Theory, Signaling/Impression Theory, and Agenda-Setting Theory, we understand that the combined influence of strategic positioning, identity development, strategic signaling, and media coverage disseminates portrayals of companies that shape stakeholder perceptions of the relative strengths and weaknesses of these companies. The net effect of these stakeholder perceptions is to make companies more or less appealing to consumers, partners, investors, creditors, and employees. Aggregated across relevant stakeholders, these perceptions crystallize as corporate reputations and provide firms with more or less status, legitimacy, visibility, celebrity, and reputation (Fombrun, 1996).

Resource-Based Theory tells us that corporate reputations generate economic value by creating stakeholder support, loyalty, and advocacy: Potential employees are more attracted to working for better regarded companies, consumers are more likely to purchase their products, bankers are more likely to give them credit at lower cost, and investors are more likely to purchase their shares. From enjoying stronger stakeholder support, reputed companies attract more and better resources, operate more efficiently, have higher productivity, and can price their offerings at a premium—all of which convert to more attractive bottom lines. Past investments in generating goodwill from social initiatives also cushion firms from resource depletion by creating a "reservoir of goodwill"—being perceived as socially responsible, those firms are less likely to face boycotts and lawsuits, and so have lower cost structures and faster recovery times when faced with crisis events (Fombrun et al., 2000; Porter & Kramer, 2006; Jones et al., 2000).

The net effect of the context–strategy–identity–reputation–support–performance causal sequence is to erect mobility barriers—barriers too difficult for rivals to imitate or overcome—that generate superior sustainable results for better regarded companies. They manifest themselves in the form of intangible assets whose value is crystallized in the excess market capitalizations that publically traded companies enjoy, and which secure for them a continuing license to operate (Deephouse & Carter, 2005; Porter & Kramer, 2006).

Conclusion: Enhancing Theory-Building about Corporate Reputations

A "reputation" is only one of the many components of the complex cognitive, social, institutional, and ecological systems in which organizations are embedded. Reputations are therefore co-determined by many other constructs with established interpretive structures and linguistic traditions. In our efforts to develop a theory of corporate reputations, a variety of rich conceptual frameworks have been applied to the field by well-intentioned scholars with different disciplinary roots.

Despite these creative contributions, scholars and practitioners remain plagued with self-doubt and insecurity about the field. If corporate reputations are to make a genuine, value-added contribution to the growing body of work on strategic positioning and value-creation, scholars and practitioners will have to agree on how to address a variety of issues that have plagued research in this area. This chapter sought to illuminate some of those issues, with particular emphasis on core questions about (1) how to define and frame corporate reputation and (2) how to address questions about research and analysis.

Little advance can be made without agreement about the basic definitions of corporate reputation and related constructs. Despite efforts to do so, there remains a degree of plasticity about the definitions in use today—and that's a significant weakness researchers must address. Other chapters in this *Handbook* examine the complementary constructs of image, identity, celebrity, status, and legitimacy—and their ties to the reputation construct. In this chapter, I have focused on the reputation construct itself, and suggested a revised definition that removes from the construct all mention of its antecedents and consequences. More specifically, I proposed that a corporate reputation can be construed simply as a collective assessment of the attractiveness of a firm to a specific stakeholder group relative to a reference group of peers. The definition has both scholarly and empirical roots that can facilitate developing both a research thread and a measurement program, and thereby enable the accumulation of findings in this area. If the definition finds adherents, it will facilitate ongoing conversations and reduce the proliferation of arguments that are, at base, epistemological in nature and, at worst, are distractions for the core tasks at hand.

Based on this definition, I suggest that core questions of reputation research will involve (1) understanding the antecedents of the collective assessments that stakeholders make of a firm's attractiveness, as well as (2) understanding their consequences internally and externally for firms, individuals, industries, and societies. There are countless antecedents that we have yet to examine closely. Many theoretical frames can be applied to develop specific hypotheses linking causal drivers to reputational outcomes. Likely as not, these hypotheses will draw on institutional and strategic theories to explain the organizational behaviors that ultimately shape stakeholder perceptions of firms. A rich field of inquiry—and recommendations for practice—can develop from this line of work.

But as practitioners are wont to remind us, reputations are not an end in themselves. To be relevant to practice, scholars must help practitioners understand and dissect the contributions that reputations make to short-term performance outcomes and to long-term value-creation for all stakeholders and societies. Robust theories grounded in an understanding of processes of resource acquisition and strategic advantage-building are likely to remain among the most helpful in shedding light on how intangible assets and economic value are created from reputation-building initiatives. Various chapters in this *Handbook* can help further crystallize the ways through which reputations contribute to driving resource flows, whether in the capital markets or labor markets, or in attracting favor from analysts, regulators, publics, and other important stakeholder groups.

Since practitioners are also active contributors to analysis and writing about corporate reputations, practitioners themselves can help eliminate confusion and improve theory development if: (1) they resist the temptation to misappropriate terminology from different disciplines; (2) they collaborate with researchers whose access to relevant data for hypothesis testing is limited; and (3) they encourage documentation of reputation dynamics by exploring, explaining, and revealing the roles that senior executives play in the selection and management of corporate symbols and the creation of perceptions and meanings in the macro-cultures in which firms are embedded.

Ultimately, positivist research is not the only vehicle through which we can grow knowledge about corporate reputations. Understanding also develops from contextualized case studies, thick descriptions, and other forms of knowledge-building. The field of reputation research is a discipline that demands continuing dialogue between the worlds of scholarship and practice. Carefully constructed theoretical frameworks, adherence to endorsed definitions, and empirical measurements are a necessary cornerstone for establishing a base of useable knowledge from which a continuing dialogue between scholarship and practice about corporate reputations can bear fruit.

Corporate Reputation: Definitions, Antecedents, Consequences

Reference	Key Frame/ Concepts	Key Predictions & Findings
Barnett et al. (2006) Walker (2010)	Defining Reputation	A corporate reputation is a collective judgment about a company based on assessments of its financial, social, and environmental impacts over time.
Albert & Whetten (1985) Whetten & Godfrey (1998)	Identity Theory	Organizational identity describes the features of companies that are central, enduring, and distinctive.
Spence (1974) Weigelt & Camerer (1988) Schlenker (1980)	Signaling/ Impression Theory	Companies signal their features in order to influence the behavior of competitors and stakeholders. Reputations are attributes ascribed to a firm based on its past actions.
Carroll & McCombs (2003) Carroll (2010)	Agenda-Setting Theory	The media influence the perceptions of companies by affecting their visibility and the salience of features consumers associate with those companies.
Barney (1991) Amit & Shoemaker (1993) Roberts & Dowling (2002)	Resource-Based Theory	The foundation of competitive advantage lies in a company's ability to control unique bundles of material, human, and locational resources
DiMaggio & Powell (1985) Oliver (1997) Scott (2003)	Institutional Theory	A firm's sustainable advantage depends on its ability to manage the institutional context of its resource decisions.
Freeman (1984)	Stakeholder Theory	Stakeholders are interested parties who stand to lose or gain by the success or failure of a firm
Rindova, Pollock & Hayward (2006) Rao (1994)	Social Construction Theory	Reputations are socially constructed: Stakeholders make sense of strategic signals emanating from companies seeking to influence observers.
Fombrun & Shanley (1990) Fombrun (1996) Fombrun & van Riel (2004) Gardberg & Fombrun (2006)	Reputation, Performance, and Intangible Assets	Reputation is influenced by advertising, profitability, citizenship, diversification, and is inversely related to financial risk.
Van Riel & Fombrun (2007)	Corporate Communication & Reputation	An integrated view of corporate communication theories and their relationship to reputation
Aaker (1991) Keller (1998) Hatch, Schultz & Larsen (2000)	Brand, Identity, and Culture	Companies build distinctive reputations and positions through 'expressiveness'

Reference	Key Frame/ Concepts	Key Predictions & Findings
Abrahamson & Fombrun (1994) Rindova & Fombrun (1999)	Macro-Culture & Cognitive Competitive Advantage	Companies inhabit socio-cultural environments from which they draw legitimacy and which they influence to create distinctiveness, attract resources, and build competitive advantage
Suchman (1985) Deephouse & Carter (2005) King & Whetten (2008)	Legitimacy and Reputation	Legitimacy emphasizes the social acceptance that comes from adhering to social norms and expectations, whereas reputation emphasizes comparisons among organizations

REFERENCES

Abrahamson, E. & Fombrun, C. J. (1994). "Macrocultures: Determinants & consequences." *Academy of Management Review*, 19: 728–755.

Albert, S. & Whetten, D. (1985). "Organizational identity." In L. L. Cummings & B. M. Staw (Eds.), *Research in Organizational Behaviour*, Vol. 7. Greenwich, CT: JAI Press, 263–295.

Amit, R. & Schoemaker, P. (1993). "Strategic assets & organizational rent." *Strategic Management Journal*, 14(1): 33–46.

Barney, J. (1991). "Firm resources & sustained competitive advantage." *Journal of Management*, 17: 99–120.

Bryant, J., Zillman, D., & Oliver, M. B. (2002). *Media Effects: Advances in Theory & Research*. UK: Routledge.

Burt, R. (1980). "Models of network structure." *Annual Review of Sociology*, 6: 79–141.

Carroll, C. (2010). *Corporate Reputation and the News Media*. UK: Routledge.

—— & McCombs, M. (2003). "Agenda-setting effects of business news on the public's images & opinions about major corporations." *Corporate Reputation Review*, 6(1): 36–46.

Caves, R. E. & Porter, M. E. (1977). "From entry barriers to mobility barriers." *Quarterly Journal of Economics*, 19: 421–434.

Corley, K. G. & Gioia, D. A. (2004). "Identity ambiguity & change in the wake of a corporate spin-off." *Administrative Science Quarterly*, 49: 173–208.

Czarniawska, B. (1997). *Narrating the Organization: Dramas of Institutional Identity*. Chicago: University of Chicago Press.

Daft, R. & Weick, K. (1984). "Toward a model of organizations as interpretation systems." *Academy of Management Review*, 9: 284–295.

Dierickx, I. & Cool, K. (1989). "Asset stock accumulation & sustainability of competitive advantage." *Management Science*, 35: 1504–1511.

DiMaggio, P. & Powell, W. (1984). "The iron cage revisited: Institutional isomorphism & collective rationality in organizational fields." *American Sociological Review*, 48: 147–160.

Dowling, G. R. (1994). *Corporate Reputations: Strategies for Developing the Corporate Brand*. UK: Kogan Page.

Dutton, J. E. & Dukerich, J. M. (1991). "Keeping an eye on the mirror: Image & identity in organizational adaptation." *Academy of Management Journal*, 34: 517–554.

——, Dukerich, J. M. & Harquail, C. V. (1994). Organizational images & member identification. *Administrative Science Quarterly*, 39: 239–263.

Elsbach, K. (1994). "Managing organizational legitimacy in the California cattle industry: The construction & effectiveness of verbal accounts." *Administrative Science Quarterly*, 39: 57–88.

Fiol, C. M. (2001). "Revisiting an identity-based view of sustainable competitive advantage." *Journal of Management*, 27: 691–699.

Fiske, S. & Taylor, S. (1990). *Social Cognition*. New York: McGraw-Hill.

Fombrun, C. J. (1996). *Reputation: Realizing Value from the Corporate Image*. Boston: Harvard Business School Press.

—— (2001). "Reputations as economic assets." In M. Hitt, R. E. Freeman, & J. Harrison (Eds.), *Handbook of Strategic Management*. Oxford, UK: Blackwell.

—— & Shanley, M. (1990). "What's in a name? Reputation-building & corporate strategy." *Academy of Management Journal*, 33: 233–258.

Fombrun, C. J. & van Riel, C. B. M. (2004). *Fame & Fortune*. New York: Financial Times/ Prentice-Hall.

——, Gardberg, N. & Barnett, M. (2000). "Opportunity platforms & safety nets: Corporate citizenship & reputational risks." *Business & Society*, 105(1): 75–106.

Freeman, R. E. (1984). *Strategic Management: A Stakeholder Approach*. Boston, MA: Pitman.

Gardberg, N. A. & Fombrun, C. (2006). "Corporate citizenship: Creating intangible assets across institutional environments." *Academy of Management Review*, 31(2): 329–346.

Gioia, D. A., Schultz, M., & Corley, K. (2000). "Organizational identity, image & adaptive instability." *Academy of Management Review*, 25: 63–82.

Goffman, E. (1959). *Presentations of Self in Everyday Life*. Garden City, NY: Doubleday.

Hall, R. (1992). "The strategic analysis of intangible resources." *Stategic Management Journal*, 13(2): 135–144.

Hatch, M. J. & Schultz, M. (2002). "The dynamics of organizational identity." *Human Relations*, 55: 989–1019.

Helm, S. (2007). "The role of corporate reputation in determining investor loyalty and satisfaction." *Corporate Reputation Review*, 10(1): 22–37.

Jones, T. (1995). "Instrumental stakeholder theory: A synthesis of ethics & economics." *Academy of Management Review*, 20: 404–437.

Jones, G. H., Jones, B. H., & Little, P. (2000). "Reputation as reservoir: Buffering against loss in times of crisis." *Corporate Reputation Review*, 3(1): 21–29.

Keller, K. L. (1998). *Strategic Brand Management: Building, Measuring, and Managing Brand Equity*. Upper Saddle River, NJ: Prentice-Hall.

King, B. G. & Whetten, D. A. (2008). "Rethinking the relationship between reputation and legitimacy: A social-actor conceptualization." *Corporate Reputation Review*, 11(3): 192–207.

Mahoney, J. & Pandian, J. R. (1992). "The resource based view within the conversation of strategic management." *Strategic Management Journal*, 13(5): 363–380.

Nahapiet, J. & Ghoshal, S. (1998). "Social capital, intellectual capital, & the organizational advantage." *Academy of Management Review*, 23: 242–266.

Oliver, C. (1997). "Sustainable competitive advantage: Combining institutional & resource-based views." *Strategic Management Journal*, 18(9): 697–713.

Peteraf, M. (1993). "The cornerstones of competitive advantage: A resource-based view." *Strategic Management Journal*, 14(2): 179–191.

Pfarrer, M. D., Pollock, T. G., & Rindova, V. P. (2010). "A tale of two assets: The effects of firm reputation and celebrity on earnings surprises and investors' reactions." *Academy of Management Journal*, 53(5): 1131–1152.

Pfeffer, J. & Salancik, G. (1978). *External Control of Organizations*. New York: Harper & Row.

Ponzi, L., Fombrun, C., & Gardberg, N. A. (2011). "RepTrak pulse: Conceptualizing and validating a short-form measure of corporate reputation." *Corporate Reputation Review*, 14(1): 15–35.

Porter, M. (1985). *Competitive Advantage*. New York: Free Press.

—— & Kramer, M. (2006). "The link between competitive advantage and corporate social responsibility." *Harvard Business Review*, December: 1–13.

Prahalad, C. K. & Bettis, R. (1986). "The dominant logic: A new linkage between diversity & performance." *Strategic Management Journal*, 7(6): 485–501.

Pratt, M. G. (2000). "The good, the bad, & the ambivalent: Managing identification among Amway distributors." *Administrative Science Quarterly*, 45: 456–493.

Rao, H. (1994). "The social construction of reputation: Certification contests, legitimation, & the survival of organizations in the American automobile industry: 1895–1912." *Strategic Management Journal*, 15(Winter): 29–44.

Rindova, V., Pollock, T., & Hayward, M. (2006). "Celebrity firms: The social construction of market popularity." *Academy of Management Review*, 31(1): 50–71.

Roberts, P. & Dowling, G. R. (2002). "Corporate reputation and sustained superior financial performance." *Strategic Management Journal*, 23(12): 1077–1093.

Rumelt, R., Schendel, D., & Teece, D. (1991). "Strategic management & economics." *Strategic Management Journal*, 12(Winter Special Issue): 5–29.

Schlenker, B. R. (1980). *Impression Management*. Monterey, CA: Brooks/Cole.

Scott, W. R. (2003). *Organizations: Rational, Natural, & Open Systems*. Upper Saddle River, NJ: Prentice-Hall.

Scott, S. G. & Lane, V. R. (2000). "A stakeholder approach to organizational identity." *Academy of Management Review*, 25(1): 43–62.

Shapiro, C. (1983). "Premiums for high-quality products as returns to reputations." *Quarterly Journal of Economics*, 98: 659–681.

Suchman, M. (1995). "Managing legitimacy: Strategic & institutional approaches." *Academy of Management Review*, 20(3): 571–611.

Tedeschi, J. T. (Ed.). (1981). *Impression Management Theory & Social Psychological Research*. New York: Academic Press.

Thompson, L. & Fine, G. (1999). "Socially shared cognition, affect, & behavior: A review & integration." *Personality & Social Psychology Review*, 3(4): 278–302.

Walker, K. (2010). "A systematic review of the corporate reputation literature: Definition, measurement, & theory." *Corporate Reputation Review*, 12(4): 357–387.

Wartick, S. L. (1992). "The relationship between intense media exposure & change in corporate reputation." *Business & Society*, 31: 33–49.

CHAPTER 6

A SURVEY OF THE ECONOMIC THEORY OF REPUTATION: ITS LOGIC AND LIMITS

THOMAS NOE

The chapter will explain the standard economic framework for analyzing corporate reputation, consider its validity, and suggest new directions for advance. I first contrast and compare the informal concept of reputation with the definition used in standard economic models of reputation formation. Next, I consider the theory in the light of the empirical evidence and conclude that, on the subset of reputation related issues the theory addresses, its qualitative predictions are broadly consistent with the empirical evidence. However, the scope of application of the economic model is very narrow relative to the breadth of reputation related activities and concerns of corporations. I conclude by sketching out a number of directions in which the economic modeling could be broadened to better encompass corporate reputation related activity while retaining its essential paradigm of rational choice and equilibrium.

INTRODUCTION

APPLIED researchers, consultancies, and senior managers devote considerable attention to developing practical tools for corporate reputation protection and enhancement. Their consensus view is that a good reputation is a very significant driver for corporate value and, at the same time, reputation is an intangible 'soft' concept, difficult to quantify and evaluate. One might imagine that economics, given its own reputation for an aversion to all things soft and non-quantifiable, would have little to contribute to this discourse. However, in fact, a large independent literature on 'reputation formation' has developed within economics. Can the discourse in economics inform the reputation discourse in applied management or are the two discourses simply using the same word 'reputation' to refer to different and fundamentally distinct concepts? For example, media researchers and point-set topologists both use the same term—'connectedness' in their research discourse. Yet it is doubtful that understanding the discourse on connectedness in one of these fields would be of much use in advancing progress in the other. Can the same be said of the reputation discourse in theoretical economics and management practice?

In order to answer this question, we will first explain and evaluate the economic theory of reputation and relate this theory to the "vernacular" concept of corporate reputation, that is, corporate reputation as understood by the business press and corporate practitioners. The aim is to produce a simple yet accurate account of how the economic theory of reputation works. We will argue that the economic concept of reputation tracks the definition in use by practitioners and management researchers fairly closely. Next, we will argue that in a broad sense, there is strong support for many of the predictions made by economic theory. However, the formalization of the reputation concept imposed by economic theory has encouraged modelers to focus their analysis on a very limited set of reputation determinants. Fortunately, this limited menu is not a necessary feature of economic modeling of reputation formation. To conclude, we provide some guidance to creative theorists for extending the limits of economic analysis and thereby close the gap between economic theory and business practice.

We have mapped out a long journey and have but limited time. Thus, we will have to forgo many detours which lead to interesting attractions. Hundreds of economic theories have been developed over the last 30 years rationalizing reputation formation. It is not possible to explain or critique each one. Moreover, as we shall see, most of the thorny issues surrounding applying the economic theory of reputation stem not from specific features of the reputation model but from underlying standard rational choice perspective of human behavior.

1 REPUTATION DEFINED

We shall first relate standard rational choice perspective to the vernacular concept of "reputation," first by developing the vernacular concept and then, by contrasting and comparing it with the concept of reputation used by economic theorists. Next, we will explain the concept of equilibrium and how it both specifies and restricts the predictions of the economic framework concerning reputation formation.

"Reputation" is derived from the Latin verb *reputare* to reckon. Thus, a reputation is an assessment made by some economic agents about the characteristics of other agents. Firm reputation is an assessment of economic agents regarding the characteristics of a firm. Following the standard conventions in the management literature, we will call the agents who form reputation about the firm, the firm's "stakeholders." Stakeholders care about those aspects of a firm's behavior that may affect their welfare broadly defined. Thus, we will focus on those firm characteristics that are payoff relevant to stakeholders—for example, commitment to product quality, trustworthiness of business dealings. Firms may of course have reputations regarding many characteristics that are payoff irrelevant, but economic analysis abstracts from these facets of a firm reputation.

An important implication of this definition is that reputation is not a single property that a firm does or does not have; rather, the firm has a reputation with specific stakeholders regarding specific characteristics. Consider a simple example. A firm raises money from the debt market to manufacture widgets. The two payoff relevant characteristics of the firm are *upright* and *green*. "Upright" represents the characteristic that the firm will not misreport its income or illicitly convey corporate assets and so on, even when such misreporting and conveyance is in the interest of shareholders. "Green" represents an inherent preference for protecting the environment which will lead the firm to choose the most environmentally friendly "green" widget production technology, even when the green technology is more expensive than a "brown" technology which poses more environmental hazards. In our contrived example, reputation for this firm can be represented by a matrix:

Table 6.1 Reputation Matrix

	Characteristic	
Stakeholder	Upright	Green
Consumers	o	x
Creditors	x	x

In the matrix, "x" represents the presence of a reputation and "o" its absence. In this example, our firm is reputed to be sound and green by its creditors and is reputed to be green by its consumers. The firm does not have a reputation for financial soundness with its consumers. This lack of reputation does not imply that consumers view the firm's management as crooked, for it is also consistent with consumers not taking any "view" on the firm's uprightness. Assuming that consumers value green production and creditors value uprightness, the firm's reputation regarding these characteristics with these stakeholders should enhance value. However, assuming that creditors are neutral toward environmental effects, a firm's reputation for greenness amongst creditors might be detrimental, as it will lead creditors to believe that the firm will use more expensive green technology even when it can "get away" with the cheaper brown alternative, thus potentially impairing debt value. Perhaps an ideal reputation matrix for a cynical firm would be as follows:

Table 6.2 "Cynical ideal"

	Characteristic	
Actor	Sound	Green
Consumers	o	x
Creditors	x	o

As we will see in the subsequent discussion, economic theory, through the concept of equilibrium, will place rather severe limitations on the ability of firms to attain reputation matrices such as this one. However, the point of this example is simply that reputation, for a given firm is a relation between firm characteristics and reputing stakeholders. Moreover, the effect of reputation on the firm can vary not only with characteristic but also with the stakeholder.[1] How does a firm affect its reputation with stakeholders? Stakeholders typically cannot directly observe the reputed characteristic and instead look to the firm's actions to make their assessments. For example if our firm was caught having two sets of books (the firm action) the creditors might not consider it upright any longer. If a firm produces shoddy products now, its may lose its reputation regarding the future quality of its products. Thus, any theory of reputation has to develop some theory of belief revision, that is, how firm actions revise stakeholders' beliefs and then explain how these belief revisions affect stakeholders' treatment of the firm.

2 REPUTATION IN ECONOMICS

Economic models of reputation formation consider this process of stakeholder belief revision in response to firm actions and the resulting change in stakeholder behavior toward the firm. These models feature interaction over more than one period, with the history of past interactions affecting stakeholders' current beliefs about the firm's characteristics. Through this process firms "build reputations." In these reputation formation models, the history of firm/stakeholder interactions may not reveal the firm's characteristics completely. Moreover, in economic models of reputation formation, stakeholders use the information from history predictively in that past history affects their current disposition only through its ability to shed light on future firm behavior.

These two characteristics—multiperiod imperfect revelation and predictive information use—distinguish economic reputation formation from related approaches to the question of how firm actions affect stakeholder responses to firms—the signaling and stigma frameworks. In the signaling framework the firm takes an *observable* action which in and of itself "proves" the firm has a characteristic of interest to stakeholders.[2] Thus, signaling can take place without repeated interaction and such signalling perfectly reveals the firm's characteristics. For example, a green firm might signal its greenness by committing a share of all its future profits to an environmental NGO, a share so large that no brown firm could increase its value by making the same commitment. In a repu-

---

[1] The practical difficulties associated with measuring the components of an actual firm's reputation matrix are enormous. For a discussion of the current state of research on applied reputation measurement (see Dowling & Gardberg Chapter 3, this volume).

[2] For a classic paper on signaling, see Spence (1973); for a comprehensive survey of signaling models see Spence (2002).

tation formation equilibrium, green firms will embrace green technology, and brown firms will also sometimes adopt this technology in order to avoid being revealed to environmentally conscious consumers as being more likely to endanger the environment. Reputation equilibria in which brown firms act green suppresses information about their inherent lack of environmental concern. In signaling equilibria, in contrast, this information is revealed.

The second characteristic, an exclusively predictive use of history, distinguishes the economic model of reputation formation from the stigma framework. Given stigma, stakeholder treatment of the firm may vary with past actions of the firm even if those actions are not predictive of future behavior. For example, a firm that undertakes a reprehensible action in a stigma framework might be shunned by consumers even if consumers knew that the firm has subsequently implemented control systems that will prevent the future occurrences of actions of the same type. In a reputation equilibrium, stakeholders' treatment of the firm would not be affected by past reprehensible behavior which they know to be not predictive of future actions. In contrast to the signaling framework, the volume of research on firm behavior within the stigma framework is very small. However, Mishina & Devers (Chapter 10, this volume) provides an interesting conceptual analysis of sigma from a management perspective and contrast the reputation and sigma in a systematic fashion.

How is stakeholder belief revision based on past history, a defining characteristic of economic reputation models, specified? The standard economics framework imposes structure on the nature of beliefs and the process of belief revision. First, agents in economic models are Bayesian in that they make decisions consistent with Bayesian decision theory. Bayesians, instead of simply affirming or denying the presence of characteristic, assign a probability to the truth of the proposition that the characteristic is present. For example, "the firm being green" has a 90 percent probability of being a true statement. Moreover, Bayesians assign probabilities to the truthfulness of all well-formed propositions. Thus, such agents always "take a view" on the characteristic, even though this view might reveal considerable uncertainty, that is, "a 0.50 probability that the firm is green." For this reason, formalizing the intuitive model presented above in the context of Bayesian decision theory, requires that we replace assent with probabilistic assessments.[3] A formalization of reputation in an economic model, in the context of our example might take the following form:

Table 6.3 Reputation and Bayesian Probabilities

	Characteristic	
Actor	Upright	Green
Consumers	0.50	0.875
Creditors	0.875	0.875

---

[3] Economists have developed decision theories that relax or abandon the Bayesian model. See, for example, Erev & Roth (1998); Gilboa & Schmeidler (1995); Gilboa (1987).

Note that, in this example, consumers and creditors assign different probabilities to the firm being sound. What is the basis for the difference? In the standard economic model, differences in beliefs are based on differences in information. In reputation framework, this information is produced by firm actions. In our example, perhaps creditors have observed that the firm has never been cited for fraudulent actions while consumers may not have observed the firm's financial history.

This brings us to the second bit of structure imposed by the economic mode— Bayesian belief revision. Economic theory assumes that stakeholders impound information using the laws or probability, more specifically they use "Bayes rule." The most transparent statement of this rule for our purposes is as follows: suppose a stakeholder is computing the odds that a firm has characteristic C. Consider the creditor in our example, and let the characteristic be uprightness. Suppose the creditor, after observing the firm's credit history, believes that the probability that the firm is upright is 0.875. In which case the odds of the firm being upright are $7:1$ (the calculation from the probabilities in Table 6.2, is $0.875/(1 - 0.875) = 7/1$), that is, it is 7 times more likely that the firm is honest than it is dishonest. When the creditor receives information from some firm action, call it A (in our example A is the firm's credit history of no fraud), Bayes rule implies that:

$$\text{NewOdds}(C \text{ given } A) = \text{OldOdds}(C) \times \frac{\text{Probability}(A \text{ given } C)}{\text{Probability}(A \text{ given not } C)}. \qquad (6.1)$$

In our example

$$\text{NewOdds}(Upright \text{ given } NopastFraud) =$$
$$\text{OldOdds}(Upright) \times \frac{\text{Probability}(NoPast\ Fraud\ given\ Upright)}{\text{Probability}(NoPast\ Fraud\ given\ not\ Upright)} \qquad (6.2)$$

Assume in our example that, before dealing with the firm and observing its actions, all stakeholders assign even odds ($1:1$) to uprightness. We know from Table 6.2 that the odds currently assigned by creditors of honesty are $7:1$. From Bayes rule (equation 6.1) we see that creditor odds before observing the firm's behavior, "Old Odds," and after observing the firm's behavior, "New Odds," are related as follows:

$$7 = \text{NewOdds}(Honest \text{ given } NoPastFraud) =$$
$$1 \times \frac{\text{Probability}(NoPastFraud\ given\ Honest)}{\text{Probability}(NoPastFraud\ given\ not\ Honest)}$$

Thus, from 2 we see that it must be the case that

$$\frac{\text{Probability}(NoPastFraud \text{ given } Honest)}{\text{Probability}(NoPastFraud \text{ given } notHonest)} = 7$$

that is, creditors' confidence in firm uprightness can be rationalized by an assessment on the creditors' part that an upright corporation is seven times more likely to have reported honestly than a non-upright firm over the given period.

In general, Bayes rule, given in 1, places considerable restrictions on agent beliefs. First, note that an agent places either infinite or 0 initial odds on the characteristic C, the agent's beliefs will never be changed by *any* information received. Thus, agents who are certain about a characteristic remain convinced regardless of what they observe in the future. Second, what matters is *relative* likelihood of the action with and without the reputed characteristic. For example, a history of no accounting fraud over a rough period in the firm's history provides much more persuasive evidence of uprightness than no restatements over a smooth patch. Third, if an action is never undertaken by the non-upright firms and sometimes undertaken by upright firms, the odds of uprightness are infinite, that is, undertaking the action will completely convince the creditors that the firm is upright.

The third restriction that the standard economic framework imposes is *maximization*, namely, that the firm as well as the stakeholders act in a way that maximizes their own welfare under a well-defined objective function. Welfare need not simply represent personal monetary gains, it could for example include the conjectured social effects of actions, monetary gains to third parties and so on. What is required is that all the players have definite preferences over all possible outcomes, and if queried as to which of two outcomes they prefer, they will answer one or the other or that they are indifferent. They will never respond by saying "I don't know."[4]

3 REPUTATION IN EQUILIBRIUM

Armed with well-defined preferences and the Bayesian probability calculus, we can begin to make predictions regarding firm and stakeholder actions. Predicted behavior is assumed to be the outcome of perfect Bayesian equilibrium. In a perfect Bayesian equilibrium, each agent maximizes her own welfare based on her conjecture about the actions

---

[4] At a technical level, additional assumptions are required which ensure that agents' preferences are "continuous." These assumptions are required so that we can represent agent preferences by a number, "utility," with the larger numbers representing the more preferred action. Further assumptions are then required to ensure that agents maximize the expected value of utility. See Myerson (1997: ch. I) for a complete development. Economic theories of choice have been developed outside this framework. See, for example, Fishburn & Lavalle (1993) and Ok (2002).

of the other agents and each conjecture about the actions of the other agents is correct. In models of reputation formation, firms undertake actions that will influence the future actions of the other stakeholders. For example, invest in green technology today to increase green reputation in the future. Thus, reputation models are per force dynamic, with agents acting in more than one period.

Why do firms care about reputation in the economic framework? The vast majority of work on reputation assumes that a reputation for "good" characteristics is pursued because reputation enhances firm value, by leading other economic stakeholders to transact with the firm at more favorable terms.[5] There are two types of reputation models, complete information models and incomplete information models. Complete information models are rooted in the work of Klein & Leffler (1981). In this strand of research, firms' preferences are known by consumers and the reputed characteristic is not the firm's inherent taste for the reputed characteristic but rather whether the firm will actually act reputably. In the incomplete information models, first developed by Kreps & Wilson (1982) and Milgrom & Roberts (1982), stakeholders are unsure about a firm's intrinsic *type*, that is, its preference for reputable behavior; the firm's actions change the stakeholders' beliefs about the firm's type and this, in turn, changes their beliefs about the likelihood the firm will act reputably.

Reputation with Complete Information

In complete information models the firm's time horizon is unbounded, either because the firms have an infinite life or because their end point is unknown. In this genus of models, a firm makes a decision that affects the welfare of stakeholders. If the firm makes an opportunistic decision in the current period, maximizing its current profit at the expense of stakeholders, stakeholders believe that it will act opportunistically in the future, and adjust their behavior accordingly—they may refuse to lend to the corporation, lower the price they will pay for its goods. If the long-term gains from reputation exceed the short-term profits from opportunism, the firm will protect its reputation by eschewing opportunism. The classic paper in this genre is Klein & Leffler (1981), which states that a firm has an opportunity to provide high or low quality goods for consumers. High quality goods cost more to produce than low quality goods but the consumers' value premium for high quality exceeds the additional cost. Thus, if product quality could be costlessly verified before purchase, it would be in the interest of both consumers and firms for high quality to always be produced. Reputation is relevant because Klein & Leffler assume that consumers cannot verify quality before purchase. However, after purchasing a good, consumers learn its quality. The firm's choice: produce high quality or "cheat" consumers by producing low quality goods when consumers anticipate high quality.

---

[5] Recently, Benabou & Tirole (2006) have proposed a different motivation for reputation formation: firms, or at least their owners, have intrinsic preferences concerning their reputation, independent of its effect on value. This is an interesting line of research but beyond the scope of this chapter.

Klein & Leffler find an equilibrium in which the firm produces high quality in every period. This equilibrium is supported by the following strategies: So long as the firm produces high quality, consumers pay the higher price associated with high quality. If the firm ever deviates from its equilibrium strategy of producing high quality, consumers offer only the low quality price thereafter, regardless of the firm's subsequent behavior, and, in response, the firm subsequently produces low quality. Thus, the gain to the firm from opportunism, that is, deviating from the high quality to low quality, is the immediate cost savings, the cost is that in the future it will be restricted to producing the less profitable low quality product. When the long-term gains are sufficiently large, maintaining reputation is advantageous to the firm. Consumers, at the same time, are willing to pay the high quality price before they are cheated because they correctly conjecture that the firm will provide the high quality good. If consumers were ever cheated, subsequently, they would be willing to pay only the low quality price. The firm thus knows that if it ever were to produce low quality, it would be regarded as a low quality producer thenceforth regardless of its subsequent actions. Thus, the firm recognizes that its best strategy, if it ever produces low quality, would be to keep producing low quality thereafter. In summary, consumer and firm beliefs are consistent with the actual actions taken by the other, and each party is maximizing its own welfare—that is this behavior represents an equilibrium.

Three aspects of this equilibrium are worth noting. First, reputation formation both requires and creates market power. It is only because firms can earn economic rents from high quality production that they are willing to forgo the gains from opportunistic short-run behavior. In a purely competitive market, firm profit net of capital charges is zero. Thus, in such an environment, there is no incentive to maintain reputation. Moreover, not only is market power required for reputation formation, the need for reputation formation itself creates market power. If reputation was not required to assure high quality production, which would be the case if, for example, consumers could verify quality before purchase, a new entrant with the same production costs as the incumbent could enter the market for high quality production and earn a profit at a price lower than the reputation-equilibrium price. Thus, the incumbent firm's market, absent the need for reputation, is contestable. However, an entrant offering a lower price in Klein & Leffler's world would not have sufficient economic profits in the long run to deter short-term opportunism. Thus, consumers would rationally conjecture that the entrant would cheat and thus they would only be willing to buy from the entrant at the lower price. In short, the need for reputation both makes the market incontestable and thus generates the market power required for reputation formation.

Second, the punishment to failing to maintain a quality reputation is grim, unrelenting, and literally eternal. Once a firm produces low quality, it is forever considered a cheating firm regardless of its subsequent behavior. Such punishment is rational in that the consumers' commitment to viewing the firm as a cheating firm makes reverting to high quality following a lapse irrational for the firm, and thus confirms the consumers' belief that the firm is a cheating firm. In fact, the very grimness of the threatened punishment deters the firm from ever acting opportunistically in the first place, much as the threat of nuclear war might prevent two nuclear adversaries from ever engaging in any combat and thus produce less combat casualties than would have occurred if the adversaries were armed with swords and spears.

Third, complete information models require an unlimited time horizon. Suppose for example, that a firm is going to be dissolved at a fixed future date. At the ultimate date, the firm would not have any future rents and thus would act opportunistically. Consumers would anticipate opportunism and be willing to pay only the low price for its low quality goods. Thus, at the penultimate period, the corporation would realize that regardless of whether it produces high quality, its goods will be priced as low quality at the ultimate date. Hence, the firm would have no reason to eschew opportunism at the penultimate date. Consumers anticipate this in an equilibrium and would thus offer the low price at the penultimate date. Now, at the anti-penultimate date, the firm would know that regardless of its choice at the ultimate and penultimate date, it will receive the low price and, by the same logic, the firm will never produce high quality at the anti-penultimate date and so on. Thus, with a fixed time horizon, the reputation formation strategy unravels through backward induction.

Reputation Formation with Incomplete Information

As we have noted, reputation formation under complete information requires market power and an unlimited horizon. Kreps & Wilson (1982) and Milgrom & Roberts (1982) developed models that allow reputation formation without requiring an unlimited horizon. These authors modeled monopoly entry deterrence, where the reputed characteristic is the willingness of a monopolist to resist entry by a challenger. In order to keep the focus of our analysis closer to Klein & Leffler (1981), we will consider a version of the model developed in Maksimovic & Titman (1991) that, like Klein and Leffler's, relates to product markets. Reputation formation works in the Maksimovic & Titman despite the limited horizon because of a new source of uncertainty—*type uncertainty*. Some firms have an intrinsic preference for high quality production (or revulsion to cheating consumers). These firms are called "high types". Other firms do not have this preference and will cheat whenever it is profitable, these are called "flexible types." Consumers cannot identify a firm's type but they can observe the firm's actions. Flexible types have an incentive to induce consumers to believe they are likely to be high types. The only way they can convince consumers that they are high types is by acting like high types for some period of time, and thereby build up their reputation. Of course, in the last period, flexible firms will always cheat. But they can only cheat the last period if they have produced high quality in all previous periods. Consumers are rational and they will reflect the probability that the firm is flexible, and thus may cheat, in the price they are willing to pay. This implies that, in the last period, flexible firms will receive a price above good value and high types will receive a price below value and that, on average, price will equal value.

Flexible firms cheating in the end game is not surprising. What is surprising is that in this model universal cheating by flexible firms *never* occurs in any period before the last period regardless of how small the initial probability is of the firm being a high type. The key to understanding this result is to understand the constraints imposed by Bayesian updating discussed in Section 2. To establish this result, I will only consider cheating at the penultimate date. At this date, the incentive to cheat is the greater than at any previous date since the incentive to cheat grows as the ultimate date is approached. If all flexible types who have not yet cheated, cheat at the penultimate date, then at the ultimate date, consumers, using Bayes rule, would have to assign 0 probability of being flexible to any firm which has not yet cheated.[6]

Thus, if all flexible firms cheat in the penultimate period, then each flexible firm would know that it changed its strategy to not cheating in this period, consumers, in the ultimate period, would be convinced with certainty that it was a high type. Since high types do not cheat, the price received by firms not cheating in the previous periods would equal the value of the high quality good. Thus, the gain from high quality production in the ultimate period would equal the entire value differential between high and low quality goods. Since consumers do not observe cheating at the penultimate date until the ultimate date, prices in the penultimate date are the same regardless of whether the firm cheats consumers at this date. Thus, the penultimate date gain from cheating equals the cost savings from producing low quality. By assumption, the cost savings are less than the value differential. Thus, if all flexible firms cheat, each flexible firm gains from not cheating now and waiting to cheat later. Thus universal cheating before the last date is not maximizing and thus cannot occur in equilibrium.

Thus, an interesting characteristic of incomplete information models is that the introduction of even a small number of "ethical" firms, that is, firms with an inherent preference for the reputed characteristic, has a great deal of influence on the behavior of opportunistic firms. Absent any ethical firms, the backward induction argument we gave when discussing Klein & Leffler (1981) would lead to universal cheating by opportunists in every period. The introduction of even a small nucleus of ethical firms blocks universal cheating by opportunists at least before the last period. Equilibria can exist where some opportunists cheat in every period and gradually such firms are thus identified. However, the increase in proportion of ethical firms always reduces total cheating by an even larger proportion. This follows because an increase in the proportion of ethical firms increases the reward to opportunists from emulating such firms. This increases the willingness of opportunists to eschew cheating. Hence each ethical firm introduced into the pool both lowers the proportion of cheaters directly by not cheating and also lowers the likelihood that opportunistic firms cheat.

Sadly, however, in this model, virtue is not its own reward. Flexible firms are always more profitable than upright firms. Upright firms need not earn economic rents in this model. However, since ethical firms must at least break even to survive and opportunistic firms are more profitable than ethical firms, opportunistic firms always earn economic rents. Moreover, as in the analysis of Klein & Leffler (1981) the punishment for

---

[6] In order to apply Bayes rule, use equation 1. Let the characteristic, C, be being a flexible type, and the action, A, be not cheating the consumer in any previous period.

cheating is grim, once cheating occurs, the cheater is identified as a flexible opportunist with certainty, and by Bayes rule and, once certain, consumers remain convinced that the firm is a flexible opportunist.

Qualitative Predictions of the Economic Reputation Framework

Despite their differences, the two approaches to modeling reputation have yielded some basic common predictions:

- The loss of reputation imposes substantial long-term costs on firms.
- The loss of reputation through opportunistic actions increases the likelihood of future opportunist actions.
- The ability to earn economic rents, that is, profits exceeding the normal rate of return, is correlated with reputation formation.
- Reputation constraints can set a floor on firm profits, blocking entry by competitors offering the same good at a lower price.

These insights apply quite generally to economic models of reputation formation. Moreover, they are the basis for research on how firms' internal structure and exterior environment affect their propensity to follow reputation building strategies. For example, Maksimovic & Titman (1991) consider the effect of firms' capital structure on reputation formation. The key to their results is that debt claims, by increasing bankruptcy risk, can shorten the horizon of stockholders. Consider a firm which is able to satisfy its creditors in the current period but faces a high likelihood of default in the future. For such a firm, the short-term gains from opportunism will be reaped by shareholders alone but some of the long-term gains from reputation formation will be captured, in the event of default, by creditors. Thus, debt shortens the horizon of shareholders and encourages opportunistic actions. This effect can be mitigated if shareholders are prevented from extracting short-term gains from the firm, for example, by the imposition of dividend payout restrictions. In a similar fashion, an adverse economic shock related to future demand for a firm's products can foreshorten its cash flow horizon and thus increases its propensity to opportunistic behavior. Thus, the reputation framework predicts opportunistic (reputation destroying) actions around adverse turning points in firms' histories, when firms realize, but stakeholders yet do not, that the long-run profits from reputation formation are no longer sufficient to support reputation forming behavior. These results yield insights into the relation between economic conditions and reputation formation:

- The decision on whether to build a reputation is a trade-off between short-term costs and long-term gains.

- The longer the time horizon for firm cash flows, the more likely the firm is to engage in reputation forming activities.
- Firms are most likely to lapse into opportunistic behavior right after a negative shock which was preceded by favorable business conditions.

4 APPLYING THE REPUTATION FRAMEWORK

In addition to forming reputations for being a tough competitor and developing quality reputation, the economic reputation framework has been applied to a number of other characteristics and stakeholders. Balvers, McDonald, & Miller (1988) model investment-banker reputation formation for fair IPO pricing with investors. In their model, the investment bank's choice of auditing firm is used by investors to infer the accuracy of the investment bank's IPO price. Abreu & Gul (2000) model reputation in bargaining games, in this model an agent is bargaining with another agent for the division of the gains from trade. The reputed characteristic is "toughness" in negotiations, an unwillingness to accept "low" offers from the other agent even when acceptance would yield a higher payoff. Even soft agents have an incentive to build a reputation with counterparties for toughness by rejecting "low" offers and thereby increase the odds the other party assigns to them being tough. Diamond (1989) models debt repayments and shows that firms increase their reputation for profitability with creditors through a history of debt repayment and thereby lower their cost of repayment.

The reputation framework has also been applied to non-corporate actors. Shapiro & Stiglitz (1984) uses one of the basic insights from Klein & Leffler (1981)—that reputation can only be sustained by agents earning economic rents—to develop a model of involuntary unemployment. In this model, workers can either shirk or work diligently for employers. The disincentive to shirking is firing. In order for this disincentive to be sufficient for workers to eschew shirking, wages must rise above the workers' minimum reservation for accepting employment so as to make the long-term losses from firing greater than the short-term gains from shirking. Unemployed workers are willing to undercut this higher wage but employers know that, at the lower wage they are willing to accept, the value of employment to them, while positive, is not sufficient to offset the short-term gains from shirking. Thus, such workers will not be hired, resulting in involuntary unemployment. The reputation framework has also been applied to sovereign states by Grossman & Huyck (1988). They explain sovereign debt repayment, which cannot be enforced contractually, as a product of states attempting to build reputations as reliable debtors in order to maintain their access to global capital markets.

The papers described above show economics has considered many possible reputable characteristics and stakeholders. However, in each of these papers we have one characteristic and one stakeholder. Noe, Rebello, & Rietz (2011) consider a corporation that has two stakeholders: consumers and outside investors. The characteristic is product quality. The tension in the model is that an unflagging commitment to product quality even at the expense of profit, for any fixed set of consumer beliefs about product quality, lowers firm value and thus requires corporate owners to raise financing at less favorable terms. Were it possible, opportunistic firms would like to convince consumers that they are quality fanatics and investors that they are flexible profit maximizers. Bayesian rationality vetoes the alluring possibility. Outside investors have the same information as consumers and thus must have the same beliefs about the firm's type. This implies that, when a flexible firm contemplates opportunistic behavior, it knows that this deviation to opportunism, not being immediately observed, will not be reflected in the financing terms outside investors will accept. Thus, if it deviates to opportunism, its short-term cash flows will be undervalued by markets. Because short-term gains are undervalued, shareholders, if they defect, will be compelled to issue claims whose value exceeds their fair value. Thus, when the firm raises funds with short-term claims (e.g., short-term debt) from outsiders, defection to opportunism has an additional cost—a partial transfer of the gains from opportunism to outside investors. This effect deters opportunism, and leads to higher quality levels and more reputation formation by flexible firms. Noe, Rebello, & Rietz (2011) considers multiple stakeholders and shows that the presence of one stakeholder (in their case investors) affects the willingness of firms to build reputation with another stakeholder (in their case consumers).

5 VALIDITY

It is apparent from our earlier discussion that the economic definition of reputation is a fairly faithful formalization of the vernacular definition and that the economic model of reputation formation is internally consistent. Thus, our evaluation of the economic model will turn on its external validity. Are its theoretical predictions consistent with actual firm behavior? Does economic theory "work" in predicting agent behavior in the sort of reputation formation situations that it models? "Working" can be defined either broadly or narrowly. In contrast to qualitative social science models, economic theory makes precise numerical predictions regarding outcomes. The economic framework work in the narrow sense if the numerical predictions of models built within the framework can be validated statistically. In contrast, broad validity requires only that the qualitative and directional predictions of the framework be validated. These qualitative implications were outlined in Section 4.

Narrowly Defined Validity

We will first consider validity narrowly defined and then turn to the question of broad validity. In general, the evidence is negative on narrow validity. Because the numerical predictions of reputation models depend on the details of the model's specification, in order to test the narrow validity of economic models it is required to establish an environment in which the assumptions of the given model are satisfied exactly. This is only possible in a laboratory experiment with human subjects. Laboratory experiments in economics consist of specifying a game structure and recruiting subjects to play the game. Subjects are provided monetary payoffs consistent with the game's structure. There have been many laboratory experiments of economic reputation models. To understand the results of these experiments we need to invoke the constraints economic theory imposes on agent behavior discussed in Section 2. Here, we showed that the key restrictions on subject behavior were Bayesian probability assessment and rational maximization over a well defined set of preferred outcomes. In the laboratory setting, preferences are fixed by the monetary payoffs assigned by the investigator.[7] Thus, the key background behavioral constraints are Bayesian updating and rational maximization. Rational maximization entails using backward induction to solve the decision problem, that is, working backward from the end point, and using the solution at each stage to form optimal strategies in the previous stage of the game.

A considerable body of laboratory research has shown that human subjects do not use backward induction in problems featuring many stages and that, when the updating problem is subtle, subjects do not update their assessments in a fashion consistent with Bayes rule. Ho, Camerer, & Weigelt (1998) estimates that the median experimental subject applies only one or two step backward induction, implying that in reputation formation games which feature many time periods and thus require many backward induction steps, backward induction reasoning is unlikely to be applied by most subjects. Bayesian updating is also problematic as a description of subject belief revision. Kluger & Wyatt (2004) and Ganguly, Kagel, & Moser (2004) both document striking failures of Bayesian reasoning on the part of subjects for decision problems involving subtle calculations. Given these results, it would be surprising if laboratory experiments on reputation formation resulted in behavior perfectly consistent with model predictions.

The expected lack of consistency has been documented in a number of experiments. Camerer & Weigelt (1988) analyze an experiment implementing a reputation formation game. They find that subject behavior deviates from theoretical predictions. However, they also find that most of the deviation can be accounted for by "home-made priors." In other words, subject behavior closely conformed to model predictions under the assumption that subjects used a different initial probability distribution over types than

---

[7] The issue of controlling subject payoffs is a bit more involved. Berg et al. (1986) show that, provided subjects' endowed preferences are consistent with expected utility maximization, monetary payoff schemes can be used to simulate any expected utility based objective function. However, as Hey & Orme (1994) document, expected utility maximization, while a relatively good descriptor of subject behavior, is not always the best model. Also, even granting expected utility maximization, subjective psychological costs to subjects of evaluating decisions may overwhelm monetary incentives especially when the difference between utility under the optimal policy and suboptimal policies is small (see Harrison (1992)).

the one specified by the experimenters. However, Brandts & Figueras (2003) document more troubling deviations from the equilibrium solution. They perform a reputation formation experiment in which the number of rounds is varied across treatments. They find that homemade priors cannot explain subject behavior even in the short (three round) treatments. This result is interesting in that a three-round game requires only two stages of backward induction to solve, and as shown by Ho, Camerer, & Weigelt (1998) two-stage induction is commonly used by experimental subjects. Thus, it is unlikely that the failure of backward induction or homemade priors is the primary cause of experimental discrepancies from theory. Results more consistent with theory were obtained by Brandts & Figueras in their long (six round) treatments. On the one hand, this is to be expected given the qualitative predictions of the reputation model discussed in Section 4. Increasing the number of periods increases the incentives for reputation formation. On the other hand, as discussed above, longer chains of backward induction usually lead to more deviations of subject behavior from equilibrium predictions.

Reputation Broadly Defined

The failure of the predictions of specific implementations of the reputation model in laboratory experiments has led researchers to consider the question of whether the qualitative predictions of the model hold. A number of studies using both laboratory and field data answer this question in the affirmative. Brandts & Figueras (2003) documents "that" reputation formation behavior is most pronounced in the early stages of their game, where the number of future stages is greatest. Moreover, increasing the proportion of "high-types," types inflexibly committed to reputation forming behavior, decreases the frequency of opportunism amongst opportunistic types. In a laboratory experiment, Dejong, Forsythe, & Lundholm (1985) document that, consistent with the reputation framework, excess profits are associated with reputation acquisition and that opportunistic behavior leads to large reductions in future profits. Agents also tend to follow the strategy of first forming a reputation and by providing high quality services and then, as the end of the game approaches and future rents from reputation attenuate, switch to opportunistic cheating behavior.

The qualitative predictions of the economic framework have also been tested in the field. Melnik & Alm (2002) document a small but significant cross-sectional relation between seller reputation and prices received in eBay auctions. Cabral & Horta (2010) find a much stronger price/reputation relation using panel data to account for dynamics and unobserved heterogeneity between sellers. They find that, subsequent to negative buyer feedback, sellers' average weekly sales growth rate falls from 5 percent to –8 percent. Moreover, sellers are much more likely to drop out of eBay after negative feedback and sellers more likely to drop are more likely to receive negative reports. These results are consistent with (a) reputation loss being very costly and (b) opportunistic behavior leading to more opportunistic behavior, exactly as the reputation model predicts. Fang & Yasuda (2009) find that analysts' personal reputation is positively related to forecasts quality and are associated with much better forecasting in the presence of conflicts of interest. Gorton (1996) examines the effect of reputation on the pricing of bank notes issued by banks in the US during the nineteenth century, when banks were free to issue notes that circulated as currency. He shows that the notes issued by new banks were more heavily discounted by markets. Karpoff & Lott (1993) document a severe reputation cost from corporate fraud, they show that on average, corporate fraud charges are associated with 1.3 percent reduction in firm market value. Consistent with the predictions in Section 4, Wang, Winton, & Yu (2010) show that corporate fraud is most likely at the start of economic downturns which were preceded by booms.

6 Extending the Limits of the Framework

The overall impression reached thus far is that the economic reputation framework is very relevant to the practical discourse on corporate reputation. The economic definition of reputation is a formalization, albeit somewhat confining, of the vernacular definition. This confining definition has its reward as it permits the development of a number of sharp characterizations of the prerequisites and effects of reputation forming activities. These characterizations appear to be broadly supported by the evidence and they can be applied to practice.

At the same time, most economic modeling of reputation is limited in that it abstracts from factors that business leaders, consultants, and the management literature deem highly relevant to reputation formation. In the vast majority of economic models, corporate reputation for a given attribute is founded only on stakeholder perception of corporation exhibiting the attribute, for example, firms build reputations with consumers for making good widgets by selling them good widgets. Most economic modeling of reputation formation ignores the determinants of reputation formation posited by identity theory, signalling/impression theory, and agenda setting theories prominent in the management literature.[8] To the extent that these effects are of first-order importance, expanding the limits of economic analysis is required for closing the gap between economic models and reputation formation economic theory. This will require a more serious engagement by economic theorists with both the management literature and corporate practice.

Efforts to enrich theory face real obstacles. Economic theorists have good reasoning for keeping their models lean and "limited." Economic theory embeds reputation in a formal model of belief formation and rational action in which factors affect reputation through their effect on the welfare of agents and the diffusion of information. Thus, the introduction of a new factor requires formalizing how the given factor affects the utility or information endowments of agents. The tariff for including a factor in a formal

---

[8] See Fombrun, Chapter 5, this volume for a detailed review of these theories.

model of reputation formation is inversely proportional to the plausibility of the assumptions linking the factor to stakeholders' preferences and information endowments and proportional to the increase in the opacity and complexity of the resulting model. This tariff is higher for some factors in reputation formation process than others. Including widget quality in a model of reputation for widget quality has a very low tariff. The modeller only needs to assume that consumers care about the quality of the goods they purchase and that they observe quality. Both assumptions seem non-controversial. Other determinants of reputation formation, such as social interactions between the company and stakeholders, public relations, impose a higher tariff because the assumptions required to link these factors to stakeholder assessments will be less obvious and more problematic. Because of this differential tariff, low-tariff reputation determinants are emphasized much more than high tariff determinants. However, a priori, there is no reason that economic theory cannot assimilate these high-tariff factors into its formal analysis.

The exact approach taken incorporating a broader range of reputation factors will depend on the sort of reputation being modeled and the tastes and ingenuity of the modeler. However, it is possible to sketch out some economic frameworks that might be used to connect economic models with the reputation factors considered in the more general management literature. Consider first identity theory. This theory posits the importance of stability and coherence in shaping the different reputations corporations form with distinct stakeholder groups. One way this coherence constraint can be reflected in economic modeling is through the ability of stakeholders to observe corporate interactions with other stakeholders and use the quality of these interactions to make inferences about the corporations' attractiveness to them. As discussed earlier, Noe, Rebello, & Rietz (2011) develop a model where a corporation must maintain a reputation both with consumers and investors. Because consumers observe the credit market and investors observe the product market, the firm's reputation in one market is linked to its reputation in the other. This informational link imposes a degree of coherence or "identity" on the firm's reputation across markets. Or consider the role of the media endorsement in agenda-setting theories of reputation articulated in the management literature. One interpretation for the importance of media endorsement is that the media are high-status social actors. Experimental economics research by Eckel & Wilson (2007) has empirically documented that the effect of observing the play of a given agent on the ability of a group of agents to coordinate to payoff-dominant equilibria is proportional to the observed agent's status. There is no reason these status effects, which have been explored in economics in the context of coordination games, could not be incorporated into reputation models. The effect of interpersonal relations on reputation identified by signaling/impression theories in the management literature is consistent with models of influence behavior. Modeling influence behavior has become a staple in economic models of corporate governance and executive compensation. For example Wulf (2009) models influence as the ability of one agent to alter the perceptions of another agent's assessment of quality of a project. In her analysis, all agents are rational and thus influenced agents realize that they may be being influenced. Nevertheless, influence activities can still be effective. There is no reason why this sort of influence analysis could not be applied to the analysis of corporate reputations.

As well as addressing the reputation determinants identified in the management literature, the economic models could be enriched by considering determinants identified by executives and the business press, notably reputation control systems and reputation redemption. Reputation control systems ensure that the firm intent to follow a reputation building program is implemented. Reputation control includes reporting and intelligence protocols, staff training, reputation audits, and so on. Investments in control systems are not explicitly mentioned in most economic models of reputation but they are implicitly present because they represent part of the cost of implementing reputable behavior, such as part of the cost of producing high quality goods. Whether new insights would be gained from making these costs more explicit in theoretical analysis depends on how such costs would be rendered explicit. Simply adding a cost variable is of questionable value but more sophisticated modeling of the incentives of employees to follow corporate policy might prove interesting.

The second limitation of the model in explaining practical reputation management relates to reputation repair. This lacuna in the economic modeling cannot be explained by insignificance of reputation repair activity. A great deal of managerial effort and consulting advice is devoted to the question of what a firm should do after it has undertaken an action that reveals the absence of the reputed trait. Moreover, management research on the topic of redemption is extensive. In fact, in this handbook, Rhee and Kim (Chapter 22, this volume) provide a conceptual framework for considering reputation repair activities, dividing them between superficial repair and substantive repairs. Superficial repair focuses on managing stakeholder perceptions while substantive repair involves organization changes aimed to eliminate the causes of the reputation damaging behavior. Rhee & Kim provide a behavioral interpretation of both superficial and substantive repair activities which appears to encompass a significant portion of observed corporate reputation repair actions.

Is it possible to also explicate reputation repair within the economic framework? To elucidate this question consider the following example. Suppose that the reputed trait is quality commitment and the stakeholders are consumers and that the firm is caught selling shoddy products. In the standard economic reputation models discussed thus far, such an action would render consumers certain that the firm was untrustworthy and no subsequent actions by the firm could change this assessment. Thus, at first glance, it seems the search for a rationale for repair within the economic reputation formation framework will be futile. The difficulty is that once an agent is identified as lacking the reputed trait, the logic of backward induction eliminates any incentive for the agent to "pretend" to possess the trait by acting reputably. As long as we consider the firm to be a unitary monolith with unchanging characteristics, we are indeed trapped by the logic of rational choice. However, there is no inherent reason economic models must model the firm as a monolith. Firms are organized groups of agents and the reputed characteristic is typically associated with specific agents within the firm. When those agents are removed and replaced, the inferences made by consumers relating to the firm based on the replaced agents' actions will rationally change. Thus, redeeming a firm's reputation by "cleaning house" and firing agents who committed reputation-destroying actions is not difficult to accommodate within the economic model. If we further posit that firms can take actions that change the character and preferences of their employees, then corporate investment directed to actually propagating a commitment to quality could rationally lead consumers to believe that despite the previous lapse, the company had changed its ways (i.e., its type) and this could restore a firm's reputation after a lapse. Thus, an interesting and plausible direction for future economic research could be to model substantive reputation repair under the assumption that firms themselves are collections of interacting agents.

Superficial repair could also be rationalized in such a model. Despite the fact that the model would not attribute actions or characteristics to the firm per se but only to its constituent agents, firm identity and thus the control and transmission of information concerning the firm could still prove important. Firm identity would stem from imperfect information which prevents stakeholders from making accurate attributions of corporate decisions to specific factors or agents associated with the firm. In our example, shoddy products might be caused by deliberate costs cutting mandated by the board, an act of nature, or the decisions of an already terminated employee. If consumers are unsure regarding which of these causes are operative, a firm could repair its reputation by revealing or suppressing information regarding the causal structure of the quality lapse. In summary, an interesting avenue for future research would be to extend the boundaries of the economic reputation model to encompass repair, both superficial and substantive, perhaps following the approaches suggested above.

In addition to extending the depth of economic reputation by considering a larger range of reputation-related firm actions, another promising direction for new modeling efforts is extending economic analysis laterally by using the insights from reputation theory to model the closely related but little explored concept of corporate stigma. At the level of inference, the problem of a firm facing the threat of stigma is parallel to the problem of a firm facing the threat of reputation loss. As in a reputation model, firms would undertake actions in each period. Stakeholders would observe these actions and form inferences regarding the firm's likelihood of having a stigmatized trait or engaging in stigmatized activities. Inference would be governed by the process of Bayesian inference discussed above. However, modeling stigma would present some new conceptual challenges to the modeler. The first would be to identify the locus of the stigma. Would stigma be associated with actions of the firm or with firm traits? For example, would consumers stigmatize a firm if they discovered that the firm had no inherent concern for the environment even if it had never caused environmental damage? Second, if stigma was generated by actions not traits, would the actions per se provoke stigma, or would their consequences? For example, would exposing workers to harmful toxins stigmatize the exposing firm even if, unexpectedly, medical researchers discovered a painless treatment which eliminated the toxin's effects? The third issue that would need to be resolved is to locate stigma: is the firm as a whole stigmatized or just the agents engaging in stigmatized actions? Finally, the modeler would need to consider how stigma will affect stakeholder preferences for dealing with the firm. With regard to the final question, the existing literature provides a great deal of guidance. Over the last ten years, economic theories have developed a substantial body of theory and experimental evidence on social preferences: preference agent have over the pay-offs received by other agents.[9] The theory has been deployed primarily to examine issues relating to fair division and justice. However, there is no reason it could not be drafted to model negative dependence between the utility of consumers and the payoffs to stigmatized firms. Such a negative dependence would cause consumers to shun such firms or at least demand more favorable terms of trade in dealing with them. This would impose a cost on stigma. In contrast, little in economic theory will aid us in making modeling choices related to the first three questions. Here, casual empiricism and the management and psychology literature will have to form the basis of pioneering modeling attempts. One may hope that models could later be refined based on empirical test of these pioneering models.

Developing models such as these will require a certain boldness in assumption formation and a willingness to rely on evidence and insights from the broader management literature, practitioner experience, and other areas of economics research. Of necessity, such models will have to have many moving parts and thus, to retain tractability, will probably have to be parametrically fairly simple. However, precisely because these models will incorporate different factors, they should be able to answer questions pertaining to the interactions between the different factors which cannot be addressed by existing theory. For example, is the value of influence activities highest for firms who are in fact the most reputable? Do personal influence activities enhance or reduce the marginal effect of media endorsement? Properly formulated models addressing these questions would enrich the corpus of economic reputation models formation, provide useful predictions for empirical research, and new insights for practitioners.

Acknowledgment

I would like to thank Mike Barnett, Cynthia Devers, and Yuri Mishina for helpful comments on earlier drafts of this chapter. All errors and omissions are the author's responsibility.

[9] Fehr & Gachter (2000) and Fehr & Schmidt (1999) are important exemplars of this literature.

Economic Analysis of Reputation Formation Finding and Key Insights

Reference	Findings
Abreu & Gul (2000)	A formal theoretical model which shows that, when there is a positive probability that some bargainers are irrationally tough, i.e., rejecting offers even when accepting offers would yield higher payoffs, rational bargainers will mimic the irrationally tough bargainers' behavior to build a reputation for toughness and thereby receive higher offers.
Armour et al.	An empirical study of the market valuation effect of enforcement actions by the UK's Financial Services Authority and London Stock Exchange. The study documents that the cost reputation loss exceeds the direct cost of penalties by a factor of almost 9. However, reputation costs are limited to enforcement actions related to misconduct toward agents who trade with the firm. Enforcement actions related to misconduct against third parties (e.g., competitors) do not result in reputation-related losses on average.
Balvers, McDonald, & Miller (1988)	Formal theoretical model and empirical study which shows that high auditor and investment banker reputation reduces underpricing of initial public offerings. Auditor and investment banker reputations are substitutes so that using highly ranked auditors has the largest effect on underpricing when the investment banker's rank is low.
Brandts & Figueras (2003)	Laboratory experiment on reputation formation where student subjects play a formalized game representing bank and borrower relations and receive monetary rewards based on their performance. The authors show that in treatments with more periods of bank/borrower interaction, aggregate subject behavior is qualitatively consistent with economic equilibrium model of reputation formation although exact numerical predictions of model fail to describe individual subject behavior. In treatments with shorter periods of interaction, the equilibrium model had less predictive success. Thus, the increased scope for profiting from reputation formation afforded by a longer time horizon trumps the greater transparency of equilibrium solutions in short-horizon treatments.
Cabral & Horta (2010)	An econometric analysis of the effect of reputation on eBay sellers. Findings indicate that the loss of reputation through negative reviews is very costly to sellers. The loss of reputation leads sellers to act less reputably subsequently and exit the eBay market much more rapidly than more reputed sellers.
Camerer & Weigelt (1988)	A laboratory experiment on reputation formation. The authors test the equilibrium predictions of a formal game theoretic model with human subjects who receive performance-based monetary rewards. Results of experiments are consistent with the model's prediction under the assumption that opportunistic subjects overestimate the probability that other subjects are nonopportunistic.
Dejong, Forsythe, & Lundholm (1985)	Laboratory implementation of a game with sellers having the opportunity to "rip-off" buyers by promising services but then failing to apply the effort required to generate these services. Subject payoffs are based on earning in the game. In about half of the treatments, reputations failed to form. In the others, reputation sustained service provision to some extent and unscrupulous sellers profited by first developing a reputation for service and then ripping off customers toward the end of the game.

(Continued)

Table Continued

Reference	Findings
Diamond (1989)	A formal theoretical model of reputation formation in capital markets. The paper shows that, when the time horizon is long enough, borrowers with risky investment options forgo the short-term gains from taking in risky projects in order to mimic the project choices of borrowers without such options and thus protect their access to capital markets.
Fang & Yasuda (2009)	Empirical study which provides evidence that, while conflicts of interest cause a deterioration in the accuracy of most financial analysts' reports, they do not affect the accuracy of the reports of the most reputed "AA" financial analysts. The author concludes that this indicates that the highly rated analysts protect their reputation capital by providing objective reports even in the presence of conflicts of interest.
Dowling & Gardberg (2012)	Conceptual analysis of the practical problems associated with reputation measurement. Topics considered include the unit of analysis, the type of data used in measurement and the design of measurement instruments.
Gorton (1996)	Empirical econometric study of the effect of reputation on notes issued by US banks during the free banking period. Paper shows that notes issued by reputed banks traded at much better terms than notes issued by less reputable banks.
Grossman & Van Huyck (1988)	Theoretical model of bank lending to sovereign countries. The authors show that even without recourse to legal sanctions, reputation concerns of sovereign borrows can induce repayment. Repayment by sovereign borrowers is enforced by the threat of losing access to capital markets.
Karpoff & Lott (1993)	Empirical study of the effect of reputation loss to corporations from fraud convictions. This paper shows that corporate value losses from fraud conviction far exceed the size of legal penalties. Authors conjecture that, in many cases, reputation costs alone are sufficient to deter fraudulent behavior even without monetary penalties.
Rhee & Kim (2012)	A conceptual analysis of reputation repair activities by firms. These activities are categorized into superficial and substantive activities. The willingness of firms to undertake substantive repair activities as opposed to superficial is considered in a behavioral framework.
Klein & Leffler (1981)	Formal theoretical model which shows that, in an infinite horizon game, the threat of reputation loss alone is sufficient to deter opportunistic behavior by firms even in the absence of legal sanctions and scruples. Sufficient economic rents to incumbent firms are sufficient to support reputable behavior. At the same time, consumers' rational conjecture that new market entrants charging lower prices cannot be trusted sustains high price and thus the required economic rent of incumbent firms.
Kreps & Wilson (1982)	Classic formal theoretical model on reputation formation when time horizon is limited. Theoretical model shows that even rational competitors have an incentive to build reputations for being irrationally tough competitors and that such reputation forming behavior can sustain monopoly even in the presence of free market entry.

Maksimovic & Titman (1991)	A formal theoretical model of reputation for product quality and corporate debt policy. Model shows that in some cases, high corporate leverage can increase the incentive of firms engaging in opportunistic actions which generate short-term cash flows at the expense of the firm's long-term reputation.
Melnick & Alm (2002)	An early econometric analysis of the effect of reputation on eBay sellers. Findings somewhat weaker than Cabral & Horta's perhaps because of a less sophisticated econometric approach that failed to control for unobserved seller heterogeneity.
Milgrom & Roberts (1982)	Classic formal theoretical model of reputation formation when the time horizon is limited. Similar insights to Kreps & Wilson (1982), i.e., rational competitors have an incentive to build reputations for being irrationally tough competitors.
Mishina & Devers (2012)	A conceptual analysis of stigma and reputation. The authors argue that the two concepts are fundamentally different. In addition, the authors sketch out how the social psychology concepts upon which the theory of stigmatization was developed, can be applied to corporations.
Noe, Rebello, & Rietz (2011)	Formal theoretical model of the relation between reputation formation and firm financial policy. The paper demonstrates that short-term claims held by outsiders, e.g., short-term debt, can increase firm incentives to invest in reputation formation.
Shapiro & Stiglitz (1984)	Formal theoretical model for reputation formation in labor markets. Shows that workers applying high effort is only sustainable if workers' compensation when employed exceeds the minimum required to induce the worker to accept employment and there is some chance the worker will become involuntarily unemployed if sacked. Equilibrium wages in the excess of the minimum required to induce unemployed workers to accept employment is sustainable because, at sub-equilibrium wages, employers know that workers will not exert high effort.

References

Abreu, D. & Gul, F. (2000). "Bargaining and reputation." *Econometrica*, 68(1): 85–117.

Balvers, R. J., McDonald, B., & Miller, R. E. (1988). "Underpricing of new issues and the choice of auditor as a signal of investment banker reputation." *The Accounting Review*, 63(4): 605–622.

Bénabou, R. & Tirole, J. (2006). "Incentives and prosocial behavior." *The American Economic Review*, 96(5): 1652–1678.

Berg, J. E., Daley, L. A., Dickhaut, J. W., & O'Brien, J. R. (1986). "Controlling preferences for lotteries on units of experimental exchange." *The Quarterly Journal of Economics*, 101(2): 281–306.

Brandts, J. & Figueras, N. (2003). "An exploration of reputation formation in experimental games." *Journal of Economic Behavior & Organization*, 50(1): 89–115.

Cabral, L. O. & Horta, A. (2010). "The dynamics of seller reputation: Evidence from EBay." *The Journal of Industrial Economics*, 56(1): 54–78.

Camerer, C. & Weigelt, K. (1988). "Experimental tests of a sequential equilibrium reputation model." *Econometrica*, 56(1): 1–36.

Dejong, D. V., Forsythe, R., & Lundholm, R. J. (1985). "Ripoffs, lemons, and reputation formation in agency relationships: A laboratory market study." *The Journal of Finance*, 40(3): 809–820.

Diamond, D. W. (1989). "Reputation acquisition in debt markets." *The Journal of Political Economy*, 97(4): 828–862.

Dowling, G. & Gardberg, N. (2012). "Keeping score: Measures of corporate reputation." In M. Barnett & T. Pollock (Eds.), *Oxford Handbook on Corporate Reputation*. Oxford: Oxford University Press, 34–68.

Eckel, C. & Wilson, R. (2007). "Social learning in coordination games: Does status matter?" *Experimental Economics*, 10: 317–329, 10.1007/s10683-007-9185-x.

Erev, I. & Roth, A. E. (1998). "Predicting how people play games: Reinforcement learning in experimental games with unique, mixed strategy equilibria." *The American Economic Review*, 88(4): 848–881.

Fang, L. & Yasuda, A. (2009). "The effectiveness of reputation as a disciplinary mechanism in sell-side research." *The Review of Financial Studies*, 22(9): 3735–3777.

Fehr, E. & Gachter, S. (2000). "Cooperation and punishment in public goods experiments." *The American Economic Review*, 90(4): 980–994.

—— & Schmidt, K. M. (1999). "A theory of fairness, competition, and cooperation." *The Quarterly Journal of Economics*, 114(3): 817–868.

Fishburn, P. C. & Lavalle, I. H. (1993). "On matrix probabilities in nonarchimedean decision theory." *Journal of Risk and Uncertainty*, 7(3): 283–299.

Fromburn, C. (2012). "The building blocks of corporate reputation: Definitions, antecedents, consequences." In M. Barnett & T. Pollock (Eds.), *Handbook of Corporate Reputation*. Oxford: Oxford University Press, 94–113.

Ganguly, A. R., Kagel, J. H., & Moser, D. V. (2004). "Do asset market prices reflect traders' judgment biases?" *Journal of Risk and Uncertainty*, 20: 219–245.

Gilboa, I. (1987). "Expected utility with purely subjective non-additive probabilities." *Journal of Mathematical Economics*, 16(1): 65–88.

—— & Schmeidler, D. (1995). "Case-based decision theory." *The Quarterly Journal of Economics*, 110(3): 605–639.

Gorton, G. (1996). "Reputation formation in early bank note markets." *The Journal of Political Economy*, 104(2): 346–397.

Grossman, H. I. & Huyck, J. B. V. (1988). "Sovereign debt as a contingent claim: Excusable default, repudiation, and reputation." *The American Economic Review*, 78(5): 1088–1097.

Harrison, G. W. (1992). "Theory and misbehavior of first-price auctions: Reply." *The American Economic Review*, 82(5): 1426–1443.

Hey, J. D. & Orme, C. (1994). "Investigating generalizations of expected utility theory using experimental data." *Econometrica*, 62(6): 1291–1326.

Ho, T.-H., Camerer, C., & Weigelt, K. (1998). "Iterated dominance and iterated best response in experimental 'p-beauty contests'." *The American Economic Review*, 88(4): 947–969.

Karpoff, J. M., Lott, J., & John, R. (1993). "The reputational penalty firms bear from committing criminal fraud." *Journal of Law and Economics*, 36(2): 757–802.

Klein, B. & Leffler, K. B. (1981). "The role of market forces in assuring contractual performance." *The Journal of Political Economy*, 89(4): 615–641.

Kluger, B. D. & Wyatt, S. B. (2004). "Are judgment errors reflected in market prices and allocations? Experimental evidence based on the Monty Hall problem." *The Journal of Finance*, 59(3): 969–997.

Kreps, D. M. & Wilson, R. (1982). "Reputation and imperfect information." *Journal of Economic Theory*, 27(2): 253–279.

Maksimovic, V. & Titman, S. (1991). "Financial policy and reputation for product quality." *The Review of Financial Studies*, 4(1): 175–200.

Melnik, M. I. & Alm, J. (2002). "Does a seller's ecommerce reputation matter? Evidence from eBay auctions." *The Journal of Industrial Economics*, 50(3): 337–349.

Milgrom, P. & Roberts, J. (1982). "Predation, reputation, and entry deterrence." *Journal of Economic Theory*, 27(2): 280–312.

Mishina, Y. & Devers, C. (2012). "On being bad: Why stigma is not the same as a bad reputation." In M. Barnett & T. Pollock (Eds.), *Oxford Handbook on Corporate Reputation*. Oxford: Oxford University Press, 201–20.

Myerson, R. (1997). *Game Theory: Analysis of Conflict*. Boston: Harvard University Press.

Noe, T., Rebello, M., & Rietz, T. (2011). "Product market efficiency: The bright side of myopic, uninformed, and passive external finance." University of Oxford working paper.

Ok, E. A. (2002). "Utility representation of an incomplete preference relation." *Journal of Economic Theory*, 104(2): 429–449.

Rhee, M. & Kim, T. (2012). "After the collapse: A behavioral theory of reputation repair." In M. Barnett & T. Pollock (eds.), *The Oxford Handbook of Corporate Reputation*. Oxford: Oxford University Press, 445–64.

Shapiro, C. & Stiglitz, J. E. (1984). "Equilibrium unemployment as a worker discipline device." *The American Economic Review*, 74(3): 433–444.

Spence, M. (1973). "Job market signaling." *The Quarterly Journal of Economics*, 87(3): 355–374.

—— (2002). "Signaling in retrospect and the informational structure of markets." *The American Economic Review*, 92(3): 434–459.

Wang, T., Winton, A., & Yu, X. (2010). "Corporate fraud and business conditions: Evidence from IPOs." *Working Paper*, University of Minnesota, forthcoming in the *Journal of Finance*.

Wulf, J. (2009). "Influence and inefficiency in the internal capital market." *Journal of Economic Behavior & Organization*, 72(1): 305–321.

CHAPTER 7

MEETING EXPECTATIONS: A ROLE-THEORETIC PERSPECTIVE ON REPUTATION

MICHAEL JENSEN
HEEYON KIM
BO KYUNG KIM

In this chapter, we combine reputation theory from economics with role theory from sociology to develop a rigorous framework for studying reputation. We begin with a critique of the dominant reputation perspectives in management research and examine why their common definition of reputation as an overall actor-level assessment may not be the most constructive way to advance reputation research. We argue that reputation can be more usefully theorized as an attribute- and audience-specific prediction of future behaviors that is based on assessments of how past behaviors meet the role expectations associated with particular social statuses. Based on our role-theoretic perspective on reputation, we identify three important research areas—the multidimensionality of reputation, the embeddedness of reputation, and reputation as a mechanism for social mobility—and discuss promising avenues for future research in each area.

INTRODUCTION

REPUTATION has emerged as an important theoretical construct in management research as witnessed by the burgeoning literature on the reputation of individuals and organizations. Despite the increased interest in reputation, there is less agreement in management research on how to define and measure reputation, which has resulted in considerable uncertainty and confusion about the reputation construct itself (Lange,

Lee, & Dai, 2011). Several scholars have tried to remedy the proliferation of reputation definitions by identifying the core aspects of the most widely used definitions and then developing their own *integrative* definitions of reputation (Fombrun & van Riel, 1997; Wartick 2002; Barnett, Jermier, & Lafferty, 2006). Although minor differences exist in these integrative reputation definitions, most definitions resemble the definition offered by Fombrun (1996) that reputation is an overall assessment of the ability of an organization to deliver value to all stakeholders (Walker, 2010). We argue that defining reputation as overall actor-level assessments limits the theoretical power and validity of reputation by confusing it with other actor-level constructs including status, identity, image, and celebrity. We take as our theoretical point of departure the simple definition from economics of reputation as attribute-specific assessments based on prior behaviors (Wilson, 1985; Jensen & Roy, 2008) and use role theory from sociology to contextualize reputation by embedding reputation assessments in social systems (Sarbin & Allen, 1968; Montgomery, 1998).

We seek to accomplish three objectives in this chapter. First, to develop our own role-theoretic perspective on reputation, we begin with a discussion of the proliferation of reputation definitions in management research and why defining reputation as overall actor-level assessments is not the most constructive way forward for reputation research. Second, we draw on reputation research in economics to understand the purpose of reputation in theory development and to provide a theoretical foundation for arguing that reputation is more usefully understood as disaggregate attribute-specific assessments. We draw next on sociological role theory to argue that audience-specific assessments based on past behaviors are best understood in terms of role expectations and role performances, which anchors our reputation perspective in social systems and provides a theoretical foundation for the multidimensional nature of reputation. Third, having outlined our role-theoretic perspective on reputation, we show that anchoring reputation in roles provides new theoretical insights and we offer three different ways in which our perspective on reputation can inform future research on reputation. We conclude by summarizing how integrating reputation theory and role theory helps to advance both theoretical and empirical research on corporate reputation, as well as discussing some of the most important methodological challenges posed by a role-theoretic perspective on reputation.

Reputation in Management Research

Before developing our role-theoretic perspective on reputation, it is useful to discuss other perspectives on reputation in order to justify why yet another perspective on reputation is needed. To accomplish this objective and avoid unnecessary repetition, we rely on the broad range of excellent reviews of reputation research published in recent years, such as Fombrun & van Riel (1997); Wartick (2002); Barnett, Jermier, & Lafferty (2006); Walker (2010); Lange, Lee, & Dai (2011); and Bitektine (2011).

Proliferation of Reputation Definitions

Reputation research has taken different paths in economics, sociology, and management. In economics, research converged quickly around the definition of reputation as a prediction about future behaviors based on past observed behaviors (Wilson, 1985) and has subsequently focused on how reputation affects various economic transactions (Bar-Isaac & Tadelis, 2008). In sociology, reputation has received little systematic attention. Most early research equated reputation with being known for "something" and used reputation for influence in questionnaires to identify community leaders (see Wolfinger, 1960). More recent research draws from economics and defines reputation as a prediction about future behaviors based on past behaviors, mostly without paying explicit attention to the social context of reputation (Raub & Weesie, 1990; Podolny, 1993; Kollock, 1994). In management, reputation has received considerable attention, but there is nevertheless little agreement on how to define reputation. Some use the narrow definition from economics (Weigelt & Camerer, 1988; Washington & Zajac, 2005; Jensen & Roy, 2008), whereas others use reputation more broadly as overall appeal (Fombrun, 1996), social identity (Rao, 1994), admiration (Staw and Epstein, 2000), organizational identity (Whetten & Mackey, 2002), and prestige, legitimacy, and image (King, 2008). Not surprisingly, Lange, Lee, & Dai (2011: 154) noted that management research is "marked by uncertainty about [reputation] definitions, dimensionality, and operationalizations."

Reflecting the proliferation of reputation definitions, attempts to unify different streams of reputation research to develop an integrative reputation definition have proliferated as well. Fombrun & van Riel (1997: 10), for example, reviewed research in economics, strategy, marketing, organisation theory, sociology, and accounting to define reputation as "a collective representation of a firm's past actions and results that describes the firm's ability to deliver valued outcomes to multiple stakeholders." Rindova et al. (2005: 1033) used a similar approach to define reputation as "stakeholders' perceptions of an organization's ability to create value relative to competitors." They argued that it is important to integrate an emphasis on reputation as perceived quality in economics with an emphasis on reputation as prominence in institutional theory. Barnett, Jermier, & Lafferty (2006: 34) reported that 17 of 49 reviewed studies defined reputation exclusively in terms of "assessments," whereas fewer studies defined reputation exclusively in terms of "awareness" (15) or "asset" (6). They used the frequency of assessment-based reputation definitions to define reputation as "[o]bservers' collective judgments of a corporation based on assessments of the financial, social, and environmental impacts attributed to the corporation over time." Despite minor differences in the integrative definitions (see also Fombrun, Chapter 5, this volume; Rindova and Martins, Chapter 2, this volume), they mostly agree that reputation is best defined in terms of "overall assessments" or even "generalized favorability" (Lange, Lee, & Dai, 2011).

Integrative Reputation Definitions

We argue that integrative reputation definitions limit reputation research in at least three different ways.

First, the emphasis on integrating reputation definitions from different disciplines and research traditions has resulted in integrative definitions that are vague and indistinguishable from other related theoretical constructs. It is therefore not surprising that subsequent theory development has focused on clarifying the distinctions between reputation and, for example, status, legitimacy, identity, image, and stigma (Washington & Zajac, 2005; Jensen & Roy, 2008; Whetten & Mackey, 2002; Mishina and Devers, Chapter 10, this volume). The emphasis on integrating different reputation definitions has also resulted in reputation definitions being isolated from broader established theoretical frameworks that are necessary to provide guidance and rigor in empirical applications of a particular reputation definition. Specifically, most integrative definitions invoke different theoretical constructs from different theoretical frameworks and research traditions including status, identity, image, organizational field, sense-making, mobility barrier, and social responsibility (Fombrun & van Riel, 1997). The result is, ironically, that integrative definitions often are disconnected from any one of the invoked theoretical frameworks, which raises questions about the exact use of integrative definitions and how they relate to each of the invoked theoretical frameworks. We begin, alternatively, with the specific functions served by the reputation construct in theory development, and emphasize theoretical parsimony in developing a role-theoretic definition of reputation that can advance theory development and guide empirical research.

Second, regardless of the approach to developing reputation definitions, defining reputation in terms of an overall assessment is itself questionable. Jensen & Roy (2008) argued that reputation is more usefully defined as an attribute-specific assessment of an actor. When reputation is viewed as attribute specific, an actor may simultaneously be ascribed a positive reputation with regard to a specific attribute and a negative reputation with regard to another attribute by the *same* audience. An accounting firm, for example, may have developed a positive reputation for the quality of its audit services but a negative reputation for its tax advice services, or developed a positive reputation for auditing large firms but a negative reputation for auditing small firms. Reputation is, accordingly, always a reputation *for* something such as quality, fairness, or timeliness, even if the attribute to which the reputation refers is not explicitly specified (as is often the case in everyday use of reputation). Defining reputation in terms of attribute-specific assessments does not rule out that attribute-specific assessments in some situations can be meaningfully aggregated to actor-level assessments. Moreover, a particular attribute can occasionally dominate the other attributes, which suggests that assessments of the dominant attribute meaningfully could be the only relevant assessments for reputation. In contrast, defining reputation in terms of actor-level assessments makes it harder to disaggregate reputation because actor-level assessments typically mask the underlying attributes, which makes actor-level assessments a less useful starting point.

Walker (2010) added that defining reputation as an "integrative perception of all stakeholders" is problematic because actors may have different reputations with *different* audiences. To align his definition of reputation with prior definitions, Walker (2010: 370) nevertheless suggested that each attribute-specific reputation represents the aggregate perception of *all* stakeholders and defined reputation as "[a] relatively stable, issue specific aggregate perceptual representation of a company's past actions and future prospects compared against some standard." We argue instead that reputation is best defined as an attribute-specific *and* audience-specific assessment of an actor because it allows for more nuanced assessments and therefore more specific and rigorous applications of the reputation construct in empirical research. Reputation definitions that aggregate assessments across all attributes and audiences are, in contrast, not only empirically unmanageable (as discussed below), but also, typically result in assessments that at best represent diffuse general impressions or sentiments among diverse audiences and at worst a meaningless average of different assessments that is not assignable to any particular audiences. It rarely makes sense, for example, to refer to a firm as having an average reputation for fairness in promotion practices if the firm has a positive reputation for fairness in promotion practices among majority employees but a negative reputation for fairness among minority employees.

Third, the integrative definition of reputation as overall assessments almost guarantees disconnects between how reputation is defined and how it is measured in empirical research. The most used measure of corporate reputation is *Fortune's* "Most Admired Companies" (FMAC) (Walker, 2010; Lange, Lee, & Dai, 2011). FMAC is an aggregate measure based on surveys of three stakeholder groups, executives, directors, and security analysts, on eight attributes including financial performance and product quality (see Dowling and Gardberg, Chapter 3, this volume, on reputation measurement). Research shows, however, that FMAC is mainly determined by the financial performance of the surveyed corporations. Fryxell & Wang (1994), for example, reported that financial performance not only was the dominant factor in explaining the variance in FMAC, but also influenced perceptions of other factors including quality of management and the innovativeness of the company (see also Brown & Perry, 1994). The finance bias is not surprising because FMAC is based on a narrow set of stakeholders for whom financial performance is the main concern. It points, as Walker (2010) noted, nevertheless to an interesting paradox: The dominant definition of reputation as overall assessments aggregated over *all* attributes and *all* stakeholders is incompatible with the dominant measure of reputation because the dominant measure does not aggregate over *all* attributes and *all* stakeholders (it is hard to imagine doing this in a single empirical study). Our reputation definition is not troubled by these issues because it focuses on attribute-specific (which could be finance), audience-specific (which could be executives, directors, and analysts) assessments.

We suggest that defining reputation from the role-theoretic perspective in terms of *attribute- and audience-specific* assessments, a definition that will be presented in greater detail in the next section, helps resolve the aforementioned problems. First of all, while the integrative definitions of reputation result in a vague concept that is indistinguishable from other related constructs, our perspective provides strong disciplinary backgrounds from economics and sociology to ensure theoretical simplicity and empirical applicability of the reputation construct. Second, defining reputation as overall assessments fails to capture the complexity of reputation and, more importantly, is less useful when it comes to studying and managing reputation across different attributes and audiences. By bringing role theory into reputation research, however, our reputation perspective provides a theoretically informed approach to contextualizing reputation across different attributes and audiences. The role-theoretic reputation construct, then, can be more easily distinguished from related actor-level theoretical constructs, such as status and identity, and can be applied more rigorously in different empirical settings. Third, integrative reputation definitions tend to result in disconnects between the reputation definition and its empirical measurement. The role-theoretic perspective on reputation, with its explicit focus on specific attributes, audiences, and contexts, tightens the connection between theory development and empirical research.

Status, Roles, and Reputation

We now develop our role-theoretic perspective on reputation by first identifying the purpose of reputation in social exchange and then using role theory to properly embed reputation in social context.

Reputation in Social Exchange

Despite disagreement about reputation definitions, there is widespread agreement that the main function of reputation is to facilitate decision-making and concurrent social exchange. The function of reputation is clearly articulated in research in economics on reputation for quality in product markets (Bar-Isaac & Tadelis, 2008; Noe, Chapter 6, this volume). A buyer faces two types of uncertainty about a seller when product quality, abstractly the level of some desirable characteristics of a product (Klein & Leffler, 1981), is difficult to determine prior to being exchanged and exchanges cannot be perfectly contracted. First, uncertainty about quality can result from the "type" of seller being unobserved, which can result in adverse selection-related problems (Akerlof, 1970). A buyer may be unable to determine whether a seller can deliver a product at the promised quality, for example, because the resources and capabilities of the seller are unknown to the buyer. Second, uncertainty about quality can result also from the "effort" of the seller being unobserved, which can result in moral hazard-related problems (Williamson, 1991). A buyer may know that a seller *can* deliver a high-quality product, for example, but is unable to determine whether the seller *will* deliver high quality and not shirk opportunistically in the exchange. Reputation facilitates social exchange by reducing these two types of uncertainty (Bar-Isaac & Tadelis, 2008): The seller may rely on reputation to signal quality and the buyer may rely on reputation to differentiate between sellers.

The reason that reputation reduces uncertainty about quality is that reputation links discrete, independent behaviors together over time and space. Shapiro (1983) suggested that a firm has a positive reputation for quality if consumers believe that the quality of the products produced by the firm in the past can be used as an indicator of future quality. The formation of reputation through investments in product quality is therefore a signaling activity: The quality of the products produced in the past serves as a signal of the quality of future products, thus providing temporal and spatial continuity in discrete behaviors and transactions. Shapiro (1983) showed also that firms have an incentive to maintain a positive reputation for quality because a positive reputation allows firms to charge a premium for their products as long as the long-term value of the premium is higher than the short-term cost savings from reducing quality (see also Klein & Leffler, 1981). Reputation, in other words, facilitates social exchange by providing strong temporal and spatial linkages between otherwise discrete behaviors, thus allowing assessments of unobservable future behaviors to be based on observable past behaviors (Wilson, 1985). According to this perspective, reputations can, of course, reflect both positive assessments (assets) and negative assessments (liabilities) of actor attributes: A positive reputation helps decide whom to choose, a negative reputation whom to avoid.

Although the function of reputation is clearly articulated in economics, the actual processes through which assessments of past behaviors shape expectations about future behaviors are not well understood. We argue that expectations to future behaviors are shaped not only by assessments of past behaviors, but also by the social systems in which both past and future behaviors are embedded (Granovetter, 1985). Indeed, Stiglitz (2000) called for integration between economics, psychology, and sociology to examine how individuals form expectations and how signaling conventions are created. Role theory, with its emphasis on role expectations and role performances, provides an answer to the call for theoretical integration and a useful framework for theorizing the social contexts of reputation.

A Role-Theoretic Perspective on Reputation

Role theory shares a concern for behavioral expectations with reputation research but suggests further that behavioral expectations are anchored in a social system that is composed of statuses and roles (Sarbin & Allen, 1968; Biddle, 1986; Callero, 1994). A role is the enactment of the set of expectations directed at the actors that occupy a particular position, that is, have a particular status, in the social system (Linton, 1936; Merton, 1957; Jensen, 2010; Jensen, Kim, & Kim, 2011). We argue that role theory is important to reputation research because roles bridge social-level status and individual-level reputation through *social* role expectations and *individual* role performances. See the summary table of core literature at the end of the chapter for key reviews of role theory.

Role expectations refer to cognitions, such as beliefs, norms, and rules, and emotions, such as affective reactions, associated with different status positions and they are shared by the occupants and external audiences of a given social status. Role performances refer to the congruence between individual role enactments and social role expectations, and role performances are not necessarily the same for all the occupants of a social status. Similarly, the performances of different aspects of a particular role are also not necessarily the same for each individual actor: A father may do well in terms of providing material support for his children, for example, but do poorly in terms of providing emotional support. According to role theory, a reputation for quality is therefore not simply an evaluation of the past quality of an actor, but more accurately an evaluation of past quality based on the role expectations to an actor of a particular status. The status-based role expectations provide the *shared standards* for evaluating past behaviors that are missing in most theoretical and empirical reputation research. The formation of reputation is accordingly rarely based only on an isolated series of behaviors, but more typically based on an explicit or implicit comparison of these behaviors to a set of shared role expectations. A reputation for something is, in other words, always relative to the occupied status position: It takes a higher level of quality, for example, for a high-status auto manufacturer to develop a differentiating reputation for quality than it does for a low-status auto manufacturer.

Role theory provides a foundation for theorizing the social context of reputation without constraining actors to specific behaviors only or ruling out individual agency. Agency refers to the ability of actors to exert some degree of control over, and act *independently* of, the social structures in which they are embedded, even if they cannot transform these structures completely (Sewell, 1992; Emirbayer & Mische, 1998). Roles facilitate agency because most actors participate in different social systems that provide access to different transposable cultural schemas for expected behaviors that can be invoked by actors outside the statuses and roles in which they originated (Sewell, 1992). Most roles encompass not only different behavioral expectations but also different cognitions and emotions such as cultural beliefs and affective reactions that require selective attention and experimentation in different situations (Callero, 1994; Emirbayer & Mische, 1998). Finally, roles are resources that help actors create new positions and relationships, and therefore should be regarded as tools that can be used in competitive struggles to control other resources including gaining access to more attractive status positions (Baker & Faulkner, 1991; Callero, 1994). The availability of different roles shapes, in other words, not only the repertoires of actions available to actors in a social system, but also provides a mechanism for actors to shape the social system and therefore the roles themselves (Swidler, 1986).

We are not the first to argue that behavioral expectations depend on social contexts. Montgomery (1998) argued that role theory is important to understand the structural embeddedness of actors. Departing from rational choice theory and its focus on repeated games and utility maximization in explaining social relationships, Montgomery (1998) argued that actors should not be viewed as unitary actors with complete and coherent preferences (actors as "fixed transsituational types"). Actors should instead be viewed as collections of social roles that contain the rules of behavior that are evoked in different situations: A situation evokes one or more roles that contain the rules of behavior that guide appropriate behavior (Montgomery, 1998). Following this "logic of appropriateness" (March, 1994), an actor may act in some situations as a businessperson and therefore be guided by utility maximization, and in other situations act as a friend and therefore be guided by different behavioral rules such as compassion (see also Akerlof & Kranton, 2000). Our role-theoretic perspective on reputation complements a role-theoretic perspective on embeddedness: Whereas the role-theoretic conception of embeddedness emphasizes that roles guide appropriate behaviors in a particular situation, the role-theoretic conception of reputation emphasizes that roles also guide how other actors evaluate these behaviors. Roles are not only the social context of behaviors but also their evaluation and therefore the social context of reputation: Meeting expectations is the key inflection point from which positive or negative reputations are formed.

We can now summarize our role-theoretic perspective on reputation: *Reputation is a prediction of future behaviors that is based on an assessment of how past behaviors meet the role expectations that follow occupying a particular social status.* Our role-theoretic perspective helps clarify the reputation construct in three different ways: First, reputation is a uniquely individual construct because reputation differentiates individuals within a status (Jensen & Roy, 2008), whereas status is a uniquely social construct because role expectations are shared within a status position. Reputation is not an overall assessment of actors because actors play different roles that relate them to different audiences, and because each role comprises different role expectations that allow actors to have multiple reputations with the same audience. Second, reputation is nevertheless related to status through roles because actors always are surrounded by role expectations and reputation is built around status-based role expectations. Thus, identical behaviors have different reputational consequences depending on the status-based role expectations, and reputation is most salient and informative when reputation and status are in disequilibrium and reputation reflects a positive or negative violation of role expectations. Third, reputation facilitates agency by providing a mechanism for status mobility through individual role performances that meet the role expectations of higher statuses: Because role expectations interlock the status positions within a social system, actors can make selective investments that exceed the expectations of their current position to move to a higher position. We discuss next more specifically how our role-theoretic reputation perspective can inform future reputation research in these three areas.

The Role-Theoretic Reputation Perspective and Future Research

The Multidimensionality of Reputation

As argued above, the role-theoretic perspective on reputation suggests that reputation is most accurately defined in terms of attribute- and audience specific assessments because actors play different roles that relate them to different audiences, and each role comprises different role expectations that allow multiple reputations to coexist within the same audience. Although not explicitly theorized in terms of role theory, some scholars have begun fruitful research on the multidimensionality of reputation. Dollinger, Golden, & Saxton (1997), for example, argued that a firm can have multiple reputations in terms of product quality and its innovativeness, management integrity, and financial soundness. Using an experimental research design with MBA students as subjects, they showed that reputational damage in one dimension does not necessarily affect the reputation in other dimensions. Defining reputation as a global perception of an actor, Roberts & Dowling (2002) divided reputation into financial and residual reputation and showed that residual reputation of firms listed on FMAC is linked to sustainable superior performance. And Greenwood et al. (2005) theorized the difficulty of transferring reputation from one product or service to another one within the same organization. They argued specifically that reputation sticks to individual service departments within an accounting firm such as audit and accounting, tax advice, managerial advisory services, and outsourcing, thus illustrating the importance of multidimensional reputation constructs.

While the aforementioned studies theorize the multidimensionality of reputation, they are less consistent in incorporating their theoretical arguments in the measurements of reputation. Greenwood et al. (2005), for example, measured audit firm reputation by the count of audit clients listed by the US Securities and Exchange Commission (SEC) and the number of positive media reports. These measures do not distinguish between the different services offered by audit firms, but capture, at most, some vague notion of favorability and ultimately seem more like an indicator of audit firm size and visibility. Jensen & Roy (2008) used a different approach to operationalize the unobservable dimensions of reputation in their study of how client firms select auditing firms. They argued that while status, as overall assessments of entire firms, is important as a first-stage screening mechanism, reputation is important in the actual selection of a partner because it helps match the idiosyncratic resource needs of the focal firm. Jensen & Roy (2008) showed next that client firms tend to choose auditing partners within a given status group depending on how the reputation of an audit firm matches their own unique needs. They operationalized the reputational matching process between client and audit firms in terms of the fit between the resource needs of the client firms and the technical skills and business integrity of audit firms, as measured by industry specialization and media coverage of audit failures, respectively.

We suggest that future reputation research should examine the different dimensions of reputation that coexist not only within a single actor but also within the same audiences. First, we propose examining how organizations handle conflicting role expectations and therefore have to balance positive and negative reputations across attributes and audiences. Research on role conflicts (Merton, 1957; Goode, 1960) helps theorize when and how organizations can or cannot balance different role expectations. A focus on role conflicts implies identifying which role expectations are most important to which audiences before analyzing the extent to which reputations formed around these expectations balance and represent acceptable compromises. The second research question asks whether reputational consistency across multiple attributes affects the overall assessment of a specific actor. Some research shows that multiple category spanning by an organization can have a negative effect on how the organization is perceived by its audiences (Zuckerman, 1999; Hsu, 2006). We suggest, analogously, studying both the consequences of reputational value (how positive or negative) and the consequences of reputational consistency across different dimensions of reputation. Third, it is important to examine the transferability of reputation between audiences and attributes in order to understand the full value of reputation: Can a reputation in one attribute or audience, for example, be leveraged to another attribute or audience in the same way that status can be leveraged from one market to another (Jensen, 2003)?

Reputation and Role Expectations

Another important implication of our role-theoretic perspective is that because actors are embedded in status-based role expectations, role expectations provide the foundation for evaluating specific behaviors. Reputation is, in other words, rarely or never built from nothing but is always built around status-based role expectations. In economics, most research modeling reputation assumes, implicitly or explicitly, that reputation is created only through observations of behavioral patterns. Actors are assumed to have no reputation before commencing a sequence of behaviors and reputation is therefore disembedded from its broader social context and presumed built from nothing (Milgrom & Roberts, 1982; Shapiro, 1983). A similar argument is made in the management literature that external audiences treat organizations as reputation neutral if their reputation is unknown or their past behavior is unobservable (Bitektine, 2011): Due to the lack of information about organizations, no predictions, positive or negative, can be made about their future behaviors. This assumption, however, is problematic because actors are always situated in a particular social system, and thus surrounded by role expectations. Even if little or no information exists about a newly hired employee, for example, other employees still have expectations about what constitutes appropriate behavior (work and social) for the new employee based on the role the new employee is to fulfill in the organization.

The embeddedness of reputation in role expectations has two implications. First, reputations are formed when external audiences evaluate how individual actors meet specific role expectations, which means that actors do not have full control over their reputations and that reputations are difficult to change once formed. The embeddedness of role expectations in social statuses adds an extra layer of inertia to the reputation of individual actors. Reputation emerges in the interplay between role expectations and past behaviors, but reputation also feeds back into role expectations such that the role expectations themselves change. An auto manufacturer, for example, can invest in quality to differentiate its products from those within the same status group, thereby motivating other auto manufacturers to also invest in quality, which may eventually change the role expectations by making quality a baseline expectation rather than a differentiating factor. Some research focuses on the discrepancies that may arise between internal reputation-building efforts and the external perception by the audience. Carmeli & Tishler (2004), for example, defined reputation as the belief held by outsiders about what distinguishes an organization and found that it is not always coherent with what top managers believe about the organization. And Martins (2005) showed that US business schools attempted to improve their reputation on the attributes relevant for the *Business Week* ranking when their actual ranking was below their own perceived rank. The reciprocal relationship between role expectations and reputations has, however, been neglected in empirical research, thus representing an important area for future research.

Second, reputation and reputational consequences become most salient when behavior is not coherent with role expectations. Reputation is related to status through roles and thus, depending on the status of an actor, role expectations differ. Consequently, identical behaviors may have different reputational consequences for different actors. Specifically, even if two actors behave in the same manner, one may be acting in accordance with their role expectations, while the other may be positively or negatively violating such expectations. Since the reputational consequences of behaviors are determined by role expectations, reputation becomes most salient and informative when reputation and status are in disequilibrium and reputation reflects a positive or negative violation of role expectations. Rhee & Haunschild (2006) reported that auto recalls led to more market share decline for firms with a stronger reputation for quality. In other words, audiences had higher expectations of firms with a positive reputation for quality, and thus a negative deviation from reputation-based expectations became more salient and led to more severe punishment. An important implication is that reputation is most informative when there is an incongruence between role enactments and role expectations. A high-status position comes with an expectation of high quality, for example, which means that delivering a high-quality product provides little additional information, whereas delivering a low-quality product provides more information because it is incongruent with the high-status role expectations (Jensen, 2006).

Empirical research rarely links role expectations to reputation or acknowledges that reputation is always evaluated based on role expectations, which suggests that research in the following three areas is important. First, based on their status, actors are always surrounded by role expectations, even if they are new to a particular status. While actors may continue to sustain their behavioral patterns after moving into a new status position, they are evaluated based on a different set of role expectations. We ask, therefore, how status mobility affects actors in terms of reputation-building when actors move into a new status position and are introduced to new role expectations. Second, since reputation is constructed by the assessment of external audiences, it is important to explore how actors adhere to role expectations when they are accountable to multiple audiences with conflicting expectations. Because industry experts and consumers sometimes have conflicting expectations for a firm, for example, firms can manage their reputation by trying to meet the role expectations of both audiences or by focusing on their reputation with a single audience (Kim & Jensen, 2011). Third, it is also important to examine whether positive reputations in some attributes function as buffers when an actor's behaviors violate the role expectations of another attribute or if the negative impact spills over and influences the reputation of other attributes. Would auto recalls, for example, have less negative impact for auto manufacturers with a positive reputation in other attributes, or would the violation in quality expectations damage reputation in other dimensions?

Reputation as a Mechanism for Status Mobility

Our role-theoretic perspective also informs future research by emphasizing the importance of reputation as a source of agency that allows actors to behave more autonomously and even change social status. Some research has begun exploring the relationship between reputation and agency. Hayward & Boeker (1998), for example, showed that having developed a reputation for accuracy allows security analysts and their investment banks to act autonomously and rate their client firms less favorably when warranted. While theorizing reputation as an agency-granting mechanism, Hayward & Boeker (1998) still relied on an actor-level measure of reputation, overall ranking in the *Institutional Investor* survey, thus making it difficult to distinguish between reputation and status and to specify the exact source of analyst reputation. As a result, little is known about how individual attribute-specific reputations can function as a mechanism that successful actors can use to gain at least some autonomy from the role expectations shaping appropriate behavior. Even less research views reputation as a mechanism for status mobility. Bielby & Bielby (1994) are an exception. They viewed positive reputation as a status-enhancing mechanism and showed empirically that programmers relied on the reputations of individual producers and celebrities for commercial success to legitimize a new prime-time television series. The status of the entire television series was, in other words, enhanced through the specific reputations of the individual components. It is necessary, however, to examine more explicitly how status entails expectations that provide the foundation for reputation, which, in turn, aggregates to define a status.

   While it is important to distinguish between reputation and status, it is also important to theorize how they are linked. Our perspective implies that role expectations and role performances allow reputation to function as a mechanism that can lead to status mobility. First, can a positive reputation in one attribute lead to enhancement in another attribute and ultimately lead to increased overall status? Toyota, for example, was initially considered a low-status automaker in the US market, but was able to enhance its status through targeted investments in quality. It is unlikely, however, that consistent improvements in quality *alone* would ever allow Toyota the membership of the same high-status group as, for example, Mercedes-Benz, hence leading to the creation of the Lexus division. Second, although reputation is defined at the attribute level, some attributes are likely to be more important for status mobility than other attributes, which makes it particularly important to understand the relationship between different attributes and their relative importance. In the automobile industry, for example, quality may be a core attribute and a necessity for upward status mobility, whereas design may be relatively less important. Third, future research should examine how organizations exert agency by creating new reputational dimensions to change the evaluation criteria of the existing audiences. For low-status organizations, status mobility through investments in existing attributes is hard because incumbents with higher status already possess better resources and capabilities. In this case, creating new evaluative dimensions may be a better strategy, such as *USA Today* emphasizing convenience instead of journalistic quality in the newspaper market (Kim, 2011).

CONCLUSION

In this chapter, we have focused on the integration of reputation and role theory. We argued that reputation is most usefully defined as a prediction of future behaviors that is based on an assessment of how past behaviors meet the role expectations that follow occupying a particular social status. By integrating reputation theory from economics with role theory from sociology, we intend to draw attention to three potential areas for future theoretical research, as discussed in the section above:(1) the multidimensionality of the reputation construct, (2) the embeddedness of reputation in role expectations, and (3) reputation as a potential mechanism for status mobility. We believe that by developing an embedded, multidimensional reputation construct we can simultaneously enrich reputation research and differentiate it from research on status. We stress also that by emphasizing the embeddedness of reputation through role expectations and performances in social systems, we do not rule out individual agency. In fact, role expectations and performances connect social structure and individual action, thus emphasizing the importance of individual role performances that build reputation which may, in turn, provide a mechanism for status mobility. Our role-theoretic approach to reputation research obviously increases the theoretical and empirical demands for future research in terms of identifying the role expectations necessary to understand and evaluate the role performances that undergird reputation.

Theoretically, research on role theory has pointed to a number of issues that may complicate clearly identifying the relevant role expectations. Specifically, research has focused on potential complications such as the lack of consensus about role expectations, ambiguity of role expectations, and how to define the relevant audiences and draw the boundaries between different audiences (Sarbin & Allen, 1968). Role expectations, for example, can sometimes be difficult to define because situations exist in which multiple roles can be invoked, possibly leading to role conflict, whereas other situations may evoke no roles, creating a state of anomie for the actors (Montgomery, 1998). Because a role-theoretic approach to reputation requires identifying the applicable roles in order to specify the relevant role expectations that undergird reputation formation, the usefulness of reputation as a mechanism to distinguish between actors depends not only on past behaviors but also on the clarity and stability of role expectations. Drawing clear boundaries between different audiences is also important because audiences ultimately set role expectations and evaluate subsequent role performances (Sarbin & Allen, 1968). Due to the differences across contexts in the formation of role expectations, audiences, and the evaluation of role performances (Biddle, 1986), an important theoretical and empirical challenge for future research is to clearly identify the relevant roles and role expectations in a given research context.

Empirically, to complement the theoretical identification of relevant role expectations requires a detailed understanding of the research setting, including the relevant audiences, the critical set of role expectations, and the related dimensions of reputation. Roles and role expectations may, however, be clearly defined in some contexts but more difficult to define in other contexts. The roles of producer, director, and screenwriter, for example, reflect a relatively clear and well-defined division of labor in film production, thus providing an ideal context for studying the implications of combining different roles (Baker & Faulkner, 1991). Carroll & Swaminathan (2000), in contrast, explored a market in which the diverging role expectations of mass brewers and microbrewers were still being formed, thus making the role expectations of each type of brewery open to interpretation and contestation. Their study of the microbrewery movement allowed them, however, to identify some of the emerging role expectations of microbreweries such as using traditional production methods and providing products with special color, foam, and taste. Other scholars have carefully identified differences in role expectations and used them to distinguish between different subcategories of firms. Rao, Monin, & Durand (2003), for example, examined the role expectations of French chefs and found that they are expected to provide a long menu of choices in classical French cuisine but only a very narrow menu or even no menu in nouvelle French cuisine.

Despite the differences between the aforementioned studies, they all point to the value of grounding research in a single industry or context to fully understand the role expectations within that context. Some early role theorists suggested that the nuanced nature of role expectations makes empirical research other than anthropological field research or qualitative case studies difficult (Neiman & Hughes, 1951). We do not advocate this extreme position. Indeed, all the aforementioned studies combine quantitative and qualitative research and test specific hypotheses using large-scale samples. We believe that large-sample quantitative research on corporate reputation can provide meaningful insights when research is grounded in a specific context, and traditional archival and survey research methods are used to identify the implicitly and explicitly expressed role expectations of a particular actor by its different audiences. Having identified the important role expectations, generating quantitative indicators of role performance can be as simple as matching the industry of a client firm to the industry specialization of an auditor (Jensen & Roy, 2008), or matching identity claims of breweries to their production methods and size (Carroll & Swaminathan, 2000). We believe that integrating role theory into reputation research is an effort well worth undertaking to provide reputation research with a stronger theoretical footing and empirical direction.

Key Articles on Role Theory

Reference	Type of Article	Basic Ideas of Role Theory	Key Concepts
Linton (1936)	Theoretical foundation	Roles as the dynamic aspect of status: Putting into effect the rights and duties that constitute the status (performing a role) (p. 114)	Social systems, status, role
Merton (1957)	Theoretical foundation	Roles as the behavior oriented to the patterned expectations of others based on status; each social status involves an array of roles (p. 110)	Role-set, status-set
Sarbin and Allen (1968)	Review of role theory	Roles as duties and obligations expected of any occupant of a particular social position in a social structure (p. 497)	Role enactment, role expectations, role location, role demands, role skills
Biddle (1986)	Review of role theory	(i) Patterned and characteristic social behaviors; (ii) Parts or identities that are assumed by social participants; (iii) Scripts or expectations for behavior that are understood by all and adhered to by performers (p. 68)	Consensus, conformity, role conflict, role taking
Callero (1994)	Review and extension of role theory	Resource perspective of role theory: (i) Roles as tools in the establishment of social structure; (ii) Agency is expressed through the use of roles as resources (p. 229)	Role as cultural object, social structure as set of schemas and resources

References

Akerlof, G. A. (1970). "The market for 'Lemons': Quality uncertainty and the market mechanism." *Quarterly Journal of Economics*, 84: 488–500.

—— & Kranton, R. E. (2000). "Economics and identity." *Quarterly Journal of Economics*, 115: 715–753.

Baker, W. E. & Faulkner, R. R. (1991). "Role as resource in the Hollywood film industry." *American Journal of Sociology*, 97: 279–309.

Bar-Isaac, H. & Tadelis, S. (2008). "Seller reputation." *Foundations and Trends in Microeconomics*, 4: 273–351.

Barnett, M. L., Jermier, J. M., & Lafferty, B. A. (2006). "Corporate reputation: The definitional landscape." *Corporate Reputation Review*, 9: 26–38.

Biddle, B. J. (1986). "Recent developments in role theory." *Annual Review of Sociology*, 12: 67–92.

Bielby, W. T. & Bielby, D. D. (1994). "'All hits are flukes': Institutionalized decision making and the rhetoric of network prime-time program development." *American Journal of Sociology*, 99: 1287–1313.

Bitektine, A. B. (2011). "Towards a theory of social judgments of organizations: The case of legitimacy, reputation, and status." *Academy of Management Review*, 36: 151–179.

Brown, B. & Perry, S. (1994). "Removing the financial performance halo from Fortune's 'Most Admired' Companies." *Academy of Management Journal*, 37: 1347–1359.

Burt, R. S. (1977). "Positions in multiple network systems, part one: A general conception of stratification and prestige in a system of actors cast as a social topology." *Social Forces*, 56: 106–131.

Callero, P. L. (1994). "From role-playing to role-using: Understanding role as resource." *Social Psychology Quarterly*, 57: 228–243.

Carmeli, A. & Tishler, A. (2004). "The relationships between intangible organizational elements and organizational performance." *Strategic Management Journal*, 25: 1257–1278.

Carroll, G. R. & Swaminathan, A. (2000). "Why the microbrewery movement? Organizational dynamics of resource partitioning in the U.S. brewing industry." *American Journal of Sociology*, 106: 715–762.

Dollinger, M. J., Golden, P. A., & Saxton, T. (1997). "The effect of reputation on the decision to joint venture." *Strategic Management Journal*, 18: 127–140.

Dowling, G. R. & Gardberg, N. (2012). "Keeping score: Measures of corporate reputation." In M. Barnett & T. Pollock (Eds.), *The Oxford Handbook of Corporate Reputation*. Oxford: Oxford University Press, 34–68.

Emirbayer, M. & Mische, A. (1998). "What is agency?" *American Journal of Sociology*, 103: 962–1023.

Fombrun, C. (1996). *Reputation: Realizing Value from the Corporate Image*. Boston, Massachusetts: Harvard Business School Press.

—— (2012). "The building blocks of corporate reputation: Definitions, antecedents, consequences." In M. Barnett & T. Pollock (Eds.), *The Oxford Handbook of Corporate Reputation*. Oxford: Oxford University Press, 94–113.

—— & van Riel, C. (1997). "The reputational landscape." *Corporate Reputation Review*, 1: 5–13.

Fryxell, G. E. & Wang, J. (1994). "The Fortune corporate 'reputation' index: Reputation for what?" *Journal of Management*, 20: 1–14.

Goode, W. J. (1960). "Norm commitment and conformity to role-status obligations." *American Journal of Sociology*, 66: 246–258.

Granovetter, M. (1985). "Economic action and social structure: The problem of embedded-ness." *American Journal of Sociology*, 91: 481–510.

Greenwood, R., Li, S. X., Prakash, R., & Deephouse, D. L. (2005). "Reputation, diversification, and organizational explanations of performance in professional service firms." *Organization Science*, 16: 661–673.

Hayward, M. L. A. & Boeker, W. (1998). "Power and conflicts of interest in professional firms: Evidence from investment banking." *Administrative Science Quarterly*, 43: 1–22.

Hsu, G. (2006). "Jacks of all trades and masters of none: Audiences' reactions to spanning genres in feature film production." *Administrative Science Quarterly*, 51: 420–450.

Jensen, M. (2003). "The role of network resources in market entry: Commercial banks' entry into investment banking, 1991–1997." *Administrative Science Quarterly*, 48: 466–497.

—— (2006). "Should we stay or should we go? Accountability, status anxiety, and client defections." *Administrative Science Quarterly*, 51: 97–128.

—— (2010). "Legitimizing illegitimacy: How creating market identity legitimizes illegitimate products." *Research in the Sociology of Organizations*, 31: 39–80.

—— & Roy, A. (2008). "Staging exchange partner choices: When do status and reputation matter?" *Academy of Management Journal*, 51: 495–516.

——, Kim, B. K., & Kim, H. (2011). "The importance of status in markets: A market identity perspective." In J. L. Pearce (Ed.), *Status, Organization and Management*. Cambridge, UK: Cambridge University Press, 87–117.

Kim, B. K. (2011). "New wine in old bottles: The role of status and market identity in creating a 'digital media' category." Ph.D. dissertation, Ross School of Business, University of Michigan, Ann Arbor, MI.

——& Jensen, J. (2011). " How product order affects market identity: Repertoire ordering in the U.S. opera market." *Administative Science Quarterly*, 56: 238–56.

King, B. G. (2008). "A political mediation model of corporate response to social movement activism." *Administrative Science Quarterly*, 53: 395–421.

Klein, B. & Leffler, K. B. (1981). "The role of market forces in assuring contractual performance." *Journal of Political Economy*, 89: 615–641.

Kollock, P. (1994). "The emergence of exchange structures: An experimental study of uncertainty, commitment, and trust." *American Journal of Sociology*, 100: 313–345.

Lange, D., Lee, P. M., & Dai, Y. (2011). "Organizational reputation: A review." *Journal of Management*, 37: 153–184.

Linton, R. (1936). *The Study of Man*. New York: D. Appleton-Century Company.

March, J. G. (1994). *A Primer on Decision Making*. New York: The Free Press.

Martins, L. L. (2005). "A model of the effects of reputational rankings on organizational change." *Organization Science*, 16: 701–720.

Merton, R. K. (1957). "The role-set: Problems in sociological theory." *British Journal of Sociology*, 8: 106–120.

Milgrom, P. & Roberts, J. (1982). "Predation, reputation, and entry deterrence." *Journal of Economic Theory*, 27: 280–312.

Mishina, Y. & Devers, C. (2012). "On being bad: Why stigma is not the same as reputation." In M. Barnett & T. Pollock (Eds.), *The Oxford Handbook of Corporate Reputation*. Oxford: Oxford University Press, 201–20.

Montgomery, J. D. (1998). "Toward a role-theoretic conception of embeddedness." *American Journal of Sociology*, 104: 92–125.

Neiman, L. J. & Hughes, J. W. (1951). "The problem of the concept of role: A re-survey of the literature." *Social Forces*, 30: 141–149.

Noe, T. (2012). "The effects of financial policy on corporate reputation." In M. Barnett & T. Pollock (Eds.), *The Oxford Handbook of Corporate Reputation*. Oxford: Oxford University Press, 114–39.

Podolny, J. M. (1993). "A status-based model of market competition." *American Journal of Sociology*, 98: 829–872.

Rao, H. (1994). "The social construction of reputation: Certification contests, legitimation, and the survival of organizations in the American automobile industry: 1895–1912." *Strategic Management Journal*, 15: 29–44.

——, Monin, P., & Durand, R. (2003). "Institutional change in Toque Ville: Nouvelle cuisine as an identity movement in French gastronomy." *American Journal of Sociology*, 108: 795–843.

Raub, W. & Weesie, J. (1990). "Reputation and efficiency in social interactions: An example of network effects." *American Journal of Sociology*, 96: 626–654.

Rhee, M. & Haunschild, P. R. (2006). "The liability of good reputation: A study of product recalls in the U.S. automobile industry." *Organization Science*, 17: 101–117.

Rindova, V. P. & Martins, L. (2012). "Show me the money: What makes reputation an intangible asset." In M. Barnett & T. Pollock (Eds.), *The Oxford Handbook of Corporate Reputation*. Oxford: Oxford University Press, 16–33.

——, Williamson, I. O., Petkova, A. P., & Sever, J. M. (2005). "Being good or being known: An empirical examination of the dimensions, antecedents, and consequences of organizational reputation." *Academy of Management Journal*, 48: 1033–1049.

Roberts, P. W. & Dowling, G. R. (2002). "Corporate reputation and sustained superior financial performance." *Strategic Management Journal*, 23: 1077–1093.

Sarbin, T. R. & Allen, V. L. (1968). "Role theory." In G. Lindzey & E. Aronson (Eds.), *The Handbook of Social Psychology*. New York: Random House, 488–567.

Sewell Jr., W. H. (1992). "A theory of structures: Duality, agency, and transformation." *American Journal of Sociology*, 98: 1–29.

Shapiro, C. (1983). "Premiums for high quality products as returns to reputations." *Quarterly Journal of Economics*, 98: 659–679.

Staw, B. M. & Epstein, L. D. (2000). "What bandwagons bring: Effects of popular management techniques on corporate performance, reputation, and CEO pay." *Administrative Science Quarterly*, 45: 523–556.

Stiglitz, J. E. (2000). "The contributions of the economics of information to twentieth century economics." *Quarterly Journal of Economics*, 115: 1441–1478.

Swidler, A. (1986). "Culture in action: Symbols and strategies." *American Sociological Review*, 51: 273–286.

Walker, K. (2010). "A systematic review of the corporate reputation literature: Definition, measurement, and theory." *Corporate Reputation Review*, 12: 357–387.

Wartick, S. L. (2002). "Measuring corporate reputation: Definition and data." *Business and Society*, 41: 371–392.

Washington, M. & Zajac, E. J. (2005). "Status evolution and competition: Theory and evidence." *Academy of Management Journal*, 48: 282–296.

Weigelt, K. & Camerer, C. (1988). "Reputation and corporate strategy: A review of recent theory and applications." *Strategic Management Journal*, 9: 443–454.

Whetten, D. A. & Mackey, A. (2002). "An actor conception of organizational identity and its implications for the study of organizational reputation." *Business Society*, 41: 393–414.

Williamson, O. E. (1991). "Comparative economic organization: The analysis of discrete structural alternatives." *Administrative Science Quarterly*, 36: 269–296.

Wilson, R. (1985). "Reputations in games and markets." In A. E. Roth (Ed.), *Game-theoretic
Models of Bargaining*. Cambridge: Cambridge University Press, 27–62.

Wolfinger, R. E. (1960). "Reputation and reality in the study of 'community power'." *American
Sociological Review*, 25: 636–644.

Zuckerman, E. W. (1999). "The categorical imperative: Security analysts and the illegitimacy
discount." *American Journal of Sociology*, 104: 1398–1438.

CHAPTER 8

IT AIN'T WHAT YOU DO, IT'S WHO YOU DO IT WITH: DISTINGUISHING REPUTATION AND STATUS

DAVID N. BARRON

MEREDITH ROLFE

The benefit to a firm of possessing a good reputation is generally held to be in the influence this can have on decision-makers who are considering entering into or continuing with an economic transaction with an actor about whom they have limited information. In this chapter we argue that status, a concept that is related to but distinct from reputation, can function in a similar way. We describe the nature of status, and how it is related to reputation. We discuss empirical research that has attempted to disentangle the effects of both reputation and status on important organizational outcomes.

INTRODUCTION

WHEN scholars and managers turn their attention to corporate reputation and its close relatives, which include status, they do so from a desire to understand the factors that influence actors when they are deciding whether to enter into an economic transaction, or other kind of relationship, with a firm. The problem facing such decision-makers is a lack of information. How do potential customers, suppliers, investors, or employees form evaluations about the organizations that they are considering as potential exchange partners? In this chapter we consider how people might evaluate the status of an organization, how this might differ from their evaluation of the organization's reputation, and why this might matter to the organization concerned.

Evaluations about reputations are often said to be based on the previous actions of a firm (Benjamin & Podolny, 1999; Uzzi, 1996; Fombrun, Chapter 5, this volume). Insofar as past behaviour provides useful information to decision-makers who are concerned about the future actions of a firm, reputation is therefore of value to decision-makers in the presence of uncertainty about the future. For example, a firm's credit rating is in part a summary of the history of its record of paying creditors in a timely fashion. A decision-maker might be influenced by this because he might think this is a signal that this is the type of firm that can be trusted to pay its bills on time. In addition, a decision-maker might reason that this credit rating is a valuable asset to the firm, and hence it will do its best to protect this asset by paying future bills on time. In this sense, reputation is often thought of as providing a rational basis for decision-makers.

However, there may be situations in which this source of information is not available, or where it would be too costly for decision-makers to obtain. For example, start-ups will have no established track record. Alternatively, decision-makers may be influenced by other pieces of information in addition to those that contribute to a firm's reputation, even though that additional information is not directly related to the economic transaction under consideration. For example, one might look at a bio-tech firm's record of registering patents (which would be part of its reputation) and in addition find out the universities that granted its leading scientists their doctoral degrees (which would be an element of its status). This additional information might either amplify or dampen the effect of reputation on decision-makers. Finally, decision-makers may, in some situations, be influenced by information even though there is no rational basis for this, in the sense that the information has no direct relationship to firm attributes of concern to the decision-maker. For example, the location of a firm's head office in a prestigious part of a major city may positively influence status judgments.

In this chapter we argue that status is a type of evaluation that can and does influence decision-makers independently of evaluations of reputation. We will suggest that, while reputation might usually be a more potent source of economic advantage to a firm than status, there are situations in which status will be more important than reputation. We will begin by discussing the nature of status, and then describe its similarities to and differences from reputation. We will then review recent empirical research that demonstrates independent effects of reputation and status.

THE CONCEPT OF STATUS

What is status? The concept has a long history in sociology, dating back at least to the work of Max Weber (Stern et al., 2010; Turner, 1988; Weber, 1956), who defined status as

> "an effective claim to social esteem in terms of positive or negative privileges" (Weber, 1956: 305).

The most important aspect of status, and status groups, in Weber's work was the contrast that he drew between status and class as bases of social ordering. The latter, already well established in Weber's time through the work of Marx, is essentially an economic basis of social grouping; a person's class position is determined by his or her relationship to the economic means of production (particularly land, capital, and labor). For Weber, though, these economic considerations alone could not explain all the significant forms of social distinction that operate in society. For him, status was a separate form of social distinction, determined by, *inter alia*, style of life, formal education, and hereditary or occupational prestige. Money and entrepreneurial position, he stressed, are not "in themselves status qualifications, although they may lead to them." Weber could therefore explain the existence of people who had high social status despite being in a low economic class (for example, members of the clergy) and also people who had low status even though they were members of the capitalist class (the nouveau riche).

(Turner, 1988: 13) explains the distinction between class and status by reference to two "related but distinctive properties of social stratification":

> Societies are either dominated by economic relations through the market-place, which produce predominantly economic forms of inequality, or they are structured around certain legal-political definitions of privilege, which are articulated through cultural systems of distinction.

In the "ideal type," or theoretically pure, economic form of society, competition for resources is the dominant mode of social interaction. Convention, etiquette, or norms have little part to play in determining the behaviour of *homo economicus*. More or less anything goes in this type of society, so long as it leads to a profitable outcome. The logical result would be endless use of "force and fraud" (Turner, 1988) to reach one's desired ends. A well-known idea for how this undesirable side effect could be minimized was introduced by Hobbes. He argued that rational actors could see that it would be in their best interests to voluntarily give up some of their individual rights to a political authority such as the state. This is known as a *social contract*. The enforcement of the rule of law actually creates opportunities for greater profit because it makes it more likely that an economic actor will be able to keep the fruits of his or her enterprise, rather than being defrauded of them by other, profit-hungry actors. In some ways, modern institutional economics can be seen as deriving from the tradition of the social contract, in that it deals with supra-organizational institutions that influence the behavior of economic actors. Certainly, both institutional economics and social contract theory place the emphasis on individualism and individual rationality.

The alternative approach to understanding the structure of society is based on culture and tradition. As Turner (1988: 20) puts it, "In a society based on tradition rather than upon the market, the standing or status of the person depends not upon what they happen to own, but upon what they are as defined in legal or cultural terms...A person's [status] depends upon birth, membership of particular families, education and training in appropriate cultural patterns, and the acquisition of respected and respectful attitudes and dispositions." The status of a person matters, because it has an influence on the ability of an individual to be successful in keeping or acquiring economic wealth.

It is worth noting that embedded in the list of bases of status mentioned above, there are two broad categories. Status that is associated with family one might think of as being more or less fixed. Elevation to or demotion from the aristocracy, for example, is rare. On the other hand, the acquisition of attitudes and dispositions implies attributes that are not fixed and hence could be seen as a means of social mobility. Indeed, many societies do see "education" as an important means of enhancing life chances. One reason is no doubt that an individual acquires knowledge and skills that enable them to command a higher wage on the labor market. However, there is also a widespread belief that attendance at elite educational institutions, such as the Ivy League universities in the US, Oxbridge in the UK, or the Grandes Ecoles in France, confers an additional prestige on a graduate that provides advantages to them in the labor market over and above those deriving from acquired human capital. Although this creates opportunities for social mobility, it is also the case that people from high-status backgrounds are much more likely to gain entry to elite educational institutions, and hence they can be seen as tending to preserve the status quo.

Although Weber and other early social theorists were not generally concerned with the status of *organizations*, nevertheless the important dimensions of the concept as it has come to be applied in the organizational domain can be seen in this early work. Like scholars of individual status, organizational scholars also see status as socially and culturally, rather than economically, determined. As with individual status, organizational status is nevertheless capable of "leading to" the accumulation of monetary wealth. Just as social status might not reflect actual differences in abilities or merit, the advantages, or "privileges" (Washington & Zajac, 2005), of high organizational status are not necessarily earned, for example by being based on previous high-quality performance. Furthermore, as Weber identified separate, though related, economic and sociological bases for the structuring of societies, contemporary scholars often distinguish economic and sociological bases for the structuring of markets. Just as the structuring factors in societies are important because they affect the distribution of income and wealth, the factors that create market structures are important because they can influence the distribution of profit among the organizations that constitute the market.

In the context of organizational research, there have been a number of authors who have defined status and discussed the mechanisms by which status is linked to a firm's economic performance. This work falls into two broad categories. First, we have scholars who consider status to be the outcome of the relations and associations firms have with other actors. This line of work often takes its lead from Podolny's definition, which holds that status is

> an actor's position in a hierarchical order. That position reflects some diffuse sense of better or worse that is indirectly tied to past behaviours, but it is more directly tied to the pattern of relations and affiliations in which the actor does and does not choose to engage. (Podolny, 2005: 13)

Similarly, Bothner, Godard, & Lee (2010: 2) define status as a

> zero-sum intangible asset possessed by social actors insofar as they are highly
> regarded by highly-regarded others.

These definitions repay some closer scrutiny. First, they emphasize that status is generated by *relations and affiliations* to other actors. A high status is the result of associations
with high-status actors and the avoidance of associations with low-status actors. If a
high-status organization does engage in an association with a lower-status firm, the
result will be a reduction in the status of the higher-status organization and an increase
in the status of the other firm. Podolny describes this process as involving a flow of *defer-
ence* between the different status actors.

Second, status is considered to be zero-sum, implying that one organization cannot
increase its status without one or more other actors losing status. This might occur in
part because of the status flow that we have just described, but also follows from the idea
that status is similar in nature to what Hirsch calls a positional good (Podolny, 2005).

> The positional economy…relates to all aspects of goods, services, work positions, and
> other social relationships that are either (1) scarce in some absolute or socially imposed
> sense or (2) subject to congestion or crowding through extensive use. (Hirsch, 1977: 27)

An example of the second characteristic might be an exclusive designer label, the status
of which is undermined by it becoming too common (as happened to Burberry as a
result of the extensive pirating of their well-known check-patterned clothing, for example). The point here is that it is impossible (by definition) for all members of a set of
organizations to have the qualities associated with high status without those very qualities becoming devalued. Essentially, this is a strategic issue; a quality that is common
cannot be a source of competitive advantage, and therefore cannot mark out an organization as being of higher status than its rivals.

Status is, by definition, conferred on an organization by some external audience. The
zero-sum nature of status comes about because this audience is—implicitly or
explicitly—making comparisons and placing organizations in rank order. If one organization loses status relative to others, then it follows logically that those other organizations must increase in their relative status. As a result, status is inherently hierarchical.
The same is not true of reputation. If all firms had the same flawless record of paying
their suppliers within 30 days, they would all have equivalent reputations for being good
credit risks. However, although there may be a logical difference, in practice, among any
reasonably large group of organizations, we would expect there to be differentiation in
both reputation and status, implying that it should be possible to construct a hierarchy
of both. Given Podolny's statement that status is "indirectly tied to past behaviours," we
would expect firms' positions in status and reputation hierarchies to be positively correlated, but for this correlation to be less than perfect.

The second category of definitions sees status as being broader in origin that associations with other actors, and thus employs definitions that are closer to classical sociological definitions, such as that of Benoit-Sumullyan:

> [Status is] an inferiority-superiority scale with respect to the comparative degree to which [actors] possess or embody some socially approved or generally desired attribute or characteristic. (Benoit-Smullyan, 1944: 151)

This leads to the following definition of status, used by Washington & Zajac (2005: 284):

> A socially constructed, intersubjectively agreed-upon and accepted ordering or ranking of individuals, groups, organizations, or activities in a social system. Status generates social esteem and special, unearned (i.e., non-merit-based) benefits known as privileges, which are granted to and enjoyed by high-status actors in a social system.

This definition overlaps with that of Podolny (2005) and Bothner, Godard, & Lee (2010) in that it specifies that status produces a hierarchy or ranking. However, it is less specific about the origin of an actor's position in this hierarchy. Essentially, status can be conferred on the basis of any characteristic that a particular social group perceives to be associated with high status. In particular, this definition implies that the characteristics associated with high status may have nothing to do with "perceived quality," and hence in this sense the "privileges" that flow from high status may not be merited.

To summarize, we are considering situations in which decision-makers have to make choices among a set of competing alternative organizations. They lack full information about all the relevant characteristics of these organizations and therefore have to rely on indirect indicators of these characteristics. Reputation is one such indicator. Decision-makers may also form evaluations of the relative status of these competing organizations based, among other possible markers, on the status of the organizations with which they interact. Organizations that are viewed by most decision-makers as high status will have an advantage over low-status rivals, other things being equal.

Reputation and Status

Having considered some definitions of status, we are now in a position to consider how status and reputation are linked. Reputation is considered by authors such as Podolny (2005) to be an economic characteristic of organizations in the sense that economic theory has often considered reputation to be an important factor in explaining firm behavior (see Noe, Chapter 6, this volume). As Bothner, Godard, & Lee (2010) have pointed out, reputation in this context typically derives from specific traits, such as honesty, treating employees well, or repaying loans on time. This leads to reputations *for* these specific traits (see also Jensen, Kim, & Kim, Chapter 7, this volume). Some authors have suggested that this specificity is a characteristic that distinguishes reputation from status, which by contrast is held to "arise from factors that are more numerous and diffuse" (Bothner, Godard, & Lee, 2010: 8). However, a number of studies have found strong evidence of a "halo" effect in reputation (Brown & Perry, 1994). In particular, firms that have demonstrated strong financial performance over a number of years tend to be seen has having strong reputations in other areas, so this may not be such an important distinguishing feature in practice.

INFORMATION

We have argued that both status and reputation are important in the context of decision-making that involves an information asymmetry. When deciding whether or not to engage in an economic exchange or on the terms of the exchange, both parties clearly need information. If a customer is in the market for a diamond ring, for example, he or she will want to know that the stone the jeweler is selling is in fact a diamond, that the price is a fair one given the quality and size of the stone, that the setting is 18 carat gold, and so on. How is a customer supposed to make these judgments?

There are a number of possibilities. One is the existence of institutions that provide external evaluation and certification. An example of that—indeed, one of the earliest examples of consumer protection legislation—is the hallmarking of gold. In these cases, instead of trusting the jeweler, the customer trusts the institution. One assumes that the quality control institution has no reason to try to cheat by, for example, hallmarking gold that is lower in quality than it purports to be. Hence customers can reasonably rely on the judgment of these third parties to provide them with information that it would be difficult and costly to obtain for themselves.

Such institutional arrangements do not always exist, however. This is the sort of information problem that many, if not all, economic exchanges involve. How can an employer be sure that a potential employee is telling the truth about their skills and experience? How can a supplier know that the promise of a customer to pay his or her debts on time will be fulfilled? And so on. In the absence of an institutional solution, one could engage the services of an independent consultant—a firm that carries out psychometric testing of job applicants, for example. Alternatively, one might rely on legal redress if the information provided turns out to be inaccurate. However, all of these would incur costs, and in some cases they merely replace one information asymmetry with another: How does one judge the level of expertise of the consultant?

Reputation provides an alternative to institutions as a means of forming a judgment about an organization (Bitektine, 2011). We might make a judgment about a jeweler on the basis of our own experiences if we have been a customer before. Alternatively, we might again turn to the judgment of third parties, such as consumer organizations or websites that allow customer ratings. There are many situations where third parties provide us with information about the past behaviors of organizations. These sources enable us to evaluate the reputation of an organization.

Status is a third way in which we might evaluate an organization. A jeweler might enhance its status by association with other high-status actors; for example, displaying a royal warrant over the door. It might enhance its status by being in a location associated with high-status jewelers, such as London's Bond Street, gaining status by geographical

proximity to other high-status jewelers. Even branches in other cities might make reference to the location of its "flagship" store. Alternatively, it might attempt to enhance its
status by displaying symbols that are culturally associated with high-status retailers,
such as a uniformed doorman.

These three examples are useful as they show the similarities, but also the differences,
between these three forms of evaluation. In the first case, third parties perform a formal
certification. In the second case, third parties collect information for me. In the case of
status, evaluations are based on observation of the status symbols displayed by the
organization. The display of a royal warrant is something of a hybrid between the three,
as a potential customer might think that some kind of "due diligence" is done by the
warranting organization (so it has some of the features of an institution), and assume
that the member of the royal family concerned has experience with the organization (so
it has some of the features of reputation). This alerts us to the fact that these various
forms of evaluation do not have hard boundaries. Nevertheless, it also shows that there
are distinctions among them.

SIGNALING

We have argued that status is established by, among other things, the display of symbols.
This naturally raises the possibility of a connection with theories of *signaling* (Chok &
Kennedy, 2010). The most well-known signaling theory was developed by the economist
Michael Spence (Spence, 1974). According to this theory, an attribute can act as a signal
if it is correlated in some way with the valued characteristic (for example, reliability) *and*
if it would be more costly for an actor poorly endowed with this characteristic to be able
to send the signal than for an actor that is richly endowed. In Spence's original formulation, the process of obtaining the signal does not enhance the attribute being signaled.
The classic example is of a job applicant who wants to signal his or her quality to a potential employer. Obtaining a credential such as a university degree will be less costly for
someone who is intelligent and diligent, and hence this can act as a signal of these qualities. Therefore, a university degree will be a valuable asset on the labor market, even if
what is learnt in the course of study does not directly improve the ability of a graduate to
perform well at work. Similarly, it will be less costly for a firm whose products are reliable to offer warranties to consumers than it will be for a firm that makes less reliable
products, and hence warranties can be an effective signal of reliability.

It is important to note that in these examples, we assume that the attributes the
employer or consumer desire in an employee or good are hard to observe directly. If an
employer could discover in a direct way which job applicant best fits the desired specifi-
cations, perhaps by the use of psychometric tests and interviews, then signals would be
unnecessary and hence worthless to job applicants. The signaling model developed by
Spence requires a number of other assumptions. First, the process of producing the signal does not have to improve the quality being signaled. For example, it is not necessary

to assume that the educational process that precedes the awarding of a credential increases a potential employee's productivity. Second, the attributes being signaled must be at least somewhat stable. Although Spence does not say so, presumably the more stable the attribute, the more useful the signal. For example, the reliability of a consumer durable is fixed once it is delivered to the customer. Third, there must be some sense in which the signal is accurate; it must be confirmed by experience.

Signals, then, are of value when the quality in question is difficult to observe directly, and hence there is uncertainty about it. Under these circumstances it will be rational for actors to invest in signaling their quality and it will be rational for actors to take into account such signals when deciding whether, and with whom, to engage in an economic exchange.

Can reputation act as a valuable signal? That will depend on whether or not it meets the various criteria listed above. Consider the various components of reputation that are included in measures such as the *Fortune* Most Admired Corporations ranking. Might a reputation for good people management, for example, send a signal to potential employees and hence improve the ability of a firm to hire talented people? If so, how could a firm develop a reputation for being a good employer that would send a convincing signal to potential employees? The obvious first step for a company wanting to develop such a reputation is actually to *be* a good employer, but this just leads us back to the information asymmetry problem; unless this quality can be appreciated by good potential employees, it will be difficult for a firm to benefit from this behavior in the face of competition from firms that are merely pretending to be good employers. The difficulty for firms is that attempts they make to present themselves as good employers, for example on their websites, in brochures, at recruitment events, and so on, are likely to be viewed with skepticism by the target audience, in part because the cost of such "signals" is the same for good and bad employers, and hence the signal will not work effectively. The increasing trend for employees to post information about their employers on the Internet, either on personal blogs, on social media such as Facebook and Twitter, or on specialist websites such as glassdoor.com, does have the potential to create an effective signal. Glassdoor.com has been attracting good reviews largely because it does take some trouble to ensure that the views expressed by its contributors are indeed from bona fide employees. The site can be consulted by anyone, but it also publicizes an annual ranking of employers based on the reviews submitted to its website. However, even websites such as this might be prone to having reviews posted on them by managers posing as employees, and so the extent to which this is viewed as a credible signal of employer quality by potential recruits may well be limited.

In this type of situation, then, there is uncertainty as to the quality of an organization in the minds of a potential exchange partner (employee, customer, supplier, etc.). It is hard to find the information necessary to resolve this uncertainty. In some cases, a firm might be able to establish a reputation, particularly where the reputation is based on credible sources of information that have been verified by objective third parties, such as auditors or credit-rating agencies. In other cases, it might be hard for a reputation to be created; it will be difficult for good firms to distinguish themselves from bad firms.

Under these conditions, potential exchange partners might look to other characteristics of organizations in an attempt to separate the good from the bad; one candidate for such a characteristic is a firm's status.

Can status also act as a signal? For it to be a signal in the strict sense implied by Spence, it is necessary that the level of status associated with an organization is correlated with the attribute that potential exchange partners are uncertain about. As we have seen, this is not necessarily the case, given the origins of status implied by the definitions discussed above. However, an alternative formulation of the theory has been suggested by Podolny (2005) that might rescue the possibility of status acting as a signal. As we have seen, Spence required that for something to be an effective signal, it must be cheaper for organizations that have the quality about which there is uncertainty to produce the signal than it would be for firms lacking that quality. Podolny argues that, logically, a signal would also be effective if "the costs of producing a good of a given quality are inversely correlated with status" (2005: 30). If potential exchange partners grant high-status organizations certain "privileges," then this condition will be met. An example, cited by Podolny, is the preference of firms and non-profit organizations for high-status auditors, even if lower-status auditors have exactly the same technical abilities and charge lower fees (Stevens, 1991). Organizations are aware that certain auditors are perceived by the world as being in the highest status category, and given the importance of having unimpeachable auditors, these firms have a huge competitive advantage over lower-status rivals, who find breaking in to this elite group almost impossible because the transaction and marketing costs they would incur in doing so are prohibitively high.

In a sense, then, status reduces risk for a potential exchange partner by making their choice of partner more understandable to the outside world. In the 1970s and 1980s it was common to hear the phrase "nobody ever got fired for choosing IBM" in the context of IT purchasing decisions. A purchasing manager would not have to justify to his or her boss the choice of IBM—then the highest-status supplier—but if a risk had been taken on a lower-status provider and this had proved problematic, then being fired would be a much greater possibility. Other significant advantages are not hard to imagine; some are discussed by Podolny (2005: 26–30).

It is this characteristic of status that results in its association with the so-called Matthew Effect, introduced into the sociological literature by Merton (1968). Once a firm has achieved high status, it is difficult for lower-status rivals to compete on equal terms, and hence the "rich get richer." Notice that this also takes us back to an important reason why Weber introduced the concept of status into his theory of social structure: It is a significant barrier to social mobility.

In summary, while reputation can be thought of as a signal in the sense described by Spence, status does not meet those strict criteria in a straightforward way. However, if we adopt Podolny's generalization of the concept we can see that high status can enable firms to have lower costs and/or charge premium prices relative to firms with lower status, *even if the basis of the high status is not related to the quality of the good or service provided.* Both reputation and status, then, can confer significant economic benefits on a firm, and as a result we would expect firms to want to protect both their reputation and their status.

EMPIRICAL EVIDENCE

The discussion so far has attempted to maintain that reputation and status are separate, if related, concepts. If the distinction is as meaningful as we have argued, then it should be possible to detect independent effects of both reputation and status on important organizational outcomes. In this section of the chapter, therefore, we review four recent empirical studies that have included separate measures of reputation and status in an attempt to see if it is indeed possible to detect such independent effects. Although this is a short list, there have so far been very few studies that have looked at both reputation and status. The articles we will discuss are summarized in the table at the end of this chapter.

Treatment of Reputation

We have argued that evaluations of a firm's reputation are based on past behavior. This is the approach taken in all of the studies that we review. Dimov, Shepherd, & Sutcliffe (2006), for example, look at the syndication of venture capital (VC) firms' investments. A firm's reputation, in their study, is determined by previous investment success. Firms that have a track record of successful investments are shown to be more desirable syndication partners. Similarly, Washington & Zajac (2005) investigate determinants of college basketball teams receiving invitations to the annual National Collegiate Athletic Association (NCAA) postseason basketball tournament. Their measure of reputation is a team's historical performance record.

The research of Stern, Dukerich, & Zajak (2010) also uses past performance as a measure of reputation. They studied the effects of status and reputation on alliance formation in technology-driven industries. Alliances between incumbent firms and start-ups are common, and generally seen as a way in which established firms can benefit from the entrepreneurial activity of new entrants. However, the lack of "unambiguous and objective information" about small, new organizations means that decisions about alliance formation with such firms are "fraught with considerable uncertainty" (Stern, Dukerich, & Zajak, 2010: 4).

Previous research has demonstrated that under such conditions, the scientific credentials of a new firm's founders are an important consideration. Stern, Dukerich, & Zajak (2010) suggest that a new firm's reputation is a product of the scientists' track record of publications and citations. Similarly, Jensen & Roy (2008) argue that the reputation of audit firms is based on observations of their previous performance, positive or negative. Reports in the media of an auditor's involvement in an audit failure, for example, would reduce that firm's reputation.

Finally, we turn to Bowman & Bastedo (2009), who study reputation and status effects on the choice of university made by potential undergraduate students in the US. This is of particular interest, as published rankings—particularly *Fortune*'s Most Admired Corporations ranking—are a very common way of measuring reputation in the academic literature. Bowman and Bastedo's approach provides an example of how a trusted third party's collection and analysis of information can influence people's evaluation of an organization's reputation. They point to strong evidence that college choice is influenced by a number of key rankings, such as the America's Best Colleges section of the *US News and World Report*. The study begins with a careful consideration of the mechanisms by which someone's decision to apply to a particular college might be influenced by its position in a published ranking, based particularly on Ajzen's theory of planned behavior (Azjen, 1985, 1991). College rankings, they suggest, can affect perceptions of a school in two distinct ways. First, applicants might think of the rankings as an objective source of expert opinion reflecting specific attributes of an educational institution. Second, it might contribute to a more diffuse sense of particular institutions being "prestigious" and therefore conferring future benefits on their alumni, for example by enhancing their ability to obtain good jobs after graduation. Rindova et al. (2005) make a similar distinction between the *perceived quality* of specific aspects of an organization and its *prominence*, which is a "broad, subjective norm."

Bowman and Bastedo (2009) go on to point out that position in a college ranking meets the criteria that we discussed above for something to be an effective signal of quality. Presumably it is easier for colleges that offer high-quality education to achieve an elevated position in a ranking than it is for colleges whose educational provision is of a lower standard. However, they also point out that the correlation between the two may be very loosely coupled; indeed, the ability of colleges to tailor their activities to achieve high rankings may in part reflect the suspicion with which they are often viewed by university academics and administrators.

The result of these considerations leads Bowman and Bastedo to consider a college's position in the *US News* rankings to be a measure of its *reputation*. The ranking is determined by certain organizational characteristics that are held to be correlated with the quality of education that a student at that college will experience, so it is a *signal of quality* in the normal sense. One could, therefore, see this as a departure from our assumption that reputation is associated with past performance. Here, the argument seems to be that current characteristics of the organization are expected to be associated with high performance in the future. Nevertheless, at least some of the "characteristics" are really previous organizational outcomes, such as the SAT scores of previous years' freshmen.

Treatment of Status

In our earlier discussion of the ways in which status is conceptualized in the literature, we pointed out that one common theme is that status is determined by the patterns of associations a firm has with high-status organizations. Dimov, Shepherd, & Sutcliffe (2006) adopt this approach. They define status in terms of the position of an organization in the network of VC firms. We will describe the measure in some detail, as this has become a common means of operationalizing status in organizational research. The measure is based on Bonacich (1987). It is defined as:

$$c_i(\alpha, \beta) = \sum_j (\alpha + \beta c_j) R_{ij},$$

where R_{ij} is the number of companies in which i and j have both invested during the period of the study. The intuition behind this measure is that its value depends on the strength of the direct ties between two firms and the centrality of those firms. In other words, a tie to a highly central firm increases status more than a tie to a peripheral firm. The parameter α is an arbitrary scaling factor, but the value of the parameter β requires a little more attention, as it determines how important are the centralities of the firms to which i is attached in determining their status. Normal practice is to set β to be less than the reciprocal of the largest eigenvalue of R. Dimov, Shepherd, & Sutcliffe follow convention by setting β to three-quarters of the reciprocal of the largest eigenvalue.

Washington and Zajac also use network position as a measure of centrality. They look at the pattern of associations in the form of the number of games a team played against high-status and low-status opponents. The former is expected to increase a team's status and hence its probability of being invited to the final tournament; the latter is hypothesized to have the opposite effect.

Stern, Dukerich & Zajac (2010) similarly determine a firm's status by association with other high status organizations. However, in this case the high status organizations are not in the same industry. They argue that the status of a start-up technology company is determined by the prestige of the universities from which they obtained their doctoral degrees. This is an important generalization of the principle that status is affected by the status of a firm's associates: these associates need not be in the same industry or even be businesses at all. Notice as well that the prestige of the degree granting university might well be associated with the quality of the scientist, but it is quite different from the scientist's actual track record of performance.

Bowman & Bastedo's (2009) study of college choice is the exception to the use of associations as the basis for an organization's status. We have already seen that they measure college reputation by its position in a published ranking. However, they point out that the significance of a position in a ranking hierarchy as an influence on college applicants is not linear. In particular, they argue that being in the top, elite group (however defined) will be disproportionately beneficial. It is in fact common for rankings to highlight membership of such an elite group. As a result, the form in which rankings are presented will be important. In the case of the US News rankings, there is indeed an explicitly identified elite group of universities: the top fifty appear on the front page. It is easy to imagine that the difference between being ranked 50 and 51 is much greater than the difference between, say, 400 and 401.

The result of these considerations leads Bowman and Bastedo to consider that being a member of the elite group of colleges in the rankings confers the additional benefit of high status. In this study, then, the "status hierarchy" essentially has only two positions: elite and non-elite. In a similar way, Jensen & Roy (2008) argue that there are two positions in the status hierarchy of auditors: the Big Four (the high-status group) and all other audit firms.

Hypotheses and Findings

The most straightforward hypothesis is that both reputation and status have independent, additive effects on the performance outcome. Bowman and Bastedo make such a hypothesis, specifically that reputation and status will have independent, positive effects on the ability of colleges to attract high-quality students, as measured by the average SAT scores of those admitted.

The results of their empirical analyses show that the status effect—that is, being on the front page of the rankings—on the quality of students admitted is considerably higher than that of moving up or down the rankings on the front page. The authors speculate that the elite, front page group of colleges acts as a short list for potential high-quality applicants, who then narrow down their choice from among that group. This is an interesting result, as it suggests not only independent effects of reputation and status, but that decision-makers use reputation and status in different ways. It is tempting to speculate that status, which might well often be more easily observed by decision-makers than reputation, is used as a way of narrowing down the options that will then be subjected to a more thorough analysis.

A similar process is posited by Jensen & Roy (2008) in their analysis of the choice of audit firms made by ex-clients of Arthur Andersen in the aftermath of that firm's demise in 2002. They argue that firms first decide which status bracket they want to select an auditor from: a firm in the Big Four or a firm outside that elite group. So, status is the main factor in the first stage of decision-making. Subsequently, reputation becomes more important as firms narrow down their choices to specific auditors within their chosen status bracket. As the authors put it, "… auditors' reputations for industry expertise and business integrity affected exactly which high-status auditors firms used" (Jensen & Roy, 2008: 512).

Washington and Zajac (2005) also hypothesize independent, additive effects. Results show support for the authors' hypotheses. Despite explicit denials on the part of NCAA officials, they find clear evidence that "historically high-status entities continued to enjoy the privileges of such a status" (Washington & Zajak, 2005: 293). In addition, a team's record of playing against high-status opponents during the regular season increased the probability of a tournament invitation independently of that team's actual results against these high-status teams. Similarly, playing against many low-status teams reduces a team's chances of an invitation, regardless of results.

Stern, Dukerich, & Zajac's (2010) hypotheses are more complex. They do begin by predicting independent, additive effects of reputation and status on the likelihood of a start-up being selected at an early stage by an incumbent firm as an alliance partner. However, an interesting additional component of their argument is that when reputational and status signals are congruent with each other, there should be an additional effect. The two different signals act to confirm each other, meaning the credibility of each signal is enhanced by corroborating evidence. Therefore, there should be an interaction effect of reputation and status in addition to their main effects. The outcome variable in the study is the stage in the commercialization process at which an alliance occurs.

The results of the analysis are supportive of the authors' hypotheses. Main effects of status and reputation are in the expected direction and are statistically significant. The amplifying effect of congruent reputation and status is also shown to be significant. Interestingly, when both reputation and status are low, the negative amplification is stronger than the positive amplification enjoyed by firms with high reputation and status. Firms in the former situation find it particularly difficult to find alliance partners early in the commercialization process.

The hypotheses of Dimov, Shepherd, & Sutcliffe (2006) are again less straightforward, as they are less concerned with the effects of status on performance than on how they mediate a VC firm's decision-making process. The authors argue that VC firms with a high level of finance expertise among their management team will tend to avoid early stage investments. This is confirmed by their results. However, this association is mediated by reputation and status effects. The effect is reduced in firms with a strong reputation, but strengthened when a firm is high in status. The latter effect is due, the authors argue, to the reluctance of high-status firms to jeopardize that status with high-risk investments.

In conclusion, we can see that the limited number of studies that have attempted to identify independent effects of reputation and status on important organizational outcomes do indeed find evidence of their existence. This supports our contention that there is a good reason to be aware of the difference between these two concepts.

FUTURE RESEARCH

The foregoing discussion shows that there have been very few studies that have investigated reputation and status effects together. There is therefore considerable scope for useful research in this area in the future. Bitektine (2011) provides a useful discussion of possible future research in this area; I build on his discussion in this section.

One clear gap in the literature is a lack of understanding of what one might call the microfoundations of reputation and status. That is, researchers typically make assumptions about how decision-makers will be influenced by possible indicators of reputation and/or status, search of evidence of an association between these indicators and a measure of organizational performance, and, if they find such an association, conclude that the mechanism linking them is via their effect on reputation and status judgments of individual decision-makers. However, it would be possible to make the formation of reputation and status judgments itself the object of empirical investigation. We know comparatively little about how attitudinal judgments about organizations are created, reinforced, or changed. Such studies would require quite a different sort of research design to those typically used in the field, with individual decision-makers being the units of analysis rather than firms. As such, it is likely that methods such as surveys and experiments would need to be employed in order to explore these issues. Specific questions that might be addressed include: what is the impact of different kinds of information and different sources of information on reputation and status judgments; what makes some kinds of information salient while other information has little impact; are the effects on judgments short-lived or enduring; and does having a high status protect firms against damage to their reputation and vice versa, or are the two factors independent?

At a different level of analysis, future research could move from studies of a single industry or organizational type (colleges, VC firms, and so on) to compare reputation and status effects across industries. Useful insights into the mechanisms by which reputation and status affect organizational outcomes could be gained by investigating whether reputation and status effects are more important in some industries or for some types of organizations than others, or whether there are more general differences in their relative importance. For example, reputations, because they are more specific and because they have to be earned by demonstrating consistent kinds of behavior over an extended period of time, may be more robust than status. Alternatively, as status may be related to symbols and characteristics that are less directly related to behavior, they may be less prone to damage than reputation, or might provide some protection against reputational damage.

Another possibility is that the importance of reputation and status varies over an organization's life cycle. For example, Petkova (Chapter 19, this volume) argues that affiliations with established industry players are an important way in which young, entrepreneurial firms can enhance their reputation (or what we would call their status).

DISCUSSION

In this chapter, we have discussed the relationships between the key organizational concepts of reputation and status. We have seen that status is typically viewed as being essentially hierarchical. Status is determined by association with other high-status organizations or by the possession and display of attributes that are culturally associated with high status. Reputation, on the other hand, is typically determined by previous behavior. High status can have considerable benefits for organizations, benefits that can be additional to those that are associated with a good reputation.

We have accepted that the distinction between reputation and status is not always going to be clear cut; they are closely related concepts and it might well be the case that in some specific situations it is not possible to differentiate between them or to identify independent effects. Some scholars go further than this, and treat the two as synonyms. For example, Burt (2005: 134) uses the term reputation to discuss Podolny's work, even though the latter describes the concept he is interested in as status, which he explicitly distinguishes from reputation.

In fact, the concept of status as we have been defining it in this chapter is close to some authors' definition of reputation. For some authors, reputation is sometimes inferred not from behavior but from characteristics of the firm or the network in which it is embedded. For example, professional service firms' reputations might be based on a list of their blue-chip clients. This type of reputation is in fact what we have been describing as status, and our contention is that it is useful to maintain the distinction. In future it will be important to learn more about the different mechanisms by which decision-makers of different types arrive at evaluations of reputation and status, and the mechanisms by which these evaluations affect their decision-making. We believe that being careful about defining our concepts is crucial to this project.

Key Literature Concerning Status and Reputation

Reference	Key concepts and definitions
Podolny (2005)	Hierarchy; deference; uncertainty; pattern of associations; status important when there is uncertainty about quality, and when reputation does not eliminate that uncertainty.
Washington and Zajac (2005)	Status is "unearned ascription of social rank" and refers to a socially constructed, inter-subjectively agreed-upon and accepted ordering or ranking of individuals, groups, organizations, or activities in a social system.
Dimov et al. (2006)	Status based on the structural position that a firm occupies in its wider network of inter-organizational relationships. It is an "unearned ascription of social rank."
Rindova et al. (2006)	Explain how the media construct firm celebrity by creating a "drama-tized reality" in reporting on industry change and firms' actions. Firms contribute to this process by taking nonconforming actions and proactively seeking to manage impressions about themselves.
Jensen and Roy (2008)	Status (prestige accorded to firms based on their hierarchical positions in a social structure) used to arrive at a "short list" of partners. Reputation (prestige based on past performance) fine tunes the choice.
Bowman and Bastedo (2009)	Status equated with position in published rankings. Particularly important to be in "top tier."
Bothner et al. (2010)	Status is a zero-sum intangible asset possessed by social actors insofar as they are highly regarded by highly regarded others. Signal of quality.
Stern et al. (2010)	Status has symbolic value. Comparison between "signaling value" of reputation and "status value" of status.

REFERENCES

Azjen, I. (1985). "From intentions to actions: A theory of planned behavior." In J. Kuhl & J. Beckman (Eds.), *Action-Control: From Cognition to Behavior*. Heidelberg: Springer, 11–39.

—— (1991). "The theory of planned behavior." *Organizational Management and Human Decision Processes*, 50: 179–211.

Benjamin, B. A. & Podolny, J. M. (1999). "Status, quality, and social order in the California wine industry." *Administrative Science Quarterly*, 44: 563–589.

Benoit-Smullyan, E. (1944). "Status, status types, and status interrelations." *American Sociological Review*, 9: 151–161.

Bitektine, A. (2011). "Toward a theory of social judgments of organizations: The case of legitimacy, reputation, and status." *Academy of Management Review*, 36(1): 151–179.

Bonacich, P. (1987). "Power and centrality: A family of measures." *American Journal of Sociology*, 92: 1170–1182.

Bothner, M. S., Godard, F. C., & Lee, W. (2010). *What is Social Status? Comparisons and Contrasts with Cognate Concepts*. Chicago: University of Chicago.

Bourdieu, P. (1986). *Distinction: A Social Critique of the Judgement of Taste*. London and New York: Routledge and Kegan Paul.

Bowman, N. A. & Bastedo, M. N. (2009). "Getting on the front page: Organizational reputations, status signals and the impact of U.S. news and world report on student decisions." *Research in Higher Education*, 50(5): 415–436.

Brown, B. & Perry, S. (1994). "Removing the financial performance halo from Fortune's 'Most Admired' Companies." *Academy of Management Journal*, 37(5): 1347–1359.

Burt, R. (2005). *Brokerage and Closure*. Oxford: Oxford University Press.

Chok, J. I. & Kennedy, M. T. (2010). "Scientists as signals: Social and human capital in the pricing of life sciences IPOs." University of Southern California. Unpublished manuscript, available at http://www-bcf.usc.edu/~markkenn/papers/ChokKennedy_WP.pdf.

Dimov, D., Shepherd, D., & Sutcliffe, K. (2006). "Requisite expertise, firm reputation, and status in venture capital investment allocation decisions." *Journal of Business Venturing*, 22(4): 481–502.

Hirsch, F. (1977). *Social Limits to Growth*. London: Routledge & Kegan Paul.

Jensen, M. & Roy, A. (2008). "Staging exchange partner choices: When do status and reputation matter?" *Academy of Management Journal*, 51: 495–516.

Merton, R. K. (1968). "The Matthew effect in science." *Science*, 159: 56–63.

Podolny, J. M. (2005). *Status Signals: A Sociological Study of Market Competition*. Princeton, NJ: Princeton University Press.

Rindova, V. P., Williamson, I. O., Petkova, A. P., & Sever, J. M. (2005). "Being good or being known: An empirical examination of the dimensions, antecedents, and consequences of organization reputation." *Academy of Management Journal*, 48(6): 1033–1049.

——, Pollock, T. G., & Hayward, M. L. A. (2006). "Celebrity firms: The social construction of market popularity." *Academy of Management Review*, 31: 50–71.

Spence, M. (1974). *Market Signalling: Informational Transfer in Hiring and Related Screening Processes*. Cambridge, MA: Harvard University Press.

Stern, I., Dukerich, J. M., & Zajak, E. (2010). *Unmixed Signals: How Reputation and Status Affect Alliance Formation*. Working paper, Kellogg School of Management.

Stevens, M. (1991). *The Big Six: The Selling Out of America's Top Accounting Firms*. New York: Simon & Schuster.

Turner, B. S. (1988). *Status*. Minneapolis: University of Minnesota Press.

Uzzi, B. (1996). "The sources and consequences of embeddedness for the economic performance of organizations: The network effect." *American Sociological Review*, 61: 674–698.

Washington, M. & Zajac, E. J. (2005). "Status evolution and competition: Theory and evidence." *Academy of Management Journal*, 48(2): 282–296.

Weber, M. (1956). *Economy and Society*. Berkeley, CA: University of California Press.

CHAPTER 9

AN IDENTITY-BASED VIEW OF REPUTATION, IMAGE, AND LEGITIMACY: CLARIFICATIONS AND DISTINCTIONS AMONG RELATED CONSTRUCTS

PETER O. FOREMAN
DAVID A. WHETTEN
ALISON MACKEY

Recognizing the conceptual confusion surrounding the reputation construct, this chapter seeks to clarify the distinctions between reputation, image, and legitimacy. We employ a social actor view of organizational identity as a foundational construct and develop a framework around the notion of "reputation for something with someone." Our organizational identity-based framework allows us to highlight the different types and sources of stakeholder expectations ("for something") as well as the factors affecting stakeholder perceptions ("with someone"), which provides a means of distinguishing reputation from its related constructs. Our framework and the conceptual distinctions it affords suggest several potentially significant implications for future research on reputation.

THE notion of reputation, as a reading of the various chapters in this volume would demonstrate, can be defined and operationalized in a variety of ways. Moreover, there is significant confusion around the reputation construct, as well as between it and related constructs—particularly identity, image, and legitimacy. As noted in prior reviews, reputation shares common conceptual ground with these other constructs, and organizational scholarship has frequently blurred the distinctions between them (Brown et al., 2006; Cornelissen, Haslam, & Balmer, 2007; Deephouse & Suchman, 2008; Pratt & Foreman, 2000b; Price, Gioia, & Corley, 2008). Some scholars have engaged in focused attempts at clarifying the similarities and differences between reputation and related concepts: for example, legitimacy (Deephouse & Carter, 2005), identity and image (Whetten & Mackey, 2002), identity and legitimacy (King & Whetten, 2008), and legitimacy and status (Bitektine, 2011). This chapter aims to draw on these and other works to provide a coherent and integrative framework of this conceptual terrain, as a means of sharpening the boundaries of reputation's distinctive domain.

One way to sort out differences and similarities among related constructs is to examine them from the perspective of a related, arguably more fundamental, construct. Following the lead of Whetten & Mackey (2002) and King & Whetten (2008), we have elected to use *organizational identity* in this capacity—that is, seeing identity as underlying or foundational to the other concepts. We believe this to be a propitious vantage point because it is consistent with the "functional" nature of reputation. As recent reviews have pointed out, reputation is a multidimensional construct, serving several key functions for the organization (Lange, Lee, & Dai, 2010; Love & Kraatz, 2009; Rindova et al, 2005). First, reputation acts as a signaling device. Built on stakeholders' aggregate assessments of the organization's past actions, it provides a means of predicting present and future behavior (Clark & Montgomery, 1998; Weigelt & Camerer, 1988). Given this key function, the most reliable predictor of an organization's conduct, arguably, is its identity. Taken as the self-defining elements of the organization, identity can be seen as the progenitor of reputation—an organization generally acts in ways that are consistent with its "self-view." Another key function of reputation is that it serves as a means of recognition and representation. Reflecting the "collective knowledge" that stakeholders have of the organization's character and activities, reputation is symbolic—providing external entities with an efficient mechanism for identifying and categorizing the organization (Martins, 2005; Navis & Glynn, 2010; Rao, 1994). In this sense, reputation is an external manifestation of identity—that is, a reflection of "who" the organization is.

In addition to its consistency with the functional properties of reputation, the identity construct has functional utility in and of itself. As the following discussion will show, identity is a parsimonious way to distinguish reputation from image and legitimacy. Several scholars have linked identity to image (Dutton & Dukerich, 1991; Elsbach & Kramer, 1996; Hatch & Schultz, 2002), reputation (Dukerich & Carter, 2000; Fombrun, 1996; Martins, 2005), and legitimacy (Hsu & Hannan, 2005; Kraatz & Block, 2008; Zuckerman, 1999). In fact, all three of these constructs are the products of social comparison processes that incorporate outsiders' perceptions of the identity of the organization. Thus, identity provides us with a common theoretical vocabulary and conceptual framework for the task. Furthermore, identity is a multilevel construct, having currency in theories of individual, organizational, and institutional behavior. This ability to travel across and connect levels proves to be especially useful in discussing concepts like reputation, which inherently incorporate multiple levels of analysis.

It is important to note that we presume a social actor view of organizational identity, and hence of image, reputation, and legitimacy (Whetten, 2006; King, Felin, & Whetten, 2010). That is, the empirical referent for all of these concepts is a particular organization—a distinct, recognizable entity, with agentic properties like other types of social actors (individuals, states). As King, Felin, & Whetten (2010) articulate, a view of "organizations as social actors" assumes that other actors view the organization as capable of taking action, and that such action is seen as fully intentional (i.e. deliberate and self-directed). An important corollary is that other social actors hold the organization accountable for its actions. This perspective of organizations is particularly salient to the concept of reputation—a social assessment of an organization's behavior.

We begin by providing a brief survey of the conceptual landscape, starting with our framing perspective: organizational identity. Our intention is not to provide a comprehensive review of the literature.[1] Rather, we focus on discussing each of the constructs in terms of, or with respect to, organizational identity—as a means of establishing a common foundation for explicating the similarities and differences between them. With this conceptual underpinning in place, we then provide a theoretical framework for clarifying the relationships between image, reputation, and legitimacy.

A CONCEPTUAL OVERVIEW

Organizational Identity

To lay the groundwork for our model, we discuss the identity construct and note certain key properties. Organizational identity consists of the self-definitional beliefs of members regarding the character or essence of the organization. It is most commonly manifested in the form of descriptive statements about "who or what we are." An organization's identity reflects *central* and *enduring* characteristics that establish its *distinctiveness* as a social entity (Albert & Whetten, 1985). By central, we mean that identity is concerned with those things that are core rather than peripheral. By enduring, we mean that identity is focused on those core elements that endure over time, rather than those that are ephemeral. By distinctive, we mean that identity consists of a set of core features and characteristics that stake out how the organization is both similar to and different from others. This corporate "self-view" facilitates several critical organizational functions, including interpreting the environment, identifying objectives, developing strategies, and acquiring resources (Dutton & Dukerich, 1991; Elsbach & Kramer, 1996; Foreman & Whetten, 2002; Gioia & Thomas, 1996; Whetten, 2006).

These central, enduring, and distinctive (CED) properties of identity are key to our subsequent model and argument. It is the CED nature of identity that makes it fundamental to understanding the character of an organization. Identity serves as the shared cognitive framework (Weick, 1995) for what the organization does, how it is structured, and how it interacts with its environment. As such, an organization's

---

[1] Given the intent of this chapter, and recognizing the wealth of work done by others in reviewing these concepts, we provide only a digested overview, with merely representative citations. Where appropriate, we note more exhaustive reviews containing more extensive references to extant work.

reputation would logically be a reflection of its identity. Furthermore, the property of distinctiveness—and its inherent similarity–difference duality—is particularly critical in our explication of the distinctions between constructs. Reflecting the twin needs for assimilation and individuation, the expression of this similarity–difference tension varies greatly across the related constructs.

Organizational identity has its roots in individual-level theories of identity, and as such embodies elements of social identity theory (SIT) and role identity theory (RIT), which we discuss in turn. Social identity theory postulates that the self is defined in part by the social groups that one affiliates with—and the expectations accompanying those affiliations (Tajfel, 1978; Turner, 1982). From an SIT perspective, an organization's identity is derived from the collectives or categories it is associated with. It is from a cultural-specific menu of social categories that founders construct a fledgling organization's shared identity (Foreman & Parent, 2008; Whetten, 2006). This "social" identity follows from the organization's similarity with others in the same group/category and highlights distinctions between groups—that is, denoting "who" and "what" the organization is and is not.

In addition, an organization's identity must denote how the organization distinguishes itself positively from like others within its group. Once a shared identity has been recognized and accepted by external stakeholders, the organization then seeks to create distance between its identity and the identity of the group or category (King & Whetten, 2008; Navis & Glynn, 2010). Extrapolating further from SIT, an organization seeks to position itself in a subjective "middle ground," offering an optimal level of distinctiveness (Brewer, 1991; Deephouse, 1999). That is to say, its identity would embody both shared elements, with the resulting degree of similarity to other organizations providing recognition and acceptance, and distinguishing elements, with the consequential degree of uniqueness providing individuation and competitive distinction.

Complementing SIT, role identity theory argues that an individual's self-view consists of a number of roles—structurally determined patterns of behavior in a given social setting (McCall & Simmons, 1978; Stryker, 1987); and thus an actor embodies multiple identities that match the various roles it plays. These role identities provide stability and predictability as the social actor interacts with others. Recently, scholars have begun theorizing about organizational-level analogs of such roles (Jensen, Kim, and Kim, Chapter 7, this volume; Pratt & Kraatz, 2009; Zuckerman, 1999). Similar to how role identities shape the individual self, an organization's identity is defined, at least in part, by the structural–functional requirements associated with the operational roles or tasks that it performs (Foreman & Parent, 2008; Zuckerman et al., 2003). To the degree that the organization's mission may have several distinct facets, or that the organization must interact with an array of diverse stakeholders, its identity will reflect these different role-related expectations about "who we are" and "what we do" (Foreman & Whetten, 2002; Glynn, 2000; Pratt & Foreman, 2000a; Scott & Lane, 2000).

Absent the kind of physical or inherited attributes (e.g., gender, ethnicity) that are identity-defining social categories for individuals, it is often difficult to distinguish between the social group and role elements of an organization's identity. While acknowledging this complication, we see two key benefits to including RIT in our application of organizational identity to the study of reputation: compared with social categories, roles tend to carry more specific expectations, and roles imply more clearly a specified self–other relationship, for example teacher–student or parent–child (Hogg, Terry, & White, 1995; Stets & Burke, 2000).

Organizational Image

More than any of the other concepts discussed here, organizational image suffers from extreme definitional plurality. The term "image" refers to an array of distinct (even incompatible) cognitions or cognitive devices. As others have noted (Brown et al., 2006; Cornelissen, Haslam, & Balmer, 2007; Price, Gioia, & Corley, 2008; Whetten & Mackey, 2002), there are three main ways in which the concept has been framed: (1) how insiders want outsiders to see the organization—intended or *projected* image; (2) how outsiders actually view the organization—refracted or *perceived* image; and (3) insiders' perceptions about how outsiders view the organization—construed or *reflected* image.

Scholars conceptualizing image as a *projection* focus on messages sent out from the organization regarding how they want to be viewed externally. These images are often intentional, even strategically crafted, and are typically reflections of the organization's actual identity—a projection or expression of the self-view. Scholars have varyingly framed this as corporate identity, corporate image, desired external image, or desired future identity (Cornelissen, Haslam, & Balmer, 2007; Gioia & Thomas, 1996; Scott & Lane, 2000). It is important to note that this notion of image is most closely related to organizational identity.

Alternatively, researchers employing the notion of image as a *perception* (or collection of perceptions) are concerned with the impressions that outsiders have of the organization. In this sense, image represents the externally perceived self-view, or the other-view. Given that what external audiences perceive about the organization is often filtered through third parties (especially the media), these images are frequently distorted, in a sense "refracted"—not entirely accurate (Dukerich & Carter, 2000; Foreman & Parent, 2008). These stakeholder perceptions of the organization have been labeled as identity impressions, corporate image, intercepted image, and reputation (Dutton & Dukerich, 1991; Hatch & Schultz, 2002; Price, Gioia, & Corley, 2008). More so than the other conceptualizations of image noted here, this external perception-oriented notion is what is most frequently meant by the term "organizational image."

Finally, scholars framing image as a *reflection* or construal concentrate on external stakeholders' mirrored perceptions of the organization—and internal members' interpretations of those external assessments (Dutton, Dukerich, & Harquail, 1994; Hatch & Schultz, 2002; Scott & Lane, 2000). The key issue emphasized here is the degree to which outsiders' perceptions of the organization are consistent with those of internal members (Dutton & Dukerich, 1991; Elsbach & Kramer, 1996).

Legitimacy

The concept of legitimacy in organizational studies dates as far back as the origins of the field in the writings of scholars like Weber, Barnard, Selznick, and Parsons (see Deephouse & Suchman, 2008, and Bitektine, 2011, for comprehensive reviews). The traditional definition of legitimacy has a distinctly moral flavor and is essentially an evaluative judgment—of a person, organization, institution, and so on—based on conformity to social norms or values, as well as compliance with legal requirements. However, more recently legitimacy has been conceptualized in broader and particularly more cognitive terms, especially in neo-institutional theory (Scott, 1995). Subsequent theoretical development has recognized the multidimensional nature of the construct, such that legitimacy is framed as an assessment based on any number and type of criteria—the most common forms being cognitive, moral/normative, rational/pragmatic, and regulative/socio-political (Deephouse & Suchman, 2008).

In what is perhaps the most widely recognized of these conceptual frameworks, Suchman identifies three types of legitimacy: pragmatic (does this benefit me?), moral (is this the right thing to do?), and cognitive (is this how it usually is?). These are similar to Scott's (1995) three "pillars" of institutions and their corresponding bases of legitimacy—regulative, normative, and cognitive, and they parallel Aldrich & Fiol's (1994) socio-political and cognitive forms of the construct. Suchman has proposed a fairly inclusive definition of legitimacy, encompassing these multiple dimensions:

> Legitimacy is the generalized perception or assumption that the actions of an entity are desirable, proper, or appropriate within some socially constructed system of norms, values, beliefs, and definitions. (1995: 574)

Thus, legitimacy is a judgment of the appropriateness of the organization as an example of a social type, form, category, or role. This evaluation of "correctness" is guided by the criteria of fit or similarity—that is, the degree to which an organization's attributes and behaviors are consistent with its pronouncements about "what kind of organization we are." Thus, in identity terms, legitimacy is an evaluative statement about the appropriateness of the organization's CED features, relative to a self-defining set of social requirements. Said another way, legitimacy is an assessment of identity with respect to what is *required*—what every organization of a particular form, or performing a particular role, must do (King & Whetten, 2008; Polos, Hannan, & Carroll, 2002; Zuckerman, 1999).

Reputation

Reputation is similar to legitimacy in that both represent external stakeholders' evaluations of the organization. However, a reputational assessment focuses not on the appropriateness of an organization's characteristics and conduct, but on the effectiveness of its performance—as a predictor of that organization's ability to meet future performance-related expectations. And the frame of reference is not the organization's similarity to type, but rather its uniqueness or difference—that is, the ways in which it distinguishes itself positively from similar others as a specific example of that type (Deephouse & Suchman, 2008; King & Whetten, 2008). In terms of identity, reputation is an evaluative statement about the quality of the organization's nature and behavior—that is, "how well you are doing what you do." It is an assessment of identity with respect to what is desired by external constituents—what the organization ideally should look and behave like (Fombrun, 1996; King & Whetten, 2008; Whetten & Mackey, 2002).

However, as the aforementioned reviews have noted, this assessment of organizational quality and effectiveness can take several forms. The reputation construct has been defined, conceptualized, and operationalized in a variety of manners (Lange, Lee, & Dai, 2011; Love & Kraatz, 2009; Rindova et al., 2005). Interestingly, *Webster's Dictionary* provides two definitions of reputation:

a. overall quality or character as seen or judged by people in general;
b. recognition by other people of some characteristic or ability.

The first definition frames reputation broadly—as an overall assessment of the character of the organization. The second definition frames the construct as something more specific—the perceptions of certain people about certain aspects of the organization. Recent scholarship on reputation has begun to make a similar distinction between general versus specific conceptualizations (e.g. Lange, Lee, & Dai, 2011; Martins, 2005; Rindova et al., 2005): in the words of Rindova et al. (2005), reputation as "collective knowledge and recognition" versus "assessments of relevant attributes." Lange et al. (2011) identify three forms of reputation: a broad sense of "being known" or prominence, a specific evaluation of "being known for something," and an aggregate perception of "generalized favorability."

The general conceptualizations are consistent with the long-standing notion of reputation as a comprehensive and cumulative assessment—external stakeholders' collective perceptions and evaluations of an organization's character and activities over time (Fombrun, 1996). In contrast, the specific view of reputation is reflected in competitive strategy research—as stakeholders' beliefs of expected performance, given their past knowledge of and experience with the organization in a particular arena or series of events (Clark & Montgomery, 1998; Weigelt & Camerer, 1988).

Taken together, these differing conceptualizations of reputation suggest several clarifying questions. What exactly is the content of reputation—what is it that stakeholders are evaluating? What is the focus of the evaluation—are constituents concerned more with similarities or differences? What are the standards or criteria for evaluation—and where did these expectations come from? Where do these assessments reside—who owns the perceptions and evaluations? How widely are they shared—is there room for disagreement among constituents? These and other questions naturally follow as we recognize the lack of clarity in the reputation construct.

These questions also reflect a growing tendency to add qualifiers to the reputation construct, for example, framing it as a *reputation for something with someone* (Lang, Lee,

& Dai, 2011). We take this particular catchphrase as a motif for orienting our conceptual framework (see Figure 9.1). That is, we first seek to clarify the reputation construct by examining the "for something" aspect. We employ a social actor view of identity to discuss the content, focus, and criteria of stakeholders' evaluations, leading to a greater distinction between reputation and *legitimacy*. We then turn our attention to the "with someone" aspect, examining the locus and scope of the evaluation. The resulting model provides a clearer understanding of the interrelationships and distinctions between reputation and *image*.

REPUTATION FOR SOMETHING

We begin our application of identity to the "for something" aspect of reputation by discussing a fundamental property of the reputation construct. While recognizing the conceptual confusion surrounding reputation, there is general agreement that the construct reflects an assessment of the organization—particularly with respect to the degree to which it is fulfilling expectations. That is, reputation is essentially an evaluation of some aspect(s) of the organization by some stakeholder(s), consisting of comparisons of perceptions and expectations (see Figure 9.1). Importantly, this comparative and evaluative nature of the reputation construct sets it apart from identity as purely a declarative statement.

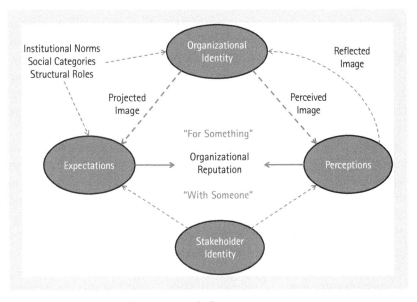

FIGURE 9.1 Organizational identity, image, & reputation.

Given this recognition of reputation as a judgment, we then ask—of what? What is it that is being evaluated, what is the focus of that evaluation, and what are the evaluation criteria? These questions come down to the issue of expectations—what is expected of a given social actor and why. The content and source of expectations are complex and problematic in the organizational studies literature. Scholars have posited several bases of social actor expectations, including (but not limited to) role standards, group norms, and institutionalized structures and routines (Bitektine, 2011; Deephouse & Carter, 2005; Hsu & Hannan, 2002; King & Whetten, 2008; Love & Kraatz, 2009; Rao, 1994; Zuckerman, 1999). Conveniently, these can be discussed and understood in terms of identity theory.

As noted above, organizational identities are fashioned from self-selected, self-defining sets of social roles, categories, and forms. That is, an organization seeks to establish an identity by and through its association with a particular set of functional roles, its placement in certain groups or categories, and its adoption of a given institutionalized form (see Figure 9.1). These identities embody specific standards in the form of attributes and behaviors, serving as a shared set of social expectations for organizational decision-makers and relevant audiences (Czarniawska & Wolff, 1998; Polos, Hannan, & Carroll, 2002). Organizations encounter serious difficulties in changing categories and standards (Rao, Monin, & Durnad, 2003) and meet sanctions for violating these standards (Hsu & Hannan, 2005; Zuckerman, 1999). Moreover, many organizations face the challenge of managing multiple identity-related expectations, stemming from the variety of functional roles they perform (Pratt & Foreman, 2000a; Zuckerman et al., 2003), their associations with different groups of organizations (Navis & Glynn, 2010; Zuckerman, 2000), and their instantiations of one or more organizational forms (Foreman & Whetten, 2002; Kraatz & Block, 2008).

Of course, these three bases of identity and sources of expectations are somewhat overlapping and interrelated. For example, Goldman Sachs' identity is a function of its legal structure (as a specific instance of an investment banking entity), its elite categorization (as one of the five largest investment banks), and its role in financing public offerings (a core function of major investment banks). And yet, as we alluded to earlier, an organization's role set carries with it a somewhat more specific series of implications for its identity than its group affiliations or archetypal forms. As scholars comparing SIT and RIT have acknowledged (Hogg, Terry, & White, 1995; Stets & Burke, 2000), role identities draw attention to the individual's behavior within a given social context, while social identities highlight intergroup relations and group processes. Additionally, while social identities emphasize the similarity or uniformity of perception and action within the group, role identities point to the uniqueness inherent in an actor's particular role set and their relationship to other actors in the group. Thus, a role-identity perspective underscores the function that audiences, their interactions with the organization, and their specific expectations for an organization's behavior, have in shaping social judgments like legitimacy and reputation.

Legitimacy and Reputation

As the prior discussion suggests, legitimacy and reputation share important similarities and yet have distinct differences. In that legitimacy constitutes an external stakeholder evaluation of the organization based on certain identity-related expectations, it is similar to reputation. But that is largely where the resemblance ends. As noted in recent reviews, while legitimacy is an up or down evaluation of conformity with established norms or standards, reputation is an assessment of relative standing vis-à-vis other organizations (Bitektine, 2011; Deephouse & Carter, 2005; Deephouse & Suchman, 2008; King & Whetten, 2008). Legitimacy represents a judgment regarding the *appropriateness* of an organization, or, more precisely, of it as an example of an organizational form, social category, or type of role. External observers are evaluating the organization through a lens of similarity and isomorphism. Does the organization meet the identity requirements associated with its kind (King & Whetten, 2008; Rao, Monin, & Durand, 2005; Zuckerman, 1999)?

Reputation, on the other hand, reflects an assessment of the *effectiveness* of the organization. The focus is on the organization's identity attributes that distinguish it from its rivals. Moreover, inherent to this assessment is an emphasis on the organization's conduct. Outsiders are evaluating the organization in comparison with the ideal—or how constituents would ideally like to see a particular type of organization behave (Whetten & Mackey, 2002). As such, a firm's past performance, taken as a signal of its capabilities and effectiveness, is more relevant to its reputation than to its legitimacy (Deephouse & Carter, 2005).

Thus, we are arguing that, while organizations face expectations that have a variety of identity-related origins, these expectations are not necessarily equivalent in their nature and consequences. Specifically, certain identity-based expectations reflect essential requirements upon which the survival of the organization depends. For example, if a particular local bank is no longer insured by the Federal Deposit Insurance Corporation (FDIC) or stops abiding by the Fair Lending Act, it loses its right to exist. These identity requirements are invariant and non-negotiable. Such violations of the institutional identity codes result in a loss of legitimacy and perhaps even the death of the organization (Hsu & Hannan, 2005). Furthermore, that bank's legitimacy will be challenged if it attempts to position itself in a distinctly different social category, say as a social service agency, with conflicting identity-related norms (Rao, Monin, & Durand, 2005; Zuckerman, 2000), or if it is viewed by some of its key stakeholders as failing to perform a core role-related activity, like making loans (Pratt & Kraatz, 2009; Zuckerman, 1999). In sum, organizations must fulfill the minimum identity-related requirements if they are to be deemed legitimate.

On the other hand, that same bank may choose to modify or adapt its business model or activities in ways that do not violate, contradict, or compromise its identity standards—as a means of positively distinguishing itself from other banks and thereby enhancing its reputation. For example, that bank may choose to position itself in one or more related industry categories or subcategories—for example "regional," "privately owned," "savings-and-loan"—as a way of differentiating themselves (Foreman & Parent, 2008; Zuckerman et al., 2003). Similarly, that bank may change how it prioritizes and performs some of its key roles, or even modify the makeup of its role-set altogether— like emphasizing certain types of lending or expanding into other financial services—so as to mark out new territory and distance itself from competition (Gioia & Thomas, 1996; Pratt & Foreman, 2000a).

Such shifts in an organization's distinctive set of roles or social categories carry with them potentially significant changes in identity-related standards, with somewhat different stakeholders holding different expectations. However, to the degree that these kinds of identity modifications do not result in contradictory or incompatible category-related norms or conflicting role requirements, that there is "identity synergy" among them (Pratt & Foreman, 2000a), they are a potentially effective means of improving that bank's distinctive competitive position. In sum, we want to draw attention to the difference between an organization complying with the fundamental shared identity requirements inherent to its form, category, or role, and actions that seek to distinguish the organization's identity within its given type.

REPUTATION WITH SOMEONE

We now turn our attention to applying identity to the "with someone" aspect of reputation. Given the stakeholder-situated nature of the reputation construct, it is logical to consider issues related to its locus. Where does reputation reside—in what stakeholders and why? Who is doing the evaluating and what is the scope of the assessment? Here the concept of identity—and its role as a sense-making device in these stakeholders—is particularly relevant. At this point we introduce individual-level identities into our model (see Figure 9.1).

We have noted the role of perceptions and expectations in reputation assessments. Research on identity would argue that both of these organizationally related cognitions are significantly influenced by an individual's own identities. We begin with the issue of expectations. Social identity theory recognizes that a person's identification with their organization is driven by an evaluation of the relative consistency between the individual's identity and the identity of the organization (Dutton, Dukerich, & Harquail, 1994; Pratt, 1998). Foreman & Whetten (2002) built on this logic and argued that an individual's identity would be expressed in their preferences for the ideal identity of their organization—that is, its "expected identity"; thus identification could be conceptualized as the congruence between a member's perceptions of, and expectations for, their organization's identity. The study's findings demonstrated that identity congruence operated at two levels, significantly affecting both commitment to the organization and legitimacy of the organizational form. Other research has shown similar connections between the identities of different social groups and the particular expectations those groups have of the organization (e.g., Glynn, 2000). Therefore, we argue, a stakeholder's expectations are influenced by their identity.

The effect of individual identity on perceptions of the organization is the second part of our argument. Theory and research on the self has argued that the self-view fundamentally shapes how an individual perceives and interprets their environment (Baumeister, 1998; Gecas, 1982; Mead, 1934). Given that the construct of identity is an expression of the self, it is reasonable to expect that identity would influence perceptions. Moreover, the same body of research on the self recognizes that individuals have "multiple selves"—a reflection of the varied roles, relationships, and responsibilities that are the reality of any person's life. Thus, perceptions of an organization may vary both between individuals (due to differences in their role-sets and social groups) and within a person (as a function of the multiple facets of their own identity) (Hogg, Terry, & White, 1995; Stets & Burke, 2000). In sum, we are arguing that individual identity has significant effects on how organizations are perceived and interpreted.

The impact of identity on both perceptions and expectations of organizations is perhaps clearest in terms of attention—what aspects of the social environment are most salient and important to the individual. As noted, the RIT view of the self focuses on an individual's set of role-related identities—which are arranged in a salience hierarchy (McCall & Simmons, 1978; Stryker, 1987). The SIT view of the self emphasizes an individual's affiliations with various social groups or categories (Tajfel, 1978; Turner, 1982). Both RIT and SIT are similar in that the structure of the social context evokes a particular role or group and thus a particular aspect of an individual's self-view. Such variation in activated identities would have consequences for both perceptions and expectations of the organization. How stakeholders view the organization, and what they expect from it, is shaped by their identity—that particular aspect of their self-view that is salient in a given situation. Therefore, reputation, as an evaluation based on a comparison of perceptions and expectations, is influenced by individual identity.

It is important to note that the effects of individual-level identities on reputation are in addition to or in conjunction with those of organizational identity. Given our argument regarding the dominant role that organizational identity plays in delineating expectations, the effect of individual-level identity is less significant (thus bolder lines for the effects of organizational identity in Figure 9.1). That is, the organization's institutional form, its social groups and categorizations, and the set of functional roles it assumes, combine to determine the essence of stakeholder expectations. Individual-level identities then act primarily as a driver of salience—making certain aspects of the organizationally determined expectations more contextually relevant and important than others to certain stakeholders.

Image and Reputation

This introduction of individual-level identities and their role in stakeholders' perceptions and expectations of the organization allows us to make a distinction between image and reputation. As noted, there is considerable confusion and lack of clarity in the literature on the concept of organizational image. Scholars have framed this in a variety of ways with a corresponding array of terms: desired, intended, projected, perceived, reflected, construed, and so on (see Brown et al., 2006; Price, Gioia, & Corley, 2008; Whetten & Mackey, 2002). We focus here on what we will refer to as projected (or intended) and perceived image.

To summarize our discussion above, projected image consists of the symbols and messages sent by an organization to external stakeholders as indicators of its identity, and perceived image consists of the impressions that those stakeholders then form of the organization. To the degree that these perceptions are then publically expressed by stakeholders, they take the form of reflected images—outsiders' impressions that are mirrored back to the organization. As such, it becomes difficult to make a distinction between "perceived" and "reflected" images, and our subsequent discussion treats the two as essentially equivalent, referred to hereafter as perceived image.[2]

Reputation has often been defined or employed in a similar manner to perceived image, and therefore the two constructs are often confused with one another or simply seen as coequal terms (Brown et al., 2006; Whetten & Mackey, 2002). However, our framework provides a means of distinguishing between the two, as well as clarifying the relationship between these concepts and projected image. Recall that reputation is a comparative and evaluative construct. That is, more than just how external constituents "see" the organization, reputation consists of stakeholders' assessments of the organization, based on comparisons of their perceptions and expectations of that organization.

In contrast to reputation, the concept of perceived image captures a given external constituent's observations and impressions of the organization—thus closely related to the "perceptions" part of reputation. Given that they are situated in and particular to the individual external observer, there may be significant variance in perceived/reflected images. Projected image, meanwhile, is an externally directed indication of the organization's desired or intended identity. This form of image represents an internally generated message, uniform or consistent across the organization, designed to inform outsiders of how the organization wishes to be defined. These desired definitions include descriptive statements about the organization's roles and categorizations—emphasizing points of differentiation or distinctiveness. As such, they signal to stakeholders certain organization-preferred "expectations." Said another way, projected image is "how we want external constituents to see us and what we want them to expect from us"; while perceived image is then "how outsiders actually see us" (cf. Brown et al., 2006; Hatch & Schultz, 2002; Pratt & Foreman, 2000b; Price, Gioia, & Corley, 2008).

---

[2] Construed image, or insiders' beliefs about how external constituents view the organization, is an altogether different construct, involving the views of both insiders and outsiders (Brown et al., 2006; Price, Gioia, & Corley, 2008). Because this form of image is less likely to be confused with reputation, we do not include it in our framework.

CONTRIBUTIONS AND IMPLICATIONS

Our objective for this chapter was to provide an identity-grounded conceptual framework and rhetoric, through which reputation scholars can systematically consider similarities and differences among reputation, image, and legitimacy. Structured around the theme of "reputation for something with someone," we discuss several key contributions and implications of this framework for reputation scholarship.

Contributions to Theory and Methods

To begin with, the social actor view of organizational identity provides a conceptual framework for the distinction between "being known" and "being known for something" recently emphasized in the reputation literature (Love & Kraatz, 2009; Lange, Lee, & Dai, 2011; Rindova et al., 2005). More specifically, with regard to the "for something" aspect of reputation, we see three significant benefits to using identity as a common frame of reference. First, it explicitly situates relevant perceptions and evaluations of an organization in attributes that are central, enduring, and distinctive (CED)—as opposed to those features that are peripheral or ephemeral. By extension, these CED features thus constitute a common foundation and rhetorical reference point for related perceptions and assessments of the organization's character. That is, the CED properties of identity allow us to discriminate between reputation and legitimacy and provide a way of viewing the interrelationships among a set of highly related constructs: projected image, perceived image, reflected image, and reputation. Importantly, this social actor perspective of organizational identity affords a way to bring legitimacy and reputation together in the same conversation without confusing the two.

A second benefit of using the proposed framework is that a social actor view assumes agentic intentional action—and accountability for such action. Such a perspective of organizations is consistent with the notion of reputation as being "for something." If stakeholders are to monitor an organization's behavior and make judgments accordingly, it stands to reason that the organization must be seen as a social actor. A third and related benefit of our framework is that it focuses attention on two sets of organizational expectations, or evaluation criteria, core to the concept of identity: between-group categorical membership requirements (legitimacy) and within-group individuating strategies (reputation). An obvious benefit of this distinction is that it helps center conceptualizations of legitimacy and reputation within corresponding empirical referents—group norms versus specific ideals.

The "with someone" component of reputation draws attention to the varied sources of these expectations and by extension highlights the challenges that organizations face in responding to conflicting expectations (Glynn, 2000; Kraatz & Block, 2008;

Zuckerman et al., 2003). We used the multilevel property of identity to link the organization with the individual within the reputation construct. This draws attention to the role of individual perceptions and expectations in reputational assessments—and thereby emphasizes the issue of stakeholder differences. This line of inquiry offers a promising link between reputation scholarship and stakeholder theory (Foreman & Parent, 2008; Scott & Lane, 2000). In particular, recent work has proposed frameworks for analyzing which stakeholders' expectations are more consequential than others (Mitchell, Agle, & Wood, 1997; Rhee & Valdez, 2009). This vein of work opens the door to a stakeholder-focused approach to reputation scholarship, studying, for example, how and why some groups have greater impact on an organization's reputation than others. Such investigations might examine the types or sources of external influences that are most significant, including the component of an organization's reputation that is impacted, the legitimacy of the stakeholders, and the nature of their relationship(s) to the organization.

The framework proposed here also informs the literature with respect to how organizational reputation is measured. As noted, a social actor perspective is more congruent with the "specific" (being known for something) than the "broad" (being known) approaches to organizational reputation. By extension, it is important for reputation scholarship to specify the focal organization's relevant comparators—roles, groups, categories, or forms—as the basis for stakeholder expectations. Researchers need thus to recognize that measures of reputation are specific to a referent group—for example "compassionate" is a critical quality for a hospital but not for a bank. It is equally important to document how measures of reputation constitute generally accepted ideals, as opposed to requirements, for organizations. For example, while "courtesy" and "helpfulness" are ideal characteristics for a bank, they are not fundamental requirements like "financial solvency" and "fiduciary trust."

Implications and Directions for Future Research

The social actor view of organizational identity taken in this chapter has several implications for future research on reputation. To begin with, work is needed to examine how specific organizational decisions impact reputation and legitimacy. Here we have in mind two kinds of actions taken to achieve competitive distinction: differentiation within a social category (Czarniawska & Wolff, 1998; Foreman & Parent, 2008), and shifting from one social category to another (Navis & Glynn, 2010; Rao, Monin, & Durand, 2005). While theories of competitive advantage recognize the value of organizations creating within-group distinctions, less is known about the upper limits of distinctiveness—might too much differentiation threaten legitimacy (Rao, Monin, & Durand, 2003; Zuckerman et al., 2003)? Furthermore, the potential loss of legitimacy is an obvious deterrent to organizations switching social categories or spanning multiple categories (Foreman & Parent, 2008; Kraatz & Block, 2008). But what of the consequences of this type of action on organizational reputation, as stakeholders hold on to old category-specific ideals while learning how to apply new ones (Corley & Gioia, 2004; Navis & Glynn, 2010; Rao, Monin, & Durand, 2003)? It would be instructive to explore whether and how different causes or types of identity-category switches impact organizational reputation differently.

The issue of multiplicity of organizational identity, and the corresponding dynamics within reputation, suggests the opportunity of studying reputation among identity hybrids (Albert & Whetten, 1985)—organizations that belong to multiple categories or forms, the characteristics of which are generally deemed to be incompatible (e.g., what it means to be a family versus a business). The obvious difficulty hybrids face is satisfying the conflicting legitimacy requirements associated with two equally important types (Foreman & Whetten, 2002; Kraatz & Block, 2008). However, among "surviving hybrids" a possibly more pressing task is establishing and maintaining a strong "hybrid reputation" (Pratt & Foreman, 2000a). Given that some research indicates that multifaceted identities often enhance legitimacy across multiple stakeholders (e.g., Zimmerman, et al., 2003), and yet other research suggests that identity plurality may lead to skepticism and rejection (e.g. Glynn, 2000), the reputations of identity hybrids likely face significant challenges. Understanding the conditions under which hybrid reputations are positively or negatively impacted would shed new light on an important, understudied challenge of this organizational form, while enhancing our understanding of reputation.

In addition, our explication of the sources of stakeholders' expectations implies that future work examine the ways in which these sources interact. Consistent with institutional theory, we suggest that the identity standards related to an organization's form are often primary in importance for legitimacy. But how then do the role and social group sources of expectations interact with the institutional when making assessments of legitimacy? What happens when there is conflict? And with respect to reputation, how do stakeholders sort and prioritize different expectations? Are some types of expectations more prominent in their minds? In the end, further research is needed to examine whether, when, and why certain types and/or sources of expectations may be more influential than others.

Finally, our identity-based framework has implications for the notion of reputation management. It is common for scholarship to suggest that organizations can and should manage their image and/or reputation (Dukerich & Carter, 2000; Elsbach, 2003; Gioia & Thomas, 1996; Rhee & Valdez, 2009). The framework set forth herein raises three fundamental concerns regarding this. At a minimum, the "for something, with someone" view of reputation makes reputation management an extremely complex and uncertain undertaking. Not only is reputation a logical property of "specific some ones" and not the organization, but actions taken to manipulate "particular some things" might be appealing to one group but appalling to another. Moreover, when reputation-management initiatives are decoupled from considerations of identity, they are likely to be short-lived and/or ill-fated (Dutton & Dukerich, 1991; Foreman & Parent, 2008; Whetten & Mackey, 2002).

In addition, organizational leaders need to understand the identity-relevant ideals that external audiences are using to evaluate the organization and seek to eliminate gaps between leaders' and evaluators' views of prevailing social norms, roles, and categories. While studies have examined how discrepancies between internal and external views of the organization result in actions to reduce such incongruence (e.g. Elsbach & Kramer, 1996; Martins, 2005), there is an implicit assumption that both parties have a similar understanding of expectations. This chapter problematizes such assumptions and draws attention to the need to ensure that organizational leaders fully understand the nature and sources of stakeholders' expectations.

Third, our framework suggests that a firm seeking to enhance their reputation would be better served by clarifying or changing constituents' expectations, rather than worrying about inaccuracies in their perceptions (cf. Dukerich & Carter, 2000; Elsbach, 2003; Rhee & Valdez, 2009). As we have argued, expectations largely follow from the self-identifying choices a firm makes—that is, what forms to adopt, what groups to affiliate with, and what roles to take on. As a result, organizations have a significant degree of control over stakeholder expectations. In contrast, stakeholder perceptions are shaped by a range of factors beyond the reach of organizational influence—for example differences in salience and relevance inherent to the unique set of an individual's roles and social groups. As such, managing reputation may, paradoxically, be more of an internal issue than an external one.

Core Research on Identity, Image, Reputation, and Legitimacy

Reference	Relevant Arguments and/or Findings
Albert & Whetten (1985)	Foundational article delineating the organizational identity construct as that which is central, distinctive, and enduring about an organization. Introduces concept of hybrid identity organizations (e.g. family–business; church–university).
Dutton & Dukerich (1991)	Finds that organization image and identity guide and activate individuals' interpretations of organizational issues/motivations for action. Develops conceptual interaction between organizational identity and image (impression management) to explain how organization and its environment interrelate over time.
Scott & Lane (2000)	Model of organizational identity as emerging from complex, dynamic, and reciprocal interactions among internal and external stakeholders. Organizational identity conceptualized as negotiated images, embedded within different systems of organizational membership and meaning, shaped by stakeholders' reflected images through an iterative process between managers and stakeholders.
Elsbach & Kramer (1996)	Examines how members respond to external events that challenge defining characteristics of their organization and threaten the organization's identity. Findings demonstrate identity management activities in response to identity threats—specifically, emphasizing membership in selective categories that highlighted favorable identity dimensions and inter-organizational comparisons.
Whetten & Mackey (2002)	Conception of organizational identity that is unique to identity and uniquely organizational—the "social actor" view. Conceptual domains of organizational identity, image, and reputation are defined with identity-congruent definitions of image and reputation.
Rao (1994)	Defines reputation as an outcome of the complementary processes of legitimation and creating an organizational identity; exploring the interplay of identity, legitimacy, and reputation in development of an organizational field. Findings suggest that intangible resources (e.g. reputation) underlie performance differences between firms but do not affect legitimacy and organizational survival.

Deephouse & Carter (2005)	Argues that despite similar antecedents, social construction processes, and consequences, there are important differences between legitimacy and reputation.
	Legitimacy emphasizes conformity via adherence to norms and expectations, whereas reputation emphasizes distinctions via comparisons among organizations.
	Empirical examination of antecedents of legitimacy and reputation demonstrates that isomorphism improves legitimacy, but effects on reputation are moderated by quality of reputation.
	Also, higher performance increases reputation but not legitimacy.
King & Whetten (2008)	Applies a social actor view of organizational identity to examine the distinction between legitimacy and reputation.
	Legitimacy and reputation are both perceptions of approval of an organization's actions, but legitimacy focuses on the need for inclusion (conformity to group standards), and reputation on the need for distinction (positive differences within the peer group).
	Reputation and legitimacy are modeled as complementary, reciprocal concepts, linked to the dual identification requirements: who is this actor similar to and how is this actor different from all similar others.
Foreman & Whetten (2002)	An empirical test of identity-based models of organizational identification in which a member's identification is conceptualized as a cognitive comparison between what they perceive the identity to be and what they think it should be.
	Extends scholarship in organizational identification to include multiple identities ("hybrid" identity organization forms).
	Results show that organizational identity congruence significantly affects member commitment, and form-level identity congruence significantly affects legitimacy, supporting the use of identity as a multilevel construct.
Hsu & Hannan (2005)	Role of identity in conceptualization and identification of organizational forms is explored (e.g. specification and differentiation of forms in terms of identity) and more broadly the role of identity within the organizational ecology literature.
	Research questions/issues core to an ecological approach to organizations are proposed: (1) the emergence of identities, (2) the persistence of identities, and (3) the strategic trade-offs among different types of identities.
Zuckerman (1999)	Explores the role of identity in establishing and maintaining legitimacy; focuses on social processes that produce penalties for illegitimate role performance in markets where stakeholders significantly influence market outcomes.
	Results demonstrate that failure to gain attention of key evaluators creates confusion over the firm's identity and legitimacy, thereby creating a stock price discount.

REFERENCES

Albert, S. A. & Whetten, D. A. (1985). "Organizational identity." In L. L. Cummings & B. M. Staw (Eds.), *Research in Organizational Behavior*, Vol. 7. Greenwich, CT: JAI, 263–295.

Aldrich, H. E. & Fiol, C. M. (1994). "Fools rush in?: The institutional context of industry creation." *Academy of Management Review*, 19: 645–670.

Baumeister, R. F. (1998). "The self." In D. T. Gilbert, S. T. Fiske, & G. Lindzey (Eds.), *The Handbook of Social Psychology*. Boston: McGraw-Hill, 680–740.

Bitektine, A. (2011). "Toward a theory of social judgments of organizations: The case of legitimacy, reputation, and status." *Academy of Management Review*, 36(1): 151–179.

Brewer, M. B. (1991). "The social self: On being the same and different at the same time." *Personality and Social Psychology Bulletin*, 17: 475–482.

Brown, T. J., Dacin, P. A., Pratt, M. G., & Whetten, D. A. (2006). "Identity, intended image, construed image, and reputation: An interdisciplinary framework and suggested terminology." *Journal of the Academy of Marketing Science*, 34(2): 99–106.

Clark, B. & Montgomery, D. (1998). "Deterrence, reputations, and competitive cognition." *Management Science*, 44(1): 62–82.

Corley, K. G. & Gioia, D. A. (2004). "Identity ambiguity and change in the wake of a corporate spin-off." *Administrative Science Quarterly*, 49: 173–208.

Cornelissen, J. P., Haslam, S. A., & Balmer, J. M. T. (2007). "Social identity, organizational identity, and corporate identity: Towards an integrated understanding of processes, patternings and products." *British Journal of Management*, 18: S1–16.

Czarniawska, B. & Wolff, R. (1998). "Constructing new identities in established organization fields: Young universities in old Europe." *International Studies of Management and Organization*, 28: 32–56.

Deephouse, D. L. (1999). "To be different, or to be the same? It's a question (and theory) of strategic balance." *Strategic Management Journal*, 20: 147–166.

—— & Carter, S. M. (2005). "An examination of differences between organizational legitimacy and organizational reputation." *Journal of Management Studies*, 42: 329–360.

—— & Suchman, M. C. (2008). "Legitimacy in organizational institutionalism." In R. Greenwood, C. Oliver, R. Suddaby, & K. Sahlin-Andersson (Eds.), *Handbook of Organizational Institutionalism*. London: Sage, 49–77.

Dukerich, J. M. & Carter, S. M. (2000). "Distorted images and reputation repair." In M. Schultz, M. J. Hatch, & M. H. Larsen (Eds.), *The Expressive Organization: Linking Identity, Reputation, and the Corporate Brand*. Oxford, UK: Oxford University Press, 97–112.

Dutton, J. E. & Dukerich, J. M. (1991). "Keeping an eye on the mirror: Image and identity in organizational adaptation." *Academy of Management Journal*, 34(3): 517–554.

——, Dukerich, J. M., & Harquail, C. V. (1994). "Organizational images and member identification." *Administrative Science Quarterly*, 39(2): 239–263.

Elsbach, K. D. (2003). "Organizational perception management." In *Research in Organizational Behavior*, Vol. 25, 297–332.

—— & Kramer, R. M. (1996). "Members' responses to organizational identity threats: Encountering and countering the business week rankings." *Administrative Science Quarterly*, 41(3): 442–476.

Fombrun, C. J. (1996). *Reputation*. Boston, MA: Harvard Business School Press.

Foreman, P. O. & Parent, M. M. (2008). "The process of organizational identity construction in iterative organizations." *Corporate Reputation Review*, 11(3): 222–245.

—— & Whetten, D. A. (2002). "Members' identification with multiple-identity organizations." *Organization Science*, 13: 618–635.

Gecas, V. (1982). "The self-concept." *Annual Review of Sociology*, 8: 1–33.

Gioia, D. A. & Thomas, J. B. (1996). "Identity, image, and issue interpretation: Sensemaking during strategic change in academia." *Administrative Science Quarterly*, 41(3): 370–403.

Glynn, M. A. (2000). "When cymbals become symbols: Conflict over organizational identity within a symphony orchestra." *Organization Science*, 11(3): 285–298.

Hatch, M. J. & Schultz, M. J. (2002). "The dynamics of organizational identity." *Human Relations*, 55(8): 989–1018.

Hogg, M. A., Terry, D. J., & White, K. M. (1995). "A tale of two theories: A critical comparison of identity theory with social identity theory." *Social Psychology Quarterly*, 58: 225–269.

Hsu, G. & Hannan, M. T. (2005). "Identities, genres, and organizational forms." *Organization Science*, 16: 474–490.

King, B. G. & Whetten, D. A. (2008). "Rethinking the relationship between reputation and legitimacy: A social actor conceptualization." *Corporate Reputation Review*, 11: 192–207.

——, Felin, T., & Whetten, D. A. (2010). "Finding the organization in organizational theory: A meta-theory of the organization as a social actor." *Organization Science*, 21(1): 290–305.

Kraatz, M. S. & Block, E. S. (2008). "Organizational implications of institutional pluralism." In R. Greenwood, C. Oliver, R. Suddaby, & K. Sahlin-Andersson (Eds.), *Handbook of Organizational Institutionalism*. London: Sage, 243–274.

Lange, D., Lee, P. M., & Dai, Y. (2011). "Organizational reputation: A review." *Journal of Management*, 37(1): 153–184.

Love, E. G. & Kraatz, M. (2009). "Character, conformity, or the bottom line? How and why downsizing affected corporate reputation." *Academy of Management Journal*, 52(2): 314–335.

Martins, L. L. (2005). "A model of the effects of reputational rankings on organizational change." *Organization Science*, 16: 701–720.

McCall, G. J. & Simmons, J. L. (1978). *Identities and Interactions: An Examination of Associations in Everyday Life*. New York: The Free Press.

Mead, G. H. (1934). *Mind, Self, and Society*. Chicago: University of Chicago Press.

Mitchell, R. K., Agle, B. R., & Wood, D. J. (1997). "Toward a theory of stakeholder identification and salience: Defining the principle of who and what really counts." *Academy of Management Review*, 22: 853–886.

Navis, C. & Glynn, M. A. (2010). "How new market categories emerge: Temporal dynamics of legitimacy, identity, and entrepreneurship in satellite radio, 1990–2005." *Administrative Science Quarterly*, 55(3): 439–471.

Polos, L., Hannan, M. T., & Carroll, G. R. (2002). "Foundations of a theory of social forms." *Industrial and Corporate Change*, 11: 85–115.

Pratt, M. G. (1998). "To be or not to be? Central questions in organizational identification." In D. A. Whetten & P. C. Godfrey (Eds.), *Identity in Organizations: Building Theory Through Conversations*. Thousand Oaks, CA: Sage, 171–207.

—— & Foreman, P. O. (2000a). "Classifying managerial responses to multiple organizational identities." *Academy of Management Review*, 25: 18–42.

—— & —— (2000b). "The beauty of and barriers to organizational theories of identity." *Academy of Management Review*, 25(1): 141–143.

—— & Kraatz, M. S. (2009). "E pluribus unum: Multiple identities and the organizational self." In J. E. Dutton & L. M. Roberts (Eds.), *Exploring Positive Identities and Organizations: Building a Theoretical and Research Foundation.* New York: Routledge, 385–410.

Price, K. N., Gioia, D. A., & Corley, K. G. (2008). "Reconciling scattered images." *Journal of Management Inquiry*, 17(3): 173–185.

Rao, H. (1994). "The social construction of reputation: Certification contests, legitimacy, and the survival of organizations in the American automobile industry: 1895–1912." *Strategic Management Journal*, 14: 29–44.

——, Monin, P., & Durand, R. (2003). "Institutional change in toqueville: Novelle cuisine as an identity movement in French gastronomy." *American Journal of Sociology*, 108: 795–843.

——, ——, & —— (2005). "Border crossing: Bricolage and the erosion of categorical boundaries in French gastronomy." *American Sociological Review*, 70: 968–991.

Rhee, M. & Valdez, M. (2009). "Contextual factors surrounding reputation damage with potential implications for reputation repair." *Academy of Management Review*, 34(1): 146–168.

Rindova, V. P., Williamson, I. O., Petkova, A. P., & Sever, J. M. (2005). "Being good or being known: An empirical examination of the dimensions, antecedents, and consequences of organizational reputation." *Academy of Management Journal*, 48: 1033–1049.

Scott, W. R. (1995). *Institutions and Organizations.* Thousand Oaks, CA: Sage.

Scott, S. G. & Lane, V. R. (2000). "A stakeholder approach to organizational identity." *Academy of Management Review*, 25(1): 43–62.

Stets, J. E. & Burke, P. J. (2000). "Identity theory and social identity theory." *Social Psychology Quarterly*, 63: 224–237.

Stryker, S. (1987). "Identity theory: Developments and extensions." In K. Yardley & T. Honess (Eds.), *Self and Identity: Psychological Perspectives.* New York: John Wiley & Sons, 89–103.

Suchman, M. C. (1995). "Managing legitimacy: Strategic and institutional approaches." *Academy of Management Review*, 20: 571–610.

Tajfel, H. (1978). "Social categorization, social identity, and social comparison." In H. Tajfel (Ed.), *Differentiation Between Social Groups: Studies in the Social Psychology of Intergroup Relations.* London: Academic Press.

Turner, J. C. (1982). "Towards a cognitive redefinition of the social group." In H. Tajfel (Ed.), *Social Identity and Intergroup Relations.* Cambridge, UK: Cambridge University Press, 15–40.

Weick, K. E. (1995). *Sensemaking in Organizations.* Thousand Oaks, CA: Sage.

Weigelt, K. & Camerer, C. (1988). "Reputation and corporate strategy: A review of recent theory and applications." *Strategic Management Journal*, 9(5): 443–454.

Whetten, D. A. (2006). "Albert and Whetten revisited: Strengthening the concept of organizational identity." *Journal of Management Inquiry*, 15(3): 219–234.

—— & Mackey, A. (2002). "A social actor conception of organizational identity and its implications for the study of organizational reputation." *Business & Society*, 41: 393–414.

Zuckerman, E. W. (1999). "The categorical imperative: Securities analysts and the illegitimacy discount." *American Journal of Sociology*, 104(5): 1398–1438.

—— (2000). "Focusing the corporate product: Securities analysts and de-diversification." *Administrative Science Quarterly*, 45(3): 591–619.

——, Kim, T. Y., Ukanwa, K., & von Rittman, J. (2003). "Robust identities or non-entities? Typecasting in the feature film market." *American Journal of Sociology*, 108: 1018–1074.

....

CHAPTER 10

ON BEING BAD: WHY STIGMA IS NOT THE SAME AS A BAD REPUTATION

....

YURI MISHINA

CYNTHIA E. DEVERS

Scholars often characterize negatively evaluated organizations as stigmatized, having a bad reputation, or both. Despite the appeal of treating bad reputation and stigma equivalently, such characterizations obscure the boundaries between these theoretically distinct constructs. In this chapter, we explicate the similarities and differences between organizational reputation and stigma. We then explore the complex interrelationships between them by examining how an existing reputation may prevent or exacerbate the infliction and diffusion of a stigma. We conclude by offering a research agenda designed to allow scholars to discuss, measure, and evaluate these social evaluation constructs more effectively.

WHEN an organization or an organizational act is evaluated negatively, scholars often characterize the organization in question as having a bad or negative reputation (e.g., Dollinger, Golden, & Saxton, 1997; Rhee & Valdez, 2009), as stigmatized (e.g., Devers et al., 2009; Hudson, 2008; Hudson & Okhuysen, 2009; Sutton & Callahan, 1987), or both (e.g., Fiol & Kovoor-Misra, 1997). Indeed, both terms are often applied to organizations synonymously. While there is intuitive appeal in treating bad reputation and stigma equivalently or using the terms interchangeably, we caution that such characterizations limit effective discussion, measurement, and estimation of these similar, but theoretically distinct, social evaluation constructs. In this chapter, we explicate the similarities and differences between organizational reputation and stigma, with the purpose of allowing each to function as a more complete and descriptive social evaluation construct in the organizational literature.

First, we examine what an organizational stigma is and how it has been studied. Second, we discuss several dimensions along which organizational stigma differs from organizational reputation. Third, drawing on these differences, we explore the complex interrelationships between the two constructs by explicating how an existing reputation may prevent or exacerbate the infliction and diffusion of a stigma, and how the presence of a stigma may influence an organization's existing reputation. We conclude by offering a research agenda designed to allow scholars to discuss, measure, and analyze these constructs more completely and effectively.

Organizational Stigma Defined

Although considerable research has examined stigma at the individual level, organizational-level stigma research is fairly nascent. Initial studies have tended to conceptualize stigma fairly abstractly, often paraphrasing Goffman's (1963: 3) definition that a stigma is "an attribute that is deeply discrediting" and that reduces the individual "from a whole and usual person to a tainted, discounted one." More recently, however, scholars have begun to offer definitions of stigma that are more explicitly organizational in nature. Collectively, this work characterizes an organizational stigma as a label that audience members affix to an organization through a socio-political process (Pozner, 2008) that evokes a group-specific, collective perception that the organization "possesses a fundamental flaw that de-individuates and discredits the organization" (Devers et al., 2009: 157). Hudson (2008) offered a more nuanced view, by proposing that two distinct types of organizational-level stigmas exist: event stigmas that result from a "discrete, anomalous, episodic" event (p. 253) and core stigmas that are based on the "nature of the organization's core attributes—who it is, what it does, and whom it serves."

Conceptual organizational stigma research has largely centered on delineating the differences between individual- and organizational-level stigmas, outlining the different strategies stigmatized organizations can use to survive (Hudson, 2008), theorizing about how a new stigma category arises (Devers et al., 2009), and the different factors that might influence why and how certain organizational actors might be assigned additional blame and culpability for organizational failures (Pozner, 2008; Wiesenfeld et al., 2008). The few empirical studies examining organizational stigmas have focused on the effects of events such as financial distress and bankruptcy on organizational members' perceptions, actions, and outcomes. This work has focused on organizational audiences' reactions to the stigma of bankruptcy (Sutton & Callahan, 1987), the labor market consequences for executives who flee or stay at a financially distressed firm (Semadini et al., 2008), and how organizations may try to prevent stigma transfer to their stakeholders (Hudson & Okhuysen, 2009). The summary table at the end of the chapter provides the key definitions and findings of the organizational stigma studies.

In comparison with stigma, organizational reputation has been studied more extensively. Yet for all of its scholarly attention, this research has focused almost exclusively on the positive or favorable end of the reputation continuum (Hirsch & Pozner, 2005;

Mishina, Block, & Mannor, forthcoming).[1] In the few studies that specifically mention bad or negative reputations, the "bad" or "negative" refers to the valence attached to the reputation construct—that is, that the reputation is unfavorable (Rhee & Valdez, 2009). Perhaps because research is so scarce on both negative reputations and organizational stigmas, scholars often conflate the two. However, this confusion is problematic for at least three reasons.

First, despite (or perhaps because of) the tremendous scholarly interest, reputation is often defined in a variety of different ways, leading to a debate that is yet to be fully resolved (e.g., Barnett et al., 2006; Fombrun & Van Riel, 1997). Second, and perhaps as a consequence, a proliferation of reputation measures (positive or negative) exists (e.g., Brown & Perry, 1994; Fryxell & Wang, 1994; Fombrun, 1996). Conversely, given the scarceness of empirical research on organizational stigma, scholars virtually have no validated conceptualizations or measures of organizational stigma to draw on. Therefore, equating bad reputation with stigma only exacerbates the definitional and measurement problems inherent in the reputation literature.

Finally, reputation and stigma operate through very different mechanisms. While reputation entails a unique assessment of an organization (e.g., Deephouse & Suchman, 2008; Jensen & Roy, 2008), a stigma is, by nature, deindividuating (Devers et al., 2009). Thus, conflating the two constructs introduces the possibility that researchers could ultimately study processes and outcomes that may be relevant for one of the constructs but not to the specific construct of interest. In the next section, we start to address these issues by explicating how organizational reputation and organizational stigma differ across six key dimensions (see Table 10.1 for a summary).

THEORETICAL ROOTS

The first key dimension along which reputation and stigma differ is in their theoretical roots. The primary theoretical roots of reputation are signaling theory (Milgrom & Roberts, 1986; Shapiro, 1982; Shapiro, 1983; Spence, 1974) and game theory (Kreps & Wilson, 1982; Milgrom & Roberts, 1982) from economics. From its initial economic roots, others have infused reputation research with a variety of theories from multiple disciplines, resulting in a proliferation of reputational definitions (Barnett et al., 2006; Fombrun & Van Riel, 1997).

The primary theoretical basis for stigma is labeling theory from the sociology of deviance (Erickson, 1962; Gibbs & Erickson, 1975; Kitsuse, 1962) and mental illness (Scheff, 1974). The basic notion is that "[f]orms of behavior per se do not differentiate deviants from non-deviants; it is the responses of the conventional and conforming members of the society who identify and interpret behavior as deviant which sociologically transforms persons into deviants" (Kitsuse, 1962: 253). Following this work, the majority

---

[1] Fine and colleagues (Ducharme & Fine, 1995; Fine, 1996, 2002a, 2002b) have studied what they call "difficult reputations" at the level of individuals but not organizations.

Table 10.1 Comparison of Reputation and Stigma

	Reputation	Stigma
Theoretical Roots	Signaling theory	Labeling theory
Dimensionality and Range	Multidimensional and continuous	One-dimensional and dichotomous
Levels of Analysis	Organizational level	Category level
Antecedents	Organization's historical pattern of consistent and reliable behaviors and/or outcomes	A group's collective perception that the organization threatens the existing social order
Ease of Acquisition and Removal	Easy to develop and maintain favorable reputation regarding capabilities and performance. Difficult to develop or maintain favorable reputation regarding organizational character. Easy to acquire unfavorable organizational character reputation.	Easy to acquire stigma, removal requires challenging and redefining stigmatizing label or reindividuating the firm, and then convincing audiences that the organization does not pose a threat to the existing order.
Social Uses	A signal of quality and future behavior.	Social control
Consequences	Unfavorable reputations lead to difficulty in sustaining financial performance, price discounts, decreased attractiveness as a transaction partner, and difficulty in improving one's reputation.	Stakeholder disidentification, client defection, counter-organizational actions, survival is threatened

of the stigma work has occurred within social psychology (for reviews see e.g., Link & Phelan, 2001; Major & O'Brien, 2005).

DIMENSIONALITY AND RANGE

A second important difference between reputation and stigma is in their dimensionality and range. Reputations form as multiple stakeholders try to make sense of the firm's characteristics, activities, and outcomes along a variety of dimensions (Fombrun & Shanley, 1990). Because different types of stakeholders have different priorities and, thus, attend to different aspects of the firm, reputation is necessarily multidimensional (Fombrun, 1996). For example, some stakeholders may focus on financial performance, others on social responsibility, and still others might focus on how the organization treats its employees.

Reputation is also continuous (e.g., Deephouse & Suchman, 2008; Fombrun & Shanley, 1990) and valenced, ranging from highly favorable to highly unfavorable (e.g.,

Brooks et al., 2003; Deephouse, 2000; Deephouse & Carter, 2005). A variety of related terms are used to discuss the valence of a reputation, including good/bad, positive/negative, and favorable/unfavorable. Importantly, however, good and bad are merely relativistic terms used for convenience, not "absolute, dichotomous reputational evaluation[s]," but rather a "relative, nonbinary evaluation" (Rhee & Valdez, 2009: 157). Due to its multidimensional nature, an organization may have a favorable reputation along one dimension and simultaneously have an unfavorable one along another (Rhee & Valdez, 2009; cf. Jensen, Kim, and Kim, Chapter 7, this volume).

Unlike reputation, organizational stigma is inherently one-dimensional, as it reflects that an organization possesses a "fundamental, deep-seated flaw" (Devers et al., 2009: 157). Although stigmatization may derive from a particular practice, structure, or action, as Goffman (1963) notes, a stigma is not about that particular practice, structure, or action, but rather about the negative attributions that observers make about the organization's core essence. These inferences permeate every aspect of the organization's being, such that once stigmatized, the organization is no longer viewed as having "merely behaved in a problematic manner," but is seen as "a dangerous deviant" that is "the embodiment of everything that the stakeholder group considers 'wrong'" (Devers et al., 2009: 162). A stigma thus deindividuates, by stripping the organization of its unique identity and imputing an alternative one based on the stereotypes ascribed to the stigmatized category. Thus, even though the organization might be objectively unique along many dimensions, stakeholders will view stigmatized organizations primarily in terms of those stereotypes.

Organizational stigma, then, is a dichotomous evaluation—those lacking a stigma are viewed as normal or usual, and those possessing a stigma are viewed as tainted and less than whole (Pozner, 2008). This is not to say that organizations cannot differ in the number of different types of audiences that stigmatize them or in the severity of the sanctions they face (Fiol & Kovoor-Misra, 1997; Hudson, 2008; Hudson & Okhuysen, 2009). Nevertheless, an organizational stigma is an all-or-nothing proposition—the organization is either stigmatized or not in the eyes of a particular audience or audiences, but an organization cannot be stigmatized along only a single dimension and not others.

LEVELS OF ANALYSIS

A third way in which organizational reputation and stigma differ is in the level of analysis at which each is applied. Organizational reputation (which, as Graffin and colleagues discuss, in Chapter 11, this volume, differs from executive reputation) entails a unique assessment of a specific organization in terms of its ability to meet the financial and social expectations of various constituents over time (Fombrun, 1996; Fombrun & Shanley, 1990). Although some evidence suggests that organizations within the same strategic group may have similar reputations (Ferguson, Deephouse, & Ferguson, 2000), reputations tend to set an organization apart from others, allowing it to be perceived as a unique entity with distinct characteristics and behaviors (Deephouse & Suchman, 2008; Jensen & Roy, 2008).

An organizational stigma, on the other hand, is not about any particular organization per se, but instead about whether or not the organization belongs to a larger, stigmatized category, such as bankrupt firms (Wiesenfeld et al., 2008). Hence, while reputations are based on distinctness from other organizations, stigmas are based on broad categorizations of sameness (Frable, 1993). In this regard, an organizational stigma bears some resemblance to Barnett and King's (2008) "reputations commons" problem, in which all firms in a particular industry may be painted with a negative brush due to the actions of one firm (Yue & Ingram, Chapter 14, this volume; see also Newburry, Chapter 12, this volume on the influence of country of origin). In the case of a reputations commons problem, a firm may be viewed as a member of a negatively evaluated industry, and yet retain its uniqueness in the eyes of its audience. In contrast to the reputations commons problem, however, because an organizational stigma tears away the uniqueness of the organization and imputes a deindividuated identity based on the stereotypes associated with the stigmatized category, stigmatized category membership and its associated stereotypes become the only relevant and salient reflection of the organization in the minds of stigmatizing stakeholders (Devers et al., 2009).

ANTECEDENTS

Reputations and stigma also differ in their antecedents. Reputations form as stakeholders use existing industry recipes (Spender, 1989) and competitive ontologies (Porac et al., 1995) to make sense of the organization and its activities (Porac, Ventresca, & Mishina, 2002). In order to develop a favorable reputation, firms must demonstrate performance and quality (Deephouse & Carter, 2005; Rindova et al., 2005), consistent and reliable behavior (Clark & Montgomery, 1998; Fombrun, 1996), and fulfill stakeholders' expectations over time (Barnett et al., 2006; Fombrun & Shanley, 1990; Fombrun & Van Riel, 1997).

Conversely, an organizational stigma does not necessarily develop from a history of behaviors or outcomes. Instead, as Kitsuse (1962: 255) notes, "the critical feature of the deviant-defining process is not the behavior of individuals who are defined as deviants, but, rather, the interpretations others make of their behaviors, whatever those behaviors may be." Hence, an important antecedent of organizational stigma is that stakeholders perceive that an organization threatens the existing social order because its values are globally and completely incongruent with the stakeholder group's values (generalized value incongruence; Sitkin & Roth, 1993). However, given that it is a collective phenomenon, in order for a stigma to arise, the perception that the focal organization is a dangerous deviant must diffuse across a critical mass of members to the point at which it becomes self-sustaining within the stakeholder group (Devers et al., 2009).

The process by which stakeholders perceive generalized value incongruence may be fairly automatic for a pre-existing stigma category, such as organizational failure (Semadini et al., 2008; Sutton & Callahan, 1987; Wiesenfeld et al., 2008). However, particular organizational characteristics or outcomes may also trigger the application of a stigma (Hudson, 2008; Hudson & Okhuysen, 2009) if those attributes, or what they symbolize, are or become viewed as deviant or threatening to an existing social structure (Goffman, 1963). Even in these instances, however, stigma emergence is less about whether or not an organization has actually experienced a particular outcome or possesses a particular characteristic and, instead, more about the inferences made by observers (Kitsuse, 1962).

EASE OF ACQUISITION OR REMOVAL

A good reputation takes time to develop because it requires a consistent ability to satisfy stakeholder concerns (Barnett et al., 2006; Fombrun, 1996; Fombrun & Shanley, 1990). However, research documents that good reputations are fragile and fleeting (Hall, 1993; Love & Kraatz, 2009; Rhee & Haunschild, 2006) because they "sit on the slippery ground of their constituents' fickle interpretations" (Fombrun, 1996: 388). Therefore, a favorable reputation can shift from good to bad much more quickly than it can shift from bad to good (Nichols & Fournier, 1999) because stakeholders assess new signals with the expectation that a questionable organization will behave in a questionable manner (Fombrun, 1996). Recently, however, some research has suggested that not all types of reputations are equally difficult to build or equally fragile—it may be easy to develop and maintain a favorable reputation regarding organizational capabilities and how the firm can perform, while it may be very difficult to develop or maintain a favorable reputation regarding an organization's values and character (Mishina et al., forthcoming).

Organizational stigmas are somewhat similar to bad character reputations in this regard because both bad character reputations and stigmas can be acquired fairly easily and are difficult to remove, although the specific reasons differ in important ways. Bad character reputations are easy to acquire and difficult to remove due to the presumption that bad behavior is more indicative of underlying character than good behavior, which may merely be an indication of conformance to societal norms (Hamilton & Huffman, 1971; Hamilton & Zanna, 1972). Stigmas are easy to acquire because they only depend on collective perceptions of generalized value incongruence (Devers et al., 2009), which may be activated by a particular event or a specific organizational characteristic (Hudson, 2008). Just as repairing a reputation is more difficult than ruining a reputation, stigma removal is also more difficult and involved than the initial stigmatization. For example, the two primary ways in which an organization can attempt to remove a stigma are by challenging and transforming societal definitions and assumptions surrounding a stigmatizing label (Fine, 1995; Gamson, 1989; Johnston, Laraña, & Gusfield, 1994; Kaplan & Xiu, 2000; Kitsuse, 1980) and/or by demonstrating to the stigmatizing stakeholder group that the organization was or is inappropriately categorized. The social movement literature in sociology discusses the difficulties inherent in changing societal definitions, but even the latter option of claiming that the organization was inappropriately categorized is likely to be very difficult, precisely because of the way in which a stigma operates.

First, because a stigma deindividuates the organization and removes its unique characteristics in the eyes of the stigmatizing stakeholder group, the organization must take steps to be viewed as something other than an anonymous, undifferentiated member of the stigmatized category—it must reindividuate itself. In doing so, the goal is to get the stigmatizing stakeholder group to view the organization as a unique entity again, perhaps by engaging in a variety of actions to gain visibility (Rindova et al., 2007). If an organization can reindividuate itself, then it is technically no longer stigmatized per se, as stigmatization implies deindividuation, but it may still be stuck with stereotyped negative characteristics as residual baggage. In other words, the organization will be viewed as an unfavorably evaluated, but unique, entity.

Additionally, because stigmas are not confined to the stigmatizing aspect but are about the inferences made regarding the underlying fundamental characteristics and core essence (Goffman, 1963) of the organization, merely changing surface structures or behavior may not be enough for redemption—a stigmatized organization is likely to be viewed in an unfavorable light unless it is able to change stakeholders' interpretations and beliefs about its very nature. As a result, although more avenues exist for organizations to remove stigmas relative to individuals (e.g., isolating and removing the problematic parts or members of the organization—Devers et al., 2009), once applied, stigmas at any level are often "almost irreversible" (Erickson, 1962: 311).

SOCIAL USES AND ORGANIZATIONAL CONSEQUENCES

Although there is some debate about how exactly reputation should be defined (see e.g., Barnett et al., 2006; Fombrun & Van Riel, 1997), in general reputation represents a firm-specific evaluation organizational audiences use to infer quality and likely behavior when more specific information is unavailable or too costly (Fombrun & Shanley, 1990; Shamsie, 2003; Weigelt & Camerer, 1988). In this sense, reputation answers the question: "How will the organization perform/behave in the future relative to other organizations?" (Bitektine, 2010: 163). Hence, the primary function of reputation is to reduce uncertainty in the minds of stakeholders by providing them with relevant expectations about the firm (Rindova et al., 2005). Reputations are thus likely to play a central role in any potential interactions that both individuals and other parties consider with the focal organization. Consequently, organizations with an unfavorable reputation have difficulty sustaining financial performance (Roberts & Dowling, 2002), may suffer price discounts relative to organizations with similar quality products (Nichols & Fournier, 1999; cf. Rindova et al., 2005), be viewed as a less attractive transaction partner (Dollinger et al., 1997), and find it difficult to improve their unfavorable reputations (Mishina et al., forthcoming).

The primary social use for an organizational stigma, however, is social control (Erickson, 1962; Kitsuse, 1962). By demonstrating the differences between acceptable and unacceptable behavior and characteristics, audience members can use organizational stigmas to promote social stability (Erickson, 1962). As a consequence, as an organization becomes stigmatized, many of its stakeholders begin cognitively to dis-identify with the organization (Bhattacharya & Elsbach, 2002; Elsbach & Bhattacharya, 2001), leading both clients (Jensen, 2006) and organizational members (Semadini et al., 2008) to defect from the organization, as well as to act in a specifically counter-organizational manner. In a study on the stigma of chapter 11 bankruptcy filings, for example, Sutton and Callahan (1987) found that various stakeholders reduced the quantity and quality of interactions with the stigmatized organization, bargained for more favorable exchange relationships, spread malicious rumors, and even directly insulted the organization and its managers, all of which threatened organizational survival and success. Additionally, certain organizational members are often blamed for the stigma and, thus, singled out for punishment (Pozner, 2008; Wiesenfeld et al., 2008). In this way, stigmas and their aftermath unfold through a socio-political process, driven by a variety of factors, including a desire for social justice, *schadenfreude*, and self-serving behavior (Wiesenfeld et al., 2008), and often result in various types of symbolic activity, including impression management and scapegoating (Fiol & Kovoor-Misra, 1997; Pozner, 2008; Sutton & Callahan, 1987). Thus, an organizational stigma can lead to a variety of social and economic sanctions for the organization and its members.

Interrelationships between Organizational Reputation and Stigma

The differences discussed above can have important implications for the interrelationships between organizational reputation and stigma. In this section, we examine how those interrelationships may affect how susceptible an organization is to a stigmatizing claim, how a stigma influences an organization's existing reputation, and if, and how broadly, an organizational stigma might spread.

Reputation and Susceptibility to Stigmatizing Claims

Actors who are held in high regard are able to engage in some deviant behaviors without fear of sanction (Goffman, 1963; Hollander, 1958, 1960). This suggests that an organization's existing reputation influences the stickiness of a stigmatizing claim. This largely results because stakeholders use the focal organization's existing reputation as a filter to determine whether or not a stigmatizing claim appears to be consistent with what they "know" about the firm (Fiol & Kovoor-Misra, 1997). Given the presumption that reputable organizations will behave in reliable, credible, trustworthy, and responsible ways (Fombrun, 1996; Love & Kraatz, 2009), a strong positive reputation may bolster an organization's ability to defend itself against a stigmatizing label.

Nevertheless, because reputation is comprised of stakeholder evaluations along a multitude of dimensions, an organization's reputation is only likely to influence its credibility if it is relevant to the domain of the potentially stigmatizing claim (e.g., environmental responsibility, product quality). If the targeted organization's reputation is supportive of its counterclaims then it is likely to be viewed as more credible, while a reputation that is contrary to its counterclaims (or is supportive of the labeler's claims) increases the likelihood that stakeholders will accept the validity of the stigmatizing label.

Stigma and Reputational Loss

Once an organization is stigmatized, the reputational penalty is severe. Specifically, a stigmatized organization's uniqueness, in the eyes of its stakeholders, is completely stripped away and obliterated (Link & Phelan, 2001). As a result, the stigmatizing stakeholder group collectively views the target solely as representing the attributes of the negatively evaluated category in which it now resides. Thus, by definition, stigmatization deindividuates an organization, thereby eradicating any existing positive or negative reputation.

During this process members of the stigmatizing stakeholder group will reinterpret the target organization's characteristics and previous actions through the lens of the stigmatizing category (Ducharme & Fine, 1995). In doing so, the stigmatizing stakeholder group selectively recasts the target organization's actions, characteristics, and outcomes to impute nefarious motives and structures to that organization as *proof* that the organization is "fully, intensely, and quintessentially evil" (Ducharme & Fine, 1995: 1311). For example, strong performance of a stigmatized firm might be recast as resulting from blind luck or unethical activities (Mishina et al., 2010), and corporate social responsibility behaviors might be viewed as instrumental attempts at ingratiation (Godfrey, 2005).

Reputation and the Spread of Stigma

A targeted firm's pre-stigma reputation may also influence whether other groups perceive it as deviant, and whether, and how broadly, the stigma may spread. Specifically, although a stigma is both stakeholder- and context-specific (Devers et al., 2009), the organization's reputation is likely to affect its symbolic value as a target, as well as the reactions of other actors, and thereby influence whether or not it is stigmatized by a wider range of stakeholder groups or in multiple contexts.

On the one hand, because public attention is a scarce resource (Hilgartner & Bosk, 1988), anything that captures attention increases the symbolic value of a target. If a targeted organization has a favorable reputation, the potential for a compelling, dramatic conflict increases, thereby enhancing its symbolic value. On the other hand, because the reactions of other actors depend on political considerations and *schadenfreude* (Pozner, 2008; Wiesenfeld et al., 2008), a favorable reputation may also help to protect the firm. As Feather and Sherman (2002) found, *schadenfreude*, or pleasure at another's misfortune, is based on resentment about an actor's undeserved favorable outcomes, and hence a desire to correct the injustice. If an organization has a favorable reputation, other actors may believe that the stigma has been unjustly applied, and thus refrain from acting against the organization. If the organization is already viewed in an unfavorable light, however, observers may naturally conclude that any misfortune that befalls the organization is justified and that it deserves sanctioning (Feather & Sherman, 2002), thereby increasing 'piling on' behavior (Wiesenfeld et al., 2008).

Bad Reputation and Organizational Stigma: A Research Agenda

Despite scholars sometimes conflating bad reputation with stigma, we believe that the literatures on reputation and organizational stigma can and should coexist. As detailed earlier, the two constructs differ along a number of important dimensions, which may lead to interesting interrelationships between the two. We now discuss several steps that we believe are necessary for reputation and stigma research to advance, followed by several areas that may generate productive future research.

NECESSARY NEXT STEPS

Unless and until scholars begin to sufficiently resolve the debates that currently exist within both literatures, we believe that there exists the likelihood for continued and increased confounding of the bad reputation and organizational stigma constructs. To advance the reputation literature, we suggest scholars attempt to build consensus around one or two common definitions of reputation (e.g., Barnett et al., 2006; Fombrun & Van Riel, 1997). We also urge a focus on identifying and validating reputation measures capable of adequately capturing the complexities of the construct.[2] Unless scholars can identify measures that are both multidimensional (cf. Brown & Perry, 1994; Fryzell & Wang,

[2] Recently, Rindova and colleagues (2007) have suggested that reputation has multiple components, prominence, evaluative favorability, strategic content, and exemplar status, thereby adding additional complexity to the reputation construct.

1994) and capture the evaluations of the entire range of a firm's constituents (e.g., Fombrun, 1996), the debate regarding whether reputations should be stakeholder-specific or aggregated across stakeholders cannot be resolved.

The majority of extant organizational stigma literature has been conceptual (Devers et al., 2009; Fiol & Kovoor-Misra, 1997; Hudson, 2008; Pozner, 2008; Wiesenfeld et al., 2008). Further, the few empirical studies that exist have inferred that organizations that have experienced failure were stigmatized, as opposed to directly measuring stigma per se (Semadini et al., 2008; Sutton & Callahan, 1987). However, a notable exception is Hudson and Okhuysen's (2009) study of gay men's bathhouses, in which these authors used census data, congressional voting records, and local and state legal statutes as proxies for hostility toward gay and lesbian individuals, and consequently, the likelihood that a bathhouse would become stigmatized. As they illustrate, the choice of measures is likely to be highly context-specific, although Hudson (2008) notes that surveys may be a less context-specific way to obtain information on stigmatization. For stigma research to advance, scholars must determine how to effectively measure organizational stigmas more directly (Hudson, 2008) and we suggest that scholars might benefit from building on Hudson and Okhuysen's (2009) methods to develop and validate such measures.

Once researchers begin to uncover appropriate ways of measuring stigma, they may be able to begin to resolve some existing debates in the organizational stigma literature. For example, the exact relationship between stigma and legitimacy,[3] as well as other social evaluations (Devers et al., 2009; cf. Foreman, Whetten, and Mackey, Chapter 9, this volume), can be explored, perhaps following an approach similar to Jensen and Roy's (2008) study on how status and reputation influenced auditor firm selection. Improved measures may also allow researchers to examine which factors might determine differences in the number and/or range of stigmatizing stakeholder groups, as well as how stigmatization impacts the survival of organizational forms. Finally, researchers could compare stigmas based on events versus those that are based on core characteristics to determine whether they play out differently (Hudson, 2008; Hudson & Okhuysen, 2009). Specifically, are they viewed as differentially controllable or preventable (Goffman, 1963)? Is one more or less likely to diffuse to additional contexts than the other? Is one more likely to lead to a courtesy stigma (Page, 1984) than the other? Because we see the core/event distinction as meaningful primarily as antecedents rather than as distinct types of stigma, our intuition is that most differences are likely to come into play before the stigma arises; nevertheless, these are important questions to consider.

---

[3] Hudson equates stigma with the "farther end of the spectrum of illegitimacy" and "negative legitimacy" (2008: 255) for illustrative purpose, but he criticizes the illegitimacy construct as "poorly defined, inconsistently operationalized, and genuinely overbroad in usage," thus suffering from, "1) the lack of a consistent definition or operationalization and 2) a confounded definition" (p. 252).

New Research Directions

First, because most studies on reputation and stigma have examined the consequences of these social evaluations for organizations and their members, a fertile new direction for research may be to explore how organizations gain a new reputation or stigma. Although Rindova and colleagues (2007) have moved toward uncovering how new reputations develop by examining the media reputations of several companies, there is room for more research. For example, because an existing organization's reputation is often used to interpret subsequent information (Fombrun, 1996; Mishina et al., forthcoming), the process by which an organization's existing reputation can be improved or damaged may be very different from the way in which an organization develops a reputation in the first place, when stakeholders may not hold set expectations.

Similarly, the process by which a firm is stigmatized or avoids such a fate has not been studied empirically. Although Sutton and Callahan (1987) examined the emerging reactions of various internal and external stakeholders to the stigma of bankruptcy, it may also be worthwhile to examine the labeling contests (Ashforth & Humphrey, 1997) that organizations engage in when trying to stigmatize or avoid stigmatization. Such work may illuminate why, out of a group of organizations that are all at risk, some firms are able to avoid stigmatization, while others become stigmatized. Research into these processes is also likely to be informed by, and have implications for, the work on industry reputation (Yue & Ingram, Chapter 14, this volume) and/or reputations based on country of origin (Newburry, Chapter 12, this volume) as well, since firms are often inflicted with the baggage of unfavorable reputations based solely on perceived industry membership and/or their home country. In a related vein, Graffin, Pfarrer, and Hill (Chapter 11, this volume) suggest that factors such as executive tenure and unexpected positive or negative events can cause executive reputations to converge or diverge with the organizational reputation. This suggests that it may also be important to continue empirical examinations of how and why executives may be able to avoid stigma transfer from their organizations (Semadini et al., 2008), or in some instances, when organizations may be able to avoid being tainted by the presence of a stigmatized executive. Additionally, although Devers and colleagues (2009) theorized about the process by which a new category of stigma might emerge, scholars have yet to empirically confirm or disconfirm this theorizing. The subprime mortgage industry may be a fertile context in which to test this argument.

We see a second productive avenue of research in examining how organizations rid themselves of bad reputations or stigmas. Rhee & Valdez (2009) theorized about how a firm may be able to repair a bad reputation (see also Rhee & Kim, Chapter 22, this volume), but this has largely escaped the notice of reputational theorists, who have examined how negative events may damage reputations (Love & Kraatz, 2009; Rhee & Haunschild, 2006) but not how reputations are repaired. Similarly, how can a stigmatized organization remove the stigma? Scapegoating (Boeker, 1992) and other forms of decoupling (Elsbach & Sutton, 1992) are often *ex ante* stigma prevention tactics, but these and other tactics may be much less effective once the stigmatizing label sticks.

A third area ripe for future research involves uncovering the unanticipated consequences (Merton, 1936; Selznick, 1949) of both reputations and stigma. Ely & Välimäki (2003) argued that concerns about maintaining a good reputation and avoiding a bad one might cause actors to engage in behaviors that are not socially optimal. Additionally, Rhee & Haunschild (2006) found that severe automobile recalls caused more market share damage to high- than low-reputation firms. While this research underscores the unforeseen negative effects of a positive reputation, it is possible that there may be unforeseen positive implications for possessing a bad reputation and/or a stigma. Indeed, research on stigma at the individual level has suggested that stigmas can sometimes have positive consequences. Shih (2004) suggests that stigmatization may result in empowerment of a stigmatized individual if he or she utilizes certain types of processes to overcome the consequences of stigmatization, and members of "dirty work" professions may actually form a stronger occupational culture as a result of having to deal with the stigma attached to their occupations (Ashforth & Kreiner, 1999; Ashforth et al., 2007). Stigmas may also precipitate action that challenges and transforms societal definitions and assumptions surrounding a stigmatizing label (Fine, 1995; Gamson, 1989; Johnston, Laraña, & Gusfield, 1994; Kaplan & Xiu, 2000; Kitsuse, 1980). Whether and how these processes might play out for organizational stigmas is an open question, however. Thus, exploring these processes may offer greater understanding of the unanticipated consequences of organizational reputations and stigmas.

Finally, we believe that scholars may find value in considering positively deviant organizations. Although the stigma literature provides insight on the causes and consequences of negative deviance, some stigma researchers have noted that "[p]eople may…mark others in favorable, nonstigmatizing ways," and certain people are marked with "medals and awards, indicating that the individual is to be respected and adulated" (Neuberg, Smith, & Asher, 2000: 31). In essence, these authors suggest that there may be a positive counterpart to a stigma, what one might think of as a "mark of distinction" that serves as an aspirational ideal to the "normals." To our knowledge, this notion of a "mark of distinction" has not yet been examined in the stigma or related literatures. The existing stigma literature applies to the presence or absence of deviant behavior that is viewed negatively (Goffman 1963), and the neo-institutional literature examines the presence or absence of conformity to accepted norms, values, and definitions (Dimaggio & Powell, 1983; Meyer & Rowan, 1977). The relatively new concept of firm celebrity comes closest to this notion of positive deviance, since celebrity is about deviations from the norm (over- or under-conformance) and a positive evaluation of that deviance (Rindova, Pollock, & Hayward, 2006). However, Rindova and colleagues (2006) are careful to point out that the same deviance that the celebrity firm engages in might be viewed as problematic for any other actor—the celebrity is viewed as not subject to the ordinary rules and constraints that others face (cf. Wade et al., 2006). Consequently, it may be worthwhile to consider whether a mark of distinction is even possible, and, if so, what the antecedents and consequences of such a mark might be.

Research on Organizational Stigma

Reference	Key Constructs and Findings
Devers et al. (2009)	• Conceptual • Organizational stigma as "a label that evokes a collective stakeholder group-specific perception that an organization possesses a fundamental, deep-seated flaw that de-individuates and discredits the organization" (p. 157). • Distinguishes organizational stigma from reputation, status, celebrity, and legitimacy, as well as individual stigmas. • Theorizes about how a new organizational stigma emerges.
Hudson (2008)	• Conceptual • Core stigma: based on the "nature of the organization's core attributes—who it is, what it does, and whom it serves" (p. 253). • Event stigma: results from a "discrete, anomalous, episodic" event (p. 253). • Discusses different strategies by which core-stigmatized organizations can survive.
Hudson & Okhuysen (2009)	• Qualitative study of men's bathhouses • Organizations that are core-stigmatized appear to engage in various boundary management processes in order to prevent the transfer of stigma to their stakeholders, but these varied somewhat by the nature of their environment (condemning, tolerant, or accepting).
Pozner (2008)	• Conceptual • Stigma as "an emergent property, determined through the process of social interaction, whereby specific meanings are attached to categories of behavior and individuals" and "forms the basis for reduced social interaction" (p. 144). • Organizational stigma *only* when the normative violation is viewed as being endorsed by the organization or attributable to the failure of organizational systems—i.e., the organization has to be viewed as being at fault. • Stigmatization and subsequent *ex post* settling up affected by impression management, scapegoating, and organizational politics.
Semadini et al. (2008)	• Study of executives of public and private Texas banks that received FDIC intervention, and a matched sample from non-failed banks. • Examined labor market consequences to executives for remaining at or fleeing financially distressed firms. • Those who jumped ship from a failing bank prior to failure seemed to suffer less demotion or city change, but jumping from a non-failing bank resulted in demotions and city changes.

(Continued)

Table Continued

Reference	Key Constructs and Findings
Sutton & Callahan (1987)	• Qualitative study of Chapter 11 computer firms. • "spoiled images resulting from the Chapter 11 label" (p. 406). • Stigma of Chapter 11 may cause key organizational audiences to react in five ways: disengagement, reduction in the quality of participation, bargaining for more favorable exchange relationships, denigration by rumor, and denigration by confrontation. • Managers engage in several behaviors to reduce stigma: concealing, defining, denying responsibility, accepting responsibility, and withdrawing.
Wiesenfeld et al. (2008)	• Conceptual • Stigmatization as a social process mediated by social, legal, and economic arbiters that begins with a corporate failure. Arbiters collect evidence and derive an interpretation or judgment that they disseminate to others. One or more individuals may be singled out as being particularly culpable, based on perceived ethical lapses, *schadenfreude*, and a desire to correct perceived injustices, although these effects may be mitigated by social capital.

References

Ashforth, B. E. & Humphrey, R. H. (1997). "The ubiquity and potency of labeling in organizations." *Organization Science*, 8: 43–58.

—— & Kreiner, G. E. (1999). "'How can you do it?': Dirty work and the challenge of constructing a positive identity." *Academy of Management Review*, 24(3): 413–434.

——, Clark, M. A., & Fugate, M. (2007). "Normalizing dirty work: Managerial tactics for countering occupational taint." *Academy of Management Journal*, 50(1): 149–174.

Barnett, M. L. & King, A. A. (2008). "Good fences make good neighbors: A longitudinal analysis of an industry self-regulatory institution." *Academy of Management Journal*, 51(6): 1150–1170.

——, Jermier, J. M., & Lafferty, B. A. (2006). "Corporate reputation: The definitional landscape." *Corporate Reputation Review*, 9(1): 26–38.

Bhattacharya, C. B. & Elsbach, K. D. (2002). "Us versus them: The roles of organizational identification and disidentification in social marketing initiatives." *Journal of Public Policy & Marketing*, 21(1): 26–36.

Bitektine, A. (2010). "Toward a theory of social judgments of organizations: The case of legitimacy, reputation, and status." *Academy of Management Review*, 36(1): 151–179.

Boeker, W. (1992). "Power and managerial dismissal: Scapegoating at the top." *Administrative Science Quarterly*, 37(3): 400–421.

Brooks, M. E., Highhouse, S., Russell, S. S., & Mohr, D. C. (2003). "Familiarity, ambivalence, and firm reputation: Is corporate fame a double-edged sword?" *Journal of Applied Psychology*, 88(5): 904–914.

Brown, B. & Perry, S. (1994). "Removing the financial performance halo from Fortune's 'Most Admired' companies." *Academy of Management Journal*, 37: 1347–1359.

Clark, B. H. & Montgomery, D. B. (1998). "Deterrence, reputations, and competitive cognition." *Management Science*, 44: 62–82.

Deephouse, D. L. (2000). "Media reputation as a strategic resource: An integration of mass communication and resource-based theories." *Journal of Management*, 26(6): 1091–1112.

—— & Carter, S. M. (2005). "An examination of the differences between organizational legitimacy and organizational reputation." *Journal of Management Studies*, 42(2): 329–360.

—— & Suchman, M. (2008). "Legitimacy in organizations." In R. Greenwood, C. Oliver, K. Sahlin, & R. Suddaby (Eds.), *The SAGE Handbook of Organizational Institutionalism*. Thousand Oaks, CA: Sage, 49–77.

Devers, C. E., Dewett, T., Mishina, Y., & Belsito, C. A. (2009). "A general theory of organizational stigma." *Organization Science*, 20(1): 154–171.

DiMaggio, P. & Powell, W. W. (1983). "The iron cage revisited: Institutional isomorphism and collective rationality in organizational fields." *American Sociological Review*, 48: 147–160.

Dollinger, M. J., Golden, P. A., & Saxton, T. (1997). "The effect of reputation on the decision to joint venture." *Strategic Management Journal*, 18: 127–140.

Ducharme, L. J. & Fine, G. A. (1995). "The construction of nonpersonhood and demonization: Commemorating the traitorous reputation of Benedict Arnold." *Social Forces*, 73(4): 1309–1331.

Elsbach, K. D. & Bhattacharya, C. B. (2001). "Defining who you are by what you're not: Organizational disidentification and the National Rifle Association." *Organization Science*, 12(4): 393–413.

Elsbach, K. D. & Sutton, R. I. (1992). "Acquiring organizational legitimacy through illegitimate actions: A marriage of institutional and impression management theories." *Academy of Management Journal*, 35(4): 699–738.

Ely, J. C. & Välimäki, J. (2003). "Bad reputation." *Quarterly Journal of Economics*, 98(3): 785–814.

Erickson, K. T. (1962). "Notes on the sociology of deviance." *Social Problems*, 9: 307–314.

Feather, N. T. & Sherman, R. (2002). "Envy, resentment, schadenfreude, and sympathy: Reactions to deserved and undeserved achievement and subsequent failure." *Personality and Social Psychology Bulletin*, 28: 953–961.

Ferguson, T. D., Deephouse, D. L., & Ferguson, W. L. (2000). "Do strategic groups differ in reputation?" *Strategic Management Journal*, 21: 1195–1214.

Fine, G. A. (1995). "Public narration and group culture: Discerning discourse in social movements." In H. Johnston & B. Klandermans (Eds.), *Social Movements and Culture*. Minneapolis: University of Minnesota Press, 127–143.

—— (1996). "Reputational entrepreneurs and the memory of incompetence: Melting supporters, partisan warriors, and images of President Harding." *American Journal of Sociology*, 101(5): 1159–1193.

—— (2002a). *Difficult Reputations: Collective Memories of the Evil, Inept, and Controversial*. Chicago: University of Chicago Press.

Fine, G. A. (2002b). "Thinking about evil: Adolf Hitler and the dilemma of the social construction of reputation." In K. Cerulo (Ed.), *Culture in Mind: Toward a Sociology of Culture and Cognition*. New York: Routledge, 227–237.

Fiol, C. M. & Kovoor-Misra, S. (1997). "Two-way mirroring: Identity and reputation when things go wrong." *Corporate Reputation Review*, 1: 147–151.

Fombrun, C. J. (1996). *Reputation: Realizing Value from the Corporate Image*. Boston, MA: Harvard Business School Press.

—— & Shanley, M. (1990). "What's in a name? Reputation building and corporate strategy." *Academy of Management Journal*, 33: 233–258.

—— & van Riel, C. (1997). "The reputational landscape." *Corporate Reputation Review*, 1(1/2): 5–13.

Frable, D. E. S. (1993). "Dimensions of marginality: Distinctions among those who are different." *Personality and Social Psychology Bulletin*, 19: 370–380.

Fryxell, G. E. & Wang, J. (1994). "The Fortune corporate 'reputation' index: Reputation for what?" *Journal of Management*, 20(1): 1–14.

Gamson, J. (1989). "Silence, death, and the invisible enemy: AIDS activism and social movement 'newness.'" *Social Problems*, 36(4): 351–367.

Gibbs, J. P. & Erickson, M. L. (1975). "Major developments in the sociological study of deviance." *Annual Review of Sociology*, 1: 21–42.

Godfrey, P. C. (2005). "The relationship between corporate philanthropy and shareholder wealth: A risk management perspective." *Academy of Management Review*, 30(4): 777–798.

Goffman, E. (1963). *Stigma: Notes on the Management of Spoiled Identity*. Englewood Cliffs, NJ: Prentice Hall.

Hall, R. (1993). "A framework linking intangible resources and capabilities to sustainable competitive advantage." *Strategic Management Journal*, 14: 607–618.

Hamilton, D. L. & Huffman, L. J. (1971)."Generality of impression formation processes for evaluative and nonevaluative judgments." *Journal of Psychology and Social Psychology*, 20(2): 200–207.

Hamilton, D. L. & Zanna, M. (1972). "Differential weighting of favorable and unfavorable attributes in impressions of personality." *Journal of Experimental Research in Personality*, 6: 204–212.

Hilgartner, S. & Bosk, C. L. (1988). "The rise and fall of social problems: A public arenas model." *American Journal of Sociology*, 94: 53–78.

Hirsch, P. M. & Pozner, J. E. (2005). "To avoid surprises, acknowledge the dark side: Illustrations from securities analysts." *Strategic Organization*, 3(2): 229–238.

Hollander, E. P. (1958). "Conformity, status, and idiosyncrasy credit." *Psychological Review*, 65(2): 117–127.

—— (1960). "Competence and conformity in the acceptance of influence." *Journal of Abnormal and Social Psychology*, 61: 365–369.

Hudson, B. A. (2008). "Against all odds: A consideration of core-stigmatized organizations." *Academy of Management Review*, 33(1): 252–266.

—— & Okhuysen, G. A. (2009). "Not with a ten-foot pole: Core stigma, stigma transfer, and improbable persistence of men's bathhouses." *Organization Science*, 20(1): 134–153.

Jensen, M. (2006). "Should we stay or should we go? Accountability, status anxiety, and client defections." *Administrative Science Quarterly*, 51: 97–128.

—— & Roy, A. (2008). "Staging exchange partner choices: When do status and reputation matter?" *Academy of Management Journal*, 51(3): 495–516.

Johnston, H., Laraña, E., & Gusfield, J. R. (1994). "Identities, grievances, and new social movements." In E. Laraña, H. Johnston, & J. R. Gusfield (Eds.), *New Social Movements*. Philadelphia: Temple University Press, 3–35.

Kaplan, H. B. & Liu, X. (2000). "Social movements as collective coping with spoiled personal identities: Intimations from a panel study of changes in the life course between adolescence and adulthood." In S. Stryker, T. J. Owens, & R. W. White (Eds.), *Self, Identity, and Social Movements*. Minneapolis: University of Minnesota Press, 215–238.

Kitsuse, J. I. (1962). "Societal reaction to deviant behavior: Problems of theory and method." *Social Problems*, 9: 247–256.

—— (1980). "Coming out all over: Deviants and the politics of social problems." *Social Problems*, 28(1): 1–13.

Kreps, D. & Wilson, R. (1982). "Sequential equilibria." *Econometrica*, 50: 863–894.

Link, B. G. & Phelan, J. C. (2001). "Conceptualizing stigma." *Annual Review of Sociology*, 27: 363–385.

Love, E. G. & Kraatz, M. S. (2009). "Character, conformity, or the bottom line? How and why downsizing affected corporate reputation." *Academy of Management Journal*, 52(2): 314–335.

Major, B. & O'Brien, L. T. (2005). "The social psychology of stigma." *Annual Review of Psychology*, 56: 393–421.

Merton, R. K. (1936). "The unanticipated consequences of purposeful social action." *American Sociological Review*, 1: 894–904.

Meyer, J. W. & Rowan, B. (1977). "Institutionalized organizations: Formal structure as myth and ceremony." *American Journal of Sociology*, 83: 340–363.

Milgrom, P. R. & Roberts, J. (1982). "Predation, reputation, and entry deterrence." *Journal of Economic Theory*, 27: 280–312.

—— & Roberts, J. (1986). "Price and advertising signals of product quality." *Journal of Political Economy*, 94: 796–821.

Mishina, Y., Dykes, B. J., Block, E. S., & Pollock, T. G. (2010). "Why 'good' firms do bad things: The effects of high aspirations, high expectations and prominence on the incidence of corporate illegality." *Academy of Management Journal*, 53(4): 701–722.

——, Block, E. S., & Mannor, M. J. (forthcoming). "The path dependence of organizational reputation: How social judgment influences assessments of capability and character." *Strategic Management Journal*.

Neuberg, S. L., Smith, D. M., & Asher, R. (2000). "Why people stigmatize: Toward a biocultural framework." In T. F. Heatherton, R. E. Kleck, M. R. Hebl, & J. G. Hull (Eds.), *The Social Psychology of Stigma*. New York: The Guilford Press, 31–61.

Nichols, M. W. & Fournier, G. M. (1999). "Recovering from a bad reputation: Changing beliefs about the quality of U.S. autos." *International Journal of Industrial Organization*, 17: 299–318.

Page, R. (1984). *Stigma*. London: Routledge.

Porac, J. F., Thomas, H., Wilson, F., Paton, D., & Kanfer, A. (1995). "Rivalry and the industry model of Scottish knitwear producers." *Administrative Science Quarterly*, 40: 203–227.

——, Ventresca, M., & Mishina, Y. (2002). "Interorganizational cognition and interpretation." In J. A. C. Baum (Ed.), *Companion to Organizations*. Oxford: Blackwell, 579–598.

Pozner, J. E. (2008). "Stigma and settling up: An integrated approach to the consequences of organizational misconduct for organizational elites." *Journal of Business Ethics*, 80: 141–150.

Rhee, M. & Haunschild, P. R. (2006). "The liability of good reputation: A study of product recalls in the U.S. automobile industry." *Organization Science*, 17(1): 101–117.

—— & Valdez, M. E. (2009). "Contextual factors surrounding reputational damage with potential implications for reputation repair." *Academy of Management Review*, 34(1): 146–168.

Rindova, V. P., Williamson, I. O., Petkova, A. P., & Sever, J. M. (2005). "Being good or being known: An empirical examination of the dimensions, antecedents, and consequences of organizational reputation." *Academy of Management Journal*, 48(6): 1033–1049.

——, Pollock, T. G., & Hayward. M. L. A. (2006). "Celebrity firms: The social construction of market popularity." *Academy of Management Review*, 31(1): 50–71.

——, Petkova, A. P., & Kotha, S. (2007). "Standing out: How new firms in emerging markets build reputation in the media." *Strategic Organization*, 5: 31–70.

Roberts, P. W. & Dowling, G. R. (2002). "Corporate reputation and sustained superior financial performance." *Strategic Management Journal*, 23: 1077–1093.

Scheff, T. J. (1974). "The labeling theory of mental illness." *American Sociological Review*, 39: 444–452.

Selznick, P. (1949). *TVA and the Grass Roots*. Berkeley: University of California Press.

Semadini, M., Cannella, A. A., Fraser, D. R., & Lee, D. S. (2008). "Fight or flight: Managing stigma in executive careers." *Strategic Management Journal*, 29: 557–567.

Shamsie, J. (2003). "The context of dominance: An industry-driven framework for exploiting reputation." *Strategic Management Journal*, 24: 199–215.

Shapiro, C. (1982). "Consumer information, product quality, and seller reputation." *The Bell Journal of Economics*, 13(1): 20–35.

—— (1983). "Premiums for high quality products as returns to reputations." *Quarterly Journal of Economics*, 98: 659–679.

Shih, M. (2004). "Positive stigma: Examining resilience and empowerment in overcoming stigma." *Annals of the American Academy of Political and Social Science*, 591: 175–185.

Sitkin, S. B. & Roth, N. L. (1993). "Explaining the limited effectiveness of legalistic 'remedies' for trust/distrust." *Organization Science*, 4(3): 367–392.

Spence, A. M. (1974). *Market Signaling: Informational Transfer in Hiring and Related Processes*. Cambridge, MA: Harvard University Press.

Spender, J. C. (1989). *Industry Recipes: The Nature and Source of Managerial Judgment*. Cambridge, MA: Blackwell.

Sutton, R. I. & Callahan, A. L. (1987). "The stigma of bankruptcy: Spoiled organizational image and its management." *Academy of Management Journal*, 30: 405–436.

Wade, J. B., Porac, J. F., Pollock, T. G., & Graffin, S. D. (2006). "The burden of celebrity: The impact of CEO certification contests on CEO pay and performance." *Academy of Management Journal*, 49: 643–660.

Weigelt, K. & Camerer, C. (1988). "Reputation and corporate strategy: A review of recent theory and applications." *Strategic Management Journal*, 9: 443–454.

Wiesenfeld, B. M., Wurthmann, K., & Hambrick, D. C. (2008). "The stigmatization and devaluation of elites associated with corporate failures: A process model." *Academy of Management Review*, 33(1): 231–251.

CHAPTER 11

UNTANGLING EXECUTIVE REPUTATION AND CORPORATE REPUTATION: WHO MADE WHO?

SCOTT D. GRAFFIN
MICHAEL D. PFARRER
MICHAEL W. HILL

Research examining executive reputation remains in its early stages. Despite much progress, the field has yet to coalesce around a definition of executive reputation, its antecedents, its relationship with other individual-, firm-, and industry-level constructs, and how it interacts with organizational reputation. In this chapter, we review recent research on executive reputation, explicating definitions, measures, and findings. Working from past studies, we provide a definition of executive reputation and examine its relationship to organizational performance, CEO celebrity, executive compensation, and organizational reputation. Further, we discuss how executive reputation is similar to, and different from, organizational reputation, and we posit how the two can coexist. Under normal circumstances, it appears that organization-level and executive-level reputations will converge and co-evolve over time. However, when shocks occur, the differences between these two constructs become more apparent. For example, amid a CEO succession, earnings surprise, or organizational crisis, executive and organizational reputation may diverge.

INTRODUCTION

THEORETICAL and empirical research on reputation as a firm-level construct is nuanced and rich. What has received less attention is executive-level reputation within the firm, and how the reputation of top managers may interact with corporate reputation.

In this chapter, we first provide a review of executive-level reputation research, its related theories, and empirical findings. Subsequent to the review, we provide a definition of executive-level reputation; discuss how it is similar to, and different from, firm-level reputation; and posit how the two coexist within the firm. Superficially, it appears that firm-level and executive-level reputations would move in tandem, co-evolve over time, and that the two would be very difficult to differentiate. However, we suggest that when shocks—both positive and negative—to the firm occur, the differences between these two constructs should become more apparent. Using a shock as our impetus, we first examine the general relationship between firm-level and executive-level reputations. We then examine specific contexts in which the firm's reputation and the reputation of its executives may or may not move in tandem.

REPUTATION IN ORGANIZATIONS

Whereas research on executive reputation is still nascent, theoretical and empirical scholarship on organizational reputation has increased in breadth and depth over the last three decades (see Barnett, Jermier, & Lafferty, 2006; Rindova et al., 2005; and Lange, Lee, & Dai, 2011 for reviews). As such, a brief review of key insights in organizational reputation can assist us in better understanding executive reputation, its antecedents, and how it may interact with organizational reputation.

An organization's reputation is an outward manifestation of its past actions and future expectations (Fombrun, 1996). It signals to its stakeholders that the organization is able to produce quality goods over time (Rindova & Fombrun, 1999; Rindova et al., 2005). Thus, stakeholders perceive organizations with high reputations as being durable and consistent, and stakeholders know what to expect based on the organization's past actions (Clark & Montgomery, 1998). As the organization's reputation grows, it reduces stakeholders' uncertainty about its future, thereby encouraging stakeholders to engage in transactions with it (Rindova et al., 2005). In turn, this increases access to resources under stakeholder control and, ultimately, the chances for economic success (Rindova & Fombrun, 1999). Indeed, numerous studies have empirically uncovered a positive relationship between organization reputation and organization performance (e.g., Deephouse, 2000; Fombrun & Shanley, 1990; Rindova et al., 2005; Roberts & Dowling, 2002).

As theoretical and empirical work has grown over the past three decades, a definition of organization-level reputation has coalesced among organizational scholars. Thus, an organization's reputation may best be described as the collective judgment of the consistent quality of its activities and outputs over time (Barnett, Jermier, & Lafferty, 2006; Deephouse, 2000; King & Whetten, 2008; Rindova et al., 2005).

Executive Reputation: Consistently Delivering Quality over Time?

Like an organization's reputation, an executive's reputation can be an important signal of the quality he or she delivers over time. Executive reputation is also thought to be influential due to the evaluative uncertainty associated with assessments of executive quality. Thus, executive reputation can be similarly conceptualized as a collective judgment of an executive's ability to consistently deliver value over time; something that reduces stakeholders' uncertainty in predicting an executive's future behavior; and an asset that also may have a positive impact on organizational performance.

Assessing the quality of an executive at any given point in time is difficult for a number of reasons. First, unlike its relationship with organizational reputation, organizational performance appears to be only loosely coupled with executive quality (Bok, 1993; March, 1984). Indeed, Holmstrom (1982) noted that an organization's performance is driven not only by executive decisions, but also by industry and environmental factors. Second, organization performance is often team-based (Hambrick & Mason, 1984). Thus, even if the portion of organizational performance that is directly attributable to executive quality could be delineated, it may be difficult to link this outcome to the specific decisions or acumen of individual executives.

Third, organizational research suggests that executives may have only a limited impact on organization-level outcomes (Salancik & Pfeffer, 1977). Informational and legitimacy concerns may constrain the strategic options that executives pursue (Hannan & Freeman, 1984), and the success or failure of an organization may be attributable to past decisions made by executives who are no longer employed at the organization (Stinchcombe, 1965). Together, these arguments suggest that assessing executive quality is a difficult and uncertain matter. Thus, an executive's reputation may be an important source of information to inform assessments of executive quality. We next review the current state of executive reputation research.

RESEARCH ON EXECUTIVE REPUTATION

A recent review of executives' impact on organizational outcomes concluded that there are no consistent links between specific executive characteristics and organizational performance (Finkelstein, Hambrick, & Cannella, 2009: 164–226). Khurana (2002: 102) highlighted this problem in noting that because "it is difficult, if not impossible, to know *ex ante* what characteristics in a CEO are needed to improve performance, directors are left to guess about which criteria are likely to be associated with success."

However, despite the high level of evaluative uncertainty ascribed to executives' ability to generate consistent value over time, several studies have attempted to generate proxies for executive quality and reputation. Such studies have examined management style (Guest, 1962), executive personality (Peterson et al., 2003), charisma (Flynn & Staw, 2004), and the fit between executive characteristics, such as functional background and education level, and industry conditions (Datta & Rajagopalan, 1998).

Additionally, numerous studies have examined external assessments of executive quality while directly or indirectly invoking the construct of executive reputation (see summary table at the end of the chapter). The most common outcome examined in relation to executive reputation is compensation. Milbourn (2003) examined the linkage between a CEO's reputation and CEO pay-for-performance sensitivities. Consistent with our contention, Milbourn (2003) theorized that, as a result of the evaluative uncertainty associated with assessing executive quality, a CEO's reputation serves as a proxy for managerial ability. Interestingly, Milbourn's (2003) is the only study we found that employs multiple measures to capture an executive's reputation. These measures included CEO tenure, whether the CEO was hired from inside or outside of the organization, a count of press articles that mention the CEO's name, and the organization's stock performance. Milbourn argued that the amount of media coverage a CEO receives as well as the CEO's tenure increase the perceived likelihood that the CEO will continue to lead the company going forward. He thus asserted that, to the extent that the CEO is expected to remain in office, the organization's stock price becomes an informative basis for compensating the CEO over the long term. Milbourn found support for this argument in observing that the sensitivity of a CEO's pay to stock performance was more than twice as high for CEOs with high levels of press coverage than it was for CEOs with low amounts of press coverage. Milbourn concluded that "pay sensitivities offered to CEOs in practice are strictly increasing in CEO reputation" (2003: 258).

Executive Reputation and Celebrity

The next set of empirical studies examining executive quality and reputation have focused on what the authors have referred to as superstar CEOs (Malmendier & Tate, 2009) or celebrity CEOs (Graffin et al., 2008; Wade et al., 2006). While the labels differ slightly, each of these studies examined the role of CEOs' winning "CEO of the Year" certification contests in various magazines. A certification contest is a "competition in which actors in a given domain are ranked based upon performance criteria that are accepted by key stakeholders as being credible and legitimate" (Wade et al., 2006: 644). Such certification contests are thought to allow observers to distill myriad data points into one ranking, and to allow observers to make clear and comparable attributions of an actor's relative capabilities or standing (Elsbach & Kramer, 1996; Fombrun & Shanley, 1990; Graffin & Ward, 2010). The resulting certifications signal the relative quality of an actor within a given domain (e.g., industry, organizational field, or time period) and, in turn, create a hierarchical ordering of the actors under consideration (Elsbach & Kramer, 1996; Podolny, 2005; Wade et al., 2006). Thus, such certifications help to inform overall assessments of a firm's or executive's quality, which is consistent with our conceptualization of executive reputation.

How executive reputation and celebrity differ. Executive reputation and CEO celebrity share many common aspects (see Table 11.1). Executive reputation and CEO celebrity each (1) are formed by the judgment of observers, (2) help inform assessments of executive quality, and (3) are informed by organization-level outcomes. The chief metric by which CEO quality is inferred is organization performance (Finkelstein, Hambrick, & Cannella, 2009; Meindl, Ehrlich, & Dukerich, 1985). As such, a necessary antecedent to an executive garnering a high reputation—or becoming a celebrity CEO—is strong organization-level performance.

However, there are some notable differences between these constructs. First, CEO celebrity focuses only on a sub-population of executives, whereas we postulate that executive reputation can pertain to any high-ranking executive. Hayward, Rindova, and Pollock (2004) theorized that to be singled out by the media and exalted as a celebrity CEO, executives must engage in distinctive behaviors so that they will clearly be viewed by journalists as the chief causal mechanism behind positive organizational outcomes. Thus, to the extent that executive reputation is informed by positive organizational outcomes and third-party assessments (Wade et al., 2006), a high executive reputation may be a necessary, but not sufficient, condition for an executive to be considered a celebrity CEO. Accordingly, we suggest that celebrity CEOs are a particular group of high-reputation CEOs who have been singled out by the media because of some idiosyncratic behavior or management practice that has made them more noteworthy than other high reputation CEOs in the eyes of the media or public.

While some studies have referred to CEO "celebrity status" colloquially, we consider this to be a misnomer. Indeed, as we conceive of CEO celebrity as a subset of executive reputation, we see celebrity as an assessment of a given CEO's quality, which is different from status. A CEO's status[1] is inferred through affiliations and not direct assessments

Table 11.1 Key Characteristics of CEO Celebrity and CEO Reputation

Characteristic	Reputation	Celebrity
Formed by observer judgment	√	√
Inform assessments of executive quality	√	√
Positive organizational outcomes	√	√
Distinct CEO behaviors lead to organizational outcomes chiefly attributed to CEO action		√
Media coverage reporting CEO as responsible for positive organizational outcomes		√

[1] Graffin and Ward (2010: 344–345) make a clear distinction between individual reputation and status in noting: "Status is conceived as 'a fundamentally relational concept' (Washington & Zajac 2005: 286) that is not simply an atomistic attribute of an isolated actor but is rather 'directly tied to the

of a CEO's capabilities. Such indicators of CEO status may include attending an elite university, being a member of a particular social club, or even being employed by an organization that has a history of employing high-quality CEOs. Assessments of status may be of particular importance when metrics of a CEO's quality are not directly observable, such as early in a CEO's tenure (assuming he or she had not been a CEO previously) or when he or she is being evaluated for promotion to CEO for the first time. Consistent with this distinction, Graffin et al. (2008) found that executives who affiliate with a celebrity CEO may benefit from this association because status is tied to the relations and affiliations an actor maintains and there is a lack of objective evidence regarding their quality as a CEO going forward (Podolny, 2005).

CEO Celebrity and compensation. Similar to Milbourn's (2003) study on executive reputation, executive celebrity is commonly linked to compensation. Across studies there is robust support that winning certification contests positively impacts CEO compensation (Malmendier & Tate, 2009; Wade et al., 2006). Specifically, Wade et al. (2006) find that award-winning CEOs receive approximately a 10 percent increase in pay relative to non-award-winning CEOs, which translates into roughly a $250k raise. Consistent with Milbourn (2003) and Malmendier and Tate (2009), Wade et al. (2006) also found that celebrity CEOs' compensation is more tightly coupled with subsequent organizational performance. An interesting implication of these findings is that becoming a celebrity CEO, as evidenced by wins in certification contests, leads to positive increases in compensation if the executives' organizations subsequently perform well, but is also associated with lower levels of pay if the organizations subsequently perform poorly. These findings relating to celebrity CEOs are consistent with Fombrun's (1996) suggestion that strong reputation brings with it heightened performance expectations for the future, what he labeled the "burden of celebrity" and what other organizational scholars have labeled the "double-edged sword" associated with higher reputation, visibility, and social approval among stakeholders (cf. Ashforth & Gibbs, 1990; Rhee & Haunschild, 2006). Thus, becoming a celebrity CEO seems to engender both compensatory benefits and burdens that also accompany a strong reputation.

CEO celebrity and the TMT. Top management team (TMT) members who work with celebrity CEOs have also been found to receive increased compensation (Graffin et al., 2008). Further, despite the fact that members of the TMT seem to share in the rewards that accompany being a celebrity CEO, CEOs extract the lion's share of such rents as evidenced by the increasing pay gap between celebrity CEOs and the TMT in the year subsequent to the CEO winning a certification contest (Malmendier & Tate, 2009; Graffin et al., 2008). Graffin et al. (2008) described this phenomenon as "winner-take-most."

pattern of relations and affiliations in which the actor does and does not choose to engage' (Podolny 2005: 13). Thus, status is gained through association with other high-status actors, and, as Washington and Zajac (2005: 282) noted, is 'not based on traditional performance considerations' and can be influential 'irrespective of performance.' On the other hand, reputation does not focus on affiliations, but rather on the evaluation of the quality of an actor." Thus, we do not perceive CEO celebrity as being an indicator of status.

That is, celebrity CEOs enjoy the majority of compensatory spoils, but they also share a portion with the TMT. The authors speculated that celebrity CEOs may share these rewards "because of their desire to maintain cooperative relationships with their senior managers and the wish to retain senior managers who might themselves become more attractive in the external labor market" (2008: 461). Consistent with this contention, Carpenter and Sanders (2002) suggested that large pay gaps between CEOs and other TMT members are negatively associated with subsequent organization performance, and that resentment and a lack of information-sharing are the underlying causes for this relationship.

TMT members who work with celebrity CEOs are also more likely to become CEOs themselves as a result of this relationship (Graffin et al., 2008). Graffin and colleagues found that TMT members were more likely, internally and externally, to be promoted to CEO when they were part of a celebrity CEO's TMT. Thus, employing a celebrity CEO may have the unintended organizational consequence of making TMT members more attractive to other firms.

CEO Celebrity and Other Behaviors. Studies also suggest that CEOs who win certification contests are also more likely to engage in certain behaviors than non-winners. Malmendier & Tate (2009) found that award-winning CEOs were more likely to engage in activities outside of their companies, such as writing books. Specifically, they found that winning one CEO of the Year contest doubles the likelihood of authoring a book, while winning five or more contests increased this likelihood tenfold. Malmendier & Tate (2009) also found that organizations employing award-winning CEOs were more likely to report quarterly earnings that exactly match their quarterly earnings forecasts. Consistent with previous studies (e.g. DeGeorge, Patel, & Zeckhauser, 1999), they suggested that exact matches between actual and forecasted earnings are indicative of earnings manipulation. Relatedly, while not directly studying celebrity CEOs, Hayward & Hambrick (1997) found that the size of the premium organizations paid for acquisitions was positively associated with the amount of media coverage their CEOs received. While the authors used this media coverage as an indicator of executive hubris, such media accounts have subsequently been used as an indicator of CEO reputation (e.g. Milbourn, 2003).

Executive reputation and organizational performance. Finally, several studies have examined the impact of employing celebrity CEOs on subsequent organizational performance. These studies reveal that, much like its influence on executive compensation, CEO celebrity brings with it both benefits and burdens; however, the benefits appear to be very short-lived. In terms of benefits, Wade et al. (2006) found that organizations that employ an award-winning CEO enjoyed positive abnormal stock returns in the days following the announcement of the winners. At the same time, however, they found that these same organizations showed negative stock market returns in the subsequent year relative to organizations that did not employ award-winning CEOs. These negative returns to winning a CEO of the Year contest were also found by Malmendier & Tate (2009). Specifically, they found that organizations that employed award-winning CEOs experienced declines in both accounting-based and market-based performance measures in the three years following the winning of an award. However, a recent study by

Koh (2010) found that employing first-time winners of CEO of the Year contests is positively associated with organization performance.

While the negative performance results may also be consistent with regression to the mean, prior studies attempted to control empirically for this alternative explanation. For example, in predicting subsequent organization performance, Wade et al. (2006) employed an Arellano-Bond dynamic panel model, which included a lagged organizational performance measure as an instrument. Employing this alternative model did not change the results which suggested negative performance returns for organizations that employ award-winning CEOs. Additionally, Malmendier & Tate (2009) constructed a matched-pair sample of similarly performing organizations and compared subsequent performance of this matched pair with the organizations employing medal-winning CEOs. Their results were also unchanged. Thus, there appears to be strong evidence of negative performance returns related to employing celebrity CEOs.

Extending the Executive Reputation–CEO Celebrity Link

One potentially interesting path for future research is investigating what processes cause organizations that employ celebrity CEOs to experience negative performance consequences. Currently two distinct causal mechanisms have been suggested: (1) CEO hubris and (2) higher expectations associated with executive reputation (i.e., the "burden of celebrity"). The hubris hypothesis, initially suggested by Hayward & Hambrick (1997) and elaborated by Hayward, Rindova, and Pollock (2004), suggests that media coverage leads CEOs to become overconfident in their own managerial acumen. This overconfidence is then thought to lead CEOs to underestimate the impact of external factors on organizational outcomes (Hayward, Rindova, & Pollock, 2004). Such biased decision-making is then thought to lead to lower levels of performance. Hayward & Hambrick (1997) found support for the hubris hypothesis by showing that media coverage led CEOs to pay higher premiums for acquisitions and that these acquisitions generated losses for shareholders.

A second potential process involves the increasing expectations that accompany becoming a celebrity CEO. These high expectations, which Fombrun (1996) referred to as "the burden of celebrity," are thought to accompany CEO celebrity as well as a high reputation. Merton recognized long ago that as actors become increasingly renowned, "more and more is expected of them" (1968: 57). This perspective thus suggests that the riskier strategies undertaken by celebrity CEOs may not necessarily be due to executive overconfidence, but rather by high reputation effectively pushing them into pursuing high-risk, high-reward strategies to meet the ever-increasing expectations of board members and shareholders.

While each process may lead to a similar outcome, the causal mechanisms differ. Hubris is an internal bias that causes CEOs to lead their organizations down a risky path, while the burden of celebrity results from CEOs' becoming cornered by their own success and being forced to make increasingly riskier decisions in order to live up to the escalating expectations of their constituents. By teasing out when each process is occurring, future research may provide a better understanding of how executive reputation influences the internal processes of organizations that employ high-reputation executives.

Extending the Executive Reputation–Organization Performance Link

Another area of study that warrants further examination is the impact of CEO celebrity and reputation on subsequent organizational performance. Despite fairly consistent support for negative returns for organizations that employ award-winning CEOs (e.g. Malmendier & Tate, 2009; Wade et al., 2006), Koh's (2010) recent findings provide evidence counter to past research. However, measurement differences of celebrity CEOs across these studies may help to explain these seemingly contradictory results. While Wade et al. (2006) and Malmendier & Tate (2009) assessed organizations that employed single and multiple CEO award winners, Koh (2010) only examined the performance implications for first-time winners.

Thus, to the extent that media attention is actually diagnostic of CEO quality, it may be the case that an initial victory in such contests may give talented CEOs the additional power and discretion that allows them to implement more effectively their superior strategic decision-making. However, as CEOs accumulate additional notoriety, they may fall victim to their own hubris or the burden of celebrity, either of which could force them to implement increasingly riskier strategies. Thus, it may be the case that there is an inverted U-shaped relationship between CEO reputation and organization performance. Further research may attempt to disambiguate how CEO reputation may have differing impacts as it accumulates.

Extending the Executive Reputation–Executive Compensation Link

Authors have also proposed, but not directly explored, differing causal mechanisms that mediate the linkage between CEO reputation and compensation. On the one hand, some authors argue that media attention becomes a form of power that the CEO can leverage in negotiating subsequent compensation packages (e.g. Malmendier & Tate, 2009; Wade et al., 2006). Wade and colleagues (2006) assert that high-reputation executives may have greater prestige power (Finkelstein, 1992) and therefore can positively influence this sort of power by building a positive reputation among observers (Dalton, Barnes, & Zaleznik, 1968). In support of this position, Malmendier & Tate (2009) note that only CEOs who were powerful were able to extract additional income subsequent to winning CEO of the Year contests.

On the other hand, other scholars have theorized that executive reputation may be a signal of managerial ability and that this signal may simply make high-reputation executives more valuable (e.g. Graffin et al., 2008). Fombrun (1996) argued that employing a high-reputation CEO may reduce the uncertainty associated with the quality of the executives leading the organization, which, in turn, may attract more talented employees and allow it greater access to capital. Hayward, Rindova, & Pollock (2004) also noted that the same media attention that leads to a CEO accumulating reputation also reinforces the idea that the CEO is the chief causal mechanism behind the organization's success. This attention will undoubtedly make sitting CEOs more attractive candidates to lead other organizations, which may also force organizations to increase the pay of high-reputation CEOs to ensure they are retained. Future studies may attempt to test which process may actually be occurring.

Advancing Organizational Research on Executive Reputation

As we can see, there have been several recent articles on CEO celebrity and executive reputation, but the field has yet to coalesce around a working definition of it or of those factors that influence it. We have defined executive reputation as a signal of quality to stakeholders. Thus, like organizational reputation, executive reputation is the general perception that an executive is consistently producing value over time (cf. Graffin & Ward, 2010). Working from this definition, we examine those factors that influence executive reputation and suggest some potential avenues for future research.

Organizational Performance

The first factor that influences executive reputation is recent organizational performance. Meindl, Ehrlich, & Dukerich (1985) noted the well-known bias known as the "romance of leadership," which results in observers over-attributing organizational outcomes to executive decision-makers and causes observers to consider them the chief causal agent of firm performance. However, it is not necessarily the level of performance that influences executive reputation, but rather recent performance relative to historical performance. Consistent with attribution theory (Kelley, 1973), we contend that executives will receive the largest attributional benefit or blame when the performance level to which they lead their firms is distinct from the firm's past performance. This contention is consistent with the findings of Meindl, Ehrlich, & Dukerich (1985) that executives were even more likely to be viewed as the primary causal agent when firm performance was extreme. We therefore expect that when organizational performance deviates from expected (i.e., historical) levels, sitting executives will be viewed as the primary cause of this deviation (Hayward, Rindova, & Pollock, 2004).

Organizational Reputation

A second factor that influences the reputation of executives is the reputation of the firm for which they work. As sustained high performance, or the ability to deliver quality, is a key antecedent of organizational reputation, this factor will likely be highly correlated with executive reputation. Indeed, the primary metric by which organization quality is assessed is financial performance and, at the same time, the primary metric by which CEO quality is assessed is organizational performance (Finkelstein, Hambrick, & Cannella, 2009; Kesner & Sorba, 1994). This suggests that, over time, the reputation of an organization and its executives will converge. As we mentioned earlier, Meindl, Ehrlich, & Dukerich (1985) recognized that CEOs receive a disproportionate share of the blame and credit for organization outcomes. Meindl and colleagues noted that observers tend to prefer the simplified attribution of executives directly causing organizational outcomes. Hayward, Rindova, & Pollock (2004) posited that the media attention that leads to a high reputation for executives reinforces and amplifies this well-known bias and results in celebrity CEOs receiving even more credit and blame for subsequent performance. Thus, media attention may cause executive- and organization-level reputations to become even more tightly coupled over time.

Executive and Organizational Reputation Divergence

Whereas many of the factors that can influence executive reputation are similar to those that influence organizational reputation, they also differ in at least three significant ways. A first important difference is the time horizon over which executive reputation is built. While organizational reputation can be built over decades or even centuries, executives have a much shorter period of time over which to build their reputations. For instance, a survey by Booz Allen Hamilton found that the average tenure for CEOs is only 7.6 years (Charan, 2005). Because of this short time frame, each piece of performance information will be weighted more heavily for executives.

Second, executive reputation may be less stable than an organization's reputation. Given the shorter time horizon over which executive reputation is developed, new information that is inconsistent with an executive's reputation may be more salient than it would be for an organization that has developed a reputation over multiple decades. A third distinct characteristic of executive reputation is that it is portable. Indeed, executives with high reputations can take a distinct reputation with them when they leave an organization, even if that organization was where their reputation was built.

Our reading of the current state of the literature on executive reputation is that some of the most fruitful paths for future research will involve those studies that examine organizational and executive reputations simultaneously. To date, we could not find any studies that have attempted to do so: every study we examined measured executive reputation or celebrity, but none included a control for organizational reputation.

Given the tight coupling between executive and organization reputations we described above, attempting to parse out differences may be a difficult task under normal operating circumstances. If an organization has performed well or poorly over time, we suggest that this performance will largely inform the type of reputation its executives will enjoy. However, we suggest that there may be times when executive and organizational reputations diverge, thus allowing us to study these two constructs independently. We now focus on two "shocks" where executive and organizational reputations move in separate directions: (1) during or immediately following executive succession; and (2) following an unexpected positive or negative event.

Executive succession. Executive and organization reputations are most likely to be distinct early in an executive's tenure at the organization. Thus, the period immediately following the promotion of an executive may be the best time to examine these constructs simultaneously—and independently. While measures of organization reputation are fairly well established (Dowling and Gardberg, Chapter 3, this volume), there may be a number of available measures to assess executives' reputations early in their tenures. These measures could include previously serving as a CEO, being an "heir apparent" to the current CEO, CEO age, and previous media attention. If an individual is hired from outside the organization, one could consider if he or she worked under a celebrity CEO, worked at a high-reputation organization, or had previously won a CEO of the Year contest.

Once the assessment of a newly appointed CEO's reputation has been made, a number of interesting research paths are available. We suggest that one potentially fruitful avenue of research is to examine how quickly these two constructs converge. First, we expect that the reputation of a newly appointed executive who is already well known will converge more slowly with organizational reputation than that of a less well-known executive. Individuals who have previously served as a CEO or who sit on numerous boards may already have well-developed reputations, which will converge more slowly with that of their employer. Conversely, if newly appointed CEOs have not developed a reputation, we expect that their and the organization's reputations will quickly converge because the CEOs' current successes or failures are the only sources of information regarding their executive competence.

These ideas suggest a number of potential research questions. For instance, will an executive's existing reputation provide some sort of buffer early in his or her tenure, or will it bring with it higher expectations that may lead to higher performance expectations? For instance, if a well-known CEO stumbles early on in his or her tenure, he or she will more likely be given "the benefit of the doubt," because his or her ability to act as a competent CEO is better known. On the other hand, how quickly will an organization's reputation influence an executive who has already developed his or her own reputation? A recent study by Graffin, Carpenter, & Boivie (2011) begins to address some of these questions. The authors found that when a newly appointed CEO had never previously served as a CEO, organizations engaged in impression management techniques to minimize the potential negative market reaction to this individual's promotion. This finding suggests that board members are aware of the fact that the perceived quality of new CEOs who have a lower reputation is more heavily influenced by each new piece of information about them.

Relatedly, researchers could also examine how the reputation of a prior executive may impact the early evaluation of the executive who succeeds this individual. For instance, how might following a high-reputation or celebrity CEO impact the newly appointed CEO? Does succeeding such high-reputation CEOs negatively impact the early evaluation of this individual? Does the "burden of celebrity" transfer to those who follow such high-reputation individuals, or do board members recalibrate their performance expectations after a high-reputation CEO steps down?

Another potentially interesting set of research questions could examine how the reputation of a newly appointed executive may interact with the relative reputation of his or her organization. For instance, how might an executive with a high reputation who becomes the CEO of an organization with a low reputation influence the early evaluations of both? For example, James Kilts was hired as the CEO of Gillette in 2001 (Kanter, 2003; Symonds & Forester, 2001). Gillette was suffering from poor performance, with declining market share, lack of sales growth, and declining share prices (Kanter, 2003; Symonds & Forester, 2001). Despite Gillette's poor performance, Kilts, who already possessed a high executive reputation as CEO of Nabisco, took the position of CEO at an organization whose reputation had clearly been diminished (Symonds & Forester, 2001). In this particular case, Kilts possessed such a high executive reputation that observers predicted that Gillette would turn around its performance easily and quickly (Symonds & Forester, 2001). During Kilts' tenure as CEO, Gillette improved its performance and was eventually sold to Procter and Gamble (Kanter, 2003; Colvin, 2005). Media coverage of the improved performance at Gillette attributed the gains to Kilts' performance and strategic decisions that he made as CEO (Kanter, 2003).

Due to the linkage of the executive with previous successes, observers expect the fortunes of the organization to improve immediately (Symonds & Forester, 2001). These expectations for improved performance may translate into immediate gains in the organization's reputation. When the organization demonstrates improvements, and those improvements are attributed to the executive with the high executive reputation, the result is both improved organizational reputation and improved executive reputation. Future studies could examine how this situation might play out.

Future research could also examine the circumstances in which a relatively unknown manager joins an organization that has a high reputation. Initially, consistent with our expectation that the executive and firm reputations will converge over time, we expect that the manager's reputation will be enhanced simply by being selected for a managerial position at an organization with a high reputation. This is similar to the initial positive enhancement of an organization's reputation from hiring a manager with a high reputation. This effect will be most noticeable when an organization hires a top manager without a well-known reputation. Certain organizations, particularly large publicly traded organizations, are under substantial pressure to avoid hiring executives who do not have well-known, positive executive reputations (Khurana, 2002). Despite this fact, organizations will sometimes choose executives who do not have an established reputation. When initially hired, an executive's reputation will begin to form where one previously did not exist. If the organization has a positive organizational reputation, a halo or positive spillover effect may occur from the organization to the new executive.

After this initial halo has occurred, observers will monitor the organization where the executive is working. If the organization maintains its high reputation, and continues to perform well, then the executive's reputation may increase. Whether this affects the reputation of the executive will depend again on what actions observers attribute to maintaining the organization's high level of reputation. If stakeholders attribute the organization's continued success to the executive, then his or her reputation will be enhanced. If not, then the executive's reputation will not change. Overall, we expect that the context of executive succession is an interesting time during which to attempt to tease out the interplay between executive and organization reputations.

"*Surprises.*" An additional context in which researchers could attempt to separate executive and organization reputations may be after a significant unexpected occurrence. Examples of such surprise events are lawsuits, mergers or acquisitions, divestitures or plant closures, product recalls, earnings surprises, and financial restatements (cf. McWilliams & Siegel, 1997; Pfarrer, Pollock, & Rindova, 2010; Pfarrer et al., 2008). Consistent with our contention that executive reputation is less stable than organizational reputation, and thus has less of a buffer or "reservoir of goodwill" associated with it (Jones, Jones, & Little, 2000; Pfarrer, Pollock, & Rindova, 2010), we expect that in response to an unexpected occurrence that is positive, executive reputation would receive a bigger boost. In contrast, executive reputation would be more negatively impacted than organization reputation in light of a negative occurrence.

We thus expect that changes in executive and organization reputations would have significantly different slopes in response to an unexpected occurrence. While Fombrun recognized that reputations "sit on the slippery ground of their constituents' fickle interpretation" (Fombrun, 1996: 388), we expect that executive reputation is more volatile. This is due to a number of factors we have mentioned above, including the relatively shorter time over which executive reputation is formed, making new information more salient, and its greater reliability on the positive effect it generates among constituents (Pfarrer, Pollock, & Rindova, 2010; Rindova, Pollock, & Hayward, 2006). Also, while organizational performance may be assessed in multiple ways, very few (if any) direct measures of executive quality are available. As such, new information will be more heavily weighted for executives than it is for organizations.

Limitations and Future Research Directions

An important limitation of studies examining executive reputation or CEO celebrity is that all such studies have been tested using samples of large public companies from the United States. This limitation suggests two avenues for future research. First, how might executive reputation influence outcomes for start-up companies (Petkova, Chapter 19, this volume)? It may be the case that hiring a high-reputation celebrity CEO may be particularly influential in terms of access to resources or the valuation of an initial public offering (IPO) for newly formed companies. Consistent with this idea, Sanders and Boivie (2005) found that observable governance characteristics influenced IPO valuations. The authors assert that observable firm characteristics are particularly influential when other performance metrics may not be publically available. Thus, given the uncertainty associated with assessing start-up firms, the impact of high-reputation CEOs may be amplified.

Future studies may also wish to examine the impact of executive reputation on organizational outcomes across national contexts (Newburry, Chapter 12, this volume). On the one hand, it may be the case that the influence of executive reputation may be idiosyncratic to the United States because American CEOs receive a higher level of compensation and media attention than their counterparts in other parts of the world. However, we performed an Internet search and found that numerous locations outside of the United States hold various CEO of the Year awards and devote a great deal of media attention to CEOs. Thus, future studies may wish to examine how executive reputation dynamics may play out in different national contexts.

Lastly, all previous studies have focused on how external parties perceive the reputation of an executive. However, an executive's internal reputation among his or her subordinates or colleagues may diverge significantly from his or her external reputation. Indeed, as a CEO accumulates media attention, his or her colleagues may be proud of the recognition brought to their organization, and press coverage may lead to more positive assessments of a sitting CEO. However, as a CEO is repeatedly exalted in the media and treated as the chief causal agent behind positive firm outcomes, those same individuals may begin to resent the simplified account of organizational success that is typically presented in the press. Thus, it could be that, over time, the internal and external reputations of executives may diverge.

Conclusion

In this chapter, we first reviewed recent research on executive reputation, explicating definitions, measures, and findings. Working from past studies, we then provided a working definition of executive reputation and examined its relationship to organizational performance, CEO celebrity, executive compensation, and organizational reputation. Further, we discussed how it is similar to, and different from, organizational reputation, and we posited how the two can coexist. Under normal circumstances, it appears that organization-level and executive-level reputations would converge and co-evolve over time. However, when shocks occur, the differences between these two constructs become more apparent. For example, amid a CEO succession, earnings surprise, or organizational crisis, executive and organizational reputations may diverge.

Research on executive reputation remains in the early stages. Despite much progress, the field has yet to coalesce around a definition of executive reputation, its antecedents, its relationship with other individual-, firm-, and industry-level constructs, and how it interacts with organizational reputation. In this chapter, we have attempted to address many of these issues, and we hope that our arguments have laid the groundwork for several exciting avenues of future research.

Core Research on Executive Reputation

Reference	Key Constructs and Findings
Milbourn (2003)	Higher CEO reputation leads to greater stock-based pay sensitivity.
Wade et al. (2006)	• When CEOs become certified as experts, stockholders value certification initially but effects dissipate and become negative.
	• Certification has positive effect on CEO compensation; effect larger than performance differences between CEOs who win and those who do not
	• Certification has positive effect on CEO pay-for-performance sensitivity for CEOs.
Graffin et al. (2008)	• Managers who work for high-status CEOs obtain higher compensation.
	• "Burden of celebrity": with star CEOs, linkage increases pay-for-performance sensitivity. Linkage tightest for CEOs.
	• Subordinates who work for star CEOs more likely to become CEOs themselves.
Malmendier & Tate (2009)	• CEOs more likely to engage in earnings management after winning an award.
	• The performance of winners' firms declines compared with predicted winners.
	• Despite firm performance declining after an award is won by the CEO, their compensation increases significantly over next three years compared with predicted winners.
	• Increased CEO compensation and firm performance decreases only found in firms with poor corporate governance.
	• After winning, CEOs change behavior, and spend more time engaged in activities outside the firm.
Graffin & Ward. (2010)	• Even when there is essentially no technical uncertainty, certifications influence reputation.
	• Two types of uncertainty influence one's reputation: technical uncertainty and performance standard uncertainty. Certification influences reputation by reducing both uncertainties.
	• When actor's technical performance nears the desired performance standard, certifications are more influential.
Koh (2011)	• Celebrity CEOs positively impact financial reporting quality and firm performance.
	• After CEO wins first award, firm performance increases (accounting and market returns).
	• Capital markets view firm's long-term performance after celebrity CEOs win awards.

REFERENCES

Ashforth, B. E. & Gibbs, B. W. (1990). "The double-edge of organizational legitimation." *Organization Science*, 1(2): 177–194.

Barnett, M. L., Jermier, J. M., & Lafferty, B. A. (2006). "Corporate reputation: The definitional landscape." *Corporate Reputation Review*, 9(1): 26–38.

Bok, D. (1993). *The Cost of Talent: How Executives and Professionals are Paid and How it Affects America*. New York: Free Press.

Carpenter, M. A. & Sanders, W. G. (2002). "Top management team compensation: The missing link between CEO pay and firm performance?" *Strategic Management Journal*, 23(4): 367–375.

Charan, R. (2005). "Ending the CEO succession crisis." *Harvard Business Review*, 83(2): 72–81.

Clark, B. H. & Montgomery, D. B. (1998). "Deterrence, reputations, and competitive cognition." *Management Science*, 44(1): 62–82.

Colvin, G. (2005). "Targeting CEO comp." *Fortune* (Europe), 152(11): 30

Dalton, G. W., Barnes, L. B., & Zaleznik, A. (1968). *The Distribution of Authority in Formal Organizations*. Boston: Harvard University Press.

Datta, D. K. & Rajagopalan, N. (1998). "Industry structure and CEO characteristics: An empirical study of succession events." *Strategic Management Journal*, 19(9): 833–852.

Deephouse, D. (2000). "Media reputation as a strategic resource: An integration of mass communication and resource-based theories." *Journal of Management*, 26(6): 1091–1112.

DeGeorge, F., Patel, J., & Zeckhauser, R. (1999). "Earnings manipulation to exceed thresholds." *Journal of Business*, 72(1): 1–33.

Elsbach, K. D. & Kramer, R. M. (1996). "Members' responses to organizational identity threats: Encountering and countering the business week rankings." *Administrative Science Quarterly*, 41(3): 442–476.

Finkelstein, S. (1992). "Power in top management teams: Dimensions, measurement, and validation." *Academy of Management Journal*, 35(3): 505–538.

——, Hambrick, D. C., & Cannella, A. A. (2009). *Strategic Leadership: Theory and Research on Executives, Top Management Teams, and Boards*. Oxford: New York.

Flynn, F. J. & Staw, B. M. (2004). "Lend me your wallets: The effect of charismatic leadership on external support for an organization." *Strategic Management Journal*, 25(4): 309–330.

Fombrun, C. J. (1996). *Reputation: Realizing Value from the Corporate Image*. Boston: Harvard Business School Press.

—— & Shanley, M. (1990). "What's in a name? Reputation building and corporate strategy." *Academy of Management Journal*, 33(2): 233–258.

Graffin, S. D. & Ward, A. J. (2010). "Certifications and reputation: Determining the standard of desirability amidst uncertainty." *Organization Science*, 21(2): 331–346.

——, Wade, J. B., Porac, J. F., & McNamee, R. C. (2008). "The impact of CEO status diffusion on the economic outcomes of other senior managers." *Organization Science*, 19(3): 457–474.

Graffin, S., Carpenter, M., & Boivie, S. (2011). "What's all that (strategic) noise? Anticipatory impression management in CEO successions." *Strategic Management Journal*, 32(7): 748–770.

Guest, R. J. (1962). "Managerial succession in complex organizations." *American Journal of Sociology*, 68(1): 47–56.

Hambrick, D. & Mason, P. (1984). "Upper echelons: The organization as a reflection of its top managers." *Academy of Management Review*, 9(2): 193–206.

Hannan, M. & Freeman, J. (1984). "Structural inertia and organizational change." *American Sociological Review*, 49(2): 149–160.

Hayward, M. L. A. & Hambrick, D. C. (1997). "Explaining the premiums paid for large acquisitions: Evidence of CEO hubris." *Administrative Science Quarterly*, 42(1): 103–127.

——, Rindova, V. P., & Pollock, T. G. (2004). "Believing one's own press: The causes and consequences of CEO celebrity." *Strategic Management Journal*, 25(7): 637–653.

Holmstrom, B. (1982). "Moral hazard in teams." *The Bell Journal of Economics*, 13(2): 324–340.

Jones, G. H., Jones, B. H., & Little., P. (2000). "Reputation as reservoir: Buffering against loss in times of economic crisis." *Corporate Reputation Review*, 3(1): 21–29.

Kanter, R. M. (2003). "Leadership and the psychology of turnarounds." *Harvard Business Review*, 81(6): 58–67.

Kelley, H. H. (1973). "The processes of causal attribution." *American Psychologist*, 28(2): 107–128.

Kesner, I. F. & Sebora, T. C. (1994). "Executive succession: Past, present and future." *Journal of Management*, 20(2): 327–372.

Khurana, R. (2002). *Searching for a Corporate Savior: The Irrational Quest for Charismatic CEOs*. Princeton, NJ: Princeton University Press.

King, B. G. & Whetten, D. A. (2008). "Rethinking the relationship between reputation and legitimacy: A social actor conceptualization." *Corporate Reputation Review*, 11(3): 192–208.

Koh, K. (2011). "Value or glamour? An empirical investigation of the effect of celebrity CEOs on financial reporting practices and firm performance." *Accounting & Finance*, 51(2): 517–547.

Lange, D., Lee, P. M., & Dai, Y. (2011). "Organizational reputation: A review." *Journal of Management*, 37(1): 153–184.

Malmendier, U. & Tate, G. (2009). "Superstar CEOs." *Quarterly Journal of Economics*, 124(4): 1593–1638.

March, J. G. (1984). "Notes on ambiguity and executive compensation." *Scandinavian Journal of Management Studies*, 1(1): 53–64.

McWilliams, A. & Siegel, D. (1997). "Event studies in management research: Theoretical and empirical issues." *Academy of Management Review*, 40(3): 626–657.

Meindl, J. R., Ehrlich, S. B., & Dukerich, J. M. (1985). "The romance of leadership." *Administrative Science Quarterly*, 30(1): 78–102.

Merton, R. K. (1968). "The Matthew effect in science." *Science*, 159(3810): 56–63.

Milbourn, T. T. (2003). "CEO reputation and stock-based compensation." *Journal of Financial Economics*, 68(2): 233–262.

Petersen, T. (1993). "Recent advances in longitudinal methodology." *Annual Review of Sociology*, 19: 425–454.

Peterson, R. S., Smith, D. B., Martorana, P. V., & Owens, R. D. (2003). "The impact of chief executive officer personality on top management team dynamics: One mechanism by which leadership affects organizational performance." *Journal of Applied Psychology*, 88(5): 795–808.

Pfarrer, M. D., Smith, K. G., Bartol, K. M., Khanin, D. M., & Zhang, X. (2008). "Coming forward: The effects of social and regulatory forces on the voluntary restatement of earnings subsequent to wrongdoing." *Organization Science*, 19(3): 386–403.

——, Pollock, T. G., & Rindova, V. P. (2010). "A tale of two assets: The effects of firm reputation and celebrity on earnings surprises and investors reactions." *Academy of Management Journal*, 53(5): 1131–1152.

Podolny, J. M. (2005). *Status Signals: A Sociological Study of Market Competition*. Princeton, NJ: Princeton University Press.

Rhee, M. & Haunschild, P. R. (2006). "The liability of good reputation: A study of product recalls in the U.S. automobile industry." *Organization Science*, 17(1): 101–117.

Rindova, V. P. & Fombrun, C. J. (1999). "Constructing competitive advantage: The role of firm-constituent interactions." *Strategic Management Journal*, 20(8): 691–710.

——, Williamson, I. O., Petkova, A. P., & Sever, J. M. (2005). "Being good or being known: An empirical examination of the dimensions, antecedents, and consequences of organizational reputation." *Academy of Management Journal*, 48(6): 1033–1049.

——, Pollock, T. G., & Hayward, M. L. A. (2006). "Celebrity firms: The social construction of market popularity." *Academy of Management Review*, 31(1): 50–71.

Roberts, P. & Dowling, G. (2002). "Corporate reputation and sustained superior financial performance." *Strategic Management Journal*, 23(12): 1077–1093.

Salanick, G. & Pfeffer, J. (1977). "Constraints on administrator discretion: The limited influence of mayors on city budgets." *Urban Affairs Quarterly*, 12(4): 475–498.

Stinchcombe, A. L. (1965). "Social structure and organizations." In J. G. March (Ed.), *Handbook of Organizations*. Chicago: Rand McNally, 142–193.

Symonds, W. C. & Forester, J. (2001). "Can James Kilts put a new edge on Gillette?" *Businessweek.com* (26 January 2001) <http://www.businessweek.com/bwdaily/dnflash/jan2001/nf2001026_543.htm>, accessed 29 June 2010.

Wade, J. B., Porac, J. F., Pollock, T. G., & Graffin, S. D. (2006). "The burden of celebrity: The impact of CEO certification contests on CEO pay and performance." *Academy of Management Journal*, 49(4): 643–660.

Washington, M. & Zajac, E. J. (2005). "Status evolution and competition: Theory and evidence." *Academy of Management Journal*, 48(2): 281–296.

···

CHAPTER 12

WAVING THE FLAG: THE INFLUENCE OF COUNTRY OF ORIGIN ON CORPORATE REPUTATION

···

WILLIAM NEWBURRY

Country of origin (COO) effects refer to "the impact which generalizations and perceptions about a country have on a person's evaluations of the country's products and/or brands" (Lampert & Jaffe, 1996: 29). In comparing large, multi-business corporations, it is hard to consider all corporation aspects. As a result, COO works as a simplifier that encompasses many other attributes. Limited information about multinational corporations (MNCs) and bounded rationality in a host country may lead to stereotypical judgments based on organizational classes to which MNCs are perceived to belong, such as a home country (Kostova & Zaheer, 1999). While COO has been studied extensively with respect to firm products, the impact of country on a firm's overall reputation and the dimensions forming a country's reputation are less well understood. In this chapter, we examine these issues. Understanding the impact of home country reputations on firm reputations in a host country, and which factors contribute to these impacts, is particularly important to managers of multinational firms. Knowing the degree to which firms benefit from or are hindered by their home country's reputation will allow firms to better manage their overall reputations as well as reputations amongst particular constituency groups.

INTRODUCTION

···

THE importance of location is one of the central tenets of the international business field (e.g., Dunning, 2009). Location characteristics impact a multitude of decisions by multinational firms, such as foreign direct investment (FDI), partner selection, and entry mode choice (e.g., Caves, 1974; Chandra & Newburry, 1997). Moreover, the location of a firm's headquarters impacts numerous key areas within the firm, such as management practices (Newburry, Gardberg, & Belkin, 2006), strategy (Zhang et al., 2010), marketing (Li & Wyer, 1994), finance (Chacar, Newburry, & Vissa, 2010), human resource management (HRM) (Mezias, 2002), corporate social responsibility practices (Maignan & Ralston, 2002), and more. Most location studies focus on more tangible aspects of a target host country, such as its GDP, market size, institutional development, or culture. However, locations also impact the perceptions and supportive behaviors of local stakeholders, such as product consumers, investors, and employees (Newburry, 2010). A major interest of these studies is the intangible component associated with a firm's or product's home country, which aids as a simplifying device in making firm supportive behavior decisions. This component is often referred to as a country of origin (COO) effect, which refers to "the impact which generalizations and perceptions about a country have on a person's evaluations of the country's products and/or brands" (Lampert & Jaffe, 1996: 29). Limited information about MNCs and bounded rationality in a host country may lead to stereotypical judgments based on organizational classes to which MNCs are perceived to belong, such as a home country (Kostova & Zaheer, 1999). While COO has been studied extensively with respect to firm products, the impact of country on other aspects of a firm's overall reputation is less well understood. In this chapter, we review the literature on COO and other effects related to the reputations of countries, with the aim of better understanding the degree to which firm reputations are determined by the reputations of the countries from which they hail.

LITERATURE REVIEW, SUMMARY, AND EVALUATION

Corporate reputation refers to the overall knowledge and esteem about a corporation held by the public (Fombrun, 1996). Reputation has been demonstrated to be associated with numerous important firm outcomes (Dowling, 2006), and is well established as an area of significant research interest (Fombrun & Shanley, 1990; Basdeo et al., 2006). However, the impacts of country reputations have been studied less directly, although several literature streams related to the importance of home countries provide guidance regarding possible country reputation effects. Thus, before proceeding to examine the potential impacts that country may have on a firm's overall reputation, we first review the existing literature relating to home country effects on supportive behaviors by individuals toward firms. We start by reviewing the country of origin (COO) literature, the area most developed in terms of country-level impacts. We then examine related areas, such as the liability of foreignness literature and the more recent country reputation literature. Important terms associated with these literature streams are found in the summary table at the end of the chapter.

Country of Origin (COO)

Consistent with location as a central component of the international business field, the term "country of origin" has been used in multiple circumstances in relation to multinational corporations (Noorderhaven & Harzing, 2003). As such, this literature seems an appropriate starting point in understanding country reputation. Two major literature strands seem important in analyzing country of origin effects—studies that examine how home country characteristics impact the actions of firms, and studies that examine local stakeholder perceptions of firms headquartered in other countries.

First, COO has been used to predict how the actions of MNCs differ based upon the home country where they are headquartered. For example, Grosse & Trevino (1996) used COO to predict investment patterns of companies into the United States. Wang, Clegg, & Kafouros (2009) found differences among foreign direct investors based upon COO with regard to whether they targeted the local or export market in China. Elango & Sethi (2007) examined how a company's home country influenced the relationship between internationalization and performance. Zhang et al. (2010) found that diversity with respect to FDI country origins facilitates FDI spillovers in a domestic market. With respect to employment practices, although MNCs often adapt strategic HR orientations to local conditions (Schuler, Dowling, & Decieri, 1993; Taylor, Beechler, & Napier, 1996), some home nation elements generally remain (e.g., Hayden & Edwards, 2001; Robinson, 1995) as companies manage the tensions between adapting to local institutional environments and HQ control (Yu & Zaheer, 2010). Overall, studies in this category find that home countries significantly impact MNC actions. These actions are highly related to the institutional environment of the home country (e.g., Deephouse, Li, & Newburry, 2009; Chacar, Newburry, & Vissa, 2010), the subject of a separate chapter in this *Handbook* (see Brammer and Jackson, Chapter 15, this volume).

While the above studies focus on COO impacts on the competitive actions of firms from particular home countries, a separate strand of COO literature focuses on perceptions of stakeholders in local host markets regarding firms from particular countries. Within this literature, it is observed that country characteristics imprint on their firms, leading firms to be associated with their country of origin (Li & Wyer, 1994). Herein, COO is most often studied from a marketing lens, and more specifically in relationship to products (Li & Wyer, 1994). Additionally, both the positive and the negative associations of products from particular countries have been noted. For example, Johansson, Ronkainen, & Czinkota (1994) noted negative associations for products from the former Soviet Union. Country of origin effects can also differ between product categories associated with a country, such that the term *product–country image* has been used to note the interrelationship between product and country (e.g., Knight, Holdsworth, & Mather, 2007; Papadopoulos & Heslop, 1993). Moreover, perceptions of a particular country's products may vary between countries (Gurhan-Canli & Maheswaran, 2000), as well as between different demographic groups within a country (Meng, Nasco, & Clark, 2008).

Li & Wyer (1994) found that COO affects product perceptions in at least three related and often overlapping ways. First, COO can act as one of a corporation's attributes (Hong & Wyer, 1989), which consumers combine with other attributes when evaluating products. Second, COO can work as a signal (Li, Leung, & Wyer, 1993), which consumers use to infer more specific information about manufactured products from a particular country. Finally, Li & Wyer (1994) found that COO may be used as a standard against which products from a particular country are compared. Verlegh & Steenkamp (1999), in their meta-analysis of COO research, found that COO has a larger effect on the perceived quality of a product than on attitudes toward the product or on intentions toward product purchase. Jo (2005), echoing earlier research, found that COO effects are lower when information about other product attributes is available. Sharma (2011) recently found that the influence of COO on behavioral intentions is moderated by consumer ethnocentrism, materialism, and value consciousness, and that the nature of these moderations differs depending upon whether the potential purchaser is in a developed or developing country. From a legitimacy perspective, limited information about MNCs and bounded rationality in a host country may lead the legitimization process to stereotypical judgments based on organizational classes to which MNCs are perceived to belong, such as industry or home country (Kostova & Zaheer, 1999).

While the bulk of COO studies have referred to product evaluations, this concept can be applied to corporations as well. Firms are founded in a particular context, which can be associated with their country of origin. Countries differ in many aspects, such as culture, economic systems, political conditions, technology, development, and regulatory systems. Each of these aspects has a great effect on the characteristics, worldviews, and missions of firms from a country. Meyer (1995) discussed how regulatory policies differ substantially within and between regions. Differences among countries will be reflected in their corporations, which, over time, will lead to variations in perceptions of firms from different countries. For example, Maignan & Ralston (2002) found that European and US firms adopt different strategies to communicate their corporate social responsibility (CSR) activities. Within *post hoc* analyses, Newburry, Gardberg, & Belkin (2006) examined the country of origin of firms in their sample, and found differences between countries in terms of relative workplace attractiveness.

Liability of Foreignness

Related to the country of origin literature is the literature on the liability of foreignness (LOF). Dating back to the work of Hymer (1976) and Kindleberger (1969), it is commonly suggested that foreign firms face costs of doing business abroad (CDBA) that put them at a competitive disadvantage relative to local firms. Zaheer (1995) argued that these costs, which she referred to as the liability of foreignness, are mainly due to spatial distances between parents and subsidiaries, a subsidiary's unfamiliarity and lack of root in a host country, the host country environment (e.g., lack of legitimacy), and the home country environment (e.g., regulations). In essence, this literature argues that firms from

foreign countries (regardless of the particular home country) will face negative consequences, including lower reputations, due to their lack of embeddedness within the local
operating environment.

Organizational legitimacy is an important contributor to LOF. Kostova & Zaheer
(1999) noted three factors shaping this legitimacy. First is the difference between home
and host country institutional characteristics, including regulative, normative, and cognitive institutions (Scott, 1995). Second are organizational characteristics that influence
both internal legitimacy (among MNC subunits) and external legitimacy (subunit legitimacy in a host environment). Finally, the legitimization process itself affects organizational legitimacy, and thus, foreign firms can gain or lose legitimacy over time, making
LOF a dynamic concept (Zaheer & Mosakowski, 1997).

Empirical evidence generally supports the view that foreign firms do indeed face liabilities, particularly within developed country contexts. For example, Mezias (2002)
found foreign-headquartered firms more likely to litigate labor lawsuits than domestic
firms in the US, and less knowledgeable about US labor practices and legal systems. Also
in the US, Newburry, Gardberg, & Belkin (2006) found foreign firms as less attractive
places of employment. Similarly, Gardberg & Schepers (2008) found that foreign-headquartered firms were perceived as having lower corporate social performance than their
domestic counterparts. Newburry (2010) also found significant differences between foreign and domestic firms in the degree to which local populations stated an intention to
pursue the supportive behaviors of product purchase, investment, and workplace attractiveness. However, a few recent scholars have challenged the assumption that foreignness is always a liability and suggested that under some conditions foreignness can be an
asset. For example, Nachum (2003, 2010) found multinationality advantages amongst
London banks and financial institutions, and Perez-Batres & Eden (2008) found a liability of localness in the Mexican banking industry. Given that institutional conditions
vary between developed and developing countries, it seems imprudent to assume that
liability of foreignness theory will necessarily apply in developing country contexts.

Country Reputation

While COO and LOF have relatively long histories of academic attention, the topic of
country reputation is a much more recent area of interest.

Anholt (2003, 2010) has focused extensively on the brand images of countries, which
he equates with their reputations, and later, cities and regions as well. Since 2005, he has
published the Anholt-GfK Roper Nation Brands Index, which surveys approximately
20,000 individuals in 20 countries regarding their perceptions of 50 countries with
respect to: exports, governance, culture and heritage, people, tourism, and investment
and immigration—six dimensions which he labels the "hexagon of competitive
identity" for national brands and reputations (Anholt, 2007).

The Reputation Institute (2009) recently began measuring country reputations via its
CountryRep™ index in terms of 11 attributes within 3 dimensions related to whether the

country had an effective government, an advanced economy, and an appealing environment. In 2009, approximately 22,000 consumer interviews were conducted online in the G8 countries (Canada, France, Germany, Italy, Russia, United Kingdom, and United States) to produce these ratings for 34 country brands. Additionally, country reputations were also rated in terms of self-perceptions within a country (i.e. Spain's rating of Spain) within 33 of the 34 countries. Foreman, Whetten, and Mackey (Chapter 9, this volume) examine organizational identity and related concepts such as image and legitimacy. Embedded within their chapter, and particularly in terms of image scholars, they note the distinction between approaches that examine a projected or self-view of an organization versus a reflected or external view. These scholars note that organizations need to manage the degree of consistency between outside perceptions and self-perceptions (Dutton & Dukerich, 1991; Elsbach & Kramer, 1996). This desire for consistency would seem to apply to country reputations as well. Overall, there was a 0.445 correlation between the CountryRep™ external scores and self-image scores for 2009, suggesting that while these are related, there are significant differences between the way residents of countries see themselves and how they are seen by others. As a separate part of the Reputation Institute study, country reputations were found to be empirically related to whether a person would pursue supportive behaviors related to whether that person would recommend visiting, living in, working in, or investing in a country (Reputation Institute, 2009).

In an early precursor to the Reputation Institute's country reputation measurement, Passow, Fehlmann, & Grahlow (2005) worked with the Reputation Institute to develop a measurement tool to examine the reputation of Liechtenstein using the following dimensions: emotional appeal, physical appeal, financial appeal, leadership appeal, cultural appeal, and social appeal. Yang et al. (2008) relabeled social appeal as global appeal in their study, while also adding political appeal to the measure. Kang & Yang (2010) found that country reputations influenced attitudes towards South Korean products, along with purchase intentions. Moreover, they found that country reputations were influenced by corporate reputations. Also working with the Reputation Institute, Alloza (2009) found evidence of Spanish firms' negative business reputations in Latin America, despite the fact that Spanish investment in Latin America is largely driven by historical and cultural ties (Galan, Gonzalez-Benito, & Zuniga-Vincente, 2007). He also noted that the negative reputations of Spanish firms did not necessarily apply to other non-business aspects of Spain's country reputation. These results are consistent with other studies finding that Spanish MNCs tend to have negative images in Latin America, often associated with a poor quality image (Guillen, 2005; Noya, 2004). For example, Casilda-Bejar (2002) argued that Latin American countries tend to consider the Spanish brand as distant, arrogant, and unfriendly.

Newsweek recently developed a measure of "The World's Best Countries" based upon five categories with multiple submeasures: education, health, quality of life, economic dynamism, and political environment (*Newsweek*, 2010). Deviating from the methodology of Country RepTrak™ and the Nation Brands Index, the *Newsweek* ratings rely on secondary data collected by sources such as the CIA's *World Factbook*, the World Health

Organization, the World Bank, and the United Nations Development Program (UNDP), among others. As such, it is much more a measure of actual country characteristics, as opposed to country reputations.

Table 12.1 lists the top-rated countries in CountryRep™, the Nation Brands Index (NBI), and the *Newsweek* ratings. While the majority of the top countries are the same throughout the various rankings, there are nonetheless strong differences in the relative country rankings. Excluding the CountryRep™ self-assessments, virtually all of the top 20 country brands are developed countries, with the exception of Brazil, which comes in at number 20 in both the CountryRep™ external and the NBI ratings. Within the CountryRep™ self-assessments, however, several developing countries are present, including India, China, Chile, Thailand, Russia, and Poland. Overall, there is a 0.702 correlation between the CountryRep™ external scores and the Nation Brands Index (NBI) scores, suggesting that these measures tap into similar constructs. Additionally, the *Newsweek* ratings correlate at 0.763 and 0.707 with the CountryRep™ and NBI scores, respectively, suggesting that a large proportion of the reputation ratings are based on actual country performance. By contrast, there are correlations of only 0.207 and 0.363 between the CountryRep™ self-assessment scores and the NBI and *Newsweek* scores, respectively, suggesting large differences between self-perceptions and external perceptions.

Contemporary Issues, Debates, and Unanswered Questions

With respect to country reputation, many key questions remain unanswered. Some crucial ones are highlighted in the following subsections, with a focus on direction of causality, liability of foreignness versus country of origin, country reputation dimensions, management of country reputation, industry and other moderating effects, and developing versus developed market impacts.

Direction of Causality

Convincing arguments can be made that company reputations influence their home country reputations, and also that company reputations are influenced by the reputations of their home countries. Untangling the conditions under which one reputation level influences the other would be of both academic and practical benefit. A general depiction of the interrelated nature of these relationships is contained within Figure 12.1.

Consistent with the relationships depicted at the top of Figure 12.1, Kang & Yang (2010) found that company reputations influence country reputations based on the

Table 12.1 Top Countries Across Country Rankings

	CountryRep™—External View[1]	CountryRep™—Self-Assessment[1]	Nation Brands Index (NBI) 2009[2]	Newsweek "World's Best Countries"[3]
1	Switzerland	Australia	United States	Finland
2	Canada	Canada	France	Switzerland
3	Australia	Finland	Germany	Sweden
4	Sweden	Austria	United Kingdom	Australia
5	Norway	Norway	Japan	Luxembourg
6	Finland	Denmark	Italy	Norway
7	Denmark	Singapore	Canada	Canada
8	Netherlands	India	Switzerland	Netherlands
9	Austria	Switzerland	Australia	Japan
10	Spain	China	Spain	Denmark
11	Ireland	France	Sweden	United States
12	Italy	Spain	Holland	Germany
13	United Kingdom	Sweden	Austria	New Zealand
14	Greece	Ireland	Scotland	United Kingdom
15	Belgium	Chile	New Zealand	South Korea
16	Germany	United States	Denmark	France
17	Japan	Netherlands	Finland	Ireland
18	France	Thailand	Belgium	Austria
19	Portugal	Russia	Ireland	Belgium
20	Brazil	Poland	Brazil	Singapore

[1] Reputation Institute, 2009. *CountryRep*™ 2009. www.reputationinstititute.com.

[2] The Anholt-GfK Roper Natio¹ Brands IndexSM 2009 Report.

[3] http://www.newsweek.com/2010/08/15/interactive-infographic-of-the-worlds-best-countries.html.

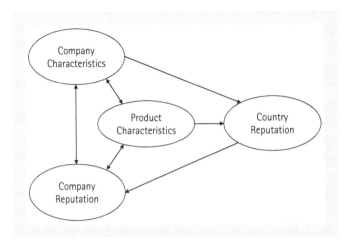

FIGURE 12.1 Relationship between country and company reputation.

logic that consumer experience with foreign products and their companies is a key source of information regarding the home countries of these companies since they often have little direct exposure to the countries themselves. Thus, this study suggests both a direct relationship between company characteristics in general and country reputations, along with an indirect relationship occurring through a company's products and services offered in the local market. Anholt (2007) suggests a similar relationship when describing a virtual cycle where nations should first have something meaningful or innovative to say before advertising their identity. While not limited to business, since these types of innovations are often associated with businesses, it follows that favorable company characteristics will lead to favorable country reputations. Similarly, the degree to which a country has an advanced economy is also a component of the CountryRep™ developed by the Reputation Institute (2009). Since reputation has often been associated with financial performance (e.g., McGuire, Sundgren, & Schneweiss, 1988; Fombrun & Shanley, 1990), to the degree that advanced economies have better performing companies, this suggests that country reputation is partially determined by company characteristics.

Embedded in the above logic is the fact that the most direct exposure that individuals have with a country and its associated companies is through the companies' products and services, which provide information cues and signals regarding both the company and its home country. Additionally, it is noteworthy that company characteristics and company reputation are treated as distinct but related variables within Figure 12.1. While it is beyond the scope of this chapter to discuss this matter in depth, the figure suggests that company characteristics influence a company's reputation, while reputation itself is an important company characteristic.

In contrast to the case above, other authors suggest that the reputations of countries influence the reputations of their firms, and the products of these firms in a particular market. This relationship is indicated in the bottom portion of Figure 12.1. In effect, country reputation produces a halo effect (e.g., Milgrom & Roberts, 1986; Roberts & Dowling, 2002) which influences perceptions of a country's companies. These arguments are more consistent with the country of origin literature, which notes that a country's characteristics imprint on its firms (Li & Wyer, 1994) and that COO acts as a heuristic base for judgment (Bodenhausen & Lichtenstein, 1987) and as a simplifier or a factor that encompasses many other attributes. For example, in their *post hoc* analyses, Newburry, Gardberg, & Belkin (2006) found that firms from different countries in their sample were systematically more or less attractive than others. Similarly, Alloza (2009) and Newburry & Gardberg (2010) found that Spanish firms had particularly poor reputations in the context of Latin America.

While it is beyond the scope of this chapter (or current research) to develop a full understanding of the factors that influence the reputation halos of certain countries, existing literature suggests a number of contributing factors. First, complex historical relationships between countries are certainly influential. For example, as noted earlier, Spanish reputations in Latin America are partially driven by colonial ties. Certainly, the reputations of British firms in many countries of the world stem from Britain's role in the Commonwealth of Nations. Past war and conflict between countries, and the degree to which a conflict involved direct contact, also has an influence, such that Japan is currently perceived much more negatively by Chinese than the US in response to the more direct and extensive Japanese occupation of China in World War II. Håkanson & Ambos (2010) found that cultural, geographical, political, and economic factors all influenced the psychic distance between countries, with geographical distance having the greatest explanatory power. All these factors would undoubtedly influence the reputations of countries as well.

Overall, by combining the two alternative relationships suggested above, Figure 12.1 presents a longitudinal process that may be, in effect, where country characteristics impact company reputations, which in turn feed back on country reputations through their interactions with product quality and as an important company characteristic. While the model may appear relatively simple in terms of number of variables, testing these relationships would necessitate a longitudinal analysis to tease out the interrelated effects. Moreover, an added level of complexity would come into play when considering the dimensions of country reputations (as discussed below). While company reputations would inherently have a more direct relationship with country reputation dimensions related to the business environment, country characteristics related to the broader country environment could be simultaneously impacting both company characteristics and country reputations. Thus, for example, various elements of the institutional environment (see Brammer & Jackson, 2002) in Germany could influence both the specific characteristics of German companies (e.g., their efficiency and reliability, or the types of products that they make) as well as the overall reputation of Germany (or German business) as a whole. Specific efforts by countries to intercede in these causal relationships by influencing specific dimensions over time become important as well, as can be seen in the case of Japan emphasizing both math and science education and promoting electronic goods manufacturing from the 1960s onwards, or more recently in China's opening up specific segments of its economy to encourage technological capability development (Chen, Newburry, & Park, 2009). Knowing the trigger points to influence a reputation cycle then becomes an important consideration for emerging markets. Such variables could be seen as important moderators of the country reputation–company reputation relationship.

Using firm-level data from the 2009 Reputation Institute Global Pulse study of firm reputations, we conducted basic correlation analyses and some basic regressions using country reputation to predict firm reputations. Interestingly, the CountryRep™ external score is negatively related to firm reputations (p<.001), while the CountryRep™ self-score is positively related to firm reputations (p<.001). These effects hold whether the two CountryRep™ scores are entered simultaneously or separately. While the limited number of countries involved in the CountryRep™ study make generalizing from these results dangerous, it nonetheless suggests that these relationships are worthy of much further examination.

Foreignness vs. Country of Origin Reputation Effects

A second area of debate where additional research is needed is the relationship between LOF and COO effects. As noted earlier, numerous past studies suggest that foreign firms primarily face negative reputation effects when they enter new markets, although some recent evidence suggests that in some instances, foreignness can be an asset. Similarly, an extensive literature notes that a firm's home country impacts the attractiveness of a firm. A component in both of these relationships is that foreignness and COO serve as heuristic devices to assist in evaluating companies and their products. However, the specific situations when foreignness dominates in reputation assessments versus specific country characteristics are less well understood.

Possible factors impacting which influence will dominate in country evaluations may include knowledge regarding a country, nationalism, and relative country development level. Regarding *knowledge* explanations, as both foreignness and country of origin serve as heuristic devices when knowledge is limited, foreignness may dominate COO when less country-specific information is available to an evaluator. Likewise, the greater the availability of country-specific information, the more likely that COO effects will dominate. *Nationalism*-based explanations, by contrast, may suggest that foreignness impacts will dominate COO impacts since nationalism generally involves preferring the home country versus outsiders. The *relative development level* of the country being evaluated compared with the country where a reputation is evaluated may also matter. Developing countries may tend to lump all developed countries together when forming reputation assessments, leading to less differentiation based upon a specific country of origin. Likewise, developed countries may tend to lump all developing countries together, again leading to a lower COO impact.

Country Reputation Dimensions

Another area of meaningful future research is the dimensions of country reputation. With regard to the two major existing measures reviewed above, CountryRep™ measures three dimensions: whether a country has an effective government, an advanced economy, and an appealing environment; the Anholt-GfK Roper Nation Brands Index measures six dimensions: exports, governance, culture and heritage, people, tourism, and investment and immigration. While there is some obvious overlap between the two sets of country reputation measures, both are relatively new and potentially in need of further development and testing. Additionally, the question of whether and when country reputation should be considered as a whole or in terms of its specific dimensions needs greater study. Looking more closely at the different potential influences on country reputation examined above, it may be the case that certain influences impact certain country reputation dimensions more than others. For example, institutional development factors may have a greater impact on a country's governance reputation than on its reputation for tourism. Thus, certain countries, for example the United States, may have generally strong reputations for certain dimensions (e.g., an appealing environment), while weaker reputations for others (e.g., effective governance). Moreover, these measures may change over time, either dramatically, as in the case of a government change or some other time-specific event, or more gradually, as in the case of emerging market products gradually infiltrating the global economy, or as populations migrate from one country to another. Additionally, the degree to which country reputations as a whole, or specific dimensions, correlate with other institutional features of countries, such as the varieties of capitalism "coordination" index (see Jackson & Deeg, 2008), the "rule of law" index, or various country development measures, is worth examining.

Management of Country Reputations

A related research direction is the degree to which country reputations can be meaningfully managed. Simon Anholt (2003, 2007, 2010) is the current leader in this area of research, with his books on the brand management of nations, cities, and regions. However, additional academic studies are warranted—particularly in terms of the effectiveness of reputation management efforts. Given the relative newness of this research area, the long-term impacts of country reputation management efforts are still not well understood. Numerous examples of country efforts to manage their reputations exist both in terms of long-term efforts, such as the establishment of Japan External Trade Organization (JETRO) offices to promote trade and investment around the world, or more short-term, dramatic efforts, such as the sponsorship of an Olympics or a World Cup which provide extensive focus on a country for a brief time period.

Industry and Demographic Moderating Effects

Recent research has highlighted the importance of industry and individual demographic characteristics as moderators of company reputation effects. Similarly, these variables might also impact the degree to which country reputations are influential. *Industry* has been established as an important component of reputation management (Winn, Macdonald, & Zietsma, 2008; Barnett & Hoffman, 2008). Along these lines, Newburry (2010) found strong industry effects for the telecom, financial, and energy industries in terms of moderating the relationship between company reputation and supportive behavior towards a company in Latin America. Thus, the degree to which industries are associated with particular countries may also imprint on overall country reputations, to the point where industry and country reputations become highly interconnected.

Similar to the case of industry moderations, Newburry & Gardberg (2010) found that workplace reputations of foreign versus domestic firms were moderated by *demographic characteristics* associated with an individual evaluator. In particular, they found that marginalized demographic groups were relatively more attracted to foreign firms that operate outside of the local system than their less marginalized counterparts in the developing world context of Latin America. These results were often opposite to those found in developed world settings (Newburry, Gardberg, & Belkin, 2006). Similar dynamics may be occurring with respect to which individuals are more likely to assess particular country reputations more positively.

Developed versus Emerging versus Developing Market Impacts

As alluded to earlier, the development level of a country may also play an important role in the establishment of country reputations. The summary table strongly suggests that developed countries have higher reputations than their developing country counterparts. In developed countries, where there are higher financial potential, higher research and development capabilities, more advanced technologies, higher competition, more institutionalized attention toward human rights and CSR, and more mature CSR regulations and incentives (Jamali, 2007; Wanderley et al., 2008), certain characteristics may be highly embedded into a country's fabric, and likewise influence the reputations of all firms from that country. However, in developing countries with less history of attending to these issues, these activities are less embedded in firms. These differences are observable by the general public in other countries through public media and information disseminated by firms in annual reports, campaigns, websites, and advertisements, influencing public perceptions along with the legitimacy of firms.

For example, it was noted earlier that CSR practices differ between European and US firms. European and US firms differ in the means they use to convey their social responsibility image (Maignan & Ralston, 2002), in corporate donations (Bennett, 1998), and in the usage of codes of ethics (Langlois & Schlegelmilch, 1990). However, CSR practices in both Europe and the US are often considered more advanced than those in most of the developing world. Recent evidence also suggests that developing, emerging, and developed countries use different lenses and possess different expectations when evaluating companies (Chen, Newburry, & Park, 2009; Deephouse, Li, & Newburry, 2009). These differences would likely extend to country reputation assessments, although empirical verification is needed.

New and Emerging Directions for Future Research

As a final discussion area, this section addresses some emerging future research directions which may assist in resolving some of the conflicts highlighted above. In particular, the inclusion of multilevel research, longitudinal research, and research involving emerging markets may be beneficial.

Multilevel Analysis

Many of the issues highlighted point to the fact that reputation assessments occur at multiple analysis levels. This is consistent with Barnett & Hoffman (2008) and Newburry (2010), all of whom have recently noted the multilevel nature of reputation. As such, it seems appropriate that a greater percentage of future research designs include multilevel models in their conceptualizations and empirical testing. As analyses of these types will naturally involve hierarchical data structures with nested data (Hitt et al., 2007), software programs with capabilities to handle these data types, such as the hierarchical linear modeling program HLM6 (Raudenbush et al., 2004), will become more necessary to compute these models. For example, Newburry (2010) used this program to compute a model predicting individual-level reputation assessments based upon predictors at three data levels (individual, within company, within country).

Longitudinal Research

A second issue highlighted earlier is that the relationship between country and company reputations most likely has longitudinal dimensions. As such, understanding their interrelationship will inherently necessitate the usage of data over a significant period of time to determine the nature and direction of causality. A study of this nature may allow for a better determination of which factors impact causality in a specific direction.

New Research Contexts

A third important issue is the understanding of new research contexts, and how country and firm reputation assessments may differ between these contexts. For example, as emerging market investment continues to gain interest among both scholars and practitioners (Hoskisson et al., 2000; Meyer, 2004), a better understanding of how the reputations of emerging market countries impact the operations and performance of their firms is becoming increasingly necessary (Newburry, 2010). As noted earlier, firm legitimacy (Deephouse & Suchman, 2008) is a major factor impacting the success of MNCs doing business in foreign countries, and much of this legitimacy stems from country of origin effects associated with the reputations of a firm's home country. However, our understanding of the country reputations of emerging and developing countries is limited in comparison with their developed market counterparts, leaving a large area of important, yet unexplored territory.

SUMMARY AND CONCLUSION

The relationship between reputation and country is of growing importance to both reputation and international business scholars. As multinational corporations and international trade continue to grow, understanding the impact of home country reputations on the reputations of companies and their products and services will become increasingly important. Within this chapter, we have tried to review some of the existing theoretical bases that predict country reputations, along with the most prevalent country reputation measures. Additionally, we have attempted to describe the relationship between country reputation and company reputation, while also highlighting some important developing trends and future research areas.

ACKNOWLEDGMENT

I gratefully acknowledge the support of the Reputation Institute for this research. In particular, I thank Charles Fombrun, Leonard Ponzi, and Sebastian Taciak. Additionally, I wish to thank Abrahim Soleimani for research assistance.

Core Research on Country Reputation

Reference	Key Constructs and Findings
Hymer (1976)	• **Cost of Doing Business Abroad:** Costs that put foreign firms at a competitive disadvantage relative to local firms. • Dichotomous Measure: Foreign or Domestic. • Prediction: Foreignness negatively related to performance.
Zaheer (1995)	• **Liability of Foreignness:** Costs due to spatial distance between parents and subsidiaries, a subsidiary's unfamiliarity and lack of root in a host country, the host country environment, and the home country environment. • Dichotomous Measure: Foreign or Domestic. • Prediction: Foreignness negatively related to performance.
Li & Wyer (1994)	• **Country of Origin:** "the impact which generalizations and perceptions about a country have on a person's evaluations of the country's products and/or brands" (Lampert & Jaffe, 1996: 29). • Measured via series of dichotomous variables based on home country. • Prediction: Country of origin predicts product purchase (or other supportive behavior).
Papadopoulos & Heslop (1993)	• **Product Country Image:** "the multidimensional nature of the images of products and brands, together with the multiplicity of places that might be involved in the design, manufacture and assembly of products" (Knight, Holdsworth, & Mather, 2007: 107).
Passow, Fehlmann, & Grahlow (2005)	• **Country Reputation:** "The aggregate of stakeholders' images of *(a country)* over time" (p. 311). • Measured via emotional appeal, physical appeal, financial appeal, leadership appeal, cultural appeal, and social appeal.
Anholt (2003)	• **Anholt–GfK Roper Nation Brands Index:** "Brand image is the perception of the brand that exists in the mind of the consumer or audience—it's virtually the same thing as reputation" (Anholt, 2007: 5). • Measured via six dimensions: exports, governance, culture and heritage, people, tourism, and investment and immigration.
Reputation Institute (2009)	• **CountryRep™:** "the degree to which people trust, admire, respect, and have a good feeling for a place" (p. 3). • Eleven items measuring three dimensions: whether a country has an effective government, an advanced economy, and an appealing environment. • Prediction: Higher country reputations predict greater supportive behavior with respect to recommending visiting, working in, living in, and investing in a country.

REFERENCES

Alloza, A. (2009). *La Reputation de España en el Mundo*. Madrid: Instituto de Análisis de Intangibles.

Anholt, S. (2003). *Brand New Justice: How Branding Places and Products Can Help the Developing World*. Oxford: Butterworth Heinemann.

—— (2007). *Competitive Identity: The New Brand Management for Nations, Cities and Regions*. Hampshire and New York: Palgrave MacMillan.

—— (2010). *Places: Identity, Image and Reputation*. Hampshire and New York: Palgrave MacMillan.

Barnett, M. L. & Hoffman, A. J. (2008). "Beyond corporate reputation: Managing reputational interdependence." *Corporate Reputation Review*, 11: 1–9.

Basdeo, D. K., Smith, K. G., Grimm, C. M., Rindova, V. P., & Derfus, P. J. (2006). "The impact of market actions on firm reputation." *Strategic Management Journal*, 27: 1205–1219.

Bennett, R. (1998). "Corporate philanthropy in France, Germany and the UK: International comparisons of commercial orientation towards company giving in European Nations." *International Marketing Review*, 15(6): 458–475.

Bodenhausen, G. V. & Lichtenstein, M. (1987). "Social stereotypes and information-processing strategies: The impact of task complexity." *Journal of Personality and Social Psychology*, 52(5): 871–880.

Brammer, S. & Jackson, G. (2012). "Balancing reputation and regulation: Cross-country comparisons." In M. Barnett & T. Pollock (Eds.), *The Oxford Handbook of Corporate Reputation*. Oxford: Oxford University Press, 297–319.

Casilda-Bejar, R. (2002). *La Década Dorada: Economía e Inversiones Españolas en América Latina 1990–2000*. Alcala, Spain: Universidad de Alcala servicio de publicaciones.

Caves, R. (1974). "Multinational firms, competition and productivity in host-country markets." *Economica*, 41: 176–193.

Chacar, A., Newburry, W., & Vissa. B. (2010). "Bringing institutions into performance persistence research: Exploring the impact of product, financial and labor market institutions." *Journal of International Business Studies*, 41: 1119–1140.

Chandra, R. & Newburry, W. (1997). "A cognitive map of the international business field." *International Business Review*, 6(4): 387–410.

Chen, D., Newburry, W., & Park, S. (2009). "Improving sustainability: An international evolutionary framework." *Journal of International Management*, 15(3): 317–327.

Deephouse, D. L. & Suchman, M. C. (2008). "Legitimacy in organizational institutionalism." In R. Greenwood, C. Oliver, K. Sahlin, & R. Suddaby (Eds.), *The SAGE Handbook of Organizational Institutionalism*. Oxford, UK: Sage, 49–77.

Deephouse, D., Li, L., & Newburry, W. (2009). "Institutional and national culture effects on corporate reputation." *Academy of Management Best Paper Proceedings*, August: 1–6.

Dowling, G. (2006). "How good corporate reputations create corporate value." *Corporate Reputation Review*, 9(2): 134–143.

Dunning, J. H. (2009). "Location and the multinational enterprise: A neglected factor?" Journal of International Business Studies, 40: 5–19.

Dutton, J. E. & Dukerich, J. M. (1991). "Keeping an eye on the mirror: Image and identity in organizational adaptation." *Academy of Management Journal*, 34(3): 517–554.

Elango, B. & Sethi, S. P. (2007). "An exploration of the relationship between country of origin (COE) and the internationalization-performance paradigm." *Management International Review*, 47(3): 369–392.

Elsbach, K. D. & Kramer, R. M. (1996). "Members' responses to organizational identity threats: Encountering and countering the business week rankings." *Administrative Science Quarterly*, 41(3): 442–476.

Foreman, P., Whetten, D. A, & MacKey, A. (2012). "Making sense of the grab bag of concepts: The interplay amongst image, identity, legitimacy, reputation." In M. Barnett & T. Pollock (Eds.), *The Oxford Handbook of Corporate Reputation*. Oxford: Oxford University Press, 179–200.

Fombrun, C. (1996). *Reputation: Realizing Value from the Corporate Image*. Boston, MA: Harvard Business School Press.

Fombrun, C. & Shanley, M. (1990). "What's in a name? Reputation building and corporate strategy." *Academy of Management Journal*, 33: 233–256.

Galan, J. I., Gonzalez-Benito, J., & Zuniga-Vincente, J. A. (2007). "Factors determining the location decisions of Spanish MNEs: An analysis based on the investment development path." *Journal of International Business Studies*, 38: 975–997.

Gardberg, N. A. & Schepers, D. H. (2008). "Do stakeholders detect corporate social performance signals?" *Academy of Management 2008 Annual Meeting Proceedings*.

Grosse, R. & Trevino, L. J. (1996). "Foreign direct investment in the United States: An analysis by country of origin." *Journal of International Business Studies*, 27(1): 139–155.

Guillen, M. (2005). *The Rise of Spanish Multinationals. European Business in the Global Economy*. New York, NY: Cambridge University Press.

Gurhan-Canli, Z. & Maheswaran, D. (2000). "Cultural variations in country of origin effects." *Journal of Marketing Research*, 37(3): 309–317.

Håkanson, L. & Ambos, B. (2010). "The antecedents of psychic distance." *Journal of International Management*, 16(3): 195–210.

Hayden, A. & Edwards, T. (2001). "The erosion of the country of origin effect: A case study of a Swedish multinational company." *Industrial Relations*, 56(1): 116–140.

Hitt, M. A., Beamish, P. W., Jackson, S. E., & Mathieu, J. E. (2007). "Building theoretical and empirical bridges across levels: Multilevel research in management." *Academy of Management Journal*, 50: 1385–1399.

Hong, S. & Wyer, R. S., Jr. (1989). "Effects of country-of-origin and product-attribute information." *Journal of Consumer Research*, 16(2): 175.

Hoskisson, R. E., Eden, L., Lau, C. M., & Wright, M. (2000). "Strategy in emerging economies." *Academy of Management Journal*, 43: 249–267.

Hymer, S. H. (1976). *The International Operations of National Firms: A Study of Direct Investment*. Cambridge, MA: MIT Press.

Jackson, D. & Deeg, R. (2008). "Comparing capitalisms: Understanding institutional diversity and its implications for international business." *Journal of International Business Studies*, 39: 540–561.

Jamali, D. (2007). "The case for strategic corporate social responsibility in developing countries." *Business and Society Review*, 112(1): 1–27.

Johansson, J. K., Ronkainen, I. A., & Czinkota, M. R. (1994). "Negative country-of-origin effects: The case of the new Russia." *Journal of International Business Studies*, 25: 157–176.

Jo, M.-S. (2005). "Why country of origin effects vary in consumers' quality evaluation." *Journal of Global Marketing*, 19(1): 5–25.

Kang, M. & Yang, S. (2010). "Comparing effects of country reputation and the overall corporate reputations of a country on international consumers' product attitudes and purchase intentions." *Corporate Reputation Review*, 13(1): 52–62.

Kindleberger, C. (1969). *American Business Abroad*. New Haven, CT: University Press.

Knight, J. C., Holdsworth, D. K., & Mather, D. W. (2007). "Country-of-origin and choice of food imports: An in-depth study of European distribution channel gatekeepers." *Journal of International Business Studies*, 38: 107–125.

Kostova, T. & Zaheer, S. (1999). "Organizational legitimacy under conditions of complexity: The case of the multinational enterprise." *Academy of Management Review*, 24(1): 64–81.

Lampert, S. & Jaffe, E. (1996). "Country of origin effects on international market entry." *Journal of Global Marketing*, 10(2): 27–52.

Langlois, C. C. & Schlegelmilch, B. B. (1990). "Do corporate codes of ethics reflect national character? Evidence from Europe and the United States." *Journal of International Business Studies*, 21(4): 519–539.

Li, W. & Wyer, R. S., Jr. (1994). "The role of country of origin in product evaluations: Informational and standard-of-comparison effects." *Journal of Consumer Psychology*, 3(2): 187–212.

Li, W. K., Leung, K., & Wyer, R. S. (1993). "The roles of country of origin information on buyers' product evaluations: Signaling or attribute?" *Advances in Consumer Research*, 20: 684–689.

Maignan, I. & Ralston, D. A. (2002). "Corporate social responsibility in Europe and the U.S.: Insights from businesses' self-presentations." *Journal of International Business Studies*, 33(3): 497.

McGuire, J., Sundgren, A., & Schneweiss, T. (1988). "Corporate social responsibility and firm financial performance." *Academy of Management Journal*, 31: 854–877.

Meng, J. G., Nasco, S. A., & Clark, T. (2008). "Measuring country-of-origin effects in Caucasians, African-Americans and Chinese consumers for products and services." *Journal of International Consumer Marketing*, 20(2): 17–31.

Meyer, S. (1995). "The economic impact of environmental regulation." *Journal of Environmental Law and Practice*, 3(2): 4–15.

Meyer, K. E. (2004). "Perspectives on multinational enterprises in emerging economies." *Journal of International Business Studies*, 35: 259–276.

Mezias, J. M. (2002). "Identifying liabilities of foreignness and strategies to minimize their effects: The case of labor lawsuit judgments in the United States." *Strategic Management Journal*, 23(3): 229–244.

Milgrom, P. & Roberts, J. (1986). "Relying on information of interested parties." *Rand Journal of Economics*, 17: 18–32.

Nachum, L. (2003). "Liability of foreignness in global competition? Financial service affiliates in the city of London." *Strategic Management Journal*, 24: 1187–1208.

—— (2010). "When is foreignness an asset or a liability? Explaining the performance differential between foreign and local firms." *Journal of Management*, 36(3): 714–739.

Newburry, W. (2010). "Reputation and supportive behavior: Moderating impacts of foreignness, industry and local exposure." *Corporate Reputation Review*, 12(4): 388–405.

—— & Gardberg, N. (2010). "Marginalization and attraction to foreign and international firms." Presentation at the *Academy of Management Annual Meeting*, Montreal, Canada, August.

——, Gardberg, N., & Belkin, L. (2006). "Organizational attractiveness is in the eye of the beholder: The interaction of demographic characteristics with foreignness." *Journal of International Business Studies*, 37(5): 666–686.

Newsweek. (2010). *The World's Best Companies*. http://www.newsweek.com/2010/08/15/interactive-infographic-of-the-worlds-best-countries.html. Accessed 28 August.

Noorderhaven, N. G. & Harzing, A. (2003). "The 'country-of-origin effect' in multinational corporations: Sources, mechanisms." *Management International Review*, 43(2): 47–66.

Noya, J. (2004). "La Imagen de España y sus inversiones en América Latina." *Universia Business Review*, 3(3): 46–61.

Passow, T., Fehlmann, R., & Grahlow, H. (2005). "Country reputation—From measurement to management: The case of Liechtenstein." *Corporate Reputation Review*, 7(4): 309–326.

Perez-Batres, L. A. & Eden, L. (2008). "Is there a liability of localness? How emerging market firms respond to regulatory punctuations." *Journal of International Management*, 14: 232–251.

Papadopoulos, N. & Heslop, L. (1993). *Product-Country Images: Impact and Role in International Marketing*. New York: International Business Press.

Raudenbush, S., Bryk, A., Cheong, Y. F., Congdon, R., & du Toit, M. (2004). *HLM6: Hierarchical Linear and Nonlinear Modeling*. Lincolnwood, IL: Scientific Software.

Reputation Institute. (2009). *CountryRep™ 2009*. www.reputationinstititute.com.

Roberts, P. W. & Dowling, G. R. (2002). "Corporate reputation and sustained superior financial performance." *Strategic Management Journal*, 23: 1077–1093.

Robinson, P. (1995). "Structural interdependence and practice conformity: An empirical examination of American MNEs and their subsidiaries in Japan." *Academy of Management Best Paper Proceedings*, 192–196.

Schuler, R., Dowling, P., & DeCieri, H. (1993). "An integrative framework of strategic international human resource management." *International Journal of Human Resource Management*, 4: 717–764.

Scott, W. R. (1995). *Institutions and Organizations*. Thousand Oaks, CA: Sage Publications.

Sharma, P. (2011). "Country of origin effects in developed and emerging markets: Exploring the contrasting roles of materialism and value consciousness." *Journal of International Business Studies*, 42: 285–306.

Taylor, S., Beechler, S., & Napier, N. (1996). "Toward an integrative model of strategic international human resource management." *Academy of Management Review*, 21: 959–985.

Verlegh, P. W. J. & Steenkamp, J.-B. E. M. (1999). "A review and meta-analysis of country-of-origin research." *Journal of Economic Psychology*, 20: 521–546.

Wanderley, L., Lucian, R., Farache, F., & Sousa Filho, J. M. (2008). "CSR information disclosure on the web: A context-based approach analysing the influence of country of origin and industry sector." *Journal of Business Ethics*, 82(2): 369–378.

Wang, C., Clegg, J., & Kafouros, M. (2009). "Country-of-origin effects of foreign direct investment: An industry level analysis." *Management International Review*, 49(2): 179–198.

Winn, M., MacDonald, P., & Zietsma, C. (2008). "Managing industry reputation: The dynamic tension between collective and competitive reputation management strategies." *Corporate Reputation Review*, 11(1): 35–55.

Yang, S., Shin, H., Lee, J., & Wrigley, B. (2008). "Country reputation in multidimensions: predictors, effects, and communication channels." *Journal of Public Relations Research*, 20(4): 421–440.

Yu, J. & Zaheer, S. (2010). "Building a process model of local adaptation of practices: A study of six sigma implementation in Korean and US firms." *Journal of International Business Studies*, 41: 475–499.

Zaheer, S. (1995). "Overcoming the liability of foreignness." *Academy of Management Journal*, 38: 341–357.

—— & Mosakowski, E. (1997). "The dynamics of the liability of foreignness: A global study of survival in financial services." *Strategic Management Journal*, 18: 439–463.

Zhang, Y., Li, H., Li, Y., & Zhou, L. (2010). "FDI spillovers in an emerging market: The role of foreign firms' country origin diversity and domestic firms' absorptive capacity." *Strategic Management Journal*, 31(9): 969–989.

CHAPTER 13

··

CORPORATE REPUTATION AND REGULATION IN HISTORICAL PERSPECTIVE

··

CHRISTOPHER McKENNA
ROWENA OLEGARIO

Historians have long been preoccupied with the subject of corporate reputation and its role in governance, even if they have not formulated it as such. This chapter outlines four areas where a significant or growing body of historical works exists: reputation mechanisms and self-regulation, the reputation of the corporate form, the reputation of regulatory bodies, and reputational capital within markets and hierarchies. Shortcomings in the historical literature are the poorly understood distinctions between fact and reputation, and the tendency to take for granted the power of reputation and to view it as an uncomplicated phenomenon. Reputation intermediaries and stakeholder theory offer historians promising new directions for research.

DESPITE the importance of reputation in regulating corporations, the subject has not been well investigated by historians. Few have taken on explicitly the research questions we expound in this chapter—namely, what has been the relationship between corporate reputation and regulation over time? What have been the regulatory functions of corporate reputations, and how have these reputations been created, sustained, rebuilt, and/or destroyed? A number of historical works have, of course, touched on these subjects, but only tangentially.[1] Rarely has the role of corporate reputation in the regulatory process constituted either a topic in its own right or functioned as a lens through which to analyze the evolution of regulatory regimes. Most often, historians have simply taken for granted that reputation can direct market behaviors and influence regulation, without probing precisely how or why this happens.

---

[1] A full-text search of historical journals in JSTOR using the term "corporate reputation" turned up only one article.

We define "regulation" broadly, drawing on economic historian Douglass North's theoretical distinction between formal and informal institutions as "the humanly devised constraints that structure political, economic and social interaction." Such institutions "consist of both informal constraints (sanctions, taboos, customs, traditions, and codes of conduct), and formal rules (constitutions, laws, property rights)" (North, 1990). North's formulation of institutions as constraints is especially useful in the kind of historical investigations that concern us here—the areas of regulation, enforcement, rationing, and monitoring. Like him, we understand regulation to include the forces that bring market actors into conformity not only with formal laws, but also with norms, conventions, and other informal restraints. Unlike North, however, we also allow that norms can be positive as well as negative—that they can inspire as well as restrain (McCloskey, 2009). Individuals and corporations can feel pressured not simply to "do no evil," as Google's informal corporate motto succinctly states, but also to contribute positively to society. But whether a corporation aims to prevent malfeasance among its members or to affect society in positive ways through the funding and implementation of social programs, its success requires self-regulation and the often subtle coercion of employees and other group members.

The following topics in the history of reputation and regulation cover broad areas in which a reasonable body of historical work exists. In most cases, the authors did not originally conceive of their work as falling within the rubric of corporate reputation and regulation. Nevertheless, their collective insights form the basis of this nascent field of inquiry and suggest directions for future research.

REPUTATION MECHANISMS AND SELF-REGULATION

According to the accepted historical narrative, the revival of trade during the Middle Ages in Europe led to a reordering of the institutions that underpinned commerce. Progressively more complex formal mechanisms came to replace the informal ones that were based on individual reputations, allowing overseas and other long-distance merchants to enlarge the scale and scope of their trading ventures. Whereas commercial trust previously inhered in groups tied together by kinship, ethnicity, or religion, the establishment of formal institutions—most importantly, the legal infrastructure that supported contracting and protected private property—enabled traders to reach beyond geographical constraints to transact with people whom they did not know well, and with whom they shared few if any biological and social ties (North & Thomas, 1973; Lopez, 1976). This historical paradigm has proved useful in explaining developments in Europe and the United States in the seven centuries since the late Middle Ages. In one such narrative, the expansion of grain cultivation in the US during the mid-nineteenth century led American merchants to store wheat in large grain elevators and transport it in railroad cars. Mixing the wheat meant that the reputation for quality of individual farmers could no longer be relied upon. The Chicago Board of Trade attempted to solve the problem by devising a three-tier grading system, substituting weight for volume as the standard measurement, and providing inspectors. When these arrangements proved deleterious (because some farmers adulterated their grain, secure in the knowledge that their actions could no longer be traced back to them), and further regulations by the Board of Trade turned out to be futile, the Illinois legislature created a new regulatory body—the Railroad and Warehouse Commission—that was responsible for inspecting the wheat. In this narrative, the process of guaranteeing the quality of Midwestern wheat that previously was reliant on the reputation of individual farmers was gradually replaced by an inspection and grading system created by the Illinois state government (Lamoreaux, et al., 2003; Cronin, 1992).

The earliest mechanisms for building trust and enforcing trading contracts were word-of-mouth reputation mechanisms that used the threat of a bad reputation to deter malfeasance in circumstances where individuals have short-term incentives to cheat. Their internal dynamics limit their effectiveness to situations where individuals expect to have repeated interactions, or where cheating would have grave consequences that are not purely economic, such as the social ostracization of the cheating parties or their heirs. Additionally, the mechanisms work only when information can flow in a reliable fashion to all members of a trading group. Reputation mechanisms are an integral part of the phenomenon referred to as private ordering: the use of extralegal mechanisms to induce compliance (Richman, 2004).Recent scholarly interest in them was fueled by the development of online commerce sites starting in the mid-1990s. The most important auction site, eBay, developed an online feedback mechanism that collates pairs of ratings provided by buyers and sellers of their experiences transacting with one another. Although some scholars have identified a bias toward positive reviews, the mechanism has proved highly effective in inducing commercial trust and discouraging fraudulent trades (Dellarocas, 2003; Jøsang, et al., 2007; Gürtler & Grund, 2006). With the spread of online feedback mechanisms, there now exist "two types of reputation-bond-based extralegal contractual regimes: the homogeneous group regime that is generally associated with repeat transactions among members of small geographically concentrated and ethnically homogeneous groups, and the information-intermediary regime in which technology links markets and secures the rapid and low-cost dissemination of information about reputation" (Bernstein, 1992). Although there are important differences, most studies stress that the principles underlying both types of reputation mechanisms are largely identical. Similar questions can therefore be asked about all reputation mechanisms, including: how did the individuals who ran the mechanism (a) identify the bad behavior, (b) make the mechanism's power credible, so people were inhibited from cheating, and (c) persuade everyone using the mechanism to pay for it (because mechanisms are not costless)?

Avner Greif's studies of the trade among the Maghribi in North Africa, and among the Genovese, Pisans, and Venetians in Italy from the eleventh to the fourteenth centuries, were among the first attempts by an economic historian to theorize enforcement mechanisms and the role of reputation. He conceived of mechanisms as both informal (gossip within social networks of family and associates) and formal (merchant guilds, courts, and the like). Using the insights of institutional and game theory, Greif demonstrated how the Maghribi's closed circle enabled them to ostracize cheaters effectively, while the more heterogeneous Italian city-states were driven to invent more formal organizations to enforce contracts (Greif, 1989). Greif's work was well received by economic historians, who saw great promise in his elegant melding of game theory with deep analyses of particular historical episodes. In *Institutions and the Path to the Modern Economy*, Greif attempted to build a more rigorous theoretical framework to help researchers determine "what to look for in considering and evaluating the self-enforceability of institutional elements in a given environment" by outlining some of the forces that influence how reputation-based, private-order institutions evolve (Greif, 2006). Approaching historical problems through the twin lenses of game theory and institutional theory, he argued, encouraged questions to come to the fore that otherwise would not arise at all—questions such as: what might induce someone to refrain from cheating when the reputational consequences are negligible? How does knowledge of what others are likely to do affect the actions of a particular individual or group? Under what conditions is the threat of punishment credible? What information is necessary for a reputation mechanism to function? (Greif, 2006).

In scenarios where the scale of trade overwhelmed the regulatory capacity of simple word-of-mouth reputation mechanisms, certain well-placed individuals could exploit the power of their own reputations to remedy the mechanisms' failings. Such was the role of the private judges in the *lex mercatoria* (merchant law), the body of private laws that evolved among merchants during the medieval period. Paul R. Milgrom et al. argued that the system of private judges was a response to the costliness of information in a trading environment that had expanded greatly in both scale and geographical reach. In addition to adjudicating disputes, the judges were able to impart important information about dishonest traders to interested parties and provided an incentive for injured parties to disclose their grievances. Such information was necessary for the reputation system to function but was not being disseminated effectively in the normal course of trade (Milgrom et al., 1990). In similar fashion, mutual protection societies could step in to augment the oral dissemination of information. London's Society of Guardians for the Protection of Trade Against Swindlers and Sharpers, founded by the city's merchants in 1776 to formalize the sharing of information on debtors, provided a model that eventually spread throughout the United Kingdom. Groups like these built reputations for reliability and effectiveness that were critical to expanding the reach of older, word-of-mouth reputation mechanisms (Finn, 2003; Olegario, 2006). In some instances, closed groups that were known to have well-functioning mechanisms could exploit their joint reputation to surmount deficiencies in the regulatory environment. This was how some Mexican textile firms were able to overcome the reluctance of banks to lend, despite the poor enforcement of property rights in Mexico between 1878 and 1913 (Maurer & Sharma, 2001). Similarly, prior to the creation of the US Federal Reserve (1913–14), the New York Clearing House Association overcame the negative effects of bank panics by pressuring its members to act prudently (Yue and Ingram, Chapter 14, this volume).

Much of the historical literature on guilds and other corporate bodies can be classified as belonging to the field of reputation and regulation studies. These bodies were voluntary, collective attempts at self-regulation that can be placed on the spectrum between informal reputation mechanisms at one end and formal state regulations at the other. Even into the late twentieth century, the US diamond industry relied heavily on such a body (the bourse) to enforce the extralegal contracts that are the norm for that closed, secretive industry (Bernstein, 1992). Guilds, associations, and professional groups do not simply try to deter malfeasance among their members but also encourage a sense of corporate identity by emphasizing the social good that flows from their groups' activities. They self-consciously engage in building their own reputations for a variety of purposes, including the ability to pre-empt or replace more stringent government regulations. Formal constitutions and codes of conduct often govern these groups, specifying the standards of a particular craft, profession, industry, or occupation, and promoting good citizenship and/or civic pride among members (for example, Lurie, 1979). By the late Middle Ages, corporate bodies in Europe had achieved reputations for legitimacy that permitted them to engage in quasi-public regulatory functions. Communes and merchant groups in particular made and enforced their own laws (Najemy, 1979). By regulating their members, merchant guilds enabled the rulers of commercial centers throughout Europe to commit to safeguarding these merchants' security, even though they hailed from outside the rulers' realms (Greif et al., 1994). Studies of European guilds demonstrate that self-regulation and state regulation interacted in an ongoing and fluid process, and that the aim of building and protecting the reputations of products and towns often united corporations and government authorities in common objectives (Smith, 1999).

In more modern times, the nascent professions sought to improve the reputations of their members, among them lawyers, medical practitioners, and accountants, by restricting membership and using state certification to bolster their position. Through selective use of their power, professionals were able to secure higher wages in exchange for an implicit bargain that professional control could successfully police practitioners and thus relieve consumers of the need to distinguish good from poor providers in the opaque market of professional services. Whether the ultimate aim of professionalization was to drive out the incompetent providers by imposing licenses and certification as a signal of quality or simply to raise prices through control over the market, the effect was the same, as professional reputation served to link the processes (von der Crone & Vetsch, 2009).

Studies like those on the diamond industry demonstrate that self-regulation continues to thrive, even in the midst of growing formal regulation. Not all self-regulation is completely voluntary, and some forms of "self-regulation" in fact do nothing more than pressure group members to comply with existing government regulation. Skeptics point to the desire to pre-empt or replace more stringent state regulations or to erect barriers to entry as primary motivations, yet the ability to influence public opinion must also be counted as a strong inducement. (Indeed, the desire of firms to project legitimacy by conforming to existing norms and regulations is one of the cornerstones of institutional theory (Fombrun, Chapter 5, this volume). Burnishing the reputation of an entire industry gives it competitive advantages. For example, the attempts of direct sellers to acquire legitimacy in the minds of the public and regulators were directly related to their desire to compete more effectively with brick-and-mortar retailers (Wotruba, 1997).

The Reputation of the Corporate Form

The late seventeenth century saw the emergence of the corporate organizational form, a mechanism for control whose evolving reputation has been documented by historians on both sides of the Atlantic (Micklethwait & Wooldridge, 2005; Lipartito & Sicilia, 2004). In the Anglo-American world, people first used the corporate form to manage cities (for example, "the City of London Corporation"), tradesmen (via guilds), and charities like universities and hospitals (through ecclesiastical corporate bodies). When, during the "Tudor Revolution" of 1485–1603 administrators sought charters to legitimate their special privileges, they incorporated their existing legal status through special Acts by the Crown or Parliament (Elton, 1953). And so, through the end of the eighteenth century in Britain, the legitimacy of the corporation rested in the exclusive legal right of Parliament to charter corporations. For hundreds of years, corporations remained extraordinary acts created by the state to enable the creation of social goods.

The fact that the corporate form could only be created by an Act of Parliament may have established the corporation's legal basis, but its civic reputation was another matter. Historians have traced the dual attempts in the Anglo-American world by various interest groups both to empower and constrain the potentially dangerous new form. Within the limited scope and intent of Parliament, corporations were largely a political device to promote broad economic and civic aims within society, not an instrument solely for the commercial gain of the corporation's owners. In the seventeenth and eighteenth centuries, the most controversial charters granted by the English Parliament were for the creation of foreign trading corporations—including the East India Company and the infamous South Sea Company—in order to promote international trade and the growth of overseas colonies (Brenner, 1993). The corporate charters that the English Parliament granted allowed these corporations to accumulate profits in exchange for operating as quasi-governments within their geographic boundaries. Given that the potential financial profits from overseas trade were so lucrative, it is not surprising that corporate charters were eagerly sought and bid up by speculators in the colonial era.

Whether in legal corporate entities like the East India Company or smaller, entrepreneurial ventures like coal mines and regional banks, the rapid growth of commercial projects engendered a general suspicion of the corporation (Harris, 2000). These fears culminated in the failure of the South Sea Bubble in the 1710s, and subsequent legal Acts, including the Bubble Act of 1719, that restricted the spread of corporations in Britain for more than a century. Yet by the middle of the eighteenth century, despite continuing distrust of the role of corporations in civic life, the English courts and business people had come to view the corporation not simply as a state instrument imbued with monopoly control, but as a private trading company organized for economic gain. The evolution of the corporation from a political charter to an economic entity, as legal historian James Willard Hurst has described it, "helped generate a diffuse distrust of the corporate form" in Britain (Hurst, 1969). Distrust of the corporate form would continue into the nineteenth century, even if pragmatic concerns led to the increased use of limited companies prior to the repeal of the Bubble Act in 1825. As James Taylor has shown, the English Companies Acts of 1844 and 1855 were passed against the backdrop of public debates about corporate fraud and malfeasance, so that even as their legal legitimacy was being established, the public reputation of corporations remained severely hampered (Taylor, 2007). By the mid-nineteenth century, after more than two hundred years of widespread use, the public reputation of the corporation remained dubious at best.

As a colony, and later as an independent nation, the status of the corporation in the United States was derived from the traditions and laws of England, most prominently in the chartered companies that first colonized North America. It is interesting, therefore, that for much of the late eighteenth and nineteenth centuries, the United States chartered new corporations at a much faster pace than the English, shifting the development of the American corporation from an act of special privilege to one of general utility by the end of the nineteenth century (Hurst, 1969). Although Americans distrusted them, corporations quickly became part of the American economic landscape.

Debates in England over the value of corporations, and their role in economic development, were concerned with the inability of the state to prevent fraud or reduce uncertainty. American legislators and public commentators, in contrast, were obsessed with the emergence of national corporations that dominated the production of basic goods and transportation, and later with the consolidation of these national industries during the great merger movement of the late nineteenth and early twentieth century (Galambos, 1975). In the United States, where the corporation became the preferred vehicle for economic development, the reputation of the corporate form soon revolved around its presumed monopolization of the national market. Business historians continue to debate the scale and scope of American corporations versus their European rivals. But they generally agree that the state increasingly replaced the regulatory power of reputation by enacting industry regulations to control corporations.

THE REPUTATION OF REGULATORY BODIES

Regulation of the marketplace, whether through oversight of economic transactions or supervision of associations, has been a central role of the state from classical times to the present. With the rise of general incorporation and the broader influence of corporate power during the second industrial revolution (c.1870–1914), however, state regulation grew in scale and influence. State control of the corporate charter gave way to direct oversight of corporations via the broader regulation of industries. As economies of scale led to the widespread consolidation of industries into monopolistic or oligopolistic corporate structures, Anglo-American corporations resisted public attempts to enforce competition through breakup by acceding to regulatory oversight and internal reorganization (Chandler, 1990; Keller, 1963, 1990). Yet if corporate regulation seemed to offer an alternative to corporate reputation as a means to monitor behavior and provide oversight, it also generated two perennial questions: Who would oversee the regulators? And what reputations did those regulatory bodies themselves have?

In this regard, it is worth charting the changing reputation of corporations and their regulators in three distinct industries over the past century: pharmaceuticals, banks, and airlines. In all three industries, corporate reputation was vital to commercial success, but all three would also be increasingly regulated by the state, despite concerted attempts to deregulate them in the late twentieth century. Regulation, and the reputation of both the companies and their national regulators, became transnational, with standards, agreements, and corporate reputation increasingly negotiated at the global level.

The modern pharmaceutical industry originated in the leading economies of the late nineteenth century. In Germany, where pharmaceutical research and development emerged from the organic chemical industry, the creation of high production standards and drugs targeting specific illnesses led to the introduction by Bayer, for example, of two different wonder drugs, aspirin and heroin, in 1899. These two examples illustrate the problems for pharmaceutical companies in exercising control over their products: the patent for aspirin was seized in the United States in World War I, and the recreational use of heroin was subsequently criminalized. Welcome in the UK and Merck in the US transformed the reputation of pharmaceuticals from homeopathic remedies of dubious quality to powerful lifesaving remedies. Yet the reputational ascendance of the global pharmaceutical giants was twinned with state regulation of pharmaceutical claims. Regulators in the UK, the US, and Germany took action against the dubious claims of patent medicines, like Lydia Pinkham's, that were little more than mixtures of alcohol and opiates. In all three jurisdictions, the combination of tight state regulation, strong intellectual property laws, and strong commercial interests led to widespread public trust both in the oversight of the pharmaceutical industry and in the major manufacturers (Carpenter, 2010). So high was public trust in the regulation of pharmaceuticals that, by the end of the twentieth century, not only were drugs often manufactured overseas, but domestic regulatory agencies relied on the judgment of overseas agencies (usually the US Federal Drug Administration (FDA)) for approval, in effect ceding their own regulatory power to another jurisdiction. Similarly, the rise of generic drugs, where the corporate reputation of the manufacturer was supplanted by the presumed reputation of the regulatory body, has had an overwhelming impact in the marketplace over the last few decades.

In banking, too, the public reputation of firms has grown in tandem with the perceived power of regulators to oversee their behavior (Calomiris, 2000). In the caveat emptor system of commercial banking that predominated in the nineteenth century in Britain and the United States, not only were bank failures common, but the lack of common banking standards meant that credit was difficult to secure and economic markets were extraordinarily volatile (Jones, 1993). By the 1930s, following the Great Crash, the growing power of central banking, in tandem with Keynesian economic tools, to regulate the macroeconomy resulted in the creation of deposit insurance in the United States, with the result that depositors no longer had to rely on the individual reputation of banks to secure their savings (Cleveland & Heurtas, 1985). While credit-rating agencies and specialized bank analysts verified the soundness of banks, the American system of insuring personal deposits through the Federal Deposit Insurance Corporation (FDIC) prevented individuals from removing their deposits at the first hint of trouble. Faith in the financial regulators increasingly replaced dependence on the corporate reputations of financial institutions. The widespread adoption of deposit insurance in the UK and the recent creation of the Consumer Financial Protection Bureau in the US illustrate how financial markets have become increasingly regulated by the state.

Finally, in aviation, where corporate reputation signals a life-or-death calculation, regulation has always been a constant both to secure the value of flag-carriers and to guarantee commercial standards. Although there have been notable failures—a few problematic airlines that chose not to repair their planes or secure their facilities—the reputation for safety that airlines have achieved during the jet era is a testament to the public's belief in the power of regulators to secure their safety. From the very start, traffic in the skies came under state supervision, and safety standards were a matter not simply of corporate profits but of civic regulation. Remarkably, even as passenger fares and state sanction routes have been deregulated, safety standards have remained under tight regulatory watch (Vietor, 1994). Because of the success of international regulatory agencies, air passengers treat plane travel as a largely homogeneous good not merely in terms of baggage allowances and meals, but also in terms of personal safety.

Reputational Capital within Markets and Hierarchies

The transition to the modern era was characterized by the spread of bureaucracies and institutions that enabled more impersonal interactions and the enlargement of trade. As Mark Granovetter has argued, however, even the most "modern" and ostensibly impersonal of economic forces remain embedded in social relations. These relations, moreover, are not general and static: they change over time, and researchers must understand the specific contexts in which they operate in order to explain the sources of their efficacy and power (Granovetter, 1985). Generally referred to as social capital, such relations also have a strong reputational component, in that the extent to which they function or don't function can be heavily determined by the reputational capital of the parties within the relationships: Do they have legitimacy? Can they be counted on to fulfill both the letter and spirit of contracts? In the case of firms, reputational capital encompasses their intangible assets, which include ethical (not just legal) compliance, innovation, quality, safety, sustainability, and security.[2] When any of these are compromised, a firm can be said to have lost some of its reputational capital, which could render economic transactions more difficult.

Historians have readily discerned the importance of reputation in the early modern era, where a number of investigations have documented the persistence in economic relations of much older notions of social identity that were linked to reputation and honor (Muldrew, 1998; Fontaine, 2001). Yet historians of the latter half of the twentieth century have also profitably explored how reputations form and operate within social relations—most obviously, in business and corporate networks. Networks control scarce resources, with jobs, capital, information, and security being the most important. They determine who participates in market activities and delineate the extent of those individuals' participation, or non-participation. Networks are characterized by mutual expectations about who is reliable and what is to be delivered by all parties. These expectations, in turn, are shaped by the reputations of individuals within these networks. Moreover, the collective reputation of groups such as elite country clubs and well-respected service organizations can transfer to the individuals within that group and ease their access to resources. Inclusion in these elite groups necessitates the simultaneous exclusion of individuals who do not share the elite memberships' profile. Pamela W. Laird documented how membership in a particular cohort (male and white), reinforced by memberships in the organizations they dominated, ensured social mobility for some individuals while decidedly excluding others (Laird, 2006). Laird writes that the "natural" social capital that was so critical to the success of Andrew Carnegie, J.P. Morgan, and Bill Gates has been supplemented since the 1960s with "synthetic" social capital, including affirmative-action programs and institutionalized mentoring. Through regulation and social pressure, more formal networks were created that served minorities and women, allowing them to build positive and economically advantageous reputations within and among organizations.

As Naomi Lamoreaux et al. argue, the reputational capital of individuals within hierarchies and markets continues to be essential to economic transactions, which cannot occur without coordination, enforcement, and access to information. These are achieved in part through recourse to social ties, especially during periods of uncertainty. Long-term connections "constituted…a third major type of coordination mechanism [along with markets and hierarchies] whose significance has waxed as well as waned over time." For instance, the close social ties that developed among the owners and managers of firms in the Philadelphia textile sector during the 1870s helped them to act collectively to exploit market opportunities, respond more flexibly to style changes, and keep better

---

[2] This list is from the Intangible Assets Finance Society, available at http://iafinance.org/ (accessed 30 April 2011).

control of wholesalers. Fear of losing social and reputational capital meant that cheating and unfair dealing among group members were kept to a minimum (Lamoreaux et al., 2003; see also Bernstein, 2001).

In the same way, family firms can function as an antidote to uncertainty in unregulated markets, especially those with a great deal of transactional frictions such as high-information-gathering and contract-enforcement costs. Many historical accounts document how family ties provided, until well into the nineteenth century, a vital social framework for increasingly complex commercial transactions at a time when national and international regulation were still in their infancy. Harold James's works demonstrate how family ties helped to overcome a number of impediments to economic growth. Among these was their ability to serve as an intermediary between states and markets by bringing order to the latter, especially when the state was too weak or, at the other extreme, too heavy-handed to order transactions effectively (James, 2006).

Family firms' ability to use reputation to fill holes in regulation is perhaps best illustrated by recent studies in banking. Through most of the nineteenth century, the Rothschild brothers and cousins not only dominated finance but actually shaped the financial architecture of the times (Ferguson, 1998). Although some of their vast influence was due to their fairly advanced communication and contractual arrangements, they also helped establish an international "regulatory" framework by pushing for currency convertibility and stability, free trade, liberal-democratic politics, and peaceful competition. For nearly one hundred years, the Rothschilds' reputation with international investors was such that the mere association of their name with companies and transactions served as the equivalent today of a combined US Securities and Exchange Commission (SEC) filing and AAA credit rating.

Several other banking houses bridged the international governance gap, reducing uncertainty for European investors in the United States, for example. In the late nineteenth and early twentieth centuries, the Warburgs (Kuhn Loeb), Speyers, and Morgans dominated international financial transactions because they could operate more easily across borders than larger public banks and because their reputation among wealthy clients, individuals, and joint-stock banks inspired trust. In several countries, the huge fees they earned came not from extraordinary technical skill, but from their capacity to convince well-heeled private investors of their ability to provide accounting and management expertise on the spot, which served as a substitute for weak regulatory assurances. Reputation had its price, however. For those who detested as well as those who welcomed the "ascent of money," the Rothschilds symbolized a new era. Their caricatures adorned the writings of those who attacked capitalism from both the left and right. The criticisms threatened both the House of Rothschild and the international financial order, and help explain the family's relative decline in the latter part of the nineteenth century. In the middle of the twentieth century, distrust of the private power of international banks led to broad public support for regulation to encourage greater and fairer financial access. By century's end, technology and regulation reduced the role of reputation in finance and confined it to the private guarantee of only a few small intermediaries like venture capitalists, who still attract capital by promising high returns and careful scrutiny of transactions beyond the scope of standard regulation and governance (Kobrak, 2009).

PROBLEMS WITH THE EXISTING LITERATURE

It is perhaps premature to speak of problems, when a recognized historical literature on corporate reputation does not yet exist. Nonetheless, two areas merit attention.

The first is the *poorly understood distinctions between reputation and factual information.* Reputation is the perception that others hold about an individual, group, or corporation, based on opinion and hearsay. In this view, reputation is important and powerful in situations where information asymmetry persists (Fombrun, Chapter 5, this volume) But once an individual's or firm's past behaviors and performance can be independently verified, they become part of the factual record. The question that then arises is whether such a record can properly be considered as "reputation" (Silberstein-Loeb, 2010). From a purely pragmatic consideration, why should stakeholders bother about something as nebulous as a company's reputation if reliable and specific information on how it behaved in the past were easily obtainable? The definitional confusion between reputation and fact, moreover, suggests larger questions about how information is constructed and disseminated within economic systems. Most scholarly literatures assume that the regulating power of reputation is determined by how effectively information moves within a market. But one can argue that markets that facilitate the movement of verifiably true information should be far less dependent on reputation than markets where information asymmetry is rife.

There is also the puzzle of why the emphasis on reputation has flourished, even in societies that have made access to information easier for citizens and regulators. Is this because even the freest and most efficient of markets experience substantial information asymmetries that oblige citizens to rely on reputation to fill the information gaps? Or, ironically, do citizens feel so overwhelmed by the volume of available information that they choose to fall back on reputation, however nebulous, rather than do the arduous work of analyzing for themselves the reams of data at their fingertips? As Rindova and Martins explain (Chapter 2, this volume), the rankings of firms produced by intermediaries like *Fortune* are used as "cognitive shortcuts" by both firms and their stakeholders to assess quality. Do some corporations exploit the lack of reliable information to deliberately build false reputations that hinder the effective working of the market? (Enron is a recent example, but history provides many others.) If this is the case, historians must explain the developments that hindered a supposedly free market from working effectively; or, more ambitiously, to explain why the structure of the market may be such that it is impossible for information to move freely, thus opening up space for reputations to form. Of course, the continuing importance of reputation, even in data-rich societies, may point to another line of inquiry: that the concern about reputation is so common among corporations because it transcends the merely economic and is instead a symptom of social, cultural, and even existential anxieties.

A second shortcoming of the historical literature is *the tendency to take for granted the power of reputation and to depict it as an uncomplicated phenomenon,* rather than as a complex process whose power to regulate may be weak or indeterminate. As other chapters in this volume attest, there is plentiful research on the benefits of a good reputation. But equally, scholars are building more rigorous theories that aid our understanding of when reputation has consequences for a corporation or industry, and when it does not. Historians have much to contribute to the ongoing debate about whether a good reputation consistently facilitates transactions, reduces transaction costs, or holds corporations to account. Clearly, reputation is a social device that at times facilitates transactions, and as a signaling device it undoubtedly lubricates the wheels of commerce in certain instances. But reputational penalties alone are sometimes not powerful enough to deter opportunism. Reputation can deter bad behavior if, and only if, an individual or firm perceives its loss as undesirable. Yet firms sometimes have been willing to lose their short-term reputations with regulators for quick gains—as, for example, in the crisis that struck the world's financial system beginning in 2008 (Lewis, 2010).

J. Bradford DeLong's work on J.P. Morgan and Kuhn, Loeb & Co. suggests that in the early twentieth century the two largest American investment banks understood that their reputations were non-replicable assets that were worth protecting. High market shares, combined with expectations of longevity, gave these firms an incentive to behave honestly. John Moody, founder of the eponymous credit-rating agency, endorsed the notion that having "Morgan's men" on corporate boards served as an informal guarantee of those firms' quality. Yet the value of reputation for these large players suggests the converse: that for firms with small market shares, the temptation to cheat to achieve very high profits—as, for example, during an economic bubble—is greater because the hit on their reputations would have less devastating effects. Such firms may therefore choose to sacrifice their reputations in a particular area in order to achieve short-term gains. Moreover—and this is a critically important element of how reputation mechanisms function—DeLong argued that clients knew this, which explains why they were more inclined to trust a large player like Morgan, who they assumed would be in the market for the long term and therefore had much stronger incentives to avoid reputational damage (DeLong, 1991. See also Morrison & Wilhelm, 2007). The behavior of some banks and mortgage companies in the first decade of the twenty-first century suggests that the willingness to incur reputational damage is not limited to smaller players (Lewis, 2010). By providing detailed explanations of such events, historians can contribute to more robust theories about when reputational sanctions are effective and when they are not.

In the same vein, the desire of regulators to create and maintain good reputations for themselves and/or their agencies must be understood as a phenomenon with multiple dimensions that over time has had profound effects on the firms and industries being regulated (Gilad and Yogev, Chapter 16, this volume). Understanding these dynamics may explain (for instance) why some industries—consumer finance being among the most flagrant modern examples—managed to retain their ability to regulate themselves despite having poor reputations with regulators and the public (Warren, 2008).

DIRECTIONS FOR FURTHER RESEARCH

The oscillating relationship between reputation and regulation continues to offer a fruitful area for historical research, as do cross-country analyses that focus on institutional and cultural contexts to explain how reputation may have regulated and constrained business corporations (Newburry, Chapter 12, this volume; Brammer and Jackson, Chapter 15, this volume). Two other areas hold the promise of producing exciting new research in the history of corporate reputation:

Reputation intermediaries. To understand how corporate reputations emerge, spread, gain traction, and are dislodged, it helps to consider how the principal intermediaries responsible for disseminating information about companies operate, and what influence they may have on regulation. Other chapters in this book speak of "institutional intermediaries" such as the media and various specialized organizations (Fombrun, Chapter 5, this volume; Rindova and Martins, Chapter 2, this volume). Historically, we can conceive of intermediaries more broadly, to include nearly all organizations and individuals responsible for creating, maintaining, mediating, and sometimes destroying corporate reputations. In addition to the media, these include advertising, marketing, and public relations professionals, and lobbyists—intermediaries who exist because the market for information is highly imperfect and provides arbitrage opportunities (Ewen, 1996; Miller & Dinan, 2008; Laird, 1998). When behavior and perception are at odds, a company may rely on internal and external corporate communications to perpetuate, or correct, unreliable opinions, and the extent to which these are effective depends largely upon the status of the intermediaries responsible for relaying the message. Intermediaries can also include regulators, celebrity endorsers and critics of corporations, non-governmental organizations (NGOs), business schools, and professional service providers such as auditors, the legal profession, and consultants (Khurana, 2007; McKenna, 2006). Intermediaries are concerned with the construction and management of their own reputations. The process can profoundly affect the way information about company activities moves within markets, as well as the quality of this information. Studying how intermediaries interact with corporations and their various constituencies is crucial to understanding how reputations form.

Corporations' multiple reputations with different groups (stakeholders). Historians can learn much from stakeholder theory, which posits that multiple interest groups have a stake in the actions of firms and the outcomes that these produce (Fombrun, Chapter 5, this volume). On the most elementary level, historians should distinguish among a firm's multiple reputations—with whom, and for what?—and note that these can be at odds with one another. Sorting out the interplay of a company's different reputations with its multiple stakeholders, and the way these change over time, can produce far more satisfying accounts of firm behavior over time.

CONCLUSION

Historians have long relied on intuitive concepts of corporate reputation. Consciously making use of the frameworks described here, and devising additional ones inspired by other chapters in this volume, can lead to fresh questions and make the "super-thick descriptions" that characterize the historical field more relevant to scholars in other disciplines. For their part, institutional scholars can incorporate historical ways of thinking to ground their theory-building more firmly in the specifics of time and place, pay greater attention to path-dependence, embeddedness, and context, and make the concept of change over time an integral part of their investigations.

Core Research on Corporate Reputation and Regulation in Historical Perspective

Reference	Key Constructs and Findings
Hurst (1969)	Distrust of the corporate form in the United States did not prevent its rapid growth but led to the strong regulatory and legal restrictions on its powers.
North & Thomas (1973)	The development of formal regulatory structures enabled economic agents to move beyond local markets and small trading networks to promote regional development in the modern world.
Greif (1989)	Among the first attempts by an economic historian to theorize enforcement mechanisms and the role of reputation.
	Demonstrated how the Maghrabi's closed circle enabled them to ostracize cheaters.
Keller (1990)	Economic and social regulation was a hallmark of the Progressive era in America.
	Those regulatory frameworks connected urban growth with the second industrial revolution.
DeLong (1991)	The corporate reputation of J.P. Morgan was valuable both to his firm and to their investors as initial public offering (IPO) results demonstrate.
	J.P. Morgan's reputation not only increased the value of the associated companies but decreased active oversight by regulators.
	Smaller or newer firms may have fewer incentives to protect their reputations in particular markets.

Reference	Key Constructs and Findings
Lamoreaux et al. (2003)	Regulatory bodies substituted for personal reputation as the marketplace expanded.
	Reputational capital within social relations can act as a third type of coordination mechanism, in addition to hierarchies and markets.
Greif (2006)	Game theory can be applied to understand reputational enforcement in historical trading networks.
Carpenter (2010)	Details how the American FDA rose to become the most important regulatory agency in the world for medicine, effectively supplanting regional and state authority.

References

Bernstein, L. (1992). "Opting out of the legal system: Extralegal contractual relations in the diamond industry." *Journal of Legal Studies*, 21(1): 115–157.

—— (2001). "Private commercial law in the cotton industry: Creating cooperation through rules, norms, and institutions." *Michigan Law Review*, 99(7): 1724–1790.

Brenner, R. (1993). *Merchants and Revolution: Commercial Change, Political Conflict, and London's Overseas Traders, 1550–1653*. Princeton, NJ: Princeton University Press.

Calomiris, C. W. (2000). *U.S. Bank Deregulation in Historical Perspective*. Cambridge: Cambridge University Press.

Carpenter, D. (2010). *Reputation and Power: Organizational Image and Pharmaceutical Regulation at the FDA*. Princeton, NJ: Princeton University Press.

Chandler Jr., A. D. (1990). *Scale and Scope: The Dynamics of Industrial Capitalism*. Cambridge, MA: Belknap Press.

Clay, K. (1997). "Trade without law: Private-order institutions in Mexican California." *Journal of Law, Economics & Organization*, 13(1): 202–231.

Cronin, W. (1992). *Nature's Metropolis: Chicago and the Great West*. New York: W.W. Norton.

Dellarocas, C. (2003). "The digitization of word of mouth: Promises and challenges of online feedback mechanisms." *Management Science*, 49(10): 1407–1424.

DeLong, J. B. (1991). "Did J.P. Morgan's men add value? An economist's perspective on financial capitalism." In P. Temin (Ed.), *Inside the Business Enterprise: Historical Perspectives on the Use of Information*. Chicago: University of Chicago Press.

Elton, G. (1953). *The Tudor Revolution in Government: Administrative Changes in the Reign of Henry VIII*. Cambridge: Cambridge University Press.

Ewen, S. (1996). *PR! A Social History of Spin*. New York: Basic Books.

Ferguson, N. (1998). *The World's Banker: The History of the House of Rothschild*. London: Weidenfeld & Nicolson.

Finn, M. (2003). *The Character of Credit: Personal Debt in English Culture, 1740–1914*. Cambridge: Cambridge University Press.

Fontaine, L. (2001). "Antonio and Shylock: Credit and trust in France, c. 1680–c. 1780." *The Economic History Review*, New Series, 54(1): 39–57.

Galambos, L. (1975). *The Public Image of Big Business in America, 1880–1940*. Baltimore, MD: The Johns Hopkins University.

Granovetter, M. (1985). "Economic action and social structure: The problem of embeddedness." *American Journal of Sociology*, 91(3): 481–510.

Greif, A. (1989). "Reputation and coalitions in medieval trade: Evidence on the Maghribi traders." *Journal of Economic History*, 49(4): 857–882.

—— (2006). *Institutions and the Path to the Modern Economy: Lessons from Medieval Trade*. Cambridge: Cambridge University Press.

——, Milgrom, P., & Weingast, B. R. (1994). "Coordination, commitment, and enforcement: The case of the merchant guild." *Journal of Political Economy*, 102(4): 745–776.

Gürtler, O. & Grund, C. (2006). "The effect of reputation on selling prices in auctions." *Discussion Paper No. 114*, Governance and the Efficiency of Economic Systems.

Harris, R. (2000). *Industrializing English Law: Entrepreneurship and Business Organization, 1720–1844*. Cambridge: Cambridge University Press.

Hurst, J. W. (1969). *The Legitimacy of the Business Corporation*. Charlottesville, VA: University of Virginia Press.

James, H. (2006). *Family Capitalism: Wendels, Haniels, Falcks, and the Continental European Model*. Cambridge, MA: Harvard University Press.

Jones, G. (1993). *British Multinational Banking, 1830–1990*. Oxford: Oxford University Press.

Jøsang, A., Ismail, R., & Boyd, C. A. (2007). "A survey of trust and reputation systems for online service provision." *Decision Support Systems*, 43(2): 618–644.

Keller, M. (1963). *The Life Insurance Enterprise: A Study in the Limits of Corporate Power*. Cambridge, MA: Harvard University Press.

—— (1990). *Regulating a New Economy: Public Policy and Economic Change in America, 1900–1933*. Cambridge, MA: Harvard University Press.

Khurana, R. (2007). *From Higher Aims to Hired Hands: The Social Transformation of American Business Schools and the Unfulfilled Promise of Management as a Profession*. Princeton, NJ: Princeton University Press.

Kobrak, C. (2009). "Family finance: Value creation and the democratization of cross-border governance." *Enterprise and Society*, 10(2): 38–89.

Laird, P. (1998). *Advertising Progress: American Business and the Rise of Consumer Marketing*. Baltimore, MD: Johns Hopkins University Press.

Laird, P. W. (2006). *Pull: Networking and Success Since Benjamin Franklin*. Cambridge, MA: Harvard University Press.

Lamoreaux, N., Raff, D. M. G., & Temin, P. (2003). "Beyond markets and hierarchies: Toward a new synthesis of American business history." *American Historical Review*, 108(2), online version.

Lewis, M. (2010). *The Big Short: Inside the Doomsday Machine*. New York: W.W. Norton.

Lipartito, K. & David, B. S. (Eds.). (2004). *Constructing Corporate America: History, Politics, Culture*. Oxford: Oxford University Press.

Lopez, R. S. (1976). *The Commercial Revolution of the Middle Ages, 950–1350*. Cambridge: Cambridge University Press.

Lurie, J. (1979). *The Chicago Board of Trade, 1859–1905: The Dynamics of Self-Regulation*. Champaign, IL: University of Illinois Press.

Maurer, N. & Sharma, T. (2001). "Enforcing property rights through reputation: Mexico's early industrialization, 1878–1913." *Journal of Economic History*, 61(4): 950–973.

McCloskey, D. N. (2009). "The institution of Douglass North," from *Bourgeois Dignity and Liberty: Why Economics Can't Explain the Modern World*, Vol. 2 of *The Bourgeois Era*, under review. University of Chicago Press.

McKenna, C. D. (2006). *The World's Newest Profession: Management Consulting in the Twentieth Century*. Cambridge: Cambridge University Press.

Micklethwait, J. & Wooldridge, A. (2003). *The Company: A Short History of a Revolutionary Idea*. New York: Modern Library.

Milgrom, P. R., North, D. C., & Weingast, B. R. (1990). "The role of institutions in the revival of trade: The law merchant, private judges, and the champagne fairs." *Economics and Politics*, 2(1): 1–23.

Miller, D. & Dinan, W. (2008). *A Century of Spin: How Public Relations Became the Cutting Edge of Corporate Power*. London: Pluto Press.

Morrison, A. D. & Wilhelm, W. J. (2007). *Investment Banking: Institutions, Politics, and Law*. Oxford: Oxford University Press.

Muldrew, C. (1998). *The Economy of Obligation: The Culture of Credit and Social Relations in Early Modern England*. New York: St. Martin's Press.

Najemy, J. M. (1979). "Guild republicanism in Trecento Florence: The successes and ultimate failure of corporate politics." *American Historical Review*, 84(1): 53–71.

North, D. C. (1990). *Institutions, Institutional Change, and Economic Performance*. Cambridge: Cambridge University Press.

—— & Thomas, R. P. (1973). *The Rise of the Western World: A New Economic History*. Cambridge: Cambridge University Press.

Olegario, R. (2006). *A Culture of Credit: Embedding Trust and Transparency in American Business*. Cambridge, MA: Harvard University Press.

Richman, B. D. (2004). "Firms, courts, and reputation mechanisms: Towards a positive theory of private ordering." *Columbia Law Review*, 104(1): 2328–2367.

Silberstein-Loeb, J. (2010). "Reputation or: How I learned to stop worrying and love the market." In J. Klewes & R. Wreschniok (Eds.), *Reputation Capital: Building and Maintaining Trust in the 21st Century*. Heidelberg, Germany: Springer-Verlag.

Smith, D. K. (1999). "Learning politics: The Nîmes hosiery guild and the statutes controversy of 1706–1712." *French Historical Studies*, 22(4): 493–533.

Taylor, J. (2007). "Company fraud in Victorian Britain: The Royal British Bank scandal of 1856." *English Historical Review*, 122(497): 700–724.

van Cleveland, H. B. & Huertas, T. (1985). *Citibank, 1812–1970*. Cambridge, MA: Harvard University Press.

Vietor, R. H. K. (1994). *Contrived Competition: Regulation and Deregulation in America*. Cambridge, MA: Harvard University Press.

von der Crone, H. & Vetsch, J. (2009). "Reputation and regulation." In J. Klewes & R. Wreschniok (Eds.), *Reputation Capital: Building and Maintaining Trust in the 21st Century*. Springer-Verlag.

Warren, E. (2008). "Product safety regulation as a model for financial services regulation." *Journal of Consumer Affairs*, 42(3): 452–460.

Wotruba, T. R. (1997). "Industry self-regulation: A review and extension to a global setting." *Journal of Public Policy & Marketing*, 16(1), International Issues in Law and Public Policy: 38–54.

CHAPTER 14

INDUSTRY SELF-REGULATION AS A SOLUTION TO THE REPUTATION COMMONS PROBLEM: THE CASE OF THE NEW YORK CLEARING HOUSE ASSOCIATION

LORI QINGYUAN YUE
PAUL INGRAM

The performance of organizations depends partly on the reputations of their industries. Such reputations are "intangible commons." Interest in protecting mutual welfare motivates members of an industry to engage in self-regulation. However, the current literature tends to have a pessimistic view of the efficacy of self-regulation in solving the problem of reputational commons. We argue that the obstacles forecasted by such pessimistic reasoning are context-bound and can be overcome if industry self-regulation includes effective sanctions and exclusion strategies. We investigate the case of the New York Clearing House Association, a community-based self-regulatory program, which, by promoting prudence among members, successfully ameliorated the negative spillover effect on market confidence during bank panics. We then identify five conditions that account for the efficacy of this self-regulation. We conclude by showing how research on institutional solutions to the problem of reputation commons can be extended.

INTRODUCTION

THE performance of organizations depends partly on the reputations of their industries. These reputations are "intangible commons" because organizations share both the penalties and rewards associated with the reputations of their industries. Interest in protecting mutual welfare motivates members of an industry to engage in self-regulation. However, current literature tends to hold a pessimistic view of self-regulation's ability to solve the problem of industry reputational commons. This pessimistic view is rooted in three lines of reasoning: (1) competitive relations within the same industry will undermine the willingness of organizations to cooperate; (2) a collective solution will suffer from opportunism and is thus unlikely to be successful; (3) a collective solution is likely to be exploited by a group of organizations in order to create unfair market competition, which, in turn, will reduce social welfare. Moreover, critics point out that when it comes to solving the problem of reputation commons, self-regulation is likely to serve as a smokescreen since reputation can be improved simply by impressing outsiders without changing the behaviors of organizations. Thus, it is important to investigate whether self-regulation can solve the problem of reputation commons by disciplining the behavior of members effectively. We argue that obstacles forecasted by these pessimistic lines of reasoning are context-bound and that they can be overcome if industry self-regulation includes effective sanctions and exclusion strategies.

To justify this claim, we first review the literature on industry reputation commons. We argue that reputation exists beyond the level of individual organizations and that the problem of reputation commons originates in the interdependence of outsiders' perception of an organization and that of its peers. All organizations within an industry face sanctions from stakeholders when social expectations are violated. At the same time, all organizations within an industry also enjoy better access to resources when their industry gains cognitive and social political legitimacy. Sharing motivates organizations to cooperate, build a good collective reputation, and protect that reputation from harm. Thus, the emergence of rules and norms to govern the commons is motivated by the self-interested decisions of organizations, as self-regulatory institutions allow organizations to gain the benefits of coordinated activity.

We then examine the case of the New York Clearing House Association (NYCHA), a community-based, self-regulatory program among commercial banking organizations. We show that the effects of negative spillover on market confidence created a reputation commons for banks during times of panic, and that the NYCHA was founded as a collective institutional solution for ameliorating the problem of reputation commons. We have identified five conditions that result in the NYCHA's efficacy in solving the commons problem: (1) previous cooperative experience created a foundation from which self-regulation could take root; (2) a transaction-based mechanism for measuring contributions and consumption offered incentives for good performers to contribute and discouraged poor performers from consuming the common good; (3) formal mechanisms for inspection, sanction, and exclusion could be enforced to exclude free-riders; (4) a close-knit community further facilitated monitoring and increased the cost of defection; and (5) antitrust legislations and the advance of the state constrained the legitimacy of self-regulation.

We end the chapter by discussing ways to extend research beyond the hurdles that self-regulation must overcome in order to solve the problem of reputation commons. We suggest that future research should examine alternative means of enforcement, such as independent third-party certification, and hybrid forms of regulation that partner with the government. Future research should also test the efficacy of self-regulation by separating the question as to whether industry self-regulations can, in theory, be effective, from legal and political contexts that have inhibited such efforts. Finally, future research should explore the consequence of changes in community structures and information diffusion mechanisms on self-regulation in order to solve reputation commons in new industries.

Reputation Commons: Concept and Type

Corporate reputation is defined as "observers' collective judgments of a corporation based on assessments of the financial, social, and environmental impacts attributed to the corporation over time" (Barnett, Jermier, & Lafferty, 2006: 34). In general, reputation is a judgment that is formed through the observation of past behaviors, but also shapes future expectations. Reputation seldom develops in isolation. Since observers can only evaluate the actions of an organization by considering those of its peers, reputations of organizations are interdependent. A downward social comparison can easily boost one's reputation. Yet standing within a group of dirty peers can hardly make one look clean if observers perceive every organization as one of *the dirty ones*. The thorny interdependence of reputation between an organization and its industry includes both competitive and communal dimensions. Wade, Swaminathan, & Saxon (1998) have observed this interdependence in the brewing industry. According to their study, the passage of prohibition laws in one state resulted in the proliferation of breweries in neighboring states, though too many prohibitions in neighboring areas dampened the number of local breweries because their legitimacy was threatened. The communal view of corporations' reputation argues that the reputation of an organization depends not only on its actions, but also on the reputation of the industry in which it occurs. If organizations depend on collective perceptions of their industry, all of them face sanctions when one severely violates the expectations of stakeholders. Thus, organizational reputation exists beyond the level of individual organizations and has its roots in an interorganizational context (Barnett & Hoffman, 2008). In this sense, industry reputation is an intangible *commons* (Barnett & King, 2008).

There are at least three reasons why the reputations of organizations share a communal feature. First of all, organizations within an industry share a reputation because they share similar attributes. Since organizations within the same industry tend to utilize similar resources, employ similar technologies, and adopt similar management practices, the actions of one are often perceived as emblematic of an entire industry. Being tarred by the same brush is not rare. In the case of the recent Gulf oil spill, for example, while the accident was unique to BP, it put all oil companies under public scrutiny because it "caused consumers to question whether a similar incident could happen to other companies" (Market Strategies International, 2010). As a result, the market index of the reputation of the energy industry plummeted by 25 percent (Market Strategies International, 2010). Second, observers use collective reputations to judge an individual firm due to the problem of information asymmetry. Outsiders may not be equipped with specialized knowledge to distinguish between the behaviors of the industry's individual members. Even if they are, the cost of making an informed judgment may be prohibitively high, especially when the source of information is distant in terms of geography, culture, and language. As a result of information asymmetry, newcomers to an industry can still bear the stigma of their predecessors long after the latter are gone (Tirole, 1996). Third, an individual organization's actions can significantly affect the reputation of an entire industry. Research in psychology has shown that salient events caused by certain group members are represented disproportionately in impressions of the group formed by observers because the availability heuristic makes it easier for extremes to be overestimated (Rothbart et al., 1978). As a result, severe accidents and catastrophes caused by an individual organization can have devastating effects on the reputation of an entire industry.

Corporate social responsibility is one instance of an industry-reputation common, as the public has become increasingly concerned about the role of corporations as responsible citizens in society. Besides pursuing profits, corporations are expected to comply with labor, environmental, human rights, or other standards of accountability. Researchers have documented numerous cases in which an entire industry is sanctioned when one or a small group of organizations violate the expectations of social responsibility. In the chemical industry, all firms were punished by shareholders due to one individual firm's accident (Barnett & King, 2008). In the coffee, athletic shoes, and apparel industries, sweatshops and other unfair labor practices have agitated widespread boycotts by consumers (Malkin, 1996; Hornblower, 2000). In the diamond industry, conflict diamonds mined in African war zones poisoned the glamour linked to the industry and caused drops in sales (Zoellner, 2006). In the early movie industry, the excessive portrayal of sex and violence by some producers drew fire from America's moral guardians, and incurred a crusade that jeopardized the future of this nascent industry (Walsh, 1996).

To be sure, industry reputation commons is not limited to the domain of social responsibility or the shared fate occasioned by shared penalties. A good collective reputation can also lead to shared rewards, such as enlarged growth opportunities or expanded resource space. As a collective perception, reputation is socially constructed and can be enhanced through a legitimation process (Rao, 1994). When organizations' actions are perceived as desirable, proper, and appropriate to the social system of norms and beliefs, they obtain a good reputation, and lead to easier resource access. Consider the necessary legitimation process at the early stage of new industries. Aldrich & Fiol (1994) argue that the essential task of industry pioneers is to construct a favorable reputation for the industry by demonstrating that it is economically viable, cognitively cogent, and morally defensible. In the case of French nouvelle cuisine, for example, endorsement by star chefs ameliorated the pressure of the culinary movement being perceived as abnormal by traditional food critics (Rao, Monin, & Durand, 2005). Similarly, in the case of American hotels, the founding of the Cornell School of Hotel Administration elevated the image of the hotel industry by presenting it as a profession that attracts talent (Ingram, 1998). When more and more people follow the steps of pioneers, a fledgling industry not only grows in size but gradually achieves a taken-for-granted status. In this constitutive legitimation process, each member contributes by its mere existence.

Another positive effect of sharing an industry reputation is regional industry clusters. The reputation of industry clusters attracts talent and customers from a wide radius. This concentration of talent catalyzes innovations that, in turn, benefit all industry members through the diffusion of learning and knowledge. In the nineteenth century, the reputation of Clyde River as a shipping capital helped shipbuilders in the area secure orders from all over the world (Ingram & Lifschitz, 2006). The fair-trade reputation enjoyed by merchants in Champagne during the Middle Ages helped the region become a trading center in Europe (Milgrom, North, & Weingast, 1990). Similarly, in the modern age, industry clusters such as Silicon Valley function as a magnet that attracts entrepreneurs, scientists, and venture capitalists (Saxenian, 1994).

COLLECTIVE SOLUTIONS TO REPUTATION COMMONS

Central to the problem of reputation commons is the interdependence of the reputation of an individual organization and that of its industry. If an individual organization can successfully distinguish itself from the rest of its industry, then no commons problem will arise. However, with limited resources, an individual firm may not be able to generate enough differences to stand out. Empirical evidence has demonstrated that even industry leaders such as Nike, Gap, and Starbucks are not immune to the backlash against their industries, despite offering superior working conditions than their peers do (Malkin, 1996; Hornblower, 2000). In fact, firms that hold high standards of accountability are more likely to be targeted by social activists, who see responsible firms as soft targets that are likelier to respond to their requests (Barron & Diermeier, 2007). Thus, they prey on these firms to generate momentum for their movements.

If individual firms have limited capacity to solve the problem of reputation commons, it is in the interest of organizations to cooperate, set enforceable standards, and impose a rationalized system to discipline their actions and those of their competitors. The emergence of a self-regulatory institution is motivated by the self-interest of organizations, and incentives to cooperate are grounded in the belief that such an institution will allow organizations to gain the benefits of coordinated activity. This concept of an institution as a "cooperation-for-collective-benefits" (Knight, 1992) is a fundamental argument of both institutional economics (North, 1990) and rational-choice institutionalism (Nee & Ingram, 1998). Industry self-regulation provides a way to solve the problem of reputation commons by providing collective benefits unattainable through the actions of an individual organization. This is also the strategy that Barnett & Hoffman (2008) called "teaming up" with peers.

The difficult fact in protecting reputational commons is that it requires many direct competitors in an industry to cooperate. Organizations that share a common reputation are also those that researchers and practitioners classify as direct competitors. Yu & Lester (2008) find that reputational spillovers occur among structurally equivalent parties. However, structural equivalence, too, has been used to define competitors because structural equivalents serve as substitutes for each other. Similarly, Barnett (2006) argues that reputation spillover is stronger among homogeneous firms. Hannan, Polos, & Carroll (2007) echo this and claim that a population's legitimacy is directly tied to the degree of similarity among its members. Yet the more similar an organization is to its rivals, the more competitive is their relationship due to overlap in shared resources (McPherson, 1983). In addition, when competition is localized, staying close to an industrial center means staying close to many competitors. Sorensen & Audia (2000) have shown that proximity to competitors significantly increases the chances of an individual organization's mortality.

The dark shadow of competition is the first obstacle in the formation of a collective solution to industry reputation commons. Competition dampens mutual trust. Without trust, institutional initiators are hesitant to act because they risk placing themselves at a disadvantage if their rivals fail to follow them. Furthermore, other organizations may suspect the intentions of rivals that initiate a regulatory institution and may thus refuse to participate for fear of being trapped in an institution that favors initiators. For example, after the scandal of the El Monte sweatshop in 1995, apparel firms in California faced a reputation-commons problem. Some of them attempted to reach out to their primary competitors to establish an anti-sweatshop alliance. But none of these efforts were productive because competitors suspected that they simply constituted another sort of "backroom competition" (Bartley, 2007: 29). In addition to reducing trust, competition also forces organizations to focus on short-term goals such as survival, whereas the improvement of industry reputation takes time. Organizations, uncertain as to whether they will still be in business the following year, are unwilling to make long-term investments in improving industry reputation.

The second obstacle facing self-regulation lies in the legitimacy of cooperation among competitors. Inherent in the theory of perfect competition is the Darwinian notion that purely competitive markets are good for society because they force firms to reach maximum efficiency. Beyond the calculation of total social welfare, another aspect of the legitimacy of self-regulation involves distributional justice, that is, whether self-regulation serves private at the expense of public interests. Some critics claim that self-regulation is simply a means by which to fend off government regulation. They criticize self-regulation for its weak standards, ineffective enforcement, and secret and mild punishments (Waguespack & Sorenson, 2010). Howard, Nash, & Ehrenfeld (2000) also contend that self-regulation is a smokescreen aimed more at improving public image than at generating real improvement, much as the globe's worst human rights violators are the most likely to sign treaties that protect human rights (Hafner-Burton & Tsutsui, 2005). Supporting such critiques, King & Lenox (2000) report that Responsible Care, a self-regulatory program established after the Bhopal accident in order to mend the reputation of the chemical industry, was incapable of reducing its members' pollution emissions.

Researchers have also expressed concern over the distributional justice of benefits for direct participants of self-regulation. For example, Barnett (forthcoming) finds that large firms exert control over industry communal organizations to advance their own interests rather than those of an entire industry. A related problem is that access to a self-regulation program is controlled by institutional incumbents who can deploy self-regulation to disadvantage their economic rivals by denying them equal rights of participation.

Besides legitimacy concerns, scholars have also been skeptical of the viability of self-regulation, specifically whether self-regulation can overcome the free-rider problem. The key to providing any common good is to induce contributions or protect it from being exploited by those who do not contribute. At least since the publication of Mancur Olson's *The Logic of Collective Action* in 1965, social scientists have been dubious of the idea that voluntary associations tend to form and take collective action whenever members jointly benefit. The reasoning behind Olson's idea is similar in structure to the dilemma of an n-person game (Hardin, 1971): if each individual can access benefits of the public good that are funded by others' contributions without payment, then in a finite number of rounds a rational actor will contribute zero. If participation in a private cooperation is voluntary and unenforced by a central authority, then each actor has an incentive to defect from agreements and to free-ride on the efforts of others.

Another concern related to the free-rider problem is the situation of adverse selection. Since organizations with lower levels of performance benefit more from an improvement in industry reputation, they have more incentives to join in coordinated action. Moreover, bad performers may use participation in industry self-regulation to disguise their poor performance. Without effective mechanisms to exclude these bad apples, self-regulation may be downgraded in a way similar to that of the market for lemons (Akerlof, 1970). King & Lenox (2000) observed the adverse selection problem in the Responsible Care program and found that firms in heavy pollution sectors were more likely to join the self-regulation program.

These obstacles have recently been re-evaluated through a series of investigations of real-life voluntary associations. Based on her research of private institutions that help pool common resources such as fisheries, forests, and water resources, Ostrom (2000) argued that when a small group of actors makes a credible commitment, engages in effective monitoring, and sanctions against deviations, self-organized cooperative institutions can protect participants' common interests, and the benefits derived from such collective action can spur efforts to create and maintain these private institutions. Can the conditions that Ostrom applied to the governance of physical commons be extended to govern reputation commons?

The depletion of physical commons such as clean water, shared fisheries, and stable climate has a direct impact on the welfare of relevant parties. The conditions of these physical commons can hardly be improved if relevant parties do not reduce water pollution, promote sustainable fisheries, or curb carbon dioxide emissions. However, reputation commons differs from physical commons in that reputation is a set of perceptions that can be decoupled from actual behavior. Thus collective solutions for improving reputation commons can work indirectly by influencing perception without touching the real problem. In support of this view, Barnett & King (2008) have found that rather than acting as a means of disciplining the actions of members, self-regulation deploys impression management practices to forestall industry-wide sanctions. The difference between physical and reputation commons raises the question about the efficacy of self-regulation in solving real problems that concern outside stakeholders. If self-regulation is simply an effort to manipulate impressions, its efficacy is greatly reduced. It thus remains an important task to investigate whether, and under what conditions, self-regulation can effectively discipline the behavior of participants in solving the problem of reputation commons. We address these problems by illustrating the case of the New York Clearing House Association (NYCHA), an industry self-regulatory institution that solved the problem of reputation commons in the banking industry before the founding of the Federal Reserve.

The Case of the New York Clearing House Association

Banks are professionally managed. Ordinary depositors cannot easily judge the health of an individual bank. Due to information asymmetry, depositors use information revealed about certain banks to evaluate the soundness of others. As a result, negative investment news about a few banks or some isolated bank failures can damage confidence in a banking market. If depositors worry that their own banks are, or might become, insolvent, they will rush to withdraw their deposits, leading to runs on many banks at the same time. Bank runs can make originally solvent banks fail. To satisfy depositors' demand for cash, these banks may be forced to liquidate their assets in a short time period, often at steep discounts. When discounted assets are inadequate to compensate for debts, a bank becomes insolvent and is likely to fail. Thus, bank runs are contagious, and the problem of reputation commons is at the center of bank panics (Calomiris & Gorton, 1991).

In the US, before deregulation in the late 1970s and early 1980s, banks in most states could only branch within their headquarter state or within the area of their headquarter cities. Localized operation made the effect of reputation spillover especially strong because banks were not diversified geographically. One cooperative arrangement through which banks could unite their actions was the clearing house. The first clearing house in the country was the New York Clearing House Association founded in 1853. Before the Federal Reserve was founded in 1914, there were more than 200 clearing houses in the country. The clearing house was a city-based voluntary association among banks. The function of the clearing house can be broken down into two categories, clearing and regulation (Cannon, 1910). To fulfill the clearing function, the clearing house provided centralized clearing services for its members over notes, drafts, checks, and bills of exchange. To fulfill the regulation function, the clearing house prescribed rules and norms for the control of its members, through which the clearing house ameliorated the problem of reputation commons. It is important to note that the clearing function preceded the regulation function. Cooperation in the clearing process brought bankers together and created a forum in which innovative self-regulation took root.

Early in its operation, the clearing house adopted a strategy of pooling the reserves of members. Pooling was not popular, however, because more conservatively managed banks had no rewards to contribute to this reserve pool, while opportunistic banks were allowed to pursue high-risk and high-return operations. From the 1870s on, the clearing house abandoned the practice of pooling reserves and adopted transaction-based loan certificates. Once a bank panic struck, member banks could borrow loan certificates from the clearing house and use them in place of currency in the clearing process. They could thus inflate the adequacy of cash that they needed to satisfy depositors' demands. These loan certificates were interest-based, and borrowing banks paid lending banks interest rates ranging from 6 to 10 percent—high enough to encourage reserve-abundant banks to share their bounty and to discourage reserve-deficient banks from borrowing more frequently than when absolutely necessary. In this way, the clearing house provided a selective incentive for banks to contribute to collective solvency, and to refrain from threatening that solvency. Serving as a credit intermediary, the clearing house enabled a more efficient use of resources during panics, when banks hoarded money.

Was the clearing house an effective regulatory institution? Yue, Luo, & Ingram (2009) have studied the efficacy of the New York Clearing House Association—the largest clearing house in the nation—in reducing the failure rate and operational risk of member banks. They found that the NYCHA reduced the failure rate of member banks by 56 percent after controlling the endogeneity of self-selection in membership. Moreover, they found that NYCHA member banks were relatively prudent and avoided highly risky operations. Yue, Luo, & Ingram (2009) also show that the NYCHA was successful in imposing self-regulation and organizing cooperative arrangements. What, however, was the welfare implication? As Yue, Luo, & Ingram (2009) demonstrate, survival benefits did not remain solely with NYCHA members but spread to all Manhattan commercial banks. The overall failure rate of this population during the regulation of the NYCHA

was significantly lower than in the previous period, which had had no private regulation. Moreover, the overall failure rate of this population under the regulation of the
NYCHA was no higher than that under the government regulation after 1914. Although
the NYCHA only rescued its members, its efforts at dampening waves of bank panics
stabilized the market and allowed the whole bank population to flourish. The number of
commercial banks located in Manhattan increased from 51 in 1853, when the NYCHA
was founded, to about 100 in 1913, when the NYCHA ceased to regulate the market.
More impressively, the total assets of these banks grew 1,400 percent during this period.
Contrary to what antitrust proponents might predict, under the regulation of the
NYCHA, New York developed into the most competitive and vibrant banking market in
the country. It is hard to exaggerate the role that the NYCHA played, and in an era without a central bank, the NYCHA was regarded as "a most important and beneficial part in
the general economic health of the nation" (Gilpin & Wallace, 1905: 5).

The success of the NYCHA in mitigating panics was a result of the system of loan certificates, and, most importantly, of the monitoring and sanctioning regime that backed
the system. First of all, the clearing house provided *club goods*, accessible only to clearing
house members. Key to the provision of club goods was that free-riders had to be
excluded from the club (Potoski & Prakash, 2009). The clearing house had a special
committee in charge of member admission. In addition, new members had to be
approved by the majority of existing members. The clearing house also adopted an
exclusion strategy. Banks that refused to share the burden of other members during a
financial crisis were suspended from the privileges of the clearing house or were even
expelled (Cannon, 1910). Second, to prevent the moral hazard problem, the clearing
house required banks to keep a high level of reserves (Hammond, 1957). The clearing
house closely monitored the balance sheets of member banks and required them to
report their condition every week. Moreover, the clearing house had the authority to
audit members' books at any moment, which it could do in response to rumors about
the state of a particular member.

Third, as a form of local self-regulation, the clearing house was relatively small, but its
modest size made close monitoring feasible and coordination relatively easy. Due to
prohibitions on bank branching, banks were locally based. Even the largest clearing
houses, such as the NYCHA, maintained a size of 50–60 members during the years they
regulated the market. Moreover, a shared market made mutual monitoring relatively
easy. Gorton & Mulleaux (1987) argue that monitoring within the clearing house was
especially effective because member banks had the specialized knowledge to value each
other's assets.

Fourth, besides formal strategies, the embeddedness of the clearing house in a close-
knit community also offered informal mechanisms for excluding free-riders.
Geographical proximity facilitated the diffusion of information and increased the stake
of sanctions. Within a small geographical region, monitoring was strong because information could easily be transferred and defectors easily identified. Moreover, actors were
less likely to defect because the stake of losing various types of connections was too
high. Geographical proximity also facilitated social interactions between community

members. Bankers within such dense community networks faced strong peer pressure to act responsibly. Informal constraints thus significantly reduced the cost of coordination within the clearing house.

It is useful to compare the clearing house with Responsible Care, an industry self-regulation program aimed at solving the problem of reputation commons in the modern chemical industry. In terms of formal control, the clearing house had a set of inspection, sanction, and exclusion strategies to control risk-taking activities among its members. As King & Leonx (2000) have pointed out, however, the Responsible Care program is unable to expel any of its members who fail to meet the standards and has only limited power to monitor members' implementation of the codes. In addition, the Responsible Care program does not inspect members' adherence but relies on their self-reporting. Having no "iron fist," this program is, not surprisingly, more attractive to bad performers and has no effect disciplining the behaviors of its members. In terms of informal control, industry self-regulation can create a code of responsible behavior to discipline members by forming and diffusing norms within the moral community of organizational peers. However, the formation of norms requires community-wide consensus, while the diffusion of norms requires dense networks. A small close-knit community did exist among commercial banks in Manhattan in the 1800s, but is obviously absent in many modern industries. Instead, a modern industry, such as the chemical industry, is composed of multinational corporations, the operations of which are globally dispersed. It is nearly impossible for these corporations to monitor each other. Finally, if members cannot identify with a moral community, informal coercion simply does not work.

If the clearing house was so successful, why did it eventually fail? The internal operation of the clearing house never really failed. Before the panic of 1907, the NYCHA issued loan certificates eight times and not a dollar was lost (Gilpin & Wallace, 1905). For the clearing houses in the rest of the US, "the losses from all the various note issues, spurious and otherwise, *were negligible!* The only loss reported in any of the accounts here considered was $170,000 in Philadelphia in 1890 out of an issue of 9.7 million—1.8 percent of that total" (Timberlake, 1993: 210; italics in original).

To understand the final episode of the clearing house as a private regulation program, we must take into account changes in economic and political contexts. From the end of the 1890s on, more and more trust companies, originally chartered to manage the wealth of the affluent, began to compete with banks in the deposit and loan market. Market competition intensified the rivalry between banks and trust companies, and trust companies were excluded from the NYCHA. During the panic of 1907, the NYCHA—as a self-regulation program for banks—refused to extend assistance to trust companies. This deepened the market crisis significantly. The serious consequences of the panic revealed the limitations of the NYCHA as a market regulator and created political opportunities for other social and political interest groups to initiate banking regulation reform.

The political environment also changed. The clearing house as industry self-regulation flourished in an era of laissez-faire. Before the founding of the Federal Reserve, the government supplied few institutional solutions to bank panics. The clearing house was founded in the Era of Free Banking (1837–1862). During this time, states were the sole authority to charter and regulate banks. The Michigan Act passed in 1837 automatized the chartering of banks, reduced state supervision, and created shakier banks. Relaxed regulation caused market chaos; the average lifespan of a bank in this era was five years; about half of the banks failed—a third because they could not redeem their notes. Many banks in this era earned the reputation of being *wildcat banks*. Although the National Banking Act of 1863 created a system of national banks that required higher standards of reserves than state banks, the government still offered no solution to the problem of reputation spillovers during panics. The rise of clearing houses was the banking industry's spontaneous response to the need for restoring market confidence and constructing an ordered market. Instead of being founded to fend off public regulation, the clearing house played an important role in filling the institutional vacuum created by the government.

The legitimacy of the clearing house in regulating the market was not challenged until the 1890s, especially after loan certificates of small denomination were circulated in place of currency during panics. The debate focused on whether loan certificates were loans or currency. Populists accused the clearing house of issuing illegal money and infringing the authority of the federal government. By 1907, a large portion of the clearing house issues had become recognizably illegal (Timberlake, 1993). Seeking to restrain big business and perceiving the institutions designed by business as serving their own interests, the progressive movement advanced the state as a legitimate market regulator allegedly for egalitarian reasons. The creation of the Federal Reserve in 1914 marked the end of the era of the clearing house as a regulator of commercial banks.

Despite its limitation in regulating an entire market, the NYCHA does prove that self-regulation can solve the problem of reputation commons by disciplining the behavior of organizations effectively. We have identified five conditions critical to the clearing house's success. First, cooperation within the non-regulatory function of clearing created a foundation in which self-regulation took root. Previous cooperation had enabled banks to leave the shadow of competition and explore opportunities that protected their common interests. Second, interest-bearing loan certificates created a transaction-based mechanism that encouraged contribution and discouraged opportunism. Third, the clearing house adopted a set of formal strategies based on inspection, sanction, and exclusion to prevent banks from taking high risks. Fourth, a close-knit community further facilitated monitoring and increased the cost of defection. Such a social structure also formed a moral community that encouraged banks to act responsibly. Fifth, the economic and political atmosphere outside the clearing house constrained the legitimacy of self-regulation. While the institutional vacuum left by the government provided fertile ground for self-regulation to flourish, the subsequent advance of progressive legislation legitimatized the state rather than private actors as regulator.

These conditions also set up boundaries for self-regulation to discipline the behavior of members effectively. For example, one limitation of the clearing house was that when the scale of the economy exceeded the boundaries of local communities, the means of exerting control were weakened. In this respect, the success of local clearing houses stood in sharp contrast to the failure of the emergence of a nationwide clearing house. Another limitation that arises when applying clearing house principles to modern industry self-regulation is the barrier set up by antitrust laws. Below we discuss ways to extend research beyond the constraints of self-regulation's efficacy in solving the problem of reputation commons.

IMPLICATIONS AND DIRECTIONS
FOR FUTURE STUDY

Our review has two goals. One is to point out that a firm's reputation is affected by factors beyond its control. The interdependence of organization and industry reputations creates a challenging problem of commons. The other is to suggest that given the communal nature of industry reputation commons, collective strategies such as industry self-regulation provide a solution to reputation commons. The case of the clearing house clearly illustrates that the reputation of an individual organization depends on that of its residing industry, and that under certain conditions self-regulation can be organized effectively to discipline industry peers' behaviors. We list the literature reviewed in this chapter regarding the concept and management of industry reputation commons in the summary table at the end of the chapter.

Regarding our first goal, the current literature can be expanded in at least three ways. First, despite growing scholarly interest in corporate reputation, most research has treated organizations as autonomous entities and ignored their mutual dependence. Future research should pay more attention to the externality between organizations and, in their analysis of organizational outcomes, take into account the commons problem. Second, the current literature on reputation commons has focused mostly on the negative interdependence between organizations. Future research should look more carefully at positive externality between organizations. As our review of the literature reveals, organizations can also benefit from the positive reputation attributed to their peers' legitimation efforts or to the effect of industry clustering. In fact, a good industry reputation can serve as a unique competitive advantage for an industry as well as for its members. It may be fruitful for future researchers to reveal how organizations create and maintain their positive industry reputation. Finally, future research can also benefit from investigating how the boundaries of reputation commons are defined. Organizations can be grouped by means other than industries. They can be grouped by geographies or other common features. Within each group or category, there are subgroups and subcategories. The interdependence of organizational reputation degenerates with the expansion of category scope. Thus effective definitions of the borders of reputation commons have important implications for the success of collective mobilization aimed at addressing problems of commons. In addition, different audiences may pick up different cognitive cues when defining a category. Future research on reputation commons should address questions such as who are the key stakeholders and from whose perspective is corporate reputation addressed.

Regarding our second goal—how to resolve the problem of reputation commons— we suggest that in order to discipline the behavior of members effectively, any self-regulation program has to be equipped with an "iron fist" that allows it to monitor and sanction. But modern antitrust laws prevent self-regulation from directly controlling and sanctioning the behavior of members. Future research should explore alternative means that self-regulation could adopt to resolve the problem of reputation commons. One direction to take is to put intra-industry efforts such as the NYCHA in context with third-party-led private regulation, of which a typical form is certification. Non-governmental organizations (NGOs) codify standards of action and certify organizations' adherence to these standards through independent inspections. An early example of such third-party certification is the Motion Picture Association of America (MPAA), which solved the reputation commons in the movie industry by certifying films accord-ing to five different categories. In the last few decades, concerns over corporate social responsibility such as sweatshops, child labor, blood diamonds, food safety, environ-mental sustainability, and other issues have spurred the foundation of dozens of non-governmental certification institutes (Bartley, 2007).

Certification is essentially a signaling strategy. By conferring certification, certifiers endorse a signal that those who are certified are superior to others who are unable or uninterested in obtaining certification. But certification is limited in its ability to sanc-tion, and thus it may be a weak solution for reputation commons. When norms are breached, a certifier's response is often limited to withdrawing or downgrading certifi-cation. This type of sanctioning has limited power because outsiders may or may not observe the change of signal. Another issue that adds to the weak sanction is fragmenta-tion within the field of certifiers themselves. Field fragmentation makes it difficult for outsiders to follow any single certifiers closely. Moreover, the proliferation of certifiers and the differentiation strategies they pursue enable opportunistic organizations to shop for certifiers. Competition within the field of certifiers speaks to another problem that arises from relying on a third party to regulate, namely, how to motivate those inde-pendent regulators who do not have a direct interest in the results of regulation. When certifiers adopt a for-profit model, competition may lead regulatory standards and enforcement to evolve along a different trajectory. When facing conflicts of interest, cer-tifiers intentionally create ambiguities in evaluating categories (Fleischer, 2009). Similarly, when certifiers begin to receive payment for their work, it is difficult for them to remain impartial while issuing certification, as was the case with bond-rating agen-cies in the recent subprime mortgage crisis (Lucchetti, Ng, & Hitt, 2010). Future research should investigate how to motivate independent third parties and how to protect their reputation (see also Gilad and Yogev, Chapter 16, this volume).

The other direction that researchers have taken is towards a hybrid form of public and private institutions in which private regulators produce the standards of regulation but outsource enforcement to the government. In the nuclear industry in the US, the

Institute of Nuclear Power Operations (INPO), a trade association, sponsors industry standards, and a state-run regulatory body, the Nuclear Regulatory Commission (NRC), enforces these standards. Rees (1994) found confirmative evidence of the efficacy of this type of hybrid form. While it raises questions about the blurriness of the boundary between public and private regulation, it does touch on one key issue concerning the success of regulation: an effective regulator must have good knowledge of an industry. Along this line of reasoning, researchers can also explore other ways in which public and private regulations can be connected.

The trend of globalization in recent decades offers new opportunities for studying industry self-governance as a solution for reputation commons. One reason is that anti-trust laws may have limited application within the global market. An obvious case of this is the US antitrust law which does not apply to any activities of American companies that affect only foreign markets. The other reason is that the increased flow of capital across national borders creates a demand for global regulatory schemes that transcend the sovereignty of any single nation. However, international conflicts add barriers to intergovernmental agreements and consequently afford private actors with unique opportunities to act as institutional entrepreneurs (Bartley, 2007). Researchers have noted that transnational regulatory programs have emerged in manufacturing and nat-ural resource-extracting industries to manage reputation problems in environmental protection and labor disputes.

Finally, advances in information technology have profoundly changed the way people communicate and have seeded various new forms of communities. When the boundaries of online communities move beyond the constraint of geography, the expanded space offers opportunities for organizing self-regulation in new domains. In addition, informa-tion technology industries offer new opportunities for investigating collective solutions for reputation commons. For example, the popularity of online social media has created a US$23 billion-a-year online-advertising industry that tracks consumers' web-surfing habits for ad targeting. But this industry is fiercely attacked by advocates of consumer privacy. To protect the reputation of the industry as well as to ward off potential public regulations, a coalition representing advertisers and Internet companies released a set of voluntary guidelines in July 2009, calling for voluntary disclosure of tracking and data use. Without an enforcement authority, this coalition encourages adherence only through peer pressure and the threat of public exposure (Steel, 2010). Future research should investigate whether advances in monitoring technology in cyberspace and amplified public exposure due to networking online can deter opportunism.

Literature Review of the Concept and Management of Industry Reputation Commons

Reference	Key Constructs & Findings
Barnett & Hoffman (2008)	This article argues that organizations' reputations and performance are not solely determined by their individual behaviors but also by interorganizational dependence.
Barnett & King (2008)	This article develops the key definition of reputation commons to describe the interdependence in organizational reputation. Organizations in an industry share sanctions thanks to shared reputation.
Wade, Swaminathan, & Saxon (1998)	There are both competitive and communal interdependences between an organization's reputation and that of its peers.
Bartley (2007); Barnett & King (2008); Malkin, (1996); Hornblower (2000); Zoellner (2006); Walsh (1996)	These articles study industry reputation commons in the domain of corporate social responsibility. The violation of social accountability by an individual organization can result in penalties for an entire industry.
Aldrich & Fiol (1994); Rao, Monin, & Durand (2005); Ingram (1998)	These articles study industry reputation commons in the domain of legitimation. There are three types of legitimation: cognitive legitimation, social–political legitimation, and constitutive legitimation. A good reputation helps all organizations within an industry to acquire resources.
Ingram & Lifschitz (2006); Milgrom, North, & Weingast (1990); Saxenian (1994)	These articles study industry reputation commons in the domain of industry clusters and regional advantage. Good reputation of an industry cluster benefits all organizations by attracting talent and customers from a wide radius.
Barnett (2006); Ingram & Yue (2008)	These articles study the collective strategy that firms can adopt to enhance their competitive positions through cooperation with their industry peers. These articles suggest that collective strategy can serve as a means of managing the communal problems, such as reputation commons, that face an entire industry.
Ostrom (1990); Ostrom (2000)	Ostrom's work shatters the belief that government regulation or pure market transaction (i.e., property rights) is the only solution to the problem of commons. Ostrom proposes that self-regulation programs can serve as a viable alternative.
Potoski & Prakash (2009)	This article proposes private clubs as a solution to the problem of commons. Clubs can mitigate the reputation commons problem by conferring a signaling benefit to firms and allowing their stakeholders to reward them for producing the social externality that club membership requires.

References

Akerlof, G. A. (1970). "The market for 'lemons': Quality uncertainty and the market mechanism." *Quarterly Journal of Economics*, 84(3): 488–500.

Aldrich, H. E. & Fiol, C. M. (1994). "Fools rush in? The institutional context of industry creation." *Academy of Management Review*, 19(4): 645–670.

Barnett, M. L. (2006). "Finding a working balance between competitive and communal strategies." *Journal of Management Studies*, 43(8): 1752–1773.

—— (Forthcoming). "One voice, but whose voice? Exploring what drives trade association activity." *Business & Society*.

—— & Hoffman, A. J. (2008). "Beyond corporate reputation: Managing reputational interdependence." *Corporate Reputation Review*, 11: 1–9.

—— & King, A. (2008). "Good fences make good neighbors: A longitudinal analysis of an industry self-regulatory institution." *Academy of Management Journal*, 51(6): 1150–1170.

——, Jermier, J. M., & Lafferty, B. A. (2006). "Corporate reputation: The definitional landscape." *Corporate Reputation Review*, 9(1): 26–38.

Baron, D. P. & Diermeier, D. (2007). "Strategic activism and nonmarket strategy." *Journal of Economics and Management Strategy*, 16(3): 599–634.

Bartley, T. (2007). "How foundations shape social movements: The construction of an organizational field and the rise of forest certification." *Social Problems*, 54(3): 229–255.

Calomiris, C. W. & Gorton, G. (1991). "Origins of banking panics: Models, facts, and bank regulation." In G. Hubbard (Ed.), *Financial Markets and Financial Crises*. Chicago: University of Chicago Press, 93–163.

Cannon, J. G. (1910). *Clearing House*. U.S. National Monetary Commission. Washington: Government Print Office.

Fleischer, A. (2009). "Ambiguity and the equity of rating systems: United States brokerage firms, 1995–2000." *Administrative Science Quarterly*, 54: 555–574.

Gilad, S. & Yogev, T. (2012). "How reputation regulates regulators: Illustrations from the regulation of retail finance." In M. Barnett & T. Pollock (Eds.), *The Oxford Handbook of Corporate Reputation*. Oxford: Oxford University Press, 320–40.

Gilpin, W. J. & Wallace, H. E. (1905). *New York Clearing House Association, 1854–1905*. New York: Moses King.

Gorton, G. & Mullineaux, D. (1987). "The joint production of confidence: Endogenous regulation and nineteenth century commercial bank clearing houses." *Journal of Money, Credit and Banking*, 19(4): 458–468.

Hafner-Burton, E. M. & Tsutsui, K. (2005). "Human rights practices in a globalizing world: The paradox of empty promises." *American Journal of Sociology*, 110(5): 1373–1411.

Hammond, B. (1957). *Banks and Politics in America*. Princeton: Princeton University Press.

Hannan, M. T., Pólos, L., & Carroll, G. R. (2007). *Logics of Organization Theory*. Princeton, NJ: Princeton University Press.

Hardin, R. (1971). "Collective action as an agreeable n-prisoners' dilemma." *Science*, 16: 472–481.

Hornblower, M. (2000). "Wake up and smell the protest." *Time*, 155(15): 58.

Howard, J., Nash, J., & Ehrenfeld, J. (2000). "Standard of smokescreen? Implementation of a voluntary environmental code." *California Management Review*, 42(2): 63–82.

Ingram, P. (1998). "Changing the rules: Interests, organizations and institutional change in the U.S. hospitality industry." In M. Brinton & V. Nee (Eds.), *The New Institutionalism in Sociology*. New York: Russell Sage Foundation, 258–276.

—— & Lifschitz, A. (2006). "Kinship in the shadow of the corporation: The inter-builder network in Clyde river shipbuilding, 1711–1990." *American Sociological Review*, 71: 334–352.

—— & Yue, L. Q. (2008). "Structure, affect and identity as bases of organizational competition and cooperation." *Academy of Management Annals*, 2: 275–303.

King, A. A. & Lenox, M. J. (2000). "Industry self-regulation without sanctions: The chemical industry's responsible care program." *Academy of Management Journal*, 43(4): 698–716.

Knight, J. (1992). *Institutions and Social Conflict*. Cambridge: Cambridge University Press.

Lucchetti, A., Ng, S., & Hitt, G. (2010). "Rating agencies face curbs." *Wall Street Journal*, May 12.

Malkin, E. (1996). "Pangs of conscience: Sweatshops haunt U.S. consumers." *Business Week*, July 29: 46.

Market Strategies International (2010). "Oil industry reputation hit by gulf oil spill, survey shows." Available at: http://www.marketoracle.co.uk/Article20709.html (accessed 26 May 2011).

McPherson, M. (1983). "An ecology of affiliation." *American Sociological Review*, 48: 519–532.

Milgrom, P. R., North, D. C., & Weingast, B. R. (1990). "The role of institutions in the revival of trade: The law merchant, private judges, and the champagne fairs." *Economics and Politics*, 2(1): 1–23.

Nee, V. & Ingram, P. (1998). "Embeddedness and beyond: Institutions, exchange, and social structure." In M. C. Brinton & V. Nee (Eds.), *The New Institutionalism in Sociology*. Stanford, CA: Stanford University Press, 19–45.

North, D. C. (1990). *Institutions, Institutional Change and Economic Performance*. Cambridge: Cambridge University Press.

Olson, M. (1965). *Logic of Collective Action: Public Goods and the Theory of Groups*. Cambridge, MA: Harvard University Press.

Ostrom, E. (1990). *Governing the Commons: The Evolution of Institutions for Collective Action*. Cambridge: Cambridge University Press.

—— (2000). "Collective action and the evolution of social norms." *Journal of Economic Perspectives*, 14(3): 137–158.

Potoski, M. & Prakash, A. (2009). "A club theory approach to voluntary programs." In M. Potoski & A. Prakash (Eds.), *Voluntary Programs*. Boston: MIT Press, 17–39.

Rao, H. (1994). "The social construction of reputation: Certification contests, legitimation, and the survival of organizations in the American automobile industry: 1895–1912." *Strategic Management Journal*, 15: 29–44.

——, Monin, P., & Durand, R. (2005). "Border crossing: Bricolage and the erosion of categorical boundaries in French." *American Sociological Review*, 70(9): 868–991.

Rees, J. V. (1994). *Three Mile Island*. Chicago: University of Chicago Press.

Rothbart, M, et al. (1978). "From individual to group impressions: Availability heuristics in stereotype formation." *Journal of Experimental Social Psychology*, 14: 237–255.

Saxenian, A. (1994). *Regional Advantage: Culture and Competition in Silicon Valley and Route 128*. Cambridge: Havard University Press.

Sorenson, O. & Audia, P. G. (2000). "The social structure of entrepreneurial activity: Geographic concentration of footwear production in the United States, 1940–1989." *American Journal of Sociology*, 106(2): 424–462.

Steel, E. (2010). "To stem privacy abuses, industry groups will track web trackers." *Wall Street Journal*, June 24, 2010.

Timberlake, R. H. (1993). *Monetary Policy in the United States*. Chicago: University of Chicago Press.

Tirole, J. (1996). "A theory of collective reputations (with applications to the persistence of corruption and to firm quality)." *Review of Economic Studies*, 63: 1–22.

Wade, J. B., Swaminathan, A., & Saxon, M. S. (1998). "Normative and resource flow consequences of local regulations in the American brewing industry, 1845–1918." *Administrative Science Quarterly*, 43: 905–935.

Waguespack, D. M. & Sorensen, O. (2010). "The ratings game: Asymmetry in classification." *Organization Science*, 22: 541–553.

Walsh, F. (1996). *Sin and Censorship: The Catholic Church and the Motion Picture Industry*. New Haven: Yale University Press.

Yu, T. & Lester, R. H. (2008). "Moving beyond firm boundaries: A social network perspective on reputation spillover." *Corporate Reputation Review*, 11(1): 94–108.

Yue, L. Q., Luo, J., & Ingram, P. (2009). "The strength of a weak institution: Clearing house, federal reserve, and Manhattan banks." In *Best Paper Proceedings of the Academy of Management Meeting*. Chicago.

Zoellner, T. (2006). *The Heartless Stone: A Journey Through the World of Diamonds, Deceit, and Desire*. New York, NY: St. Martin's Press.

CHAPTER 15

HOW REGULATORY INSTITUTIONS INFLUENCE CORPORATE REPUTATIONS: A CROSS-COUNTRY COMPARATIVE APPROACH

STEPHEN BRAMMER

GREGORY JACKSON

Corporate reputations are inherently subjective and relative phenomena, and yet prior research has not given significant consideration to the factors that frame actors' perceptions of companies or those that establish benchmarks for corporate conduct. In this chapter, we introduce an institutional perspective on corporate reputation that addresses these issues. Specifically, we focus on the role played by country regulatory institutions in shaping the formation, management, and functions of corporate reputation. Our discussion emphasizes the importance for corporate reputations of the variety present in nations' regulatory institutions, as embodied in the different capacity of states to regulate, the diversity of countries' regulatory styles, and the distinctive patterns of economic organization seen across countries. We argue that these variations have significant implications for how actors construct reputations and for the patterns of firm conduct that are deemed legitimate in particular circumstances, and establish an agenda for future research on corporate reputation that embraces a comparative institutional approach.

INTRODUCTION

IN this chapter we explore the role played by regulatory institutions in the formation, character, and management of corporate reputations. Since regulatory institutions are a primary feature of nation states, and because there is considerable variation across countries in the overall strength and detailed features of regulatory institutions, our analysis will emphasize cross-country comparisons. Rather than emphasizing the importance of countries of origin for firms' reputations (a subject addressed by Newburry in Chapter 12, this volume), or the nature and historical development of regulatory institutions within a particular country (addressed by McKenna and Olegario in Chapter 13, this volume), this chapter addresses the notion that there are "institutionalized social standards that make systematic comparison between organisations possible and meaningful" (King & Whetten, 2008: 193), by exploring comprehensively how different institutional contexts shape corporate reputations in a cross-nationally comparative perspective.

In so doing, our aim is to bring to the fore the importance of a comparative institutional perspective for corporate reputation by arguing that corporate reputation research has largely under-emphasized the potential for institutional phenomena (structures, processes, norms, rules, etc.) to play a role in shaping the formation, management, and functions of corporate reputations. To meet this objective, we review recent research on different forms of statehood and comparative capitalism, which address how formal and informal regulatory institutions differ across countries. In particular, we attempt to address how these institutional differences matter for corporate reputation based on theoretical synthesis and motivating examples.

We begin our analysis by introducing the implications of adopting an institutional perspective for understanding corporate reputation and briefly reviewing extant research that has addressed related issues. We develop our discussion by highlighting the role of the regulatory state in shaping the conditions in which reputations are formed. Subsequently, we explore the importance of different types of economic systems for corporate reputation, drawing upon the varieties of capitalism approach. Having done so, we consider the importance of contexts with less well-developed institutions for corporate reputations, including some consideration of the particular issues that arise in the context of the multinational firm. A final section concludes.

CORPORATE REPUTATION AND INSTITUTIONS

In this section, our aim is to briefly review existing research relating to the relevance of institutions in general, and regulatory institutions in particular, for firm reputations. We do this with the aid of the summary table at the end of the chapter, which identifies several strands of previous research that are relevant to our objectives. For each strand of thinking, we identify its relevance to an institutionally grounded conception of firms' reputations and a set of questions that our analysis seeks to shed light on. Our starting point is Fombrun's classic article (1996: 165) in which he defines corporate reputation as "a perceptual representation of a company's past actions and future prospects that describe the firm's appeal to all of its key constituents." While early literature conceptualized reputation as a summary or aggregated perception of multiple stakeholders, reputation is now usually seen as being multiple—a reputation for what and to whom (Carter & Deephouse, 1999)?

The first two themes identified in the summary table relate to the definition and formation of firm reputations. As the table shows, central to reputational research has been the recognition that reputations are socially constructed through the actions of firms, on the one hand, and the perception and evaluation of stakeholders, on the other (Rao, 1994; Fombrun & Rindova, 1994; Lahdesmaki & Siltaoja, 2010). So far, research has tended to emphasize how firms' actions shape their reputations, while relatively little attention has been given to how stakeholders form their reputational assessments. Recognizing the socially constructed nature of reputations, we argue, raises important questions regarding the origins of the frames that stakeholders use to interpret firms' actions, and of the role played by institutions in shaping stakeholders' expectations of firms. A second significant theme in extant reputational research is the observation that reputation is inherently comparative in the sense that "firms are being compared to some explicit or implicit standard" (Brown & Logsdon, 1997: 184). Regarding the particular standards by which firms are evaluated, one simple but useful approach is to conceptualize stakeholders as making reputational assessments in relative terms, by comparing the actions of a firm relative to other peer organizations (Deephouse & Carter, 2005).

A third theme present in the summary table relates to the interconnectedness of the reputations of particular firms with those within relevant communities of peers. For example, research has suggested that comparisons between firms within sectors, industries, or organizational fields are very important for reputation. If stakeholders are only weakly able to differentiate between particular companies, a significant reputation-altering event may have important spillover effects (Winn, Macdonald, & Zietsma, 2008; Barnett, 2006). Hence reputation may be a shared attribute of organizations within a given field, giving rise to what has been termed a "reputation commons problem" (King et al., 2002). For example, Hoffman (1997) shows how other oil companies faced significant collective reputational harm following the Exxon oil spill. This research raises questions regarding the scope and definition of the organizational fields within which such interdependence in firm reputations exists.

Moreover, the social comparisons involved in reputational assessments by stakeholders raise a more general issue of how reputation relates to wider sets of social institutions. For example, Rao (1994: 30) notes, "organizations acquire standing when they use environmentally preferred symbols and their actions conform to institutionalized rules." More recently, Love and Kraatz (2009: 316) argue that stakeholders "confer good reputations on firms that exemplify cultural stipulations and ideals and . . . penalize firms that fail to display appropriate symbols." Reputation assessments are thus linked with institutionalized rules and taken-for-granted assumptions that confer legitimacy, understood by Suchman (1995: 574) as "a generalized perception or assumption that the actions of an entity are desirable, proper, or appropriate within some socially constructed system of norms, values, beliefs, and definitions."

Reflecting this discussion, the fourth theme identified in the summary table focuses on recent attempts to clarify the meaning of corporate reputation and differentiate it from the related concept of legitimacy (Deephouse & Carter, 2005; Fombrun & Shanley, 1990; Whetten & Mackey, 2002; Rindova, Pollock, & Hayward, 2006; Barnett, 2006; Bitektine, 2011). Legitimacy is assessed by stakeholders in relation to conformity with some minimum set of common social expectations within the broader institutional environment. Legitimacy is focused on "similarity" across organizations, and about belonging to a common accepted category. Meanwhile, reputation is focused on "difference," and how an organization distinguishes itself from its peers. While the distinction between reputation and legitimacy is clear on a conceptual level, the two concepts overlap in practice—both are externally conferred assessments of an organization (Thomas, 2007) and substantial overlap may exist in the criteria applied in making these assessments (Bitektine, 2011). Legitimacy may be seen as a necessary but not a sufficient condition for a good reputation (Doh et al., 2010). While this link between legitimacy and reputation is established in the literature, the implications thereof have not been fully explored.

King and Whetten (2008) develop this distinction further to argue that institutionalized forms of legitimacy provide an institutional benchmark for understanding reputation. The standards of legitimacy within a field do not just define membership as a legitimate organization, but also provide an institutional frame within which corporations may seek to build their reputations. In this way, reputation is nested within legitimacy—beyond their similarity with institutionalized forms, firms may competitively aspire to differentiate themselves within this in relation to ideal standards, and thus build positive corporation reputations.

The final theme identified in the summary table relates to the observation that specifically regulatory and legislative standards have been identified as playing an important role in shaping firm reputations in previous research. At the same time, most work addressing institutional aspects of reputation focuses on single countries. However, notions of legitimacy often differ between sectors and countries, as well as over time. In particular, comparative theories have shown how differences in institutions lead to a diversity of organizational forms across fields or, more broadly, across countries (Biggart, 1991). These differences relate to both formal regulatory institutions, as well as broader conventions regarding business conduct. Institutional diversity, understood as the different forms of legitimate corporate behavior across countries, is likely to provide different institutional frames for corporate reputation.

REGULATION ACROSS COUNTRIES AND ITS INFLUENCE ON CORPORATE REPUTATION

Existing literature has established that legitimate and institutionalized forms of organization provide a frame within which firms develop good or bad reputations based on stakeholders' perceptions of relative differences among organizations within a certain field or domain. Institutional theorists acknowledge the importance of state regulation as a driver of institutionalization. By regulation, we consider here the formal rules of the game, often grounded in law and enforced by the administrative apparatus of the state as a third party.[1] In particular, regulation is often associated with so-called "coercive iso-morphism" (DiMaggio & Powell, 1991), where firms adopt similar structures and prac-tices due to the power of the state to impose these under threat of coercive sanction. This section looks at the implications of formal regulation and the role of the state in different countries for corporate reputation.

Literature addressing the interface between regulation and reputation is scant. Thus, an important research agenda remains in developing new theoretical approaches to rep-utation that incorporate the role of regulation. In suggesting a future agenda for theo-retical development, we identify at least two distinct types of linkages that exist between regulatory institutions and reputation.

In the first sense, *reputation may substitute for regulation*, albeit somewhat partially and imperfectly. Particularly where formal institutions are weak due to the lack of capac-ity of states to enforce rules, informal institutions may play a greater role in coordinating economic activity. Since actors may not trust the state to uphold property rights or enforce contracts, economic exchange is dependent upon and shaped by the presence or absence of more or less particularistic forms of trust rooted in social networks and related reputational mechanisms. Historical studies of regulation in Western economies also find similar mechanisms at play. Early corporate regulation in nineteenth-century Britain relied strongly on informal, reputation-based networks among "gentlemen" as a basis of trust and self-regulation of economic exchange, such as regarding relations between stockholders and company directors, as discussed at length by McKenna and Olegario (Chapter 13, this volume). Slowly, these informal sets of institutions came to be replaced by more formal types of regulation.

In a second sense, *regulation may provide a frame for evaluating reputation*. Here reputation does not replace or substitute for regulation, but acts more as a comple-ment or extension of regulation. Stakeholder expectations are shaped by the institu-tionalized norms and taken-for-granted ideas embodied within formal regulatory frameworks. Consequently, corporate compliance with regulatory standards is an important benchmark by which stakeholders assess corporate reputation. To the extent that corporations simply conform and comply with taken-for-granted rules, they are likely to attain legitimacy but not develop any (positive or negative) reputa-tion with a particular stakeholder. Rather, positive reputation arises where firms act in ways that are consistent with institutional norms, but exceed the level of standards required by regulation.

In developing this distinction between substitution and framing, this section reviews some of the broader cross-nationally comparative literature on state capacity and regu-latory styles. The diversity of regulatory institutions across countries is likely to help understand both why reputation sometimes substitutes for regulation, as well as how regulation frames reputation in different ways.

---

[1] While we focus here on formal state regulation, the analysis can be extended to include informal forms of regulation or self-regulation grounded in market mechanisms.

State Capacity

Adopting a cross-national comparative perspective, a large body of research has documented the vast diversity in the form and content of regulation across countries. The origins of the modern state can be traced back to the consolidation of centralized sovereignty and growing organizational capacity, which emerged as both a consequence of war-making in Europe and the economic effects of competition over external trade (Spruyt, 2002; Tilly, 1990). A broader comparison of state formation across Europe, the Americas, Asia, and Africa suggests that the modern state was not realized to the same extent everywhere. Different varieties of statehood have adopted different forms of economic regulation.

One general observation is that states have different capacities to regulate economic behavior within their territories (Evans, Skocpol, & Rueschemeyer, 1985). Modern states are organized as bureaucratic agencies that form and implement policy. States differ greatly in their capacity to enforce formal rules due to the power differentials between state bureaucracies relative to other domestic elites, social movements, labor unions, international agencies, and so forth (Levitsky & Murillo, 2009; Fligstein, 2001). States may have low enforcement capacity due to the absence of a professional and independent civil service, or lack of infrastructure to monitor noncompliance with rules (Gonzales & King, 2004). If the state lacks a credible commitment to sanction noncompliance, actors may have insufficient incentive to follow official rules (Herbst, 2000). Consequently, the "rule of law" in different countries (La Porta et al., 1998) is associated with a wide range of different economic and political outcomes (Haggard, Macintyre, & Tiede, 2008).

Variation in state capacity may influence corporate reputation in complex ways. Where state regulation is weak or absent, firms have greater strategic scope to adopt policies to enhance corporate reputation toward stakeholders. Here, reputation substitutes for formal regulation. Such strategies may be firm-specific efforts to differentiate the reputation of the individual firm, or more collective strategies, such as the development and adoption of codes of conduct. Moreover, some corporate codes are explicitly designed to pre-empt state regulation by promoting a more favorable political environment (Sethi, 2002). At the same time, strong state capacity increases pressure for firms to adopt voluntarily measures that may enhance their reputation. For example, financial institutions were more likely to adopt the equator principles in promoting "green" project finance if they came from countries with strong states and high levels of governance effectiveness (Wright & Rwabizambuga, 2006). Here, reputation acts as a complement to state regulatory capacity.

At the extreme, states with low capacity may fail to maintain the monopoly over the means of coercion, degenerate into a pattern of predatory behavior toward citizens, and face growing competition between different armed and potentially violent groups (Bates, 2008). Situations of limited statehood (Magan, Risse, & McFaul, 2009) or so-called "institutional voids" (Khanna & Palepu, 2006) increase the potential salience of informal institutions in filling the gap left by the state in regulating economic activity. Where states lack the capacity to instill generalized formal institutions and "rule of law," economic transactions are likely to depend on more particularistic forms of trust. Here, corporation reputation may play an important role as a substitute for formal regulation, since stakeholders create and maintain economic relationships with the firm based on relative reputational assessments of the particular firm. We will return to discuss the distinct implications for corporate reputation in relation to this important case of institutional voids later in the chapter.

Regulatory Styles

The political economy literature has also documented a diversity of regulatory traditions and modes of intervention across states of the advanced industrialized world. Since state capacity reflects long-term political settlements and their renegotiation over time, states often have distinctive "regulatory styles" embedded in the structure of state agencies, existing sets of laws, and characteristic means of influence (Dobbin, 1994; Ziegler, 1997). One key dimension of variation concerns the distinction between regulatory and interventionist states (Fligstein, 2001: 42). Regulatory regimes create agencies to enforce general rules in the marketplace, but refrain from substantive intervention in the decisions of market actors. In short, the state plays the role of umpire or referee, as in the case of the Securities and Exchange Commission (SEC) in the United States. By contrast, interventionist states involve state officials more directly in decisions about investment and in the control of firms. Another dimension of regulatory style concerns the possibility of regulatory "capture" by particular interest groups. Capture occurs when a particular group gets one-sided control of a policy domain (Fligstein, 2001: 43).

Whitley has provided a useful summary of these various dimensions within a single typology distinguishing between regulatory and developmental states (Whitley, 2005, 2007). Regulatory states are focused on establishing the "rules of the game," but leave economic actors to pursue their own objectives in the market. By contrast, developmental states take a more active role in coordinating the behavior of firms by structuring incentives, giving direct financial support, and directly controlling firms through public ownership or the like. In addition, Whitley goes beyond existing distinctions between regulatory and interventionist states by proposing subtypes of developmental states: dominant developmental states, business corporatist states, and inclusive corporatist states. The key concept here concerns the extent to which the state tolerates or supports independent intermediary organizations, such as those representing business or labor, within a policy field. Dominant developmental states, such as South Korea, tend to limit the independence and role of autonomous interest associations. This approach contrasts with the more business corporatist approach of Japan, where the state works more collaboratively with business associations. However, the Japanese "corporatism without labor" tends to exclude trade unions from the policy process (Pempel, 1998). More inclusive corporatist states, such as Sweden, use state power to actively involve the interest groups of both business and labor, thus delegating policy responsibility to some extent but actively encouraging social partnership and compromise between these groups.

What do different types of states imply for the development and use of reputations? One important observation by Whitley is that whereas corporatist states tend to promote consensus and homogeneity of organizational practices, regulatory states are often associated with greater variability of organizational forms across firms and sectors. In our view, these different types of regulatory style may frame reputation in very distinct ways.

Regulatory states provide formal rules that serve as minimum standards for all firms, but leave considerable scope for voluntary adoption of higher standards. Here, corporations can aspire to build reputations by adopting practices that are consistent with but exceed regulatory standards. In these contexts, reputation is likely to be framed in terms of deviation from the average. Good reputation takes on a form of "celebrity" in that firms are known for their star quality or difference from other firms (Rindova, Pollock, & Hayward, 2006). For example, European firms were more likely to adopt corporate social responsibility (CSR) policies aimed at social standards in countries with low levels of employment protection than in more regulated economies (Jackson & Apostolakou, 2010). The converse side of reputations concerns the high emphasis on individual liability within regulatory states, such as the US. For example, the strong threat of legal liability means that US executives are unlikely to apologize over mistakes or manage reputation by openly acknowledging errors (Tyler, 1997). The emphasis on strict liability means that reputation remains more specific to individual firms, whereby reputational damage to one firm within an organizational field has less spillover onto other firms.

Meanwhile, corporatist states place a greater emphasis on regulation through collective forms of self-organization in industry. In this case, rules may be more substantive and place greater constraints on firm behavior, thus promoting greater homogeneity across organizations. Also, corporations may aspire to build reputations either by having a strong leadership role and being an important player in establishing consensus or by participating in collective norms and regulatory standards. In these contexts, reputation is more strongly vested within the status quo and upholding of common standards, rather than in deviation from these. Put differently, reputation may be more about "citizenship" in a specific sense of participation by civil society (Matten & Crane, 2005) rather than celebrity. Reputation has a stronger collective character, and remains more "implicit" within the wider field of institutions (Matten & Moon, 2007). Reputational damage may be more contagious across organizations. One consequence of the emphasis on collective reputation-building in corporate states may be a stronger exclusion of outsiders and favoring of insiders. For example, Li and Samsell (2009) find that trade flows are greater for countries with more rule-based governance institutions than for countries with more relation-based governance institutions.

REPUTATION IN DIFFERENT VARIETIES
OF CAPITALISM

Institutional diversity goes beyond the capacity and style of the state regulation across societies. The notion of distinct national varieties of capitalism or business systems has gained considerable currency in the last two decades in economics (Aoki, 2010), business studies (Jackson & Deeg, 2008a), and the wider social sciences (Morgan et al., 2010). This comparative approach to the study of capitalisms (CC) has focused on institutionalized forms of coordination among private economic actors (Hollingsworth, Schmitter, & Streeck, 1994; Crouch & Streeck, 1997). Beyond the traditional distinction between markets and hierarchies, the framework examines the role of communities, the state, networks, and associations (Hollingsworth & Boyer, 1997; Crouch, 2005). The CC approach compares how such institutions influence the comparative institutional advantage of firms for different kinds of economic activities, as well as why such institutions have emerged and change over time.

Mapping the Institutional Diversity of Capitalism

A central distinction found in the CC literature is between countries governed largely by markets and hierarchies (market capitalism) and those using a richer variety of coordination mechanisms (institutional capitalism) (Crouch & Streeck, 1997). This distinction on the relative strength of the market as an institutional form reappears in the later, but highly influential, "Varieties of Capitalism" (VoC) approach of David Soskice and Peter Hall (2001). Focusing on the Organisation for Economic Co-operation and Development (OECD) countries of the mid-1980s to mid-1990s, the authors distinguish two basic types of production regimes (capitalisms): *liberal market economies* (LMEs) and *coordinated market economies* (CMEs). This typology is based on the relative extent of market coordination through investment in transferable assets (LMEs) versus non-market or strategic coordination through investment in specific assets (CMEs). The four institutional domains are thus characterized in terms of long-term (CME) versus short-term (LME) finance, regulated (CME) versus deregulated (LME) labor markets, general (LME) versus vocational (CME) training, and strong inter-firm competition (LME) versus inter-firm coordination (CME). Comparative institutional advantages exist in each system, whereby CMEs excel at incremental innovation and LMEs at radical innovation (Hall & Soskice, 2001: 32).

The simple twofold categorization of institutions in the VoC approach has been widely criticized and led to the development of various alternative comparative typologies of institutions (Whitley, 2007; Aoki, 2010; Schmidt, 2002; Jackson & Deeg, 2008b). While this debate is vast, we differentiate between two aspects that should be explored in future research—the external view of how outsiders perceive corporate reputation based on the comparative institutional advantage of a particular country of origin, and the internal view of how reputation acts as social capital for stakeholders in more market-oriented or coordinated forms of capitalism.

Reputation as a Mirror of Comparative Institutional Advantage

A key contribution of the CC literature has been to map and explain the competitive institutional advantages of different countries. Firms in LMEs have greater institutional support for market-based coordination, and thus tend to specialize or succeed in business segments that are cost-sensitive or characterized by radical innovation. Conversely, firms in CMEs receive greater institutional support for longer-term investment in specific assets, and thus have advantages where innovation is incremental. Here, stable organizational routines and the skills of a core workforce are centrally important. This approach lends greater theoretical substance to the popularized observations regarding the strength of US venture capital and biotechnology, on the one hand, and that of German engineering or Japanese automobile production, on the other hand (Porter, 1990). A substantial literature has sought to further refine and test the implications of institutional diversity for economic performance (Hall & Gingerich, 2004; Kenworthy, 2006; Taylor, 2004; Akkermans, Castaldi, & Los, 2009; Boyer, 2004; Schneider, Schulze-bentrop, & Paunescu, 2009).

These patterns of competitive advantage can give some insights into how country of origin influences corporate reputation (see Newbury, Chapter 12, this volume). While many factors influence nation brands (Anholt, 2006; Fetscherin, 2010), institutional factors related to specific varieties of capitalism may have a reputational influence on nation brands in ways that mirror or even reinforce comparative institutional advantages. First, the positive perception of a nation may influence the collective reputation of all firms in a country in a collective or aggregate sense. Second, country of origin may influence the frame of how corporate reputations are understood. Nation brands give corporations a particular reputation *for something* by association—German engineering, Swiss watchmaking, and so forth. In this case, nation brand may extend its influence to the reputation of particular firms. These associations are, in fact, highly correlated with patterns of competitive institutional advantage, as discussed above.[2]

Reputation as a Competitive or Collective Form of Social Capital

The role of reputation as a form of social capital is also shaped by institutions. Given the different institutional modes of coordination between LME and CME economies,

---

[2] Here we make no claims on the causal direction—whether reputation reflects such advantages, or whether reputation of particular firms shape the collective national image.

corporate reputation may take on different forms and functions in these different settings. Here, we draw on the distinction between competitive and collective forms of reputation management (Winn, Macdonald, & Zietsma, 2008; Barnett, 2006). Competitive reputation management refers to single firms' efforts to enhance their reputation vis-à-vis others in the industry, whereas collective reputation management entails efforts to alter judgments about the reputation of a collective—be it based on a network of firms or other form of association.

In LME economies, positive reputation is likely to be associated with competitive forms of reputation management.[3] Reputation is based on "deviance" or celebrity in the sense of differentiation from average, taken-for-granted forms of practice (Rindova, Petkova, & Kotha, 2007). For example, firms in LME countries rely strongly on external labor markets to recruit employees, and these markets may place a premium on firms with a reputation for paying above-average wages or offering fast-track promotion relative to other competing firms. Similarly, in capital markets, reputation for outperforming market indices or exceeding analyst expectations may generate self-reinforcing positive momentum within the market. Since investors make no specific commitments to firms, the role of corporate reputation is strongly framed around positive or negative deviation from market expectations. Consequently, reputation is strongly shaped by market intermediaries and other gatekeepers, such as auditors, accountants, and analysts. These actors essentially use their own reputation as a proxy for the trustworthiness of market information, thereby supplementing formal regulation and facilitating more "pure" market-led transactions. In Silicon Valley, the reputation of venture capitalists plays an important role in coordinating investment by financiers into new entrepreneurial industries characterized by high levels of uncertainty (Podolny, 2001).

This importance of corporate reputation for understanding market dynamics in LME countries can be illustrated in various ways. In their study of CSR among top European firms, Jackson and Apostolakou (2010) find that firms from LMEs most frequently adopt "explicit" forms of CSR in contrast to firms from CMEs. The high importance of reputation in LMEs may also be a liability. For example, the high variability of reputation for quality among US automobile firms also creates vulnerability for high reputation firms to suffer greater market penalties for product recalls than low-reputation firms (Rhee & Haunschild, 2006).

By contrast, reputational capital in CMEs is more strongly associated with conformity and participation in collective or collaborative endeavors. Given the dominance of non-market modes of coordination, firms must be sure to cultivate and protect social capital vested within collective institutional life. In countries like Japan, coordination takes place through various forms of horizontally segmented networks and particularistic ties—as suggested by the term "alliance capitalism" (Gerlach, 1992). Saving face and

---

[3] A further link here concerns the elective affinity between LME-type economies and the regulatory form of states, as discussed in the previous section (Whitley, 2007). Strong regulatory rules ensured by a state allow market actors to trust in the wider set of rule-based institutions with less need to make assessments about the trustworthiness of particular firms based on their specific reputation as a firm.

maintaining an unblemished reputation are of central concern, and key elements of long-term, trust-based relationships within these networks. Here, corporate reputation of one firm is less easy to differentiate from that of other firms. Members of the Mitsubishi *keiretsu* share a common corporate image,[4] and negative perceptions by stakeholders are likely to carry across to other group firms. The situation of "mutual hostages" within network-based forms of governance (Williamson, 1996; Powell, 1991) creates strong peer pressure to conform, including both upward pressure to "not let the side down" in maintaining standards and downward pressure to not "show up" other members.

Given the strong inward orientation toward corporate groups, Japanese firms have faced a particular set of challenges regarding reputation management in crisis situations. In the case of corporate scandals, Japanese top executives have been known to apologize and resign more quickly than their Western counterparts. While often attributed to "culture," a more institutional explanation might stress the relatively low likelihood of criminal prosecution for white-collar crime in Japan, as well as the strong responsibility to the group of corporate insiders, and relative proximity to retirement within the system of "lifetime employment" (West, 2006). But, conversely, this strong relationship orientation to the firm can lead to a strong disjuncture between the perceptions of corporate insiders and expectations of the general public (Chikudate, 2009a). The food poisoning scandal at Snowbrand in 2000 was aggravated by the slow response of executives, and the overconfident trust in the company's own technologies (Wrigley, Ota, & Kikuchi, 2006). The train crash of a Western Japan Railway train in 2005, which killed 105 people, can be linked to the myopic reputational concerns of individual employees among their peer group, who were forced to undergo highly punitive "learning" processes in case mistakes were detected (Chikudate, 2009b).

Among CMEs, the specific form of coordination remains important in understanding reputation. Here, Germany represents a parallel but somewhat distinct case of reputation relative to Japan. In Germany, coordination is based on relatively public forms of associational governance, rather than the Japanese network-based relations. Accordingly, reputation is linked more to good citizenship within formal associations and the capacity for external influence that goes with positive reputation. For example, relative to US firms, corporate reputation in Germany is shaped by a number of distinct dimensions: the greater salience of fairness, in terms of pricing or conflict resolution, and the importance of reciprocity and transparency in dealing with stakeholders (Walsh & Wiedmann, 2004). These dimensions stress that good reputation may not be based on relative differentiation among competitors, as in the case of liberal markets, but on conformity with certain institutionalized norms related to commitment and cooperation with other stakeholders. Non-cooperation may have strong reputational consequences in the form of diminished capacity to obtain compromise in the future. Other studies of reputation management in Germany show that firms in competitive export sectors characterized by high levels of coordination and incremental innovation (e.g. machine tools,

---

[4] A keiretsu is a group of companies with interlocking business relationships and shareholdings.

automobiles, or chemicals) attribute very low salience to the management of corpora-tion reputation (Wiedmann & Buxel, 2005). Reputational concerns are primarily directed toward domestic consumers, and firms tend to adopt collective strategies of reputation management, such as product quality certification (ibid). Meanwhile, German firms undertake CSR of a more "implicit" form relative to their counterparts in LME countries (Jackson & Apostolakou, 2010; Habisch et al., 2004).

In sum, national institutions shape how firms are likely to invest in reputation-building. Put simply, the institutional patterns of CMEs may make it more likely that firms invest in building strong relational capital with employees, financiers, consumers (through strong product quality and innovation), and society more broadly. Meanwhile, the institutional features of LMEs may mean that firms invest in reputational assets that are locally valuable and help to differentiate their position within the market. In other words, institutional settings help to shape the desirable features of firm behavior that are consistent with a "good reputation"—and the same actions/outcomes in different places might be viewed differently.

REPUTATION WITHIN INSTITUTIONAL VOIDS AND ACROSS INSTITUTIONAL VARIETY

In the previous sections we have argued that institutional characteristics of countries play an important role in shaping the formation and management of corporate reputations. However, we have thus far largely restricted our attention to the variety in institutional features exhibited among countries with well-developed and reasonably stable institu-tional environments. In this section, we turn our attention to the role played by institutions in influencing reputations within countries with less developed institutional frameworks. Such contexts, introduced above as being characterized by limited statehood (Magan, Risse, & McFaul, 2009) and by relatively underdeveloped state capacity to regulate actors' actions in many spheres of economic and social life, provide for many of the most chal-lenging aspects of reputation management, and many of the most significant reputational risks that firms face. For example, international labor standards remain an important rep-utational issue for multinational firms. Scandals involving sweatshop working conditions have famously affected Nike, Gap, and Disney, among others (Jenkins, 2005; O'Callaghan, 2007; Eweje, 2009). Significant reputational issues have also arisen in relation to environ-mental harms, impacts upon indigenous populations, and involvement in bribery and corruption (Frynas, 2005; O'Callaghan, 2007; Davis & Ruhe, 2003).

Research in strategy and international management has shown that emerging and developing economies have very different institutional characteristics to those found in developed economies (Meyer & Peng, 2005; Wright et al., 2005; Gelbuda, Meyer, & Delios, 2008; Meyer & Tran, 2006). In particular, emerging and developing economies are characterized by highly volatile institutional landscapes that accompany rapidly changing market structures and macroeconomic performance (Meyer & Tran, 2006), and situations where "the absence of [strong formal] institutions is conspicuous" (McMillan, 2007). Imperfections and absences in the institutional landscapes of developing and emerging economies give rise to "institutional voids" (Khanna & Palepu, 2000) that play important roles in shaping the strategic choices of multinationals and local companies alike. The phrase "institutional voids" is understood broadly as describing situations in which the institutional "rules of the game" are uncertain and in which features of a country's institutional landscape, such as reliable legal institutions, the financial or education systems, and transport and communication infrastructure, are poorly developed (Khanna & Palepu, 1997, 2006).

In respect of corporate reputations, the primary consequence of operating in contexts characterized by low levels of institutional development is that the approach of benchmarking of desirable conduct by reference to social expectations is less viable because "the outcomes generated by an emergent institution are still subject to evaluation" (Henisz & Zelner, 2005) since they lack the "taken for granted" (Suchman, 1995) status of institutionalized expectations seen in countries with more well-developed and stable institutions. Furthermore, because of the political and social unpredictability associated with many such contexts, institutionalized expectations regarding corporate conduct are a moving target, generating considerable uncertainty in reputation formation. Given difficulties in determining, and consequently adhering to, local rules and norms, how should firms approach the management of their reputations? As argued above, the lack of clear and clearly enforced regulatory institutions lends considerable support to the centrality of firm reputations for firm success within broader systems founded upon relational processes of exchange and coordination. For example, research has shown that reputational assets play an important role in facilitating inter-firm collaborations that foster innovation and market access in emerging and developing economies (Mesquita & Lazzarini, 2008), and that socialized systems of coordination, such as guanxi, gwangye, and blat, within which firm, and individual, reputations play an important role are especially prevalent in contexts with weak formal institutions.[5] At the same time, the tendency for reputation to play an important role in economic and social exchange itself requires a certain level of economic stability, without which investments in reputational capital, based on anticipated future benefits, carry little value.

The Multinational Company: Managing Reputation across Multiple Institutional Frames

In the previous section, we highlighted that operating in arenas characterized by low state capacity generated difficulties in establishing firm reputations that stem from

---

[5] Guanxi describes personalized networks of influence, and is a central feature of Chinese business and society. Gwangye is a similar concept in Korean society, and Blat is a Russian term denoting the use of informal agreements, exchanges of services, connections, Party contacts, or black market deals in business.

uncertainties regarding norms and expectations of conduct. At the same time, the void left by the absence of regulatory institutions meant that reputations were central to economic coordination, provided the level of uncertainty wasn't so great that it undermined the value of investing in reputational assets. In this section, we focus on the issues raised for the formation and management of reputation within the multinational company. As previous research has noted, multinational companies have a variety of distinctive characteristics in addition to the observation that they are typically larger than firms operating in a single country (Westney & Zaheer, 2001; Doz & Prahalad, 1991). In the current context, the main distinguishing feature of multinational companies stems from the variety of country contexts that they operate within. As Kostova, Roth, and Dacin (2008: 997) indicate, this provides multinational corporations (MNCs) with "diverse, non-monolithic, fragmented, and possibly conflicting sets of external environments".

For MNCs, conflicting institutional pressures suggest a number of possible implications for corporate reputation. First, MNCs must cope with different images and associations of their country of origin across the world. Second, MNCs may find it hard to build and maintain reputation as social capital when operating in both LME- and CME-type institutional environments simultaneously. A classic example here was the merger of Daimler and Chrysler, and the very different norms of executive pay in the two countries. The high value of stock options was seen as a credible commitment to capital markets in the US, but as a violation of legitimate norms of equality and corporatist institutions in Germany. Third, MNCs may face a particular asymmetry regarding high regulatory standards in home countries from the advanced industrial and democratic world, but increasingly operate in countries characterized by very low levels of formal regulation or "institutional voids." In such circumstances, MNCs face difficult choices between adopting relatively homogeneous "global" standards across all the domains they operate in, perhaps reflecting "global hyper-norms," and adapting to local needs and conditions on a case-by-case basis. As has been noted, the former approach entails significant costs (Sharfman, Shaft, & Tihanyi, 2004) and substantial difficulties in implementation across varied institutional contexts (Helin & Sandström, 2008), while the latter risks actors in one context adopting a local institutional frame to interpret an MNC's conduct in a different context in ways that undermine the firm's reputation and success (Matten & Moon, 2008).

DIRECTIONS FOR FUTURE RESEARCH

Having developed the argument that institutions, particularly those associated with regulatory states, importantly shape corporate reputations, we now turn our attention to briefly outlining some areas that we see as promising for future research. In order to frame this analysis, we draw upon Figure 15.1, which summarizes three arenas in which we expect adopting an institutionalized perspective on corporate reputations might be particularly fruitful.

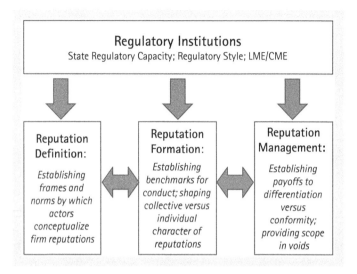

FIGURE 15.1 Regulatory institutions and corporate reputation.

The first arena in which an institutionalized perspective is likely to contribute significantly to thinking in respect of corporate reputation relates to the role of institutions in shaping the definition and conceptualization of firm reputation in particular contexts. As Rindova and Martins (2011) highlight, reputation research is increasingly seeing firm reputations as being specific—a given firm has a reputation for something, in the eyes of a particular group of actors. Some ways in which institutions affect how actors construe the reputations of firms relate to the role of institutions in shaping organizational identities (and thence the values and goals they project), and the role of institutionally shaped cognitive frames in influencing how actors understand the reputations of firms. Future research could make significant contributions by exploring how firm reputations are differently framed by actors across varied institutional contexts.

A second arena where institutional thinking is likely to contribute substantially to our understanding of firm reputation relates to institutionally established normative standards by which the expectations and evaluations of companies are made. This suggests that the implications for firm-level reputations of any given business strategy, decision, or investment, are likely to be highly sensitive to the character of the wider institutional contexts within which firms operate. Most clearly, regulatory institutions define behaviors that are compliant and noncompliant with mandated standards and thereby establish the range of behaviors in particular domains that are consistent with maintaining firm reputations. More broadly, institutions define legitimate conduct and through this, establish points of reference against which organizations acquire status relative both to those normative and cognitive expectations and peer organizations. Alongside establishing benchmarks for conduct, we have also argued that institutional contexts play an important role in shaping whether reputations are construed as individual versus collective phenomena. Put differently, we argued that the institutional context shapes the extent of interdependencies between the reputations of individual companies.

A third arena in which an institutional perspective offers productive opportunities for future research lies in relation to how companies use and manage their reputations in given contexts. On the one hand, we have argued that the payoffs to particular strategic decisions are likely to be highly sensitive to the nature of prevailing institutional norms. For example, the reputational harm associated with making layoffs might be particularly substantial within a coordinated market economy where there is a comparatively strong orientation toward collective aspects of firm reputations. On the other hand, the variation across countries in the character of national institutions provides for substantial managerial challenges and for considerable strategic scope for how organizations deal with contexts characterized by limited statehood. Exploring how firms cope with institutional variety when managing their reputations provides for a particularly interesting avenue for research in our opinion.

CONCLUSION

In this chapter we have highlighted the importance of regulatory institutions for firm reputations, within a cross-country comparative perspective. We have argued that while some research has begun to explore the importance of institutions for reputation, particularly in recognizing the inherently comparative nature of firm reputations, their perceptual character, and the role of socially constructed legitimacy in providing a lower bound to reputation, extant research on corporate reputation has broadly failed to embrace a central place for institutions. In light of this recognition, we have attempted to show that the variety and specific features of regulatory institutions present in different countries play an important role in shaping the functions and formation of firm reputations in important ways. Reputations are, we argue, differently construed and constructed, derived from distinctive patterns of conduct vis-à-vis economic and social actors, and put to different competitive and collaborative uses depending upon the properties of the wider institutional context within which firms operate.

Inevitably, given the limitations of the space available, it has been necessary to limit the scope of our analysis. In particular, while we have focused here on the significance of regulatory institutions for reputations, we see the general arguments we have proposed as having wider implications for future research that seeks to "institutionalize" our understanding of the character, formation, and use of firm reputations. Our hope is that scholarship in the area of corporate reputation will increasingly address the importance of institutions for reputation and that this will yield numerous major theoretical and empirical contributions.

Institutions and Reputation in Prior Research—Core Themes and Emerging Questions

Authors	Suggestion regarding the relationship between institutions and reputation	Questions raised that are relevant for our comparative institutional perspective on reputation
Rao (1994); Fombrum & Rindova (1994); Lahdesmaki & Siltaoja (2010)	Firms' reputations are socially constructed by stakeholders and represent a summative view of how successful firms are in meeting stakeholders' expectations	What are the origins of the frames used by stakeholders to shape their assessments? What role do institutions play in shaping these frames and stakeholders' expectations of firms' conduct?
Brown & Logsdon (1997); Deephouse & Carter (2005)	Reputational assessments of firms inherently involve a comparative element whereby firms are evaluated relative to peers and external standards	What are the origins of the standards by which firms are assessed? Are these standards different in different settings?
Barnett (2006); Winn et al. (2008); King et al. (2002); Hoffman (1997)	The reputation of a firm is strongly linked in the minds of stakeholders to firms in the same industry sector such that firms in an industry to a substantial extent share a common reputation	Do similar "spillover effects" in stakeholder evaluations of firms occur at the level of the nation state? Are firms within particular national settings subject to similar expectations and assessments?
Doh et al. (2010); King & Whetten (2008)	Legitimacy, while distinct from reputation, provides a lower bound to stakeholders' expectations of firms and therefore minimum standards for reputation-building	How do institutions shape what is interpreted by stakeholders as legitimate conduct? How do standards by which legitimate conduct is judged vary systematically across country contexts?
Sethi (2002); Wright & Rwabizambuga (2006)	Firms' actions in respect of specific local regulatory and legislative standards play an important role in shaping stakeholders' assessments of them	How do different regulatory and legislative styles shape firm reputations?

REFERENCES

Akkermans, D., Castaldi, C., & Los, B. (2009). "Do 'liberal market economies' really innovate more radically than 'coordinated market economies'?: Hall and Soskice reconsidered." *Research Policy*, 38(1): 181–191.

Anholt, S. (2006). *Competitive Identity: The New Brand Management for Nations, Cities and Regions*. Hamphire and New York: Palgrave Macmillan.

Aoki, M. (2010). *Corporations in Evolving Diversity: Cognition, Governance, and Institutions*. Oxford: Oxford University Press.

Barnett, M. L. (2006). "Finding a working balance between competitive and communal strategy." *Journal of Management Studies*, 43(8): 1753–1773.

Bates, R. H. (2008). "State failure." *Annual Review of Political Science*, 11: 1–12.

Biggart, N. W. (1991). "Explaining Asian economic organization. Toward a weberian institutional perspective." *Theory and Society*, 20: 199–232.

Bitektine, A. (2011). "Toward a theory of social judgements of organizations: The case of legitimacy, reputation, and status." *Academy of Management Review*, 36(1): 151–179.

Boyer, R. (2004). "New growth regimes, but still institutional diversity." *Socio-Economic Review*, 2(1): 1–32.

Brown, B. & Logsdon, J. M. (1997). "Factors influencing Fortune's corporate reputation for 'community and environmental responsibility'." In J. Weber & K. Rehbein. (Eds.), *Proceedings of the 8th Annual Meeting of the International Association for Business and Society*, 184–189.

Chikudate, N. (2009a). "Collective hyperopia and dualistic natures of corporate social responsibility in Japanese companies." *Asian Business and Management*, 8(2): 169–184.

—— (2009b). "If human errors are assumed as crimes in a safety culture: A lifeworld analysis of a rail crash." *Human Relations*, 62(9): 1267–1287.

Crouch, C. (2005). *Capitalist Diversity and Change. Recombinant Governance and Institutional Entrepreneurs*. Oxford: Oxford University Press.

—— & Streeck, W. (1997). *Political Economy of Modern Capitalism: Mapping Convergence and Diversity*. London; Thousand Oaks, Calif.: Sage.

Deephouse, D. L. & Carter, S. M. (2005). "An examination of differences between organizational legitimacy and organizational reputation." *Journal of Management Studies*, 42(2): 329–360.

DiMaggio, P. J. & Powell, W. (1983). "'The iron cage revisited': Institutional isomorphism and collective rationality in organizational fields." *American Sociological Review*, 48: 147–160.

—— & Powell, W. W. (1991). "The iron cage revisited: Institutional isomorphism and collective rationality in organization fields." In W. W. Powell & P. J. Dimaggio (Eds.), *The New Institutionalism in Organizational Analysis*. Chicago, IL: University of Chicago Press, 63–82.

Dobbin, F. (1994). *Forging Industrial Policy. The United States, Britain, and France in the Railway Age*. Cambridge, UK: Cambridge University Press.

Doh, J. P., Howton, S. D., Howton, S. W., & Siegel, D. S. (2010). "Does the market respond to an endorsement of social responsibility? The role of institutions, information, and legitimacy." *Journal of Management*, 36(6): 1461–1485.

Dowling, G. (2001). *Creating Corporate Reputations: Image, Identity, and Performance*. Oxford: Oxford University Press.

Evans, P. B., Skocpol, T., & Rueschemeyer, D. (1985). *Bringing the State Back In*. New York: Cambridge University Press.

Fetscherin, M. (2010). "The determinants and measurement of a country brand: The country brand strength index." *International Marketing Review*, 27(4): 466–479.

Fligstein, N. (2001). *The Architecture of Markets: An Economic Sociology of Capitalist Societies.* Princeton: Princeton University Press.

Fombrun, C. J. & Rindova, V. (1994). "Reputational rankings: Institutionalizing social audits of corporate performance." In S. Wartick & D. Collins (Eds.), Proceedings of the Fifth Annual Meeting of the International Association for Business and Society, 216–221.

—— & Shanley, M. (1990). "What's in a name? Reputation building and corporate strategy." *Academy of Management Journal*, 33(2): 233–258.

Gerlach, M. L. (1992). *Alliance Capitalism: The Social Organization of Japanese Business.* Berkeley: University of California Press.

Gonzales, F. & King, D. (2004). "The state and democratization: The United States in comparative perspective." *British Journal of Political Science*, 34: 193–210.

Habisch, A., Jonker, J., Wegner, M., & Schmidpeter, R. (2004). *Corporate Social Responsibility Across Europe.* Berlin: Springer.

Haggard, S., MacIntyre, A., & Tiede, L. (2008). "The rule of law and economic development." *Annual Review of Political Science*, 11: 205–234.

Hall, P. A. & Gingerich, D. W. (2004). "Varieties of capitalism and institutional complementarities in the macroeconomy: An empirical analysis." *Max-Planck-Institut für Gesellschaftsforschung, Discussion Paper.*

—— & Soskice, D. (2001). "An introduction to varieties of capitalism." In P. A. Hall & D. Soskice (Eds.), *Varieties of Capitalism: The Institutional Foundations of Comparative Advantage.* Oxford: Oxford University Press, 1–70.

Halsall, R. (2008). "From 'business culture' to 'brand state': Conceptions of nation and culture in business literature on cultural difference." *Culture & Organization*, 14(1): 15–30.

Helin, S. & Sandström, J. (2008). "Codes, ethics, and cross-cultural differences: Stories from the implementation of a corporate code of ethics in a MNC subsidiary." *Journal of Business Ethics*, 8(2): 281–291.

Henisz, W. J. & Zelner, B. A. (2005). "Legitimacy, interest group pressures and change in emergent institutions: The case of foreign investors and host country governments." *Academy of Management Review*, 30(2): 361–382.

Herbst, J. (2000). *States and Power in Africa: Comparative Lessons in Authority and Control.* Princeton, NJ: Princeton University Press.

Hoffman, A. (1997). *From Heresy to Dogma: An Institutional History of Corporate Environmentalism.* San Francisco, CA: The New Lexington Press.

Hollingsworth, J. R. & Boyer, R. (1997). *Contemporary Capitalism: The Embeddedness of Institutions.* Cambridge; New York: Cambridge University Press.

——, Schmitter, P. C. & Streeck, W. (1994). *Governing Capitalist Economies.* Oxford: Oxford University Press.

Jackson, G. & Apostolakou, A. (2010). "Corporate social responsibility in Western Europe: An institutional mirror or substitute?" *Journal of Business Ethics*, 94(3): 371–394.

—— & Deeg, R. (2008a). "Comparing capitalisms: Understanding institutional diversity and its implications for international business." *Journal of International Business Studies*, 39(4): 540–561.

Jackson, G. & Deeg, R. (2008b). "From comparing capitalisms to the politics of institutional change." *Review of International Political Economy*, 15(4): 680–709.

Kenworthy, L. (2006). "Institutional coherence and macroeconomic performance." *Socio-Economic Review*, 4: 69–91.

Khanna, T. & Palepu, K. (2006). "Stategies that fit emerging markets." *Harvard Business Review*, 84 (June): 60–69.

King, B. G. & Whetten, D. A. (2008). "Rethinking the relationship between reputation and legitimacy: A social actor conception." *Corporate Reputation Review*, 11: 192–207.

King, A., Lenox, M., & Barnett, M. (2002). "Strategic responses to the reputation commons problem." In A. Hoffman & M. Ventresca (Eds.), *Organizations, Policy, and the Natural Environment: Institutional and Strategic Perspectives*. Stanford, CA: Stanford University Press, 393–406.

Kostova, T., Roth, K., & Dacin, T. (2008). "Institutional theory in the study of MNCs: A critique and new directions." *Academy of Management Review*, 33(4): 994–1007.

Lähdesmäki, M. & Siltaoja, M. (2010). "Towards a variety of meanings—Multiple representations of reputation in the small business context." *British Journal of Management*, 21: 207–222.

La Porta, R., Lopez-de-Silanes, F., Schleifer, A., & Vishney, R. W. (1998). "Law and finance." *Journal of Political Economy*, 106(6): 1113–1155.

Levitsky, S. & Murillo, M. V. (2009). "Variation in institutional strength." *Annual Review of Political Science*, 12: 115–133.

Li, S. & Samsell, D. P. (2009). "Why some countries trade more than others: The effect of the governance environment on trade flows." *Corporate Governance: An International Review*, 17(1): 47–61.

Love, E. G. & Kraatz, M. (2009). "Character, conformity, or the bottom line? How and why downsizing affected corporate reputation." *Academy of Management Journal*, 52: 314–335.

Magan, A., Risse, T., & McFaul, M. A. (2009). *Promoting Democracy and the Rule of Law: American and European Strategies (Governance and Limited Statehood)*. Houndsmill: Palgrave Macmillan.

Matten, D. & Crane, A. (2005). "Corporate citizenship: Toward an extended theoretical conceptualization." *Academy of Management Review*, 30(1): 166–179.

—— & Moon, J. (2007). "'Implicit' and 'explicit' CSR—A conceptual framework for a comparative understanding of corporate social responsibility." *Academy of Management Review*, 33(2): 404–424.

Mesquita, L. F. & Lazzarini, S. G. (2008). "Horizontal and vertical relationships in developing economies: Implications for SMEs' access to global markets." *Academy of Management Journal*, 51(2): 359–380.

Morgan, G., Campbell, J. L., Crouch, C., Pedersen, O. K., & Whitley, R. (2010). *The Oxford Handbook of Comparative Institutional Analysis*. Oxford: Oxford University Press.

Pempel, T. J. (1998). *Regime Shift. Comparative Dynamics of the Japanese Political Economy*. Ithaca, NY: Cornell University Press.

Podolny, J. M. (2001). "Networks as the pipes and prisms of the market." *American Journal of Sociology*, 107(1): 33–60.

Porter, M. E. (1990). *The Competitive Advantage of Nations*. New York, NY: The Free Press.

Powell, W. W. (1991). "Neither market nor hierarchy: Network forms of organization." In G. Thompson, J. Frances, R. Levacic, & J. Mitchell (Eds.), *Markets, Hierarchies, and Networks*. London: Sage.

Rao, H. (1994). "The social construction of reputation: Certification contests, legitimation, and the survival of organizations in the American automobile industry: 1895–1912." *Strategic Management Journal*, 15(Winter Special Issue): 29–44.

Rhee, M. & Haunschild, P. R. (2006). "The liability of good reputation: A study of product recalls in the U.S. automobile industry." *Organization Science*, 17(1): 101–117.

Rindova, V. P., Pollock, T. G., & Hayward, M. L. A. (2006). "Celebrity firms: The social construction of market popularity." *Academy of Management Review*, 31: 50–71.

——, Petkova, A. P., & Kotha, S. (2007). "Standing out: How new firms in emerging markets build reputation." *Strategic Organization*, 5(1): 31–70.

Schmidt, V. A. (2002). *The Futures of European Capitalism*. Oxford: Oxford University Press.

Schneider, M., Schulze-Bentrop, C., & Paunescu, M. (2009). "Mapping the institutional capital of high-tech firms: A fuzzy-set analysis of capitalist variety and export performance." *Journal of International Business Studies*, 41(2): 246–266.

Sethi, S. (2002). "Standards for corporate conduct in the international arena: Challenges and opportunities for multinational corporations." *Business and Society Review*, 107(1): 20–40.

Sharfman, M., Shaft, T., & Tihanyi, L. (2004). "A model of the global and institutional antecedents of high-level corporate environmental performance." *Business & Society*, 43(1): 6–36.

Spruyt, H. (2002). "The origins, development, and possible decline of the modern state." *Annual Review of Political Science*, 5(5): 127–149.

Taylor, M. Z. (2004). "Empirical evidence against varieties of capitalism's theory of technical innovation." *International Organization*, 58: 601–631.

Thomas, D. E. (2007). "How do reputation and legitimacy affect organizational performance?" *International Journal of Management*, 24(1): 108–116.

Tilly, C. (1990). *Coercion, Capital, and European States, AD 990–1992*. London: Wiley-Blackwell.

Tyler, L. (1997). "Liability means never being able to say you're sorry: Corporate guilt, legal constraints, and defensiveness in corporate communication." *Management Communication Quarterly*, 11: 51–73.

Walsh, G. & Wiedmann, K.-P. (2004). "A conceptualization of corporate reputation in Germany: An evaluation and extension of the RQ." *Corporate Reputation Review*, 6(4): 304–312.

West, M. K. (2006). *Secrets, Sex, and Spectacle: The Rules of Scandal in Japan and the United States*. Chicago: University of Chicago Press.

Whetten, D. A. & Mackey, A. (2002). "A social actor conception of organizational identity and its implications for the study of organizational reputation." *Business & Society*, 41: 393–415.

Whitley, R. (2005). "How national are business systems? The role of states and complementary institutions in standardizing systems of economic coordination and control at the national level." In G. Morgan, R. Whitley, & E. Moen (Eds.), *Changing Capitalisms? Internationalization, Institutional Change, and Systems of Economic Organization*. Oxford: Oxford University Press, 190–234.

—— (2007). *Business Systems and Organizational Capabilities: The Institutional Structuring of Competitive Competences*. Oxford: Oxford University Press.

Wiedmann, K.-P. & Buxel, H. (2005). "Corporate reputation management in Germany: Results of an empirical study." *Corporate Reputation Review*, 8(2): 145–163.

Williamson, O. (1996). *The Mechanisms of Governance*. Oxford: Oxford University Press.

Winn, M. I., MacDonald, P., & Zietsma, C. (2008). "Managing industry reputation: The dynamic tension between collective and competitive reputation management strategies." *Corporate Reputation Review*, 11(1): 35–55.

Wright, C. & Rwabizambuga, A. (2006). "Institutional pressures, corporate reputation, and voluntary codes of conduct: An examination of the equator principles." *Business & Society Review*, 111(1): 89–117.

Wright, M., Filatotchev, I., Hoskisson, R., & Peng, M. (2005). "Strategy research in emerging economies: Challenging the conventional wisdom." *Journal of Management Studies*, 42(1): 1–33.

Wrigley, B. J., Ota, S., & Kikuchi, A. (2006). "Lightning strikes twice: Lessons learned from two food poisoning incidents in Japan." *Public Relations Review*, 32(4): 349–357.

Ying, F. (2006). "Branding the nation: What is being branded?" *Journal of Vacation Marketing*, 12(1): 5–14.

Ziegler, J. N. (1997). *Governing Ideas: Strategies for Innovation in France and Germany*. Ithaca, NY: Cornell University Press.

···

CHAPTER 16

HOW REPUTATION REGULATES REGULATORS: ILLUSTRATIONS FROM THE REGULATION OF RETAIL FINANCE

···

SHARON GILAD

TAMAR YOGEV

Positive reputation is a strategic asset that regulatory agencies seek to develop and preserve. However, in order to build a positive reputation, regulators need to manage successfully multiple needs of various actors. Among these actors are politicians, consumers and the public at large, the media, and other governmental and regulatory bodies. These actors hold conflicting expectations, interests, and views with which the regulators are expected to deal effectively. How do regulators manage these potentially conflicting demands in light of their own reputational risk? Based on a case study of the British Financial Ombudsman Service (FOS), we argue that reputation plays a key role in regulatory processes and decisions. By examining multiple interactions of the FOS with different actors, such as financial firms, the media, consumers, politicians, and the Financial Services Authority (FSA), we reveal the mechanisms through which reputation regulates regulators. We further highlight how regulators' pursuit of a positive reputation leads them to take actions that enhance or diminish the reputations of the companies they regulate.

INTRODUCTION

···

REGULATORS are constantly observed and judged by multiple audiences, including political and judicial overseers, the media, regulated firms, organized consumer groups, other regulated agencies, and government departments (e.g. Carpenter, 2001, 2002,

2004, 2010; NOLL, 1985; Olson, 1995, 1996, 1997; Vogel, 2003; Krause & Corder, 2007; Krause & Douglas, 2005; Maor, 2010a). Their reputation is shaped and readjusted in interaction with these multiple stakeholders. Because of the diverse, and sometimes conflicting, expectations of their audiences, regulators may seek to highlight different aspects of their roles and capabilities in their interaction with different stakeholders (Yeung, 2009). Moreover, at times regulators may have to undermine one aspect of their reputation and standing vis-à-vis one group of stakeholders in order to protect another aspect of their reputation that is valued by other key audiences (Gilad, 2009; Maor, 2007). Thus, regulatory reputation is continuously forged and strategically defended.

Regulators' strategies in crafting, communicating, and defending their reputations are the main focus of this chapter. Our analysis of regulators' strategies is guided by two perspectives within political science research: the notion of "regulatory reputation" and the scholarship on public officials' "blame avoidance."

A secondary focus of this chapter is to explore how regulators' reputation management leads them to take actions that enhance or diminish the reputations of the companies they regulate. Regulators are among the key mediators of industries' and individual firms' reputations (Bosch & Lee, 1994; Davidson, Worrell, & Cheng, 1994; Ehasn et al., 1991; Karpoff, Chapter 18, this volume). Studies show that firms, particularly large and well-recognized ones, perceive noncompliance and the threat of regulatory enforcement primarily as a reputation risk (Braithwaite, 1989; Fisse & Braithwaite, 1983; Gunningham, Thornton, & Kagan, 2005; Parker, 2002). Thus, when regulators interpret and manage risks to society in order to minimize their own reputational risks (Black, 2005; Rothstein, Huber, & Gaskell, 2006; Power, 2009), they influence the corporate reputation of regulated firms. This chapter explores the nature of such processes by reference to existing literature and a case study of the British Financial Ombudsman Service (FOS), a semi-regulatory public body that handles consumer complaints regarding the selling of retail financial products.

FORGING REPUTATION AND AVOIDING BLAME: THEORETICAL FRAME

Two key streams in the regulatory and public administration literature analyze regulators' management of the attitudes of external stakeholders. One, most notably associated with the work of Daniel Carpenter, examines regulators' forging and maintenance of their reputation. Another, led by the writings of Christopher Hood, focuses on regulators' (and other officeholders') strategies for avoiding blame. To date, these streams of research have developed independently of each other. Juxtaposing these literatures for the first time, as we do in this section, highlights different aspects of regulators' management of externals' perceptions of their organizations, namely their reputations.

Forging and Maintaining Regulatory Reputation

We take "regulatory reputation" to signify externally held beliefs regarding an agency's efficacy in pursuing its formal and informal mandate, its technical expertise, and the legitimacy of its aims and the means it employs (Carpenter, 2010). This conceptualization of reputation is compatible with established notions in organizational theory (e.g. Albert & Whetten, 1985; Foreman, Whetten, and Mackey, Chapter 9, this volume), according to which reputation is the external manifestation of an organizational identity, as interpreted and understood by those outside the organization. The literature on regulatory reputation is still in its infancy. It has not yet systematically conceptualized the spectrum of strategies that regulators employ in order to forge and maintain their reputation. Below are three reputation-management strategies that we identify within extant literature.

Constructing a Distinct Reputation

The long-term survival of a regulatory agency and the success of its claims for public resources depend, to some extent, on its reputation for the proficient execution of a *unique* function (Carpenter, 2001, 2010; Maor, 2007, 2010b). Consequently, reputation-sensitive regulators seek a niche role, which is sufficiently differentiated from that of other agencies in their environment, and resist tasks outside their constructed domain (Carpenter, 2001, 2010; Gilad, 2008a; Wilson, 1989). They attempt expansion to new territories only when new tasks fall squarely within their constructed role, and when failure to claim jurisdiction could undermine their distinctive reputation (Maor, 2010a). Finally, regulators' inclination to cooperate with other agencies is shaped by the extent to which this supports or endangers their success in fulfilling their unique task (Gilad, 2009; Wilson, 1989).

Shaping Public Expectations

Regulatory bodies continuously seek to manage the gap between their self-perception—their role, adequate means of operation, the constitution of success/failure—and the way the public perceives their role, develops expectations of them, and accordingly assesses their performance (Gilad, 2008b). The smaller the gap between the regulatory body's self-perception and public expectations, the more likely that the regulator will maintain its positive reputation. The aim of regulatory expectations management goes beyond damping expectations so as to avoid blame for future failure. It is an attempt to align internal and external conceptualizations of the regulatory task. These dynamics are evident in Black's (2005) study of the British regulator—the Financial Services Authority (FSA)—"risk-based regulation," and its underlying assumption that risk has to be managed but cannot and should not be eradicated. As Black (2005) shows, the risk-based regulation framework was both an inward-looking means for homogenizing the FSA's organizational culture and an outward-looking "attempt to…define the parameters of responsibility, and thus the parameters of blame; to reshape public and political expectations of what [the regulator]…can and should do, and conversely, of what it cannot and should not do." However, as recent events have shown, regulators' ability to manage public expectations is limited. The FSA's Chief Executive acknowledged this in a post-crisis public lecture:

> There remains the perennial problem of a mis-match regarding what a regulator can do—and indeed what it is charged to do—and what society expects. Events have shown that society never really accepted or understood a "non zero failure" [risk-based] regulatory regime. (Sants, 2010)

Striking a Balance Between Conflicting Bases for Reputation

Within their constructed domain, regulators need to balance between different, sometimes conflicting, facets of their reputation. For example, Carpenter (2002, 2004) proposes that regulators who process pharmaceutical companies' applications for new drug approval strike a balance between the reputation benefits of repeat clinical testing, which reduces the risk of harm from drug side effects, and the reputational cost of regulatory delay in the authorization of a new drug. Similarly, Maor and Sulitzeanu-Kenan (forthcoming) find that the Food and Drug Administration was inclined to risk prompt recourse to enforcement action, over the safer option of further collection of evidence and/or negotiation with regulated firms when facing media criticism for under-enforcement. These studies suggest that regulators strike a balance between alternative bases for reputation in light of relative threats posed by their external environment.

Regulatory Blame Avoidance

Regulatory "blame avoidance" (Hood, 2002, 2007; Hood & Rothstein, 2001; Hood, Rothstein, & Baldwin, 2001; Sulitzeanu-Kenan & Hood, 2005) regards strategic behavior that is intended to avoid or limit damage to agencies' reputations and/or to restore their reputations in the aftermath of crisis.[1] The key assumption underlying the literature on "blame avoidance" is that officeholders, regulators included, are primarily concerned with avoiding blame for failure, whereas claiming credit for successful operations is a residual motivation (Weaver, 1986). Christopher Hood and colleagues have developed a coherent categorization of the strategies that politicians, bureaucrats, and regulators employ in order to avoid blame. They distinguish between three types of strategies

---

[1] The word "reputation" is not used explicitly in this scholarship, which refers to "blame" or "blamability."

as follows. Whilst this literature regards officeholders in general, below we discuss its implications for regulators.

Agency Strategies

Agency strategies pertain to regulators' pursuit of formal jurisdiction that will minimize their likelihood to attract blame. The literature on blame avoidance predicts that regulators will resist tasks that carry high risk of damage to their reputation (Hood & Rothstein, 2001; Wilson, 1989[2]). Equally, regulators may seek to diffuse potential blame by collaborating and sharing responsibility with other agencies (Hood & Rothstein, 2001; Hood, Rothstein, & Baldwin, 2001). This latter strategy implies that blame avoidance may sometimes override regulators' pursuit of an exclusive domain.

Presentational Strategies

Presentational strategies refer to regulators' post-crisis management of external perceptions, involving denial of the problem and/or responsibility for a blameful event, attempts to shift blame to others, provision of excuses, and so forth. Regulatory agencies' deployment of presentational strategies in the aftermath of crisis is, to the best of our knowledge, little researched.

Policy Strategies

"Policy strategies are attempts by officeholders or institutions to avoid or limit blame by the substance or content of what they do" (Hood, 2007: 200). Most notably, in response to external threats, regulators may choose to set and follow strict rules for their use of discretionary powers in order to be in a position to provide coherent explanation for their actions, and inactions, in the event of failure. Black (2005) demonstrates this with regard to the FSA's development of a formalized "risk-based" approach to its internal allocation of resources to supervision. Such formalization and rationalization of regulation is also consistent with the findings of Hood and Rothstein (2001) and Hood, Rothstein, & Baldwin (2001), which show that increasing external scrutiny drove regulators to adopt "more formal written procedures or checklists for risks assessment," which had the potential for "limiting blame by forming the basis of a procedural defence for officials" in the event of failure (Hood & Rothstein, 2001: 29). More generally, risk-based regulation is consistent with the current vogue amongst regulators and other public bodies, at least in the UK, to adopt formal risk-management techniques to manage risks to their reputations (Power, 2007; Power, 2009; Rothstein, Huber, & Gaskell, 2006).

Are the above theoretical streams employing different labels for the same phenomena? Yes and no. We would suggest that these literatures highlight complementary aspects of regulators' reputation management. The summary table at the end of the

---

[2] To be accurate, Wilson suggests that bureaucrats tend to avoid "learned vulnerabilities" and "tasks that will produce divided and hostile constituencies" (191).

chapter presents the main predictions and findings of the above literatures (please note that some of the references in this table are discussed later in this chapter).

Forging and Defending Reputation: Empirical Illustrations

The data presented in this section are based on nonparticipant observation at the FOS, which was conducted between November 2003 and December 2004.[3] The data include (a) a random sample of complaint files, (b) over 40 interviews within and outside the FOS, (c) FOS internal correspondence and guidance, and (d) observations at the FOS offices, including internal talks and training sessions.

The FOS was formed in 2000 to complement regulation by the FSA. By 2005, the end of the research period, the FOS had handled over 110,000 complaints and employed nearly 900 people. The FOS operated a two-tier complaint-handling process. All complaints were initially handled by low-level complaint handlers, named "adjudicators" (during the research period, the FOS employed over 400 adjudicators). When adjudicators found a complaint to be prima facie valid, they issued an initial assessment and recommendation to the firm to offer compensation to the complainant without further formal decision. These recommendations became final and binding only if accepted by both parties to the dispute. About 90 percent of the FOS's overall complaints caseload was concluded on this informal basis.

Firms and complainants were entitled to challenge adjudicators' assessments by requesting their further review by an "ombudsman," of which there were 19 at the time of this research. The ombudsmen's decisions were legally binding upon firms, whereas complainants could pursue their cases anew via the civil courts (although, in practice, the costs and burden of proof involved in legal proceedings rendered this option extremely unlikely). Both firms and complainants were further entitled to challenge the ombudsmen's decisions via appeals for judicial review, which were infrequent but occurred nonetheless.

Constructing a Distinct Reputation

The FOS provides a good illustration of regulators' pursuit of a reputation for a distinct function and expertise (Gilad, 2008a). To differentiate itself from the civil courts, the FOS emphasized the quick and informal nature of its decision-making and interaction with complainants. Additionally, to distinguish itself from the FSA, the FOS stressed the restriction of its role to *individual* dispute resolution, as opposed to regulatory standard-

---

[3] For a detailed description of the sample and case study background see Gilad (2010).

setting and enforcement. For example, in one of many similar identity-reputation claims, the FOS asserted:

> We perform our function in a different way to the courts... using quicker and more informal procedures... ours is a distinct role, separate from the FSA. We make decisions on one-off cases... we do not carry out regulatory functions. (FOS annual report 2006: 7)

The FOS's above construction of its role in terms of quick and informal dispute resolution had some important implications for its relationship with the FSA, with ramifications for firms' corporate reputations. As long as firms were inclined to settle complaints quickly and informally, complaint handlers were much less likely to systematically collate, analyze, and pass to the FSA information regarding a firm's poor selling or complaint-handling practices. In contrast, when firms persistently contested adjudicators' decisions, complaint handlers tended to use their ability to pass information to the FSA as a threat, and, where necessary, to actually pass such information to the FSA (Gilad, 2009).

In addition, loyal to its conceptualization of its role as distinct from the FSA's regulatory functions, the FOS was disinclined to "name and shame" individual firms and resisted consumer groups' requests to publish statistics regarding the volume and result of complaints per firm. Among the reasons for this policy was the FOS's assumption that firms would be more amenable to settling complaints informally and quickly if granted confidentiality. An executive of the FOS explained this policy in a personal interview:

> We are always keen to point out that all we do is organise redress for consumers... [Naming and shaming firms] could be creating all sorts of problems as to "what exactly does the Ombudsman do? Why have you [the Ombudsman] been telling us [the industry] for the last 10 years we are not a regulator, we provide redress not regulation when you suddenly do something which is quintessentially regulatory?"

It is noteworthy that since the research period the FOS has dramatically changed its policy regarding publication of complaints statistics. As of September 2009 the FOS publishes, twice a year, comparative data regarding the number and outcome of complaints per firm. What is most relevant for our purposes is that the FOS justified this policy change as aligned with its legal mandate and core identity-reputation, namely, quick and informal dispute resolution, thus:

> A number of public-interest arguments have been put forward in favour of publishing business-specific complaint data. But the key consideration is that... we believe that publishing the data will facilitate the resolution of disputes quickly and with minimum formality. (FOS, March 2009)

Moreover, to distinguish its publication of complaints data from FSA regulation, the ombudsman further asserted:

> The published [complaints] data will include comparatively positive information as well as comparatively negative information. This is not an exercise in "naming and shaming." Dealing with financial businesses that behave badly is a matter for

the regulators. Parliament has given the role of handling individual complaints to the Ombudsman service and the role of consumer protection to the FSA. (FOS March 2009)

The FOS's above conceptualization of the division of labor between its individual dispute resolution and FSA regulation was threatened during the research period by a series of industry scandals, which gave rise to a high volume of consumer complaints. The ombudsman's decisions on these cases attracted media and political attention, and tainted the industry's reputation. This, in turn, resulted in industry allegations that the FOS was acting as a de facto regulator, making decisions with broad applications and costly implications. In private negotiations, the FOS executives sought to shift responsibility to the FSA, requesting the regulator to require firms to settle the relevant complaints before they reach the FOS. Such FSA action would have liberated the FOS from making decisions on these cases. Yet the FSA was generally reluctant to issue guidance regarding the relevant cases, and the FOS was disinclined to publicly shame the FSA into action because this would have jeopardized their relationship. Consequently, the FOS was left with a reputation-sensitive task, which it would have preferred to avoid. As discussed further below, the reputation risk involved in handling these cases drove the FOS to adopt a standardized complaint-handling strategy, which was alien to its identity.

In sum, we suggest that regulators seek a differentiated reputation as an agency that specializes in the execution of role X (and not in role Y) using Z (and not W) means. Consequently, regulators focus on mitigating certain risks to society, while overlooking other risks. Ultimately, regulators' conceptualization of their role—for example their appetite to name and shame—further shapes their impact upon the reputation of regulated firms. Yet, regulators' ability to strategically select their domain and nurture a reputation within it is limited by the interests and expectations of their multiple stakeholders and overseers.

Shaping Realistic Expectations

Complaint handlers, in interviews, asserted that many complainants had unrealistic expectations regarding the FOS's role and the prospects for redress, which were forged by the media. The type of coverage that the FOS was, paradoxically, concerned about encouraged *everyone* to pursue their complaints with the FOS, thereby creating unrealistic expectations for redress, which could eventually result in complainants' disappointment and dissatisfaction with FOS proceedings.

Certainly, positive media publicity for the FOS had the potential advantage of bringing the FOS and the public value of its services to the attention of larger audiences. Yet, as explained by the head of an FOS support unit in a personal interview, positive media exposure could give readers false expectations regarding the likely resolution of their complaints through stories of successful customers' cases:

Media exposure...has two impacts. The first is it gets more people in here, obviously more people hear about us and they know they've got a problem...[at the same time, the press] increasingly print stories which are pretty optimistic about what we do and the prospects. So, the impact of that, those people are more disappointed [if we reject their complaints]. However, what we've also found, sometimes, is when I send out a survey, if there's been some good press report about what we're doing, then suddenly, everyone says, "Yeah, they're doing a good job."

The following example, from the *Daily Mail*, epitomizes the type of positive coverage that complaint handlers castigated and feared:

If you believe you were mis-sold [a financial product] or misled [about its nature], you should dig in and fight all the way to the Financial Ombudsman Service—the ultimate arbiter of disputes between financial companies and their customers. (Beugge, 2003)

The above article continues with another section entitled "how to complain...and to whom," in which the newspaper encourages customers to file complaints. The FOS's communication strategy was intended, among other aims, to minimize such gaps between public perceptions and the ombudsman's internal conceptualization of their role. Communication for the FOS was therefore not simply a marketing tool. It aimed simultaneously to create awareness of the ombudsman, to deliver nuanced messages to the industry, to provide answers to criticism, and to educate the public about the ombudsman's role and its limitations.

In addition to the FOS's corporate communication strategies, individual complaint handlers' daily interpersonal interactions with complainants were similarly designed to educate complainants about the FOS's role, and to reshape their expectations. More generally, adjudicators' written communication with complainants was designed to attain complainants' trust and satisfaction with the complaint-handling process, regardless of its outcome. Adjudicators sought to gain complainants' trust by demonstrating their attentiveness to complainants' allegations and their proclivity to endorse the complaint if provided with sufficient information. They were sensitive to complainants' need for individual treatment, displayed sympathy with their loss, enabled them to save face, and carefully reshaped their expectations for redress and from the FOS. These practices aimed to secure complainants' consent and satisfaction when complaint handlers' professional assessments of the complaints diverged from complainants' subjective sense that they had been treated unjustly by firms (Gilad, 2008b).

Finally, what were the effects of the FOS's communication strategies and its interpersonal interactions with complainants upon the reputation of regulated firms? Arguably, the FOS's stress that not all consumer complaints are valid and worthy of redress, could have enhanced consumers' confidence in the financial industry. Yet, as firms and the FOS have painfully learnt, the FOS's rejections of complaints and its explications that cases vary, and each complaint should be assessed according to its individual merits, are not newsworthy. In contrast, the ombudsman's decisions in favor of complainants, particularly those regarding big and salient firms, make a good story. Hence, in practice the

FOS's decisions, as reflected in the media, had substantial adverse impact on the indus-try's reputation regardless of the FOS's communication strategies.

In sum, our analysis suggests that regulators do not necessarily seek positive reputa-tions per se. They also aim to influence public expectations about what regulation can and cannot, and should and should not, achieve. Yet, it is also the case that the impact of regulators' communication strategies is limited, and that they are often unsuccessful in aligning public expectations with their internal conceptualization of their role.

Striking a Balance between Conflicting Bases for Reputation

The literature on regulatory reputation, as discussed above, suggests that regulators strike a balance between different and conflicting facets of their reputation. What current stud-ies lack, however, is an insight into regulators' internal constitution of this balance. The ethnographic data from the FOS study contributes to filling this gap by providing an insight into the evolution of the internal institutions of regulatory reputation-balancing. Below we show how the FOS's internal control and reward structure gradually formed so as to balance and mitigate risks to its reputation stemming from delays in case process-ing, poor quality, and inadequate interpersonal interaction between adjudicators and complainants. Further, we show how external threats to reputation were interpreted in light of—and used as part of—internal struggles over the FOS's organizational identity.

As already mentioned, one of the FOS's key identity-reputation claims regarded the swiftness of its decision-making. With rapidly increasing complaint volumes, the organ-ization was experiencing case backlogs that threatened this aspect of its reputation. Moreover, to manage its mounting caseload, the FOS engaged in rapid growth and staff recruitment. Therefore, in addition to its concern that delays in case processing would dampen complainants' satisfaction with its services, the FOS was also under pressure to prove to the FSA and to the industry, which ultimately funded this expansion, that it was productive in its use of existing staff and resources.

The FOS's concern with managing its caseload and case backlogs was institutional-ized in an elaborate performance-management and reward system. Each adjudicator and each team manager had a six-month case-closure target, expressed in terms of the average number of cases that the adjudicator and the team overall were expected to bring to full closure every week. Adjudicators and team managers who exceeded their targets, as measured at the end of each six-month period, were eligible for a bonus beyond their respective salaries. In addition to the overall number of cases closed, adjudicators were expected to handle *all* cases in a timely manner, and within a maximum period of 12 months. A case that had been open for over 12 months would be reported and discussed at the FOS's board meeting.

Alongside the FOS's rigorous management of its swelling caseload, was a growing anxiety, especially among ombudsmen and veteran adjudicators, that efficiency was eroding the quality of decision-making. Interviewees tended to contrast the role of

ombudsmen as "quality guardians" with operational managers' focus on managing efficiency and case backlogs. One ombudsman made the following argument, linking
ombudsmen's focus on decision quality to the risk of personal reputation damage:

> I wouldn't say that ombudsmen...are unconcerned with figures...we want to get as
> many cases out as possible, but [we] will only do it if they're to a certain quality.
> Because, our names are on the bottom [of these decisions] and if it all goes wrong,
> we're the ones who are going to end up in court [for judicial review] or in the national
> press...So, we have a certain level, which seems to be higher than other people's,
> and therefore...we get tarred with the brush of...sticks-in-the-mud and stopping
> cases from going out.

Internal concerns with quality attained higher priority during the research period due to
two salient incidents that threatened the organization's reputation. One was a critical
BBC Radio 4 *Money Box* program (broadcast on April 13, 2004), which directed public
attention to the FOS's performance-management and reward scheme. The other was an
internal investigation of mismanagement of complaints in one team. These two events
provided a stronger voice to the ombudsmen to strengthen and formalize the organization's quality assurance system. An executive linked the enhanced formalization of the
quality assurance system to both the ongoing internal debate between a focus on decision
quality and case processing, and to the organization's concerns with adverse publicity:

> The organisation is under enormous pressure to keep on top of the volume of cases
> it's dealing with, which means you have to be a bit obsessed with the numbers, but
> by the same token we have to be very mindful that if we let the standards drop it will
> be all over the press as well.

In addition to the formalization of the quality assurance system, concerns with reputation for quality impacted on the FOS's reward structure. Adjudicators' and team managers' ability to earn bonuses for case closure above target was capped. This capping was
initially introduced as a result of internal dissatisfaction with bonus disparities across
teams, and concern that allocation of large bonuses may draw external criticism from
both firms and consumer bodies. A few months later, the bonus cap was further reduced
in response to the above mentioned BBC 4 *Money Box* program.

Alongside its balancing between case-closure productivity and decision-making quality, the FOS was also concerned to maximize the satisfaction of individual complainants,
and to forgo risks to reputation due to individuals' inappropriate communication with
complainants. Thus, managers directed and monitored adjudicators' interpersonal interaction with complainants—for example their writing style, "phone manner," and so on.
Periodic charts of complainants' considerable satisfaction with the organization's decision-making processes were displayed internally on every floor, and published in the
FOS's annual reports (Gilad, 2008b).

Finally, and most importantly, the division of labor between adjudication teams
within the FOS, and the variability in the level of targets across these teams, reflected the
organization's balancing between the above multiple concerns (or reputation claims) for
productivity, decision quality, and customer satisfaction. Complaints were channeled to

different departments ("business units") and teams within the FOS according to their perceived complexity and sensitivity. Sensitive cases—such as those that were already under political, media, or judicial scrutiny, or those that were more likely to attract such scrutiny—were handled by more experienced adjudicators. Adjudicators in these teams had lower case-closure targets and a smaller component of performance-related pay. Consequently, in comparison with those handling less sensitive cases, these adjudicators had more time to investigate cases and to manage the relationship with the complainants and the firms, and thereby to mitigate the risk that their decision would cause the FOS reputation damage in the event of external scrutiny. At the same time, elsewhere within the FOS, the organization's concerns with case closure productivity were addressed by the bulk of the non-sensitive cases (i.e. those that were unlikely to reach the political or judicial sphere) being handled swiftly and informally by adjudication teams with higher case closure targets.

Hence, the FOS's control and reward structure was designed to balance its triple pursuit of swift case processing, decision quality, and complainants' satisfaction. This design took shape, and was readjusted, in response to threats posed by the organization's environment, and their deployment in internal struggles. The balance between the FOS's relative focus on efficiency, decision quality, and satisfaction was struck according to its ability to process cases rapidly, and meet high targets, at a low risk of external scrutiny and reputation damage. When the latter risks were higher, cases were handled by more experienced adjudicators, who were allowed to devote more time and resources to case investigation and to communication with firms and complainants (hereafter referred to as "full investigation").

More generally, our above analysis highlights that regulators' internal systems of control may operate as a means of balancing multiple and conflicting threats to their reputation, and as a locus of the struggle between conflicting visions of what the organization is about. This analysis underscores that the locus of regulators' management and the balancing of their reputations are not restricted to their public relations offices and to their interaction with journalists and other external overseers. Rather, from the FOS's point of view, and presumably that of other regulatory bodies, internal performance management was ultimately about forging, negotiating, and safeguarding their organizational identity and reputation.

Blame-Proofing via Rationalization

We have described how the FOS's internal control and reward system balanced the organization's multiple claims for—and risks to—reputation. In this section we go further to show how the FOS's choice of complaint-handling technologies—between case-by-case dispute resolution and standardized decision-making—oscillated in light of the risks to the organization's reputation.

High-quality decision-making, as understood within the FOS, involved judgment of each case according to its individual merits and circumstances (Gilad, 2008a). In handling complaints on a case-by-case basis, adjudicators employed individual judgment and discretion. While some guidance was available to adjudicators from the FOS's intranet, it was general and did not refer to specific firms and/or to particular products. This approach was rooted in the FOS's conceptualization of its role in terms of *individual* dispute resolution, and its differentiation of its role from that of the FSA and the civil courts.[4]

The FOS's management of complaints on a case-by-case basis had a number of potential advantages for the FOS, firms, and complainants. For firms it entailed that losing one case did not create an adverse precedent with necessary application to other complaints and transactions. Consequently, firms were generally amenable to informally settling complaints and paying redress, because each case was of relatively small consequence for them. For complainants, this approach meant that firms were more inclined to agree to informally settling complaints and paying out redress. From the FOS's point of view, insofar as case-by-case dispute resolution encouraged firms to agree to informal settlements, it lubricated the swift processing of the ombudsman's case backlogs (Gilad, 2009).

In spite of the FOS's general preference for case-by-case dispute resolution, when handling sensitive complaints of a systemic nature, complaint handlers pursued a standardized complaint-handling strategy. In these cases, adjudicators and their team managers tended to request detailed guidance from the ombudsmen and followed such guidance strictly when handling all relevant complaints (Gilad, 2009). This type of guidance would be in regard to a specific series of financial products that were sold by a particular firm. Wherever ombudsmen issued specific guidance to adjudicators, the latter tended to decide most relevant complaints in favor of the complainants (Gilad, 2010). Firms were disinclined to settle such complaints informally, and they tended to request formal ombudsman reviews of adjudicators' decisions. Firms' contestation of these decisions was rooted in their concern that the FOS's rulings, and their own agreement to settle complaints, would be interpreted by their regulator—the FSA—as an admission of liability that should apply to other similar complaints and possibly to all other transactions regarding the same products (Gilad, 2009). In other words, firms resisted the FOS's decisions in these cases due to their possible financial impact and the damage to their reputation vis-à-vis the FSA. Complaint handlers' formalization and rationalization of their handling of the relevant complaints exacerbated firms' anxiety, and therefore their resistance, as well as the industry's criticism that the FOS was acting as a de facto regulator.

While standardization exacerbated individual firms' resistance and collective industry criticism of the FOS, and thereby undermined the FOS's aim to process all complaints swiftly and informally, it protected other important aspects of the ombudsman's reputation. When handling new complaints of a systemic nature, adjudicators anticipated firms' appeals for an ombudsman's review if a complaint was upheld and they

---

[4] It can also be linked with broader ideologies of professional work as entailing judgment, which cannot be standardized (Freidson, 2001).

wanted to commit the ombudsman to their position in advance. Thus, individual adjudicators and their team managers tended to demand that ombudsmen provide them with specific guidance. Similarly, the ombudsmen were prepared to provide specific guidance, because they operated under the assumption that firms were likely to appeal for judicial review in these cases. The ombudsmen were therefore minded to avoid any inconsistent decisions regarding similar complaints, which could undermine their decisions in court. Finally, the FOS's executives anticipated political and media scrutiny of the FOS in these cases, and they therefore wanted to be able to explain the logic of the organization's decision-making. In short, the formalization and rationalization of the FOS's handling of these complaints were shaped by the concurring motivations of complaint handlers at all levels to safeguard their individual and organizational reputation vis-à-vis multiple internal and external stakeholders and formal overseers (Gilad, 2009, 2010).

In sum, we suggest that when facing or perceiving high risks to reputation, regulators are inclined to self-bind, formalize, and rationalize their use of discretion. To reiterate, the literature on blame avoidance suggests that formalization and rationalization of regulatory discretion is a prevalent phenomenon (see the discussion of "policy strategies" above). Such formalization and rationalization might be embedded in official risk-management systems (Black, 2005; Power, 2009), or in unofficial albeit institutionalized practices as in the FOS case. Rationalization tends to undermine regulators' capacity to adapt flexibly their interaction to the circumstances of individual cases, and to the specific motivations and capabilities of individual firms. It may also, as exemplified in the FOS case, pose risks to the reputations of regulated firms, thereby stirring their resistance. Yet, regulators value rationalization since it enhances their capacity to provide coherent explanations for what they are doing (and not doing) in the event of judicial, media, and/or political scrutiny.

CONCLUSION

Regulation is continuously being shaped and reshaped in light of the reputation risks that regulators face in their interactions with multiple stakeholders. Regulators' reputation-management strategies are therefore an important driver of regulatory policy and its implementation. We argue that such strategies are rooted in—and constrained by—regulators' organizational identities and in internal struggles over the aims and scope of regulation. This chapter contributes to existing regulatory literature by mapping and explicating the strategies that regulatory agencies employ in order to establish, maintain, and defend their reputations. It systematically juxtaposes, for the first time, existing categorization of blame-avoidance strategies and literature on regulatory reputation. Drawing on a case study of the British Financial Ombudsman Service (FOS) we argue that regulators' reputation-management strategies pertain to three broad spheres: regulatory task boundaries, regulatory communication, and regulatory operation.

Regulatory Task Boundaries (constructing a distinct reputation; "agency strate-gies"): Regulators seek to demarcate for themselves a reputation for the proficient execu-tion of a unique role, which is consistent with their internal identity. They might further seek to avoid tasks that carry high risk of reputation damage. However, they will not/ cannot forgo tasks that fall squarely within their constructed identity reputation, even when the execution of these tasks carries a high risk of failure and reputation damage. Resisting such tasks can itself damage their reputation. Ultimately, what falls within— and outside—the regulatory agency's domain is not a unilateral regulatory choice. It is a matter for incremental negotiation between the preferences and strategies of regulators and those of their multiple stakeholders and overseers.

Regulatory Communication (shaping public expectations; "presentational strate-gies"): Regulatory external communication serves as an integral part of regulation (e.g. providing consumers with information about firms),[5] and as a reputation-management tool. The latter includes raising public awareness of regulation, shaping stakeholders' perceptions of the value of regulation, and responding to criticism. In particular, how-ever, our analysis has highlighted that regulators use communication to shape the expec-tations of the public and politicians about what regulation can and cannot achieve. In so doing, regulators act strategically to counter future blame for failure. Yet, regulatory shaping of public expectations is not simply a matter of *external* public relations. It is rooted in regulators' internal identity regarding the appropriate boundaries of regula-tion. Nonetheless, as our analysis stresses, regulators' ability to align public expectations and perceptions (i.e. reputation) with their internal conceptualization of regulation (i.e. identity) is often limited.

Regulatory Operation (striking a balance between conflicting bases for reputation; "policy strategies"): Regulators' pursuit of reputation for the successful performance of a unique role, leads them to prioritize certain tasks over others. For instance, a regulator that conceptualizes its role and success in terms of legal enforcement will prioritize inspections and investigations of firms' breaches of regulation over education and com-munication. In addition, regulators balance between different aspects of their perform-ance (e.g. swift vs. accurate decision-making) in response to the relative reputation risks that they perceive at any one time. We have shown that this latter balancing exercise is reflected in institutional structures (e.g. control and reward structures) and triggered by internal struggles over the regulatory agency's identity.

Clearly, regulatory reputation-management strategies are not always consistent with regulatory identity. Under certain conditions, to safeguard their reputation vis-à-vis one set of audiences, regulators may act in ways that undermine their internal identity and core reputation. We have demonstrated this with regard to the FOS's formalization of its approach to the handling of new complaints of a systemic nature. This strategy was intended to protect the FOS's reputation when handling complaints that were likely to result in judicial review or in media and political scrutiny. Yet, it also exacerbated firms'

---

[5] For analysis of communication as a regulatory tool see Yeung (2005).

resistance, provoked industry criticism of the FOS, and run counter to the FOS's prefer-ence for swift and informal dispute resolution.

A further contribution of the above analysis, which goes beyond the specific field of regulation, is that it highlights the manifold spheres within which reputation manage-ment takes place. We are suggesting that the locus of reputation management is not con-fined merely to organizations' verbal communications, to their PR offices, or to their interactions with the media. Our analysis suggests that more attention should be given to the reputation-management aspects of organizations' internal controls and interper-sonal interactions with their customers and service users. For example, we have shown how the FOS's internal control system balanced the organization's competing claims for productivity, decision-making quality, and customer satisfaction in light of the relative risk that cases would end up experiencing judicial, media, or political scrutiny.

Finally, regulatory reputation-management strategies may have important implica-tions for the reputation of regulated firms. Regulators whose reputation depends on cooperative relationships with firms will focus their efforts on behind the scenes negotia-tions with firms, while keeping the threat of overt enforcement in the background. At the other end of the scale, regulators who nurture an identity reputation for firmness will put more resources into publicly visible enforcement, with adverse implications for the repu-tation of regulated firms. Nonetheless, regulators' choice between behind the scenes negotiations and visible enforcement actions is also a function of the different and changing environments within which they operate. Thus, in the aftermath of crisis and regulatory reputation damage, even regulators who put a high value on a cooperative relationship with firms may find it imperative to employ visible enforcement actions.

What is Next in the Nexus of Regulation and Reputation?

The research on regulatory reputation is still evolving, and various questions remain unanswered. The current section discusses the variety of future directions that might contribute to the scholarship of regulatory reputation and the implications for corporate reputation.

The Shaping of Regulatory Reputation Management

First, future research might look at the implications of regulatory reputation manage-ment on resource depletion and selective attention to tasks in the context of multitask regulators (or multifocal corporations). One significant research question might be: How much of regulators' attention to tasks is shaped by short-term changes in political and media signals, and how much is shaped by a relatively stable identity reputation that favors certain tasks, competencies, or traits over others? Another question might be: What shapes the variance between some regulators' responsiveness to short-term media and political signals, and others' consistent focus on certain tasks over others? For exam-ple, in the aftermath of the recent financial crisis, will reputation-anxious financial regu-lators shift their resources to the regulation of banks and mortgage selling (over firms' sale and management of insurance, deposits, and investment products)? If they do, this may result in short-term burden for certain industries relative to others, as well as in long-term neglect and regulatory failure in relation to less salient task domains (cf. May, Workman, & Jones, 2008).

Second, we have pointed to the scarcity of research regarding regulators' presentational and communication strategies. In particular, there is surprisingly little research of regulators' management of the media. Such research might ask: Under what conditions do regulators respond to stakeholders' criticism? What type of responses do they tend to offer? What is the explanation for the variance in their strategies? When are regulators' communication strategies shaped by the short-term salience of issues versus their stable concern to protect their reputation for certain competencies over others? Put differently: Do regulators respond to criticism when it is politically salient, or when it touches upon those tasks, competencies, or traits that they perceive as core to their identity and reputation?

Third, as we have shown, current literature is split between those who expect politicians, civil servants, and regulators to actively pursue a positive reputation for a unique trait or competence, in comparison with those who expect them to focus on avoiding and managing blame. More work needs to be done to unravel why some regulatory agencies cultivate a unique reputation, and why in order to do so they are willing to innovate and take risks, whereas others seek to minimize blame by shadowing similar agencies and adopting institutionalized processes and techniques regardless of their effectiveness.

Regulatory and Corporate Reputations and Cooperation

A vast literature examines corporations' multiple motivations for compliance and cooperation with (or resistance to) regulation. One shortcoming of this literature is its frequent portrayal of regulatory encounters as two-actor games between regulators and regulated firms, whilst overlooking regulators' and corporations' sensitivity to the expectations of their multiple audiences (Gilad, 2009). A reputation-centered lens on regulatory encounters calls for further exploration in two directions. The first question, which has already received some attention in extant literature, asks how the concern of regulators and corporations to build and maintain a positive reputation vis-à-vis third parties—investors, consumers, and so on—shapes their mutual cooperation. The second, less explored question asks how regulators' and corporations' conceptions of each other's reputation in the eyes of third parties shape their inclination to cooperate with or publicly challenge one another. In particular, how do firms' perceptions of the regulator's reputation in the eyes of investors, consumers, and politicians, impact upon their (dis-)inclination to comply, evade, or publicly challenge regulatory demands?

Regulatory Reputation and Public Perceptions of Regulators and Regulated Industries

The literature on regulation has largely focused on the interactions between—and the perceptions of—regulators and regulated firms. The perceptions and agency of the general public are largely missing in this literature (other than with regard to the small niche of public risk perceptions). A common assumption is to argue that regulation (or at least self-regulation) is a source of positive corporate reputation for regulated industries vis-à-vis investors and consumers. Yet the opposite can also be true inasmuch as regulatory enforcement damages the corporate reputation of individual firms, with potential spill-over for the reputation of other firms. One avenue for future research would be to assess how the reputation of regulators, in the eyes of investors and consumers, impacts upon the public's confidence or distrust in—and (dis-)inclination to transact with—regulated entities. Another research direction would be to assess the impact of regulatory reputa-tion on the public's inclination to air its dissatisfaction with regulated industries (cf. Gilad, 2008b).

Key Articles on Regulatory Reputation

References	Key findings
Regulatory Reputation	
Pursuing an exclusive and differentiated domain:	* Identity-reputation claims stress the agency's exclusive and differentiated domain
Carpenter (2001, 2010); Gilad (2008a); Maor (2011); Wilson (1989: ch. 10)	* Avoiding tasks outside the agency's asserted domain
Shaping public expectations: Gilad (2008b);	* Educating the public about the agency's role and its limitations
Black (2005)	* Managing gaps between external and internal perceptions of the agency's domain
Striking a balance between conflicting bases for reputation: Carpenter (2002, 2004); Maor & Sulitzeanu-Kenan (forthcoming)	* Regulatory outputs, as mediated via internal systems of reward and control, balance between conflicting facets of reputation
Blame Avoidance	
Agency strategies:	* Resisting tasks that carry high risk for blame
Hood, Rothstein, & Baldwin (2001); Hood (2007); Hood & Rothstein (2001); Sulitzeanu-Kenan & Hood (2005)	* Collaborating with others so as to diffuse responsibility
Blame avoidance:	* Fully or partially denying a problem exists
Hood (2007); Sulitzeanu-Kenan & Hood (2005)	* Fully or partially denying regulatory responsibil-ity for failure
Policy strategies:	* Formalizing and rationalizing regulatory discretion
Black (2005); Gilad (2009); Hood & Rothstein (2001); Hood, Rothstein, & Baldwin (2001); Hood (2007); Sulitzeanu-Kenan & Hood (2005)	* Withdrawing from performing a task within the agency's formal mandate.

References

Albert, S. & Whetten, D. (1985). "Organizational identity." *Research in Organizational Behavior*, 7: 263–295.

Beugge, C. (2003). "On the edge." *Daily Mail*, 15 October.

Black, J. (2005). "The emergence of risk-based regulation and the new public risk management in the United Kingdom." *Public Law*, 3: 512–548.

Bosch, J. C. & Lee, I. (1994). "Wealth effects of food and drug administration (FDA) decisions." *Managerial and Decision Economics*, 15: 589–599.

Braithwaite, J. (1989). *Crime, Shame, and Reintegration*. Cambridge, UK: Cambridge University Press.

Carpenter, D. P. (2001). *The Forging of Bureaucratic Autonomy: Reputations, Networks, and Policy Innovation in Executive Agencies, 1862–1928*. Princeton, NJ: Princeton University Press.

—— (2002). "Groups, the media, agency waiting costs, and FDA drug approval." *American Journal of Political Science*, 46: 490–505.

—— (2004). "Protection without capture: Product approval by a politically responsive, learning regulator." *American Political Science Review*, 98: 613–631.

—— (2010). *Reputation and Power: Organizational Image and Pharmaceutical Regulation at the FDA*. Princeton, NJ: Princeton University Press.

Davidson, W. N., Worrell, D., & Cheng, L. T. W. (1994). "The effectiveness of OSHA penalties: A stock-market-based test." *Industrial Relations*, 33: 283–296.

Feroz, E. H., Park, K., & Pastena, V. S. (1991). "The financial and market effects of the SEC's accounting and auditing enforcement releases." *Journal of Accounting Research*, 29: 107–142.

Financial Ombudsman Service (Great Britain) (2006). *Annual Review and Report & Financial Statements: 1 April 2005 to 31 March 2006*. London: Financial Ombudsman Service. Available online at http://www.financial-ombudsman.org.uk/publications/ar06/ar06-chief.htm.

Financial Ombudsman Service (Great Britain) (2009). "Publication of complaints data: What will we do." Available online at http://www.financial-ombudsman.org.uk/publications/policy-statements/complaint_data_mar09.html.

Fisse, B. & Braithwaite, J. (1983). *The Impact of Publicity on Corporate Offenders*. Albany, New York: State University of New York Press.

Freidson, E. (2001). *Professionalism: The Third Logic*. Cambridge: Polity.

Gilad, S. (2008a). "Exchange without capture: The UK Financial Ombudsman Service's struggle for accepted domain." *Public Administration*, 86: 907–924.

—— (2008b). "Accountability or expectations management? The role of the Ombudsman in financial regulation." *Law & Policy*, 30: 227–253.

—— (2009). "Juggling conflicting demands: The case of the UK Financial Ombudsman Service." *Journal of Public Administration Research and Theory*, 19: 661–680.

—— (2010). "Why the 'Haves' do not necessarily come out ahead in informal dispute resolution." *Law & Policy*, 32: 283–312.

Gunningham, N. A., Thornton, D., & Kagan, R. A. (2005). "Motivating management: Corporate compliance in environmental protection." *Law & Policy*, 27: 289–316.

Hood, C. (2002). "The risk game and the blame game." *Government and Opposition*, 37: 15–37.

—— (2007). "What happens when transparency meets blame-avoidance?" *Public Management Review*, 9: 191–210.

—— & Rothstein, H. (2001). "Risk regulation under pressure: Problem solving or blame shifting?" *Administration & Society*, 33: 21–53.

——, ——, & Baldwin, R. (2001). *The Government of Risk: Understanding Risk Regulation Regimes*. Oxford; New York: Oxford University Press.

Krause, G. A. & Corder, K. J. (2007). "Explaining bureaucratic optimism: Theory and evidence from U.S. executive agency macroeconomic forecasts." *American Political Science Review*, 101: 129–142.

—— & James, W. D. (2005). "Institutional design versus reputational effects on bureaucratic performance: Evidence from U.S. government macroeconomic and fiscal projections." *Journal of Public Administration Research and Theory*, 15: 281–306.

Maor, M. (2007). "A scientific standard and an agency's legal independence: Which of these reputation-protection mechanisms is less susceptible to political moves." *Public Administration*, 85: 961–978.

—— (2010a). "Organizational reputation and jurisdictional claims: The case of the US food and drug administration." *Governance*, 23: 133–159.

—— (2010b). "Organizational reputations and the observability of public warnings in 10 pharmaceutical markets." SSRN, Available online at http://papers.ssrn.com/sol3/papers.cfm?abstract_id=1527346.

—— (2011). "Organizational reputations and the observability of public warnings in 10 pharmaceutical markets." *Governance*, 24(3): 557–582.

—— & Sulitzeanu-Kenan, R. (forthcoming). "The Effect of Salient Reputational Threats on the Pace of FDA Enforcement Governance" (in press). *Governance*.

May, P. J., Workman, S., & Jones, B. D. (2008). "Organizing attention: Responses of the bureaucracy to agenda disruption." *Journal of Public Administration Research and Theory*, 18: 517–541.

Noll, R. G. (1985). "Government regulatory behavior—A multidisciplinary survey and synthesis." In R. G. Noll (Ed.), *Regulatory Policy and the Social Sciences*. Berkeley: University of California Press.

Olson, M. (1995). "Regulatory agency discretion among competing industries—Inside the FDA." *Journal of Law Economics & Organization*, 11: 379–405.

—— (1996). "Substitution in regulatory agencies: FDA enforcement alternatives." *Journal of Law, Economics, and Organization*, 12: 376.

—— (1997). "Firm characteristics and the speed of FDA approval." *Journal of Economics & Management Strategy*, 6: 377–401.

Parker, C. (2002). *The Open Corporation: Effective Self-Regulation and Democracy*. New York: Cambridge University Press.

Power, M. (2007). *Organized Uncertainty: Designing a World of Risk Management*. Oxford: Oxford University Press.

——, Scheytt, T., Soin, K., & Sahlin, K. (2009). "Reputational risk as a logic of organizing in late modernity." *Organization Studies*, 30: 301–324.

Rothstein, H., Huber, M., & Gaskell, G. (2006). "A theory of risk colonization: The spiralling regulatory logics of societal and institutional risk." *Economy and Society*, 35: 91–112.

Sants, H. (2010). "UK financial regulation: After the crisis: Financial services authority." Available online at http://www.fsa.gov.uk/pages/Library/Communication/Speeches/2010/0312_hs.shtml.

Sulitzeanu-Kenan, R. & Hood, C. (2005). "Blame avoidance with adjectives? Motivation, opportunity, activity and outcome." Unpublished Paper, University of Oxford.

Vogel, D. (2003). "The hare and the tortoise revisited: The new politics of consumer and environmental regulation in Europe." *British Journal of Political Science*, 33: 557–580.

Weaver, R. K. (1986). "The politics of blame avoidance." *Journal of Public Policy*, 6: 371–398.

Wilson, J. Q. (1989). *Bureaucracy: What Government Agencies Do and Why They Do It*. New York: Basic Books.

Yeung, K. (2009). "Presentational management and the pursuit of regulatory legitimacy: A comparative study of competition and consumer agencies in the United Kingdom and Australia." *Public Administration*, 87: 274–294.

CHAPTER 17

A LABOR OF LOVE? UNDERSTANDING THE INFLUENCE OF CORPORATE REPUTATION IN THE LABOR MARKET

WILLIAM S. HARVEY

TIMOTHY MORRIS

Although there is an established and growing literature on corporate reputation, our understanding of how it is shaped within the labor market is not well understood. This chapter fills this important gap through focusing on how different internal and external stakeholders affect an organization's reputation in multiple labor markets. In particular, the chapter emphasizes the way in which employees and potential employees form reputations, as well as what the consequences are for organizations. It is argued that professional service firms exemplify the type of organizations that rely particularly heavily on labor market reputation for their competitive success, through attracting and retaining talent, encouraging alumni to act as endorsers, and through building strong social ties with, and signaling, a high quality of service to clients. We argue that while the labor market is a significant space where reputation is built within professional service organizations, reputation does not necessarily hold the same level of significance in other types of markets and organizations.

INTRODUCTION

CORPORATE reputation is seen as important because it is an intangible asset that enables organizations to gain public recognition, charge premium prices, attract talented workers, enhance their access to particular markets, and attract investment (Fombrun &

Shanley, 1990; Rindova and Martins, Chapter 2, this volume). Intangible assets are diffi-cult to replicate because, as in the case of reputation, they are created over time and are a function of complex social relationships and exchanges between different stakeholders in various contexts (Mahon, 2002).

This chapter focuses on a particular area and form of reputation that has been rela-tively under-researched but is acknowledged to be important, namely reputation in the labor market. This includes the reputation of employing organizations among both potential and actual employees and vice versa. We proceed by focusing on the labor market, and in particular professional service organizations, as an exemplar of the sort of sector in which labor market reputation is said to be highly important. By considering why this is the case, we develop a broader argument about the conditions in which labor market reputation is likely to be considered critical for employing organizations.

In the context of this chapter, our working definition of corporate reputation is the reflective value that different stakeholders place on an organization based on both their preconceptions of and their direct experiences with the economic and social attributes of the organization. Of particular importance here is the fact that reputation is about what people both inside and outside of the organization think about the organization over time. In addition, these impressions are made not only by direct experiences, but also as a result of rumors and gossip through social networks. We are particularly inter-ested in the labor market and suggest that building and maintaining reputations within this space is critical for influencing the impressions of multiple stakeholders and there-fore helping organizations to gain a competitive advantage.

Labor Markets

Labor markets are the space where workers (labor supply) search for and compete with one another for paid employment, while employers search for workers (labor demand). Labor markets are where wages are determined and their scope stretches from the inter-national scale to the national, regional, and local scale. Labor markets may be structured in many different and overlapping ways, including, but not limited to, primary, second-ary, tertiary, and quaternary, and internal and external (Gospel, 2011). The structure of labor markets, arguably, may have implications for how and the extent to which they affect corporate reputation. The remainder of this section focuses on the ways in which primary and secondary labor markets, employees, as well as internal and external labor markets shape corporate reputation.

Primary and Secondary Labor Markets

Primary and secondary labor markets are understood in terms of the segmentation of employee rights (Doeringer & Piore, 1971). Primary jobs, for example, are well paid and long term, with good working conditions, employee rights, and legal support. In contrast, secondary jobs are poorly paid and short term, lacking good working conditions, employee rights, and legal support. Historically, primary jobs have been occupied by workers with high levels of skills and training, as well as groups who have been advantaged within certain countries, such as white males, whereas secondary jobs have been occupied by low-skilled workers and many groups who have been marginalized within certain countries, such as ethnic minorities, migrants and women. Typically, it can be difficult for workers to move between primary and secondary jobs.

Arguably, primary and secondary workers are not only segmented by their pay, working rights, and social mobility, but also in terms of their ability to influence corporate reputation. We show below that the structural variations in labor markets affect corporate reputation in various ways. As developed economies have shifted towards tertiary and quaternary activities, employees have, arguably, become increasingly important in shaping corporate reputation because they are directly linked to the value-added of the final product (Turban & Greening, 1997). The resource-based perspective, for example, argues that an organization's human capital contributes to its competitive advantage.

Employees

According to Hannon and Milkovich (1996), organizations with positive human resources (HR) reputations are able to attract more potential employees than organizations with lower HR reputations (see also Harvey, 2011). Organizations now also consider attracting high-quality employees as critical for their success, so much so that the term "war for talent" (Chambers et al., 1998; Guthridge, Komm, & Lawson, 2008) has been coined to describe the way in which organizations are competing with one another to attract and retain the best workers. In short, attracting and retaining employees is seen as important for generating corporate reputation and competitiveness.

Employees also affect corporate reputation in other ways, namely as ambassadors of the organization, as stipulating particular standards, and as influencing perception "from above." Gray & Balmer (1998) argue that a favorable corporate reputation in the eyes of employees is important for instilling morale and productivity within the workplace. Employees are also important because they frequently interact with external stakeholders and thus they should, arguably, be trained about how to engender a positive impression of the organization (Gray & Balmer, 1998: 700). Pruzan (2001) suggests that employees often demand high standards from their employers and in many cases will put pressure on them because they want to be proud of their workplace. Often employees consider their employer's reputation as more important than other criteria such as salary: "There is increasing evidence that the good employees demand more from their place of employment than a competitive wage, professional development, and a career path" (Pruzan, 2001: 53). Finally, senior employees of an organization can also have a strong influence on its reputation. We know, for instance, that a celebrity CEO's performance can increase an organization's reputation, at least in the short term, although this has been over-exaggerated by journalists (Hayward, Rindova, & Pollock, 2004). Graffin, Pfarrer, and Hill (Chapter 11, this volume) find that executive reputation is both similar to and different from an organization's reputation. In normal circumstances, they argue that both forms of reputation would converge over time, but when an organization experiences a "shock" such as a change in CEO or an organizational crisis then executive and organization reputation may diverge. These examples demonstrate how employees affect corporate reputation, particularly in an economic era of labor upskilling with a growing concentration on tertiary and quaternary economies.

Internal Labor Markets (ILMs) and External Labor Markets (ELMs)

ILMs have low staff turnover and encourage employee development and promotion as well as setting wages internally, whereas many ELMs have workers moving fluidly between organizations and wages are determined at a broader industry level (Lazear & Oyer, 2004). As a result, ILMs tend to have more internal control over labor markets than ELMs, which suggests that the former might also have greater control over its reputation within the labor market. An emphasis on ILMs and ELMs highlights the significance of multiple stakeholders in influencing corporate reputation. Fombrun (1996: 60), for example, argues:

> To build an enduring and resilient reputation, however, a company must establish strong relationships not only with customers but with other key constituents. After all, serving the customer goes only so far. A company also has to meet the expectations of its employees, investors, as well as the communities it serves.

He suggests that an organization's reputation derives from its relationships with seven audiences: customers, investors, employees, competitors, the local community, government, and the wider public. These relationships shape particular images that stakeholders hold of organizations, which combine to create a "reputational halo" (Fombrun, 1996: 194). Arguably, there are other important stakeholders that build an organization's reputation (see Table 17.1) and they can also be segmented into groups who have varying degrees of interaction with the organization. This is important because the level of interaction between an organization and different stakeholders is likely to influence the degree to which the latter shapes the former's reputation. Table 17.1, for instance, outlines a number of external, semi-external/internal, and internal stakeholders who are potentially important in shaping corporate reputation. Stakeholder theory suggests that there is a significant relationship between stakeholder ties and reputation. The argument that all stakeholders have value to organizations and no interests should dominate and the argument that organizations hold networks with many groups are just two examples of how internal and external labor markets are important in shaping reputation (Jones & Wicks, 2009).

Table 17.1 Segments of Stakeholders

External	Semi-external/internal	Internal
Customers	Former employees	Senior managers
Clients	Potential employees	Employees
NGOs/pressure groups	Board members	
Regulators	Shareholders	
Politicians	Subcontractors	
Competitors	Unions	
Communities	Joint venture partners	
Suppliers		
Universities/think tanks		

The issue of how far employees affect an organization's reputation can also vary significantly between internal and external labor markets. The literature on boundaryless careers suggests that workers are increasingly building their careers across multiple employers and therefore their employment choices are more influenced by ELMs than ILMs (Arthur & Rousseau, 1996). Bidwell and Briscoe (2010) argue that our understanding of how workers build careers that span multiple organizations is not well understood, and that despite the fact that the majority of workers remain within local labor markets (even if they are changing employers), there is a growing number of workers who are searching for jobs across regions and international borders. There are also a significant number of workers, namely internal company transferees, who remain within ILMs but cross international borders. Chang and Wang (1996) argue that organizations should avoid training workers with generic skills which are useful for other organizations because such workers are more likely to be poached by competitors. However, the hiring and firing of software engineers, for example, has been notorious in Silicon Valley (Arthur & Rousseau, 1996; Saxenian, 2006). Yet, it is unclear what impact high labor turnover within ELMs has for the reputations of organizations compared with low labor turnover within ILMs. Further research is needed to establish the degree to which ILMs and ELMs differ in their impact upon corporate reputation.

An important way that ILMs and ELMs are connected is through social networks because as workers build knowledge, skills, connections, and social capital, they improve their ability to be hired as well as their influence on the organization (Doeringer & Piore, 1971; Bidwell & Briscoe, 2010). As such, more senior employees, arguably, hold a strong degree of influence over an organization's reputation. This fits with the argument in the literature concerning the impact of executive reputation on organizational reputation (Graffin, Pfarrer, and Hill, Chapter 11, this volume). Rindova et al. (2005) found that US business schools increased their prestige with different stakeholders when they were affiliated with high-status actors, which highlights the significance of key individuals in bolstering institutional reputation. CEOs are also having an increasingly important role for the reputation of certain organizations. When, for example, Steve Jobs announced in

January 2009 that owing to illness he would be having a six-month leave of absence as CEO of Apple Inc., the share price of the company dropped by 10 percent. In the words of Kitchen & Laurence (2003: 116): "CEO reputation and corporate reputation are increasingly intertwined."

Labor Market Reputation

In a competitive labor market where employees are selecting among potential employers, the implication is that reputation can be a form of competitive advantage or disadvantage. The strength of this advantage or disadvantage depends on the criteria employees are using to judge employers in making employment choices (for instance, how important is reputation as opposed to location as a criterion for selecting a potential employer?), plus the general state of the labor market (loose or tight) and therefore how much choice employees have to select employers. Thus, labor market reputation is one factor that may assist organizations in becoming and remaining competitive.

Both the practitioner-based literature and academic literature note the importance of reputation in the labor market. As we discussed above, the former suggests reputation plays a part in the "war for talent" (Chambers et al., 1998; Guthridge, Komm, & Lawson, 2008) and is exemplified in ranking models such as "best employers" published by various media such as Vault. The latter focuses on the sources or antecedents of employer reputation and the effects or benefits (Fombrun, 1996; Dowling, 2001; Rindova et al., 2005). Relatively less research has been published on the extent to which, and the processes by which, organizations seek to manage their reputations in labor markets. Reputation within the labor market makes an important difference for organizations because it enables them to attract top talent, and keep employees committed and therefore hard working and less wage-sensitive.

It is worth noting why reputation concerns of potential or actual employees are distinctive from other areas of reputation. We noted above that stakeholder theory portrays labor as one of a number of groups with a legitimate interest in the activities of the organization. However, employees can be seen as both external and internal stakeholders. Externally, when potential employees are making judgments about the organization's reputation or when past employees are seen as exemplars of the organization, that is, in the terms used by Barnett, Jermier, & Lafferty (2006), where reputation is operating at the level of awareness and assessment. Internally, employees are also representatives of the organization and in that position are both upholding and creating the organization's reputation; that is, they are an asset in reputational terms (Barnett, Jermier, & Lafferty, 2006). Thus, employees can both create and evaluate the organization's reputation simultaneously. Arguably, employers can "borrow" reputation from employees and vice versa to enhance their reputation. For example, by hiring a high-status or celebrity CEO, or a star employee, there may be spillover effects such that organizations enhance their reputations among other stakeholders such as investors or clients (Khurana, 2002; Hayward, Rindova, & Pollock, 2004). Equally, within a partnership organization, a given office may use the human resources of another office as a way of borrowing reputation during a tender or when delivering a project. This means that labor market reputation is in some respects distinctive from other forms of reputation.

Research suggests that employer reputation is generated partly by the volume of publicity for an organization (Turban & Greening, 1997). However, this is not the only factor involved in decision-making by potential employees. For instance, in the market for graduate employees, while some of the key factors that drive students to apply to different organizations are understood, it is less well known how they form reputations of organizations. According to Turban & Greening (1997: 668):

> firms that were more familiar to potential applicants were larger; had more media exposure, larger advertising budgets, more positive CSP [corporate social performance], and more positive ratings for reputation and attractiveness as employers; and were more likely to recruit on campus.

Brooks & Highhouse (2006) suggest that through enhancing their name recognition, organizations can engender a "warm glow" amongst external stakeholders. Belt & Paolillo (1982) found a statistically significant correlation between organizations that had high corporate images and responses to a recruitment advertisement. In addition, those organizations that were more familiar on campus tended to have more positive reputations and were seen to be more attractive employers. Students at the University of Oxford also considered corporate reputation as very important when considering which organizations to apply to and accept jobs from (Harvey, 2011). Van Riel (1995) found that better known companies are rated higher in terms of reputation than less known organizations because their greater media visibility is often associated with a higher degree of importance perceived by the general public. McQuail (1985) found a similarly virtuous cycle, with the media providing greater coverage to organizations that they considered as being favored by the public, which leads to the public believing those organizations are more important because they receive greater media attention.

It is arguable that the value of reputation to employers varies across the labor market. Clearly, employers are not all equally concerned either to build a strong labor market reputation or devote resources to maintaining one. While some employers devote substantial resources to specific reputational strategies, for instance by creating and publicizing employee-friendly policies expressed in statements about espoused work/life balance principles, or ethical statements that are pitched at sympathetic employees as much as other stakeholders, others either do not follow such strategies or do not seek to publicize them to potential employees, that is, use them as a recruitment and retention strategy.

In short, some employers seek to compete on the basis of reputation in the labor market, even if this simply involves offering relatively high pay or career opportunities, while others do not. Understanding why this is, and the conditions under which a reputational strategy may pay off, offers a more nuanced means of conceptualizing reputation and the labor market. This variation links to the nature of the labor market and, specifically, the way it is segmented. To illustrate this, we examine an example of a sector where reputation is highly important, both in customer and in labor markets. We know that professional service organizations have a high turnover of labor (Morris & Pinnington, 1998; Løwendahl, 2005) and that quality is notoriously difficult to gauge because of informational asymmetries (Fombrun & Shanley, 1990; Rindova, Williamson, & Petkova, 2010). We also know that reputation within the labor market is particularly important within professional services because here an organization's reputation is largely predicated on the knowledge, social network, and presentational competencies of employees. Therefore, it represents a particularly good case example of the significance of labor market reputation.

> Questions of reputation are of particular concern to knowledge-based institutions like consulting firms, law firms, investment banks, hospitals, and universities; their most valuable assets—the services they provide—are largely intangible. Economists call the services of these groups "credence goods"—goods that are bought on faith, that is to say, on reputation. (Fombrun, 1996: 7)

Labor Market Reputation within Professional Service Organizations

Professional services is a sector where reputation within the labor market is particularly important. Hiring and retaining top talent, for example, is integral to the competitiveness of organizations since much of the work entails delivering knowledge-intensive services. Because knowledge is embedded in professional staff and delivered through individuals and teams of employees interacting with clients, hiring and retaining professional staff of the appropriate quality is linked to competitive success (Morris & Empson, 1998; Gardner, Anand, & Morris, 2008). Linked to this point, Greenwood et al. (2005) argue that professional staff are relatively mobile and therefore employers have to focus on policies by which they can not only attract but also retain them. Furthermore, in the process of production, professional staff not only generate customized solutions for clients but also form strong and enduring social networks with them (Greenwood et al., 2005). A lot of project-based work is secured through repeat purchase work with clients, and as a result building and enduring social ties with clients is critical for the long-term success of professional service organizations (Bolton, 1998; Chiou & Droge, 2006).

Employees may, over time, become clients meaning that numerous clients have experience with working inside professional service organizations. If managed successfully, former employees can act as ambassadors for their former employers, which is invaluable for securing work for the organization from the outside (Glückler & Armbrüster, 2003). These "alumni networks" have become a vital tool for securing projects for management consultancy organizations, given the "increased flow of consultants into managerial careers and the potential promotion of consulting practice within organizations" (Sturdy & Wright, 2008: 431). Many employees see this as a form of giving something back to their former employers, having gained important reputational capital from their experience. Taken together, these reasons mean that reputation through direct experience as well as through particular social networks is invaluable for professional service organizations seeking to gain a strategic advantage in the labor market.

Labor market reputation is also important because of the nature of the service, where quality is difficult for clients to assess directly. Von Nordenflycht (2010: 161) refers to the "opaque quality" in knowledge-intensive organizations when it is difficult for clients to judge the quality of the output. He argues that there are four ways of signaling quality to customers: bonding, reputation, appearance, and ethical codes. Bonding includes features that guarantee high quality through imposing sanctions on those that produce low quality. Reputation is a way of signaling high quality in opaque markets where quality is difficult to determine. Appearance of an organization or its employees is important because this is one of the facets that clients can more easily monitor. Ethical codes ensure that organizations maintain a certain level of conduct in order to protect the interests of the customer through professional associations.

In considering the implications of labor market reputation, Glückler and Armbrüster (2003: 276) distinguish between "spot-exchange commodities" and "knowledge-intensive services":

> In spot-exchange commodities it is the producer who takes on the risk of production measures because customers can see, compare, and often test the product prior to purchase (Levitt, 1981). Knowledge-intensive services, by contrast, are a case of deferred compliance, since the product will be generated in co-production only after the agreement is signed, and thus it is the client who takes on the primary risk.

The nature of professional services therefore means that clients take on a high degree of risk at the point of purchase. This explains why clients who are satisfied with previous projects might preference repeat purchases with the same professional service organization because it reduces the uncertainty of using a new organization. In addition, professional services are experience goods, in which there is typically an extended process of production in which the client co-produces the product and judgments about quality will entail more than technical features (Mills, Chase, & Margulies, 1983).

When clients re-engage with employees of professional service organizations, the attitude, body language, and delivery of service of the latter will either be consistent or inconsistent with the client's previous experience. If it is consistent then it will not change the view of the client and will confirm their previous beliefs and behavior. However, if it is inconsistent then clients have to make sense of any differences (Pfarrer, Pollock, & Rindova, 2010). Such a re-evaluation, which can be positive or negative, will affect the client's view of the company's reputation and will determine whether they decide to use the services of the same organization or look elsewhere. And since repeat work from clients is the most profitable for organizations because there are no marketing or other client acquisition costs, this reinforces the significance of forging and maintaining strong contacts with clients. All this is to say that employee relations with clients within the labor market are important for building corporate reputation in professional service organizations.

Greenwood et al. (2005) argue that reputation within professional service organizations is vital because it serves as a social signal in a client market that is rife with information asymmetry. Similarly, Davies & Miles (1998) argue that any gaps between the internal and external perceptions of an organization are particularly critical in service organizations when the interaction between employees and clients is an integral component of the quality of the service delivered. Dowling (1994: 92) also notes the possibility of reputational asymmetry but outlines the implications somewhat differently: organizations that identify a gap between what employees and external stakeholders think about an organization can prevent reputational crises. This highlights the significance of labor market reputation because if employees over- or under-emphasize the quality of their work compared with what clients think then this can cause a gap in perception, either positive or negative, which can have implications for the organization's overall reputation.

Uncertainty with respect to service quality, or the inability of clients to make good judgments over relative quality, has important implications for competition among professional service organizations (Starbuck, 1992). In these circumstances, clients may select an organization on the basis of its superior social ties (Glückler & Armbrüster, 2003: 280). Frequently, reputation resides with individual partners or in specific expertise-based practice groups, particularly within smaller organizations and markets, because these individuals have substantial experience of specific types of problem, understand client opportunities, and hold strong personal networks with this stakeholder group (Gardner, Anand, & Morris, 2008). Indeed, to achieve promotion to the most senior positions in these organizations, partners have to establish personal reputations, based on expertise in particular client problems and for delivering particular services (Gilson & Mnookin, 1985; Von Nordenflycht, 2010; Malhotra, Morris, & Smets, 2010). The consequence of these strong tie networks is that it is difficult for competitors and in particular new entrants to overcome the barrier of existing reputational advantages, but at the same time, it makes the professional service organization dependent upon particular individuals or groups. This emphasizes the important role of employees in shaping labor market reputation.

Within a professional service organization marketplace, information about quality at the level of the practice group or individual is complex and difficult to judge *ex ante*. "The challenge for a firm is to convince clients of its superior competence. The challenge for the client is to make sense of competing claims" (Greenwood et al., 2005: 663). Glückler and Armbrüster (2003: 280) suggest that "networked reputation" from trusted resources plays a crucial role by providing additional information about groups to whom individuals are not connected (see summary table at the end of the chapter). Similarly, Anand, Gardner, & Morris (2007) found that one means by which professionals could build new practice areas was to exploit the reputation of senior individuals for existing services or to exploit their reputations with close clients and co-create innovations that could then be marketed more widely. By contrast, organizations that have a damaged reputation experience greater difficulty obtaining new clients and maintaining existing ones (Wilson & Grimlund, 1990). Given the very specific and strategically important work of professional service organizations, as well as the difficulty in certain contexts of measuring the quality of their service, clients are often unable or unwilling to transfer reputation from one type of work to another, leading to what Greenwood et al. (2005: 665) refer to as "reputation stickiness." This suggests the vital role of employees in managing the expectations and perceptions of clients through building and establishing social networks.

To summarize, professional services are an example of a sector where reputation plays a critical role in terms of the client market and thus also the labor market. The purchasing decisions of clients are based strongly on reputation. In the literature it has been argued that this is because of information asymmetry favoring the producer about the "opaque quality" of professional services and the competence of those supplying them. The nature of the product, which is based on complex and customized solutions for clients who frequently engage with the professional service organization in the production process, makes judgments about the quality of the service beforehand difficult. The client therefore has to select among competing professional service organizations based on other factors, notably reputation in the marketplace built by transactions with other buyers.

Even if the assumption of information asymmetry does not hold for some important classes of client, such as corporations and investment banks, the reputation of individuals or expert practice groups based on experience of undertaking similar transactions or holding specific forms of know-how plays an important role in the selection of the professional service organization. Individuals or teams of professionals are therefore critical for organizational success because of the nature of the product and because of their importance in building client confidence through reputational judgments. Thus, finding and keeping individuals of appropriate quality is critical to the success of the organization and this means that its own reputation is important as an attraction device. Indeed, organizations signal this partly through the rigor of their selection policies and through the use of "up-or-out" promotion policies to select for partnership only those deemed to be of sufficient quality so that they can sustain and improve the reputation of the organization (Gilson & Mnookin, 1985; Malos & Campion, 1995; Morris & Pinnington, 1998).

CONCLUSIONS

This chapter has provided an overview of the literature on corporate reputation within labor markets. We suggest that labor market reputation is critical in helping organizations gain a competitive advantage. Attracting and retaining talent, improving brand awareness, establishing a strong reputation early, and understanding that the influence of reputation is segmented by skills, for example, are just a few areas where organizations could improve their labor market reputation, which in turn would bolster their competitiveness. Within the professional service sector, hiring and retaining talent, building strong social ties with clients, encouraging alumni to act as endorsers, maintaining reputation ownership, and highlighting the quality of service delivery to clients and non-clients in competitive markets are a few examples of how labor market reputation can help organizations to gain a strategic advantage.

Using professional service organizations as a case example, the general conclusions that can be drawn from this discussion help explain the conditions under which reputation in the labor market may be important to organizations and why. First, there are said to be general benefits for employers accruing from a strong reputation among actual or potential employees: these include lower hiring costs because the employer is operating in a buyer's market and does not have to expend the level of resources to attract a pool of candidates compared with other organizations. Second, high reputation is likely to mean that high-quality employees will seek to work with the employer, regardless of how quality is defined, because of the spillover effects of organizational reputation on individual employees. Third, the benefits of reputation offer employers resource-based advantages which they can convert into competitive superiority. These include lower labor turnover and higher commitment. Employees with high commitment expend higher discretionary effort, that is, they work harder, and show loyalty to the organization as well as sharing its values. In the case of professional service organizations, strong employee reputations are important because they are likely to attract and retain clients. Nonetheless, not all organizations can or will choose to invest in reputation formation or maintenance in order to seek these benefits.

Labor market reputation is most valuable to organizations that seek to compete on the basis of the quality of their employees or that are dependent on high-quality individuals for the delivery of particular services. These organizations are likely to operate in segments of the labor market in which individuals with relatively high skill levels and experience are located, or where the competence of the employee makes a substantial difference to product quality which is valued by customers. Examples would be service sectors which compete on the basis of customer experience or where particular forms of expertise are critical to the final product quality. On the other hand, there are many industries where employers do not seek to compete on the basis of labor quality and derive their employees from secondary sectors of the market. Or they operate with labor strategies in which they simply seek to minimize costs, for example by subcontracting and employing casual labor. Alternatively, these organizations simply do not have the resources to develop a strong labor market reputation, for example because they are not well endowed with unique resources, or are highly dependent on other organizations, or are insufficiently well connected to influential intermediaries within social networks. Many small organizations will fit into this category; others provide products or services in which reputation is simply not as important to buyers as price or convenience. In many areas of manufacturing, the labor process is designed to deskill tasks and to establish control through routines. These would be examples of areas, in contrast to those others we have discussed above, where reputation is unlikely to play an important role in the labor market.

FUTURE RESEARCH DIRECTIONS

There are a number of important implications stemming from this chapter that relate to ILMs and ELMs, different stakeholders, and professional service organizations. In terms of ILMs and ELMs, it is not clear whether internal stakeholders such as employees differ in how they form reputations of their employers. Nor is it evident to what extent external stakeholders such as potential employees vary in their attitudes towards organizations. This is important because current trends in the global economy suggest further segmentation in labor markets, with some organizations opting for expansion and recruitment from the global labor market, while others opt for consolidation and recruitment from national and local labor markets. This segmentation highlights that the labor market may influence corporate reputation in disparate ways depending upon its structure, but further research is needed to establish in what ways ILMs and ELMs shape corporate reputation.

Despite the important work of stakeholder theorists, it remains relatively unclear how various internal and external stakeholders affect an organization's reputation. *Fortune*'s influential "Most Admired Companies" survey (FMAC), for example, has been criticized for focusing on a narrow group of stakeholders (executives, directors, and securities analysts), yet few critics have explored in what ways these and other stakeholders differ in the impressions they hold towards organizations and what the economic and social impacts are. It is likely, to borrow and rephrase from George Orwell's *Animal Farm*, that "all stakeholders influence corporate reputation equally, but some influence corporate reputation more than others." However, further research is needed to determine the impact of different stakeholders on corporate reputation. This argument also applies to within stakeholder groups. Employees at various levels of an organization, for example, may hold markedly different impressions towards the same organization and therefore they should not necessarily be regarded as a homogeneous group.

Within professional service organizations, it is well known from the theoretical literature that quality is particularly difficult to judge because clients are unable to gauge quality before a project has been delivered and often have no direct comparison with other alternative services after it has been delivered because of the intangible nature of the sector. As a result, reputation is often an important dimension that clients consider when choosing a service provider because it acts as a signal of quality to many stakeholders. On the other hand, where clients hire from professional service organizations or are "educated" buyers because of their repeated experiences of selecting such organizations, this raises questions about how reputation is assessed, and, indeed, the focus of reputational assessment either at the level of the firm or the level of the individual partner who provides the service. Further work is required to explore how such judgments are made and their impact on decision-making.

Finally, this chapter has raised important questions about the transferability of reputation. A significant implication from this research is that certain internal and external stakeholders can help lend reputation. An important area for future research would be to explore the exact mechanisms and implications of borrowing reputation internally and externally, both for organizations as well as for individuals. If reputation is portable then this would suggest that it can vary over time and across geographical space, yet to date there has been little research on reputation with reference to time and/or geography.

Summarizing the Literature on Labor Markets, Reputation, and Professional Service Organizations

Reference	Key Constructs and Findings
Doeringer & Piore (1971)	Jobs are segmented into well-paid and secure (primary) and poorly paid and insecure occupations (secondary).
	Internal labor markets (ILMs) have low staff turnover and encourage employee development and promotion. External labor markets (ELMs) have workers moving between organizations and wages are set at an industry level.
Hannon & Milkovich (1996)	Organizations with positive HR reputations amongst potential employees are better able to attract talented workers.
Chambers et al. (1998); Guthridge et al. (2008)	Highly skilled professionals are essential in the war for talent. Within the marketplace, demand outstrips supply.
Pruzan (2001)	Talented employees expect a lot from their workplace and often reputation is more important than salary.
Hayward et al. (2004); Rindova et al. (2005)	The role of celebrity CEOs is significant for shaping corporate reputation, but it has been over-exaggerated by journalists.
Graffin et al. (Chapter 11, this volume)	Normally, executive and organizational reputation aligns, but during shock periods they may diverge.
Fombrun (1996)	Relationships with stakeholders lead to them holding multiple images of the organization which, when combined, create a reputational halo.
Arthur & Rousseau (1996)	Workers who have boundaryless careers build their employment experience across multiple organizations. Arguably, their impressions are shaped more by ELMs than ILMs.
Akerlof (1970); Fombrun & Shanley (1990)	Stakeholders have different levels of information. This is an important cue and signal when judging reputation, particularly when quality is difficult to gauge because of asymmetrical information.

Reference	Key Constructs and Findings
Belt & Paolillo (1982); Turban & Greening (1997); Harvey (2011)	Organizations that are publically known hold stronger reputations and therefore they receive a greater number of job applicants.
Glückler & Armbrüster (2003); Sturdy & Wright (2008)	Alumni networks are important for helping to promote professional service organizations as well as for gaining the support of former employees.
Greenwood et al. (2005)	Reputation stickiness is when clients are often unable or unwilling to transfer reputation from one practice area to another, or from one organization to another, because of the difficulty with measuring quality.

References

Akerlof, G. A. (1970). "The market for 'lemons': Quality uncertainty and the market mechanism." *The Quarterly Journal of Economics*, 84(3): 488–500.

Anand, N., Gardner, H. K., & Morris, T. (2007). "Knowledge-based innovation: Emergence and embedding of new practice areas in management consulting firms." *Academy of Management Journal*, 50(2): 406–428.

Arthur, M. B. & Rousseau, D. M. (1996). *The Boundaryless Career: A New Employment Principle for a New Organizational Era*. Oxford: Oxford University Press.

Ball-Rokeach, S. J. (1973). "From pervasive ambiguity to a definition of the situation." *Sociometry*, 36: 378–389.

Barnett, M. L. & Hoffman, A. J. (2008). "Guest editorial. Beyond corporate reputation: Managing reputational interdependence." *Corporate Reputation Review*, 11: 1–9.

—— & King, A. A. (2008). "Good fences make good neighbors: A longitudinal analysis of an industry self-regulatory institution." *Academy of Management Journal*, 51(6): 1150–1170.

——, Jermier, J. M., & Lafferty, B. A. (2006). "Corporate reputation: The definitional landscape." *Corporate Reputation Review*, 9(1): 26–38.

Belt, J. A. & Paolillo, J. G. P. (1982). "The influence of corporate image and specificity of candidate qualifications on response to recruitment advertisement." *Journal of Management*, 8(1): 105–112.

Bennett, R. & Gabriel, H. (2003). "Image and reputational characteristics of UK charitable organizations: An empirical study." *Corporate Reputation Review*, 6(3): 276–89.

Bergh, D. D., Ketchen Jr., D. J., Boyd, B. K., & Bergh, J. (2010). "New frontiers of the reputation-performance relationship: Insights from multiple theories." *Journal of Management*, 36(3): 620–632.

Bidwell, M. & Briscoe, F. (2010). "The dynamics of interorganizational careers." *Organization Science*, 21(5): 1034–1053.

Bolton, R. N. (1998). "A dynamic model of the duration of the customer's relationship with a continuous service provider: The role of satisfaction." *Marketing Science*, 17(1): 45–65.

Brammer, S. J. & Pavelin, S. (2006). "Corporate reputation and social performance: The importance of fit." *Journal of Management Studies*, 43: 435–455.

Bromley, D. B. (2000). "Psychological aspects of corporate identity, image and reputation." *Corporate Reputation Review*, 3(3): 240–252.

—— (2002). "Comparing corporate reputations: League tables, quotients, benchmarks, or case studies." *Corporate Reputation Review*, 5(1): 35–50.

Brooks, M. E. & Highhouse, S. (2006). "Familiarity breeds ambivalence." *Corporate Reputation Review*, 9(2): 105–113.

——, ——, Russell, S. S., & Mohr, D. C. (2003). "Familiarity, ambivalence, and firm reputation: Is corporate fame a double-edged sword?" *Journal of Applied Psychology*, 88: 904–914.

Campbell, A. & Alexander, M. (1997). "What's wrong with strategy?" *Harvard Business Review*, 75(6): 42–51.

Carmeli, A., Gilat, G., & Weisberg, J. (2006). "Perceived external prestige, organizational identification and affective commitment: A stakeholder approach." *Corporate Reputation Review*, 9(1): 92–104.

Chambers, E. G., Foulon, M., Handfield-Jones, H., Hankin, S. M., & Michaels, E. G. (1998). "The war for talent." *McKinsey Quarterly*, 3: 44–57.

Chang, C. & Wang, Y. (1996). "Human capital investment under asymmetric information: The Pigovian conjecture revisited." *Journal of Labor Economics*, 14(3): 505–519.

Chiou, J.-S. & Droge, C. (2006). "Service quality, trust, specific asset investment, and expertise: Direct and indirect effects in a satisfaction-loyalty framework." *Journal of the Academy of Marketing Science*, 34(4): 613–627.

Davies, G. & Chun, R. (2002). "Gaps between the internal and external perceptions of the corporate brand." *Corporate Reputation Review*, 5(2–3): 144–158.

—— & Miles, L. (1998). "Reputation management: Theory versus practice." *Corporate Reputation Review*, 2(1): 16–27.

——, Chun, R., & Kamins, M. A. (2010). "Reputation gaps and the performance of service organizations." *Strategic Management Journal*, 31: 530–546.

Dimaggio, P. J. & Powell, W. W. (1983). "The iron cage revisited: Institutional isomorphism and collective rationality in organizational fields." *American Sociological Review*, 48: 147–160.

Dirks, K. T., Lewicki, R. J., & Zaheer, A. (2009). "Repairing relationships within and between organizations: Building a conceptual foundation." *Academy of Management Review*, 34(1): 68–84.

Doeringer, P. & Piore, M. (1971). *Internal Labor Markets and Manpower Analysis*. Lexington, MA: D.C. Health.

Donaldson, T. & Preston, L. E. (1995). "The stakeholder theory of the corporation: Concepts, evidence, and implications." *Academy of Management Review*, 20(1): 65–91.

Dowling, G. R. (1994). *Corporate Reputations: Strategies for Developing the Corporate Brand*. London: Kogan Page Limited.

—— (2001). *Creating Corporate Reputations*. Oxford: Oxford University Press.

Dutton, J. E. & Dukerich, J. M. (1991). "Keeping an eye on the mirror: Image and identity in organizational adaptation." *Academy of Management Journal*, 34(3): 517–554.

Ellemers, N., Kortekaas, P., & Ouwerkerk, J. W. (1999). "Self-categorisation, commitment to the group and group self-esteem as related but distinct aspects of social identity." *European Journal of Social Psychology*, 29(2–3): 371–389.

Ferris, G. R., Perrewé, P. L., Ranft, A. L., Zinko, R., Stoner, J. S., Brouer, R. L., & Laird, M. D. (2007). "Human resources reputation and effectiveness." *Human Resource Management Review*, 17: 117–130.

Fombrun, C. J. (1996). *Reputation: Realizing Value from the Corporate Image.* Boston, MA: Harvard Business School Press.

Fombrun, C. J. & Shanley, M. (1990). "What's in a name? Reputation building and corporate strategy." *Academy of Management Journal,* 33(2): 233–258.

—— & Van Riel, C. B. M. (1997). "The reputational landscape." *Corporate Reputation Review,* 1(1/2): 5–13.

——, Gardberg, N. A., & Sever, J. M. (2000). "The reputation quotient: A multiple stakeholder measure of corporate reputation." *Journal of Brand Management,* 7(4): 241–255.

Freeman, R. E. (1984). *Strategic Management: A Stakeholder Approach.* Boston, MA: Pitman.

—— (1999). "Divergent stakeholder theory." *Academy of Management Review,* 24(2): 233–236.

Fryxell, G. E. & Wang, J. (1994). "The fortune corporate reputation index: Reputation for what?" *Journal of Management,* 20(1): 1–14.

Gabbioneta, C., Ravasi, D., & Mazzola, P. (2007). "Exploring the drivers of corporate reputation: A study of Italian securities analysts." *Corporate Reputation Review,* 10(2): 99–123.

Gardner, H. K., Anand, N., & Morris, T. (2008). "Chartering new territory: Diversification, legitimacy, and practice area creation in professional service firms." *Journal of Organizational Behavior,* 29: 1101–1121.

Gilson, R. J. & Mnookin, R. H. (1985). "Sharing among the human capitalists: An economic inquiry into the corporate law firm and how partners split profits." *Stanford Law Review,* 37(2): 313–392.

Gioia, D. A. (1999). "Practicability, paradigms, and problems in stakeholder theorizing." *Academy of Management Review,* 24(2): 228–232.

Glückler, J. (2007). "Geography of reputation: The city as the locus of business opportunity." *Regional Studies,* 41(7): 949–961.

—— & Armbrüster, T. (2003). "Bridging uncertainty in management consulting: The mechanisms of trust and networked reputation." *Organization Studies,* 24(2): 269–297.

Goins, S. & Gruca, T. S. (2008). "Understanding competitive and contagion effects of layoff announcements." *Corporate Reputation Review,* 11(1): 12–34.

Gospel, H. (2011). "Labour markets in theory and practice. Perspectives from Western industrial countries." In J. Benson & Y. Zhu (Eds.), *The Dynamics of Asian Labour Markets. Balancing Control and Flexibility.* London: Routledge.

Gotsi, M. & Wilson, A. M. (2001). "Corporate reputation: Seeking a definition." *Corporate Communications: An International Journal,* 6(1): 24–30.

Gray, E. R. & Balmer J. M.T. (1998) "Managing Corporate Image and Corporate Reputation". *Long Range Planning,* 31(5): 695–702.

Greenwood, R. & Suddaby, R. (2006). "Institutional entrepreneurship in mature fields: The big five accounting firms." *Academy of Management Journal,* 49: 27–48.

——, Li, S. X., Prakash, R., & Deephouse, D. L. (2005). "Reputation, diversification, and organizational explanations of performance in professional service firms." *Organization Science,* 16(6): 661–673.

Guthridge, M., Komm, A., & Lawson, E. (2008). "Making talent a strategic priority." *McKinsey Quarterly,* 1: 49–59.

Hall, R. (1992). "The strategic analysis of intangible resources." *Strategic Management Journal,* 13: 135–144.

Hannon, J. M. & Milkovich, G. T. (1996). "The effect of human resource reputation signals on share prices: An event study." *Human Resource Management,* 35(3): 405–424.

Hansen, M. T., Nohria, N., & Tierney, T. (1999). "What's your strategy for managing knowledge?" *Harvard Business Review,* 77(2): 106–116.

Harvey, W. S. (2011). "How do University of Oxford students form reputations of companies?" *Regional Insights*, 2: 12–13.

Hayward, M. L. A., Rindova, V. P. A., & Pollock, T. G. (2004). "Believing one's own press: The causes and consequences of CEO celebrity." *Strategic Management Journal*, 25: 637–653.

Helm, S. (2007). "One reputation or many? Comparing stakeholders' perceptions of corporate reputation." *Corporate Communications: An International Journal*, 12(3): 238–254.

——(2009). "Corporate reputation as anticipated corporate conduct—Introduction to the AMJ special issue." *Australasian Marketing Journal*, 17(2): 65–68.

Highhouse, S., Brooks, M. E., & Gregarus, G. (2009). "An organizational impression management perspective on the formation of corporate reputations." *Journal of Management*, 35(6): 1481–1493.

Jensen, M. C. (2001). "Value maximisation, stakeholder theory, and the corporate objective function." *European Financial Management*, 7(3): 297–317.

Jones, T. M. & Wicks, A. C. (1999). "Convergent stakeholder theory." *Academy of Management*, 24(2): 206–221.

Khurana, R. (2002). *Searching for a Corporate Savior: The Irrational Quest for Charismatic CEOs*. Princeton, NJ: Princeton University Press.

Kitchen, P. J. & Laurence, A. (2003). "Corporate reputation: An eight-country analysis." *Corporate Reputation Review*, 6(2): 103–117.

Lazear, E. P. & Oyer, P. (2004). "Internal and external labor markets: A personnel economics approach." *Labour Economics*, 11: 527–554.

Levitt, T. (1981). "Marketing intangible products and product intangibles." *Harvard Business Review*, 59: 94–102.

Lewellyn, P. G. (2002). "Corporate reputation: Focusing the Zeitgeist." *Business and Society*, 41(4): 446–455.

Lewicki, R. J. & Bunker, B. B. (1996). "Developing and maintaining trust in work relationships." In R. M. Kramer & T. R. Tyler (Eds.), *Trust in organizations: Frontiers of Theory and Research*. Thousand Oaks, CA: Sage, 114–139.

Løwendahl, B. (2000). *Strategic Management of Professional Service Firms*. Copenhagen: Copenhagen Business School Press.

Mahon, J. F. (2002). "Corporate reputation. A research agenda using strategy and stakeholder literature." *Business & Society*, 41(4): 415–445.

Malhotra, N., Morris, T., & Smets, M. (2010). "New career models in UK professional service firms: From up-or-out to up-and-going-nowhere?" *The International Journal of Human Resource Management*, 21(9): 1396–1413.

Malos, S. B. & Campion, M. A. (1995). "An options-based model of career mobility in professional service firms." *Academy of Management Review*, 20(3): 611–645.

Marsden, P. V. & Campbell, K. E. (1984). "Measuring tie strength." *Social Forces*, 63(2): 482–501.

McQuail, D. (1985). "Sociology of mass communication." *Annual Review of Sociology*, 11: 93–111.

Mills, P. K., Chase, R. B., & Margulies, N. (1983). "Motivating the client/employee system as a service production strategy." *Academy of Management Review*, 8(2): 301–310.

Morris, T. & Empson, L. (1998). "Organizations and expertise: An exploration of knowledge bases and the management of accounting and consulting firms." *Accounting, Organizations and Society*, 23: 609–624.

Morris, T. & Pinnington, A. (1998). "Promotion to partner in professional service firms." *Human Relations*, 51(1): 3–24.

Pfarrer, M. D., Pollock, T. G., & Rindova, V. P. (2010). "A tale of two assets: The effects of firm reputation and celebrity on earnings surprises and investors' reactions." *Academy of Management Journal*, 53(5): 1131–1152.

Podnar, K. (2004). "Is it all a question of reputation? The role of branch identity (the case of an oil company)." *Corporate Reputation Review*, 6(4): 376–387.

Podolny, J. M. (1993). "A status-based model of market competition." *American Journal of Sociology*, 98: 829–872.

Pratt, M. G. (1998). "To be or not to be? Central questions in organizational identification." In D. A. Whetten & P. C. Godfrey (Eds.), *Identities in Organizations: Building Theory Through Conversation*. Thousand Oaks, CA: Sage, 171–207.

Pruzan, P. (2001). "Corporate reputation: Image and identity." *Corporate Reputation Review*, 4(1): 50–64.

Roberts, P. W. & Dowling, G. R. (2002). "Corporate reputation and sustained superior financial performance." *Strategic Management Journal*, 23: 1077–1093.

Rhee, M. & Valdez, M. E. (2009). "Contextual factors surrounding reputation damage with potential implications for reputation repair." *Academy of Management Review*, 34(1): 146–168.

Rindova, V. P. (1997). "The image cascade and the formation of corporate reputations." *Corporate Reputation Review*, 1(1/2): 188–194.

—— & Fombrun, C. J. (1999). "Constructing competitive advantage: The role of firm-constituent interactions." *Strategic Management Journal*, 20: 691–710.

——, Williamson, I. O., Petkova, A. P., & Sever, J. M. (2005). "Being good or being known: An empirical examination of the dimensions, antecedents, and consequences of organizational reputation." *Academy of Management Journal*, 48: 1033–1049.

——, Petkova, A. P., & Kotha, S. (2007). "Standing out: How new firms in emerging markets build reputation." *Strategic Organization*, 5(1): 31–70.

——, Williamson, I. O., & Petkova, A. P. (2010). "Reputation as an intangible asset: Reflections on theory and methods in two empirical studies of business school reputations." *Journal of Management*, 36(3): 610–619.

Rowley, T. J. (1997). "Moving beyond dyadic ties: A network theory of stakeholder influences." *Academy of Management Review*, 22(4): 887–910.

Saxenian, A. (2006). *The New Argonauts: Regional Advantage in a Global Economy*. Cambridge, MA: Harvard University Press.

Starbuck, W. H. (1992). "Learning by knowledge intensive firms." *Journal of Management Studies*, 29: 713–740.

Strong, K. C., Ringer, R. C., & Taylor, S. A. (2001). "The* rules of stakeholder satisfaction (*timelineness, honesty, empathy)." *Journal of Business Ethics*, 32: 219–230.

Sturdy, A. & Wright, C. (2008). "A consulting diaspora? Enterprising selves as agents of enterprise." *Organization*, 15(3): 427–444.

Tirole, J. (1996). "A theory of collective reputations." *Review of Economic Studies*, 63: 1–22.

Turban, D. B. & Greening, D. W. (1997). "Corporate social performance and organizational attractiveness to prospective employees." *Academy of Management Journal*, 40(3): 658–672.

Turner, J. C. (1982). "Towards a cognitive redefinition of the social group." In H. Taifel (Ed.), *Social Identity and Intergroup Relations*. Cambridge: Cambridge University Press, 15–40.

Van Riel, C. B. M. (1995). *Principles of Corporate Communication*. Hemel Hempstead, UK: Prentice Hall Europe.

Von Nordenflycht, A. (2010). "What is a professional service firm? Toward a theory and taxonomy of knowledge-intensive firms." *Academy of Management Review*, 35(2): 155–174.

Walker, K. (2010). "A systematic review of the corporate reputation literature: Definition, measurement, and theory." *Corporate Reputation Review*, 12(4): 357–387.

Washington, M. & Zajac, E. J. (2005). "Status evolution and competition: Theory and evidence." *Academy of Management Journal*, 48: 281–296.

Weigelt, K. & Camerer, C. (1988). "Reputation and corporate strategy: A review of recent theory and applications." *Strategic Management Journal*, 9: 443–454.

Wilson, T. E. & Grimlund, R. A. (1990). "An examination of the importance of an auditor's reputation." *Auditing: A Journal of Practice and Theory*, 9(1): 43–59.

Zuckerman, E. W. (2000). "Focusing the corporate product: Securities analysts and de-diversification." *Administrative Science Quarterly*, 45: 591–619.

CHAPTER 18

DOES REPUTATION WORK TO DISCIPLINE CORPORATE MISCONDUCT?

JONATHAN M. KARPOFF

In theory, reputational losses can penalize and deter corporate misconduct. But do they? This chapter surveys and summarizes empirical research on the importance of reputational penalties for corporate misconduct. For some types of misconduct, including financial misrepresentation and consumer fraud, reputational losses are large—indeed, much larger than such direct costs as regulatory fines and private lawsuits. These losses manifest as costly disruptions in the firm's management, decreases in revenues, and increases in the cost of capital.

For other types of misconduct, such as environmental violations, reputational losses are negligible. These results indicate that market-based reputational losses accrue when a firm's opportunistic behavior causes its counterparties to change the terms of contract, causing the firm to lose sales and face higher input costs. Reputational losses do not accrue when the harmed parties do not have ongoing business relationships with the firm.

INTRODUCTION

FEW matters of economic policy are as contentious as the extent and consequences of business misconduct. "They lie, they cheat, they steal, and they've been getting away with it too long," claims *Fortune* magazine about financial fraud. *The Times* of London agrees: "The threat of fines…has proved laughably inadequate in producing better behaviour." Such views are at the root of recent efforts to increase government oversight of financial reporting and corporate governance, including the US Sarbanes-Oxley Act of 2002 and the US Dodd-Frank Act of 2010.

A counterargument is that even the taint of misconduct is extremely costly for firms. PricewaterhouseCooper contends that, in addition to exposing "companies, their boards of directors, and senior management to criminal and civil liability... [Fraud] can significantly damage retail & consumer companies' most valuable assets—their reputation."[1] Some researchers argue that concerns about poor reputation can encourage firms to limit the environmental impact of their activities (e.g., Kennedy, Chok, and Liu, Chapter 4, this volume).

Both arguments are at least partially correct. As Oliver Williamson (1984: 198) notes, firms sometimes "lie, cheat, steal, mislead, disguise, obfuscate, feign, distort, and confuse" to increase profits. But as Klein & Leffler (1981) and Shapiro (1983) show theoretically, firms with reputations for bad behavior can lose customers and face higher costs. In theory, the threat of lost reputation can discipline managers and provide incentives for legal and honest dealing. But does such theory work in practice?

This chapter examines the empirical research on corporate reputation. As with many contentious issues, a good starting point is with the terms of dialogue.[2] The second section proposes a definition of "business reputation" that facilitates both a theoretical basis for understanding the role that reputation plays and a way to measure its importance. Direct measures of a company's reputation remain empirically challenging, so the research literature has approached this issue indirectly, by measuring the *lost* reputation when firms lie, cheat, and steal. The third and fourth sections examine lying and cheating on corporations' financial statements, while the fifth section examines the value of lost reputation in other types of misconduct, including consumer fraud, environmental violations, and product recalls.

On the surface the evidence appears mixed, with reputational losses being important for some types of misconduct (e.g., financial misrepresentation, consumer fraud) but negligible for other types (e.g., environmental violations). In the sixth and seventh sections I argue that the results do, in fact, follow a pattern. The key to understanding such apparently mixed results is to note that reputational losses occur when a firm's counterparties—that is, its customers, suppliers, employees, and investors—change the terms by which they are willing to do business with the firm. Counterparties make such changes when they believe that the chance of being harmed by a firm's opportunistic behavior increases. Customers who discovered that BeechNut cheated consumers of its baby food products, for example, decreased their demand for BeechNut's products (see Jennings, 2006: 551). And investors who discover that a firm's financial statements are in error decrease their demands for that firm's debt and equity, raising the firm's cost of capital (see Graham, Li, & Qiu, 2008). Notice that customers and investors need not consciously seek to discipline a firm for its misconduct. Rather, by guarding their own interests against the possibility of being cheated, they offer a firm less attractive terms of trade.

---

[1] See http://www.pwc.com/us/en/retail-consumer/publications/protecting-retail-consumer-fraud.jhtml (accessed 13 December 2011).

[2] The meaning of corporate reputation is a topic of much discussion, e.g., see Barnett, Jermier, & Lafferty (2006) and Foreman, Whetten, and Mackey (Chapter 9, this volume).

This helps to explain why reputational losses are not uniformly large and important across all types of misconduct. Environmental violations, for example, harm parties other than the ones with whom a firm does business. Downstream fishermen are damaged if an electroplating company dumps toxic chemicals into a municipal storm sewer. But the fishermen do no business with the firm, and the firm's customers have no direct incentive to lower their demands for the firm's products if the dumping does not affect the quality of those products. As a result, the polluting electroplating company experiences no reputational losses.

In short, the research that I review in this chapter indicates that reputation does indeed matter, but not uniformly across all types of corporate activities. This raises several questions about how and when reputation helps to guarantee honest dealing and discipline opportunistic behavior. The concluding section in this chapter identifies six areas for future research in this area.

What is Reputation?

Merriam-Webster.com defines reputation as "overall quality or character as seen or judged by people in general." In this sense, businesses as well as people have reputations, some better than others. Much useful discussion about corporations' reputations relies on similar definitions (e.g., see Roberts & Dowling, 2002).

In this chapter I take a different approach. To judge how important reputation is, we need a way to measure it, or at least to measure its loss. This requires a more specific definition of reputation. I define reputation as the present value of the cash flows earned when an individual or firm eschews opportunism and performs as promised on explicit and implicit contracts. Stated differently, reputation is the value of the quasi-rent stream that accrues when counterparties offer favorable terms of contract because they believe the firm will not act opportunistically toward them.

This definition follows theoretical models by Klein & Leffler (1981), Shapiro (1983), and Karpoff & Lott (1993). It is consistent also with the discussion of reputation by Noe (Chapter 6, this volume), and with Rindova's and Martins's (Chapter 2, this volume) definition of reputation as a "strategic intangible asset." In Klein and Leffler's model, reputation—and reputation alone—encourages good behavior and disciplines bad behavior. The upshot is that people and businesses can invest in reputation, just as they might invest in machinery, R&D, or human capital. Viewed this way, reputation is a valuable asset. It is the present value of the improvement in net cash flow and lower cost of capital that arises when a firm's counterparties trust that the firm will uphold its explicit and implicit contracts, and will not act opportunistically to their detriment.[3]

---

[3] This definition of reputation is proposed by Karpoff & Lott (1993). Klein & Leffler (1981) do not use the term "reputation." Nonetheless, the reputation loss that is measured in the empirical research summarized below can be modeled as W2 in the Klein–Leffler model.

Reputational capital is not transparent on a firm's balance sheet, but circumstantial evidence suggests that it is important. For example, Beatty, Bunsis, & Hand (1998) find that investment banks with high reputation obtain higher fees for their services. Resnick et al. (2006) find that high-reputation sellers on eBay get higher prices than others, even for the same goods. Atanasov, Ivanov, & Litvak (2011) find that venture capital firms that are sued by their business partners subsequently lose financing and business.

Nonetheless, as Dowling and Gardberg (Chapter 3, this volume) discuss, measuring the size of a firm's reputational capital is difficult, and we have little direct evidence on its size for most firms. To get around the measurement problem, researchers have used a different kind of experiment to infer the importance of reputation to firms. This experiment examines the counterexamples—that is, instances in which people or firms *lose* reputation by lying, cheating, or stealing. To the extent that such losses are large, we can infer whether, and where, reputation matters.

One view is that a reputational loss as simply one of several types of bad consequences for business misconduct, on a par with consumer boycotts, lowered credit ratings, or stock price declines. My definition of reputational loss differs from this. If consumers boycott a firm, the loss in sales is one way in which a reputation loss occurs; likewise if a firm's credit ratings are lowered and its cost of capital increases. That is, the size of the reputation loss includes the value of the lost sales and the value impact of a change in a firm's cost of capital. Notice that, viewed this way, a stock price decline is not a sanction imposed by investors for a firm's misconduct. Rather, a stock price decline is a measure of investors' expectations of the total net costs to the firm from the news of its misconduct. Stated differently, a stock price decline is not a reputational loss, but it is a measure of a firm's total losses, which may include a reputational loss.

MEASURING REPUTATION LOSSES—AN EXAMPLE

Figure 18.1 shows the cumulative daily market-adjusted returns on Xerox common stock from 1997 through 2006. The (split-adjusted) share price closed on January 2, 1997 at $22.38, and closed on December 29, 2006 at $15.97. Returns were positive from early 1997 through most of 1999, with the share price peaking at $56.60 on May 3, 1999. But then the wheels fell off and share prices tumbled beginning in late 1999, reaching a low of $4.05 on October 9, 2002. Overall, Xerox shareholders had a bad decade.

It turns out that in early 1997 Xerox began to inflate its reported earnings by accelerating its recognition of revenue on its equipment lease contracts. Rather than recognizing revenue when lease payments were made, it booked the full stream of expected lease payments when the lease agreement was made. The effect was to increase near-term revenue and earnings. This reporting strategy helped to boost Xerox's share price through much of 1999. Xerox's revenue-accelerating reporting scheme, however, came with a built-in flaw. The only way such a scheme can work and not be discovered is if the company generates sufficiently high real growth to make up for, and to cover up, the eventual

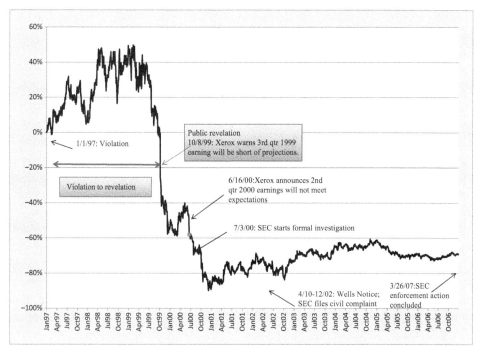

FIGURE 18.1 Xerox's cumulated market-adjusted stock return, 1997–2006.

shortfall in future periods' revenues. Xerox was unable to generate such high sales growth, and eventually it had to recognize that it would not be able to cover up its aggressive reporting practice. On October 8, 1999, the firm announced that its third-quarter earnings would not meet projections. Investors correctly inferred that the announcement was only the tip of a larger problem, and the stock price fell dramatically. In the ensuing months Xerox made additional disclosures of earnings shortfalls. The U.S. Securities and Exchange Commission (SEC) launched an investigation of Xerox's reporting practices in 2000, and eventually the firm was penalized for misrepresenting its financial statements.

As illustrated in Figure 18.1, Xerox's misleading financial reports did work—temporarily—to boost its share price. Using the measurement procedure used by Karpoff, Lee, & Martin (2008b)—and discussed below—Xerox artificially inflated its market capitalization by a total of $1.039 billion, from $15.725 billion to $16.864 billion. We should expect that when the revenue-accelerating financial reporting practice was revealed to the public, Xerox's share price should have dropped to wipe out this artificial share price inflation. This would have brought the share price back to where it would have been if the financial reports had never been in error.

As revealed in Figure 18.1, however, Xerox's share price did not simply go back to wipe out the artificial share price inflation—*it fell much further*. Again using the Karpoff, Lee, & Martin (2008b) method, the total loss in Xerox's market capitalization when investors learned about its misconduct, adjusted for market-wide price movements, was $5.0 billion. This is nearly five times the artificial share price inflation. Why did the share price fall so far?

Figure 18.2 illustrates the nature of Xerox's losses in a way that helps to answer this question. It is a stylized representation of the overall impact on Xerox's market capitalization of the misrepresentation and its discovery. During the period that Xerox misrepresented its revenues and earnings, its share values increased. This is illustrated by the upward sloping line. Immediately before Xerox announced that third-quarter 1999 earnings would be less than previously forecast, the firm's market capitalization was $16.864 billion. The cumulated loss in market capitalization, measured over the sequence of events by which investors learned of the misconduct, was $5 billion. This left the company with a market capitalization (adjusted for market-wide movements) of $11.864 billion.

Of the $5 billion loss, only $1.039 billion, or 20.8 percent, is the reversal of the artificial share price inflation. This represents the share value returning to the level at which, hypothetically, it would have been if no misrepresentation had occurred. An additional $0.523 billion of the loss can be attributed to amounts Xerox paid in fines and to settle a class action lawsuit. The rest of the loss—$3.44 billion—is due to something else. The most plausible explanation is that most of the $3.44 billion is due to impaired operations because of the revelation of misconduct—what I call "the reputational loss."

What are these impaired operations? First, the discovery of financial misconduct can impair the firm's operations if its managers are indicted, lose their jobs, or divert time and energy to the investigation rather than attending to company business. The investigation also could force the firm to adopt new monitoring and control policies that increase its cost of operations. Such higher costs of operation will lower the firm's future earnings and result in a lower current value.

Second, the news can change the company's cost of capital. The fact that the firm's officers furnished misleading financial information indicates that the company has poor internal controls, managers who behave opportunistically, or both. Such information

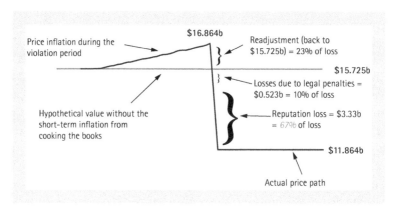

FIGURE 18.2 Xerox's loss partitioned into components for share deflation, legal penalties, and reputational loss.

can cause the firm's investors and other stakeholders to change the terms with which they are willing to do business with the firm. Graham, Li, & Qiu (2008), for example, find that lenders charge higher interest rates to firms whose financial reports or internal controls are suspect.

And third, news of firm misconduct could even change its cash flow from operations. As we will see, this is particularly relevant for firms that act opportunistically to cheat their customers or employees. They lose customers or face higher contracting costs.

All three of these effects contribute to the firm's reputational loss. The reputational loss is the present value of the higher costs and/or lower revenues when firms are discovered to have cheated their investors, suppliers, employees, or customers. It occurs because of direct impairments to the firm's ongoing operations, and also because counterparties alter the terms with which they are willing to continue to do business with the firm.

MEASURING REPUTATION LOSSES TO FINANCIAL MISCONDUCT—LARGE SAMPLE EVIDENCE

Share Price Impacts

I chose the Xerox example because it illustrates the results from a broader sample of firms. Karpoff, Lee, & Martin (2008b) measure the impact on share values of SEC enforcement actions for financial misrepresentation from 1978 through September 2006. Their sample of 585 enforcement actions represents all SEC actions for violations of requirements that firms keep accurate books and records (15 U.S.C. §§ 78m(b)(2)(A)) and maintain a system of internal accounting controls (15 U.S.C. §§ 78m(b)(2)(B)).

Most SEC enforcement actions follow a conspicuous trigger event that publicizes the potential for misconduct and attracts the SEC's scrutiny. Trigger events include self-disclosures of malfeasance, restatements, auditor departures, unusual trading, and whistle-blower lawsuits. Karpoff, Lee, & Martin report that the average one-day market-adjusted stock return on such trigger dates is −25.24 percent. Using an updated version of Karpoff, Lee, & Martin's data, Karpoff & Lou (2010) report an average abnormal return of −18.2 percent on the trigger date.

Following a trigger event, the SEC gathers information through an informal inquiry that may develop into a formal investigation of financial misconduct. The announcement of a formal investigation is associated with an average share price decline of 13.7 percent.

The SEC releases its findings and penalties in its Administrative Releases (Notices and Orders) and Litigation Releases. (Some—but not all—of these releases also receive a designation as an Accounting and Auditing Enforcement Release (AAER). Karpoff, Lee, & Martin (2008a) report that 63 percent of the regulatory releases in their sample also were assigned an AAER number.) If the SEC proceeds and imposes sanctions, the news of its initial regulatory action is associated with a further 9.6 percent decline. Subsequent releases that indicate that the matter is resolved are associated with an average decline of 4.2 percent.

This sequence of events typically takes several years to play out. Karpoff & Lou (2010) report that the median length of the violation period is 24 months, and the median length from the beginning of the violation until its initial public revelation is 26 months. From the initial public revelation until the end of the enforcement action takes an additional 41 months.

These findings are similar to those from many other studies that examine the share price reactions to disclosure of financial misconduct. The results of a number of such studies are summarized in the summary table at the end of the chapter. Using data from AAERs, Feroz, Park, & Pastena (1991) measure a two-day abnormal stock return of –12.9 percent. Dechow, Sloan, & Sweeney (1996) measure a one-day abnormal return of –8.8 percent, and Beneish (1999) reports a three-day abnormal return of –20.8 percent. Palmrose, Richardson, & Scholz (2004) examine share price reactions to news that a firm has to restate earnings, and report a mean two-day abnormal return of –9.2 percent. Using the Government Accountability Office's (GAO) (2002, 2003) database on announcements of earnings restatements, Desai, Hogan, & Wilkins (2006) report a mean three-day abnormal return of –11.07 percent, and Arthaud-Day et al. (2006) report a mean of –11.0 percent. Hennes, Leone, & Miller (2008) calculate that, among these restatements that result from material irregularities, the mean three-day abnormal return is –13.64 percent.

Announcements that a firm is the defendant in a lawsuit alleging financial fraud also are associated with large stock price declines. Francis, Philbrick, & Schipper (1994) measure a one-day abnormal stock return of –17.16 percent upon public disclosure of misconduct that prompts a lawsuit, and Gande & Lewis (2009) report a three-day abnormal stock return of –4.66 percent upon the news that a lawsuit against a firm had been filed.

Measures of Reputational Loss

As in the Xerox case, these stock price declines represent a combination of legal penalties, a reversal of the artificial share price inflation, and lost reputation. In isolated cases, the legal penalties can be quite large. For example, the SEC imposed a $250 million fine on Qwest Communications International, and $100 million fines each on Bristol-Myers Squibb Co. and the Royal Dutch/Shell Group. WorldCom initially was fined $2.25 billion for misreporting its earnings from January 1999 through March 2002 by a cumulative amount of $11 billion. This fine, however, was reduced in bankruptcy and district court negotiations to $750 million.

Despite such high-profile cases, Karpoff, Lee, & Martin (2008b) report that only 47, or 8 percent, of the 585 firms in their sample were assessed monetary penalties by regulatory agencies. The mean fine was $106.98 million, but excluding the WorldCom case, the mean fine was only $59.8 million. Monetary penalties from shareholder class action law-suits are more common; 39 percent of the firms in their sample paid class action settle-ments. The mean settlement in these cases was $37.7 million.

Although legal penalties sometimes are large, on average they are much smaller than firms' share value declines when their misconduct is revealed. In Karpoff, Lee, & Martin's (2008b) data, the mean legal penalty equals only 3.1 percent of the total loss in the mar-ket values of the targeted companies. Class action settlements account for an additional 5.4 percent of the loss. Together, these legal penalties equal only 8.8 percent of the total dollar loss associated with the enforcement actions.

To measure the reversal of the artificial share price inflation, Karpoff, Lee, & Martin report on two methods, one based on asset write-downs and the other based on earn-ings restatements. To illustrate the asset write-down approach, consider the following example:

> Suppose the Acme Company is an all-equity firm with a book value of assets of $100 and a market-to-book ratio of 1.5. The market value of the firm's assets, and its stock, is therefore $150. But then assume that Acme issues a misleading financial statement that overstates its asset values by $10. If the firm's market-to-book ratio stays the same, its share values will increase temporarily by ($10 x 1.5) to $165. But when the financial misrepresentation is discovered, Acme's book values will adjust back to $100. And if there is no other impact, the share value will fall back to $150. That is, Acme's shares will drop in value from their inflated value of $165 to their "correct" value of $150.

For each company in their sample, Karpoff, Lee, & Martin estimate the firm's market-to-book ratio by taking the median ratio of other firms in its industry. The size of the artifi-cial asset inflation is measured as the largest asset write-down in the period following the discovery of the misconduct. Using this method, Karpoff, Lee, & Martin estimate that 24.5 percent of the share price loss for firms in their sample is due to the reversal of the artificial share price inflation.

Estimation of the artificial share price inflation can become quite complicated, and, indeed, is a potentially fruitful area for future research. For example, if the market-to-book ratio is not static but depends on a firm's reported assets (say that investors' views of a firm's long-term growth depend on that firm's reported financials), the Acme exam-ple would become a more challenging estimation problem. It also might be useful to estimate the artificial share price inflation using a multiple of overstated earnings rather than overstated assets. Karpoff, Lee, & Martin (2008b) report on earnings-based esti-mates for a subset of their sample with available information. They obtain results that are similar to those based on the multiples-of-assets approach, but their earnings-based sample is small.

Using point estimates, Karpoff, Lee, & Martin (2008b) estimate that 8.8 percent of the total losses to firms in their sample were due to legal penalties and 24.5 percent to reversal of the artificial share inflation. The residual—66.6 percent—is an estimate of the amount of the total loss that is due to lost reputation. This breakdown is illustrated in Figure 18.3. This is a crude estimate. However, using median rather than mean values,

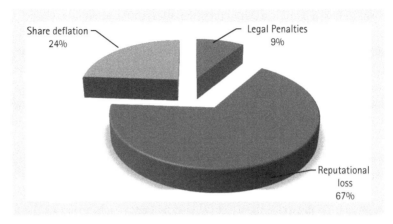

FIGURE 18.3 Sources of loss for financial misrepresentation.
Based on data for 384 cases, as reported in Karpoff, Lee, and Martin (2008b)

limiting the sample to firms that survived the enforcement process, or using alternate measures of the share deflation all yielded similar or larger measures of the reputation loss. Even extreme assumptions that generate large estimates of the share inflation effect leave a large portion of these firms' share price losses unexplained, except for the notion that they lost reputation.

Stated differently, Karpoff, Lee, & Martin's results indicate that firms can increase their share values temporarily by misrepresenting their earnings and assets. When the misrepresentation is detected, however, firm value decreases by more than the original inflation. For every dollar of inflated value during the period that the firm's books are in error, the firm loses that dollar when its misrepresentation is uncovered. In addition, the firm loses an additional $3.08. Some of this additional loss—36¢—is due to the legal penalties these firms incur. Most—$2.71—is due to lost reputation.

These results support the argument that financial reporting violations carry large penalties. The largest penalties are not from regulators or private lawsuits. Rather, they are from the firm's investors and other counterparties. It is unlikely that investors and firm counterparties intend, or are even aware, that they impose penalties on the offending firm. Rather, they are simply protecting their own interests by requiring a premium to do business with firms that are less trustworthy than they previously believed.

REPUTATIONAL LOSSES FOR OTHER TYPES OF BUSINESS MISCONDUCT

The previous discussion focused on reputational losses to firms that are revealed to have misrepresented their financial statements. Many researchers have investigated whether reputational losses occur for other types of business misconduct. Here, the results are mixed, with large measures of reputational loss for some types of misconduct but negligible loss for other types.

Panel B of the summary table gives the results from several of these investigations. Peltzman (1981), for example, finds that firms accused of false advertising by the Federal Trade Commission suffer losses in market capitalization measured over eight days of 2.42 percent. He concludes that only a small portion of these losses can be explained by such direct costs as fines and penalties, implying that investors anticipated large indirect losses to these firms—what I call a reputational loss. Jarrell & Peltzman (1985) examine the impacts of product recalls in the automobile and pharmaceutical industries. Again, they find significant share price losses, of which only about 23 percent can be explained by the direct costs of the product recall. This implies that much, even most, of these firms' total losses are due to lost reputation. Barber & Darrough (1996) also conclude that the reputational losses for automobile recalls are substantial.

Karpoff & Lott (1993), Alexander (1999), and Murphy, Shrieves, & Tibbs (2009) measure the reputational losses to frauds of related parties, including customers. News of such misconduct results in substantially smaller share price declines than for financial misconduct. Karpoff & Lott (1993), for example, report a mean two-day abnormal return for their sample of related-party fraud of –1.22 percent, and Murphy, Shrieves, & Tibbs (2009) report a mean two-day abnormal return of –2.30 percent. Both papers, however, conclude that such direct costs as legal penalties can explain only a small portion of these firms' losses. Averaging over both papers' point estimates, the portion of the overall loss that can be explained by reputational losses is 56 percent.

Another large estimate of reputational loss comes from air safety disasters. Mitchell & Maloney (1989) find that the one-day abnormal stock price reaction to an air crash that involves some oversight or pilot error is –1.68 percent. Much of this loss is attributed to lost future sales, that is, a reputational loss.

To measure the size of a reputational loss, it is important to first account for all direct costs that conceivably could explain the firms' share price losses. van den Broek et al. (2010) do this when they measure the reputational loss to Dutch firms that are subject to antitrust charges, by excluding any losses from having to abandon the conspiracy-related profits that were targeted in the antitrust action. Still, van den Broek et al. (2010) conclude that the reputational loss from antitrust actions averages 46 percent of these firms' total losses.

However, reputational losses are not uniformly large for all types of misconduct. Karpoff & Lott (1993) and Alexander (1999) find that the average stock price drop when firms are revealed to have engaged in misconduct that does not affect their counterparties—examples include check-kiting or failure to report large currency transactions—is statistically insignificant. Using a larger sample, Murphy, Shrieves, & Tibbs (2009) report that the share price reaction to news of misconduct that does not affect a firm's counterparties is negative and significant (–0.80 percent). But they find that all of this loss can be attributed to these firms' legal penalties, implying no reputational loss.

Estimates of reputational loss also are small or negligible for firms that violate environmental regulations. Jones & Rubin (2001) find that, among a sample of public utility companies, news of an environmental violation is not associated with a decline in share values. They conclude that there must be very little reputational loss for these companies. Karpoff, Lott, & Wehrly (2005) find that the average share price reaction is negative (–1.00 percent) in their broader sample of environmental violations. However, they also find that the legal penalties for the firms in their sample are of similar magnitude to the share value losses. Violations affecting air quality during the 1980s and 1990s, for example, resulted in an average fine of $31.7 million (in constant 2002 dollars). In addition, the guilty companies were required to incur costs averaging $123 million to comply with air quality rules or to remediate the damage of their pollution. Firms that were responsible for contaminated sites faced an average penalty of $11.0 million and a cleanup cost of $108 million. While firms that are caught contaminating air, water, or land resources face significant costs, these costs are all those imposed by regulators and the courts. These costs fully explain the defendant firms' losses in share values, implying that the reputational loss from violating environmental rules is negligible, on average.

WHY DO REPUTATIONAL LOSSES DIFFER?

Some types of misconduct expose companies to greater reputational losses than others. Lying to investors by misrepresenting financial statements triggers large reputational losses. So does defrauding customers, as with an incident in which BeechNut sold fake juice that was labeled "100 percent pure" apple juice (again, see Jennings, 2006: 531). In such incidents, the perpetrator reveals itself to be untrustworthy. Companies that defraud customers therefore tend to lose sales. Those that cheat employees or other suppliers face higher input costs or lost trade credit. And those that lie to their investors face higher financing costs.

Reputational losses are not uniformly high, however. This is most apparent from the empirical results regarding environmental violations. In theory, firms that violate environmental rules could suffer reputational losses if consumers and suppliers refuse to do business with them. After the 1989 *Exxon Valdez* oil spill, for example, some consumers cut up their Exxon credit cards and vowed to buy gasoline from other vendors. The data, however, show that, on average, the reputational loss from harming the environment is negligible. Jones & Rubin (2001) and Karpoff, Lott, & Wehrly (2005) argue that this is because firms that violate environmental rules do not impose costs on parties with whom they do business. Using the example stated previously, downstream fishermen are damaged if an electroplating company dumps toxic chemicals into a municipal storm sewer. But the fishermen do no business with the firm, and the firm's customers have no direct incentive to lower their demands for the firm's products if the dumping does not affect the quality of those products. As a result, the polluting electroplating company experiences no reputational costs.

A similar argument holds for violations that do not directly affect the parties with whom the firm does business. Although actions such as check-kiting are against the law, it is not evident that any of the parties with whom the firm does business are harmed by the activity. As a result, when firms are caught violating these types of rules they may face legal penalties. But since they do not directly harm their customers, investors, or suppliers, they do not suffer a reputational loss. That is, investors do not expect them to lose sales or face higher operating costs, and their share values are not substantially affected.

How Reputational Losses Show up in Firms' Operations

The evidence implies that firms engaging in many types of misconduct incur large reputational losses. This evidence is based, however, on observations that share prices decline when investors find out about the misconduct. But are investors correct? That is, do reputational losses actually show up in firms' subsequent performance? Do these firms subsequently lose business, incur higher costs, or experience a higher cost of capital?

The research on this question is still developing. But, as summarized in Panel C of the summary table, a number of findings are consistent with the event study results. For example, Karpoff & Lott (1993) find that firms charged with defrauding customers and other stakeholders do in fact have lower operating earnings over the following five years. Alexander (1999) reports that 57 percent of such firms experience termination or suspension of specific contracts. Furthermore, such business losses occur only following frauds of parties with whom the firm does business. Offenses against other parties with whom the firm does not do business do not lead to a high rate of lost sales. Similarly, Murphy, Shrieves, & Tibbs (2009) find that allegations of illegal acts are accompanied by a significant decrease in firms' earnings and an increase in uncertainty over future earnings.

There is fairly strong evidence that financial misconduct results in a higher cost of capital for a firm. Hribar & Jenkins (2004), Kravet & Shevlin (2010), and others show that the cost of equity capital increases for firms that restate earnings. And Graham, Li, and Qiu (2008) show that bank lender rates increase for restating firms.

Several papers document direct evidence of reputational losses. Beatty, Bunsis, & Hand (1998) find direct evidence of operating losses for investment bankers that are investigated by the SEC for problems in bringing initial public offering IPO firms to the public market. These firms experience sharp decreases in their shares of the IPO underwriting market after they are targeted by an SEC investigation. The share prices of these firms' client companies also decline, indicating that the decrease in an investment banker's reputation affects its clients as well. Atanasov, Ivanov, & Litvak (2011) find reputational effects are large in the venture capital business. Specifically, venture capital firms that are sued by their business partners subsequently lose financing and business.

In online auctions, buyers deal with sellers they do not know and cannot even see. So we would expect reputational effects to be very important and that sellers with high reputations would charge higher prices than others. Price premiums are the amounts that (some) buyers willingly pay for an increased guarantee that they will not be ripped off. In equilibrium, the chance to earn a price premium is sufficient to encourage high-reputational sellers to deliver on their promise not to cheat buyers.

Consistent with such expectations, evidence indicates that high-reputation sellers on eBay do in fact sell at higher prices than others, even for the same items. For example, Resnick et al. (2002) find that the prices of vintage postcards on eBay average 7.6 percent higher for sellers with a high reputation than for other sellers—even for the exact same postcards. Dewally & Ederington (2002) find similar results for comic books sold on eBay. The impact of a seller's reputation on price is particularly great when the quality of the comic book has not been certified by a third party.

Finally, several findings indicate that managers who involve their companies in financial misconduct end up losing their jobs. Jayaraman, Mulford, & Wedge (2004) find that managers of firms that are subjects of SEC Accounting and Auditing Enforcement Releases tend to be displaced at an unusually high rate. Desai, Hogan, & Wilkins (2006) and Agrawal & Cooper (2007) find that managers of firms that have to restate their earnings share similar fates. Karpoff, Lee, & Martin (2008a) report that 92 percent of managers whom the SEC identifies as involved in financial misrepresentation lose their jobs; 81 percent lose their jobs even before the SEC imposes any sanctions.

CONCLUSIONS: QUESTIONS FOR FURTHER RESEARCH

It is a truism that a firm's reputation matters. But how much does it matter? And why? To ascertain just how much reputation matters, researchers have examined instances in which firms can lose their reputations—that is, when firms are caught engaging in illegal or opportunistic activities. Firms lose market value upon the news of such misconduct. Frequently, the size of the loss far exceeds direct costs such as fines, penalties, and lawsuit settlements. The portion of a firm's loss that cannot be explained by such direct costs is a measure of that firm's reputational loss.

Using this approach, the evidence indicates that firms experience significant reputational losses when their misconduct imposes costs on their counterparties. Firms that misrepresent their financial statements face a higher cost of capital; and firms that cheat customers lose sales. For some types of misconduct, however, there appear to be small or negligible reputational losses. A notable example involves environmental violations. Firms lose value when they violate, say, Clean Air Act rules about emissions, but the size of the value loss is roughly the same as the firm's legal penalties and remediation costs. This implies that reputation plays a small role in disciplining environmental violations, and that regulations and legal penalties play a more important role.

So, does reputation work to discipline corporate misconduct? The answer is yes, but reputation is not a panacea or magical thing. It does not work to discipline all types of misconduct. Rather, firms lose reputation when their counterparties decrease their willingness to do business with them. And this happens when a firm acts in ways that increase its counterparties' concern that they will be harmed when they do business with the firm—that is, when a firm acts opportunistically in ways that hurt its customers, suppliers, employees, and investors.

The earliest papers cited in this chapter are over 20 years old. Nonetheless, the empirical research on reputational losses has only just begun to provide a well-rounded picture of reputation's role in facilitating the development of markets and economic growth. I conclude by offering a list of six questions for future research. Work on these questions can begin to fill in the gap between our theoretical understanding of reputation and the extent to which it works to encourage integrity and honest dealing in different markets.

How Important are Reputational Penalties Around the World?

Armour et al. (2011) find that reputational losses are important for financial misconduct in the UK, but most empirical research in this area has focused on US firms. We do not know if reputational losses help to discipline related-party misconduct in other markets around the world. This question is compelling for both theoretical and empirical reasons. Theoretically, the equilibrium reliance on reputation in any given market will depend on legal, institutional, and cultural factors (see Brammer & Jackson, Chapter 15, this volume; Newburry, Chapter 12, this volume; and McKenna & Olegario, Chapter 13, this volume). Where legal contracting protections are weak, for example, we might expect that buyers and sellers rely more on the informal protection provided by reputational guarantees. Indeed, Karpoff & Lott (1993) argue that, in the absence of any legal protections, sellers will provide different levels of reputational guarantee, just like they cater to other types of buyer clienteles. In markets that rely heavily on reputation to guarantee contractual performance, we should expect to see relatively large reputational penalties for misconduct.

How do Reputational Penalties Interact with Public and Private (lawsuit) Enforcement of Securities and other Laws?

Examining the securities laws in 49 countries, La Porta, Lopez de Silanes, & Shleifer (2006) conclude that governmental regulations that seek to limit financial misconduct do little to assist the development of financial markets. They argue that private enforcement, for example the threat of lawsuits, is much more important for financial market development than public enforcement. Howell & Roe (2009) use different measures of public enforcement that are based on the budgets or number of employees of the financial regulatory authority, and conclude the opposite. Both studies, however, ignore the role of reputation in disciplining financial misconduct and promoting financial market development. The empirical research indicates that reputational losses for financial misconduct exceed the explicit penalties imposed by either public or private enforcement agents. And the work summarized by McKenna and Olegario (Chapter 13, this volume) and Gilad and Yogev (Chapter 16, this volume) shows how regulators' actions affect the reputations of the firms they regulate. These results imply that a properly specified test of the effects of public and private enforcement must include reputational penalties as well.

How and When do Firms Rebuild Damaged Reputation?

The Klein-Leffler (1981) model implies that investment in reputational capital is similar to other capital investments. We should expect firms optimally to invest in reputation until the marginal investment yields zero net present value. This principle applies also to investment in reputation after the firm suffers a reputational loss. Some firms decide to reinvest in damaged reputational capital, as in the case of Johnson and Johnson after the Tylenol product tampering case (e.g., see Mitchell, 1989). Other firms, such as Arthur Andersen after the Enron financial reporting scandal, abandon their brand name, reflecting a decision not to invest in damaged reputation. Other than such anecdotes, we do not know whether firms tend to reinvest in reputation following a reputational loss, under what conditions they do so, what form the reinvestment takes, and whether the reinvestment is successful. Along these lines, Rhee and Kim (Chapter 22, this volume) and Elsbach (Chapter 23, this volume) identify some firm characteristics that affect a firm's decision to reinvest in damaged reputations.

How good are our Event-study Measures of Reputational Penalties?

Most measures of reputational loss are based on the residual approach first used by Peltzman (1981), Jarrell & Peltzman (1985), and Karpoff & Lott (1993). This measure reflects investors' expectations of the long-term cash flow consequences when firms' misconduct is revealed. To date, however, there is only limited evidence on whether such measures correspond to actual decreases in revenues or increases in costs (see, however, Murphy, Shrieves, & Tibbs, 2009). There also is limited research on the quality of the residual measures themselves. Karpoff & Lott (1993) point out that the measure of reputation loss can reflect lost cheating profits, which should not be considered a reputational loss. The measure also could reflect expectations of higher future direct costs if, for example, the firm is likely to be a repeat offender. In cases of financial misrepresentation, the measure of reputational loss is affected by the estimate of the reversal of artificial share price inflation. Karpoff, Lee, & Martin (2008b) argue that their measure of reputational loss is not much affected by alternate estimates of the artificial price inflation. But, in general, such estimates could have a large impact on the measure of reputational loss. Further research could clarify whether the reputational loss measures reported to date withstand further scrutiny.

How does Corporate Governance Affect the Likelihood and Cost of Opportunistic Behavior by Corporations?

Given the high cost of being caught—at least for many types of misconduct—one might infer that good governance would decrease the likelihood that managers would engage in misconduct. This argument, however, is incomplete. It ignores the possibility that, *ex ante*, some instances of misconduct could be expected to increase value. In such cases we should expect that well-governed firms would have incentives for managers to engage in misconduct. (If this possibility sounds unlikely, consider tax avoidance strategies. If the penalties for overly aggressive tax reporting are sufficiently low, it can behoove share-holders to incentivize managers to be aggressive in their tax reporting.)

Why do they do it?

The results surveyed here indicate that there are large consequences for firms and managers that are caught engaging in misconduct. Then why do they do it? Researchers have exam-ined several theories, including compensation incentives, poor governance, and inappro-priate expectations.[4] Most of these explanations receive empirical support. Most, however, are considered in isolation. To the extent that any one explanation (say, governance) is important, any test (say, regarding compensation incentives) that leaves it out suffers from an omitted variables problem. Future research that considers many potential factors at once could help us to understand better the forces that encourage corporate misconduct.

In short, the empirical research on the importance of reputation is still in its infancy. It is widely accepted that a firm's reputation matters. But to guide business and public policy, it is important to have some idea of how and when reputation matters, and even what we mean by the term "reputation." Attempts to investigate these questions should help to round out our understanding of the role of reputation in facilitating the development and use of markets to allocate scarce resources and encourage economic development.

ACKNOWLEDGMENT

I thank Lori Yue and Mike Barnett for helpful comments on an earlier draft of this chapter, and Alex Henning for research assistance.

[4] See, for example, Burns & Kedia (2006), Harris & Bromiley (2007), Mishina et al. (2010), and Agrawal & Cooper (2010).

Selected Empirical Studies Regarding the Costs of Corporate Misconduct

Type of misconduct or event	Reference	Reputation loss?*	Key findings
Panel A: Event studies of financial reporting violations			
Financial misrepresentation	Karpoff, Lee, & Martin (2008b)	Yes	Mean one-day stock return of −18% to −25%, including
	Karpoff & Lou (2010)	N.M.	a large reputational loss.
Accounting and Auditing Enforcement Release (AAER)	Feroz, Park, & Pastena (1991)	N.M.	Mean stock returns during one- to three-day event
	Dechow, Sloan, & Sweeney (1996)	N.M.	windows of −9% to −21%.
	Beneish (1999)	N.M.	
Earnings restatements	Palmrose, Richardson, & Scholz (2004)	N.M.	Mean stock returns during two- to three-day event
	Desai, Hogan, & Wilkins (2006)	N.M.	windows of −2% to −11%.
	Arthaud-Day et al. (2006)	N.M.	
	Hennes, Leone, & Miller (2008)	N.M.	
Lawsuits	Francis, Philbrick, & Schipper (1994)	N.M.	Mean stock returns during one- to three-day event
	Gande & Lewis (2009)	N.M.	windows of −5% to −17%.
Panel B: Event studies of other types of misconduct			
False advertising	Peltzman (1981)	Yes	Mean eight-day stock return of −2.4%.
Product recalls	Jarrell & Peltzman (1985)	Yes	Mean stock returns during 2- to 11-day event windows
	Barber & Darrough (1996)	Yes	of −0.4% to −6.1%.
Misconduct affecting related parties	Karpoff & Lott (1993)	Yes	Mean two-day stock returns of −1.2% to −2.3%.
	Alexander (1999)	Yes	
	Murphy, Shrieves, & Tibbs (2009)	Yes	
Air safety disasters	Mitchell & Maloney (1989)	Yes	Mean one-day stock return of −1.7% when some blame is assigned to pilot error.
Antitrust charges	van den Broek et al. (2010)	Yes	Mean 3-day stock return of −2.3%.
Misconduct affecting unrelated parties	Karpoff & Lott (1993)	No	Mean two-day stock returns of −0.9% to +0.4%. Two of
	Alexander (1999)	No	the three estimates are statistically insignificant.
	Murphy, Shrieves, & Tibbs (2009)	No	

Category	References		Description
Environmental violations	Jones & Rubin (2001)	No	Jones–Rubin report statistically insignificant stock returns; Karpoff et al. report a mean two-day return of −1.0%, but attribute this loss to direct penalties such as fines and remediation costs.
	Karpoff, Lott, & Wehrly (2005)	No	

Panel C: Other evidence of reputation losses

Category	References	Description
Misconduct affecting related parties	Karpoff & Lott (1993) Alexander (1999) Murphy, Shrieves, & Tibbs (2009)	Firms defrauding related parties subsequently have lower earnings, increased uncertainty over future earnings, and fewer contracts.
Earnings restatements	Hribar & Jenkins (2004) Kravet & Shevlin (2010) Graham, Li, & Qiu (2008)	The firm's cost of capital increases after earnings restatements.
Defense procurement fraud	Karpoff, Lee, & Vendrzyk (1999)	Unranked defense contractors charged with procurement fraud lose business.
Investment banks targeted by SEC actions	Beatty, Bunsis, & Hand (1998)	Investment banks investigated by the SEC lose market share.
Venture capitalist sued by business partners	Atanasov et al. (2011)	Venture capital firms that are sued by business partners lose financing and business.
eBay seller reputations	Resnick et al. (2006) Dewally & Ederington (2006)	eBay sellers with higher reputations get paid higher prices.
Financial misconduct	Jayaraman, Mulford, & Wedge (2004) Desai, Hogan, & Wilkins (2006) Agrawal & Cooper (2009) Karpoff, Lee, & Martin (2008a)	Significant managerial turnover surrounding the revelation of misconduct.

*N.M. indicates that a reputation loss was not measured.

References

Ahmed, P., Gardella, J., & Nanda, S. (2002). "Wealth effect of drug withdrawals on firms and their competitors." *Financial Management*, 31(3): 21–41.

Agrawal, A. & Cooper, T. (2009). "Corporate governance consequences of accounting scandals: Evidence from top management, CFO and auditor turnover." *Working Paper*, University of Alabama.

Alexander, C. (1999). "On the nature of the reputational penalty for corporate crime: Evidence." *The Journal of Law and Economics*, 42(1): 489–526.

Armour, J., Mayer, C., & Polo, A. (2011). "Regulatory sanctions and reputational damage in financial markets." *Oxford Legal Studies Research Paper* 62/2010: ECGI—Finance Working Paper No. 300/2010.

Arthaud-Day, M. L., Certo, S. T., Dalton, C. M., & Dalton, D. R. (2006). "A changing of the guard: Executive and director turnover following corporate financial restatements." *Academy of Management Journal*, 49(6): 1119–1136.

Atanasov, V. A., Ivanov, V. I., & Litvak, K. (2011). "Does reputation limit opportunistic behavior in the VC industry? Evidence from litigation against VCs." *The Journal of Finance*, forthcoming.

Barber, B. M. & Darrough, M. N. (1996). "Product reliability and firm value: The experience of American and Japanese automakers 1973–1992." *The Journal of Political Economy*, 104(5): 1084–1099.

Barnett, M. L., Jermier, J. M., & Lafferty, B. A. (2006). "Corporate reputation: The definitional landscape." *Corporate Reputation Review*, 9(1): 26–38.

Beatty, R. P., Bunsis, H., & Hand, J. R. M. (1998). "The indirect economic penalties in SEC investigations of underwriters." *Journal of Financial Economics*, 50(2): 151–186.

Beneish, M. D. (1999). "Incentives and penalties related to earnings overstatements that violate GAAP." *The Accounting Review*, 74(4): 425–457.

Bonner, S. E., Palmrose, Z., & Young, S. M. (1998). "Fraud type and auditor litigation: An analysis of SEC accounting and auditing enforcement releases." *The Accounting Review*, 73(4): 503–532.

Dechow, P. M., Sloan, R., & Sweeney, A. (1996). "Causes and consequences of earnings manipulation: An analysis of firms subject to enforcement actions by the SEC." *Contemporary Accounting Research*, 13(1): 1–36.

Desai, H., Hogan, C. E., & Wilkins, M. S. (2006). "Reputational consequences of aggressive accounting: Earnings restatements and management turnover." *The Accounting Review*, 81(1): 83–112.

Dewally, M. & Ederington, L. (2006). "Reputation, certification, warranties, and information as remedies for seller-buyer information asymmetries: Lessons from the on-line comic book market." *Journal of Business*, 79(2): 693–730.

Feroz, E. H., Park, K. J., & Pastena, V. S. (1991). "The financial and market effects of the SEC's accounting and auditing enforcement releases." *Journal of Accounting Research*, 29(Supplement): 107–142.

Francis, J., Philbrick, D., & Schipper, K. (1994). "Shareholder litigation and corporate disclosures." *Journal of Accounting Research*, 32(2): 137–164.

Gande, A. & Lewis, C. M. (2009). "Shareholder initiated class action lawsuits: Shareholder wealth effects and industry spillovers." *Journal of Financial and Quantitative Analysis*, 44(4): 823–850.

Grady, D. B. & Strickland, T. H. (2007). "Public information as a deterrent to environmental infractions." *Applied Economics*, 39(15): 1961–1972.

Graham, J. R., Li, S., & Qiu, J. (2008). "Corporate misreporting and bank loan contracting." *Journal of Financial Economics*, 89(1): 44–61.

Harris, J. & Bromiley, P. (2007). "Incentives to cheat: The influence of executive compensation and firm performance on financial misrepresentation." *Organization Science*, 18(3): 350–367.

Hennes, K. M., Leone, A. J., & Miller, B. P. (2008). "The importance of distinguishing errors from irregularities in restatement research: The case of restatements and CEO/CFO turnover." *The Accounting Review*, 83(6): 1487–1519.

Houser, D. & Wooders, J. (2006). "Reputation in auctions: Theory and evidence from eBay." *Journal of Economics and Management Strategy*, 15(2): 353–369.

Howell, E. J. & Roe M. J. (2009) "Public and private enforcement of securities laws: Resource-based evidence". *Journal of Financial Economics*, 93(2): 207–38.

Hribar, P. & Jenkins, N. T. (2004). "The effect of accounting restatements on earnings revisions and the estimated cost of capital." *Review of Accounting Studies*, 9: 337–356.

Jackson, H. E. & Roe, M. J. (2009). "Public enforcement of securities laws: Preliminary evidence." *Journal of Financial Economics*, 93(2): 207–238.

Jarrell, G. & Peltzman, S. (1985). "The impact of product recalls on the wealth of sellers." *The Journal of Political Economy*, 93(3): 512–536.

Jayaraman, N., Mulford, C., & Wedge, L. (2004). "Accounting fraud and management turnover." *Working Paper*, Georgia Institute of Technology.

Jennings, M. M. (2006). *Business: Its Legal, Ethical, and Global Environment*. Mason, OH: Thomson Higher Education.

Jin, G. Z. & Kato, A. (2006). "Price, quality, and reputation: Evidence from an online field experiment." *The RAND Journal of Economics*, 37(4): 983–1004.

Jones, K. & Rubin, P. (2001). "Effects of harmful environmental events on reputations of firms." *Advances in Financial Economics*, 6: 161–182.

Karpoff, J. M. & Lott, J. R. (1993). "The reputational penalty firms bear from committing criminal fraud." *Journal of Law & Economics*, 36(2): 757–802.

—— & Lou, X. (2010). "Short sellers and financial misconduct." *The Journal of Finance*, 65(5): 1879–1913.

——, Lee, D. S., & Vendrzyk, V. P. (1999). "Defense procurement fraud, penalties, and contractor influence." *Journal of Political Economy*, 107(4): 809–842.

——, Lott, J. R., & Wehrly, E. W. (2005). "The reputational penalties for environmental violations: Empirical evidence." *Journal of Law and Economics*, 48(2): 653–675.

——, Lee, D. S., & Martin, G. S. (2008a). "The consequences to managers for financial misrepresentation." *Journal of Financial Economics*, 88(2): 193–215.

——, ——, & —— (2008b). "The cost to firms of cooking the books." *Journal of Financial and Quantitative Analysis*, 43(3): 581–611.

Klassen, R. D. & McLaughlin, C. P. (1996). "The impact of environmental management of firm performance." *Management Science*, 42(8): 1199–1214.

Klein, B. & Leffler, K. (1981). "The role of market forces in assuring contractual performance." *Journal of Political Economy*, 89(4): 615.

Kravet, T. & Shevlin, T. (2010). "Accounting restatements and information risk." *Review of Accounting Studies*, 15(2): 264–294.

La Porta, R., Lopez-de-Silanes, F., & Shleifer, A. (2006). "What works in securities laws?" *Journal of Finance*, 61: 1–32.

Lei, Q. (2010). "Financial value of reputation: Evidence from the eBay auctions of gmail invitations." *Journal of Industrial Economics*, 59(3): 422–456.

Margolis, J. D., Elfenbein, H. A., & Walsh, J. P. (2007). "Does it pay to be good? A meta-analysis and redirection of research on the relationship between corporate social and financial performance." Working Paper, Harvard Business School.

Mishina, Y., Dykes, B. J., Block, E. S., & Pollock, T. G. (2010). "Why good firms do bad things: The effects of high aspirations, high expectations and prominence on the incidence of corporate illegality." *Academy of Management Journal*, 53(4): 701–722.

Mitchell, M. L. & Maloney, M. T. (1989). "Crisis in the cockpit—the role of market forces in promoting air travel safety." *Journal of Law and Economics*, 32(2): 329–55.

Murphy, D. L., Shrieves, R. E., & Tibbs, S. L. (2009). "Understanding the penalties associated with corporate misconduct: An empirical examination of earnings and risk." *Journal of Financial and Quantitative Analysis*, 44(1): 55–83.

Palmrose, Z. & Scholz, S. (2004). "The circumstances and legal consequences of non-GAAP reporting: Evidence from restatements." *Contemporary Accounting Research*, 21(1): 139–180.

——, Richardson, V., & Scholz, S. (2004). "Determinants of market reactions to earnings restatements." *Journal of Accounting and Economics*, 37(1): 59–89.

Peltzman, S. (1981). "The effects of FTC advertising regulation." *Journal of Law and Economics*, 24: 403–448.

Prince, D. W. & Rubin, P. H. (2002). "The effects of product liability litigation on the value of firms." *American Law and Economics Review*, 4(1): 44–87.

Resnick, P., Zeckhauser, R., Swanson, J., & Lockwood, K. (2006). "The value of reputation on eBay: A controlled experiment." *Experimental Economics*, 9(2): 79–101.

Roberts, P. W. & Dowling, G. R. (2002). "Corporate reputation and sustained superior financial performance." *Strategic Management Journal*, 23(12): 1077–1093.

Romano, R., (1991). "The shareholder suit: Litigation without foundation?" *Journal of Law, Economics, & Organization*, 7(1): 55–87.

Rubin, P. H., Murphy, R. D., & Jarrell, G. (1988). "Risky products, risky stocks, regulation." *Regulation* 12(1): 35–39.

Shapiro, C. (1983). "Premiums for high quality products as returns to reputations." *Quarterly Journal of Economics*, 98(4): 659–679.

Song, W. & Uzun, H. (2004). "The impact of clients' alleged financial reporting fraud on underwriter reputation." *Working Paper #04-16*, University of Pennsylvania.

van den Broek, S., Kemp, R., Verschoor, W. F. C., & de Vries, A. (2010). "Reputational penalties to firms in antitrust investigations." *Working Paper*, Erasmus School of Economics.

Williamson, O. E. (1984). "The economics of governance: Framework and implications." *Journal of Institutional and Theoretical Economics*, 140: 195–223.

CHAPTER 19

FROM THE GROUND UP: BUILDING YOUNG FIRMS' REPUTATIONS

ANTOANETA PETKOVA

This chapter discusses the processes through which young firms develop their initial reputations. A review of the main theoretical perspectives that pertain to this topic identifies three distinct mechanisms for developing reputation: reputation-borrowing through affiliations with established industry players, reputation-building through entrepreneurial actions and communications, and reputation by endowment based on the personal reputational capital of the young firms' founders and top management team (TMT). I map these perspectives on the stages in the development of reputation for young entrepreneurial firms. At the "attention-generating" stage, young firms have to overcome the lack of public awareness of their existence and activities. At the "uncertainty-reduction" stage, young firms have to handle the lack of understanding and the skepticism of stakeholders. At the "evaluation" stage, young firms have to create positive perceptions about themselves.

INTRODUCTION

REPUTATION—defined as stakeholders' perceptions about a firm's ability to deliver value (Fombrun, 1996; Rindova & Fombrun, 1999)—has been studied primarily in the context of large established organizations (Fombrun, Chapter 5, this volume; Rindova & Martins, Chapter 2, this volume). However, developing reputation is also important for all young entrepreneurial firms that aspire to transition from being small and unknown into being well known and successful. Think of Amazon.com, Google, eBay, Facebook, and the like that have introduced new technologies to drastically change our definitions of markets, transactions, and means of communication. Often such organizations need significant time, money, and other resources to develop their first products. However, in the lack of initial reputation they are unlikely to obtain these critical resources. Indeed, young firms appear trapped in a vicious circle—their future reputation depends on producing high-quality products but in order to produce any product they need to attract resources from critical stakeholders and the only way to do so is by developing some initial reputation. Unlike established firms which sometimes receive too much attention and public scrutiny (Whittington and Yakis-Douglas, Chapter 20, this volume), young firms usually struggle to get noticed. Further, instead of a history of previous performance, all they can offer is an idea, and a promise that the idea will materialize in the future. Thus, stakeholders have to form their initial perceptions of young firms based on expectations for future performance instead of demonstrated past performance. These unique challenges faced by young firms early in their lives have attracted a growing research interest in the processes through which such firms develop their initial reputations.

This chapter begins with a review of the main bodies of research that offer insights about the processes of building reputation for young entrepreneurial firms. After outlining the theoretical mechanisms identified by these perspectives, I discuss their connections to each stage in the development of reputation for young entrepreneurial firms. Comparing the three perspectives helps identify a number of issues that remain to be addressed. The chapter concludes with a discussion of some opportunities and directions for future research in this promising area.

MECHANISMS FOR DEVELOPING REPUTATION FOR YOUNG ENTREPRENEURIAL FIRMS

The emergence of reputation early in an organization's life is fundamental to reputation research, yet surprisingly few studies have addressed this question directly. In the interest of providing a richer picture of the scholarly understanding of this issue, my review includes a broad range of studies related to the reputation of young firms. Based on their assumptions about the sources of reputation and the factors that contribute to it, these studies are classified into three perspectives (roughly representing three mechanisms for developing reputation) labeled "reputation-borrowing," "reputation-building," and "reputation by endowment." Representative studies for each perspective are summarized in the summary table at the end of the chapter.

Reputation-borrowing

Studies taking a "reputation-borrowing" perspective are based on the assumption that young entrepreneurial firms that lack their own reputation can "borrow" the reputation of third parties through affiliation with them. Scholars working from this perspective have been primarily concerned with the sources of reputation—that is, the prestigious affiliates—and the benefits of having them. The research questions they address are related to the effects of affiliation on performance (Stuart, Hoang, & Hybels, 1999), and the impact of different types of affiliations at a given stage of the young organization's life cycle (Lee, Pollock, & Jin, 2011; Pollock et al., 2010) or under different market conditions (Gulati & Higgins, 2003).

These studies point to the fact that new firms lack reliable performance track records because they usually earn no profits in the first few years after founding (Gompers & Lerner, 2001), while also lacking the resources necessary to invest in other relevant reputational signals (Pollock, Porac, & Wade, 2004; Williamson, 2000). For these reasons, most new firms have to borrow reputation from already established—preferably prestigious—actors with whom they affiliate (Stuart, Hoang, & Hybels, 1999). Such prestigious affiliates include strategic alliance partners (Higgins & Gulati, 2003; Stuart, Hoang, & Hybels, 1999), customers (Reuber & Fischer, 2005), venture capital investors (Lee, Pollock, & Jin, 2011; Pollock et al., 2010), and investment banks that serve as underwriters during initial public offering (Gulati & Higgins, 2003; Pollock et al., 2010). Researchers have identified a number of benefits associated with having prestigious affiliations, including higher survival chances, ability to attract future strategic alliance partners, improved innovation, growth, and financial performance (Gulati & Higgins, 2003; Larson, 1992; Pollock & Gulati, 2007; Shane & Stuart, 2002; Stuart, Hoang, & Hybels, 1999).

The reputation-borrowing phenomenon is explained by the fact that the public evaluations of a young firm of unknown quality are influenced by the social standing of the actors associated with it (Stuart, 2000; Stuart, Hoang, & Hybels, 1999). The choices of third parties vis-à-vis a young organization, and especially their decisions to enter an exchange relationship with it, serve as an important signal of its quality and potential. Prestigious actors are believed to be more knowledgeable and capable of evaluating a young entrepreneurial firm and, therefore, the relationships with them serve as endorsements and certifications of the young firm's quality and potential (Gulati & Higgins, 2003; Stuart, 2000; Stuart, Hoang, & Hybels, 1999). For example, Powell (1996) found that biotechnology firms with more and higher quality partnerships receive higher market valuations from the market analysts. Although these studies focus on prestigious affiliations rather than reputation, the theorized mechanism through which affiliations affect performance outcomes is through the reputation borrowed from the prestigious affiliates. Overall, the reputation-borrowing perspective suggests that securing affiliations with prestigious third parties can compensate to some extent the lack of reputation young entrepreneurial firms face, because through their decision to affiliate with the new firm, prestigious third parties signal to more distant stakeholders the worthiness, quality, and potential of the new firm (Pollock et al., 2010; Stuart, Hoang, & Hybels, 1999).

Reputation-building

The studies taking a "reputation-building" perspective acknowledge the inapplicability of most strategies used by established organizations for young entrepreneurial firms and try to identify strategies that address the unique challenges faced by these firms (Petkova, Rindova, & Gupta, 2008; Rindova, Petkova, & Kotha, 2007). The main assumption underlying this perspective is that new firms, although resource constrained, can devise some unique strategies for developing their initial reputation. The research questions these studies address focus primarily on the inputs into the reputation-building process and the mechanisms through which different actions on the part of young firms affect their reputations as an outcome (Petkova, Rindova, & Gupta, 2008; Rao, 1994; Reuber & Fischer, 2007; Rindova, Petkova, & Kotha, 2007). The studies reviewed in this chapter identify specific visible actions that can set young firms apart from competitors by signaling their underlying quality and potential to various stakeholders. Such actions include innovation and new product introduction (Reuber & Fischer, 2007; Rindova, Petkova, & Kotha, 2007), winning product awards and competitions (Rao, 1994; Reuber & Fischer, 2007), investments in human and social capital (Petkova, Rindova, & Gupta, 2008), and symbolic actions and communications (Petkova, Rindova, & Gupta, 2008; Rindova, Petkova, & Kotha, 2007).

These studies emphasize the multiple challenges faced by young entrepreneurial firms at the beginning of their lives. Specifically, scholars point not only to stakeholders' uncertainty about young firms' underlying quality and potential, but also to their unawareness of the existence of a given young firm and the more fundamental lack of understanding of their innovative activities. Given the complex set of issues that a young firm has to resolve, the reputation-building activities identified by these studies are theorized to serve one or more of the following purposes: (a) attract stakeholders' attention to the young firm, (b) establish its credibility as a viable organization, and (c) provide indication of underlying quality, potential, and future prospects (Petkova, Rindova, & Gupta, 2008; Reuber & Fischer, 2007; Rao, 1994; Rindova, Petkova, & Kotha, 2007).

Given the need to attract large-scale public attention and to resolve the high levels of uncertainty regarding young entrepreneurial firms, the reputation-building perspective attributes a major role to institutional intermediaries such as the media and industry analysts who bring young firms to the focal attention of large stakeholder audiences (Kennedy, 2008; Rao, 1994; Rindova, Petkova, & Kotha, 2007). Due to their intermediation role in markets, the media, it is argued, both reflect and influence the creation of young firms' reputations (Pollock & Rindova, 2003; Rindova, Petkova, & Kotha, 2007). Further, media reports about young firms are found to reflect objectively the actions taken by those firms and to disseminate important information about their achievements (Rindova, Petkova, & Kotha, 2007), thus magnifying the relatively weak signals coming from the small-scale actions of young firms and making them visible to a large number of stakeholders (Kennedy, 2005).

The reputation-building studies pay special attention to the definition and measurement of reputation. For example, Rindova, Petkova, & Kotha (2007) conceptualize the emerging reputation of young firms as a multidimensional construct, consisting of visibility, strategic character, favorability, and esteem. In addition, Petkova, Rindova, & Gupta (2008) observe that the initial reputation of new firms emerges as either "local" (i.e., reflecting the perceptions of a small set of customers who have direct interactions with the new firm) or "generalized" (i.e., reflecting the awareness of many distant stakeholders who have no direct experience with the new firm). Rao (1994) further points to the connection between legitimacy and reputation, arguing that a new firm has to be seen as a legitimate market participant before stakeholders begin to evaluate it and develop reputational beliefs. The importance of the reputation construct is also reflected in the attempts of most studies to measure reputation directly, using various operationalizations such as the amount and content of media coverage received (Rindova, Petkova, & Kotha, 2007), the number of industry awards won (Rao, 1994), whether or not a young firm gets selected by potential customers (Reuber & Fischer, 2007), and a combination of media counts with self-reported perceptions of founder-entrepreneurs (Petkova, Rindova, & Gupta, 2008).

Reputation by Endowment

Entrepreneurship research often equates the individual reputation of the founders with the reputation of the new organization (e.g., Shane & Cable, 2002). This approach is problematic for several reasons: For one, confusing individual and firm level of analysis is problematic both theoretically and methodologically, as individual-level constructs have to be aggregated properly to infer firm-level constructs (Klein & Kozlowski, 2000). Further, new firms are often started by multiple individuals with different reputations—a fact that makes it difficult and pretty arbitrary to determine whose reputation the young firm represents. Even for firms started by a single founder, when the founder has experienced both successes and failures in the past, it is not clear what individual reputation he or she has accumulated.

What is clear, though, is that the individual has accumulated some experience—and based on it some personal reputational capital—that can be used by stakeholders as a signal of quality and underlying potential for the new firm (Petkova, 2006). I have identified a number of studies that focus on the effect of the previous experience of the founders and TMT members on the perceptions of critical stakeholders about new firms. These studies assume that the founders and TMT members endow their new firms with their personal reputation developed through education, work experience, and previous entrepreneurial success. The research questions they address focus on the effects of experience on stakeholder perceptions under different levels of uncertainty (Pollock, Fund, & Baker, 2009; Sapienza & Gupta, 1994) and at different stages of the young firms' life cycles (Beckman & Burton, 2008; Beckman, Burton, & O'Reilly, 2007).

Scholars have emphasized the critical role that the founders play in setting up the vision and identity for the new firm, creating an organizational structure with long-lasting consequences, and determining the innovation strategy that the new firm would pursue (Beckman & Burton, 2008; Burton, Sorensen, & Beckman, 2002). Experienced founders and TMTs transfer to their new firms some of their personal reputations because their experience reduces stakeholder perceptions of uncertainty with regard to the new firm by ensuring that it possesses the necessary organizational and technical expertise (Pollock, Fund, & Baker, 2009; Sapienza & Gupta, 1994). For example, venture capital investors perceive less uncertainty about firms founded by experienced entrepreneurs, as evident by less monitoring (Sapienza & Gupta, 1994) and higher chances of retention of the founder-CEO when making young firms public (Pollock, Fund, & Baker, 2009). Further, breadth and diversity of TMT experience are found to improve the young firms' access to venture capital and chances of going public (Beckman, Burton, & O'Reilly, 2007; Beckman & Burton, 2008). Overall, although these studies are not concerned with explaining the reputation of young firms per se, they point to the important need for young firms to reduce stakeholder uncertainty in order to attract resources. As discussed later in this chapter, uncertainty reduction is an important stage in the process of developing reputation for young firms.

Comparison among the Three Perspectives

A comparison between the perspectives discussed above shows that they converge on the key idea that reputation is a cognitive construct. The reputation-borrowing and reputation-building perspectives explicitly define and/or refer to reputation in terms of stakeholder perceptions about the young firm. The reputation-by-endowment perspective focuses more narrowly on stakeholder perceptions of the uncertainty inherent in the young firm (as explained later, uncertainty-reduction is a critical stage in developing reputation for young firms).

The three perspectives also differ in several important ways. First, given their different assumptions and research questions addressed, they focus to a different degree on outcomes versus process. The reputation-borrowing perspective clearly demonstrates the benefits of having prestigious affiliates (Pollock & Gulati, 2007; Pollock et al., 2010), while the processes and mechanisms through which these benefits accrue to the young firms are usually theorized. In contrast, the studies taking a reputation-building perspective focus primarily on the factors contributing to the development of reputation and the processes that lead to the desired outcomes, often taking for granted that reputation is beneficial for new firms (Petkova, Rindova, & Gupta, 2008; Reuber & Fischer, 2007; Rindova, Petkova, & Kotha, 2007). The reputation-by-endowment studies fall somewhere in between, with a strong emphasis on outcomes but also examining specific organizational trajectories and transition processes that connect the initial reputational endowments to the observed outcomes (Beckman & Burton, 2008; Pollock, Fund, & Baker, 2009).

Second, these perspectives theorize different mechanisms through which young firms obtain reputation and identify different reputation-granting authorities. The reputation-borrowing perspective considers prestigious affiliates as the reputation-granting authority, because these individuals or organizations are competent and knowledgeable about the focal new firm and arguably better evaluators than the general public. The reputation-borrowing phenomenon occurs by virtue of the young firm being selected by prestigious actors as an affiliate. The reputation-by-endowment occurs internally (i.e., no reputation-granting authority is involved): when creating a new firm its founders and TMT transfer some of their personal reputation capital to it. Both perspectives attribute a somewhat passive role to the young firm in the development of its reputation. In contrast, the reputation-building perspective attributes a lot of agency to the young firm, viewing the development of early reputation as actively initiated by its own actions and communications. This perspective identifies as major reputation-granting authorities powerful institutional intermediaries such as the media, industry experts, and analysts, who play a critical role in helping young firms reach broad stakeholder audiences.

Third, the two perspectives explicitly concerned with the concept of reputation—reputation-building and reputation-borrowing—differ in their emphasis on awareness vs. evaluations as representing a young firm's reputation (see Rindova & Martins, Chapter 2, this volume, for details on the dimensions of reputation), as well as in the ways they operationalize and measure reputation. The reputation-borrowing perspective emphasizes the evaluative dimension of reputation. Except for Pollock and Gulati (2007), studies focus strictly on the endorsement/evaluation benefits of affiliation, implicitly assuming that the relevant stakeholder audiences monitor the affiliations of young entrepreneurial firms and take them into account when making their own decisions. Further, in line with the assumption that young firms have no reputation of their own, researchers taking this perspective usually make no attempts to measure reputation directly. Instead, they theorize about the reputation-borrowing mechanism and test for effects of prestigious affiliations on the outcomes of interest, such as performance or resource acquisition (Stuart, Hoang, & Hybels, 1999). Thus, the availability of prestigious affiliates serves as a proxy for the reputation that young firms have borrowed.

The reputation-building perspective emphasizes more explicitly the need for young firms to attract large-scale public attention and to demonstrate their ability and potential to relevant stakeholder audiences. For example, Rindova, Petkova, & Kotha (2007) argue that being young and small usually means a lack of stakeholder awareness of the new firm's existence and that attracting public attention is an integral part of the reputation-building process. Overall, in this perspective awareness and evaluation appear to be equally important dimensions of reputation. Given the strong focus on the construct of reputation itself, the reputation-building studies usually measure reputation directly (Petkova, Rindova, & Gupta, 2008; Rindova, Petkova, & Kotha, 2007).

In sum, the perspectives discussed above offer different—and I believe complementary—insights into the processes through which young firms develop their initial reputation. In the next section, I identify the stages in this process and try to map the three perspectives onto each stage.

Stages in the Development of Reputation for Young Entrepreneurial Firms

An integration of the theoretical perspectives discussed above helps us understand better the role of different and possibly complementary mechanisms through which young entrepreneurial firms develop reputation. Specifically, my analysis points to three stages through which reputation emerges: At the "attention-generating" stage, young firms overcome the lack of public awareness of their existence and activities; at the "uncertainty-reduction" stage, they address the lack of understanding and the skepticism of potentially relevant stakeholders; and at the "evaluation" stage, young firms create positive perceptions about themselves by convincing relevant stakeholders of the value of their activities. Below I discuss the purpose of each stage and the activities identified by research to date as potentially relevant (see Table 19.1 for a summary).

Stage One: Generating Attention

As already mentioned, one of the major problems faced by young entrepreneurial firms is the lack of public awareness of their existence and activities. For example, Pollock and Gulati (2007) emphasize the problem of attracting attention to young firms, explicitly pointing to the fact that the reputation signals about them may not be noticed by the relevant stakeholders that are supposed to interpret those signals. The purpose of the "attention-generating" stage is to make prospective customers, partners, investors,

Table 19.1 Stages in Developing Reputation for Young Entrepreneurial Firms

Theoretical perspectives	Stage 1: Attracting attention	Stage 2: Reducing uncertainty	Stage 3: Forming evaluations
Reputation-borrowing	Affiliations with major firms in the industry	Affiliations with prestigious VCs and underwriters	Affiliations with prestigious customers Affiliations with VCs
Reputation-building	Communications	Communications	Innovation/new product introduction
	Visibility-enhancing activities	Progress towards milestones	Winning contests Communications
Reputation by endowment	Celebrity founders (???)	Founders' personal reputational capital	Founders' personal reputational capital (???)
	Location (???)	Initial organization structure	

Note: The question marks (???) indicate potentially relevant factors that have not been examined by previous research.

future employees, and other relevant stakeholders aware of the existence of the newly created organization. Attracting attention is an important precursor to the development of reputation, because an organization has to become a part of the stakeholders' consideration set before they can form perceptions and opinions about it (Pollock & Rindova, 2003). Ideally, at this stage the young firm would become widely visible in its organizational field as more and more stakeholders become aware of it (Rindova, Petkova, & Kotha, 2007). It should be noted that the benefits of a high level of visibility are not limited to young firms. My co-authors and I have found that established organizations that are prominent in their field are able to charge premium prices for their outputs as compared with less prominent competitors (see Rindova et al., 2005). Therefore, one could think of creating initial awareness as the first step that a young firm can take towards becoming prominent in its organizational field. Consider the example of Amazon.com: the early visibility it generated within a year of its founding was pretty remarkable for a young firm in an emerging industry (Rindova, Petkova, & Kotha, 2007); now, it is one of the most prominent e-commerce firms, undoubtedly enjoying the benefits of its early reputation-building efforts.

Recent studies have argued that the availability of media coverage is a major indicator of the level of public awareness generated by a young entrepreneurial firm. For example, Kennedy (2005, 2008) points to the importance of "being counted" by the media for making stakeholders aware of the existence of a young firm in an emerging market. Further, Pollock and Rindova (2003) and Pollock and Gulati (2007) provide compelling arguments for the role of the media in attracting large-scale public attention towards the few young firms selected for coverage.

How can young firms attract the attention of the media and various stakeholders? The reputation-building perspective speaks most directly to this issue by identifying communications and visibility-enhancing activities as critical attention-generating strategies. For example, in its early days Amazon.com organized interactive book-writing with celebrity writers and poetry contests to attract stakeholder attention (Rindova, Petkova, & Kotha, 2007). Other examples include presence at industry events and professional conferences (Petkova, Rindova, & Gupta, 2008), customer education efforts (Petkova, Rindova, & Gupta, 2008; Rindova, Petkova, & Kotha, 2007), and participation in certification contests (Rao, 1994). Another possible way to attract attention is the affiliation with a prestigious industry player, as suggested by the reputation-borrowing perspective (Pollock & Gulati, 2007; Stuart, Hoang, & Hybels, 1999). The effects of different affiliates for attracting stakeholders' attention have not been examined directly. However, it is conceivable that partnerships with major firms in the industry can make a young firm more noticeable to potentially relevant stakeholders. Unusual endowment in individual reputational capital is also a potentially relevant factor to consider. Stories about serial entrepreneurs or senior executives who left Microsoft to join a new firm appear periodically in the media, because journalists like to create "celebrities" (Hayward, Rindova, & Pollock, 2004). Thus, founders and/or TMT members who have already developed strong personal reputations among entrepreneurship circles can attract media attention to their new firms.

Stage Two: Uncertainty-reduction

The second problem specific to young entrepreneurial firms is the lack of understanding on the part of prospective customers and other stakeholders, which makes them skeptical and unlikely to appreciate the value of the innovative products that young firms have to offer. Uncertainty-reduction is a prerequisite for forming evaluative opinions—stakeholders need to understand, at least to some degree, the young firm and its activities before they can form evaluative opinions. At the "uncertainty-reduction" stage, young firms have to convince skeptical stakeholders that they fit with the industry norms and rules, and to explain the meaning and purpose of their innovations. This stage is particularly important for young firms introducing innovative products and technologies for which available categories and frameworks may not apply (Aldrich & Fiol, 1994). Such firms need to legitimate not only themselves and their technologies but also the emerging sector they are trying to create (Aldrich & Fiol, 1994; Rindova, Petkova, & Kotha, 2007).

Research to date has pointed to the problem of uncertainty-reduction and meaning-creation primarily in discussion of legitimacy and the legitimation of new industries (Aldrich & Fiol, 1994; Rosa et al., 1999). As far as the reputation of young firms is concerned, the fact that understanding precedes evaluations has been acknowledged (Rao, 1994) and a number of uncertainty-reduction activities have been identified. Communications in the form of entrepreneurial stories and narratives appear particularly relevant in this regard, as they can be used to explain the vision, strategy, and activities of young entrepreneurial firms (Lounsbury & Glynn, 2001; Porac, Mishina, & Pollock, 2002). Fast progress in technology development and new product introduction also help reduce stakeholders' uncertainty (Petkova, Rindova, & Gupta, 2008; Reuber & Fischer, 2007). Another potentially relevant factor is the founders' reputational capital which has been found to reduce the uncertainty of venture capitalists (VCs) and public investors with regard to young firms (Pollock, Fund, & Baker, 2009; Sapienza & Gupta, 1994). Further, starting with a fully developed functional structure (Beckman & Burton, 2008) can also assure stakeholders that the new firm is indeed a "real" organization that fits with industry practices. Finally, affiliations with prestigious VCs and underwriters can reduce the uncertainty about young firms by certifying that they meet certain investment criteria (Pollock et al., 2010).

Stage Three: Positive Evaluation

The formation of positive evaluations among stakeholders has attracted the majority of research attention to date: most studies discussed in this chapter explicitly address the evaluative stage in the formation of a young firm's reputation. At the "evaluation" stage, stakeholders form positive perceptions, which ultimately constitute the evaluative dimension of reputation, or what most people mean when saying that an organization has a "good" reputation (Rindova et al., 2005). In order to develop positive perceptions about a focal young firm, stakeholders not only have to know about its existence and to understand its purpose, but also to perceive the young firm as being able and likely to deliver products of certain value and quality. Therefore, at this stage of the reputation-formation process, the young firm has to demonstrate that it has the necessary resources and capabilities to deliver valuable products.

Scholars tend to identify one or more "signals" that can be used by stakeholders to judge the underlying quality and value-creation potential of young entrepreneurial firms. Empirical studies show that signals of the young firm's underlying quality, such as innovation and new product development (Rindova, Petkova, & Kotha, 2007; Rueber & Fischer, 2007), as well as entrepreneurs' reputational and/or social capital (Petkova, 2006; Petkova, Rindova, & Gupta, 2008), are critical inputs into the formation of positive evaluations among stakeholders. In addition to these (internal) resources, prestigious affiliations can also serve as endorsement of the young firm's underlying quality and potential (Pollock et al., 2010; Stuart, Hoang, & Hybels, 1999). Affiliations with prestigious customers (Reuber & Fischer, 2005) and VCs (Pollock & Gulati, 2007; Pollock et al., 2010) are particularly likely to help, because both of these affiliates are explicitly concerned with the quality of the young firms.

Unlike the previous two stages, where I pointed to the use of communications as a major tool for attracting stakeholder attention and reducing the uncertainty about young firms, at the evaluative stage communications alone may not be enough to address stakeholder concerns with the young firms' quality and potential. As one entrepreneur I interviewed explained, "the best quality of public relations with a lousy quality product is like the advertising that goes on for a movie before the movie comes out. But when the movie comes out, all of a sudden people know if it's any good or not…so you have to have the quality" (Petkova, 2006: 23). Consistent with this idea, in our comparative case study of Amazon.com and its competitors, my co-authors and I observed that intensive communications helped Amazon.com highlight and showcase its major innovations and resources (Rindova, Petkova, & Kotha, 2007). Overall, the limited research to date suggests that communications can lead to the formation of positive perceptions about young firms when supported by high-quality resources and innovative outputs but their stand-alone effect is not clear. Whittington and Yakis-Douglas (Chapter 20, this volume) and Elsbach (Chapter 23, this volume) offer further insights with regard to what makes for effective (or ineffective) strategic communications.

CONCLUDING REMARKS: EMERGING DIRECTIONS FOR FUTURE RESEARCH

The review of extant research on the reputation of young entrepreneurial firms and my attempts to map the three main perspectives onto the stages of reputation development show that research in this area is still in its infancy. While the studies discussed in this chapter offer important insights about the ways young firms can develop their initial reputations, these studies have answered just a few of the many important research questions regarding young firms' reputations. More importantly, they have opened several avenues for future research, as outlined below.

First, the role of young firms in developing their own reputation is yet to be fully understood. The reputation-borrowing perspective points to the fact that prestigious affiliates supposedly have access to superior information about the young firms they select to affiliate with. However, issues like why a focal young firm happens to be selected and, more importantly, what exactly a young firm can do to become selected by the prestigious affiliates, have received little attention. Some studies suggest that the young firms endowed with higher-quality reputational capital by their founders are more likely to be selected by prestigious affiliates (Hallen, 2008; Higgins & Gulati, 2003). However, entrepreneurship scholars also point to the fact that some affiliates, such as venture capital investors and alliance partners, provide mentoring, guidance, and various resources that can help the not-so-good young firms become better (Baum & Silverman, 2004; Sapienza & Gupta, 1994). Therefore, two important questions for future research are: *How can a young firm convince prestigious actors to affiliate with it? Are there any benefits (and if yes, what are they?) for the established industry players who affiliate with young firms?*

The reputation-building perspective points to the importance of being selected for consideration and coverage by institutional intermediaries, such as the media and industry analysts. However, except for the two qualitative case studies that my co-authors and I have published recently (Petkova, Rindova, & Gupta, 2008; Rindova, Petkova, & Kotha, 2007), research falling into this perspective identifies outcomes, such as winning a contest (Rao, 1994) or a product award (Reuber & Fischer, 2007), rather than particular actions to achieve these outcomes, as the inputs into the reputation-building process. The various actions and communication strategies identified from case studies are informative in terms of the repertoire of options available to young firms, but they leave open multiple questions, such as: *What are the "best practices" in building reputation for young firms? Are there certain strategies that work better earlier versus later? Are some strategies more or less effective under certain conditions?* These and other related questions can be addressed by large-sample longitudinal studies that allow for enough variation in activities and resources across the young firms studied.

A second promising area for future research is to explore the differences among young firms' founders and TMTs in their reputation-building efforts. One would expect that more experienced founders would be both more proactive and more successful in their reputation-building efforts (i.e., the endowment effect). Yet, my interviews with experienced entrepreneurs show that entrepreneurs differ widely in their personal beliefs and priorities with regard to technology development versus development of reputation and other intangible assets early in the life of the new firms they started (Petkova, 2006). While individual beliefs may explain, at least to some extent, the variations in effort and allocation of time and attention to reputation-building activities, the degree to which a young firm's reputation-building efforts are effective and indeed lead to the development of initial reputation still remains to be explained. For example, it is possible that some entrepreneurs understand the importance of reputation but lack the time, resources, or skills to develop and initiate an effective reputation-building strategy for their firms.

The gender of the founders and/or TMT members may also play a role—both in terms of priorities and success with reputation development efforts. In the male-dominated world of entrepreneurship and venture capital, being a woman may be seen both as a benefit (e.g., different, even more entrepreneurial) and as a drawback (e.g., lack of credibility, misfit with the stereotype of the high-tech founder). Scholars have also pointed to the industry and context specificity that may determine the use and effectiveness of some reputation-building strategies versus others (Fischer & Reuber, 2007; Petkova, Rindova, & Gupta, 2008). All these speculations are yet to be examined systematically in empirical settings. Examples of important questions for future research to address include: *Why do some entrepreneurs engage in reputation-building efforts for their new firms earlier than others? What factors explain the varying effectiveness of different young firms' reputation-building strategies? Are there any special skills and capabilities needed for effectively devising a reputation-building strategy for young entrepreneurial firms? How does the gender of the founders affect their reputation-building strategies and effectiveness?*

A third opportunity for future research is to develop a richer and more nuanced understanding of the various reputation-granting authorities identified by past research and the potential effects that the first reputation-granting authority may have on the reputation trajectory of a young firm. Given their focus on one reputation-granting authority at a time (e.g., affiliates, the media, industry analysts), the studies discussed in this chapter provide no indication of the relative objectivity or reliability of different reputation-granting authorities. For example, one could argue that the media and industry analysts are much more impersonal and therefore more objective than affiliates. Alternatively, affiliates can be viewed as more reliable evaluators because they have multiple chances to evaluate the young firm over the span of their relationship with it. One could speculate further which of these authorities are more or less competent in evaluating new firms. Similarly, the consequences of having a new firm's initial reputation granted by one authority versus another have not been examined to date. For example, it is clear that the media can bring a new firm to the attention of large numbers of potentially relevant stakeholders. However, these benefits may be relatively short-lived if media attention is not sustained. Moreover, having the initial reputation granted by different authorities may have qualitatively different consequences for the trajectory that a young firm's reputation will follow over its lifespan. All these speculations point to a number of questions that remain wide open for exploration by future research: *What are the consequences of having the initial reputation of a young firm granted by different authorities? Does the reputation with the media substitute for "borrowing" reputation through affiliations? Or are these two complementary paths of reputation development that add unique value to young firms' reputations?*

Finally, a potentially important factor not discussed in this chapter that may be relevant to the reputation of young firms is their geographic location. Whereas the role of location for access to resources is well understood (Saxenian, 2004), whether location in major entrepreneurship clusters (e.g., the Silicon Valley) is good or bad for attracting attention to young firms is not clear. One could argue, for example, that the proximity to potentially relevant stakeholders and the numerous networking opportunities available in the Silicon Valley provide more chances for a young firm to get noticed. Alternatively, given the hundreds of startups competing for attention, such "crowded" locations may prove challenging for young firms trying to stand out from their peers. Future research is needed to explore more carefully the potential effects of location on reputation development and especially on the attention-generating stage. In addition to location in major industrial clusters vs. other areas in the same country, cross-country differences in political, economic, social, and cultural factors can also affect a number of issues discussed in this chapter, such as mechanisms for developing reputation and factors that contribute to the process and its effectiveness. In particular, countries differ in the availability of venture capital, the policies and procedures for young firms going public, and the role that media play in influencing stakeholder perceptions about young firms. For example, the norm of featuring entrepreneurs as celebrities may be more pronounced in the US than in other countries. Thus, important questions for future research to address are: *What are the effects of location in major industrial clusters or emerging centers for entrepreneurial activities on the reputation development process for young firms? How do cross-country differences in political, economic, and socio-cultural factors affect the reputation development process of young firms?*

Summary of Key Studies

Reference	Key Predictions & Findings
Representative studies for "reputation-borrowing"	
Gulati & Higgins (2003)	The signaling value of different endorsements (relationships) depends on the type of market uncertainties that prevail during the time a firm goes public.
	Found: Endorsements by prominent venture capital firms are more beneficial in "cold" market; endorsements by prestigious investment banks are more beneficial in "hot" market.
Lee, Pollock, & Jin (2011)	Uncertainties and risks regarding young organizations make market participants use endorsements by reputable affiliates as signals of a young firm's quality and potential.
	How much a young firm benefits from affiliating with high-reputation venture capitalists depends on the timing of involvement, industry specialization, and geographic proximity of the venture capital firm.
	Found: Early involvement enhances the value of affiliation with high-reputation venture capitalists for young firms; effects of industry specialization and geographic proximity are independent of reputation.
Pollock & Gulati (2007)	A young firm's proclivity to form strategic alliances depends on its visibility within the industry, the perception that it has something useful to offer its partners, and the expectation to deliver on its commitments in the future.
	Found: Initial market response, affiliations with prestigious VCs, and analyst coverage of the firm positively affect alliance formation.
Pollock et al. (2010)	Young firms signal their quality and potential through affiliation with various prestigious third parties.
	Different types of prestigious affiliates convey different signals, depending on whether they provide certification or substantive value to the young firms.
	Found: The benefits of prestigious executives and directors accumulate in a linear fashion (cumulative effect); the benefits of affiliations with prestigious venture capital investors and underwriters accumulate in a curvilinear fashion (diminishing effect).
Reuber & Fischer (2005)	Affiliations with prestigious customers are important reputation signals under high purchase complexity.
	Large number of satisfied customers is important under low purchase complexity and customized product offerings.
	Large number of recognizable and comparable customers in the same niche is important under low complexity/standardized product offerings.

(Continued)

Table Continued

Reference	Key Predictions & Findings
Stuart (2000)	Prominent organizations are (a) likely to be selective in their choice of strategic partners in order to preserve their own reputations; (b) likely to be perceived as reliable evaluators of quality differences among potential partners. Therefore, affiliations with prominent organizations serve as endorsement of the unknown quality and potential of young firms.
	Found: Young and small firms benefit more from affiliations with prestigious alliance partners than with older and larger peers.
Stuart, Hoang, & Hybels (1999)	Faced with greater certainty about the quality of young firms, third parties rely on the prominence of affiliates to make judgments about a firm's quality.
	Found: Young firms endorsed by prominent partners perform better during IPO than those without prominent affiliates.
Representative studies for "reputation-building"	
Fischer & Reuber (2007)—theory paper	Reputation forms as the attitudes of multiple individuals in a given stakeholder group converge. This process is facilitated by coherent and consistent positive signals.
	Reputation valence is influenced by evaluations of the category to which the new firm belongs and the firm-specific information.
Petkova, Rindova, & Gupta (2008)	An exploratory case study of the reputation-building efforts and types of reputation accumulated by new firms.
	Found: Generalized reputation is built for new firms that introduce unobservable or difficult to evaluate products, through the use of symbolic activities and investments in human capital, social capital, and product development. Local reputation is built for new firms that introduce observable or easy to evaluate products, through investments in customer relationships, product quality, and human capital.
Rao (1994)	"victories in certification contests are credentialing mechanisms that…build the reputations of organizations" (p. 30). Argues that reputation and legitimacy intertwined early in a firm's life.
	Found: Victories in industry contests increase the survival chances of young firms.
Rindova, Petkova, & Kotha (2007)	Inductive case studies suggest that the reputation of new firms in emerging markets is influenced by the patterns of visible market actions that the firm takes.
	Found: Visibility is related to higher levels of action. Strategic character reflects action composition. Favorability is related to innovative actions and expectation of value-creation. Esteem is explained with a combination of innovations and symbolic actions that make the firm an exemplar of the emerging new market.
Reuber & Fischer (2007)	Dynamic effects of quality signals on reputation change.
	Found: Receiving product awards leads to positive reputational change; gaps in product announcements lead to negative reputational change; same pattern of reputation change for younger and older firms.

Representative studies for "reputation by endowment"

Beckman, Burton, & O'Reilly (2007)	Previous industry experience that TMT members bring to new firms influences stakeholder perceptions about the firms' potential and access to capital.
	Found: Diverse TMT experiences have positive effect on obtaining venture capital and going public.
Beckman & Burton (2008)	Founders' experience affects the initial organizational structure, which has long-lasting effects on subsequent executives and structures. Initial structure influences chances of venture capital funding and going public.
	Found: Starting with a more complete functional structure increases the likelihood of going public. Broadly experienced teams obtain venture capital faster. Experience and structure completeness reinforce each other's effect on obtaining venture funding and going public.
Burton, Sorensen, & Beckman (2002)	Reputational benefits accrue to employees of prominent firms: Entrepreneurial prominence reduces perceived uncertainty of the new firm
	Found: Entrepreneurial prominence and senior management experience increase the likelihood of receiving external financing at start-up. Entrepreneurial prominence and graduate degree increase the likelihood to pursue an innovation strategy.
Pollock, Fund, & Baker (2009)	Founder-CEO experience affects the uncertainty perceived by venture capital investors with regard to a young firm.
	Found: Industry-based uncertainty reduces the chances for founder-CEO retention. Founder-CEO experience and venture capital firm experience moderate the relationship between industry-based uncertainty and founder-CEO retention.
Sapienza & Gupta (1994)	Greater uncertainties regarding the start-up and its CEO lead to more monitoring on the part of venture capital investors.
	Found: CEO previous start-ups experience reduces perceived uncertainty/need for monitoring. Earlier funding stage and higher level of innovation increase need for monitoring.

REFERENCES

Aldrich, H. & Fiol, M. (1994). "Fools rush in? The institutional context of industry creation." *Academy of Management Review*, 19: 645–670.

Baum, J. A. C. & Silverman, B. S. (2004). "Picking winners or building them? Alliance, intellectual, and human capital as selection criteria in venture financing and performance of biotechnology startups." *Journal of Business Venturing*, 19: 411–436.

Beckman, C. M. & Burton, M. D. (2008). "Founding the future: Path dependence in the evolution of top management teams from founding to IPO." *Organization Science*, 19: 3–24.

——, ——, & O'Reilly, C. (2007). "Early teams: The impact of team demography on VC financing and going public." *Journal of Business Venturing*, 22: 147–173.

Burton, M. D., Sorensen, J. B., & Beckman, C. M. (2002). "Coming from good stock: Career histories and new venture formation." *Social Structure and Organizations Revisited*, 19: 229–262.

Fischer, E. & Reuber, A. R. (2007). "The good, the bad, and the unfamiliar: The challenges of reputation formation facing new firms." *Entrepreneurship Theory and Practice*, 31(1): 53–75.

Gulati, R. & Higgins, M. C. (2003). "Which ties matter when? The contingent effects of interorganizational partnerships on IPO success." *Strategic Management Journal*, 24: 127–144.

Hayward, M. L. A., Rindova, V. P., & Pollock, T. G. (2004). "Believing one's own press: The antecedents and consequences of chief executive officer celebrity." *Strategic Management Journal*, 25(7): 637–653.

Higgins, M. C. & Gulati, R. (2003). "Getting off to a good start: The effects of upper echelon affiliations on underwriter prestige." *Organization Science*, 14: 244–263.

—— & —— (2006). "Stacking the deck: The effect of upper echelon affiliations for entrepreneurial firms." *Strategic Management Journal*, 27: 1–26.

Kennedy, M. T. (2005). "Behind the one-way mirror: Refraction in the construction of product market categories." *Poetics*, 33: 201–226.

—— (2008). "Getting counted: Markets, media, and reality." *American Sociological Review*, 73: 270–295.

King, B. G. & Whetten, D. A. (2008). "Rethinking the relationship between reputation and legitimacy: A social actor conceptualization." *Corporate Reputation Review*, 11(3): 192–207.

Klein, K. & Kozlowski, S. W. J. (2000). "From micro to meso: Critical steps in conceptualizing and conducting multilevel research." *Organizational Research Methods*, 3: 211–236.

Lee, P. M., Pollock, T. G., & Jin, K. (2011). "The contingent value of venture capitalist reputation." *Strategic Organization*, 9: 33–69.

Lounsbury, M. & Glynn, M. A. (2001). "Cultural entrepreneurship: Stories, legitimacy, and the acquisition of resources." *Strategic Management Journal*, 22: 545–564.

Martens, M., Jennings, J. E., & Jennings, P. D. (2007). "Do the stories they tell get them the money they need? The role of entrepreneurial narratives in resource acquisition." *Academy of Management Journal*, 50: 1107–1132.

Petkova, A. P. (2006). "Reputation building by new ventures: Three essays on processes and performance." Doctoral Dissertation, University of Maryland, College Park, USA.

——, Rindova, V. P., & Gupta, A. K. (2008). "How can new ventures build reputation? An exploratory study." *Corporate Reputation Review*, 11(4): 320–334.

Pollock, T. G. & Gulati, R. (2007). "Standing out from the crowd: The visibility-enhancing effects of IPO-related signals on alliance formations by entrepreneurial firms." *Strategic Organization*, 5: 339–372.

—— & Rindova, V. (2003). "Media legitimation effects in the market for initial public offerings." *Academy of Management Journal*, 46: 631–642.

——, Rindova, V. P., & Maggitti, P. G. (2008). "Market watch: Information and availability cascades among the media and investors in the IPO market." *Academy of Management Journal*, 51: 335–358.

——, Fund, B. R., & Baker, T. (2009). "Dance with the one that brought you? Venture capital firms and the retention of founder-CEOs." *Strategic Entrepreneurship Journal*, 3: 199–217.

——, Chen, G., Jackson, E. M., & Hambrick, D. C. (2010). "Just how much prestige is enough? Assessing the value of multiple types of high-status affiliates for young firms." *Journal of Business Venturing*, 25(1): 6–23.

Porac, J. F., Mishina, Y., & Pollock, T. G. (2002). "Entrepreneurial narratives and the dominant logic of high-growth firms." In A. Huff & M. Jenkins (Eds.), *Mapping Strategic Knowledge*. Thousand Oaks, CA: Sage, 112–136.

Rao, H. (1994). "The social construction of reputation: Certification contests, legitimation, and the survival of organizations in the American automobile industry: 1895–1912." *Strategic Management Journal*, 15: 29–44.

Reuber, A. R. & Fischer, E. (2005). "The company you keep: How young firms in different competitive contexts signal reputation through their customers." *Entrepreneurship Theory and Practice*, 29(1): 57–78.

—— & Fischer, E. (2007). "Don't rest on your Laurels: Reputational change and young technology-based ventures." *Journal of Business Venturing*, 22(3): 363–387.

Rindova, V. P., Williamson, I. O., Petkova, A. P., & Sever, J. M. (2005). "Being good or being known: An empirical examination of the dimensions, antecedents, and consequences of organizational reputation." *Academy of Management Journal*, 48: 1033–1049.

——, Petkova, A. P., & Kotha, S. (2007). "Standing out: How new firms in emerging markets build reputation in the media." *Strategic Organization*, 5(1): 31–70.

Rosa, J. A., Porac, J. F., Runser-Spanjol, J., & Saxon, M. S. (1999). "Sociocognitive dynamics in a product market." *Journal of Marketing*, 63(Special Issue): 64–77.

Sapienza, H. J. & Gupta, A. K. (1994). "Impact of agency risk and task uncertainty on venture capitalist-CEO interaction." *Academy of Management Journal*, 37: 1618–1632.

Saxenian, A. (2004). *Regional Advantage: Culture and Competition in Silicon Valley and Route 128*. Cambridge, MA: Harvard University Press.

Shane, S. & Cable, D. (2002). "Network ties, reputation, and the financing of new ventures." *Management Science*, 48: 364–381.

Stuart, T. (2000). "Interorganizational alliances and the performance of firms: A study of growth and innovation rates in a high-technology industry." *Strategic Management Journal*, 21: 791–811.

Stuart, T. E., Hoang, H., & Hybels, R. C. (1999). "Interorganizational endorsements and the performance of entrepreneurial ventures." *Administrative Science Quarterly*, 44: 315–349.

Williamson, I. O. (2000). "Employer legitimacy and recruitment success in small business." *Entrepreneurship: Theory & Practice*, 25: 27–42.

CHAPTER 20

....

STRATEGIC DISCLOSURE: STRATEGY AS A FORM OF REPUTATION MANAGEMENT

....

RICHARD WHITTINGTON
BASAK YAKIS-DOUGLAS

This chapter addresses strategy communications as a form of reputation management. It traces the rise and variable adoption of strategy communications across large corporations globally. We review the existing literature relevant to strategy communications and identify two key research questions that emerge: why do managers adopt this reputation management practice, and how do managers perform them. On the first question of why, we propose avenues of research that build on the literatures on voluntary disclosure, strategic signaling, and institutional theory. On the second question of how, we propose both discourse analytical approaches and a dramaturgical perspective that recognizes strategy communications as a kind of praxis, involving many modalities beyond simple words and recordable through a host of new media such as webcasting, blogs, and tweets. We go on to suggest research opportunities for the reputation management field generally in exploring issues of choice and praxis. We also consider the public policy implications of strategy communications.

INTRODUCTION

....

THIS chapter considers organizations' external communications about overall strategy as a type of reputation management. These strategy communications can take many forms, including strategy briefings, corporate press releases, and annual reports, and their impact may be felt in various ways, including stock prices and analyst recommendations. Given these impacts, such strategy communications are central to the reputational question of how stakeholders regard a firm's potential to deliver value (Rindova, Pollock, & Hayward, 2006). In this chapter we review the developing literature on strategy communications, with particular attention to their symbolic content (Zajac & Westphal, 2004). Our focus is specifically on communications about the strategic plans of the firm as a whole, rather than announcements about individual strategic moves. We identify two significant research opportunities with regard to these strategy communications. First, we introduce the question of why organizations choose to adopt this practice at all, given the advantages of secrecy and surprise in strategy: here we shall particularly draw on insights from the accounting and finance literature on voluntary disclosure (Bassen, Basse Mama, & Ramaj, 2010). Second, we raise the issue of how these strategy communications are actively performed. Here we are treating strategy communications not only as a more or less institutionalized practice, but also as a form of locally enacted praxis (Reckwitz, 2002). Finally, we shall propose that questions of choice and praxis are opportunities in the reputation management literature more widely, beyond strategy communications in particular.

We start by illustrating these strategy communications with a prominent example. On 11 February 2011, Nokia's recently appointed CEO, Stephen Elop, held a "strategy and finance briefing" elaborating a new overall strategy for the struggling phone giant. The new strategy included an alliance with Microsoft, the downgrading of some of Nokia's own software programs, and the abandonment of growth in the United States. The Microsoft alliance was announced on the evening before the briefing, prompting an immediate 7 percent plunge in Nokia's stock price at market opening next morning. Thus Elop had a clear task in the briefing—to change the market's mind. Two meetings were scheduled: the first with specialist journalists at 10 a.m., the second with financial analysts at 12 p.m. The meetings took place in a large London hotel conference room and were publicly viewable via live webcast. Each meeting was divided into 20 minute presentations delivered from the stage, followed by Questions and Answers with the audience. The Nokia investor relations website provided press releases summarizing key points as well as presentation PowerPoints. Despite the coup of introducing Microsoft CEO Steve Ballmer to the first meeting, neither went well. As the meetings proceeded, bloggers and twitterers commented in real time on the lack of detail (on new phones, for example), the jargon ("ecosystems," and so on) and the theatrical "performance" itself (technological glitches and Elop's and Ballmer's suits, smiles, and physiques).[1] During the first half-hour of the journalists' meeting, Nokia's stock fell by 2 percent (about €500m), and during and immediately after the analysts' meeting the stock fell a further 4 percent, against a market as a whole that was slightly up on the day.

This example illustrates three points that we shall develop in this chapter. First of all, a company's ability to communicate a positive and plausible strategy matters to stakeholders. Nokia failed, and the loss of corporate value indicates substantial damage to its reputation. Second, strategy communication is a complex, multimodal practice, not reducible to a single text but involving several media (press releases, webcasts,

---

[1] E.G. http://blogs.ft.com/fttechhub/2011/02/nokia-live/; http://www.zdnet.com/blog/hardware/live-blog-nokia-financial-and-strategy-briefing/11357; http://www.engadget.com/2011/02/11/live-from-nokias-capital-markets-day/#disqus_thread (all accessed 2 March 2011).

PowerPoints, and direct speeches) that are ordinarily coordinated as a total package. Third, while strategy communications may often adopt the procedures of a somewhat routinized practice—the hotel conference room, the PowerPoint slides, and so on—they also demand considerable skill in the praxis of execution. Elop and Ballmer were performing on stage. As the growing skepticism of the blogosphere and the sliding stock price both showed, how they performed their roles over the course of the day had significance in itself, over and above the bare information in the initial announcement of the Microsoft alliance. Praxis makes a difference.

The chapter continues as follows. We start by introducing the emerging literature on strategy communications, in particular highlighting the importance of symbolic management for reputation and legitimacy. We then trace the spread of strategy communications (strategy reviews, strategy presentations, strategy briefings, and so on) as a practice amongst large firms globally, and explore financial market and other institutional pressures that potentially account for this. The third substantive section turns to praxis, both examining the continuing potential of traditional discourse analytical approaches to strategy communications, but also pointing to the way in which many modes of communication—discourse, artifacts, and bodies—are employed across a range of media in the symbolic management of strategy. Our final discussion summarizes research opportunities in the area of strategy communications generally and points to possible extensions in related areas. It closes by picking up on the significance of strategy communications for public policy and the support of long-term investment in market economies.

STRATEGY COMMUNICATIONS AND REPUTATION MANAGEMENT

Our focus on strategy communications implies an active orientation to the shaping of corporate reputations, with a role for choice about both whether and how to communicate. In this sense, we are not concerned with reputation as a by-product of the strategic and performance track record of organizations (Basdeo et al., 2006; Roberts & Dowling, 2002). Rather, our approach emphasizes the deliberate and discretionary use of communications to construct corporate reputations. These communications, therefore, are close to what Rindova & Fombrun (1999) have termed "strategic projections," the various kinds of statements about intended strategy issued by organizations through annual reports, press releases, and advertisements, for example. Strategic projections contribute to the formation of corporate reputations by affecting how audiences evaluate a firm and allocate the resources they control (Rindova & Fombrun, 1999). In their terms, these projections not only provide information about strategic investments, but have additional symbolic content in providing ready-made and potentially desirable interpretations of strategic moves for key audiences.

We particularly emphasize how organizations manage the symbolic rather than simply informational aspects of these communications. Symbolic management generally refers to how organizations justify their moves or performances in order to appear consistent with the social values and expectations of important audiences (Ashforth & Gibbs, 1990; Benner & Ranganathan, 2011). In this view, organizations make symbolic as well as substantive communications, with the first having a potential value over and above the second. For example, corporations may make symbolic appeals to agency theory in order to justify managerial compensation schemes, with shareholders responding positively to these justifications independently of the degree to which schemes are actually implemented (Zajac & Westphal, 2004). Symbolic management has a particularly important reassuring role in areas of inherent uncertainty, as in the control of managerial agency. Strategy, projecting into an unknowable future, also involves high uncertainty. Regardless of whether a strategy is substantively enacted, the very promise of a strategy, if couched appropriately, may have high symbolic value.

Research attention is beginning to turn to communications about strategy and particularly their symbolic content. The table at the end of the chapter summarizes the six main studies in terms of their key constructs and findings and the organizational communications media on which they focus. The focus here is on studies of strategy communications that attend to symbolic content, rather than simple factual announcements of particular strategic moves (such as the launch of a new product or an acquisition). In the table this symbolic management includes, for example, the use of charismatic language (Fanelli, Misangyi, & Tosi, 2009) and the qualified or unqualified justification of a particular kind of strategic change (Fiss & Zajac, 2006).

The small number of studies points to the neglected nature of this kind of symbolic strategic communication. The neglect is undue for, even from these few studies, it is clear that symbolic management can have material consequences. Thus Fanelli, Misangyi, & Tosi (2009) find that the use of charismatic language is associated with favorable analyst recommendations and greater consensus amongst analysts, while Martens, Jennings, & Jennings (2007) show that use of contextually familiar language can improve initial public offering (IPO) premia for entrepreneurs. In the sense that Rindova & Fombrun (1999) propose, these strategic communications are consequential for reputations in that they affect how critical audiences evaluate the enterprises in question.

But having shown that symbolic communications about strategy make a material difference, there remain at least two significant gaps. The first is one of choice. A strong orientation has been toward new ventures and firms undertaking IPOs (e.g., Martens, Jennings, & Jennings, 2007; Rindova, Petkova, & Kothari, 2007), which of course have little option about communicating their strategy: they need investors and customers (Petkova, Chapter 19, this volume). Only one study here, Fiss & Zajac (2006), considers why some firms rather than others might choose to communicate symbolically in the first place. Thus Fiss & Zajac find that it is government or family-owned enterprises that are more likely to provide a qualified rather than unqualified justification of the adoption of shareholder value measures. Second, there is the question of how such firms communicate. In this respect, following the "linguistic turn" (e.g., Martens, Jennings, & Jennings, 2007;

Kennedy, 2008), these studies have favored the discourse in written texts—annual reports, shareholder letters, prospectuses, and press releases—and typically focused on only one communications medium at a time. There are just two partial exceptions to this narrow use of media. Rindova, Petkova, & Kothari (2007) use websites as well as press releases, while Vaara & Monin (2010) manage to draw on interviews and other sources to illuminate the press releases that were their prime source for the organizations' strategic communications. Effectively, though, other media for symbolic communication are ignored.

It is plain from the research so far that the symbolic contents of strategy communications matter. They change reputations, as reflected in analyst recommendations and stock price valuations. But, from this review, we draw two significant opportunities at least. First of all, it is unclear why firms in general choose to communicate about their strategy. The predominant focus up to now has been on the effects of these communications, not which firms do communicate and which do not. Second, attention has concentrated on formal texts as the media for these communications—letters to shareholders, press releases, and the like. These are evidently influential, but, if the Nokia example at the start of this chapter is representative, such texts are just one of a whole set of communications media surrounding strategy. There is an opportunity to extend to other kinds of symbolic management, including the actual presentations as recorded by webcasts for example. As research goes beyond the written record, it becomes possible to explore the rich, micro-level dynamics of symbolic praxis, in other words, strategy communications as performance (Biehl-Missal, 2011). In the end, formal texts are like yetis' footprints in the snow: traces of larger phenomena, left behind after the action has passed.

Our proposed focus on the strategy communications of established corporations is particularly apt for exploring both choice and performance. First of all, unlike new ventures or those seeking IPOs, established corporations have a good deal of discretion about how much they should communicate in this way, with some doing so regularly, some at particular points, and many barely at all. These communications are a partially institutionalized practice, whose variable adoption is not yet understood. Second, especially for larger corporations, these strategy communications are often recorded live and attract a lot of attention, including real-time commentaries and continuous stock price movements. With webcast videos, market reactions, and simultaneous blogs and tweets, it becomes feasible to consider these communications not only as practices, but as forms of praxis. The performance of the communicators, and audience evaluations, can be followed as they happen.

WHY COMMUNICATE STRATEGY?

The kind of strategy communication made by Nokia in February 2011 is now a routinized practice amongst many corporations, including Nokia itself. Although Nokia's briefing at the start was prompted by a particular strategic move, Nokia—like companies such as BP, Shell, and Vodafone—makes such presentations about overall strategy most years. From a competitive strategy point of view, these strategy communications are initially puzzling: why inform competitors of one's strategic intentions? Why, too, invite such direct scrutiny from analysts and the media, with all the risks entailed? Nokia's strategy briefing was disastrous for its reputation, as reflected in its share price. Corporations do not have to make these communications, and most indeed do not. We propose three promising avenues for explaining such strategy communications. The first comes from finance, where strategy communications can be considered under the general rubric of "voluntary disclosures," phenomena such as earnings forecasts, business segment reporting, and new product announcements (Bassen, Basse Mama, & Ramaj, 2010: 63). The second avenue is inspired by signaling theory in the strategy literature (Farrell, 1987). The third approach to explaining strategy communications is institutionalist, taking account of different and changing sociological contexts (e.g., Rao & Sivakumar, 1999).

There is indeed a great deal of variability in the willingness of large corporations to make these strategy communications. A Factiva search suggests that exactly a quarter of Fortune Global Top 100 corporations made external strategy communications during 2009: included are consumer companies such as Procter & Gamble, Vodafone, and Nokia, financial companies such as Barclays and DeutscheBank, and BRIC and Asian companies such as Lukoil and Toshiba.[2] As Figure 20.1 suggests, the proportion of Fortune Global Top 100 corporations choosing to make these strategy communications has risen substantially since the 1990s, with a peak of 29 in 2005 and a fairly steady pattern since then. For these large global corporations, therefore, strategy communications seem to be an increasingly common but still far from universal form of reputation management. This growth of strategy communication, and the variability in take-up, needs to be explained.

For the finance and accounting literature, voluntary disclosures in general (e.g., earnings forecasts and business segment information) are a central puzzle. There are direct costs in preparing the appropriate information and presenting it effectively (Armitage & Marston, 2008; Roberts et al., 2006). There are also potential "proprietary costs" to disclosure, in particular costs imposed by the reactions of competitor and other actors to the information released (Wagenhofer, 1990; Prencipe, 2004). For example, information concerning the high potential profits of a particular strategy is liable to encourage competitors to attempt imitation and regulators to investigate potential abuses of market power (Wagenhofer, 1990). Nonetheless, while is true that only a very small part of this literature has attended to strategy communications, even obliquely (Eng & Mak, 2003; Mazzola, Ravasi, & Gabbioneta, 2006), research on voluntary disclosure does offer some pathways for understanding why some firms might communicate more about strategy than others.

---

[2] Search terms: "strategy meeting," "strategy presentation," "strategy review," "strategy update," "strategy briefing," and "strategy announcement," excluding internal events and reviewed for relevance.

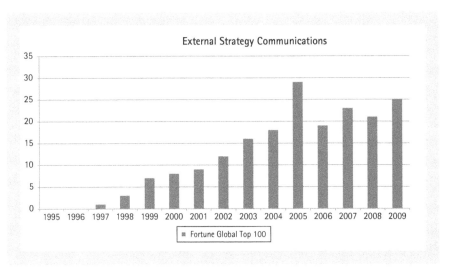

FIGURE 20.1 External strategy communications.

The finance and accounting literature propose a number of firm-specific factors that may promote voluntary disclosures about strategy. Some of these factors are structural to the firm. For instance, large size may reduce disclosure costs, by spreading the cost of information management and, perhaps, by reducing the threat of competitor reaction (Bassen, Basse Mama, & Ramaj, 2010). For complex businesses, disclosure can help mitigate the agency problem existing between corporate managements and shareholders: the reduction in uncertainty attendant on reducing information asymmetries increases the willingness of shareholders to pay more for the company's stock (Bassen, Basse Mama, & Ramaj, 2010; Healy & Palepu, 2005). Thus diversified businesses that are hard for outsiders to understand have a greater incentive to reduce information asymmetries through disclosure, as do those companies with a high market-to-book value (reflecting, for instance, high expenditures on marketing or research and development), whose assets analysts may perceive as uncertain (Hutton, 2005; Barth, Kasnick, & McNichols, 2001). Similarly, firms pursuing ambitious and innovative strategies have an incentive to disclose in order to gain shareholders' and analysts' support (Healy & Palepu, 1995). Ownership and board structure also influence patterns of disclosure, with large proportions of institutional ownership, government ownership, and low managerial ownership, for example, increasing the propensity to disclose (Eng & Mak, 2003; Hutton, 2005). Firms that have a large analyst following are more likely to disclose, though the relationship goes in the opposite direction as well, with disclosure encouraging increased analyst following too (Hutton, 2005; Barth, Kasnick, & McNichols, 2001). As well as these structural reasons for favoring disclosure, the literature identifies more contingent ones. These include prospective or recent transactions requiring shareholder support, for example acquisitions, security offerings, or debt offerings (Healy & Palepu, 2001). Poor performance, a contest for corporate control, and CEO turnover can also increase the likelihood of voluntary disclosure (Skinner, 1994). These types of urgent contingencies may help explain the number of financial institutions (six) amongst the 25 Fortune Global 100 making strategy communications during the financial crisis of 2009.

The strategy literature, too, proposes a number of factors that may encourage strategy communications specifically. Wagenhofer's (1990) warning about the danger of prompting competitor entry into attractive markets finds counterarguments in the literature on strategic interactions. Here strategy communications may actually diminish competitive rivalry. Thus incumbents trying to defend their position in an industry can signal commitment in order to deter new entry, for example by announcing ambitions with regard to market share or future capacity increments or by affirming the importance of that industry with regard to the strategy of the firm as a whole (Porter, 1985). In industries where there are large sunk costs (because of research and development (R & D) or initial capital investments), there are incentives to signal intentions clearly to competitors in order to discourage new entrants (Farrell, 1987). Similarly, in capital intensive industries such as paper and pulp, announcements of plans for new capacity help to manage aggregate investment in the industry, holding back more marginal projects, especially in competitive subsectors (Christensen & Caves, 1997). Strategy communications can thus work to reduce competitive rivalry in an industry, and are particularly likely where large investments are required. Some initial support for such industry effects is provided by the fact that eight of the 25 Fortune Global 100 corporations communicating strategy in 2009 were oil companies, working in an industry characterized by substantial and interdependent investments.

The literatures on voluntary disclosure and strategy dynamics help account for firms' relative willingness to communicate about strategy cross-sectionally, but are less able to explain the general increase in such communications since the 1990s. Here, broadly institutionalist perspectives may be more helpful. The institutional context in which large Western firms have evolved in the last two decades has seen a growing emphasis on shareholder value as the guiding norm of business, associated with the rise of large institutional shareholders such as mutual funds and an accompanying increase in the numbers of financial analysts hungry for information (Fligstein, 2001; Davis, 2009). In this institutional environment, there may be substantial penalties to corporations that are unable to "sell" strategic visions that fit the preconceptions of the analyst and shareholder community, the discount suffered by conglomerates being a case in point (Zuckerman, 2000). The result has been a parallel rise within large corporations of investor relations professionals, responsible for supplying information to shareholders and analysts (Kelly, Laskin, & Rosenstein, 2010; Sandhu, 2009). Taking an institutionalist perspective, Rao & Sivakumar (1999) find that the creation of investor relations departments by Fortune 500 firms is significantly associated with the number of financial analyses following the company, as well as the existence of board interlocks with other companies that had already instituted investor relations departments. Similar institutional factors may be at play in the decision to communicate about strategy.

Nonetheless, the implications of an institutional shift toward shareholder value are still somewhat ambiguous with regards to the decision to communicate on strategy. On the one hand, the institutional prioritization of shareholder value has increased the availability of financial information, and this commodification of quantitative data may have placed a premium on qualitative inputs, such as strategy communications, which can potentially provide more discerning analysts with an investing edge (Rogers, 2000). On the other hand, investor relations departments still struggle to get analysts to look beyond their focus on quarterly earnings in order to consider prospects for the long term (Laskin, 2009). Internally too, finance and strategy can be awkward partners. Zorn (2004) finds that the creation of the "chief finance officer" position in large corporations, linked to the rise of shareholder value concerns, is negatively associated with the presence of a strategic planning vice president (VP). Thus, there is a suggestive parallel between the general growth of strategy communications and the institutional shift to norms of shareholder value, but the exact links between these trends are not unproblematic and still need to be teased out.

Institutions may also help explain international differences in strategy communications. Again, the relationship with American-style shareholder value appears complex. Amongst the 25 Fortune Global 100 corporations making strategy communications in 2009 (Figure 20.1), it is noticeable that only three are American: Exxon Mobil, Marathon, and Procter & Gamble. At 12.0 percent, this contrasts strikingly with the 31 percent share of the Fortune Global 100 held by American companies. Here, institutionally sensitive research into patterns of international voluntary disclosure may be informative. It has been found that companies based in common law countries (such as the United Kingdom, Australia, and the United States) are generally more likely to voluntarily disclose financial information (Hope, 2003), and the same might be expected of strategy communications in particular. On the other hand, companies coming from civil law or other traditions have an increased propensity to disclose as they become more global in scope: participation in the global marketplace increases the incentives to conform to the standards of common law institutions as well (Webb, Cahan, & Sun, 2008). This emergence onto the international arena may explain the readiness of new BRIC (Brazil, Russia, India, and China) multinationals, such as LUKOIL, to communicate about strategy.

In sum, strategy communications are a form of reputation management that is used quite variably by large corporations internationally. We propose that the literatures on voluntary disclosure, competitive interaction, and institutional change all suggest paths for exploring why some firms choose to communicate, while others do not. Following these literatures, the propensity for strategy communications is likely to be influenced by institutional environment, industry effects such as the nature of strategic investments and rivalry, firm-specific structural factors such as ownership, complexity, and analyst following, and more contingent firm factors such as performance problems, CEO turnover, or the proximity of large financial transactions.

How to Communicate Strategy?

As we noted earlier, a good deal of research on strategy communications has been inspired by the so-called linguistic turn, and focused on formal documents such as press releases or letters to shareholders (Martens, Jennings, & Jennings, 2007; Kennedy, 2008). Such texts can make a material difference to corporate reputation as reflected in analyst recommendations or IPO pricing. The strategy communications on which we focus here typically involve texts too, for example the transcripts of speeches and PowerPoint presentations. The discursive content of such texts is like to be a consequential part of how strategies are communicated. However, strategy communications are also made live, where the quality of the performance—recall the unfortunate reception of Nokia's Stephen Elop—makes a difference too. This section therefore draws not only on the standalone discourse analysis of strategy communications texts (Barry & Elmes, 1997; Schriffin, Tannen, & Hamilton, 2003), but adopts a more dramaturgical perspective in which words are just one of the modes by which strategy communications are performed as praxis (Reckwitz, 2002; Whittington, 2006).

Two kinds of discourse analysis offer dimensions potentially relevant to how strategy communications are performed: linguistic and thematic. First, the language used in chief executive and strategy discourse in general has already been studied at both lexical and grammatical levels, in ways that are suggestive for strategy communications in particular. At the grammatical level, Rogers (2000) has pointed to how chief executives may use active and passive constructions in their presentations in order to claim or distance themselves from responsibility. A preponderance of passive constructions, suggestive of fatalism, is unlikely to be well received by market actors interested in backing exceptional performance. Similarly, Vaara, Sorsa, & Pälli (2010) suggest the potential significance of the balance between declarative and imperative grammars in strategic plans, with the use of imperative formulae intended to give plans more authority. The grammar of strategic plans can also show different degrees of what Vaara, Sorsa, & Pälli (2010) call "self-authorizing," in other words the attribution of a kind of natural agency to the strategy in its own right (as in "the strategy requires this or that"). Again, the grammars of the imperative and self-authorizing are likely to strike analysts and markets in particular ways.

Turning to the lexical level, Rogers (2000) proposes the potential significance of positive and negative words, the negative likely to exert a baleful influence on market confidence. More subtle is the use of words that index more widely legitimate (or illegitimate) forms of strategy discourse (Barry & Elmes, 1997). Means of constructing legitimate discourse might include invoking words associated with established "language games" such as competition as a form of warfare (Rindova, Becerra, & Contordo, 2004); endowing charismatic authority on the strategic leader through the choice of emotional and inclusive words (e.g., "our passion") (Fanelli, Misangyi, & Tosi, 2009); or referencing seemingly authoritative concepts in the strategic management discipline such as SWOT (strengths, weaknesses, opportunities, and threats) analysis (Vaara, Sorsa, & Pälli, 2010). As Fanelli, Misangyi, & Tosi (2009) propose, in particular for chief executive letters, such putatively legitimate forms of strategy discourse may be expected to win greater support in the financial markets.

The discourse of strategy communications can also be analyzed in terms of underlying themes. Barry & Elmes (1997) identify a fundamental tension in strategy discourse between the credible and the unfamiliar: strategies need to be distinctive and innovative, yet not so outlandish as to be unbelievable. Discursive approaches have therefore considered both the degree of continuity in "plot" in corporate communications (Rindova & Fombrun, 1999) and the extent of "discursive innovation" in strategic plans (Vaara, Sorsa, & Pälli, 2010), i.e. the introduction of new buzzwords and concepts. Continuity in plot may enhance credibility, while discursive innovation introduces the unfamiliar. This tension between continuity and innovation also implies the importance of time as a theme in strategy communications. Thus Bozzolan & Mazzola (2007) analyze the simple planning horizons (three years, five years, and so on) used in their Italian strategy communications, while both Fanelli, Misangyi, & Tosi (2009) and Martens, Jennings, & Jennings (2007) consider the balance of references to the past, present, and future in their documents. Also in relation to credibility, Martens, Jennings, & Jennings point to the importance of clearly elaborated rationales for IPO strategies, while Mazzola, Ravasi, & Gabbioneta (2006) develop criteria for assessing the causal texture of their Italian strategy communications. Mazzola, Ravasi, & Gabbioneta (2006) also consider that the provision of detail on strategy implementation and measures of progress is likely to enhance credibility. Other themes that are proposed to enhance analyst and shareholder support are the reliance on quantitative data, especially the provision of long time series (Bozzolan & Mazzola, 2006; Ramnath, Rock, & Shane, 2008), and the provision of detailed disaggregated data, for example on business segments (Rogers, 2000; Ramnath, Rock, & Shane, 2008).

But texts are only part of the complete performance of strategy communications. Here we make use of practice theory's distinction between practices, the routinized general form, and praxis, the enactment of such practices in a particular moment (Reckwitz, 2002; Whittington, 2006). From a praxis point of view, the texts of strategy communications are often no more than the inert residues of a much more complex and dynamic performance. Clothing, voice, and gesture are all part of strategy's symbolic repertoire too. Thus Zott & Huy (2007) have already explored how entrepreneurs use a wide range of artefacts and activities in the symbolic management of their ventures' legitimacy. They show how successful entrepreneurs are often attentive to the performance aspects of symbolic management, buying-in specialized consultants to advise on presentational skills, how to dress, how to move during meetings, and even how to talk. Likewise, Biehl-Missal (2011) characterizes chief executives' presentations as a form of "show business," where stage design, clothing, and style, as well as rhetorical content, can all make a difference. As Elsbach (Chapter 23, this volume) indicates too, the presentational skills of "über-cool" Steve Jobs have been important to the reputation of Apple and its products, his style and humour at product launches working to reinforce the corporate image. On stage, Jobs was the symbolic embodiment of Apple.

In theorizing about the praxis of strategy communications, we can draw particularly on the literature on impression management, which has already been explored as a contributor to corporate legitimacy and reputation, particularly at the level of organizational routines (Elsbach & Sutton, 1992; Elsbach, Sutton, & Principe, 1998). Here though we highlight impression management at the level of individuals' performance: that of senior managers as they communicate their strategies. This goes beyond the words that might be analyzed as spoken discourse. As Goffman (1959) originally proposed, there are both the impressions that an actor gives verbally and those which the actor gives *off* through non-verbal cues. Goffman's dramaturgical perspective points to how human interaction has elements of theatrical performance in which people manage impressions by manipulating not just speech, but bodies and a range of physical props. Communications involves a whole package of modalities, some managed more self-consciously than others.

Recent microethnographic approaches make increasing use of video analysis in order to capture the complex, multimodal nature of human practices (Streeck, Goodwin & Labaron, 2011). Microethnographers' video recordings reveal how speech is often supported by a variety of modes, both bodily (posture, gesture, gaze, and orientation) and artifactual (representational tools such as whiteboards or PowerPoint presentations). From this perspective, discourse analysis techniques are liable to "logocentricism" (Streeck et al., 2011), missing the full apparatus through which meaning is communicated and interpreted. In a business context, something of this multimodality can be recognized in Clark & Greatbatch's (2004) observation of the performances of management gurus such as Tom Peters and Gary Hamel in front of their audiences. These gurus are verbally dextrous, but they also use tone of voice, pacing of speech, facial expressions, bodily movement, and physical orientation in order to communicate their messages. It is not by words alone that they impress.

In the same way, strategy communications are staged events amenable to dramaturgical analysis. There is a reason why Stephen Elop and Steve Ballmer met together with their audience in London. They did not rely simply on a written press release; they performed on stage. Their performances did not impress: value leaked away from Nokia as they spoke. The multimodal nature of their praxis was recorded on the video of the webcast and their failure was registered instantly both on the financial markets and in the comments of bloggers and twitterers. The running commentary of the blogosphere was merciless with regard to the perceived weaknesses of Elop's and Ballmer's performances, both bodily (their apparently false smiles and large paunches) and artifactual (apparently cheap suits, inappropriate introductory soundtrack, and an awkward choice of blue as the predominant presentational color).[3] Beyond the substantive content of the

---

[3] E.G. http://www.zdnet.com/blog/hardware/live-blog-nokia-financial-and-strategy-briefing/11357; http://www.engadget.com/2011/02/11/live-from-nokias-capital-markets-day/#disqus_thread (all accessed 2 March 2011).

presentation, and beyond the actual words, there was a failure of symbolic management, whose reputational cost was manifest in Nokia's sinking stock price.

More generally, a dramaturgical view of strategic communications suggests that, given the multimodal nature of human activity, discourse needs to be explored in the light of all the means through which organizations and people express themselves. Texts, bodies, and artefacts may be all part of the same communication. Some of these media— for example, written documents—are relatively controlled means for giving messages; others—for instance, bodies in live interaction—are liable to give off impressions in a manner that is much less manageable. New technologies allow these multimodal communications and their effects to be monitored much more closely than before and without direct researcher intrusion: webcasts, live twitter feeds, blogs, and market movements are given to us on a plate. Beyond the registering of bare practices, researchers can now follow the rich multimodality of praxis in real time. As they do so, the research scope expands from simply the adoption of practices to the actual performance. At issue is the skill with which CEOs and similar perform their communications. Inappropriate jargon, false appearances, or inconsistencies between modalities can easily puncture the bubble of belief.

CONCLUSIONS

This chapter has focused on the discretionary use of strategy communications as a form of reputation management, particularly focusing on their symbolic content. Existing studies have shown that the symbolic reference of these communications can influence reputation, as measured by criteria such as valuation premia or press coverage, over and above that warranted by their substantive content. However, these studies have so far largely taken for granted the original choice to communicate about strategy and, moreover, have focused on a relatively inert form of communications: texts taken in isolation. We recap on continuing research opportunities with regard both to the adoption of strategy communications as a practice and to the performance of communications as praxis, at the same time pointing to possible extensions of these approaches.

With regard to adoption, these strategy communications allow researchers to explore issues of reputation management choice in a relatively new and discretionary domain. For organizations in crisis mode and for new ventures seeking customers and investors, communications are more or less obligatory. But for more established firms strategy communications events are both a relatively novel practice (taking off in the 1990s) and one adopted to widely varying extents: some industries (most notably oil) are much more likely to use strategy communications than others, while in any one year the great majority of large corporations choose not to communicate. Given the risks involved, the active choice to communicate on strategy needs to be explained. Here we have suggested that the finance and accounting literature on voluntary disclosure is particularly relevant. Additional insights are likely to come from the theoretical literature on strategic interaction within industries and the institutionalist literature on new practice adoption, particularly within the new shareholder value regime of Western capitalism. A better understanding of the strategic communications choices amongst these established firms may inform research on the role of voluntary communications in reputation management more widely, for example with regard to environmental or employment policies. The opportunity is to explore reputation management in general not only as a reactive phenomenon, or as a by-product of other actions, but as something involving active choice.

On communication performance, Nokia's experience suggests that praxis can make a difference to reputation, as reflected in the company's sliding share price as CEO Steve Elop performed on stage. However, the contrast with Steve Jobs (Elsbach, Chapter 23, this volume) indicates considerable variation in the effectiveness of such performance. With the contemporary availability of webcasts, blogs, and tweets, it is becoming much easier to capture the full dynamics of strategy communications praxis in real time. The new technologies make it possible now to systematically and minutely compare the performances of senior managers from different companies on the screen, and to monitor their reputation effects minute by minute. The promise is a much better understanding of what it takes to be a skilled performer of strategy communications. The same kinds of understanding can be explored in other kinds of videoed and closely monitored situations, for instance crisis management. Here the opportunity is to investigate reputation management more generally as a kind of living praxis.

While the practice and praxis of strategy communications might be important for corporate reputation, there are wider issues as well. The openness or opacity of strategy has public policy implications (Whittington, Cailluet, & Yakis-Douglas, 2011). We have already referred to the difficulties that firms may have in persuading the markets to value ambitious and innovative strategies (Healy & Palepu, 1995) and it seems that investor relations departments struggle to persuade analysts to look beyond quarterly earnings (Laskin, 2009). Financial markets, especially Anglo-Saxon ones, are frequently accused of a pernicious short-termism, one that militates against long-term strategies (Marginson & McAulay, 2008; Black & Fraser, 2002). The consequence is an unwillingness on the part of quoted firms to invest in long-term capacity building, training, or research and development, with significant implications for the sustained performance of both individual firms and the economies in which they are embedded.

As a sign of large firms' own resentment of these short-term pressures from the financial markets, a handful of companies, such as Unilever and GlaxoSmithKlein, have recently abandoned their previous practices of producing short-run earnings forecasts. Paul Polman, chief executive of Unilever, explained this shift: "I needed to create an environment where we were not chasing 20 targets for the short-term, but we were able to do the right thing for the long term" (*Financial Times*, 5 April 2010). Meanwhile, the chief executive of the Financial Services Authority (FSA), a United Kingdom regulator, Hector Sants, placed some of the blame for the recent financial crisis on poor oversight of the strategies of the major financial institutions by financial analysts and investors. Sants enjoined financial analysts and institutional shareholders to pay more attention to strategy: "as investors you should challenge management to ensure their plans are credible" (Financial Services Authority, 11 March 2009). In short, there is a concern that the long-term strategies of firms are not being adequately understood in order to serve the long-term interests of both firms and economies more widely. There is a case, therefore, for strategy communications shifting from the domain of voluntary disclosure toward more mandatory disclosure. In the light of recent theoretical understanding of sustainable competitive advantage as built on unique and inimitable resources (Barney & Clark, 2007), the threat of competitor exploitation of strategic disclosure is not necessarily severe. Societies delegate huge economic power to such large corporations as Barclays, Google, Microsoft, or the Chinese National Oil Corporation; the quid pro quo should be a greater transparency for their strategies.

To conclude, this chapter has highlighted strategy communication as a neglected concern in the corporate reputation literature and an important topic practically for corporations, for investors, and for the public interest at large. We need to understand more about both why firms adopt strategy communications practices and the praxis of how they go about it. Insights from such an understanding may inform research on other kinds of voluntary communications relevant to corporate reputation and on the praxis of corporate communications more widely. There are public policy benefits too. Greater disclosure of strategy holds the promise of reducing information asymmetries between investors and corporations, increasing both stock prices and the willingness of markets to fund long-term and innovative strategies. Beyond the immediate interests of firms and shareholders, therefore, there is a compelling public interest in conducting more research on strategy communications and testing the case for more public enforcement of such disclosures.

Research on Symbolic Management in Strategy Communications

Reference	Key Constructs and Findings	Organizational Media
Fanelli, Misangyi, & Tosi, 2009	CEO charismatic strategic visions promote favorable security analyst recommendations	Letters to shareholders
Fiss & Zajac, 2006	Qualified acceptance of strategic change (shareholder value adoption) associated with firm ownership and positive stock evaluations	Annual reports
Martens, Jennings, & Jennings, 2007	Entrepreneurial narratives influence resource acquisition (e.g., IPO value premia)	IPO prospectuses
Kennedy, 2008	New entrants benefit in terms of media attention from comparison with a few rather than many peers	Press releases
Rindova et al., 2007	Firms' symbolic actions in emerging markets influence media coverage and favorability	Press releases and websites
Vaara & Monin, 2010	Four key legitimization strategies in a controversial merger	Press releases

References

Armitage, S. & Marston, C. (2008). Corporate disclosure, cost of capital and reputation: Evidence from finance directors. *The British Accounting Review*, 40(4): 314–336.

Ashforth, B. E. & Gibbs, B. W. (1990). The double-edge of organizational legitimation. *Organization Science*, 1(2): 177–194.

Barney, J. & Clark, D. (2007). *Resource-based Theory: Creating and Sustaining Competitive Advantage*. Oxford and New York: Oxford University Press.

Barry, D. & Elmes, M. (1997). Strategy retold: Toward a narrative view of strategic discourse. *Academy of Management Review*, 22(2): 429–452.

Barth, M., Kasnick, R., & McNichols, M. (2001). Analyst coverage and intangible assets. *Journal of Accounting Research*, 39(1): 1–34.

Basdeo, D., Smith, K., Grimm, C., Rindova, V., & Derfus, P. (2006). The impact of market actions on firm reputation. *Strategic Management Journal*, 27(12): 1205–1219.

Bassen, A., Basse Mama, H., & Ramaj, H. (2010). Investor relations: A comprehensive overview. *Journal of Betriebswirtschaft*, 60: 49–79.

Benner, M. & Ranganathan, R. (2011). Offsetting legitimacy? How pressures from securities analysts influence incumbents in the face of new technologies. *Academy of Management Journal*, forthcoming.

Biehl-Missal, B. (2011). Business is show business: Management presentations as performance. *Journal of Management Studies*, 48(3): 1467–6486.

Black, A. & Fraser, P. (2002). Stock market short-termism—An international perspective. *Journal of Multinational Financial Management*, 12(2): 135–158.

Bozzolan, S. & Mazzola, P. (2007). Strategic plan presentations to financial analysts: The effect on earnings forecasts' revision and cost of capital. Unpublished working paper, University of Padova.

Christensen, L. & Caves, R. (1997). Cheap talk and investment rivalry in the pulp and paper industry. *Journal of Industrial Economics*, 45(1): 47–73.

Clark, T. & Greatbatch, D. (2004). Management fashion as image spectacle: The production of best-selling management books. *Management Communication Quarterly*, 17(3): 396–424.

Davis, G. F. (2009). *Managed by the Markets: How Finance Reshaped America*. New York: Oxford University Press.

Elsbach, K. D. & Sutton, R. I. (1992). Acquiring organizational legitimacy through illegitimate actions: A marriage of institutional and impression management theories. *Academy of Management Review*, 35(4): 699–738.

——, ——, & Principe, K. E. (1998). Averting expected challenges through anticipatory billing: A study of hospital billing. *Organization Science*, 9(1): 68–86.

Eng, L. L. & Mak, Y. T. (2003). Corporate governance and voluntary disclosure. *Journal of Accounting and Public Policy*, 22(4): 325–345.

Fanelli, A., Misangyi, V., & Tosi, H. (2009). In charisma we trust: The effects of CEO charismatic visions on securities analysts. *Organization Science*, 20(6): 1011–1033.

Farrell, J. (1987). Cheap talk, coordination and entry. *RAND Journal of Economics*, 18(1): 34–39.

Fiss, P. C. & Zajac, E. J. (2006). The symbolic management of strategic change: Sensegiving via framing and decoupling. *Academy of Management Journal*, 49(6): 1173–1193.

Fligstein, N. (2001). *The Architecture of Markets*. Princeton: Princeton University Press.

Goffman, E. (1959). *The Presentation of Self in Everyday Life*. New York: Doubleday and Co.

Healy, P. & Palepu, K. (1995). The challenges of investor communication: The case of CUC international. *Journal of Financial Economics*, 38(2): 111–140.

—— & —— (2001). Information asymmetry, corporate disclosure and capital markets. *Journal of Accounting and Economics*, 31(1–3): 405–440.

Hope, O.-K. (2003). Firm-level disclosures and the relative roles of culture and legal origin. *Journal of International Financial Management and Accounting*, 14(3): 218–248.

Hutton, A. (2005). Determinants of managerial earnings guidance prior to regulation faire disclosure and bias in analysts' earning forecasts. *Contemporary Accounting Research*, 22(4): 867–914.

Kelly, K., Laskin, A., & Rosenstein, G. (2010). Investor relations: Two-way symmetrical practice. *Journal of Public Relations Research*, 22(2): 182–208.

Kennedy, M. (2008). Getting counted: Markets, media and reality. *American Sociological Review*, 73(2): 270–295.

Laskin, A. V. (2009). A descriptive account of the investor relations profession: A national study. *Journal of Business Communication*, 46(2): 208–233.

Marginson, D. & McAulay, L. (2008). Exploring the debate on short-termism: A theoretical and empirical analysis. *Strategic Management Journal*, 29(3): 273–292.

Martens, M., Jennings, J., & Jennings, D. (2007). Do the stories they tell get them the money they need: The role of entrepreneurial narratives in resource acquisition. *Academy of Management Journal*, 50(5): 1107–1132.

Mazzola, P., Ravasi, D., & Gabbioneta, C. (2006). How to build reputation in financial markets. *Long Range Planning*, 39(4): 385–407.

Porter, M. E. (1985). *Competitive Advantage: Creating and Sustaining Superior Performance*. New York: Free Press.

Prencipe, A. (2004). Proprietary costs and determinants of voluntary segment disclosure: Evidence from Italian listed companies. *European Accounting Review*, 13(2): 319–340.

Ramnath, S., Rock, S., & Shane, P. (2008). The financial analyst forecasting literature: A taxonomy with suggestions for further research. *International Journal of Forecasting*, 24(1): 34–75.

Rao, H. & Sivakumar, K. (1999). Institutional sources of boundary-spanning structures: The establishment of investor relations departments in the fortune 500 industrials. *Organization Science*, 10(1): 27–42.

Reckwitz, A. (2002). Toward a theory of social practices: A development in culturalist theorizing. *European Journal of Social Theory*, 5(2): 243–263.

Rindova, V. P. & Fombrun, C. (1999). Constructing competitive advantage: The role of firm-constituent interactions. *Strategic Management Journal*, 20(8): 691–710.

——, Becerra, M., & Contordo, I. (2004). Enacting competitive wars: Competitive activity, language games, and market consequences. *Academy of Management Review*, 29(4): 670–686.

——, Pollock, T., & Hayward, M. (2006). Celebrity firms: The social construction of market popularity. *Academy of Management Review*, 31(1): 51–70.

——, Petkova, A., & Kotha, S. (2007). Standing out: How new firms in emerging markets build reputation. *Strategic Organization*, 5(1): 31–70.

Roberts, P. W. & Dowling, G. R. (2002). Corporate reputation and sustained superior performance. *Strategic Management Journal*, 23(12): 1077–1093.

Roberts, J., Sanderson, P., Barker, R., & Hendry, J. (2006). In the mirror of the market: The disciplinary effects of company/fund manager meetings. *Accounting, Organizations and Society*, 31(3): 277–294.

Rogers, P. (2000). CEO presentations in conjunction with earnings announcements: Extending the construct of organizational genre. *Management Communication Quarterly*, 13(3): 426–485.

Sandhu, S. (2009). Strategic communications: An institutional perspective. *International Journal of Strategic Communications*, 3(2): 72–92.

Schriffin, D., Tannen, D., & Hamilton, H. E. (2003). *Handbook of Discourse Analysis*. Oxford: Wiley-Blackwell.

Skinner, D. (1994). Why firms voluntarily disclose bad news. *Journal of Accounting Research*, 32(1): 38–60.

Streeck, J., Goodwin, C., & LeBaron, C. (2011). Embodied interaction: An introduction. In J. Streeck, C. Goodwin, & C. LeBaron (Eds.), *Embodied Interaction: Language and Body in a Material World*. Cambridge, England: Cambridge University Press.

Vaara, E. & Monin, P. (2010). A recursive perspective on discursive legitimation and organizational action in mergers and acquisitions. *Organization Science*, 21(1): 3–22.

Vaara, E., Sorsa, V., & Pälli, P. (2010). On the force potential of strategy texts: A critical discourse analysis of a strategic plan and its power effects in a city organization. *Organization*, 17(6): 686–702.

Wagenhofer, A. (1990). Voluntary disclosure with a strategic opponent. *Journal of Accounting and Economics*, 12(4): 341–363.

Webb, K., Cahan, S., & Sun, J. (2008). The effect of globalization and legal environment on voluntary disclosure. *International Journal of Accounting*, 43(3): 219–245.

Whittington, R. (2006). Completing the practice turn in strategy research. *Organization Studies*, 27(5): 613–634.

——, Cailluet, L., & Yakis-Douglas, B. (2011). Opening strategy: The evolution of a precarious profession. *British Journal of Management*, 22: 531–544.

Zajac, E. J. & Westphal, J. D. (2004). The social construction of market value, institutionalization and learning perspectives on stock market reactions. *American Sociological Review*, 69(3): 433–457.

Zorn, D. (2004). Here a chief, there a chief: The rise of the CFO in the American firm. *American Sociological Review*, 69(3): 345–364.

Zott, C. & Huy, Q. N. (2007). How entrepreneurs use symbolic management to acquire resources. *Administrative Science Quarterly*, 52(1): 70–105.

Zuckerman, E. W. (2000). Focusing the corporate product: Securities analysts and de-diversification. *Administrative Science Quarterly*, 45: 591–619.

CHAPTER 21

MANAGING CORPORATE REPUTATION THROUGH CORPORATE BRANDING

MAJKEN SCHULTZ

MARY JO HATCH

NICK ADAMS

We discuss the differences and relations between branding and corporate reputation and present three perspectives on corporate branding: A marketing perspective, an organizational perspective and a co-creation perspective. Based on an empirical study of how the Danish pharmaceutical company Novo Nordisk used its central idea of "Changing Diabetes" to co-create its corporate brand with stakeholders, and how the company uses longitudinal measures of the impact its corporate brand has on corporate reputation, we investigate ways to theorize the connection between brand and reputation. We conclude that the relationship between corporate brand and corporate reputation is moderated by management practices targeted at influencing these phenomena and point to the need to include corporate brand management in the theory and practice of corporate reputation.

INTRODUCTION

THE phenomena of corporate reputation and corporate branding are both defined as intangible assets contributing to the market value of corporations (e.g., Aaker, 1996; Fombrun, Chapter 5, this volume; Fombrun, 1996; Kapferer, 2000). Moreover, scholars suggest that they are both affected by stakeholder perceptions and that both depend on relationships between stakeholders and organizations (e.g., Balmer & Greyser, 2006; Dowling, 2006, 2001, 1994; Hatch & Schultz, 2008; van Riel & Fombrun, 2007).

Nonetheless, these concepts still need to be adequately theorized in relationship to each other as they are studied by different groups of scholars taking different approaches to their subject matter. For example, while the field of branding started out by focusing on how consumers perceive and react to products and services, corporate reputation has always been conceptualized as the aggregation of stakeholder judgments about an organization that have been amassed over time (Barnett, Jermier, & Lafferty, 2006; Fombrun & Shanley, 1990; Lange, Lee, & Dai, Y., 2011; van Riel & Fombrun, 2007; Rindova et al., 2005). Recent developments within the branding field attend to how organizations brand themselves, thus turning attention to the management of corporate brands and expanding the purview to include internal stakeholders as well as external stakeholders, while continuing to be concerned with end consumers (Aaker, 2004; Balmer, Stuart, & Greyser, 2009; Gregory, 2007; Hatch & Schultz, 2008, 2009; Heding, Knudtzen, & Bjerre, 2009; Ind, 1997; Kornberger, 2010; Merz & Vargo, 2009). However, the branding field has employed the concepts of image and corporate images to conceptualize the shifting perceptions of external stakeholders rather than corporate reputation as an aggregate of these perceptions over time (e.g., Balmer & Greyser, 2003; Keller, 2003; Keller, Apéria, & Georgson, 2008).

As a consequence of these developments within the branding field, the boundaries between corporate branding and corporate reputation have become blurred and their conceptual definitions and implications for management have converged. At the same time, the possibilities for using corporate branding to influence corporate reputation have multiplied, along with the insights and tools corporate branding brings into play at the strategic level. Thus, many reputation scholars are interested in the relationship between corporate branding and corporate reputation. For example, van Riel & Fombrun, argue that corporate reputation gained attention "because it captures the effects that brands and images have on the overall evaluations which stakeholders make of companies" (2007: 40). Meanwhile brand scholars such as Ind (1997) and Keller, Apéria, & Georgson (2008: 367–368) emphasize corporate reputation as a way to track the full impact of a corporate brand on multiple external stakeholders, thereby positioning corporate branding as an influence on reputation (see also Abratt, 1989). Still others explore the combined importance of corporate brands and corporate reputation, for example to explain variations in market-to-book value relationships (Little et al., 2009; see also Benjamin & Polodny, 1999) or to demonstrate their impact on price and perceived quality (Saxton & Dollinger, 2004).

In relation to their influence on management practice, many organizations that have formalized their corporate reputation and corporate brand management practices have assigned responsibility for branding to the marketing function, while corporate reputation is most often the responsibility of corporate communication along with media relations and reputation tracking. Even when both sit within the communication function they are often assigned to different groups. These structural practices create a silo problem for those attempting to manage cross-functionally, as pointed out by David Aaker (2008; see also Hatch & Schultz, 2008). To overcome silo problems, a few companies, such as our case company Novo Nordisk, have begun developing units dedicated to corporate branding, which often have facilitating cross-functional roles. These differences in the way they are organized pose challenges to articulating the relationship between corporate branding and reputation, even as they demonstrate the relevance of doing so.

In this chapter we discuss the origin of branding and compare branding with corporate reputation. We describe multiple perspectives on corporate branding, also found in the reputation field, and propose how corporate branding can influence corporate reputation. We then present the case of Novo Nordisk to suggest how one company managed its brand in a way it believes influenced its reputation, describing also how the company measures the impact of its efforts on different stakeholders in various markets. Our analysis of this case suggests that future conceptual developments within the corporate reputation field should include brand management practices in order to capture the ways that corporate branding and reputation are related through practice.

THE DEVELOPMENT OF CORPORATE BRANDING

In this section we focus on the main developments within the field of branding and what sets corporate brands apart from other types of branding. We suggest basic differences between corporate branding and reputation and elaborate multiple, often complementary, perspectives on corporate branding and reputation as well as on related management practices.

The Origin of Branding

The notion of "branding" emerged in the marketing discipline along with the development of trademarks. Since that time, brands have come to be formally defined as "A name, term, symbol, or design, or combination of these, which is intended to identify goods or services of one seller or group of sellers and to differentiate them from those of competitors" (American Marketing Association, cited in Kapferer, 2000: 187). Thus, from the start, branding concerned how organizations distinguished their product, services—and, in the case of corporate branding, themselves—from others, and how they made that distinction visible, relevant, and attractive to stakeholders.

When the basic definition of branding moved to the corporate level, issues of how companies express who they are, what they stand for, and how their expressions differentiate them from their competitors came into focus. Thereafter, many scholars argued that the source of a brand's distinction resides in the identity of the organization that supports it (e.g., Aaker, 2004; Aaker & Joachimstahler, 2000; Hatch & Schultz, 1997, 2008; Olins, 2003). Also, from early on scholars of branding claimed that differentiation not only resides in the functional benefits of the brand, but in the meaning that stakeholders associate with the branded product or service. As Levy (1959: 123) put it in his landmark article "Symbols for sale":

> Now it seems worthwhile to redirect attention to the ways products turn people's thoughts and feelings toward symbolic implications, whether this is intended by the manufacturer or not. If the manufacturer understands that he is selling symbols as well as goods, he can view his product more completely. He can understand not only how the object he sells satisfies certain practical needs but also how it fits meaningfully into today's culture. Both he and the consumer stand to profit.

The branding field has developed extensively since these early days, and scholars inside and outside the marketing discipline have contributed different conceptual perspectives on branding. For example, Heding, Knudtzen, & Bjerre (2009), in a recent textbook, identified seven different approaches to brand management, defined as economic, identity, consumer-based, personality, relational, community, and cultural approaches. These seven approaches represent different definitions, methods, and theories of how brand value is created. The authors relate corporate brand and corporate reputation management to the identity-based approach, arguing that both derive value from the attraction and relevance of the culture and identity of the organization to stakeholders. However, they emphasize the long-term formation of corporate reputation in relation to external stakeholders and point at differences in management practices, arguing that corporate reputation is influenced via public relations, whereas corporate branding is part of the marketing function (Heding, Knudtzen, & Bjerre, 2009: 55–61). Kornberger (2010: 31) distinguished between the production of brands, where brands are used as a management tool or corporate catalyst, and the consumption of brands, wherein brands act as signs or media. According to Kornberger, questions related to the production of brands concern how branding influences the ways in which organizations are managed and how brand meaning is constructed, while a focus on consumption addresses how brands work at the interface between stakeholders and organizations, and how stakeholders contribute to brand meanings.

In spite of the differences in perspectives on branding there is general agreement that the branding field has moved through at least three significant developmental stages:

1) A shift from focusing on the origin of brands in individual products and services to including the corporation/organization as the platform for branding.
2) A shift from focusing on consumers as passive receivers of brand messages to multiple stakeholders as active co creators of brand value.
3) A shift from branding as a subset of the marketing discipline focused on the marketing mix toward branding as a cross-disciplinary activity influenced, but not controlled, by the company.

Some of the main reasons given for these developments are: the shortening of product life cycles and difficulties of sustaining product-based differentiation; the costs involved in brand building in a global multichannel marketplace; the movement toward greater involvement of stakeholders in the creation of brands; and the shift toward a service economy where the role of employees in brand delivery has increased (Hatch & Schultz, 2009; Heding, Knudtzen, & Bjerre, 2009; Holt, 2004; Keller, Apéria, & Georgson, 2008; Merz & Vargo, 2009).

Comparing Branding and Reputation

In spite of the overlap in developments within the branding and reputation fields we find that there are fundamental differences between branding and reputation. Our discussion below refers both to the definitions of the constructs and how these phenomena are influenced by management practices. These differences are summarized in Table 21.1.

Branding scholars stress the multiplicity of stakeholder experiences evoked when stakeholders give meaning to a product, service, organization, and so on, thereby creating a brand. Branding scholars apply their ideas to multiple levels of analysis, including everything from individual products to individual people, groups, organizations, and nations, noting how any of these phenomena can be branded. In contrast, reputation is defined in terms of judgments and assessments of a corporation's attractiveness, enhancing the reflected considerations that are accumulated over time (Barnett, Jermier, & Lafferty, 2006; Fombrun & Shanley, 1990; van Riel & Fombrun, 2007; Rindova et al., 2005). Reputation is composed of judgments among external stakeholders and has most often been concerned with the reputation of corporations, business fields, and, most recently, nations. Branding arises from both internal and external stakeholders continuously giving meaning to brands as individuals, groups, or, most recently, and independently of the company's intentions, in communities.

Finally, we argue that there is a difference in how branding and reputation are influenced by management practices. Although branding and reputation are both contextualized by environmental and strategic factors (e.g., Fombrun, Chapter 5, this volume) the ways in which organizations aspire to influence their brands and reputations differ. Many companies apply what we have labeled expressive practices (Schultz, Hatch, & Larsen, 2000) in order to directly influence how internal and external stakeholders experience and interact with brand. This does not imply that stakeholders always embrace the intended meanings, for example as communicated via marketing campaigns, or that stakeholders are conceived as passive recipients of corporate intentions, but the branding field does provide a wide range of managerial practices intended to influence internal and external stakeholder experiences and their engagement with the product or company, as shown in Table 21.1.

Branding practices involve multiple business functions, such as marketing, sales, corporate communication, and human resources (HR) (Hatch & Schultz, 2008), albeit often with the aid of outside brand consultants who manage the internal process or create the external brand campaigns. In contrast, reputation only concerns external stakeholders and is often mediated by third parties without the direct inclusion of employees.

Table 21.1 Comparing Central Dimensions Between Branding and Corporate Reputation

Dimensions	Branding	Corporate Reputation
Definition	A brand arises from the emotional, cognitive, and aesthetic experiences and expressions of stakeholders (internal and external) when they (alone, in groups, or in community with others) interact with and/or use the symbols and practices associated with products, services, corporations, cities, and/or nations	"A collective assessment of a company's attractiveness to a specific group of stakeholders relative to a reference group of companies with which the company competes for resources" (Fombrun, Chapter 5, this volume)
Cognitive Dimension	Giving meaning(s) to products, services, organizations, etc. by individuals and/or collectives	Accumulated judgments about an organization
Emotional/Aesthetic Dimension	Appreciation (positive or negative) of brand-specific experiences and expressions and all that the brand represents for the stakeholder(s)	Feelings, trust, admiration, and esteem that influence accumulated judgments about an organization
Stakeholder Role	All stakeholders (internal and external to the organization) who influence brand co-creation by their engagement with the brand and/or with each other	External stakeholders provide images that aggregate over time into a reputation
Time Perspective	Ongoing construction of meaning from experiences of a brand within and among those who interact with it. Brand meaning carries traces of past meaning and experiences into the future; it is dynamic	Long-term accumulation of images
Managerial Practices	*Direct management* seeks to influence internal and external stakeholders via expressive practices and the facilitation of their activities in relation to the brand, such as: • Brand portfolio and architecture • Corporate communication, internal marketing • Marketing of the corporation, city, nation, and/or product/service using multiple channels • Visual identity, e.g., name, style, logo, tagline • Brand ambassador programs • Hosting brand community building websites or events • Branded philanthropy, sponsoring employee volunteer programs, CSR, and sustainability projects • Creating brand experiences in retail and delivery • Tracking brand loyalty and perception	*Indirect management* seeks to obtain knowledge about stakeholders and use it to intervene in reputation-creating and maintenance processes, such as: • Managing media relations/public relations • Employing lobbyists to influence analysts and investors • Reputation measurement and tracking • Mapping reputation risk, often done stakeholder group by stakeholder group

To the extent that companies engage in reputation management it concentrates on influencing judgments by significant third parties, such as media, investors, and relevant non-governmental organizations (NGOs), and obtaining deeper knowledge about reputation and the critical issues that might generate a risk of losing reputation. As such, reputation is influenced more indirectly by managerial practices than branding in general and is often located in the corporate communication function. Taking Fombrun's (Chapter 5, this volume) argument that reputations develop from three principal sources—stakeholder experiences, corporate initiatives, and third party coverage—externally oriented branding practices can be conceived as corporate initiatives aimed at influencing stakeholder experiences as well as third party interpretations of the corporate brand's attractiveness and relevance.

Perspectives of Corporate Brands

There are multiple perspectives on how to define corporate brands (similar to the perspectives on corporate reputation, e.g., Fombrun, Chapter 5; Rindova and Martins, Chapter 2, both this volume). Below, we summarize these perspectives by merging contributions that draw upon different theoretical traditions and disciplines. We suggest three principled perspectives on corporate branding and highlight their differing managerial implications: 1) A marketing perspective on corporate branding based in corporate identity and brand equity theory; 2) an organizational perspective on corporate branding based in corporate communication and organization theory; and 3) a co-creation perspective based in service marketing and consumer culture theory. These perspectives are elaborated in the tables and examples below.

In the marketing perspective (see the first summary table at the end of the chapter) a "branded house" view of corporate brands is opposed to a "house of brands" view (e.g., Aaker, 2004). This definition derives from the distinctive manifestations of the corporation that evoke associations among stakeholders (Keller, 1998; Olins, 2003). Perceptions of brand value are then thought to be shaped by brand equity (e.g., Aaker, 1996, 2004; Keller, 2003), which is measured by assessing awareness, knowledge and perceived quality, emotional bonding and purchasing intentions among consumers (for an overview of measures see van Riel & Fombrun, 2007). Together, these measurement activities track consumers' cognitive and emotional perceptions of who the organization is and how it differs from its competitors.

The marketing perspective provides extensive tool development for managers seeking to influence the brand. Tools range from brand portfolio management and the design of logos, a house style, and core values, to marketing mix strategies using different communication channels and advertising campaigns. For example, Apple's corporate brand is based on central ideas of imagination, innovation, and design, which are expressed consistently through the Apple logo, aesthetic style, and user interfaces. Furthermore, Apple communicates its brand idea consistently through highly successful advertising campaigns like "1984," "Think Different," and "I am a Mac." Also, Steve Job's ability to interact with consumers through media has created rock-star excitement in relation to new product launches.

Proponents of the organizational perspective (see the second summary table, at the end of the chapter) believe that corporate brands are based in organizational identity and culture (including the core values of the organization). This perspective emphasizes the importance of internal stakeholders and their collective or organizational culture(s) and brand heritage, *and* recognizes the importance of external stakeholders other than consumers, such as media, NGOs, collaborating partners, regulators, and so on (e.g., Cornelissen 2004; van Riel & Fombrun, 2007). The organizational perspective addresses the limitations of the marketing perspective by attempting to align external perceptions of the organization with the internal organizational culture in order to enhance the chances that the brand will be regarded as credible and trustworthy. The perspective also stresses the importance of ongoing interactions between internal and external stakeholders, which suggest a range of engaging brand management practices (e.g., Antorini & Andersen, 2005; Hatch & Schultz, 2010; Kornberger, 2010; Merz & Vargo, 2009). Development of the Apple brand, for example, reflects interactions between the organization's visionary founder and a highly innovative organizational culture that attracted Apple employees from all over the world to deliver on the desires of those who create their markets. Through the establishment of brand stores, Apple provides a meeting place between customers and employees that reflects and delivers the brand, such as an informal touch-and-feel atmosphere; employees wearing Apple t-shirts who proactively offer customers support and have a friendly, low-key demeanor; and the always buzzing and interactive Genius Bar. In its more recent development Apple has been able to extend this identity by creating an iWorld, stimulating a feeling of belonging among its growing number of customers.

The co-creation perspective (see the third summary table, at the end of the chapter) argues that corporate brands are constructed by corporations in interaction with their stakeholders, stressing the processes through which co-creation occurs (e.g., Gregory, 2007; Merz & Vargo, 2009; Payne et al., 2009). Stakeholders are not just participants in extended networks of brand relations but rather are active contributors to, instead of passive receivers of, brand meaning and value. In consumer culture studies, the cultural and societal context of brands is emphasized (e.g., for an overview see Arnould & Thompson, 2005; see also Holt, 2004; du Gay, 2000; Kornberger, 2010). Co-creation studies focus on how consumers use brands as symbolic material to construct brand meaning, operating either as individuals or as part of collectives known as brand communities (e.g., Fournier & Lee, 2009; Muniz & O'Guinn, 2001). Schau, Muñiz, & Arnould show how consumers use various social practices to "realize value beyond what which the firm creates or anticipates" (2009: 30), while Prahalad & Ramaswany (2004) describe how consumers take an active part in the value creation of companies via four "building blocks." Drawing on these co-creation studies, Hatch & Schultz (2010) showed how adult fans actively co-created the LEGO brand by engaging in innovative activities with LEGO employees, for example through the global LEGO brand community lug.net and by participating in the LEGO Ambassador Program at LEGO facilities in Denmark (see also Schultz & Hatch, 2003). Apple also engages its vast number of dedicated consumers in brand co-creation, for example through the App Store, where consumers are able to share their creations in the iWorld or create user groups through its user group program.

The above examples illustrate that the three perspectives outlined are not mutually exclusive, which suggests the possibility of developing a multidisciplinary conceptualization of corporate branding. Although each places a different emphasis on the importance and nature of brand management, they all provide insights relevant to managing organizations as corporate brands in a multi-stakeholder context and thus to the likelihood that corporate branding is a way to influence corporate reputation.

CORPORATE BRANDING IN NOVO NORDISK

In this section we illustrate how Danish pharmaceutical company Novo Nordisk embarked on a corporate brand strategy with the intention to use its corporate brand activities to influence its corporate reputation. The case is part of an ongoing longitudinal study of corporate branding activities at Novo Nordisk that we have been following since 2004 (see also Hatch & Schultz, 2008; Rubin, Schultz, & Hatch, 2008; Schultz et al., 2005). Much of this case has been written in collaboration with the third author of this chapter, Nick Adams, who has been working in and managed Novo Nordisk's corporate brand unit since 2005. Finally, data describing the Novo Nordisk corporate brand and corporate reputation among stakeholders was provided by the Reputation Institute (www.reputationinstitute.com).

The Move to Corporate Branding

Like many other pharmaceutical companies Novo Nordisk has a long tradition of extensive product branding and has in the past leveraged its corporate reputation on its core insulin products, NovoRapid and NovoMix, together with the NovoPen device. The company has always based its culture on strong corporate values, which the demerger in 2000 of its enzymes and healthcare businesses and the formulation of the Novo Nordisk Way of Management (www.novonordisk.com) brought into focus. At that time, the company also refined its corporate identity to make it more distinctive, based on the idea of "Being There" for all of its stakeholders.

In 2003 Novo Nordisk was confronted with an increase in global competition from companies such as Eli-Lilly, Sanofi-Aventis, Bayer, and Pfizer. Like other pharmaceutical companies involved in diabetes they were responding to market growth resulting from the global Type 2 diabetes pandemic. The intensification of competition was accompanied by accusations by critics and the media that the entire pharmaceutical industry was violating business ethics (e.g., Abramson, 2004; Angell, 2005; Kassirer,

2005). Thus, the context the company faced was increasing concern among multiple stakeholders, including politicians, healthcare professionals, NGOs, and citizens, to find ways to stem the explosive growth in diabetes, coupled with lack of trust in the pharmaceutical industry.

In 2004 Novo Nordisk decided to create a more differentiated identity for the company. This time it drew on the core of its well-established identity in diabetes. The company labeled this effort "corporate branding" to emphasize its strategic aspirations compared with previous corporate identity programs that had focused more on logo, tagline, visuals, and other communication materials. Although Novo Nordisk was small in size compared with its competitors, management argued it could claim leadership in the diabetes area in relation to dimensions such as global market share, resources dedicated to research, and relationships with patients. Furthermore, the company had already gained a reputation for its comprehensive engagement in social and environmental responsibility, evidenced by its top position in the Dow Jones Sustainability Index since 2001. Novo Nordisk's management decided to leverage its position as a responsibility-focused diabetes care company with the declared aspiration to promote its leadership, create a more differentiated global brand versus its competitors, and enhance its corporate reputation. Thus, the corporate brand was perceived by management as the development of an identity (i.e., a global leader in diabetes care) to create distinctive organizational experiences and expressions in the view of stakeholders that would, in turn, influence long-term stakeholder assessments of the company—its corporate reputation.

Novo Nordisk had for several years managed its corporate reputation through issues management, and media relations through its corporate communication department. When the company decided to enhance its efforts in corporate branding, it created an independent corporate branding unit as a spin-off of the corporate communication department. The branding unit was deliberately asked to involve other functions in the development of the brand in the four chosen pilot markets of China, Germany, the UK, and US, along with a number of headquarter functions including corporate communications, marketing, human resources, and research and development (R&D). This cross-functional team reported directly to executive management and established a reference group for the development of different areas of the brand.

As a first step the corporate branding team developed the central idea for the corporate brand using the metaphor of a house (see Figure 21.1). The foundation of the brand house rests on the Novo Nordisk Way of Management and the Triple Bottom Line and its roof proclaims the brand aspiration "leading the fight against diabetes." The foundation is supported by four pillars defined as: People with values, Science for people, Care for people, and Healthy communities. These pillars were used as both proof points for the company's past performance and guidelines for prioritizing future, what we would label expressive activities (see Hatch & Schultz, 2008: 212–215).

The second step involved translating these conceptual ideas into a branding platform to be used in relation to all stakeholders. After a period of testing among internal and external stakeholders and one false start on developing a platform called "Type Zero," the company

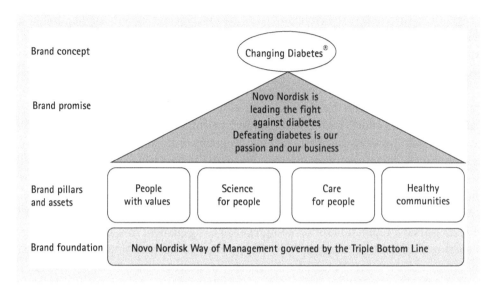

FIGURE 21.1 Corporate brand house at Novo Nordisk.

ultimately chose the central idea statement "*Changing Diabetes*" because it reflected the most fundamental needs of diabetics and the highest aspiration of the company.

Implementing Corporate Branding

Over the next several years, the corporate branding team initiated a broad range of activities based on "Changing Diabetes." Table 21.2 provides a summary of the three stages in the implementation of the corporate brand.

During stage one the headquarters team created new versions of its marketing and communication materials, aimed at both internal and external stakeholders and for use by all markets, to communicate proactively about "Changing Diabetes." These materials included brand books, corporate brochures and communication toolboxes. Further, the team engaged in a series of local workshops to support development of local brand houses in order to combine and communicate existing activities and take new brand-based initiatives.

The second stage particularly focused on global brand flagship programs as a response to market needs for large-scale brand initiatives. Several of those entailed co-creation with individuals and NGOs from the diabetes field. The Unite for Diabetes initiative offered one example of co-creation. This initiative aimed at placing concern for diabetes on the agenda of the United Nations (UN) and was initiated by a young American diabetic, Clare Rosenfeld, who came to the attention of Novo Nordisk when she joined the company's Young Voices program. Young Voices was dedicated to improve communication with the "next generation" of diabetics (http://www.novonordisk.com/about_us/

Table 21.2 Stages of Corporate Branding at Novo Nordisk

Corporate Branding Process	Corporate Initiative	Implementation to Markets	Market Feedback	Corporate Input to Next Stage
First Stage: 2004–2005 Creating Brand Platform	Corporate decision on brand concept "Changing Diabetes" and brand house platform	Brand houses are adapted and developed in key markets	Experiences from brand houses feed back to corporate headquarters	Need for overall flagship activities across markets
Second Stage: 2005–2007 Brand Flagship Programs	Development of specific corporate flagship activities: "Changing Diabetes" bus. Young Voices. Leadership forums	Roll-out of flagship initiatives in key markets	Brand and reputation tracker shows positive data in all four key markets	Need for building capacity and pushing local corporate branding activities
Third Stage: 2008–Embedding in Organization	Development of guidelines for local development and execution of corporate brand activities	Key markets develop plans with specific local activities	Experiences from markets lead to further develop-ment of the corporate brand	Extend corporate brand into product brands, employer brand, and sales. Link to strategic vision as next process

changing-diabetes/young-voices.asp; see also Hatch & Schultz, 2008: 212–215). Through engagement with Rosenfeld and the International Diabetes Federation, Novo Nordisk formed a partnership, which included other NGOs and industry partners, that eventually succeeded in creating the UN's annual World Diabetes Day (14 November). Alongside this effort, Novo Nordisk also initiated a "Changing Diabetes" project that toured the world in a bus, seeking to create awareness and give information about diabetes. Many young diabetics from the Young Voices program participated in the tour and co-created local activities along with local Novo Nordisk staff as it traveled around the world generating, in the places it visited, comprehensive media attention and political interest. The "Changing Diabetes" bus intended to end its tour parked in front of the UN building in New York City on World Diabetes Day 2006, though its popularity convinced the company to extend its life until 2012 screening more than 135,000 people for diabetes along its journey across five continents.

In the third stage the central idea of "Changing Diabetes" was further implemented on a product brand level, to create alignment between corporate and product brands. This was done through creating a brand system for diabetes product brands, and provided opportunities for even further exposure of the "Changing Diabetes" messaging. Also, the brand idea developed in relation to other areas, such as within human resources with regard to current and future employees, as expressed in the idea of "*Life changing careers*" and the elaboration of sales force storytelling and training. Finally the company had several other product areas outside of diabetes that were brought closer to the corporate brand, particularly in the case of the central idea developed for the hemophilia franchise, "*Changing Possibilities in Hemophilia*," which captured the same essence of change and used a similar brand house framework for its launch.

Applying the Three Perspectives on Corporate Branding

The above overview of how the corporate brand has been developed at Novo Nordisk during the last five years shows how the brand became more inclusive of the local affiliates as it bounced back and forth between central initiatives, local adaptations, and emerging market needs. The case illustrates how the company drew on all three perspectives of corporate branding proposed in this chapter. In line with the marketing perspective, the central idea of "Changing Diabetes" was formulated, tested, expressed, and communicated to external stakeholders, while the emergence and embedding of the idea in the identity of the company and the emphasis on internal stakeholders better fits the organizational perspective. In particular, the ongoing organization-wide dialogue between headquarters and the local affiliates neatly maps onto the organizational identity dynamics described by Hatch & Schultz (2002). Finally, many of the activities were initiated and executed through co-creation between employees and committed stakeholders, supporting the co-creation perspective, in this case with the goal of changing diabetes together. These activities may involve individual diabetic consumers or NGOs working in the diabetic field who, regardless of their partnerships, seem to enhance creativity and provide legitimacy to Novo Nordisk.

RELATING CORPORATE BRANDING AND CORPORATE REPUTATION

In this section we discuss the relations between corporate branding and corporate reputation, first based on the empirical tracking of the development in both constructs related to Novo Nordisk over a five-year period. Second, we discuss how corporate branding and reputation come together in practice, as most brand management practices also influence corporate reputation—and the other way around.

Tracking the Relationship between Corporate Branding and Reputation

One of the aspirations behind Novo Nordisk's development of its corporate brand was to influence corporate reputation. This aspiration was specified in relation to key competitors (Eli-Lilly and Sanofi Aventis); key markets (China, the US, UK, Germany), and key stakeholders (primary care health professionals, secondary care health professionals, patients). Targeting these specific groups, Novo Nordisk Marketing and Corporate Branding units collaborated with the Reputation Institute to develop a customized tracking tool that combines corporate brand goal performance measures with measures of corporate reputation. The tool allowed the company to track and compute the correlation between the perceived accomplishment of the corporate brand goal of being the world's leading diabetes care company and leading the fight against diabetes (in relation to both Type 1 and Type 2 diabetes), and corporate reputation (defined by the RepTrak™Pulse as the feeling, trust, admiration, and esteem of the company in the eyes of stakeholders; for a deeper discussion of the RepTrak measurement see Ponzi, Fombrun, & Gardberg, 2011). The brand goal focused on perceptions among external stakeholders, although internal stakeholders were included in the first two years. The tool also allowed the company to track stakeholder perceptions of its competitors' performances relative to Novo Nordisk's corporate brand goal.

Using these measures, Novo Nordisk has tracked its corporate brand and reputation since 2006. The data in Table 21.3 demonstrate correlations between brand goal performance and corporate reputation as perceived by the three key stakeholder groups aggregated across the four key markets for each year during the period 2006–2010. Data on key competitors' performances against Novo Nordisk's brand goal are not reported here, but show that competitors are not achieving Novo Nordisk's level of reputation for leadership in the field of diabetes care, something which is also reflected in the continuous growth in market share for Novo Nordisk in all key markets (annualreport. novonordisk.com).

The data in Table 21.3 show that Novo Nordisk's corporate brand goal performance and corporate reputation are correlated, but not at such a high level as to suspect that the two measures are completely entangled. The significant correlations as tested by Fisher's Z-transformation indicate that improvements in perceived corporate brand performance move in the same directions over the period measured, and this is the case for all three stakeholder groups. The exception is the last period in which data were available, when the correlation for patients increased, while that for healthcare professionals dropped slightly. Overall, the strongest correlations between perceived brand goal performance and corporate reputation occur among patients. Fisher's Z-transformation testing also revealed a significant increase in the strength of the relationship for all three target groups over the period 2006–2010, when corporate brand management was introduced in the company.

As stated already, the strong correlations between brand and reputation are not in a range that would indicate that the constructs are undifferentiated (in which case we would expect their correlation to be closer to one). The greater likelihood is that the increasing correlations over time indicate significant strengthening of the associative link between brand and reputation in the minds of those whose perceptions provide the

Table 21.3 Correlations Between Measures of Corporate Brand Goal Performance and Corporate Reputation in Novo Nordisk in 4 Key Markets 2006–2010

	2006	2007	2008	2009	2010
Secondary Care	0.556	0.679	0.605	0.698	0.653
Primary Care	0.639	0.667	0.628	0.679	0.665
Patients	0.654	0.704	0.688	0.672	0.768
AVERAGE	0.616	0.683	0.640	0.683	0.695

data. The increase in the correlations over time indicates that the association of the two constructs is intensifying in the perceptions of external stakeholders. This is most strongly the case for patients, in spite of small fluctuations year to year that may reflect various changes in their interactions with the brand's products or services. Thus it would seem that the brand goal of being perceived as a leader in the fight against diabetes is becoming more aligned with Novo Nordisk's corporate reputation as time goes on, and that this alignment effect is stronger for patients than for either primary or secondary care providers. We cannot say exactly why this alignment is occurring, it might be combinations of different direct and indirect management practices, such as continuous corporate communication of "Changing Diabetes," changes in advertising, the involvement of markets in the development of the brand house, more brand-driven sales work or increased media attention—or even an, as yet, unidentified factor driving both brand and reputation.

The company's preferred explanation for the alignment of brand and reputation is that Novo Nordisk's increased emphasis on taking the side of patients over the past decade has been intensified through the global scale of the corporate branding process. While the company has long maintained close relationships with its diabetes specialist stakeholders, the outreach to patients changed significantly during the roll-out of the "Changing Diabetes" initiative. This effect is about to be enhanced by the company's decision to feature patients in its 2011 restatement of corporate strategy, and to include patients explicitly in redrawing the Novo Nordisk brand house. For example, going forward the brand essence will be to: "defeat diabetes with patients at the heart of our actions."

It is of course possible that Novo Nordisk's strong reputation influences perceptions of the company as a leader in diabetes care (a halo effect), making it more likely that the company will be perceived as a strong leader, as stated in its brand goal. However, given that the period 2006–2010 saw the company give much greater emphasis to corporate branding, Novo Nordisk management believes the data indicate that corporate branding influenced reputation more than the other way around.

Connecting Corporate Branding and Reputation in Practice

The Novo Nordisk data also reflect differences in the company's managerial practices related to corporate branding and reputation (as illustrated in Table 21.1), as the strategic focus on corporate branding sparked the development of new management practices, initiated in part to influence the company's corporate reputation. Thus, while corporate branding and reputation are separated conceptually, we argue that they come together in practice, as the same practices have direct and indirect influences on both phenomena. In comparison with the marketing and co-creation perspectives, we realize that our position as part of the organizational perspective focused our empirical attention on how the company was seeking to manage its brand and its concern with the links between brand and reputation. Obviously, it is not a one-way relationship from brand to reputation, as practices seeking to influence corporate reputation, for example via media coverage and third party endorsement, also have significant implications for the corporate brand, just as the current reputation when initiating corporate branding contextualizes such effort. This was the case for Novo Nordisk when the tarnished reputation for many pharmaceuticals motivated the development of "leading the fight against diabetes" as the strategic aspiration for the company's brand. Here we focus on how corporate branding has become a significant organization-driven attempt to influence reputation, as corporate branding entails a wide range of expressive practices (Schultz, Hatch, & Larsen, 2000).

In Figure 21.2 we illustrate the broad range of management practices, drawing upon the analytical framework for corporate branding developed by Hatch & Schultz (see the second summary table at the end of this chapter) and arguing that alignment between strategic vision, organizational culture, and stakeholder images supports corporate brand building based in identity. Here, identity, comprising the central idea, core values, and their cognitive, emotional, and aesthetic expressions, is translated into the conceptual platform for the corporate brand.

Figure 21.2 illustrates how corporate brand management entails different kinds of practices directed at multiple stakeholders and reflecting their roles and needs. The thick arrows indicate that all practices can impact corporate reputation, whereas the thin arrows remind us that corporate reputation both contextualizes and bounces back to corporate branding, particularly over time. Figure 21.3 uses the same framework to provide an overview of corporate brand management practices from Novo Nordisk, as discussed earlier. The differences between the figures indicates the strong alignment of Novo Nordisk's corporate branding practices, that is, the extent to which these practices coherently express the identity for the brand. Whereas the arrows between vision, culture, and image in Figure 21.2 pose questions about alignment, Figure 21.3 illustrates how the managerial practices undertaken in Novo Nordisk were aligned through being based in the idea of "Changing Diabetes." The brand management practices in Figure 21.2 are labeled according to their typical intentions. Top management is most often *directing* the strategic aspiration for the brand in relation to the overall strategy and goal-setting, such as the use of Balanced Scorecard in Novo Nordisk to create company-wide

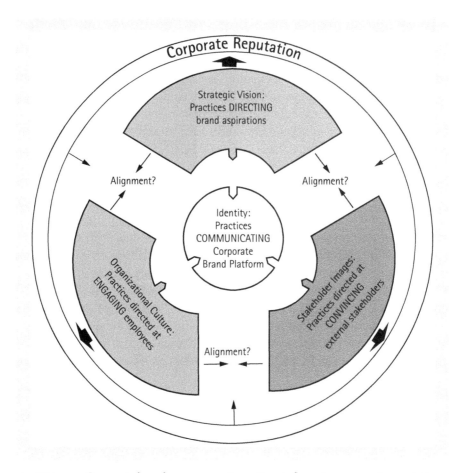

FIGURE 21.2 Corporate brand management practices influencing corporate reputation.

targets for brand goal and reputation tracking for senior managers. Having been crafted through a variety of organizational processes, such as listening to perceptions from employees and key stakeholders, a corporate platform is *communicated* to internal and external stakeholders. Such communication processes, such as responsibility for the branding unit to develop and implement the Novo Nordisk brand house(s) over time, are typically supported by the functional units, boards, and taskforces responsible for corporate branding. Often practices seeking to *engage* employees precede the development of practices toward external stakeholders, as employees are needed as ambassadors and active contributors to the brand execution, for example, implementing how "Changing Diabetes" is turned into specific action plans in local markets. As opposed to the marketing of product brands, the managerial practices directed at external stakeholders aim to *convince* external stakeholders to participate actively in the co-creation of the corporate brand rather than seducing them to buy a specific product. As illustrated by Novo Nordisk, branding practices are either deliberately co-created with

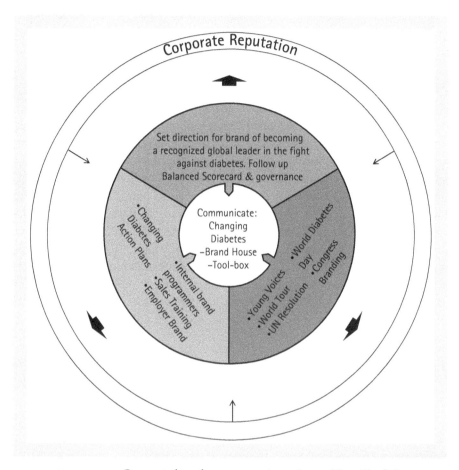

FIGURE 21.3 Corporate brand management practices at Novo Nordisk.

external stakeholders (e.g., Young Voices and UN Resolution) or invite stakeholders to participate in the ongoing development of the central idea of the brand (e.g., World Tour).

As indicated by our data, there is reason to believe that the combined outcome of these brand management practices have influenced the corporate reputation of Novo Nordisk in a positive direction. However, in their effort to influence the corporate brand, the managers of Novo Nordisk have also taken part in the processes they intended to influence, as when they joined activities already in the making within the global diabetes community, such as the push for a UN resolution. Here, the reputation of the company may have helped to attract diabetics and NGOs to participate in the brand development. Also, the corporate branding team used the brand house to highlight and support activities already taking place locally, thereby enhancing the co-creation of the brand between employees and external stakeholders. Thus, alignment between the different corporate brand management practices may foster positive synergies between brand

and reputation, as engaged employees are motivated to listen and respond to stakeholders attracted to the central brand idea. In the best situations, internal and external stakeholders together produce outcomes that are even more influential and innovative than expectations, such as the small idea of driving a bus around the world that turned into the "Changing Diabetes World Tour."

Deliberate attempts to manage a corporate brand can also develop in a negative direction. This may occur if the management practices are misaligned, for example, if there is no connection between the communication to internal and external stakeholders, or if a top management creates expectations that are not aligned with employee behavior and competences. As a consequence the company can lose its credibility and eventually create mistrust among stakeholders, damaging the corporate reputation. Also, the brand's influence on reputation is contextualized by the branding efforts by competitors and interpretations of those efforts by third parties. If competitors take advantage of positive synergies, as described above, then a company's reputation can suffer even greater erosion by unflattering comparisons. In conclusion, formal brand management practices may well work best when they complement rather than try to control existing forces at work among the stakeholders of a company. That is to say that neither corporate branding nor reputation "belong" exclusively to an organization, even though they swirl around and interpenetrate them.

Implications for Future Research

Our study suggests several areas for future research:

1) Corporate branding and reputation are interlinked via management practice, as several of the practices intended to influence corporate branding also have implications for corporate reputation and, possibly, the other way around. This opens an avenue for research that explores more fully the relevance and importance of various types of management practices to corporate reputation. These might go beyond corporate branding to include for example, HR and corporate social responsibility (CSR). Thus, future theorizing about corporate reputation should explore the role of management practice and how specific practices are co-created with stakeholders in different strategic contexts.

2) Corporate reputation is a multilevel construct in that the influences of corporate reputation are located both at the organizational level and at the field or societal level. So far the majority of research has focused on the field level, whereas our study addresses influences at the organizational level. There is a need for more research exploring the connections between the two levels of analysis in a global context. For example, a multilevel study of Novo Nordisk would have included research questions at the societal level, such as asking how global changes in the

perceptions of Type 2 diabetes as a global pandemic have influenced stakeholder reactions to "Changing Diabetes" and their willingness to participate in the co-creation of the brand.

3) Our study examined correlations between corporate branding and corporate reputation tracked over time using a customized measurement instrument. In order to enable further research on the correlations between brand and reputation and comparisons between different industries and markets, there is a need to develop a stronger conceptual framework for the relationships between corporate branding and reputation, which balance the need to measure the unique aspirations of the brand in relation to its many stakeholders against the ability to make comparisons across time and space.

ACKNOWLEDGMENT

In the writing of this chapter we want to thank managing partner Dr Leonard J. Ponzi and managing partner Kasper U. Nielsen, Reputation Institute, for help in analyzing the relations between brand and reputation. We also want to thank our editors and particularly Professor Michael Barnett for valuable comments in developing the arguments of the chapter.

Marketing Perspective on Corporate Branding

References	Key Constructs and Findings
Aaker (2004, 2004a) Aaker & Joachimstahler (2000)	• A corporate brand is a brand that represents a corporation—or, more generally, an organization—and reflects its heritage, values, culture, people, and strategy. • Brands can be described using a brand identity system, whereby corporate brands based in organizational associations differentiate themselves. • Within brand portfolio structure corporate brands come closest to the branded house. • Brand equity derives from market behavior, awareness, perceived association, differentiation, quality, and loyalty among consumers.
Olins (2008, 1995)	• A corporate brand can embrace both the organization as a whole and its products and its services. It is the complete set of tangible manifestations that make the strategy of the organization visible and palpable for all audiences to see. • A brand is based in a central idea and is transmitted through its products/service, staff behavior, environment, and communication.
Keller (1998, 2005)	• A corporate brand name may evoke associations wholly different from an individual brand. A corporate brand is more likely to evoke associations of common products and their shared attributes or benefits, people and relationships, activities and values, and corporate credibility. • A corporate image can be thought of as the associations that consumers hold with regard to the company making the product or providing the service as a whole. • A corporate or family brand can be a source of much brand equity as product brands may often relate to corporate brands.

Organizational Perspective on Corporate Branding

References	Key Constructs and Findings
Hatch & Schultz (2008, 2002, 1997)	• A corporate brand acts as a focal point for the attention, interest, and activity stakeholders bring to a corporation. It is much more than visual identity (logo, name, etc.) as it is based on the dynamics that sustain the identity of the organization. • Approach branding as an application of identity dynamics defined by the conversation a company has with its internal and external stakeholders. Identity brings organizational culture and societal culture into contact via the conversations between employees and stakeholders. • Branding is then built on the foundation of the identity conversation and adds strategic vision to organizational culture and stakeholder images to make a tripod to support branding efforts. The implication for practice is that alignment between vision, culture, and images supports corporate brand building. • Corporate brands can be assessed by identifying gaps that occur in the Vision–Culture–Image alignment of an organization.
Van Riel & Fombrun (2007) Van Riel (1995)	• The purpose of the corporate brand is to personalize the company as a whole in order to create value from the company's strategic position, institutional activities, organization, employees, and portfolio of products and services. • Corporate communication is central in defining, communicating, and negotiating corporate brands. • The positive drivers of corporate brands are creating a sense of internal coherence, demonstrating the strength and size of the organization, and exploiting economies of scale opposed to multiple product brands. • The negative drivers of corporate brands are wasting investments in product brands, giving up equity in powerful local brands, limiting distribution options, and ignoring consumers in local markets.
Balmer & Greyser (2003) Balmer, Stuart, & Greyser (2009)	• Derives from an organization's identity and is encapsulated in a branding position statement, which delineates the tangible and intangible attributes of the brand. Brand reputation serves as a company's covenant with key stakeholders. • Corporate brands emerge from the alignment of multiple types of identity: actual, communicated, conceived, ideal, and desired, called the ACID model. • Multiple identities are pervasive in public as well as private organizations. Different identities tend to inhabit different time frames. They can even co-exist comfortably within a company if they are somewhat inconsistent
Ind (1997, 2004)	• A corporate brand conveys a company's reputation to its audience. It is about far more than names and logos. A successful corporate brand links the corporate name to the company's distinctive qualities such as service or value. • There are three core attributes that define corporate brands as a distinct area: intangibility, complexity, responsibility. • The best way to develop a brand that has a high degree of relevance and consistency is to ensure that the employees of an organization understand and believe in the values of the organization. They cannot be invented—they have to come from the essence of the organization.

Co–Creation Perspective on Corporate Branding

References	Key Constructs and Findings
Merz & Vargo (2009)	Brands are constructed from the network of relationships between all the stakeholders rather than the traditional dyadic relationship. Brand values are co–created with stakeholder ecosystems and dynamically constructed through social interactions between stakeholders. • Brand comprises collaborative value–creating activities of firms and all of their stakeholders. Co–creation defines brand values in terms of the stakeholders' collectively perceived values–in–use of the brand. • Co–creation requires a process orientation in the study of brands and reflects a new brand logic based in a service–marketing perspective.
Muniz & O'Guinn (2001)	• Consumers form brand communities. A brand community is a specialized, non–geographically bound community based on a structured set of relations among admirers of a brand. Brand communities exhibit three traditional markers of community: shared consciousness, rituals and traditions, and a sense of moral responsibility. • Brand community acknowledges the social nature of brands, moving thinking away from the traditional consumer–brand dyad to the con–sumer–brand–consumer triad. • Brand community shows that consumers are actively engaged in creating the brand and that clearly affects brand equity and broadens the conception of consumer loyalty.
Prahalad & Ramaswamy (2004)	• The move from a "company–centric value creation" to the "co–creation of value" where consumers want to interact with firms. It emerges from the changing role of the consumer in the industrial system. • Companies must create environments that enable a diversity of co–creative experiences. This should motivate individuals to co–create and personalize their experiences. • Brand value is co–created between companies and stakeholders; co–creation occurs through access, dialogue, reputation, and risk.

References

Aaker, D. A. (1996). "Measuring brand equity across products and markets." *California Management Review*, 38(Spring): 102–120.

—— (2004). "Leveraging the corporate brand." *California Management Review*, 46(3): 6–18.

—— (2004a). *Brand Portfolio Strategy*. New York: The Free Press.

—— (2008). *Spanning Silos: The New CMO Imperative*. Boston: Harvard University Press.

—— & Joachimstahler, E. (2000). *Brand Leadership*. New York: The Free Press.

Abramson, J. (2004). *Overdosed America: The Broken Promise of American Medicine*. New York: HarperCollins.

Abratt, R. (1989). "A new approach to the corporate image management process." *Journal of Marketing*, 5(1): 63–76.

Angell, M. (2005). *The Truth About the Drug Companies: How They Deceive Us and What to Do About It*. New York: Random House.

Antorini, Y. M. & Andersen, K. S. (2005). "A communal approach to corporate branding." In M. Schultz, Y. M. Antorini, & F. Csaba (Eds.), *Corporate Branding: Purpose, People, Process*. Copenhagen: Copenhagen Business School Press, 79–103.

Arnould, E. J. & Thompson, C. J. (2005). "Consumer culture theory." Journal of Consumer Research, 31(March): 868–882.

Balmer, J. M. T. & Greyser, S. A. (Eds.). (2003). *Revealing the Corporation*. London: Routledge.

—— (2006). "Integrating corporate identity, corporate branding corporate communications, corporate image and corporate reputation." *European Journal of Marketing*, 40(7/8): 730–741.

——, Stuart, H., & Greyser, S. A. (2009). "Aligning identity and strategy: Corporate branding at British Airways in the late 20th century." *California Management Review*, 51(3): 6–23.

Barnett, M., Jermier, J., & Lafferty, B. (2006). "Corporate reputation: The definitional landscape." *Corporate Reputation Review*, 9(1): 26–38.

Benjamin, B. A. & Podolny, J. M. (1999). "Status, quality, and social order in the California wine industry." *Administrative Science Quarterly*, 44: 563–589.

Cornelissen, J. (2004). *Corporate Communication: Theory and Practice*. London: Sage Publications.

Dowling, G. (1994). *Corporate reputations: Strategies for Developing the Corporate Brand*. London: Kogan Page.

—— (2001). *Creating Corporate Reputations. Identity, Image and Performance*. Oxford: Oxford University Press.

—— (2006). "How good corporate reputations create corporate value." *Corporate Reputation Review*, 9(2): 134–143.

du Gay, P. (2000). "Markets and meaning: Re-imaging organizational life." In M. Schultz et al. (Eds.), *The Expressive Organization: Linking Identity, Reputation and the Corporate Brand*. Oxford: Oxford University Press, 66–77.

Fombrun, C. J. (1996). *Reputation: Realizing Value from the Corporate Image*. Boston: Harvard Business School Press.

—— & Shanley, M. (1990). "What's in a name? Reputation building and corporate strategy." *Academy of Management Journal*, 33(2): 233–258.

Fournier, S. & Lee, L. (2009). "Getting brand communities right." *Harvard Business Review*, 87(4): 105–111.

Gregory, A. (2007). "Involving stakeholders in developing corporate brands: The communication dimension." *Journal of Marketing Management*, 23(1–2): 59–73.

Hatch, M. J. & Schultz, M. (1997). "Relations between organizational culture, identity and image." *European Journal of Marketing*, 31(6): 356–365.

—— & —— (2002). "The dynamics of organizational identity." *Human Relations*, 55(8): 989–1018.

—— & —— (2008). *Taking Brand Initiative: How Companies Align Strategy, Culture and Identity Through Corporate Branding*. San Francisco: Jossey-Bass.

—— & —— (2009). "Of bricks and brands. From corporate to enterprise branding." *Organisational Dynamics*, 38(2): 117–130.

—— & —— (2010). "Towards a theory of brand co-creation with implications for brand governance." *Journal of Brand Management*, 7(8): 590–604.

Heding, T., Knudtzen, C., & Bjerre, M. (2009). *Brand Management*. London: Routledge.

Holt, D. (2004). *How Brands Become Icons: The Principles of Cultural Branding*. Cambridge, MA: Harvard Business School Press.

Ind, N. (1997). *The Corporate Brand*. London: Macmillan Business.

—— (2004). *Living the Brand*. London: Kogan Page.

Kapferer, J. N. (2000). *Strategic Brand Management*, 2nd ed. London: Kogan Page.

Kassirer, J. (2005). *On the Take: How Medicines Complicity with Big Business can Endanger Your Health*. Oxford: Oxford University Press.

Keller, K. L. (1998). *Strategic Brand Management*. New Jersey: Prentice-Hall.

—— (2003). "Brand synthesis: The multidimensionality of brand knowledge." *Journal of Consumer Research*, 29(4): 595–600.

——, Apéria, T., & Georgson, M. (2008). *Strategic Brand Management: A European Perspective*. Essex: Pearson Education.

Kornberger, M. (2010). *Brand Society*. University of Cambridge Press: Cambridge.

Lange, D. Lee, P. M., & Dai, Y. (2011). "Organizational reputation: A review." *Journal of Management*, 37: 153–185.

Levy, S. J. (1959). "Symbols for sale." *Harvard Business Review*, July–August: 117–124.

Little, P., Coffee, D., Lirely, R., & Little, B. (2009). "Explaining variation in market to book relations: Do corporate reputation ratings add explanatory power over and above brand values?" *Journal of Finance and Accountancy*, 10(1): 1–10.

Merz, M. & Vargo, S. (2009). "The evolving brand logic: A service-dominant logic perspective." *Journal of the Academy of Marketing Science*, 37(3): 328–344.

Muniz, A. M. & O'Guinn, T. C. (2001). "Brand community." *Journal of Consumer Research*, 27: 412–432.

Olins, W. (1995). *Corporate Identity*. London: Thames and Hudson.

—— (2003). *On Brand*. London: Thames and Hudson.

Payne, A., Storbacka, K., Frow, P., & Knox, S. (2009). "Co-creating brands: Diagnosing and designing the relationship experience." *Journal of Business Research*, 62(3): 379–389.

Ponzi, L. J., Fombrun, C. J., & Gardberg, N. (2011). "RepTrak™ Pulse: Conceptualizing and validating a short-form measure of corporate reputation." *Corporate Reputation Review*, 14(1): 15–35.

Prahalad, C. K. & Ramaswamy, V. (2004). *The Future of Competition: Co-Creating Unique Value with Customers*. Boston: Harvard Business School Press.

Rindova, V., Williamson, I., Petkova, A., & Sever, J. (2005). "Being good or being known. An empirical examination of the dimensions, antecedents, and consequences of organizational reputation." *Academy of Management Journal*, 48(6): 1033–1049.

Rubin, J., Schultz, M., & Hatch, M. J. (2008). "Coming to America: Can Nordic brand values engage American stakeholders?" *Brand Management*, 16(1–2): 30–39.

Saxton, T. & Dollinger, M. (2004). "Target reputation and appropriability: Picking and deploy-
ing resources in acquisitions." *Journal of Management*, 30: 123–147.

Schau, H. J., Muñiz, A., & Arnould, E. J. (2009). "How brand community practices create value."
Journal of Marketing, 73(5): 30–51.

Schultz, M. & Hatch, M. J. (2003). "The cycles of corporate branding: The case of LEGO company." *California Management Review*, 45(1): 6–26.

——, ——, & Larsen, M. H. (Eds.). (2000). *The Expressive Organization: Linking Identity,
Reputation and the Corporate Brand*. Oxford: Oxford University Press.

——, Rubin, J., Hatch, M. J., & Andersen, K. (2005). "Novo Nordisk: Focusing the corporate
brand." *(A) Case. Darden Business School Case*. UVA-BC- 0192.

van Riel, C. B. M. (1995). *Principles of Corporate Communication*. London: Prentice-Hall.

—— & Fombrun, C. (2007). *Essentials of Corporate Communication*. New York: Routledge.

....

CHAPTER 22

AFTER THE COLLAPSE: A BEHAVIORAL THEORY OF REPUTATION REPAIR

....

MOOWEON RHEE
TOHYUN KIM

In response to a call for an integrated reputation repair model, this chapter presents a behavioral theory of reputation repair with a focus on the behavioral mechanisms underlying an organization's response to a reputation-damaging event. Viewing reputation repair as a process of problem solving consisting of three steps (problem recognition, search for solutions, and implementation of solutions), we examine some inherent characteristics of problem solving, which can facilitate superficial problem solving, rather than substantive problem solving, and impede effective reputation repair. To guide future studies of reputation repair, the chapter further discusses how the characteristics of reputation-damaging events (type, attribution, and rarity), organizational characteristics (structure, culture, demography, history, and position), and the types of stakeholders create certain behavioral forces that promote or obstruct an organization's reputation repair process and performance. This chapter concludes with some theoretical and practical messages about reputation repair.

INTRODUCTION

....

As reviewed in earlier chapters in this volume, organizational reputation has been conceptualized in organizational and management literature as a signal conveying information about either an organization's behavior (Shapiro, 1983; Weigelt & Camerer, 1988), or its positions within a social system (Elsbach & Kramer, 1996; Rao, 1994), or the audiences' collective perception of it (Fombrun & Shanley, 1990; Rindova et al., 2005). In this chapter, we take a multidimensional view of organizational reputation by combining these different perspectives (see also Rindova and Martins, Chapter 2, this volume) and focus on the evolutionary process of organizational reputation, which involves mutual learning between an organization and its audiences. According to this view, an organization's reputation evolves through the interactions between the organization and the audiences, primarily its stakeholders: The organization's past behavior and positions influence the stakeholders' perceptions of the organization, which in turn affect the organization's future behavior and positions (Fombrun, 1996). Many studies on organizational reputation focus on the early stages of this evolutionary process, that is, the creation and building of an organization's reputation and its consequences for organizational performance (Rhee & Valdez, 2009). According to these studies, organizations that successfully build and manage their reputations tend to enjoy various advantages in their performance and behaviors (see Barnett, Jermier, & Lafferty, 2006; Rindova and Martins, Chapter 2, this volume). However, reputation scholars have paid relatively little attention to the potential consequences if an organization's reputation was in danger.

Unfortunately, an organization sometimes runs into various events—such as accidents or scandals—that engender the stakeholders' negative reactions toward the organization and thus damages the organization's reputation. Such an organization typically responds to the reputation-damaging event by engaging in reputation-repairing activities. If the organization's reputation-repairing activities are successful, the stakeholders would restore or renew their positive perceptions of the organization. In contrast, an inappropriate response to the event may worsen the stakeholders' perception of the organization. While a growing number of studies have begun to focus on these later stages of reputation management, that is, preventing and repairing the damages to organizational reputation (e.g., Dukerich & Carter, 2000; Heugens, van Riel, & van den Bosch, 2004; Rhee & Hadwick, 2011; Rhee & Valdez 2009), our understanding of the reputation repair process is still far from complete. In particular, the literature on impression management and strategic discourse (see Elsbach, Chapter 23; Whittington and Yakis-Douglas, Chapter 20, both this volume; and our review in the next section) certainly supports this stream of research, but reputation studies need to build on a more comprehensive research agenda for reputation repair.

In this chapter, we first review current studies on reputation repair and impression management and emphasize a need for a more integrated reputation repair model that elucidates the behavioral mechanisms underlying an organization's response to a reputation-damaging event. In response to this call, we present a behavioral theory of reputation repair and suggest future research directions. Our model views reputation repair as a process of problem solving, consisting of three steps: problem recognition, search for solutions, and implementation of solutions. More specifically, we show how some inherent characteristics of problem solving may impede effective reputation repair by facilitating superficial problem solving rather than substantive problem solving. We also provide the implications of our model for future studies by discussing how various factors surrounding an organization with a damaged reputation foster or impede the reputation repair process and performance. Those factors include the characteristics of reputation-damaging events (type, attribution, and rarity), organizational characteristics (structure, culture, demography, history, and position), and the types of stakeholders. We conclude with a call for caution among future reputation studies and corporate reputation managers.

LITERATURE REVIEW

Reputation Repair and Impression Management

Most existing studies on reputation repair tend to center on a firm's impression management by regarding it as an immediate solution to reputation damages or a crucial element in reputation repair activities. In particular, those works have presented several
case studies on reputation repair, which investigate the various strategies an organization employs to address a reputation-damaging event and repair its reputation. For
example, Fombrun's (1996) case study of Salomon Brothers notes how it recovered from
a financial scandal by accommodative impression management and substantive reorganization throughout the company. Carroll (2009) found that Cadbury Schweppes
could weather the salmonella scare involving its chocolate products by defensive impression management. In their study of four Silicon Valley computer firms that underwent
bankruptcy proceedings, Sutton & Callahan (1987) showed that these firms responded
to their stakeholders' negative reactions by employing diverse impression management
strategies, such as concealing, defining, denying responsibility, accepting responsibility,
and withdrawing. Heugens, van Riel, & van den Bosch (2004) also examined the process
in which Dutch food firms reacted to the introduction of genetically modified foods by
developing and combining various impression management capabilities.

Among such diverse impression management strategies, scholars have stressed
the importance of choosing a strategy that matches the type of reputation-damaging
event (Coombs, 1998, 2007; Dowling, 2001; Elsbach, Chapter 23, this volume;
Marcus & Goodman, 1991). For example, Marcus & Goodman (1991) categorize reputation-damaging events by the extent of causal attributions of organizational
responsibility, and argue that the events with strong attributions (e.g., scandals)
require an organization's accommodative responses while those with weak attributions (e.g., accidents) can be dealt with by defensive responses. Other scholars have
extended these arguments by further subdividing the types of events and presenting
impression management strategies relevant to each type (Coombs, 1998, 2007;
Dowling, 2001).

There is growing attention to other factors that influence an organization's choice of
impression management strategies in the face of reputation-damaging events. For example, Dukerich & Carter's (2000) theoretical model of reputation repair proposes that a
mismatch between an organization's reputation (held by outsiders) and its external
image (held by insiders) leads to the organization's misallocation of resources to impression management. While such studies advance the research scope of the reputation
repair model, their focus is still on impression management as the key reputation-
repairing activity. The table at the end of the chapter summarizes major theoretical and
empirical studies on reputation repair with a focus on the reputation-repairing activities
they discuss.

A Contemporary Issue: Toward an Integrated Reputation Repair Model

As our brief literature review shows, prior studies on reputation repair have focused primarily on (1) categorizing the types of reputation-damaging events and (2) presenting effective impression management strategies in response to those events. However, these studies tend to take a normative and suggestive viewpoint, so they are likely to ignore how an organization actually responds to its damaged reputation (Elsbach & Kramer, 1996) and how various organizational and environmental factors facilitate or hinder the organization's responses (Rhee & Valdez, 2009). To better understand the reputation repair process and performance, we need an integrated reputation repair model that includes an organization's actual behavior in the face of reputational threats and the factors influencing such behavior.

A few studies have attempted to examine various ways in which organizations respond to reputation-damaging events. For example, Elsbach & Kramer (1996) investigated the top 20 business schools' responses to the 1992 *BusinessWeek* survey rankings of US business schools. Their findings suggest that an organization's members may respond to damages in the organization's reputation by shifting their attention to the positive dimensions of its reputation in order to preserve the positive perceptions of their organizational identity. In a similar context, Martins (2005) found that some business schools engaged in organizational change in response to reputational damages and others did not, depending on the top managers' reaction to the rankings. His findings, together with those of Elsbach & Kramer (1996), imply that organizations may demonstrate divergent behaviors in the face of a similar reputation-damaging event. In his study of product recalls in the US automotive industry, Rhee (2009) examined the effect of an organization's reputation on its learning effort to reduce its product defect rate. His study suggests that damages to an organization's reputation can induce a certain learning behavior that helps the organization reduce the occurrence of subsequent reputation-damaging events.

In the meantime, there have been emerging theoretical endeavors to develop a reputation repair model that investigates multilevel, multidimensional factors affecting the process and performance of an organization's response to a reputation-damaging event. Rhee & Valdez (2009) present a model of the contextual factors that affect the difficulty of reputation repair. In particular, they present a set of theoretical propositions that address how reputational, organizational, and interorganizational factors influence an organization's perceived capability to cope with a reputation-damaging event and the external visibility of the event, which, in turn, determines the organization's susceptibility to reputational damages and the difficulty of repairing the damaged reputation. Rhee & Hadwick (2011) complement Rhee & Valdez's (2009) model by adding relational and behavioral perspectives, as the process of repairing an organization's damaged reputation is not independent of the process of restoring the stakeholders' trust in the organization and the process of managing and recovering from an organizational crisis. By reviewing prior research on trust management and crisis management and using this to draw possible implications for reputation repair studies, they present a research agenda that will help establish a more comprehensive reputation repair model.

Despite the abovementioned scholarly efforts (also see the table at the end of the chapter for a summary of those studies), reputation repair studies are still at an embryonic stage and the establishment of an integrated reputation repair model remains incomplete (Rhee & Hadwick, 2011). In an attempt to build a more complete reputation repair model, this chapter suggests a behavioral theory of reputation repair that takes into consideration the behavioral mechanisms underlying an organization's responses to reputation-damaging events. As a test of the validity of our framework as a research model, we also discuss future directions of reputation repair research by demonstrating the potential contribution of the behavioral theory to a better and deeper understanding of various factors influencing reputation repair processes.

A Behavioral Theory of Reputation Repair

Superficial versus Substantive Reputation Repair

As we reviewed above, prior studies on reputation repair have focused mainly on how an organization can influence and fix its stakeholders' negative perceptions of the organization through using impression management strategies. Such attention to the stakeholders' perceptions is quite understandable because reputations are constructed and evaluated mainly by the stakeholders and they tend to react negatively toward an organization experiencing a reputation-damaging event (Dukerich & Carter, 2000; Fombrun, 1996; Rhee & Valdez, 2009). However, the exclusive focus of researchers and practitioners on managing the stakeholders' perceptions can lock them into what we call *superficial reputation repair* in their research model and crisis management, respectively, which may temporarily conceal the essential problems in an organization's reputation-repairing activities.

Given that reputation is not static and evolves through the interactions between an organization's behavior and position and its stakeholders' perceptions over the long run, the organization should engage in *substantive reputation repair* in response to a reputation-damaging event, which involves changing the organization's behavior and position to remove the causes of the reputation-damaging event and prevent a recurrence of similar events. Without such an effort to address the root causes, an organization's impression management cannot be an effective long-term reputation repair tool as its stakeholders are less likely to be convinced of the organization's capability to recover from the event and alter their negative perceptions of the organization (Fombrun, 1996). Moreover, if a similar reputation-damaging event recurs, the organization is likely to suffer much more severe reactions from its stakeholders (Coombs, 2004). This suggests the necessity of incorporating a more evolutionary perspective in the reputation repair research and practice.

Therefore, both an organization's successful reputation repair and an ideal research program on reputation repair must encompass both the issues of (1) restoring or renewing the stakeholders' perceptions of the organization by protecting these stakeholders, physically and psychologically, from the harm of the reputation-damaging event (Coombs, 2007); and (2) identifying the root causes and restructuring or reorganizing the organization's behavior and position to prevent the recurrence of similar events (Haunschild & Rhee, 2004). We suggest that our behavioral theory of reputation repair creates an opportunity to address these two issues by focusing our attention on the behavioral mechanisms underlying an organization's reputation repair process and performance.

A Model

We view reputation repair as a process of problem solving, involving three steps: (1) problem recognition, (2) search for solutions, and (3) implementation of solutions (Carley & Harrald, 1997; Cyert & March, 1963; Tucker & Edmondson, 2003). A reputation-damaging event is considered as a problem, where an organization faces imminent failure due to a critical downturn in the stakeholders' perceptions of the organization (cf. Kim, Kim, & Miner, 2009; Kim & Miner, 2007). Such an event triggers the organization's attention and stimulates *problemistic search*, or a search for solutions to the problem at hand (Cyert & March, 1963; Greve, 2003). Ideally, the organization makes cause-and-effect inferences to find and implement the solutions that would eliminate the causes of the problem, repair its damaged reputation, and reduce the occurrence of subsequent reputation-damaging events. Organizational learning occurs at each step along the problem-solving process, contributing to a further reduction in the recurrence of similar events (Carley & Harrald, 1997; Haunschild & Rhee, 2004; Miner et al., 1999). Figure 22.1 presents a simple illustration of this behavioral model of reputation repair.

However, reputation repair is not always successful because an organization may face difficulty in problem solving at various steps for a variety of reasons (Carley & Harrald, 1997): An organization may fail to recognize the problem, identify the cause and effect, find the appropriate solutions, or implement the solutions. The reputation-repairing process will not occur if an organization does not perceive a reputation-damaging event as a problem in the first place. As we discuss in the next section, since reputation-damaging events vary in their impact and salience depending on the characteristics of the events, the organization, and its stakeholders, some organizations are not likely to recognize the problem while others do. Organizations may need to manufacture a crisis internally in order to initiate the problem-solving process (Kim, 1998).

Most importantly, some inherent characteristics of problem solving may impede an effective search for solutions, resulting in the implementation of superficial solutions, rather than substantive solutions for reputation repair (Cyert & March, 1963; Tucker &

Edmondson, 2003). Here, we highlight the three characteristics of problemistic search noted by Cyert & March, (1963: 120–22), as they provide important insights into the building of a behavioral reputation repair model, particularly the issue of substantive versus superficial responses to a reputation-damaging event:

1. An organization's search is stimulated when the organization recognizes a problem, whereas its search is depressed when the organization perceives that the problem is solved (Bromiley, 2005; Cyert & March, 1963; Greve, 2003). This characteristic may lead the organization to rely on short-term superficial solutions that temporarily conceal the root cause of problems. For example, Tucker & Edmondson (2003) found that most nurses in hospitals responded to problems by applying short-term remedies to patch the problems and did not seek to change the underlying organizational routines to remove the root causes because those short-term solutions appeared to be temporarily successful. Therefore, it is implied that if an organization perceives that its (or other organizations') damaged reputation is repaired by a short-term solution (e.g., superficial impression management), then it is less likely to search further for a longer-term solution (e.g., substantive reorganization).

2. Search is based on a simple model of causality, such as the assumptions that a cause will be found near its effect and that a new solution will be found near an old one

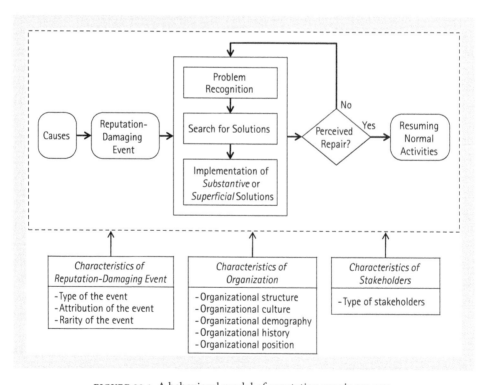

FIGURE 22.1 A behavioral model of reputation repair process.

(Cyert & March, 1963). Since the main symptom of a reputational problem is the stakeholders' negative reactions, many organizations are likely to search locally for the solutions that directly involve altering their stakeholders' perceptions, rather than to search globally for the solutions that involve identifying and removing the root causes underlying the reputation-damaging event (cf. Levinthal, 1997). Also, if an organization perceives that the implementation of a solution to a reputation-damaging event is successful, then the organization is likely to apply the same solution when another reputation-damaging event occurs. For example, Heugens, van Riel, & van den Bosch's (2004) findings show that most Dutch food companies repeatedly used defensive communication strategies in response to reputation-damaging events with little attention to the general nature of those strategies.

3. Search is biased by the expectation of the participants in an organization. One of the consequences of such biases is a decrease in the amount of problem-solving time allowed to solve a problem genuinely (Cyert & March, 1963), in favor of resuming the normal activities of pursuing the organization's initial primary goals. Argyris & Schön (1978: 2–3) also note an organization's tendency to fall into *single-loop learning*, detecting and correcting errors to carry on its present policies or achieve its present objectives, instead of engaging in *double-loop learning*, detecting and correcting errors to modify its underlying norms, policies, and objectives. That is, when an organization's normal activities are interrupted by an abnormal reputation-damaging event, the organization is likely to settle on a short-term solution by superficially managing the stakeholders' perceptions—without an effort to implement a substantive longer-term solution—in order to achieve its performance goals, which were set before the occurrence of the event (cf. Tucker & Edmondson, 2003).

Building upon the features of problemistic search and their implications for a reputation repair model, therefore, a central research question ensues: How do various factors surrounding an organization with a damaged reputation foster or impede each step of the organization's reputation repair process (shown in Figure 22.1) and result in a superficial versus substantive reputation repair? For example, some factors may facilitate an organization's recognition of a problem and reduce its resistance to the implementation of substantive solutions by increasing the external visibility of a reputation-damaging event, while the same factors can also increase the level of difficulty in the organization's reputation repair, especially in the step of searching for appropriate solutions (Rhee & Valdez, 2009). Also, the factors increasing the level of difficulty in reputation repair may motivate an organization to solve the problem at hand and to engage in substantive reputation repair, while they also interfere with the organization's regular resource management, leading the organization to reallocate its limited resources to superficial reputation repair to weather the immediate negative reactions of the key stakeholders. Some factors may influence the timing and speed of the reputation repair process by requiring rapid search and implementation, impeding deliberate cause-and-effect inferences, and facilitating superficial rather than substantive problem solving. Future studies on reputation repair should attempt to conduct a thorough investigation into those factors.

In the next section, we discuss some of those factors by examining the effects of various characteristics of the reputation-damaging events, the organizations, and the stakeholders on reputation repair process and performance (see Figure 22.1 for an illustration of those factors). This discussion will not cover a complete list of research agendas that can be derived from our behavioral model of reputation repair, but it will offer a clear direction on how our model can be applied to research on reputation repair.

FUTURE RESEARCH DIRECTIONS: MODEL APPLICATIONS

Characteristics of Reputation-Damaging Events and Problem Solving

Type of Reputation-Damaging Events

As we reviewed above, many prior studies on reputation repair have examined different types of reputation-damaging events and effective impression management strategies that match with those types (e.g., Coombs, 1998, 2007; Dowling, 2001; Marcus & Goodman, 1991). These studies tend to focus on organizational crises as reputational threats, defined as high impact events (e.g., accidents and scandals) that threaten the viability of the organization and require its immediate response (Pearson & Clair, 1998: 60). As Heugens, van Riel, & van den Bosch (2004) note, however, damages to a reputation may originate not only from a crisis, but also from an issue or trend (e.g., poor performance and low status), usually represented by gaps between the stakeholders' perceptions of the organization and their expectations. Crises and issues have different implications for the search and learning process (Heugens, van Riel, & van den Bosch, 2004) and, thus, for the reputation repair process.

Since crises are highly salient and impactful, they serve as unfreezing events (Schein, 1972), questioning the basic assumptions within an organization (Pearson & Clair, 1998) and creating a window of opportunity during which organizational changes can occur (Carley & Harrald, 1997). In this sense, crises may be seen as catalysts that are likely to motivate and enhance substantive reputation repair (Sitkin, 1992; Winter, 2000). However, under the intensive time pressure and high ambiguity that accompany a crisis situation, it may be difficult for an organization to effectively invest its time and resources in investigating and identifying the root causes of the problem, and learning from the experience (Ocasio, 1995).

On the contrary, issues tend to evolve at a relatively slow pace, allowing an organization to engage in a deliberate learning process by comparing, analyzing, explaining, and devising analogies (Heugens, van Riel, & van den Bosch, 2004; Zollo & Winter, 2002). That is, issues equip the organization with sufficient time and resources that can be devoted to substantive reputation-repairing activities. For example, consistent with the performance feedback model (Cyert & March, 1963; Greve, 2003), prior studies have found that organizations tended to engage in organizational change when they observed that their performance indicators, such as status in the marketplace, was lower than the level they aspired to achieve (Martins, 2005); such responses may help reduce subsequent reputation-damaging events (Rhee, 2009). However, since issues are not as salient as crises, organizations may fail to recognize them as problems, and even if organizations have identified the problems and found the solutions, participants in the organizations may resist implementing solutions involving reorganization, which they believe may not be necessary (cf. Carley & Harrald, 1997). Therefore, future studies should investigate how different types of reputation-damaging events influence an organization's problem-solving process and performance in its reputation-repairing activities and lead to substantive versus superficial reputation repair. While we have proposed the analytic dimension of crises vis-à-vis issues, scholars need to further explore various dimensions that would differentiate the reputation repair process (e.g., severe versus non-severe events; Haunschild & Rhee, 2004).

Attribution of Reputation-Damaging Events

Reputation-damaging events vary in terms of the extent to which they are attributed to a focal organization. If a reputation-damaging event is perceived to be the fault of the organization, there will be a stronger perception that the organization should be responsible for the event, incurring greater damages to the organization's reputation (Coombs, 1998). Therefore, Marcus & Goodman (1991) and Coombs (1998) argued that the events strongly attributed to an organization (e.g., scandals and misconducts) require more accommodative responses from the organization than those with more external attributions (e.g., accidents and natural disasters), to which the organization can demonstrate defensive responses. While a stronger perception of organizational responsibility for a reputation-damaging event provides an organization with greater difficulty in reputation repair (Rhee & Valdez, 2009), they may facilitate substantive reputation-repairing activities, rather than superficial activities, when the event triggers the organization's proactive responses. For example, studies on learning from failure suggest that a defensive approach to reputation repair is less likely to produce learning efforts than a proactive approach (Haunschild & Rhee, 2004; Kim, 1998; Rhee & Hadwick, 2011). Therefore, future studies may examine the effects of the internal vis-à-vis external attribution of a reputation-damaging event on the difficulty of repairing damaged reputations, relative to its effects on the triggering of substantive reputation repair.

Rarity of Reputation-Damaging Events

While reputation-damaging events are generally uncommon, there is still variance in the extent of rarity across different events. For example, accidents caused by natural disasters are typically rarer than product recalls. On one hand, research on organizational learning shows some behavioral underpinnings leading to the difficulty of learning from rarer events (e.g., Haunschild & Sullivan, 2002; Kim, Kim, & Miner, 2009; Lampel,

Shamsie, & Shapira, 2009; March, Sproull, & Tamuz, 1991). For example, Lampel, Shamsie, & Shapira (2009) show that organizations are less likely to recognize a rarer event as a problem as they believe that such an event is unlikely to recur. Also, it is more difficult to make a reliable cause-and-effect inference from a smaller experience sample (Haunschild & Sullivan, 2002; March, Sproull, & Tamuz, 1991). Therefore, an organization is likely to have difficulty in engaging in substantive reputation repair when faced with rare reputation-damaging events.

On the other hand, organizations may be more likely to focus their problem-solving effort on rarer events because they contain useful lessons (Lampel, Shamsie, & Shapira, 2009). That is, events may be enacted through their salience and trigger organizational attention to the unique and unusual features of the events (Weick & Sutcliffe, 2006). Such increased attention to a rare event is likely to intensify an organization's learning endeavor to accumulate knowledge about and through the event (Lampel, Shamsie, & Shapira, 2009). Hence, the rarity of an event may facilitate an organization's substantive reputation repair. Given these conflicting predictions, future research on the net effect of the rarity of a reputation-damaging event, as well as its contingency on contexts, would be valuable.

Characteristics of Organizations and Problem Solving

Organizational Structure

A tightly coordinated and centralized structure seems to enhance an organization's reputation repair performance by enabling the organization's concerted effort at recovery in the face of a reputation-damaging event that requires immediate responses under time and resource pressures. It is also possible that the centralization of authority facilitates substantive reputation repair by improving communication and coordination within an organization (cf. Mahler & Casamayou, 2009) and focusing its attention on the problem area, which triggers the organization's search for solutions and learning from experience (cf. Haunschild & Rhee, 2004). For example, Fombrun (1996) notes how Salomon, Inc., the holding company of two major operating units, Salomon Brothers and Phibro Energy, centralized its authority in order to effectively restore its damaged reputation after a scandal at Salomon Brothers in 1991.

However, Perrow (1984) argues that centralizing authority over procedures to prevent and detect errors can demotivate organizational members by forcing them to mechanically comply with rules and procedures. As Haunschild & Rhee (2004) found in their study of auto product recalls, involuntary responses to a reputation-damaging event are unlikely to result in organizational learning and improvements in subsequent performance. In this sense, a flexible, organic structure is more likely to facilitate organizational learning and adaptation, resulting in substantive reputation repair, than a tight, mechanical structure (Adler, Goldoftas, & Levine, 1999; Jennings & Seaman, 1994; Puranam, Singh, & Zollo, 2006). Therefore, future studies should be able to identify and examine the pros and cons of both organic and mechanical structures in repairing an organization's damaged reputation.

Organizational Culture

A strong organizational culture is defined as "a set of norms and values that are widely shared and strongly held throughout the organization" (O'Reilly & Chatman, 1996: 166). It can make an organization's search and learning process reliable by developing common understandings of its experience and making its interpretations public, stable, and shared (March, Sproull, & Tamuz, 1991; Sørensen, 2002), which may also enhance reputation repair process and performance.

However, stable, shared knowledge interferes with the discovery of different and contradictory interpretations of the organization's experience, from which reliable learning arises (Kim & Rhee, 2009; March, 1991; March, Sproull, & Tamuz, 1991). Strong culture may also endanger organizational members' psychological safety, something which allows their risk-taking attempts and exploratory learning (Edmondson, 1999; Tucker & Edmondson, 2003). For example, Vaughan (1997) and Mahler & Casamayou (2009) note that NASA's strong culture, emphasizing political and bureaucratic accountability, contributed to the Challenger accident in 1986 and the similar Columbia accident in 2003. Therefore, a weak and heterogeneous culture, encouraging diverse values and individual contributions, may be more likely to facilitate substantive reputation repair. In addition to the distinction of strong and weak cultures, future studies need to expand cultural dimensions and examine how various features of organizational culture contribute to substantive reputation repair vis-à-vis superficial reputation repair.

Organizational Demography

Prior studies have found that demographic diversity contributes to search and learning processes (Beckman, 2006; Taylor & Greve, 2006). These findings may imply that the knowledge and experience diversity of members in an organization helps its substantive reputation repair process because such diversity can bring diverse interpretations and perspectives to problem solving. One way of introducing diversity into an organization is by recruiting new members with new knowledge or different backgrounds (Harrison & Carroll, 2005; Kim & Rhee, 2009; March, 1991). For example, Fombrun (1996) notes that Salomon's first move in its reputation-repairing activities was to hire Warren Buffett, an esteemed leader with a personal reputation for integrity, as the interim chairman, and Deryck Maughan, an eight-year veteran of Salomon's Tokyo office, as the chief operating officer, who subsequently implemented structural, cultural, financial, and personnel changes.

However, the excessive turnover accompanied by the pursuit of organizational demographic diversity can be problematic: organizational members who have experiences with rare reputation-damaging events can leave the organization, causing organizational memory to disappear (Carley & Harrald, 1997; Mahler & Casamayou, 2009; March, 1991). For example, Carley & Harrald (1997) note that the Red Cross had difficulty in its disaster relief operations after Hurricane Andrew had destroyed South

Florida in 1992, because senior personnel who had experience with similar events, such as Hurricane Hugo in 1989, did not participate in the operation due to retirements or transfers. Therefore, future studies may investigate the optimal balance, if any, in organizational demography (e.g., between old, experienced members and new members of diverse backgrounds), which can significantly enhance an organization's substantive reputation repair.

Organizational History

Studies on organizational learning note the benefits of cumulative organizational experience. By interpreting and making inferences from its history, an organization accumulates knowledge, attempts to improve on its performance, and reduces the rate of errors and failures (Haunschild & Rhee, 2004; Levitt & March, 1988). Hence, in general, organizations with prior experience in reputation repair are likely to respond effectively to similar reputation-damaging events in the future.

As we noted above, however, problemistic search is simple-minded (Cyert & March, 1963), leading organizations to apply an old solution that they used before to a new problem. This tendency is exacerbated in the case of reputation repair because, as discussed earlier, reputation-damaging events are generally rare events, which makes it difficult to draw reliable cause-and-effect inferences (Haunschild & Sullivan, 2002; March, Sproull, & Tamuz, 1991). Therefore, research into organizational learning emphasizes the importance of both the volume and heterogeneity of organizational history in learning from rare events (Haunschild & Sullivan, 2002; Kim, Kim, & Miner, 2009; Madsen & Desai, 2010). Extending this line of thought, we can conjecture that an organization with abundant and diverse experiences of reputation repair is in a better position to prepare a pool of relevant solutions—especially in the face of diverse reputation-damaging events—and is more likely to be effective at a substantive reputation repair process. Future studies can further construct a more fruitful set of reputation repair experiences to present comprehensive links between organizational history and reputation repair process/performance.

Organizational Position

An organization's behavior and performance are enabled and constrained by its position within social hierarchies, social networks, and resource space, and so is its reputation building and rebuilding processes. Indeed, an organization's reputation itself, directly and indirectly, forms the organization's relative positions within social hierarchies (Benjamin & Podolny, 1999; Podolny, 1993) and affects its behavior (e.g., Kim, 2010; Rhee, 2009). For example, Rhee & Haunschild (2006) and Rhee (2009) found that organizations with different positions in reputational order show divergent levels of vulnerability to reputation-damaging events (i.e., product recalls) and display different levels of learning effort to avoid the recurrence of similar events, because the organizations and their stakeholders have certain expectations about the organizations based on the positions they occupy. Focusing on the multidimensionality of hierarchical positions, Rhee & Valdez (2009) and Kim (2010) suggest that the organizations' relative positions along each dimension have varying levels of salience to the organizations and their stakeholders and, therefore, have diverging effects on their reputation-repairing activities. Consequently, future studies will benefit from an investigation into how an organization's relative positions within multidimensional social hierarchies influence its efforts and abilities to implement substantive reputation repair.

An organization's position within its social networks may also influence its reputation-repairing activities. An organization's network partners are its key stakeholders, providing crucial resources, such as information, knowledge, and endorsement, to the organization (Brass et al., 2004); at the same time they form their own perceptions of the organization. Moreover, the organization's relationships with its network partners also influence other stakeholders' perception of the organization (Benjamin & Podolny, 1999; Podolny, 1993). Therefore, positive relationships with network partners based on trust may serve as a buffer to reputational threats, enabling the organization to put more resources and efforts into substantive reputation repair (Rhee & Hadwick, 2011). However, such a buffer may decrease an organization's motivation to engage in substantive reputation repair and leave the organization idle and reliant on superficial reputation-repairing activities. An organization can also learn from or imitate its network partners' experience and knowledge (Beckman & Haunschild, 2002), which may influence the organization's choice between substantive and superficial reputation repairs. Hence, future studies may examine how an organization's structural positions within social networks, its relationship with its network partners, and the characteristics of those partners enable and constrain the organization's reputation repair process and performance.

In addition, an organization's position on resource space can affect its reputation repair process (e.g., Haunschild & Rhee, 2004; Rhee & Haunschild, 2006). For example, Rhee & Haunschild (2006) found that specialist organizations, or those positioned in a narrower resource space (e.g., Porsche), are less vulnerable to reputational threats than generalist organizations covering a larger resource space (e.g., Toyota) because of their clear and focused identity. Moreover, Haunschild & Sullivan (2002) found that generalists are less likely to learn from their failures because they have to deal with a wider range of complex problems than specialists. However, Haunschild & Rhee's (2004) findings suggest that generalists may learn more from reputation-damaging events because the events have more negative consequences for generalists due to their greater visibility, and thus are perceived as more significant problems. Therefore, we suggest that future studies continue to investigate the differences in reputation repair process and performance between generalists and specialists across various industry contexts.

Characteristics of Stakeholders and Problem Solving

An organization's reputation repair process and performance may vary depending on the type of stakeholders it has. The heterogeneous nature of stakeholders' interests and the different avenues available for their information gathering may lead to variance in their reactions to reputation-damaging events and thus provide the organization with different levels of difficulty in problem solving (Rhee & Valdez, 2009). For example, Marcus & Goodman (1991) argue that shareholders tend to prefer an organization's defensive approaches to reputation repair, which protect their interests, while the victims prefer the organization's accommodative approaches. Rhee & Valdez (2009) note that some stakeholders (e.g., the public) tend to have limited access to information on an organization's reputation-damaging events and thereby display inadequate or excessive reactions to the events. When an organization's reputation-repairing activities involve dealing with such stakeholders, the organization may engage in superficial reputation repair by overreacting or underreacting to the stakeholders (cf. Dukerich & Carter, 2000). Conversely, a special group of stakeholders (e.g., watchdog agencies, mass media, and endorsers) have access to detailed information and affect other stakeholders' perception of the organization (Rhee & Valdez, 2009). Watchdog agencies' scrutiny and punishment and the mass media's reporting on an organization's reputation-damaging events, for example, make the events more visible to other stakeholders, whereas the endorsers' persistent support of the organization after the events increases other stakeholders' perception of the organization's capability to repair its reputation (Rhee & Valdez, 2009). While these stakeholders may request an organization's substantive reputation repair, the organization may still engage in superficial reputation repair by lobbying the agencies or endorsers. Future studies may categorize the stakeholders depending on the types of problem-solving approaches they demand from an organization and investigate how the organization searches for solutions to cope with their demands and repair its damaged reputation.

Conclusion

Building upon our literature review of reputation repair, we realized there was a need for a reputation repair model that can address an organization's variant responses to reputation-damaging events in a more comprehensive, systematic way. In an attempt to satisfy this goal, we presented a behavioral theory of reputation repair that views reputation repair as a process of problem solving, with a focus on the behavioral mechanisms underlying an organization's motivation and ability to engage in substantive vis-à-vis superficial reputation-repairing activities. An application of our model was presented as the form of a central research question for the study of reputation repair: What contextual factors create the behavioral forces that lead to an organization's choice of a certain reputation repair activity. Among many possible factors, we discussed the effects of various characteristics of reputation-damaging events, organizations, and stakeholders on the process and performance of problem solving for reputation repair.

Although we pointed out the emphasis of prior studies on impression management and the risk that such an emphasis can lead to exclusive research and practical focuses on superficial reputation repair, it does not mean that impression management is not important. Rather, substantive solutions to the problem of a reputation-damaging event may encompass impression management designed to protect the stakeholders psychologically from the harm of the event, as well as reorganization devised to prevent the recurrence of similar events. As Carley & Harrald (1997) note, an organization may not even benefit from its substantive problem solving unless its stakeholders recognize or appreciate the organization's responses to a reputation-damaging event. Therefore, managing the stakeholders' perceptions of the organization can serve as a key supplement to the substantive reputation repair process and a crucial part of an organization's successful reputation repair. Thus another important implication of our behavioral theory of reputation repair is that scholars and managers should pay attention to how an organization can enhance reputation repair performance through an appropriate combination of substantive problem solving and impression management.

While we emphasized the importance of substantive reputation repair in reducing the recurrence of reputation-damaging events, such an effort to reduce errors or failures should not discourage an organization's experimentation. Refinement and exploitation of successful routines tend to produce reliable outcomes with fewer errors, at the risk of causing an organization to stagnate (March, 1991). Recognizing failure as a necessary by-product of experimentation, Cannon & Edmondson (2005) suggest that organizations should actively increase their chances of experiencing failure by deliberate experimentation, which may further increase their capability to cope with reputation-damaging events (cf. Zollo & Winter, 2002). Similarly, Haunschild & Rhee (2004) find that organizations tend to proactively initiate and respond to their errors because it helps prevent further errors that cause greater damage to the organizations. We thus suggest that scholars and managers should explore the behavioral processes in which an organization attends to solving certain reputational threats while continuously experimenting with new routines and accumulating new knowledge necessary for its long-term viability amidst changing environments.

ACKNOWLEDGMENT

The authors wish to thank Tim Pollock, Mike Barnett, and the participants at Reputation Symposium 2010 for their helpful comments and suggestions on earlier drafts. This work was supported by the National Research Foundation of Korea Grant funded by the Korean Government (NRF-2010 330-B00100).

Summary of Existing Studies on Reputation Repair

Reference	Research Contexts and Reputation Repair Activities
Sutton & Callahan (1987)	Empirical context: Bankruptcy of four Silicon Valley computer firms Reputation repair activities: Impression management (concealing, defining, denying responsibility, accepting responsibility, and withdrawing)
Marcus & Goodman (1991)	Empirical context: 15 cases of organizational crises (accidents, scandals, and product safety incidents) Reputation repair activities: Impression management (defensive and accommodative signaling)
Fombrun (1996: ch. 15)	Empirical context: Financial scandal in Salomon Brothers Reputation repair activities: Impression management (accommodative approach) and reorganization (personnel, structural, and cultural changes)
Coombs (1998)	Empirical context: Experimental cases of four crises types (accident, transgression, natural disaster, and product tampering) Reputation repair activities: Impression management (attack the accuser, denial, excuse, justification, ingratiation, corrective action, and full apology)
Dukerich & Carter (2000)	Theoretical focus: Mismatch between reputation and external image Reputation repair activities: Impression management with inordinately or insufficiently allocated resources
Dowling (2001: ch. 12)	Theoretical focus: Different types of events depending on causal attributions Reputation repair activities: Impression management (hide-and-seek, fatalistic, offensive, and eye-for-an-eye)
Heugens, van Riel, & van den Bosch (2004)	Empirical context: Eight Dutch firms' introduction of genetically modified foods Reputation repair activities: Impression management (dialogue, advocacy, silence, and crisis communication)
Coombs (2007)	Theoretical focus: Different clusters of crises types (victim, accidental, and preventable) Reputation repair activities: Impression management (denial, diminish, and rebuild)
Carroll (2009)	Empirical context: Salmonella scare in Cadbury Schweppes Reputation repair activities: Impression management (defensive approach)
Elsbach & Kramer (1996)	Empirical context: Reputational ranking of US business schools Reputation repair activities: Organizational members' perceptual change
Martins (2005)	Empirical context: Reputational ranking of US business schools Reputation repair activities: Reorganization
Rhee (2009)	Empirical context: Reputation for product quality of automakers Reputation repair activities: Learning effort to reduce subsequent organizational errors
Rhee & Valdez (2009)	Theoretical focus: Contextual factors affecting the difficulty of reputation repair Reputation repair activities: Overcoming susceptibility to reputation-damaging events
Rhee & Hadwick (2011)	Theoretical focus: Reputation repair as trust and crisis management Reputation repair activities: Recovering trust relationships with stakeholders

REFERENCES

Adler, P. S., Goldoftas, B., & Levine, D. I. (1999). "Flexibility versus efficiency? A case study of model changeovers in the Toyota production system." *Organization Science*, 10(1): 43–68.

Argyris, C. & Schön, D. A. (1978). *Organizational Learning: A Theory of Action Perspective.* Reading, MA: Addison Wesley.

Barnett, M. L., Jermier, J. M., & Lafferty, B. A. (2006). "Corporate reputation: The definitional landscape." *Corporate Reputation Review*, 9(1): 26–38.

Beckman, C. M. (2006). "The influence of founding team company affiliations on firm behavior." *Academy of Management Journal*, 49: 741–758.

—— & Haunschild, P. R. (2002). "Network learning: The effects of partners heterogeneity of experience on corporate acquisitions." *Administrative Science Quarterly*, 47(1): 92–124.

Benjamin, B. A. & Podolny, J. M. (1999). "Status, quality, and social order in California wine industry." *Administrative Science Quarterly*, 44: 563–589.

Brass, D. J., Galaskiewicz, J., Greve, H. R., & Tsai, W. (2004). "Taking stock of networks and organizations: A multilevel perspective." *Academy of Management Journal*, 47(6): 795–817.

Bromiley, P. (2005). *The Behavioral Foundations of Strategic Management*. Malden, MA: Blackwell.

Cannon, M. D. & Edmondson, A. C. (2005). "Failing to learn and learning to fail (intelligently): How great organizations put failure to work to innovate and improve." *Long Range Planning*, 38: 299–319.

Carley, K. M. & Harrald, J. R. (1997). "Organizational learning under fire: Theory and practice." *American Behavioral Scientist*, 40(3): 310–332.

Carroll, C. (2009). "Defying a reputational crisis—Cadbury's salmonella scare: Why are customers willing to forgive and forget?" *Corporate Reputation Review*, 12(1): 64–82.

Coombs, W. T. (1998). "An analytic framework for crisis situations: Better responses from a better understanding of the situation." *Journal of Public Relations Research*, 10(3): 177–191.

—— (2004). "Impact of past crises on current crisis communication: Insights from situational crisis communication theory." *Journal of Business Communication*, 41(3): 265–289.

—— (2007). "Protecting organization reputations during a crisis: The development and application of situational crisis communication theory." *Corporate Reputation Review*, 10(3): 163–176.

Cyert, R. M. & March, J. G. (1963). *A Behavioral Theory of the Firm*. Englewood Cliffs, NJ: Prentice-Hall.

Dowling, G. R. (2001). *Creating Corporate Reputations: Identity, Image, and Performance*. New York: Oxford University Press.

Dukerich, J. M. & Carter, S. M. (2000). "Distorted images and reputation repair." In M. Schultz, M. J. Hatch, & M. H. Larsen (Eds.), *The Expressive Organization: Linking Identity, Reputation, and the Corporate Brand*. New York: Oxford University Press, 97–112.

Edmondson, A. (1999). "Psychological safety and learning behavior in work teams." *Administrative Science Quarterly*, 44: 350–383.

Elsbach, K. D. & Kramer, R. M. (1996). "Members' responses to organizational identity threats: Encountering and countering the *Business Week* rankings." *Administrative Science Quarterly*, 41(3): 442–476.

Fombrun, C. J. (1996). *Reputation: Realizing Value from the Corporate Image*. Boston: Harvard Business School Press.

Fombrun, C. & Shanley, M. (1990). "What's in a name? Reputation building and corporate strategy." *Academy of Management Journal*, 33(2): 233–258.

Greve, H. R. (2003). *Organizational Learning from Performance Feedback: A Behavioral Perspective on Innovation and Change*. Cambridge, UK: Cambridge University Press.

Harrison, J. R. & Carroll, G. R. (2005). *Culture and Demography in Organizations*. Princeton, NJ: Princeton University Press.

Haunschild, P. R. & Rhee, M. (2004). "The role of volition in organizational learning: The case of automotive product recalls." *Management Science*, 50(11): 1545–1560.

Haunschild, P. R. & Sullivan, B. N. (2002). "Learning from complexity: Effects of prior accidents and incidents on airlines' learning." *Administrative Science Quarterly*, 47: 609–643.

Heugens, P. P. M. A. R., van Riel, C. B. M., & van den Bosch, F. A. J. (2004). "Reputation management capabilities as decision rules." *Journal of Management Studies*, 41(8): 1349–1377.

Jennings, D. F. & Seaman, S. L. (1994). "High and low levels of organizational adaptation: An empirical analysis of strategy, structure, and performance." *Strategic Management Journal*, 15(6): 459–475.

Kim, L. (1998). "Crisis construction and organizational learning: Capability building in catching up at Hyundai Motors." *Organization Science*, 9: 506–521.

Kim, T. (2010). "Search behavior, social positions, and institutional logics: The U.S. feature film industry, 1997–2006." Unpublished Ph.D. dissertation. Honolulu, HI: University of Hawaii at Manoa.

Kim, J.-Y. & Miner, A. S. (2007). "Vicarious learning from the failures and near-failures of others: Evidence from the U.S. commercial banking industry." *Academy of Management Journal*, 50(2): 687–714.

Kim, T. & Rhee, M. (2009). "Exploration and exploitation: Internal variety and environmental dynamism." *Strategic Organization*, 7(1): 11–41.

Kim, J.-Y., Kim, J.-Y., & Miner, A. S. (2009). "Organizational learning from extreme performance experience: The impact of success and recovery experience." *Organization Science*, 20(6): 958–978.

Lampel, J., Shamsie, J., & Shapira, Z. (2009). "Experiencing the improbable: Rare events and organizational learning." *Organization Science*, 20(5): 835–845.

Levinthal, D. A. (1997). "Adaptation on rugged landscapes." *Management Science*, 43(7): 934–950.

Levitt, B. & March, J. G. (1988). "Organizational learning." *Annual Review of Sociology*, 14: 319–340.

Madsen, P. M. & Desai, V. (2010). "Failing to learn? The effects of failure and success on organizational learning in the global orbital launch vehicle industry." *Academy of Management Journal*, 53(3): 451–476.

Mahler, J. G. & Casamayou, M. H. (2009). *Organizational Learning at NASA: The Challenger and Columbia Accidents*. Washington, DC: Georgetown University Press.

March, J. G. (1991). "Exploration and exploitation in organizational learning." *Organization Science*, 2(1): 71–87.

——, Sproull, L. S., & Tamuz, M. (1991). "Learning from samples of one or fewer." *Organization Science*, 2(1): 1–13.

Marcus, A. A. & Goodman, R. S. (1991). "Victims and shareholders: The dilemmas of presenting corporate policy during a crisis." *Academy of Management Journal*, 34(2): 281–305.

Martins, L. L. (2005). "A model of the effects of reputational rankings on organizational change." *Organization Science*, 16(6): 701–720.

Miner, A. S., Kim, J.-Y., Holzinger, I. W., & Haunschild, P. R. (1999). "Fruits of failure: Organizational level failure and population level learning." *Advances in Strategic Management*, 16: 187–220.

Ocasio, W. (1995). "The enactment of economic adversity: A reconciliation of theories of failure-induced change and threat-rigidity." *Research in Organizational Behavior*, 17: 287–331.

O'Reilly, C. A. & Chatman, J. A. (1996). "Culture as social control: Corporations, culture and commitment." *Research in Organizational Behavior*, 18: 157–200.

Pearson, C. M. & Clair, J. A. (1998). "Reframing crisis management." *Academy of Management Review*, 23(1): 59–76.

Perrow, C. (1984). *Normal Accidents: Living with High-Risk Technologies*. New York: Basic Books.

Podolny, J. M. (1993). "A status-based model of market competition." *American Journal of Sociology*, 98(4): 829–872.

Puranam, P., Singh, H., & Zollo, M. (2006). "Organizing for innovation: Managing the coordination-autonomy dilemma in technology acquisitions." *Academy of Management Journal*, 49(2): 263–280.

Rao, H. (1994). "The social construction of reputation: Certification contests, legitimation, and the survival of organizations in the American automobile industry: 1895–1912." *Strategic Management Journal*, 15(Winter): 29–44.

Rhee, M. (2009). "Does reputation contribute to reducing organizational errors? A learning approach." *Journal of Management Studies*, 46: 676–703.

—— & Hadwick, R. (2011). "Repairing damages to reputations: A relational and behavioral perspective." In R. J. Burke, G. Martin, & C. L. Cooper (Eds.), *Corporate Reputation: Managing Threats and Opportunities*. Surry, UK: Gower, 305–325.

—— & Haunschild, P. R. (2006). "The liability of good reputation: A study of product recalls in the U.S. automobile industry." *Organization Science*, 17(1): 101–117.

—— & Valdez, M. E. (2009). "Contextual factors surrounding reputation damage with potential implications for reputation repair." *Academy of Management Review*, 34(1): 146–168.

Rindova, V. P., Williamson, I. O., Petkova, A. P., & Sever, J. M. (2005). "Being good or being known: An empirical examination of the dimensions, antecedents, and consequences of organizational reputation." *Academy of Management Journal*, 48(6): 1033–1049.

Schein, E. H. (1972). *Professional Education: Some New Directions*. New York: McGraw-Hill.

Shapiro, C. (1983). "Premiums for high quality products as returns to reputations." *Quarterly Journal of Economics*, 98(4): 659–680.

Sitkin, S. (1992). "Learning through failure: The strategy of small losses." *Research in Organizational Behavior*, 14: 231–266.

Sørensen, J. B. (2002). "The strength of corporate culture and the reliability of firm performance." *Administrative Science Quarterly*, 47: 70–91.

Sutton, R. I. & Callahan, A. L. (1987). "The stigma of bankruptcy: Spoiled organizational image and its management." *Academy of Management Journal*, 30(3): 405–436.

Taylor, A. & Greve, H. R. (2006). "Superman or the fantastic four? Knowledge combination and experience in innovative teams." *Academy of Management Journal*, 49(4): 723–740.

Tucker, A. L. & Edmondson, A. C. (2003). "Why hospitals don't learn from failures: Organizational and psychological dynamics that inhibit system change." *California Management Review*, 45(2): 55–72.

Vaughan, D. (1997). "The trickle-down effect: Policy decisions, risky work, and the Challenger tragedy." *California Management Review*, 39(2): 80–102.

Weick, K. E. & Sutcliffe, K. M. (2006). "Mindfulness and the quality of organizational attention." *Organization Science*, 17(4): 514–524.

Weigelt, K. & Camerer, C. (1988). "Reputation and corporate strategy: A review of recent theory and applications." *Strategic Management Journal*, 9(5): 443–454.

Winter, S. G. (2000). "The satisficing principle in capability learning." *Strategic Management Journal*, 21: 981–996.

Zollo, M. & Winter, S. G. (2002). "Deliberate learning and the evolution of dynamic capabilities." *Organization Science*, 13(3): 339–351.

....

CHAPTER 23

A FRAMEWORK FOR REPUTATION MANAGEMENT OVER THE COURSE OF EVOLVING CONTROVERSIES

....

KIMBERLY D. ELSBACH

In this chapter, I use a case study of Apple's iPhone 4 to develop a framework that extends our understanding of reputation management in the context of evolving controversies (i.e., controversies that occur over weeks or months, and are punctuated by several distinct reputation management events). This framework suggests that managers should consider several previously ignored contextual dimensions of reputation management when dealing with an evolving controversy. These contextual dimensions include: (1) the timing of reputation management (before or after each event over the course of the controversy), (2) the valence of each event (positive or negative), and (3) the sequential nature of reputation management communications over the course of the controversy. Together, these insights enhance situational theories of reputation management and provide practical guidance to managers coping with evolving controversies.

ORGANIZATIONAL reputations are *perceptions of the quality of an organization as compared to other organizations* (Elsbach, 2006; Rindova and Martins, Chapter 2, this volume). The type of quality or qualities that organizations are known for denote the *dimensions* of their reputation (e.g., quality in customer service vs. quality in creativity).[1] In turn, *reputation management* involves deliberate actions by leaders and spokespersons designed to improve, protect, or repair perceptions of the organization's quality and character (Elsbach, 2006; Fombrun & Rindova, 2000).

---

[1] Fombrun, Gardberg, & Server (2000) have proposed that there are six central *dimensions* of corporate reputations (i.e., emotional appeal, products and services, financial performance, vision and leadership, workplace environment, and social responsibility).

As was recently illustrated by BP's poor handling and communications regarding the 2010 Deepwater Horizon oil drilling accident, reputation management is a critical, yet often underappreciated, activity in today's organizations. In this chapter, I focus on the use of reputation management tactics in relation to major, critical events (e.g., corporate scandals, industry accidents, positive rankings). I refer to these tactics as "event-based" reputation management to distinguish them from everyday and ongoing actions that organizations use to build and maintain their reputations.

Much of the historical research on event-based reputation management has focused on designing effective communications in *response* to specific types of crises, such as product failures (Fombrun, 1996; Marcus & Goodman, 1991). This research suggests, in general, that damaged organizational reputations are best repaired through actions and communications that provide clear, rational explanations of an organization's actions, sensitivity to audience concerns, and a focus on visible changes the organization has instituted to prevent a similar crisis occurring in the future (Coombs, 1999).

More recent research, has also suggested that contextual variables surrounding a crisis are important in developing frameworks for event-based reputation management (see Rhee and Kim, Chapter 22, this volume). For example, Rhee & Valdez (2009) recently developed a framework illustrating how factors such as the multidimensionality of an organization's reputation and the social networks into which an organization is tied may affect how visible a crisis is to audiences, as well as audiences' perceptions of the organization's ability to respond to the crisis. Similarly, Coombs (2007) developed a situational crisis communication theory, which proposes that contextual variables—such as having a history of similar crises or having a poor prior relationship with stakeholders—will have an impact on how much responsibility for a crisis is attributed to an organization. These frameworks have received some early, but limited, empirical support from studies of crisis management (Coombs, 2007), suggesting that contextual theories may provide a more complete understanding of reputation management events.

Despite these recent improvements, none of these situational frameworks has gone beyond examinations of reparative reputation management following a single, organizational crisis event. Event-based reputation management, however, may not just relate to single crisis events, and may be more than purely remedial in nature. Organizations may use reputation management prior to anticipated negative events (such as the introduction of a controversial product), and may use reputation management both before and after significant positive events (Elsbach, 2006). For example, Whittington and Yakis-Douglas (Chapter 20, this volume) describe how strategy communications can be used to manage corporate reputations following positive events (e.g., a corporate merger).

Thus both the timing of the reputation management (before or after a significant event) and the valence of the significant event (positive or negative) comprise contextual factors that may be important to frameworks of event-based reputation management. In addition, because multiple tactics may be used over the duration of an evolving controversy (e.g., a controversy that occurs over weeks or months, and is punctuated by positive and negative sub-events—such as the evolving controversy surrounding the Deep Water Horizon oil spill), reputation management may occur over the course of several, closely related events. As a result, the sequence of event-based reputation management communications, across an evolving controversy, may constitute an additional contextual variable that is important to situational theories of reputation management.

In an effort to extend our understanding of event-based reputation management, then I examine how the effective use of reputation management, during an evolving controversy, may depend on these three previously ignored contextual variables, that is, (1) the timing of the reputation management (before or after each event), (2) the valence of each event (positive or negative), and (3) the sequential nature of reputational communications. I investigate the importance of these contextual dimensions on effective reputation management through a case study of Apple's 2010 introduction of their iPhone 4. I draw insight from this case study, as well as from a set of key extant research studies (summarized in the table at the end of the chapter), to examine event-based reputation management.

An Illustration of Reputation Management During an Evolving Controversy: The Case of the Apple iPhone 4

Over the course of four months in the spring and summer of 2010, the Apple Corporation (or simply "Apple") introduced its new iPhone 4. During this time, Apple dealt with four distinct reputation management events that took place in four distinct contexts (i.e., contexts defined by the valence of the event, the timing of reputation management, and the most recent reputation management that had taken place prior to the event). As a result, this case illustrates how these contextual variables affected the design of effective, event-based reputation management during an evolving controversy. In the following sections, I provide an overview of Apple and its reputation, and then describe the case of the iPhone 4 in four parts, corresponding the four events and contexts.

Overview of Apple Inc. and its Reputation[2]

At the time of this case study, Apple was a multinational consumer electronics company headquartered in Cupertino, California (US). Established in 1976, Apple was a worldwide leader in the production of personal electronics devices, including both laptop and

---

[2] See http://en.wikipedia.org/wiki/Apple_Inc.

desktop computers (iMacs), personal audio devices (iPods), mobile smartphones (iPhones), and most recently a tablet computer device (the iPad). Apple Inc's reputation was built on four components. First, Apple was known as "innovative"—as much for its advertising as for its electronics design and aesthetics (Joel, 2010: B5). Second, Apple Inc. was known as having products of "superior quality," and had been named to *Fortune* magazine's list of the most admired companies in the world in 2009 and 2010. Third, Apple was also perceived as a free-spirited "underdog" or disadvantaged small-fry, who took on stuffy corporate giants like IBM and Microsoft (Berkow, 2010: FP5), and had an almost evangelical following of loyal fans (Corrigan, 2010: 22). Finally, Apple had a reputation for strict control over its technology (Heining, 2010a). Apple's new products were revealed in tightly controlled and highly orchestrated media events, in which audiences were wowed by newly revealed features that were not released until perfected. For the past several decades, Apple had also been embodied by its charismatic CEO and co-founder, Steve Jobs.

In the months just preceding the release of the iPhone 4, Apple had affirmed its reputations for innovation and excellence with the launch of the iPad. On 27 January 2010 Apple issued a press release about its new iPad—the first device of its kind to allow web browsing, email, gaming, videos, e-books, and photo libraries. Apple founder, Steve Jobs, was quoted in the press release as saying "iPad is our most advanced technology in a magical and revolutionary device at an unbelievable price...iPad creates and defines an entirely new category of devices..." (quoted from "Apple Launches iPad," www.apple.com/pr/library/2010/01/27ipad.html). These comments would be important to setting the context for Apple's evolving controversy (described below) regarding the introduction of its iPhone 4.

CONTEXT I: PRIOR TO AN ANTICIPATED POSITIVE EVENT AND FOLLOWING RECENT AFFIRMATIONS OF REPUTATIONS FOR INNOVATION AND EXCELLENCE

On 19 April 2010 technology website Gizmodo published photos, videos, and extensive reviews of what it said was the yet-to-be released Apple iPhone 4 (Heining, 2010a). Claiming that they had received a prototype of the next generation iPhone from someone who found it in a bar (later revealed to have been true), Gizmodo engineers disassembled the phone to inspect its components and features (Peck, 2010). Based on their inspection, Gizmodo bloggers believed the prototype to be a genuine Apple product and revealed that the new phone had several very cool new features, including a glass-like ceramic back, improved camera with flash, an improved display, and a bigger battery

(Peck, 2010). These features and a review of the phone were posted on Gizmodo's website by blogger Jason Chen.

While these events were mildly embarrassing to Apple, which, as noted above, prides itself on tight control of its research and development (Heining, 2010a), the main problem these events produced for Apple was managing the excitement that the unanticipated pre-release had inspired in consumers. Much of this excitement was spurred on by industry analysts whose first views of the lost iPhone led them to make exciting claims about the new device. For example, one industry writer noted:

> This could be the first phone to bring video telephony to the masses... [this development] would get people very, very, excited. (Gelles, 2010: C01)

These types of comments affirmed Apple's strong reputation for innovation, but also put pressure on Apple to live up to this reputation and to manage expectations about their yet-to-be released iPhone 4. In other words, they required Apple to engage in reputation management in the context of an anticipated, positive event.

Extant research on the "labeling" of events suggests that verbal tactics can be used prior to the announcement of a positive event to frame "the meaning and importance" of the event (Ashforth & Humphrey, 1995: 453). One of the most common forms of reputation management prior to anticipated positive events is to advertise or name the goals that the organization has set for itself. In this way, the organization can both *set expectations regarding the anticipated positive event, and direct attention toward the goals that the organization perceives it is most likely to attain (or claim to attain)*. Such goal advertisement may be part of a "dialogue" approach to reputation management (Heugens, van Riel, & van den Bosch, 2004) that seeks to inform and communicate with audiences in an ongoing basis so that those audiences are prepared for anticipated events.

In particular, specific organizational goals are often advertised to audiences prior to the company's attempts at achieving them as a means of highlighting their strengths and directing attention away from their weaknesses (Heugens, van Riel, & van den Bosch, 2004). Accordingly, organizations typically advertise goals when they are fairly certain that they can meet them (e.g., goals for the release date of a highly anticipated movie sequel by a Hollywood movie studio), when they expect that other groups or organizations will set goals for them if they do not do it themselves (e.g., the Atlanta Olympic Committee's goals for upgrading city infrastructure prior to the 1996 Summer Olympic Games), or when they expect that the mere act of setting the goal would be beneficial, regardless of whether or not it is achieved.

In Apple's situation, then, extant research would suggest that the company focus audiences' attention on specific attainable goals that Apple thought its new iPhone would achieve. Yet using such goal specification to focus attention on a few, achievable goals for an upcoming event would also undermine the "surprise" of unveiling new innovations. These types of goal advertisements would be antithetical to organizational reputations characterized by frame-breaking and surprise. That is, innovative organizations, such as

Apple Inc., who are known for introducing new products or services that "surprise and delight" their customers (Apple Inc, 2010a), may find it difficult to pre-advertise goals that are meant to attenuate expectations, rather than to heighten expectations. This may have been especially true at this time, since Apple had just affirmed its reputation for innovation with the launch of the iPad. These arguments may explain why Apple did not use goal advertisement to focus audiences' attention following the preemptory release of information about its iPhone 4.

Instead, Apple took the heavy-handed approach of quieting the discussion of its unreleased iPhone. That is, they sought to affirm their reputation for "control" while avoiding actions that might undermine their reputation for innovation. Although the lost iPhone 4 was returned to Apple by Gizmodo immediately after Apple acknowledged that it was their product (Arthur & Kiss, 2010), officers from the San Mateo, California Police Department, and California's Rapid Enforcement Allied Computer Team (REACT) raided the home of Gizmodo writer, Jason Chen, on 26 April 2010—confiscating computers, hard drives, and a new iPad supposedly used in "committing a felony" (Heining, 2010b). It was later revealed that Apple Inc. executives sat on REACT's steering committee and that Apple had contacted police about potential stolen property in relation to the phone (Harris & Tobin, 2010).

Industry writers as well as mainstream media quickly denounced what they saw as oppressive persecution by Apple Inc. against a journalist engaged in free speech. Calling Apple a "behemoth" in a "David and Goliath confrontation," British web entrepreneur Nick Denton, who was associated with Gizmodo, said he was "shocked" to hear of the raid on Chen's house and that he was concerned about Apple's apparent role in the raid. As he noted:

> It's extraordinary that one would have a police force that was so aligned with corporate interests. (Quoted in Pilkington, 2010: 1)

Other journalists went farther, calling REACT "goon squads…carrying computers instead of billy clubs" (Harris & Tobin, 2010: 33), and late night television satirist Jon Stewart devoted a nine-minute slot to a parody he called "Appholes" (Harris & Tobin, 2010: 33). In that skit, Stewart complained that Apple was "becoming the Man" and pleaded to Jobs to say it wasn't so. Stewart went on to say:

> Microsoft was supposed to be the evil one, but you guys are busting down doors in Palo Alto. Come on, Steve, chill out. (Quoted in Harris & Tobin, 2010: 33)

While these events affirmed their reputation for control, they also appeared to damage Apple's reputation as the free-spirited underdog, and painted the organization as just one more big corporation. As the London *Times* reported:

> It will be hard for Apple, which recently posted record profits of $3.07 billion, to maintain its image as a company staffed by free-thinking technology buffs who prefer T-shirts and chinos to corporate suits and ties. (Harris & Tobin, 2010: 33)

CONTEXT II: FOLLOWING A POSITIVE EVENT AND RECENT AFFIRMATIONS OF REPUTATIONS FOR CONTROL, INNOVATION, AND EXCELLENCE

Three weeks after the raid on Jason Chen's home, Apple introduced the new iPhone 4 through a press release and press conference on 7 June 2010. In the press release, Steve Jobs described the new phone as follows:

> iPhone 4 is the biggest leap since the original iPhone … FaceTime video calling sets a new standard for mobile communication, and our new Retina display is the highest resolution display ever in a phone, with text looking like it does on a fine printed page. We have been dreaming about both of these breakthroughs for decades. (Apple Inc., 2010a)

Jobs also demonstrated the new FaceTime video-calling feature in a press conference at Apple's Worldwide Developer's Conference in San Francisco. Wowing the crowd, Jobs affirmed his geek identity and Apple's reputation for coolness by saying:

> I grew up with The Jetsons and Star Trek just dreaming about video calls. And it's real now. (Sarno, 2010: B1)

Jobs even showed some humor, and finally responded to the Gizmodo leak of the iPhone prototype in his introduction by joking, "Stop me if you've already seen this" (Sarno, 2010: B1).

The entertaining and über-cool unveiling by Jobs was a hit with industry writers and analysts. Calling the event a "touchdown," *Dallas Morning News* technology writer Jim Rossman said he was likely to buy the phone because of its new features (Godinez, 2010). Other writers waxed poetic about the complete coolness of the design, calling it "magically great" (Joel, 2010) and "unprecedentedly slick" (Lim, 2010). These comments reinforced Apple's reputation as an innovator, despite the recent hit to its reputation as an upstart. As one writer noted:

> You have to respect a company that iterates and innovates when what was presently in-market seemed more than above average. (Joel, 2010: B5)

Clearly, the unveiling was a huge success and enhanced Apple's reputation for innovation. Following such positive events, extant research shows that the most common reputation management tactic used is strategic re-categorization. Strategic re-categorizations are typically refinements or qualifications of publicly granted categorizations. For example, a firm may qualify its "best company to work for" categorization by claiming to be a very "family friendly" organization or have the best "culture of work–life balance." These types of re-categorizations *acknowledge a positive evaluation, but also qualify it in a way that reduces the chances that, (a) audiences may question the evaluation (e.g., how can you*

be the "best company to work for when you don't pay the highest?") or, (b) future, uncon-
trollable events may disconfirm it (e.g., a new ranking system is implemented that provides
a less positive evaluation of the organization).

In this way, organizations draw attention to their strongest attributes and increase the chances that audiences will see them live up to their high praise. Thus, following its ranking as one of the top 20 US business schools by *Business Week* magazine, the University of California, Berkeley, publicized that it was the best "value" in MBA education, as well as one of the highest ranked public universities in the United States (Elsbach & Kramer, 1996). Similarly, the University of Michigan was quick to attract attention to its high ranking in the area of executive MBA education, and also noted its overall high ranking among public institutions. These re-categorizations were publicized on their school websites, in alumni magazines, and in business school newsletters (Elsbach & Kramer, 1996).

At the same time re-categorization tends to narrow and specify the groups to which an organization belongs and should be compared against. In essence, this tactic portrays the organization as specialized (Elsbach & Kramer, 1996). While such specialization may be attractive to many organizations, it may be less so with organizations whose reputations are built on the character of "general excellence" or "overall superiority." For such organizations (e.g., Harvard University, Coca-Cola, Mercedes Benz), re-categorization into a more specialized niche may diminish their overall status, and thus, be less attractive as a reputation management tactic.

This reluctance to use re-categorization by firms identified by their general excellence (as Apple had recently affirmed in its communications about the iPad) may explain why Apple did not follow their positive iPhone 4 unveiling with more specialized categories. In this situation, Apple could have used the positive media to focus attention on its clearest design improvements and categorize itself not just as the inventor of new, framebreaking devices (such as the iPod and iPad) but as a designer of perfected features. In fact, some of the clearest improvements in the iPhone 4 were perfections of rather older technologies. For example, technology writer Christopher Lim noted in the *Singapore Times*:

> The main reason [to buy an iPhone 4] would be to invest in a rigorously-tested phone system that has a limited set of features, but ensures all of those features have the best implementation. A perfect example is the ability to copy and paste text. The humblest phones have been able to do this for well over a decade, but iPhones only gained this ability last June. That delay would be ludicrous if not for the fact that the iPhone operating system, which is now dubbed iOS, still has the best copy-and-paste implementation on the market. (Lim, 2010)

Yet Apple did not tout these improvements in its press releases or advertisements for the iPhone 4. Instead, Apple focused mostly on its breakthroughs in video-calling and high-resolution display, affirming its reputation for innovation. Further, Apple re-affirmed its reputation for general excellence in a letter to Apple consumers on 28 June 2010. In this press release, Steve Jobs was quoted as saying: "This is the most successful product launch in Apple's History." These types of claims affirmed Apple's reputation for product superiority and general excellence, but provided little wiggle room for backtracking if things went wrong. This lack of wiggle room would become a problem for Apple in the coming days and weeks.

CONTEXT III: FOLLOWING A NEGATIVE EVENT AND FOLLOWING RECENT AFFIRMATIONS OF REPUTATIONS FOR CONTROL, INNOVATION, AND EXCELLENCE

On 24 June 2010 the first iPhone 4s were finally delivered to the Apple faithful. Almost immediately, there were complaints from customers about dropped calls related to Apple's new external antenna. Apparently, holding the new iPhone in one's left hand—with one's thumb on one side and fingers wrapped around the other side—could cause the two antennae, which were embedded in the external case, to bridge, resulting in a loss of signal strength and, ultimately, dropped phone calls (Silverman, 2010).

Following these types of product failures and audience complaints, the most commonly used reputation management tactics are justifications and excuses (Marcus & Goodman, 1991; Elsbach, 2006). These remedial tactics appear effective following negative, reputation-threatening events because they *demonstrate both rationality and consideration of audience views in the decision processes that led to the negative event, and dissociate the current organization from the negative organization portrayed in the media.*

Justifications are accounts that claim there was a good reason for an action that was criticized (Tedeschi, 1981), and suggest that the outcomes of the action were not necessarily bad. These tactics suggest that the organization's actions were based, at least in part, on their attempts to satisfy audience needs (Elsbach, 1994). Such justifications are often backed up by evidence of *dissociation* between the organization's long-standing character and the complaints about the action from the popular press and media (Hearit, 1994). For example, a low cost airline that is criticized for charging passengers to use the onboard lavatory may claim that, in line with its typical strategy it was attempting to save consumers money on fares by cutting out all possible expenses. This justification suggests that the company had the consumers' interests in mind when it took the action that led to the complaints.

By contrast, excuses are claims that an organization was not responsible for a negative outcome, even while admitting that this outcome occurred. Organizations that have harmful product failures often use excuses to deny responsibility for the negative event, and back up those excuses by describing prior actions that the organization took to prevent the accident or product failure (Elsbach, 1994). Thus excuses may include claims that the negative events were due to technical failure, sabotage, or isolated human error, all of which was unforeseeable, and for which they should not be held accountable (Marcus & Goodman, 1991). These tactics are designed to show that the organization was rational and proficient in its actions and that the negative event was something, "that the company could not have foreseen or prevented … and does not reflect underlying inadequacies in either the company, its management, or its way of doing business" (Marcus & Goodman, 1991: 286).

Yet, rather than using these types of justifications or excuses following consumers' initial complaints about the iPhone 4 antenna, Steve Jobs appeared to blame the problem on consumers rather than on Apple. As several blogs noted, when one customer emailed Jobs about the antennae issue and asked if this was a design flaw, Jobs emailed back, "Nope. Just don't hold it that way" (Rose, 2010). Later, another consumer got the following, similar response from Jobs:

> Gripping the phone will result in some attenuation of its antenna performance, with certain places being worse than others depending on the placement of the antennas. This is a fact of life for every wireless phone. If you ever experience this on your iPhone 4, avoid gripping it in the lower left corner in a way that covers both sides of the black strip in the metal band, or simply use one of the many available cases. (Rose, 2010)

Jobs' disuse of remedial justifications or excuses following the initial antenna problems may have been, in part, related to Apple's desire to, once again, maintain their reputation for control. That is, for Apple, providing justifications or excuses following the initial antenna problems may have been viewed as admitting that they were not in control. While no organization maintains complete control over its destiny, some organizations, like Apple, have reputations that are more strongly built on the character of control than others. For example, "total institutions" (Goffman, 1961) that are designed to control all aspects of members' lives (e.g., armies, asylums, or prisons), often have reputations grounded in the character of control. For these organizations to claim that they were victims of forces beyond their control may be paramount to claiming they had failed in their organizational missions. Further, admitting a lack of control would have been especially hard for Apple at this time, because it had recently affirmed its control following the unauthorized release of photos of the iPhone 4 prototype (discussed earlier).

Unsurprisingly, Apple's "blaming the victim" approach to responding to consumer concerns was not met with enthusiasm. As noted earlier, following negative events, effective reputation management typically involves demonstrating the use of rational decision processes and a consideration of audience views and needs in the actions leading up to the negative event. Yet Apple showed no evidence that they considered users' concerns or views when they designed the antenna or when they responded to complaints about its faults.

In the days that followed, dozens of websites and media outlets printed comments from angry consumers who complained that Apple should have known about the problem before it released the phone (Arthur, 2010). Further, consumers were upset that they would have to purchase a $30 case to resolve the signal problem. These problems appeared to threaten Apple's reputation for superior quality. As one blogger wrote:

The [iPhone 4] has a major design flaw that threatens Apple's reputation of producing higher quality devices that justify the high costs. Usually a company of this magnitude would issue a recall, but not Apple, they blamed the issue on not holding the phone correctly. They even went so far as to make a commercial that showed everyone holding the phone "correctly." (Quoted in Electronic Urban Report, 2010)

CONTEXT IV: PRIOR TO A NEGATIVE EVENT AND FOLLOWING RECENT AFFIRMATIONS OF REPUTATIONS FOR CONTROL, INNOVATION, AND EXCELLENCE

In response to the increasing bad press, Apple issued a press release on 2 July 2010 about the iPhone 4. In it, Apple claimed that, after looking into the cause of the dropped calls reported by some iPhone users, they were "stunned" to find out that the formula they used to calculate signal strength (i.e., number of bars) was "totally wrong" and had been since the original iPhone was released in 2007 (Apple Inc., 2010b). As a result, Apple claimed that users perceived that they were losing signal strength, when in fact they had no signal strength to begin with. Apple claimed to have fixed the problem with the help of AT&T and said it was issuing a free software update that would eliminate the problem for consumers.

This response, which essentially denied the existence of an antenna problem, did not improve things for Apple. Users continued to claim that the antenna was faulty (Martin, 2010), and bloggers continued to sound the death knell of Apple's reputation for high quality and customer care (Smith, 2010). Things got even worse on 12 July 2010 when the highly respected magazine *Consumer Reports* verified that the antenna problem was legitimate, stating that "none of the [other phones tested] had the signal-loss problems of the iPhone 4" (quoted in Burrows & Guglielmo, 2010). In the end, *Consumer Reports* declined to recommend the iPhone 4—the first time the magazine had failed to recommend an iPhone.

These events made it clear that Apple had a design problem with their iPhone 4 antenna, and that it would continue to lose signal strength in the future. In anticipation of these continued problems, Apple CEO, Steve Jobs, decided to hold a multimedia press conference on 16 July 2010 to explain why these problems were likely to continue with the iPhone 4 and to announce a program to provide free phone cases for all consumers and full refunds for any dissatisfied customers.

In managing organizational reputations with regard to such anticipated negative events, extant research suggests that the most effective reputation management tactics would be anticipatory excuses (Snyder, Higgins, & Stucky, 1983; Hewitt & Stokes, 1975). These types of excuses include claims that the organization should not be held responsible for the anticipated negative outcome, because it is likely the result of factors outside of the organization's control. Such tactics appear effective in protecting organizational reputations because they help to separate, in audiences' minds, the "true" organization from the organization associated with the anticipated negative event. In these cases, organizations are attempting to send the message that an *anticipated negative event is not indicative of the stable and enduring qualities of the organization, and should be considered a rare aberration caused mainly by forces outside of the organization's control* (Elsbach, Sutton, & Principe, 1998).

In this vein, a series of organizational studies on corporate annual reports suggests that, when performance is poor, organizations design their annual reports to serve as anticipatory excuses prior to the announcement of quarterly earnings (see Staw, McKechnie, & Puffer, 1983). In these announcements, the organizations place blame on the industry or environment, rather than on themselves (e.g., they provide an environmental excuse for poor performance, such as the introduction of new regulations that hampered their performance). The message conveyed is, "our impending performance review will reflect the results of environmental influences beyond our control."

Organizations whose reputation is characterized by control (like Apple) may, however, find anticipatory accounts difficult to use. In fact, admitting up front that the organization is not in control prior to an impending negative event may be seen as more harmful to a reputation for control than admitting lack of control following a negative event. This is because the organization should, presumably, be able to prepare for the negative event and find ways to maintain control in dealing with it.

Despite these difficulties, however, Steve Jobs appeared to use anticipatory excuses to explain the anticipated, continued problems with the iPhone 4, although doing so admitted a lack of control for Apple (watch the video at: http://www.apple.com/apple-events/july-2010/). Throughout his presentation, Jobs emphasized that the signal loss issue was not unique to the iPhone 4, placing most of the blame on the Wi-Fi environment, and excusing Apple from responsibility for most dropped calls. Jobs demonstrated, through video, how phones from Blackberry, HTC, and Samsung could be made to lose signal strength by holding them in the same way as the iPhone 4. He then excused the problem as "life in the smartphone world" and claimed that "every phone has weak spots." These excuses appeared to blame the antenna problems on unforeseeable environmental issues, for which Apple should not be held responsible.

In the end, Jobs reported that Apple would give a free bumper case to all iPhone 4 purchasers and would offer full refunds to all buyers who requested them. He promised that Apple would work hard to resolve signal issues and vowed that he wanted all of Apple's users to be happy.

Based on media reports and questions during the press conference, the outcome of Apple's "antenna-gate" presentation was viewed as a draw. Consumers received a free fix for their reception problems and recognition from Apple that their concerns were valid. Further, Apple provided a reasonable excuse for future antenna problems (it's the wireless signal environment). Yet, Apple refused to apologize for blaming users for holding the phone the wrong way and didn't respond to the *Consumer Reports* issue. As a result, many industry experts remained critical of Apple's response to the antenna problems. As one industry writer commented:

> The main problem is the way [Apple's] reacted to this situation, which was far too slow, very high-handed, and very dismissive—telling owners that they're holding it wrong. Basically, they've created a PR disaster out of nothing, which is very unusual for a company that is normally so good at public relations. (Quoted in Brown, 2010: 9)

SUMMARY AND FRAMEWORK

By late July 2010, the four-month iPhone 4 saga appeared to be more of loss than a gain for Apple. On the downside, three of the four components of Apple's corporate reputation were damaged. First, Apple's reputation as the scrappy underdog had been, perhaps irretrievably, undermined. As Queen's University (Kingston, Ontario) Professor of Internet Marketing, John Pliniussen, noted:

> People tend to view Apple as being "the angels, the cool guys, the nerds who have done well and kicked the ass of the big companies...But now they're big themselves and they're turning into the "big guys" and sort of being scammy. (Quoted in Berkow, 2010: FP5)

In addition, Apple's reputation for general excellence and superior quality had taken a major hit. As columnist Berkow reported:

> When an iPhone 4 ended up in the hands of Jason Chen...Apple called the police...When problems first arose with the design of the iPhone 4 antenna...Steve Jobs...initially blamed the problem on his own customers...[and later] pushed the blame on to AT&T...Even after *Consumer Reports* confirmed there was a hardware problem caused by a design flaw in the phone's antennae, Steve Jobs still refused to apologize and admit that Apple erred...(2010: FP5)

Finally, analysts had begun to question whether or not Apple's reputation for tight control and secrecy concerning their new technology was, in fact, a good thing. As industry writer Wade Roush wrote,

> The question is whether, in the case of the iPhone 4, Apple's closed innovation style backfired on the company, resulting in the release of a form-over-function product whose performance had not been adequately tested outside the controlled conditions of Apple's Cupertino campus. (Roush, 2010)

Still, the iPhone 4's cool new features led Apple to sell over 1.7 million devices in the first weekend of its release, and caused one of its faithful fans to produce a YouTube video defending Apple against all attacks (watch it at: http://www.youtube.com/watch?v=VKIcaejkpD4). Apparently, the company's reputation for innovation had weathered the storm. As marketing executive Susanna Freedman noted, "When you build a brand like Apple, there's loyalty beyond reason" (quoted in Brown, 2010: 9).

In summary, the case of the iPhone 4 suggests that effective reputation management tactics need to be customized to fit the context in which they are used. Yet this case also demonstrates how difficult it may be for organizations to use the correct reputation management tactics if their recent reputational affirmations conflict with these tactics. I summarize these findings through a framework, illustrated in Figure 23.1, of event-based reputation management during an evolving controversy.

DISCUSSION

Organizational reputations are valuable because they send strong signals to external audiences about the status of a firm (Fombrun, 1996). Yet reputations are not immune to attack and damage, and if not managed in critical situations may diminish in favorability and strength (Elsbach, 2006). In this chapter, I have proposed a framework of effective reputation management that considers the context of reputation management over the course of an evolving controversy. I have illustrated this framework through a case study of the Apple iPhone 4. This framework and case study extend our theories of corporate reputation, as well as suggesting directions for future research.

THEORIES OF CORPORATE REPUTATION

First, the framework and case study draw attention to the importance of considering the *valence* of relevant events when designing reputation management. When managing reputation-enhancing events, for example, the framework suggests that organizations focus on strategically directing the attention of audiences (i.e., either to specific goals or specific category-memberships). By contrast, when managing reputation-threatening events, the framework suggests that organizations focus on persuading audiences through detailed arguments and accounts. This difference suggests that reputation-enhancing events are viewed as self-explanatory, merely requiring the direction of attention, while reputation-threatening events are viewed as difficult to understand and merit detailed and careful explanation. Reputation management may thus be viewed as requiring less effort and attention in positive contexts than in negative contexts. Such a perspective could explain why opportunities for enhancing reputations related to reputation-enhancing events are often missed.

Second, the framework draws attention to the importance of the timing of reputation management in relation to a reputation management event. The framework suggests, for example, that effective anticipatory tactics focus on the stable character of the

CONTEXT 1– Anticipation of release of new iPhone 4 after prototype revealed.
Type of event: Positive
Timing of rep. mgmt: Before Event
Recent rep. mgmt: Affirmed Innovation and Excellence

PRESCRIBED REPUTATION MANAGEMENT

Effective Tactics – *set expectations regarding the anticipated positive event, and direct attention toward the specific goals that the organization perceives it is most likely to attain.*

Common Forms – Goal Specification to clearly define expected goal achievement.

Conflicts with Recent Reputation Management – Goal specification may be inconsistent with recent affirmations of innovation and surprise

APPLE CASE ILLUSTRATION

Apple is connected to a police raid on the home of the blogger who had written about the lost iPhone. Apple appears to use this tactic to affirm reputation for control after photos of phone appear. This tactic damages Apple's reputation as an underdog. Apple may have not used prescribed goal specification due to recent affirmations of innovation.

CONTEXT 2 – Excitement after formal unveiling of new iPhone
Type of event: Positive
Timing of rep. mgmt: After Event
Recent rep. mgmt: Affirmed Control, Innovation and Excellence

PRESCRIBED REPUTATION MANAGEMENT

Effective Tactics – *acknowledge a positive evaluation, but also qualify it in a way that reduces the chances that audiences may question it, or future, uncontrollable events may disconfirm it.*

Common Forms – Lower level re-categorization of organization to more specifically bound organizational excellence.

Conflicts with Recent Reputation Management: Lower level re-categorization may be inconsistent with recent affirmations of excellence

APPLE CASE ILLUSTRATION

Apple touts its new technology and product superiority – affirming reputations for innovation and general excellence. This tactic provides little room for excuses if future problems arise. Prescribed re-categorizations may not have been used because of conflicts with recent affirmations of general excellence.

CONTEXT 3 – Customer complaints about antenna after release of iPhone 4.
Type of event: Negative
Timing of rep. mgmt: After Event
Recent rep. mgmt: Affirmed Control, Excellence and Innovation.

PRESCRIBED REPUTATION MANAGEMENT

Effective Tactics – *demonstrate both rationality and consideration of audience views and needs in the decision processes that led to the negative event, and dissociate current organization from negative organization portrayed in the media.*

Common Forms – Remedial Justifications and Excuses for the event

Conflicts with Recent Reputation Management – Remedial excuses may be inconsistent with recent affirmations of control.

APPLE CASE ILLUSTRATION

Apple blames antenna problem on users holding the phone wrong. This tactic does not address design issues and damages Apple's reputation for general excellence. Prescribed excuses may not have been used because they conflict with recent affirmations for control.

CONTEXT 4 – Press conference to explain anticipated, future signal problems
Type of event: Negative
Timing of rep. mgmt: Before Event
Recent rep. mgmt: Affirmed Control Innovation and Excellence

PRESCRIBED REPUTATION MANAGEMENT

Effective Tactics – *demonstrate that the anticipated negative event is not indicative of the stable and enduring qualities of the organization, and the organization should not be evaluated based on this event.*

Common Forms – Anticipatory Justifications and Excuses for the event

Conflicts with Recent Reputation Management – Anticipatory excuses may be inconsistent with recent affirmations of control.

APPLE CASE ILLUSTRATION

Apple uses prescribed anticipatory excuses, and blames past and future dropped signals on wireless environment, not iPhone. Steve Jobs shows how signal may be lost on other phones as well. Jobs says that Apple will provide free bumper case or refunds to customers. This tactic damages reputation for control but protects reputation for innovation.

FIGURE 23.1 Framework and illustration of event-based reputation management during an evolving controversy.

organization, while remedial tactics focus on the more changeable and temporary character of the environment. These findings suggest that, prior to anticipated events, organizational spokespersons focus audiences' attention on those organizational characteristics that they are most certain about (e.g., well-established goals, enduring traits) because these characteristics are likely to be positively perceived even in the face of the impending reputation-threatening event. By contrast, when an event (positive or negative) has already happened, organizational spokespersons need to refocus attention away from the organizational traits, and toward the environment that is likely to be an important organizational factor in the future. In this way, the organization may both direct attention away from negative organizational traits associated with a negative event, and moderate unrealistic future expectations based on positive organizational traits associated with a positive event.

Finally, and perhaps most interestingly, the framework highlights the importance of considering recent reputation management efforts when designing current and future reputation management regarding an ongoing and evolving controversy. As noted in the introduction, recent theorizing on crisis management, including chapters in the current volume, has suggested that the historical context in which reputation management occurs plays an important role in the design and effectiveness of reputation management strategies (Coombs, 2007; Rhee & Valdez, 2009; Yue and Ingram, Chapter 14, this volume). In particular, this research has suggested that an organization with a history of crisis events and poor relations with stakeholders will have difficulty responding effectively to reputation-threatening events.

The current framework extends this thinking by proposing that an organization's specific and recent history of reputation management tactics (i.e., the specific reputational claims and affirmations that have been made about the organization) may play a direct role in the form of reputation management that is used in regard to a current reputation management event. Specifically, the framework suggests that recent reputational affirmations may conflict with specific reputation management tactics, and thus cause organizations to choose not to use those tactics, even if they are warranted. For example, a recent affirmation of an organization's reputation for control may conflict with its use of excuses—which claim that factors outside of the organization's control were responsible for an event—as a reputation management strategy. In such a case, an organization may choose not to use excuses to manage their organizational reputation, even if excuses are the prescribed method of reputation management.

Together, the above implications suggest that organizations pay attention to the more *immediate* context in which reputation management occurs (i.e., the valence of the reputation management event, the timing of reputation management in relation to the event, and recent reputational affirmations), as well as more distant contextual influences described by extant research (e.g., the organization's history of crises and relationships with major stakeholders).

These insights also suggest some directions for future research.

DIRECTIONS FOR FUTURE RESEARCH

The current framework suggests that effective reputation management is a more dynamic and interactive effort than previously implied. As a result, it may be useful for researchers to investigate the dynamic and interactive nature of reputations and their audiences more fully. Researchers have recently suggested that reputation management be viewed as a dialogue between organizations and their audiences (Heugens, van Riel, & van den Bosch., 2004). In the same manner, Whittington and Yakis-Douglas (Chapter 14, this volume) argue for a "discourse analysis" of strategic communications, and suggest that such communications involve attention to ongoing "plots" as well as newly introduced themes and buzzwords in dialogues with external audiences. These suggestions imply that the audiences may be actively engaged in discourse with firms and their spokespersons over time, and that reputations (and reputation management) should be necessarily viewed in the light of this engagement and history.

Future research may take these ideas further by identifying specific dialogues or stories that are important to maintaining positive reputations with external audiences (e.g., stories of tradition vs. stories of innovation, dialogues about ideology vs. dialogues about rationality), as well as the types of communications most effective in telling these stories (e.g., formal reports vs. routine organizational actions). Future research might also examine how organizations may effectively (and strategically) engage audiences in the particular dialogues it wishes to have (e.g., discussions of future innovations), while disengaging audiences from dialogues it hopes to end (e.g., discussion of past scandals). As was evident in the case of the Apple iPhone 4, it may not be easy to persuade audiences to give up on one conversation (e.g., discussion of Apple's specific antenna problems) and start another (e.g., discussion of general problems with the wireless environment). Yet there may be effective tactics for guiding conversations and dialogues over time and, as Whittington and Yakis-Douglas in Chapter 20, this volume suggest, clues to these tactics may lie in research on discourse analysis and communications theory.

The current framework also highlights the constraints placed on reputation management by recent organizational communications (e.g., a firm can't claim that it had no control over a negative event if it had recently claimed to be fully in control of its future). This notion suggests that the timing of reputational claims plays an important role in reputation management. Yet it is not clear how long audiences pay attention to reputational events and how much time must pass before an organization may be free of the constraints of past claims. Future research might examine the role of time more directly in relation to reputation management.

For example, researchers may determine if there are cycles of reputational ups and downs, and if there are norms for the length of times audiences scrutinize organizations following specific types of negative events. In this vein, Yue and Ingram (Chapter 14, this volume) suggest that all oil companies may have been scrutinized more carefully follow-ing the BP oil spill of 2010, but doesn't suggest how long that scrutiny lasted and what factors affected the timing of the scrutiny. As reputation management becomes an ongo-ing exercise, identifying common time lines in the evolution of a reputation manage-ment event may be critical to effectively managing reputation management resources.

CONCLUSION

When Apple CEO Steve Jobs envisioned the release of the much anticipated iPhone 4, it is unlikely that he imagined the problem-plagued scenario that played out during the spring and summer of 2010. Yet, by following the events as they unfolded, we can iden-tify a number of contextual constraints that affected how well Apple was perceived, in spite of the problems it encountered during the new iPhone's release. If there is one les-son firms should take away from this case study it is this: in responding to a reputation-threatening event, consider not just what your audience wants to hear today, but how what you're saying today affects what audiences will expect tomorrow.

Key Studies of Event-Based Reputation Management

Reference	Key Constructs and Findings
Marcus & Goodman (1991)	Use of remedial excuses and justifications are effective in protecting reputation following accidents. Use of apologies are effective following scandals. All accounts are effective following product failures.
Elsbach & Kramer (1996)	Organizations responded to identity threat by re-categorizing at levels that showcased their most desired and positive identity characteristics.
Elsbach, Sutton, & Principe (1998)	Anticipatory accounts protect reputations by reducing scrutiny of controversial actions.
Glynn & Abzug (2002)	Organizational names that were changed to have more domain specificity and shorter length were viewed as more legitimate. Names that had higher symbolic isomorphism were rated as more legitimate.
Heugens, van Riel, & van den Bosch (2004)	Dialogue that includes others in decision processes is used as a reputation management strategy when time pressures are absent and issues are well-known.
Coombs (2007)	A past history of similar crises and poor relationships with stakeholders lead audiences to perceive the organization as more responsible for a crisis, making it harder to repair organizational reputation.
Rhee & Valdez (2009)	Reputations are harder to repair if a crisis event is closely linked to organizational reputation, if the organization has diverse stakeholders, if the organization is older and has fewer positive dimensions to its reputation.

REFERENCES

Apple Inc. (2010a). "Apple presents iPhone 4." www.apple.com, June 7.

Apple Inc. (2010b). "Letter from Apple regarding iPhone 4." www.apple.com, July 2.

Arthur, C. (2010). "Irate iPhone owners resort to nail polish to fix £499 gadget." *The Guardian*, June 26, 9.

—— & Kiss, J. (2010). "Apple demands return of iPhone 4G prototype." *The Guardian*, April 21, 7.

Ashforth, B. E. & Humphrey, R. E. (1995). "Labeling processes in the organization: Constructing the individual." In L. L. Cummings & B. M. Staw (Eds.), *Research in Organizational Behavior*, Vol. 17. Greenwich, CT: JAI Press, 413–461.

Berkow, J. (2010). "Worm in Apple's reputation." *National Post (Canada)*, July 17, FP5.

Brown, C. (2010). "Apple barely bruised by iPhone furore." *The Scotsman*, July 17, 9.

Burrows, P. & Guglielmo, C. (2010). "Apple engineer told Jobs iPhone antenna might cut calls." *Bloomberg News*, July 15.

Coombs, W. T. (1999). "Information and compassion in crisis responses: A test of their effects." *Journal of Public Relations Research*, 11: 125–142.

—— (2007). "Protecting organizational reputations during a crisis: The development and application of situational crisis communication theory." *Corporate Reputation Review*, 10: 163–176.

Corrigan, T. (2010). "Will fans risk another bite of the Apple?" *The Daily Telegraph*, July 17, 22.

Electronic Urban Report (2010). *The Gadget Guy: iPhone 4: The Good, the Bad, and the Just Plain Wrong (Blog)*. July 1.

Elsbach, K. D. (1994). "Managing organizational legitimacy in the California cattle industry: The construction and effectiveness of verbal accounts." *Administrative Science Quarterly*, 39(1): 57–88.

—— (2006). *Organizational Perception Management*. Mahwah, NJ: Lawrence Erlbaum.

—— & Kramer, R. M. (1996). "Members' responses to organizational identity threats: Encountering and countering the *Business Week* rankings." *Administrative Science Quarterly*, 41: 442–476.

——, Sutton, R. I., & Principe, K. E. (1998). "Averting expected controversies through anticipatory impression management: A study of hospital billing." *Organization Science*, 9: 68–86.

Fombrun, C. (1996). *Reputation*. Boston, MA: Harvard Business School Press.

—— & Rindova, V. P. (2000). "The road to transparency: Reputation management at Royal Dutch/Shell." In M. Schultz, M. J. Hatch, & M. H. Larsen (Eds.), *The Expressive Organization. Linking Identity, Reputation, and the Corporate Brand*. New York: Oxford University Press, 77–96.

——, Gardberg, N., & Server, J. (2000). "The reputation quotient: A multi-stakeholder measure of corporate reputation." *The Journal of Brand Management*, 7: 241–255.

Gelles, J. (2010). "Apple keeps the buzz buzzing." *The Philadelphia Inquirer*, April 22, C1.

Glynn, M. A. & Abzug, R. (2002). "Institutionalizing identity: Symbolic isomorphism and organizational names." *Academy of Management Journal*, 45: 267–280.

Godinez, V. (2010). "Apple raises its game." *The Dallas Morning News*, June 8, D1.

Goffman, E. (1961). *Asylums: Essays on the Social Situation of Mental Patients and Other Inmates*. New York: Doubleday.

Harris, M. & Tobin, D. (2010). "Apple peels off its nice-guy mask." *The Sunday Times*, May 9, 32–33.

Hearit, K. M. (1994). "Apologies and public relations crisis at Chrysler, Toshiba, and Volvo." *Public Relations Review*, 20: 113–125.

Heining, A. (2010a). "Found 'iPhone' a rare breach of Apple secrecy." *The Christian Science Monitor*, April 19.

—— (2010b). "Police raid home of Gizmodo writer over iPhone prototype." *The Christian Science Monitor*, April 26.

Heugens, P. M. A. R., van Riel, C. B. M, & van den Bosch, F. A. J. (2004). "Reputation management capabilities as decision rules." *Journal of Management Studies*, 41: 1349–1377.

Hewitt, J. P. & Stokes, R. (1975). "Disclaimers." *American Sociological Review*, 40: 1–11.

Joel, M. (2010). "One device to rule them all." *The Montreal Gazette*, June 10, B5.

Lim, C. (2010). "Looking beyond the specs; The iPhone 4's hardware is its least interesting aspect." *Business Times Singapore*, June 14.

Marcus, A. A. & Goodman, R. S. (1991). "Victims and shareholders: The dilemmas of presenting corporate policy during a crisis." *Academy of Management Journal*, 34: 281–305.

Martin, M. (2010). "Law firms suing Apple not impressed with explanation of reception issues." *TUAW (Blog)*, July 3.

Peck, T. (2010). "Apple worker leaves 'prototype of top-secret 4G iPhone' in bar." *The Independent*, April 20, 16.

Pilkington, E. (2010). "Media: Taking a bite out of Apple." *The Guardian*, May 3, 1.

Rhee, M. & Valdez, M. E. (2009). "Contextual factors surrounding reputation damage with potential implications for reputation repair." *Academy of Management Review*, 34: 146–168.

Rose, M. (2010). "Double Stevemails on iPhone reception; 'Just don't hold it that way'." prods@weblogsinc.com, June 24.

Roush, W. (2010). "Was 'Antennagate' a side effect of Apple's secrecy culture?" *Xconomy (Blog)*, July 19.

Sarno, D. (2010). "Video calling takes center stage; Apple's next iPhone hits shelves June 24." *Los Angeles Times*, June 8, B1.

Silverman, D. (2010). "Are you seeing these iPhone issues?" *TechBlog, Houston Chronicle*, June 24.

Smith, S. (2010). "Are Apple's happy days over?" *Minyanville (Blog)*, July 2.

Snyder, C. R., Higgins, R., & Stucky, R. J. (1983). *Excuses. Masquerades in Search of Grace.* New York: John Wiley & Sons.

Staw, B. M., McKechnie, P. I., & Puffer, S. M. (1983). "The justification of organizational performance." *Administrative Science Quarterly*, 28: 582–600.

Tedeschi, J. T. (Ed.) (1981). *Impression Management Theory and Social Psychological Research.* New York: Academic Press.

INDEX